TEXAS HOMEOWNERS ASSOCIATION LAW

THIRD EDITION

TEXAS HOMEOWNERS ASSOCIATION LAW

THIRD EDITION

THE ESSENTIAL LEGAL GUIDE FOR TEXAS HOMEOWNERS ASSOCIATIONS AND HOMEOWNERS

GREGORY S. CAGLE

Two Harbors Press
2301 Lucien Way #415
Maitland. FL 32751
407.339.4217
www.TwoHarborsPress.com

ISBN-13: 978-1-63413-989-2
LCCN: 2016918553

Distributed by Itasca Books

Cover Design by Jenni Wheeler

Printed in the United States of America

ACKNOWLEDGMENT AND DEDICATION

A book doesn't write itself, and though the author may get sole credit for producing the thoughts and ideas expressed within the printed text, the writing of a book requires the energy and work, and often the sacrifice and patience, of a number of people who remain anonymous except to the author himself. This is certainly true for me, and I want to thank everybody (albeit anonymously) who contributed to the third edition of this book through their encouragement, suggested topics for inclusion in the third edition, catching the rare typos from previous editions, and inquiring numerous times as to when the third edition will finally be published. I trust you know who you are.

Most importantly, I want to acknowledge and thank Avery Cagle, Hayden Cagle, and Jennifer Cunningham, who I love dearly and am forever grateful to for their patience and forgiveness as I spent time writing and editing the third edition of this book. As a full-time practicing attorney and a cofounder of a start-up software company that developed the first legal compliance software for homeowners associations, finding spare moments of time to work on this book is difficult to do and such time was often supplied by the sacrifice of time I would have spent with each of you. Though I know that my words of appreciation cannot replace time, I hope that each of you knows how much I love you and appreciate your love and support.

Finally, I want to express my utmost appreciation to my longtime assistant, Tina Gutierrez, to whom this book is dedicated. I have been practicing law for more than 18 years, and Tina has been my secretary, legal assistant, and friend for more than 15 of those years. During the course of such time, no person has had a greater impact on the success of my law practice than Tina, and I would not be able to juggle all of the spinning plates in my life and still practice law without her assistance. In addition, no other single person has had more of a direct impact on the publishing of this book than Tina. From cover design to interior layout of this book, Tina has been a constant source of invaluable advice and feedback, and she is solely responsible for creating the table of authorities in every edition of this book to date, which with more than 2,500 citations to statutes, case law, and other authorities is no small task.

Tina, I am extremely grateful for the never-ending compassion, loyalty, and friendship that you have shown to me over the last 15 years. For all of those reasons and many others, the third edition of this book is dedicated to you.

TABLE OF CONTENTS

CHAPTER 3 FORMATION AND ADMINISTRATION OF TEXAS HOMEOWNERS ASSOCIATIONS

INTRODUCTION

The fastest-growing form of housing in the United States today is "Common-Interest Developments," which include planned unit developments of single-family homes and condominiums. These Common-Interest Developments are almost always governed by a "Homeowners Association," which is a legal entity created by the real estate developer for the purpose of managing the development, maintaining development amenities and commonly owned improvements, and enforcing development restrictions.[1] In fact, the Community Associations Institute, a national organization for Association-Governed Communities, estimates that as of 2014, there are more than 333,600 Association-Governed Communities in the United States, which govern more than twenty-six million homes and sixty-six million residents, an increase of more than 3,000 percent from the same data compiled in 1970.[2]

In simple terms, Homeowners Associations are private organizations made up of the property owners in residential Common-Interest Developments. Such organizations are created by the recording of a contractual document by the real estate developer, generally called a "Declaration of Covenants, Conditions, and Restrictions," that "runs with the land" in the development and which each subsequent owner of property in the development becomes contractually obligated to comply with upon becoming owner of a lot or unit in such development. In most cases, the Declaration of Covenants, Conditions, and Restrictions will establish the powers and duties of the Homeowners Associations and will provide that each owner of property in the Common-Interest Development is an automatic mandatory member of the Homeowners Association.

---

1 Common-Interest Developments with a mandatory-membership Homeowners Association are commonly referred to as "Association-Governed Communities."

2 *See* https://www.caionline.org/AboutCommunityAssociations/Pages/StatisticalInformation.aspx. In 1970, there were only 10,000 association-governed communities in the United States, which governed more than 701,000 homes and 2.1 million residents.

In addition, most Homeowners Associations are organized as nonprofit corporations and are subject to state statutes that govern nonprofit corporations. These nonprofit corporations are always initially controlled by the developer, who usually has exclusive authority to appoint the members of the Homeowners Association's Board of Directors. In almost all cases, however, there comes a point in time when control of the Homeowners Association transitions from the developer to the homeowners in the community, from which point the members of the Homeowners Association's Board of Directors are elected from and by the homeowners themselves. According to the Community Associations Institute, more than two million Americans serve as volunteers on Homeowners Associations' Boards of Directors and/or Homeowners Association committees.[3] Often, these volunteer homeowners serving on the Boards of Directors and other various committees are not lawyers or real estate professionals, and for many it is the first time they have served as a Director of any type of corporation.

As Officers and Directors of a nonprofit corporation, these homeowners are charged with certain fiduciary duties and are responsible for carrying out their duties within the formal confines of the Homeowners Association's governing documents and all applicable laws. These responsibilities can be significant, and their implementation is governed by formal procedures that may be both new and confusing to these homeowners. With the ever-increasing number of laws governing Homeowners Associations, and the litigiousness of our society, most Homeowners Associations have found it necessary to retain legal counsel to keep them abreast of changes in the law, advise them on interpretation of their governing documents, guide them in compliance with requisite procedures and operations of nonprofit corporations, and assist them in collection of assessments and enforcement of restrictive covenants in their communities.

---

3 *See* http://www.cairf.org/research/factbook/2014_statistical_review.pdf.

The laws governing Homeowners Associations differ significantly from state to state. Despite the existence of numerous publications on laws generally applicable to Homeowners Associations, there was no publication on the laws applicable to Homeowners Associations in the State of Texas until the publication of the first edition of this book in 2010. This book is written specifically for Texas homeowners living in Association-Governed Communities and individuals serving on a Board of Directors or a committee of a Texas Homeowners Association. It is organized by topic and written in plain English, as opposed to the often confusing legalese of most statutes and legal case law, and it is intended to serve as a comprehensive reference handbook on the laws applicable to Texas Homeowners Associations and as an inexpensive resource to guide Officers, Directors, and homeowners as to their rights, duties, and responsibilities.

This book seeks to accomplish such endeavor by providing a "plain English" explanation of the legal requirements for administration and operation of a Texas Homeowners Association, including Homeowners Associations that are incorporated as nonprofit corporations and those that are unincorporated nonprofit associations. This book also seeks to provide answers to the most common questions that arise from time to time in the operation of an Association-Governed Community and includes sample form documents for use by Texas Homeowners Associations and homeowners. Finally, this book includes a detailed table of contents and a subject index to assist readers in quickly identifying applicable topics by key words or subject matter.

The main commentary on each topic is written in a manner that tries to avoid legalese and unnecessary legal terms, which are often confusing or difficult to decipher, when possible. In such effort, many statutes and case law opinions are summarized or reworded so as to clarify them or make them easier to understand, and, in some cases, superfluous or inapplicable statutory provisions have been omitted. Although not intended, it is possible that in trying to explain the applicable laws and concepts in a simpler manner, some nuances of these statutes that may be important in certain limited circumstances may be lost in translation. For such reasons, the author has included footnotes with citations to the specific statutes and case law being discussed in each chapter so that readers may go directly to the source and read the actual statute or case law opinions themselves. A table of authorities is also included in the appendix that lists all of the statutes and case law opinions cited in this book.

In addition, while the author has gone to great lengths to avoid use of legalese in this book, the use of commonly used terms of art in the context of Texas Homeowners Association law could not be avoided and are used frequently throughout this book. These commonly used terms of art have special understood meanings in the context of Texas Homeowners Association law and are often used by or incorporated into the governing documents of Texas Homeowners Associations. For these reasons, these commonly used terms of art have been incorporated into this book, as well, and are identified by the use of initial capital letters, as in the case of "Homeowners Association," or all capital letters, as in the case of the abbreviation "HOA." All such commonly used terms of art have been included in the Glossary of Terms in the appendix of this book. If a reader is unfamiliar with the meanings of these terms, he or she is encouraged to review the Glossary of Terms.

Finally, it is the author's hope that this book will assist homeowners serving in leadership roles within Texas Homeowners Associations in understanding their duties and responsibilities and the regulatory authority that governs their Homeowners Association by simplifying and clarifying the formal and technical elements of association operation under Texas and federal laws and explaining them in plain English so that it does not take an attorney to interpret it. Despite such intentions, many functions of Texas Homeowners Associations will be regulated by each Homeowners Association's particular governing documents, which can differ significantly from community to community. For such reason, this book is not intended to be a substitute for legal advice from an attorney and should not be relied upon in lieu of seeking legal advice from an attorney familiar with the laws applicable to Texas Homeowners Associations who has reviewed the governing documents applicable to a particular community. Notwithstanding, this book will serve as a useful guidebook and an exhaustive reference manual on the laws applicable to Texas Homeowners Associations and enable homeowners to better understand and interpret the governing documents applicable to their community and aid in the administration and operation of the Homeowners Association in which they serve.

CHAPTER 1 MASTER-PLANNED COMMUNITIES AND CONDOMINIUMS

CHAPTER 1 MASTER-PLANNED COMMUNITIES AND CONDOMINIUMS

1.1 The Association-Governed Community Concept

"Association-Governed Communities" can trace their roots back to late eighteenth-century England, when London instituted the practice of maintaining private parks with funds provided through subscriptions from or trusts composed of adjacent landowners.[1] And it wasn't long for the concept to travel over to America, take root, and begin to evolve.

The earliest example of the Association-Governed Community concept in America dates back to 1831 when Samuel Ruggles, a New York developer, established Gramercy Park, a private "London-style" garden square, which he conveyed to a trust for the benefit of adjacent lot owners who were charged with its maintenance and upkeep.[2] It did not take long, however, for this concept to evolve from creating a trust to maintain amenities to making property owners directly responsible for such maintenance.

In the 1840s, a developer in Boston built a neighborhood that also consisted of a centrally located private park surrounded by private residences, known as Louisburg Square.[3] The developer, though, neglected to make arrangements for the continued maintenance and upkeep of the private park. In response to this oversight, some of the homeowners organized themselves into a "Committee of Proprietors" and undertook the responsibility of maintaining the park themselves.[4] They also drew up a document binding themselves, and any future owners of such properties, to the maintenance of the park.[5]

---

1 Evan McKenzie, Privatopia: Homeowner Associations and the Rise of Residential Private Government 34 (Yale University Press 1994.

2 McKenzie, *supra* note 1.

3 McKenzie, *supra* note 1.

4 McKenzie, *supra* note 1.

5 McKenzie, *supra* note 1.

Today, this voluntary group of Louisburg Square homeowners is considered to be the founding fathers of our contemporary residential Homeowners Associations, and the document they created is thought to be a precursor to our modern restrictive covenants.[6]

In 1869, a Chicago real estate developer hired Frederick Law Olmsted and Calvert Vaux, the designers of New York City's Central Park, to create an exclusive development, called Riverside, just outside the city of Chicago. The idea was to create the illusion of a rural paradise within just a few minutes' train ride of the city, and Olmsted and Vaux's plan called for picturesque winding streets, minimum lot sizes, and setbacks from the roadway. The developer of Riverside intended to use restrictive covenants to provide for maintenance of the landscaping and parks, but on the advice of Olmsted and Vaux, the developer expanded the use of restrictive covenants to create detailed zoning regulations by writing them into the restrictive covenants applicable to the community. The developer also expanded the use of restrictive covenants to limit the rights of the homeowners' use of their property. For example, in order to maintain the illusion of wide-open spaces, the restrictive covenants applicable to the Riverside community prohibited the building of fences; and, to ensure exclusiveness of the development, the restrictive covenants also prohibited homeowners from leasing their property.

The concept of Association-Governed Communities was further expanded in the early 1900s. Beginning in 1910, a real estate developer named Jesse Clyde Nichols began to create a series of master-planned communities in Kansas City, Missouri.[7] Like the developers of the previous century, Nichols used restrictive covenants to provide maintenance of common areas, restrict ownership, control planning, and exercise some control over the homeowners' use of their property.[8] As a means of enforcing the

---

6 McKenzie, *supra* note 1.

7 McKenzie, *supra* note 1, at 39.

8 McKenzie, *supra* note 1, at 39–40.

restrictive covenants, Nichols also organized an association of the homeowners.[9] Up until this time, membership in these organizations was voluntary, and their activities were confined to maintenance and beautification of parks and other amenities.[10] In 1914, Nichols created the Mission Hills development, which for the first time made membership in the association of homeowners mandatory and thus started the trend of "mandatory membership" of homeowners in Association-Governed Communities.[11]

The United States government was also instrumental in furthering the expansion of Association-Governed Communities during the twentieth century. In 1934, the United States Congress created the Federal Housing Administration (more commonly known as the "FHA"), which, in conjunction with its mortgagee guarantee program, encouraged real estate developers to incorporate restrictive covenants and mandatory membership associations of homeowners within their developments.[12] In 1944, the United States Congress also created the Veterans Administration, which adopted similar recommendations for real estate developers.[13]

In the mid-twentieth century, the concept of Association-Governed Communities continued to evolve with the birth of a new type of common-interest development in the form of condominium ownership of real property. In 1951, the United States territory of Puerto Rico adopted the first condominium statute within the United States and its territories.[14] The Puerto Rican statute called for the creation of a council of owners to administer and maintain common areas that were to be owned in-common by all of the

---

9 McKenzie, *supra* note 1, at 39–40.

10 McKenzie, *supra* note 1, at 39–40.

11 McKenzie, *supra* note 1, at 40.

12 McKenzie, *supra* note 1, at 63–67.

13 Robert H. Nelson, Private Neighborhoods and the Transformation of Local Government 35–36 (Urban Institute Press 2005).

14 McKenzie, *supra* note 1, at 95; Nelson, *supra* note 13, at 40.

property owners in the Common-Interest Development. Thereafter, in 1962, the United States Congress enacted the National Housing Act, which made FHA mortgage insurance available to condominium unit owners.[15] Following that, the FHA published a model condominium statute, and by 1967, almost every state had adopted a legal framework for condominium ownership of real property.[16]

In the 1970s, two major events occurred that also contributed to the proliferation of Association-Governed Communities and further transformed the way real estate developers utilized Homeowners Associations in real estate developments. In 1978, voters in California approved Proposition 13, which limited the ability of local governments to raise property taxes to cover the costs created by new real estate developments.[17] As a consequence, local governments in California began to require that certain local services they previously provided be instead provided by private property owners associations.[18] This created a trend of "load shedding" by municipalities, which eventually spread to all of the other states.[19]

The second event was the enactment of the Clean Water Act of 1977 by the United States Congress. This law required all new real estate developments to detain storm water so that the flow of water runoff to adjoining properties was no greater than the pre-development rate of storm water runoff. As a result, nearly all newly created residential real estate developments were required to have detention or retention areas to hold excess storm water until it could be released at the pre-development flow level. Since these detention areas served multiple residences, they were almost always designated as a common area for the development, which resulted in the need for a Homeowners

[15] McKenzie, *supra* note 1, at 95.

[16] McKenzie, *supra* note 1, at 95–96.

[17] Nelson, *supra* note 13, at 41.

[18] Nelson, *supra* note 13, at 41.

[19] Nelson, *supra* note 13, at 41.

Association to own and maintain it. As real estate developers became forced to establish Homeowners Associations to maintain these federally mandated common areas, they began to use them to also provide other amenities home buyers desired so as to make their developments more marketable.

Nowadays, Homeowners Associations often deliver services that were once within the exclusive province of local governments, including trash pickup, street paving, and lighting, to name but a few. This transfer, or privatization, of services has become commonplace as the demand for housing has outpaced the ability of many local governments to provide services. In addition, many Homeowners Associations maintain swimming pools, tennis courts, playgrounds, and other amenities that most Americans cannot afford on their own, as well as provide security, social activities, clubhouses, walking trails, and more for the benefit of their homeowners and residents.

As real estate developers were creating Association-Governed Communities, they began to impose more and more rules upon the properties that would ensure a degree of architectural conformity in the exterior appearance of the homes in the community and restrict certain uses of property that might negatively affect the value of property in the community and homeowners' peaceful enjoyment of their homes. Some common examples of these types of rules include: restrictions on use of the property for residential purposes only; restrictions on the height, size, and placement of structures on lots; and rules requiring homeowners to maintain their yards, fences, and homes in good condition. These rules, which are generally referred to as "Restrictive Covenants," but are also synonymously known as "land-use restrictions," "deed restrictions," "restrictions," and/or "covenants," are usually found within a document entitled "Declaration of Covenants, Conditions, and Restrictions," which is generally referred to as simply the "Declaration" or "CC&Rs." The Declaration constitutes a private contractual agreement, which the real estate developer imposes upon the property in the development by recording the Declaration in the local property records prior to selling any of the property in the development to home buyers. The Declaration "runs with the land," which means subsequent purchasers become contractually obligated to comply with the Declaration upon purchasing any of the property in the development subject to the Declaration. In addition to imposing Restrictive Covenants upon homeowners' properties, the Declaration also creates the Homeowners Association, which is often charged with the duty to maintain the common areas of the community and to enforce the provisions of the Declaration against homeowners who fail to follow them.

In order for a Homeowners Association to perform such obligations and provide such services, it must have a source of income. As a result, almost all Declarations require each member of a Homeowners Association to pay dues (generally referred to as "Assessments") that are used to cover the expenses of the community at large. Some examples of these common expenses are: landscaping for the common areas; maintenance and upkeep of community amenities; insurance for commonly owned structures and areas; enforcement of Restrictive Covenants; mailing costs for newsletters and other correspondence; employment of a management company or on-site manager; security personnel and gate maintenance; and any other item delineated in the governing documents for the Homeowners Association or agreed to by its Board of Directors. The Declaration also commonly vests the Homeowners Association with tools to collect unpaid assessments and, in a lot of cases, the ability to foreclose a lien against a delinquent homeowner's property for nonpayment of Assessments.

In many ways, Homeowners Associations have become private governmental microcosms with many of the same or similar duties and powers of a local governmental entity. Homeowners Associations have the authority to enforce Restrictive Covenants that regulate construction of homes and use of property (much in the same way as zoning ordinances do), to maintain parks, amenities, and other community improvements for the benefit of its homeowners, and to tax its homeowners by levying Assessments. And in many ways, Homeowners Associations have come to be perceived by homeowners as government-like in their bureaucracy and procedures. In the best Association-Governed Communities, however, Homeowners Associations offer a real sense of community by providing important and valuable services to their homeowners and maintaining a safe, well-maintained living environment that preserves the nature of the community and protects the value of the homeowners' homes.

1.2 Common-Interest Developments in Texas

There are two basic forms of Common-Interest Developments under Texas law: "Subdivision Developments" and "Condominium Developments." These types of developments are distinguished by the type of real property ownership contemplated by the development.

Subdivision Developments are Common-Interest Developments that consist of parcels of land, usually called "Lots," that are subject to separate conveyance and exclusive ownership. In the context of real estate development, the term "Subdivision Development" generally refers to the division of a tract or parcel of land into two or more Lots or other divisions of land for the purpose, whether immediate or future, of sale or of building development in which each new Lot or divided piece of land is subject to separate fee simple ownership. In most cases, Subdivision Developments arise where a real estate developer owns a large tract of land and divides the tract into separate, individually owned Lots by filing a "Subdivision Plat" with the local governmental entity, which must then approve it. The Subdivision Plat will typically divide the parcel of land into: (1) residential Lots that are to be separately sold to and owned by homeowners; (2) "Common Areas" that are to be owned and maintained by a Homeowners Association for the benefit of the Lot Owners; and (3) streets to provide homeowners access to their Lots. The key distinguishing element of this type of development is that each Lot is a separate, exclusively owned parcel of real property, and the Common Areas of land are owned by the Homeowners Association for the benefit of the Lot Owners.

Condominium Developments are a unique form of real property ownership created by statutory law. A Condominium Development differs significantly from a Subdivision Development in that a Condominium Development generally involves a single tract or Lot, specific portions of which are designated for separate and exclusive ownership, called "Units," and the remaining portions of which are owned in common by the owners of the separately owned Units, collectively called "Common Elements." The most common example of a Condominium Development is an apartment building, where the interior of the individual apartments are exclusively owned by each respective Unit Owner, but the Lot on which the building is located, the exterior of the building, and all hallways, stairs, and elevators are owned by all of the Unit Owners in common with each other. Condominium Developments, however, come in all shapes and sizes and can include developments with detached, single-family homes that look and feel like traditional Subdivision Developments. The key distinguishing element of this type of development is that it consists of only one Lot or tract, in which specific portions are designated as separately and exclusively owned Units, and all other portions of which are Common Elements that are owned by the Unit Owners in common with each other, not by the Homeowners Association.[20]

The laws applicable to Subdivision and Condominium Developments differ significantly, and for this reason, it is important to determine what type of development a particular Common-Interest Development is. Unfortunately, it is not always very easy to determine what kind of development a particular community is by looking solely at its physical characteristics. To add to the confusion, Subdivision and Condominium Developments can go by many different common descriptions or monikers, depending on the perception the developer is trying to create, including master-planned communities,

[20] *See* Tex. Prop. Code § 82.003(a)(8). Real property is a Condominium Development only if one or more of the Common Elements are directly owned in undivided interests by the Unit Owners. Tex. Prop. Code § 82.003(a)(8). If all of the Common Elements are owned by a legal entity separate from the Unit Owners, even if the separate legal entity is owned by the Unit Owners (such as a Homeowners Association), then the real property is not a Condominium Development. Tex. Prop. Code § 82.003(a)(8).

planned unit developments, townhome communities, garden-home communities, estate communities, ranch communities, etc. In addition, Condominium Developments don't always call themselves condominiums or include the term "condominium" in the name of the community. The easiest way to determine whether a particular development is a Subdivision Development or a Condominium Development is to look at the legal description of the real property that is separately owned, which can be found within an owner's deed. If the legal description for the separately owned real property identifies it as a specific "Lot" of a platted subdivision or a tract of land described by metes and bounds, then it is a Subdivision Development. On the other hand, if the legal description of the separately owned real property describes it as a "Unit" or "Apartment," along with a proportionate ownership share or percentage in additional portions of a Lot or tract of land, then it is a Condominium Development.

1.3 Homeowners Associations in Texas

A "Property Owners Association" or "Homeowners Association" is an organization made up of owners of Lots or Units in a Common-Interest Development, which is generally vested with the management and maintenance of the community and its amenities or commonly owned property.[21] The term Homeowners Association (or "HOA") is commonly used interchangeably to refer to associations of homeowners in both residential Subdivision Developments and Condominium Developments in Texas. However, because there are many laws that apply differently to residential Subdivision and Condominium Developments, it is important to be specific in the terms used to refer to a Homeowners Association that governs a residential Subdivision Development versus a Homeowners Association that governs a residential Condominium Development. A "Condominium Association" is the proper term used in Texas to refer to a Homeowners

---

[21] The term Property Owners Association typically includes associations of Lot Owners or Unit Owners in both residential and non-residential Common-Interest Developments; whereas the term Homeowners Association typically refers exclusively to an association of Lot Owners or Unit Owners in residential Common-Interest Developments.

Association that governs a Condominium Development. Most people, however, still generally refer to Homeowner Associations governing Condominium Developments as Homeowners Associations, or simply HOAs. While it is not necessarily inaccurate to refer to a Condominium Association as a Homeowners Association or an HOA, it would be incorrect to refer to a Homeowners Association governing a residential Subdivision Development as a Condominium Association.

Unlike Condominium Associations, there is no single term designated under Texas law for Homeowners Associations that govern residential Subdivision Developments.[22] The Texas Property Code uses the term "Property Owners Association" in Chapters 202 and 205 to describe any incorporated or unincorporated association owned by, or whose members consist primarily of, the owners of property covered by a dedicatory instrument through which the property owners or a board of directors (or similar governing body) manage or regulate a residential Subdivision Development, Condominium Development, or a similar planned development. The Texas Property Code, however, uses the term "Community Association" in Chapter 206 instead of "Property Owners Association" to describe any incorporated Homeowners Association created to enforce restrictive covenants, which would necessarily include Homeowners Associations overseeing both residential Subdivision and Condominium Developments.[23] To add to the inconsistencies, the Texas Property Code uses the term "Property Owners Association" again in Chapter 209, but it defines such term as any incorporated or unincorporated association whose membership primarily consists of owners of Lots in a residential Subdivision Development that is designated as the representative of such Lot Owners and manages or regulates such residential Subdivision Division for the benefit of

[22] In fact, Chapter 204 of the Texas Property Code recognizes that a Property Owners Association overseeing a Subdivision Development may also be referred to as a "homeowners association," "community association," "civic association," "civic club," "association," "committee," or other similar name. Tex. Prop. Code § 204.004(a).

[23] Tex. Prop. Code §§ 202.001(2), 206.001(1).

such Lot Owners.[24] Accordingly, under Chapter 209, the term "Property Owners Association" expressly excludes Condominium Associations from the scope of such term (even though the scope of such term under Chapters 202 and 205 expressly includes Condominium Associations).[25]

As a result of the Texas Property Code's inconsistent use of terms to describe Homeowners Associations, most Texas attorneys practicing in this area of the law generally refer to any of these types of Homeowner Associations interchangeably as a "Property Owners Association" (or "POA") or simply as a "Community Association." These terms are typically used to describe any organization of property owners (regardless of whether it is a Condominium Association or another type of Property Owners Association) that is a "mandatory membership organization" made up of Unit or Lot Owners who become obligated to such membership as a result of their ownership of such Unit or Lot.

1.4 Statutory Laws and Governing Documents that Apply to Texas Homeowners Associations and the Hierarchy of such Authorities

Understanding the legal framework in which Texas Homeowners Associations exist is fundamental to proper leadership of them. Homeowners Associations are private organizations created by written agreement and are made up of homeowners in a residential community who become mandatory members of such organization upon acquiring ownership of their Lot or Unit. These written agreements, which create the Homeowners Association, will also generally establish the scope of the Homeowners Association's powers and duties, as well as specify the procedures for its administration and management. Such written agreements include: (1) the Declaration of Covenants,

---

24 Tex. Prop. Code § 209.002(7). Chapter 204 of the Texas Property Code also uses the term "Property Owners Association" to refer to an association that is a designated representative of owners of property in a Subdivision Development whose membership consists of the Lot Owners within such Subdivision Development. Tex. Prop. Code § 204.004(a).

25 Tex. Prop. Code § 209.002(7).

Conditions, and Restrictions for the development; (2) the Homeowners Association's "Certificate of Formation" (formerly known as "Articles of Incorporation"); (3) the Homeowners Association's "Bylaws"; and (4) any rules and regulations promulgated by the Homeowners Association under authority established by the Declaration of Covenants, Conditions, and Restrictions (generally referred to simply as the "Association Rules"). Such written agreements govern the operation and actions of a Homeowners Association and are collectively referred to as a Homeowners Association's "Governing Documents."[26] In addition to such Governing Documents, Texas Homeowners Associations are also governed by various federal, state, and local statutes and ordinances, which in some cases override any inconsistent provisions in a Homeowners Association's Governing Documents.

All of these authorities govern the day-to-day operations of a Texas Homeowners Association and can be "ranked" in order of hierarchical authority (with higher-ranking authorities overruling conflicting provisions found in lower-ranking authorities). The highest—most powerful—category affecting Texas Homeowners Associations is public law, followed by the Homeowners Association's Governing Documents.

---

[26] A Homeowners Association's Governing Documents are also referred to as its "Dedicatory Instruments" under the Texas Property Code, which defines a Dedicatory Instrument as each document governing the establishment, maintenance, or operation of a residential Subdivision Development, Condominium Development, or other type of similar planned development, and includes a Declaration or similar instrument subjecting real property to: (1) Restrictive Covenants, Bylaws, or similar instruments governing the administration or operation of a Homeowners Association; (2) properly adopted rules and regulations of the Homeowners Association; and/or (3) all lawful amendments to such Restrictive Covenants, Bylaws, instruments, rules, or regulations. Tex. Prop. Code §§ 82.003(11-a); 202.001(1). It's important to note that while Section 202.001 defines a Dedicatory Instrument as a Declaration or similar instrument subjecting real property to "Bylaws," one Texas appellate court has held that a Homeowners Association's Bylaws, itself, may not constitute a Dedicatory Instrument of the Homeowners Association. *See Storck v. Tres Lagos Property Owners Ass'n, Inc.*, 442 S.W.3d 730, 738 (Tex. App.—Texarkana 2014, pet. Denied).

1.4.1 Hierarchy of Public Law Applicable to Texas Homeowners Associations

Public law consists of all federal, state, and local statutes and ordinances enacted by federal, state, and local governmental entities. Public law generally trumps private contractual agreements, such as those constituting the Governing Documents of a Texas Homeowners Association; and, as public laws change, certain provisions of a Homeowners Association's Governing Documents may be rendered inapplicable or unenforceable.

The categories of public law have their own hierarchy among themselves, starting with federal law (the highest authority), followed by state law, and then local ordinance (the lowest authority). Examples of federal laws that govern Texas Homeowners Associations (and override inconsistent or different provisions of a Homeowners Association's Governing Documents) include the Fair Housing Act, Americans with Disabilities Act of 1990 (more commonly referred to as the "ADA"), Freedom to Display the American Flag Act, and the Federal Communications Commission's Over-the-Air Reception Devices Rule (generally referred to as the "OTARD Rule"), as well as laws governing bankruptcy and federal income tax matters.

After federal law, the next-highest authority applicable to Texas Homeowners Associations is state law. There is a significant number of state laws applicable to Texas Homeowners Associations that have a direct and indirect impact on their operations. These state laws include: (1) the Texas Nonprofit Corporation Law; (2) the Texas Business Organizations Code; (3) Chapters 5, 81, 82, and 201 through 213 of the Texas Property Code; (4) Chapters 551 and 552 of the Texas Government Code; (5) the Texas Community Homes for Disabled Persons Location Act and related provisions in the Texas Health and Safety Code; and (6) Texas's own version of the Fair Debt Collections Practices Act and Fair Housing Act. Finally, Texas Homeowners Associations are also subject to the ordinances, codes, and regulations of the cities and counties in which they are located. Some cities enact ordinances, such as fair housing ordinances, that have counterparts in state or federal law.

1.4.2 Hierarchy of Governing Documents Applicable to Texas Homeowners Associations

The next-highest authority on the hierarchy ladder is the Homeowners Association's Governing Documents, which, like public law, also have a hierarchy of their own. Of the Homeowners Association's Governing Documents, publicly recorded Subdivision Plats creating a Subdivision Development and Condominium Plats and Plans attached to a Condominium Declaration are of the highest authority. These documents establish the location of Lots, Common Areas, and Improvements. In the case of Condominium Developments, they also identify the location of Condominium Units and the Common Elements. These documents can also include easements imposed on Lots and Units, as well as development restrictions, that reign supreme over anything inconsistent in the Homeowners Association's other Governing Documents.

The second type of Governing Document, and the next-highest in authority, is a Homeowners Association's Declaration of Covenants, Conditions, and Restrictions. This is a private agreement, most commonly created by a real estate developer, that contains contractual obligations and restrictions related to the ownership and use of Lots or Units in a real estate development (called "Restrictive Covenants"). Such private agreement, and the Restrictive Covenants contained therein, are imposed upon such Lots or Units by the recording of such private agreement in the Official Public Records of the county in which the development is located prior to the developer selling any of the Lots or Units to home buyers. These private agreements usually take the form of a document entitled "Declaration of Covenants, Conditions, and Restrictions," or some similar variation thereof, and are synonymously referred to by homeowners as the "declaration," "CC&Rs," "land-use restrictions," "restrictive covenants," "deed restrictions,"

"restrictions," and/or "covenants." For simplicity, all such private agreements shall be referred to generically as the "Declaration" for the remainder of this book.

In simple terms, the Declaration constitutes a private contractual agreement between the owners of all properties subject to such Declaration that each such owner is bound by and obligated to comply with. This can sometimes be a surprise to homeowners when they learn that they are subject to a contractual agreement that regulates the use of their home, especially since they did not sign such contract and may not have even been aware of the existence of such agreement at the time they purchased their home. However, because the Declaration is recorded in the Official Public Records of the county where the development is located and "runs with the land," each homeowner is presumed to have notice of the Declaration applicable to his or her property and becomes obligated to comply with the contractual obligations of the Declaration simply upon acquiring ownership of his or her property, whether or not he or she is actually aware of the Declaration.

The Declaration is generally the most important document governing a Texas Homeowners Association. The Declaration establishes the Homeowners Association as a private organization of homeowners in the applicable development and vests the Homeowners Association with certain powers and duties over the applicable community, as well as establishes Restrictive Covenants that regulate homeowners' use of their property. To the extent of any conflicts between the provisions of a Declaration and the provisions of another Governing Document of a Homeowners Association, the provisions of the Declaration control.

If a Texas Homeowners Association is incorporated as a nonprofit corporation, then the next-highest authority of its Governing Documents after the Declaration is the Homeowners Association's Certificate of Formation (or Articles of Incorporation), followed by its Bylaws.[27] Under the Texas Nonprofit Corporation Law, a nonprofit corporation is formed by recording a Certificate of Formation (previously called Articles of Incorporation under the former Texas Non-Profit Corporation Act) in the Office of the Texas Secretary of State.[28] The Certificate of Formation for a Texas nonprofit corporation must include: (1) the name of the nonprofit corporation being formed; (2) a statement indicating such entity is to be a nonprofit corporation; (3) the purpose or purposes for which the nonprofit corporation is being formed; (4) if the nonprofit corporation is to have no members, a statement to that effect; (5) if management of the nonprofit corporation's affairs is to be vested in the nonprofit corporation's members, a statement to that effect; (6) the number of Directors constituting the initial board of Directors and the names and addresses of those Directors or, if the management of the nonprofit corporation is vested solely in the nonprofit corporation's members, a statement to that effect; and (7) if the nonprofit corporation is to be authorized on its winding up to distribute the nonprofit corporation's assets in a manner other than as provided by the Texas Nonprofit Corporation Law, a statement describing the manner of distribution.[29]

In addition to the Certificate of Formation, Texas nonprofit corporations are required to have Bylaws.[30] Bylaws are the rules adopted by a nonprofit corporation to provide for its management and administration.[31] In general, Bylaws will contain provisions for the regulation and management of the affairs of the nonprofit corporation

---

27 All Texas Homeowners Associations overseeing Condominium Developments that were created on or after January 1, 1994, are required to be organized as either for-profit or nonprofit corporations. Tex. Prop. Code § 82.101. While Condominium Associations that were created prior to January 1, 1994, and Subdivision Associations are not required to be incorporated, in practice most are incorporated as nonprofit corporations.

28 Tex. Bus. Org. Code §§ 1.002(6), 3.001(a) and 4.001.

29 Tex. Bus. Org. Code §§ 3.005(a), 3.009. Such requirements are substantially similar to the required provisions of a nonprofit corporation's Articles of Incorporation under the former Texas Non-Profit Corporation Act. Tex. Rev. Civ. Stat. Ann. art. 1396-3.02.

30 Tex. Bus. Org. Code § 22.102(a). Bylaws are required to be adopted by a nonprofit corporation's Board of Directors or, if the management of the corporation is vested in the nonprofit corporation's members, by the members of the nonprofit corporation. Tex. Bus. Org. Code § 22.102(a).

31 Tex. Bus. Org. Code § 22.001(2).

that are consistent with Texas law and the nonprofit corporation's Certificate of Formation.[32]

In general, the provisions of the Certificate of Formation (or Articles of Incorporation) of a nonprofit corporation trump any provisions of its Bylaws that are inconsistent with a provision of the Certificate of Formation (or Articles of Incorporation), except for one limited circumstance.[33] An amendment to a nonprofit corporation's Bylaws that changes the number of Director positions on the Board of Directors of the nonprofit corporation from the number of Directors stated in its Certificate of Formation will control over the number of Directors stated in the Certificate of Formation, unless the Certificate of Formation provides that a change in the number of Directors may be made only by amendment to the Certificate of Formation.[34] In other words, a nonprofit corporation can change the number of Directors on the Board of Directors by amending the Bylaws instead of the Certificate of Formation, unless the Certificate of Formation states that the number of Directors may only be changed by amendment of the Certificate of Formation.

Finally, the lowest hierarchical Governing Documents of a Texas Homeowners Association are its Association Rules. It is very common for a Declaration to authorize a Homeowners Association to adopt rules and regulations for the enforcement or implementation of the Declaration's provisions. Association Rules include any guidelines, rules, policies, and/or practices the Homeowners Association adopts under the authority granted to it by the Declaration. Association Rules generally may be promulgated, modified, and/or rescinded at the discretion of the Homeowners Association's Board of

---

32 Tex. Bus. Org. Code § 22.102(b). The contents of a nonprofit corporation's Bylaws can vary, but they typically include: (1) provisions concerning the number of Directors and Officers for the nonprofit corporation and their terms of office; (2) the manner of electing and removing Directors and Officers; (3) any qualifications to serve as a Director or Officer; (4) the time, place, and procedures for calling a meeting of the Board of Directors or members of the nonprofit corporation; and (5) the procedures for amending the Bylaws.

33 Tex. Bus. Org. Code § 22.103(a).

34 Tex. Bus. Org. Code § 22.103(b).

Directors; however, Association Rules may not conflict with the Declaration and may not impose restrictions upon homeowners that are above and beyond those imposed by the Declaration.

1.4.3 Exceptions to the General Rules of Hierarchical Authority and Other Rules Concerning the Application of Public Law and Governing Documents to Homeowners Associations

There are some exceptions to the hierarchy of authorities and other general rules that readers should be aware of. First, while there are many statutory laws regulating Texas Homeowners Associations, some of these statutes may not apply to a particular community or may not override conflicting provisions in a particular community's Governing Documents. For example, Chapters 201, 203, 204, 205, 206, 208, 210, 211, and 212 of the Texas Property Code and Chapters 551 and 552 of the Texas Government Code only apply to Texas Homeowners Associations in a few select counties within the State of Texas.

Second, different versions of certain statutes apply differently to Homeowners Associations depending on when the Homeowners Association was established. For instance, the Texas Condominium Act only applies to Condominium Developments created prior to January 1, 1994; while, the Texas Uniform Condominium Act applies to Condominium Developments created on or after January 1, 1994, and Condominium Developments created prior to January 1, 1994, whose Declaration states or has been amended to state that it is to be governed by the Texas Uniform Condominium Act.[35] To make matters more confusing, there are certain provisions of the Texas Uniform Condominium Act that apply to all Condominium Developments, regardless of when they were created.[36] Thus, depending on when a Texas Condominium Development was created, it may be governed solely by the Texas Uniform Condominium Act or it may be

[35] Tex. Prop. Code §§ 81.0011; 82.002.

[36] Tex. Prop. Code § 82.002(c).

governed by the Texas Condominium Act plus certain select provisions of the Texas Uniform Condominium Act.

Third, while state law ranks higher in authority than a Homeowners Association's Governing Documents, there are many provisions of the Texas Nonprofit Corporation Law that serve as "gap-fillers," or default rules, that apply only in the event the Homeowners Association's Certificate of Formation (or Articles of Incorporation) or Bylaws don't address an applicable issue. For such reasons, there are many instances in this book where an explanation of a statute or rule is predicated with a statement similar to: "unless otherwise provided in the Homeowners Association's Declaration, Articles of Incorporation, or Bylaws . . ." In such instances, the applicable statute or rule is a default rule and is not applicable if the substance of such statute or rule is already addressed by a Homeowners Association's Governing Documents, in which case the provision of the Governing Documents would take precedence over the default rule in the statute.[37] Accordingly, it is important to always read and understand both the Texas Nonprofit Corporation Law and a particular Homeowners Association's Governing Documents in order to determine whether a specific statutory law preempts its Governing Documents, applies in addition to its Governing Documents, or is subordinate to its Governing Documents.

Finally, it is important to make sure the statutory law being reviewed is current. Keep in mind that statutory law is ever-changing. It is subject to being rescinded, modified, and/or expanded during any legislative and congressional session. The Texas Legislature convenes once every two years, while the United States Congress is in session throughout most of each year. During a legislative or congressional session, the Texas Legislature or United States Congress may amend a particular statutory law, and in some

[37] There are also many provisions of the Nonprofit Corporation Law that apply in addition to any provisions in a Homeowners Association's Certificate of Formation or Bylaws. In such instances, an explanation of a statute or rule may be predicated with a statement similar to: "in addition to any provision in the Homeowners Association's Declaration, Articles of Incorporation, or Bylaws . . ."

cases they have been known to completely rewrite an entire statutory scheme. For example, the statutory laws governing nonprofit corporations were codified at Article 1396 of the Texas Revised Civil Statutes and were known as the "Texas Non-Profit Corporation Act." In 2005, however, the Texas Legislature enacted the Texas Business Organizations Code and recodified the statutory laws governing nonprofit corporations at Chapter 22 of such Code.[38] Chapter 22 of the Texas Business Organizations Code is known as the "Texas Nonprofit Corporation Law," and while it is substantially similar to the Texas Non-Profit Corporation Act, there are some distinct differences. In addition, in 2011, the Texas Legislature enacted landscape-changing reforms to the laws governing all Texas Subdivision Associations. Among the statutory reforms enacted by the Texas Legislature are laws that impose new comprehensive procedures and requirements concerning: (1) calling and conducting meetings of a Subdivision Association's Board of Directors and its membership, including new rules related to casting and counting ballots and election of members to the Board of Directors; (2) inspection and copying of a Subdivision Association's records; (3) collection of assessments; and (4) enforcement of Restrictive Covenants.

As with the earlier editions of this book, it is important to note that the third edition of this book will discuss and cite many statutory laws applying to Texas Homeowners Associations as those statutes exist at the time this book goes to print. Such laws are subject to change and at any given point may be substantially modified and/or rescinded. For this reason, it is very important that the actual statutes cited in this book be reviewed to ensure that they have not been modified before relying upon the information presented in the following chapters of this book.[39]

---

[38] The Texas Nonprofit Corporation Law was initially made applicable only to nonprofit corporations formed after January 1, 2006, but it became applicable to all nonprofit corporations, regardless of when they were formed, effective January 1, 2010.

[39] The author of this book intends to publish revised editions of this book as the laws applicable to Texas Homeowners Associations are modified or enlarged; however, there is no guarantee that some statutes may not be modified between publications. Therefore, the author of this book advises readers to check a cited

1.5 Synonymous Terms of Art Applicable to Texas Homeowners Associations and Use of Terms of Art in this Book

Texas Homeowners Associations are governed by many different laws, all of which have particular terms of art that are used in the context of such laws (and which are often incorporated into the Governing Documents of Homeowners Associations governed by such laws). While such statutory terms of art may differ considerably from one statute to another, in many instances, such terms have synonymous meanings in the context of Homeowners Associations and are often used interchangeably in a Homeowners Association's Governing Documents without distinction. For these reasons, in order to properly understand the statutory laws governing Texas Homeowners Associations, it is necessary to have a basic understanding of the terms of art applicable to the respective applicable statutes, as well as an understanding of which of those terms of art have synonymous meanings in the context of Texas Homeowners Associations. In addition, in order to properly summarize and explain the statutory laws governing Texas Homeowners Associations in a nonconfusing manner (and to be able to provide some measure of continuity of terms with synonymous meanings, but also to be able to distinguish such terms in certain contexts when necessary), this book utilizes certain specific terms of art in reference to Homeowners Associations, owners of real property subject to a Homeowners Association, and corporate documents applicable to a Homeowners Association within the context of this book.

1.5.1 Terms of Art Utilized in this Book in Reference to Homeowners Associations

The Texas Property Code uses the terms "Property Owners Associations" and "Community Associations" to describe both Subdivision and Condominium Associations at certain times and to describe only Subdivision Associations at other times, and it uses

statute itself to ensure that it has not been revised before fully relying upon it. Readers may also check the author's website, www.TexasHOALaw.com, where any significant modifications in laws applicable to Texas Homeowners Associations since the last publication of this book will be identified and explained.

the term "Associations" to describe only Condominium Associations. Most laypersons, however, commonly use the term "Homeowners Association" (or "HOA") to refer to an association of homeowners in both residential Subdivision Developments and Condominium Developments in Texas. All of these terms mean practically the same thing and refer to an association of homeowners in an Association-Governed Community that is governed by one or more of the same Declarations.[40]

For simplicity, and because this book is written for homeowners living in a residential Association-Governed Community and/or serving on the Board of Directors and various committees of a Texas Homeowners Association overseeing a residential Common-Interest Development, this book shall refer to all such Property Owners Associations for the remainder of this book by their most common moniker, either "HOAs" or "Homeowners Associations," and shall use such terms when no distinction is to be made between Homeowners Associations governing residential Subdivision and Condominium Developments. However, where it is necessary to distinguish between these two types of associations, this book will refer to Homeowners Associations that govern residential Condominium Developments as "Condominium Associations" and Homeowners Associations that govern residential Subdivision Developments or similar planned developments in which all of the land has been divided into two or more parts as "Subdivision Associations."

In addition, while almost all Texas Homeowners Associations are incorporated as Texas nonprofit corporations and are governed by the Texas Nonprofit Corporation Law, there are some that are not incorporated or are incorporated as for-profit corporations.[41] So as to distinguish between Homeowners Associations that are incorporated as a Texas

---

[40] While it is not necessarily inaccurate to refer to a Condominium Association as a Homeowners Association, it would be incorrect to refer to a Homeowners Association overseeing a residential Subdivision Development as a Condominium Association.

[41] This is certainly true for Condominium Associations governed by the Texas Uniform Condominium Act, which are required to be incorporated as either for-profit or nonprofit corporations. Tex. Prop. Code § 82.101.

nonprofit corporation and those that are not, when referring to Texas Homeowners Associations that are incorporated as nonprofit corporations in the context of applicable provisions of the Texas Nonprofit Corporation Law, such Homeowners Associations shall be referred to as "Nonprofit Corporation HOAs." Similarly, when referring to Texas Homeowners Associations that are not incorporated as a nonprofit corporation, but that would constitute a nonprofit association under the Texas Uniform Unincorporated Nonprofit Association Act, such Homeowners Associations shall be referred to as "Nonprofit Association HOAs."

1.5.2 Terms of Art Utilized in this Book in Reference to Property Owners

As with Homeowners Associations, property owners go by many different terms of art under Texas law and Homeowners Associations' Governing Documents. Under various provisions of the Texas Property Code applicable to Texas Homeowners Associations, homeowners are referred to as "Owners," "Unit Owners," "Lot Owners," and/or "Property Owners." As a result, most Declarations for Texas Homeowners Associations incorporate one or more of the same terms to refer to homeowners within the context of such document. Similarly, the Texas Nonprofit Corporation Law uses the term "Member" to refer to a person who has membership rights in a nonprofit corporation under its Certificate of Formation (or Articles of Incorporation) or Bylaws, and as a result, most Texas Homeowners Associations' Certificates of Formation (or Articles of Incorporation) and Bylaws generally utilize the term "Members" in reference to homeowners who are members of the Homeowners Association within the context of such corporate documents. For such reasons, alternate use of the terms "Member," "Homeowner," "Owner," "Unit Owner," "Lot Owner," and/or "Property Owner" within a Homeowners Association's Governing Documents should generally be treated synonymously as meaning an owner of real property subject to a Declaration that establishes a Homeowners Association and makes such owner a mandatory member of such Homeowners Association.

Again, for simplicity, this book shall refer to all owners of real property in a residential Common-Interest Development as "Homeowners" when no distinction is to be made between owners of Lots in a Subdivision Development or owners of Units in a Condominium Development. However, where necessary to distinguish between these two types of property owners, this book will refer to owners of Lots as "Lot Owners" and owners of Units as "Unit Owners." In addition, so as to distinguish Homeowners who are members of a Homeowners Association that is incorporated as a Texas nonprofit corporation from Homeowners who are members of a Homeowners Association that is not incorporated, the former shall be referred to as "Member-Homeowners."

1.5.3 Terms of Art Utilized in this Book in Reference to Governing Documents

Homeowners Associations are private organizations created by written agreements. The written agreements that create the Homeowners Association will also generally establish the scope of the Homeowners Association's powers and duties, as well as specify the procedures for its administration and management. Such written agreements generally include: (1) the Declaration of Covenants, Conditions, and Restrictions for the development (generally referred to simply as the "Declaration"); (2) the Homeowners Association's "Certificate of Formation" (formerly known as "Articles of Incorporation"); (3) the Homeowners Association's "Bylaws"; and (4) any rules and regulations promulgated by the Homeowners Association under authority established by the Declaration (generally referred to simply as the "Association Rules"). Such written agreements govern the operation and actions of a Homeowners Association and are often collectively referred to informally as a Homeowners Association's "Governing Documents."

A Homeowners Association's Governing Documents are also sometimes referred to more formally as its "Dedicatory Instruments." A Dedicatory Instrument is a statutory term under the Texas Property Code, which defines a Dedicatory Instrument as each document governing the establishment, maintenance, or operation of a residential Subdivision Development, Condominium Development, or other type of similar planned development, and includes a Declaration or similar instrument subjecting real property to: (1) Restrictive Covenants, Bylaws, or similar instruments governing the administration or operation of a Homeowners Association; (2) properly adopted rules and regulations of the Homeowners Association; and/or (3) all lawful amendments to such Restrictive Covenants, Bylaws, instruments, rules, or regulations.[42]

While all Dedicatory Instruments applicable to a Homeowners Association are considered to be included within its Governing Documents, not all of its Governing Documents are Dedicatory Instruments. For example, a Homeowners Association's Certificate of Formation (formerly called Articles of Incorporation) is a Governing Document, but not a Dedicatory Instrument that must be recorded in the Official Public Records of the county in which an applicable Subdivision or Condominium Development is located.[43]

For simplicity, this book will primarily use the term "Governing Documents," as opposed to "Dedicatory Instruments," when referring to the collective written agreements that create and govern a Texas Homeowners Association and the Common-Interest Development that it oversees. However, this book will use the term "Dedicatory Instrument" when such term is expressly incorporated in a statute or when referring collectively to Governing Documents that must be recorded in the Official Public Records of a county in which an applicable Subdivision or Condominium Development is located.

---

[42] Tex. Prop. Code §§ 82.003(11-a); 202.001(1).

[43] In addition, there is some debate as to whether a Homeowners Association's Bylaws constitute a Dedicatory Instrument. While Section 202.001 defines a Dedicatory Instrument as a Declaration or similar instrument subjecting real property to "Bylaws," one Texas appellate court has held that a Homeowners Association's Bylaws, itself, may not constitute a Dedicatory Instrument of the Homeowners Association. *See Storck v. Tres Lagos Property Owners Ass'n, Inc.*, 442 S.W.3d 730, 738 (Tex. App.—Texarkana 2014, pet. Denied).

1.5.4 Terms of Art Utilized in this Book in Reference to Corporate Governing Documents

Finally, as noted earlier, until recently, the statutory law governing nonprofit corporations was codified at Article 1396 of the Texas Revised Civil Statutes and known as the "Texas Non-Profit Corporation Act." In 2005, however, the Texas Legislature enacted the Texas Business Organizations Code and recodified the statutory law governing nonprofit corporations at Chapter 22 of such Code. Chapter 22 of the Texas Business Organizations Code is known as the "Texas Nonprofit Corporation Law" and became applicable to all Texas nonprofit corporations, regardless of when they were formed, effective January 1, 2010. Accordingly, all Texas Homeowners Associations that are incorporated as nonprofit corporations are now governed by the Texas Nonprofit Corporation Law, even if their Governing Documents still reference the former Texas Non-Profit Corporation Law.

While the Texas Nonprofit Corporation Law is substantially similar to the Texas Non-Profit Corporation Act, there are some distinct differences between them. One of the more confusing, but non-substantive, changes is that the document used to form a nonprofit corporation is now called a "Certificate of Formation" under the Texas Nonprofit Corporation Law, instead of "Articles of Incorporation" under the former Texas Non-Profit Corporation Act. Such terms, however, have synonymous meanings under the respective statutes.[44]

Since the Texas Non-Profit Corporation Act has now been completely phased out and replaced by the Texas Nonprofit Corporation Law, this book will cite solely to the Texas Nonprofit Corporation Law and will utilize the terms of art particular to the Texas Nonprofit Corporation Law, with one exception. Because most Homeowner-controlled Nonprofit Corporation HOAs currently existing in Texas were formed prior to January 1,

---

[44] Tex. Bus. Org. Code § 1.006(1).

2006, by the filing of (and are still governed by) a document entitled "Articles of Incorporation" instead of "Certificates of Formation," in order to avoid confusion, this book will refer to both Certificates of Formation and Articles of Incorporation as simply "Articles of Incorporation."

CHAPTER 2 CONDOMINIUM DEVELOPMENTS IN TEXAS

CHAPTER 2 CONDOMINIUM DEVELOPMENTS IN TEXAS

2.1 The Condominium Concept

There are two basic forms of real property ownership under Texas law. The most common manner of real property ownership is "fee simple" ownership. The term "fee" (from the word "fiefdom") refers to legal rights in land, and the term "simple" means unconstrained. Fee simple ownership represents absolute ownership of real property. Under fee simple ownership, the owner of the real property owns 100 percent (100%) of the Lot or legally described tract of land. Fee simple ownership is the absolute and unqualified legal title to real property, including both buildings and land, and is the most common type of real property ownership in the United States. Fee simple ownership of real property is what is generally found in Subdivision Developments.

When two or more people together are the fee simple owners of the same Lot or parcel of land, they are considered to be "tenants in common," who each own separate and distinct undivided interests in the same property. For instance, if two individuals bought a parcel of land together, with each paying 50 percent of the purchase price, each person would own an undivided 50 percent interest in all portions of such parcel of land, and neither would own any portion of such land as his or her separate property.

Condominiumn ownership of real property is a hybrid form of real property ownership that consists of both separate and common ownership of a single parcel of land by multiple owners, which is created and regulated by statute.[1] Legally defined, a "condominium" is a form of real property ownership in which specific portions of the real property are designated for separate ownership or occupancy, and the remaining portions of such real property are designated for common ownership or occupancy solely by the

[1] *Dutcher v. Owens*, 647 S.W.2d 948, 949–50 (Tex. 1983) ("In essence, condominium ownership is the merger of two estates in land into one: the fee simple ownership of an apartment or unit in a condominium project and a tenancy in common with other co-owners in the common elements.").

owners of the separately owned portions.[2] In plain English, a Condominium Development consists of one Lot or tract where specific portions of such Lot or tract are designated as "Units," which are to be separately owned and exclusively occupied by Homeowners or "Unit Owners," and the remaining portions of such Lot or tract that are not designated as Units constitute "Common Elements," which are to be owned in-common by all of the Unit Owners. The result is that each Unit Owner owns 100 percent of the specific portion of the Lot or tract that is designated as his or her specific Unit and a proportionate undivided share of all of the Common Elements in common with all of the other Unit Owners.

There is a common misconception that Condominium Developments refer to only apartment-style buildings in which each apartment or Unit is separately owned. The term "condominium" does not refer to a type of building or construction design. Rather, the term "condominium" refers to a form of ownership of real property. While some Condominium Developments look like apartments, others may look like duplexes, townhomes, or garden homes. Condominium Developments can even resemble traditional Subdivision Developments with detached, single-family homes, which are generally referred to as "Site-Condominiums."

In a Site-Condominium Development, a single tract of land is divided up between Units and Common Elements, but instead of designating particular apartments or areas of a building as the Units, specific portions of the land are designated as the Units in much the same way a Subdivision Development would be platted into separate Lots. In other words, the boundaries of the separately owned Units are defined in the same manner that the physical boundaries of Lots are delineated in a Subdivision plat, and each Unit Owner is permitted to build a detached single-family home within the boundaries of his or her Unit in the same way a Lot Owner might construct a detached home within the boundaries

2 Tex. Prop. Code § 82.003(a)(8).

of his or her Lot. Even though a Site-Condominium Development resembles a Subdivision Development in many ways, there are significant differences between a Site-Condominium Development and a Subdivision Development. From a Homeowner's perspective, however, the most significant difference between a Site-Condominium Development and a Subdivision Development is the effect it has on their ownership of property. Regardless of whether a Condominium Unit's boundaries are defined as the interior of the perimeter walls of the Unit, as in the case of an apartment building–styled Condominium Development, or as a physical line on the ground, as in the case of a Site-Condominium Development, the rights and duties of the Unit Owner are the same, and they are controlled by one of two Texas statutes and the Condominium Declaration recorded in the local property records that creates the Condominium Development. The following subchapters will identify and explain those rights and duties under the Texas Condominium Act and/or the Texas Uniform Condominium Act, as well as explain how such statutes interact with a Condominium Association's Declaration.

2.2 Application of the Texas Condominium Act and/or the Texas Uniform Condominium Act

Condominium Developments in Texas are governed by either the Texas Condominium Act (otherwise known as Chapter 81 of the Texas Property Code) or the Texas Uniform Condominium Act (otherwise known as Chapter 82 of the Texas Property Code). It is extremely important to know which Act is applicable to any given Condominium Development because there are significant variations between the two Acts.

The Texas Condominium Act was enacted in 1983 and is only applicable to Condominium Developments created prior to January 1, 1994.[3] This is because the Texas Legislature enacted the Texas Uniform Condominium Act in 1993, which took effect on

3 Tex. Prop. Code § 81.0011(a).

January 1, 1994, and became binding upon all Texas Condominium Developments created on or after January 1, 1994.[4] In addition, the Texas Uniform Condominium Act was also made binding upon all Condominium Developments created before January 1, 1994, where the owners of Units in the Condominium Development have amended the Condominium Declaration so as to make it subject to Chapter 82 of the Texas Property Code and such amendment is recorded in the Official Public Records of each county in which the Condominium Development is located.[5] In other words, the Texas Condominium Act governs all Texas Condominium Developments created prior to January 1, 1994, that have not elected to be subject to the Texas Uniform Condominium Act, and the Texas Uniform Condominium Act governs all Texas Condominium Developments created on or after January 1, 1994, and Condominium Developments created prior to January 1, 1994, that have a Condominium Declaration or amended Condominium Declaration that expressly makes such Condominium Development subject to the Texas Uniform Condominium Act.

There are some exceptions, however, to this simple dichotomy. All Condominium Associations governed by the Texas Condominium Act are also governed to some extent by the Texas Uniform Condominium Act because certain sections of the Texas Uniform Condominium Act were made applicable to all Condominium Developments, regardless of when they were created.[6] The sections of the Texas Uniform Condominium Act that are also applicable to Condominium Developments subject to the Texas Condominium Act include Sections 82.005 (entitled "Separate Titles & Taxation"); 82.006 (entitled "Applicability of Local Ordinances, Regulations, & Building Codes"); 82.007 (entitled

---

4 Tex. Prop. Code § 82.002(a). The Texas Uniform Condominium Act also applies to all Condominium Developments created prior to January 1, 1994, if its Condominium Declaration or an amendment of its Condominium Declaration that was recorded before January 1, 1994, states that Chapter 82 of the Texas Property Code will apply to the Condominium Development in its entirety on January 1, 1994. Tex. Prop. Code § 82.002(a)(2).

5 Tex. Prop. Code § 82.002(a)(1).

6 Tex. Prop. Code § 82.002(c).

"Condemnation"); 82.053 (entitled "Construction & Validity of Declaration and Bylaws"); 82.054 (entitled "Description of Units"); 82.102(a)(1)–(7), (a)(12)–(21), (f), and (g) (entitled "Powers of Unit Owners' Association"); 82.108 (entitled "Meetings"); 82.111 (entitled "Insurance"); 82.113 (entitled "Association's Lien for Assessments"); 82.114 (entitled "Association Records"); 82.116 (entitled "Management Certificate"); 82.118 (entitled "Service of Process on Unit Owners in Certain Municipalities; Change of Address Required"); 82.157 (entitled "Resale of Unit"); and 82.161 (entitled "Effect of Violations on Rights of Action & Attorneys Fees").[7] Accordingly, even if a Condominium Association is governed by the Texas Condominium Act, certain provisions of the Texas Uniform Condominium Act are still applicable to it.

While in most instances the provisions of the Texas Condominium Act and the Texas Uniform Condominium Act are similar and in many other instances the provisions of the Texas Uniform Condominium Act apply outright to all Condominium Developments (regardless of when they were created), there are still many instances where such Acts differ significantly from each other and the Texas Uniform Condominium Act does not otherwise apply to Condominium Developments created prior to January 1994. To avoid confusion, this book will cite only to the Texas Uniform Condominium Act when its provisions apply to all Texas Condominiums. In all other instances, this book will cite to the relevant provisions of both the Texas Condominium Act and the Texas Uniform Condominium Act, and where such provisions differ, this book will explain the differences.

[7] Tex. Prop. Code § 82.002(c). Such provisions of the Texas Uniform Condominium Act, however, only apply with respect to events and circumstances occurring on or after January 1, 1994, and do not invalidate existing provisions of the Condominium Declaration, Bylaws, or plats or plans of a Condominium Development for which the Condominium Declaration was recorded before January 1, 1994. Tex. Prop. Code § 82.002(c).

2.3 Understanding Condominium Terms of Art

There are many terms of art unique to Condominium Developments or that have unique or specific meanings within the context of Condominium Developments. In addition, these terms of art are often incorporated into the documents that govern Condominium Developments. Thus, it is important to know the basic terminology in order to understand the laws and concepts involved with Condominium Developments. These basic terms are found in the Texas Condominium Act (Chapter 81 of the Texas Property Code) and the Texas Uniform Condominium Act (Chapter 82 of the Texas Property Code).[8] The following is a list of such basic terms, with both their legal definitions and, where necessary, an explanation of such definitions in plain English:

Condominium Development (called simply a "Condominium" under the Texas Uniform Condominium Act) is defined as a form of real property ownership in which portions of the real property are designated for separate ownership or occupancy and the remainder of such real property is designated for common ownership or occupancy solely by the owners of those portions designated for separate ownership or occupancy.[9] In plain English, a Condominium Development is a single Lot or tract of land in which some designated portions are separately and exclusively owned (called "Units") and the remaining portions of which (called "Common Elements") are owned in-common by the owners of the separately owned Units.

---

[8] The definitions prescribed by the Texas Uniform Condominium Act apply to all Condominium Developments in the State of Texas that were created after January 1, 1994, and to those created prior to January 1, 1994, to the extent such definitions do not conflict with the Condominium Declaration of Condominium Developments created prior to January 1, 1994. Tex. Prop. Code § 82.002(c).

[9] Tex. Prop. Code § 82.003(8). The Texas Condominium Act defines the term "Condominium" as a form of real property ownership that combines separate ownership of individual apartments or units with common ownership of other elements. Tex. Prop. Code § 81.002(3).

Leasehold Condominium is defined as a Condominium Development in which all or a portion of the real property is subject to a lease, the expiration or termination of which will terminate the Condominium Development or reduce its size.[10]

Condominium Declaration (called simply a "Declaration" under the Texas Uniform Condominium Act) is defined as a written instrument, however denominated, that creates a Condominium Development and any amendment to that instrument.[11] In plain English, the Condominium Declaration is the document that creates the Condominium Development and is recorded in the Official Public Records of the county in which the Condominium Development is located.

Dedicatory Instrument is defined as each document governing the establishment, maintenance, or operation of a Condominium Regime, and includes a Condominium Declaration or similar written instrument subjecting real property to: (1) restrictive covenants, bylaws, or similar instruments governing the administration or operation of a Condominium Association; (2) rules and regulations properly adopted by the Condominium Association; or (3) all lawful amendments to the covenants, bylaws, instruments, rules, or regulations.[12]

Declarant is defined as a person, or group of persons acting in concert, who (1) as part of a common promotional plan offers to dispose of the person's interest in a Unit not previously disposed of; or (2) reserves or succeeds to any Special Declarant Right.[13] In plain English, the Declarant is the individual or entity acting as the developer of the Condominium Development. The original Declarant will be identified in the original

---

10 Tex. Prop. Code § 82.003(16).

11 Tex. Prop. Code § 82.003(11). The Texas Condominium Act defines the term "Declaration" as the instrument that establishes property under a condominium regime. Tex. Prop. Code § 81.002(5).

12 Tex. Prop. Code § 82.003(11-a).

13 Tex. Prop. Code § 82.003(10).

Condominium Declaration creating the Condominium Development. The rights of the original Declarant, however, can be assigned, and it is not unusual for a subsequent entity to become the Declarant of a Condominium Development after the original Condominium Declaration is recorded.

Special Declarant Rights is defined as rights reserved for the benefit of a Declarant to: (1) complete improvements indicated on Condominium Plats and Plans filed with the Condominium Declaration; (2) exercise any Development Right; (3) make the Condominium Development part of a larger Condominium Development or planned community; (4) maintain sales, management, and leasing offices, signs advertising the Condominium Development, and models; (5) use easements through the Common Elements for the purpose of making improvements within the Condominium Development or within real property that may be added to the Condominium Development; or (6) appoint or remove any Officer or Director of the Condominium Association during any period of Declarant control of the Condominium Association.[14]

Development Rights is defined as a right or combination of rights reserved by a Declarant in the Condominium Declaration to: (1) add real property to a Condominium Development; (2) create Units, Common Elements, or Limited Common Elements within a Condominium Development; (3) subdivide Units or convert Units into Common Elements; or (4) withdraw real property from a Condominium Development.[15]

Unit is defined as a physical portion of the Condominium Development designated for separate ownership or occupancy, the boundaries of which are described by the Condominium Declaration.[16]

---

[14] Tex. Prop. Code § 82.003(12).

[15] Tex. Prop. Code § 82.003(12).

[16] Tex. Prop. Code § 82.003(23). The Texas Condominium Act uses the term "Apartment" instead of "Unit" and defines such term as an enclosed space, regardless of whether it is designed for residential or other use,

Common Elements is defined as all portions of a Condominium Development other than the portions designated as Units.[17] Common Elements can be further subcategorized as either Limited Common Elements or General Common Elements.

Limited Common Elements is defined as a portion of the Common Elements allocated by the Condominium Declaration or by operation of Section 82.052 of the Texas Uniform Condominium Act for the exclusive use of one or more, but less than all, of the Units.[18] In plain English, Limited Common Elements are those portions of a Condominium Development that are not part of an Owner's Unit, but are used exclusively by one, or only a few, of the Unit Owners. The most illustrative example of a Limited Common Element is a balcony on the outside of an apartment-styled Condominium Development that is accessible by only a single Unit and is intended to be used by only that Unit's Owner.

General Common Elements is defined as all portions of the Common Elements that do not constitute Limited Common Elements.[19]

---

that consists of one or more rooms in a building and that has a direct exit to a thoroughfare or to a common space that leads to a thoroughfare. Tex. Prop. Code § 81.002(1).

17 Tex. Prop. Code § 82.003(5).

18 Tex. Prop. Code § 82.003(17). The Texas Condominium Act defines the term "Limited Common Elements" as a portion of the Common Elements allocated by unanimous agreement of a Council of Owners for the use of one or more, but less than all, of the Apartments, such as special corridors, stairways and elevators, sanitary services common to the Apartments of a particular floor, and similar areas or facilities. Tex. Prop. Code § 81.002(7).

19 Tex. Prop. Code § 82.003(14). The Texas Condominium Act defines the term "General Common Elements" as the property that is part of a Condominium Development other than property that is part of or belongs to an Apartment in the Condominium Development, including: (1) land on which the building is erected; (2) foundations, bearing walls and columns, roofs, halls, lobbies, stairways, and entrance, exit, and communication ways; (3) basements, flat roofs, yards, and gardens, except as otherwise provided; (4) premises for the lodging of janitors or persons in charge of the building, except as otherwise provided; (5) compartments or installation of central services, such as power, light, gas, water, refrigeration, central heat and air, reservoirs, water tanks and pumps, and swimming pools; and (6) elevators and elevator shafts, garbage incinerators, and all other devices and installations generally existing for common use. Tex. Prop. Code § 81.002(6).

Condominium Plan is defined as a dimensional drawing, which is generally attached to the Condominium Declaration and recorded in the Official Public Records of the county in which the Condominium Development is located, that identifies or describes the horizontal and vertical boundaries of the Units and Common Elements contained in the Condominium Development.[20] The Condominium Plan will also typically identify the location of each particular Unit and designated Limited Common Elements.

Condominium Plat is defined as a survey, which is generally attached to the Condominium Declaration and recorded in the Official Public Records of the county in which the Condominium Development is located, that contains the information required by Section 82.059 of the Texas Uniform Condominium Act.[21] In a Site-Condominium Development, the Condominium Plat will typically identify the location and physical boundaries of the Units and Common Elements contained in the Condominium Development.

Identifying Number is defined as a symbol or address that identifies each separate Unit in a Condominium Development.[22] In plain English, the Identifying Number is the number(s) or letter(s) or combination of numbers and letters assigned to each Unit to distinguish it from the other Units in the Condominium Development.

Condominium Association (called simply an "Association" under the Texas Uniform Condominium Act) is defined as a Unit Owners' association organized under the

---

[20] Tex. Prop. Code § 82.003(18).

[21] Tex. Prop. Code § 82.003(19). Section 82.059 of the Texas Uniform Condominium Act is discussed in more detail in subchapter 2.8 of this book. As used in the Texas Uniform Condominium Act, the term "Plat" does not have the same meaning as "plat" in Chapter 212 or 232 of the Texas Local Government Code or other statutes dealing with municipal or county regulation of property development. Tex. Prop. Code § 82.003(19).

[22] Tex. Prop. Code § 82.003(15).

provisions of the Texas Uniform Condominium Act.[23] The Texas Uniform Condominium Act requires that a Unit Owners' association be organized as a for-profit or nonprofit corporation and that the membership of the Unit Owners' association at all times consists exclusively of all the Unit Owners in the Condominium Development.[24] In plain English, a Condominium Association is a Homeowners Association, organized as a for-profit or nonprofit corporation, whose membership consists of only Unit Owners in the Condominium Development.

Board of Directors is defined as the body, regardless of name, designated to act on behalf of a Condominium Association subject to the Texas Uniform Condominium Act.[25]

Unit Owner is defined as a Declarant, or other person who owns a Unit, but does not include a person having an interest in a Unit solely as security for an obligation, such as a mortgagee or lender with a Deed of Trust Lien on the Unit.[26]

Common Expenses is defined as expenditures made by, or financial liabilities of, the Condominium Association, together with any allocations to reserves.[27]

---

23 Tex. Prop. Code § 82.003(3). The Texas Condominium Act uses the term "Council of Owners" instead of "Association" and defines such term as all the Apartment Owners in a Condominium Development. Tex. Prop. Code § 81.002(4).

24 Tex. Prop. Code § 82.101.

25 Tex. Prop. Code § 82.003(4). The Texas Condominium Act provides for management of an applicable Condominium Association by its "Council of Owners," which is defined as all of the Apartment Owners in the Condominium Development. Tex. Prop. Code §§ 81.002(4); 81.201.

26 Tex. Prop. Code § 82.003(24). A "Deed of Trust Lien" is a written instrument that is used to secure the repayment of a mortgage by placing conditional legal title to the real property securing such mortgage in a neutral third party (typically called the "trustee"), who may later exercise a power of sale to foreclose such real property in the event the borrower fails to repay such mortgage. A Deed of Trust Lien is the most common form of lien used to secure a lender who finances a homeowner's purchase of a Lot or Unit.

27 Tex. Prop. Code § 82.003(7).

Common Expense Liability is defined as the liability for Common Expenses allocated to each Unit.[28]

Allocated Interests is defined as the undivided interest in the Common Elements, the Common Expense Liability, and votes in the Condominium Association allocated to each Unit.[29]

2.4 The Condominium Declaration

A Condominium Development is created by recording a properly executed Condominium Declaration in the Official Public Records of each county in which any portion of the Condominium Development is located.[30] To be properly executed under the Texas Uniform Condominium Act, a Condominium Declaration must be executed by the owner of the real property that will constitute the Condominium Development (who is generally referred to as the "Declarant" within the Condominium Declaration).[31]

The Condominium Declaration creates the Condominium Development and establishes the property interests, rights, duties, and obligations of the Declarant, Unit

---

[28] Tex. Prop. Code § 82.003(6).

[29] Tex. Prop. Code § 82.003(2).

[30] Tex. Prop. Code § 82.051(a). Condominium Developments created prior to January 1, 1994, that are subject to the Texas Condominium Act are also properly created by the recording of a Condominium Declaration, or in lieu of a Condominium Declaration, a "Master Deed" or "Master Lease." Tex. Prop. Code § 81.101. The Texas Condominium Act defines "Master Deed" as a deed that establishes property as a Condominium Development and a "Master Lease" as a lease that establishes property as a Condominium Development. Tex. Prop. Code § 81.002(8)–(9).

[31] Tex. Prop. Code § 82.051(a). The Condominium Declaration must also be executed by every lessor of a lease, the expiration or termination of which will terminate the Condominium Development or reduce its size (also known as a "Leasehold Condominium"). Tex. Prop. Code § 82.051(a). In the event of a Leasehold Condominium, the Condominium Declaration must also state: (1) the recording data for the lease; (2) the date on which the lease is scheduled to expire; (3) a legally sufficient description of the real property subject to the lease; (4) any right of the Unit Owners to redeem the reversion and the manner in which the Unit Owners may exercise that right or a statement that the Unit Owners do not have that right; (5) any right of the Unit Owners to remove improvements within a reasonable time after the expiration or termination of the lease or a statement that the Unit Owners do not have that right; and (6) any right of the Unit Owners to renew the lease and the conditions of renewal or a statement that the Unit Owners do not have that right. Tex. Prop. Code § 82.056(a).

Owners, and the Condominium Association. In addition, the Condominium Declaration will establish the powers of the Condominium Association and impose land-use restrictions associated with construction, maintenance, and repair of Units and Common Elements.[32] The Condominium Declaration is also the highest ranking of a Condominium Association's Governing Documents. This means if there is a conflict between the Condominium Declaration and the Condominium Association's Bylaws, the Condominium Declaration prevails, except to the extent the Condominium Declaration is inconsistent with the Texas Uniform Condominium Act.[33]

The Texas Uniform Condominium Act requires that the Condominium Declaration contain the following information:[34]

(1) the name of the Condominium Development, which must include the word "condominium" or be followed by the words "a condominium" or a phrase that includes the word "condominium," and the name of the Condominium Association;[35]

---

[32] Tex. Prop. Code § 82.055.

[33] Tex. Prop. Code § 82.053(c).

[34] The requirements for a Condominium Declaration (or Master Deed or Master Lease) under the Texas Condominium Act differ slightly from those of the Texas Uniform Condominium Act. Under the Texas Condominium Act, a Condominium Declaration, Master Deed, or Master Lease for a Condominium Development must contain: (1) the legal description of the real property dedicated to the Condominium Declaration, depicted by a plat of the property that locates and identifies by letter each existing or proposed building; (2) a general description of each Apartment, including the square footage, location, number, and other information necessary for identification of the Apartment, depicted by a plat of the floor of the building in which the Apartment is located that identifies the building by letter and the floor and the Apartment by number; (3) a general description of each area not already described that is subject to individual ownership and exclusive control, such as a garage or carport, depicted by a plat that shows the area and appropriately identifies it by letter or number; (4) a description of the Limited Common Elements; (5) each Apartment's fractional or percentage interest in the entire Condominium Declaration; (6) a provision that the Condominium Declaration may only be amended at a meeting of the Apartment Owners at which the amendment is approved by the holders of at least sixty-seven percent (67%) of the ownership interests in the Condominium Development; and (7) a provision that an amendment of the Condominium Declaration may not alter or destroy a unit or a Limited Common Element without the consent of the owners affected and the owners' first lien mortgagees. Tex. Prop. Code § 81.102(a). In addition, a Condominium Declaration, Master Deed, or Master Lease for a Condominium Declaration may contain any covenants or other matters the Declarant considers appropriate. Tex. Prop. Code § 81.102(b).

[35] Tex. Prop. Code § 82.055(1).

(2) the name of each county in which any part of the Condominium Development is located;[36]

(3) a legally sufficient description of all real property included in the Condominium Development;[37]

(4) a description of the boundaries of each Unit created by the Condominium Declaration, including the Unit's Identifying Number;[38]

(5) a statement of the maximum number of Units that the Declarant reserves the right to create;[39]

(6) a description of the Limited Common Elements, other than any chute, flue, duct, wire, conduit, bearing wall, bearing column, or any other fixture that is partially within and partially outside the designated boundaries of a Unit that serves only that Unit, and any shutters, awnings, window boxes, doorsteps, stoops, porches, balconies, patios, exterior doors, and windows or other fixtures designed to serve a single Unit but are located outside the Unit's boundaries;[40]

(7) a description of any real property, except real property subject to Development Rights, that may be allocated subsequently as Limited Common Elements, together with a statement that the property may be so allocated;[41]

(8) an allocation to each Unit of its Allocated Interests;[42]

(9) any restrictions on use, occupancy, or alienation of the Units;[43]

---

[36] Tex. Prop. Code § 82.055(2).

[37] Tex. Prop. Code § 82.055(3). A description of a Unit and all rights, obligations, and interests appurtenant to such Unit that is created by the Condominium Declaration or Bylaws is legally sufficient if the description contains: (1) the name of the Condominium Development; (2) the recording data for the Condominium Declaration (including any amendments), Condominium Plats, and Condominium Plans; (3) the county in which the Condominium Development is located; and (4) the Identifying Number of the Unit. Tex. Prop. Code § 82.054.

[38] Tex. Prop. Code § 82.055(4).

[39] Tex. Prop. Code § 82.055(5).

[40] Tex. Prop. Code §§ 82.052(2) & (4), 82.055(6).

[41] Tex. Prop. Code § 82.055(7).

[42] Tex. Prop. Code § 82.055(8).

[43] Tex. Prop. Code § 82.055(9).

(10) a description of and the recording data for recorded easements and licenses appurtenant to or included in the Condominium Development or to which any portion of the Condominium Development is or may become subject by reservation in the Condominium Declaration;[44]

(11) the method or manner in which the Condominium Declaration may be amended;[45]

(12) a Condominium Plat or Plan or the recording data of a Condominium Plat or Plan that has been recorded in the Official Public Records;[46]

(13) a statement of the Condominium Association's obligation under Section 82.111(i) of the Texas Uniform Condominium Act to rebuild or repair any part of the Condominium Development after a casualty or any other disposition of the proceeds of a casualty insurance policy;[47]

(14) a description of any Development Rights and other Special Declarant Rights reserved by the Declarant, together with a legally sufficient description of the real property to which each of those rights applies, and a time limit within which each of those rights must be exercised;[48]

(15) if any Development Right may be exercised with respect to different parcels of real property at different times, a statement to that effect, together with:

(a) either a statement fixing the boundaries of those portions and regulating the order in which those portions may be subjected to the exercise of each Development Right or a statement that no assurances are made in those regards;[49] and

(b) a statement as to whether, if any Development Right is exercised in any portion of the real property subject to that Development Right, that Development Right must be exercised in all or in any other portion of the remainder of that real property;[50]

---

44 Tex. Prop. Code § 82.055(10).

45 Tex. Prop. Code § 82.055(11).

46 Tex. Prop. Code § 82.055(12).

47 Tex. Prop. Code § 82.055(13).

48 Tex. Prop. Code § 82.055(14).

49 Tex. Prop. Code § 82.055(15)(A).

50 Tex. Prop. Code § 82.055(15)(B).

(16) all matters required by the Texas Uniform Condominium Act to be stated in the Condominium Declaration;[51] and

(17) any other matters the Declarant considers appropriate.[52]

In addition, a Condominium Declaration or other recorded contract may require Unit Owners in a Condominium Development to maintain a membership in a specified private club, such as a country club. If a provision of a Condominium Declaration or other recorded contract does require Unit Owners to maintain membership in a specified private club, then such provision will be considered invalid after the tenth (10th) anniversary of the date the provision was recorded or renewed unless such provision is: (1) renewed after the ninth (9th) anniversary of such date; and (2) done so in the manner specified in the Condominium Declaration or other recorded contract for amending the Condominium Declaration and the text of such renewed provision is recorded in the Official Public Records of each county in which the Condominium Development is located.[53] A provision requiring Unit Owners to maintain membership in a specified private club may not be enacted or renewed as a Bylaw by the Condominium Association.[54]

---

51 Tex. Prop. Code § 82.055(16).

52 Tex. Prop. Code § 82.055(17).

53 Tex. Prop. Code § 82.0675(a). The provisions of the Texas Uniform Condominium Act concerning provisions mandating membership in a private club are not applicable to Condominium Developments created prior to January 1, 1994, that are subject to the Texas Condominium Act. However, the Texas Condominium Act has a similar provision. Tex. Prop. Code § 82.102. Section 81.112 of the Texas Condominium Act provides that a provision of a Condominium Declaration, Master Deed, Master Lease, or other recorded contract that requires Apartment Owners to maintain a membership in a specified private club is not valid after the tenth (10th) anniversary of the date the provision is recorded or renewed unless such provision is: (1) renewed after the ninth (9th) anniversary of such date; and (2) done so at a meeting of the Apartment Owners at which the renewal is approved by the holders of at least sixty-seven percent (67%) of the ownership interests in the Condominium Development and the text of such renewed provision is filed in the Official Public Records of each county in which the Condominium Development is located. Tex. Prop. Code § 81.112(a).

54 Tex. Prop. Code §§ 82.0675(b), 81.112(b).

2.5 Ownership of Units and Determining Unit Boundaries

Each Unit, together with its Allocated Interest in the Common Elements, constitutes a separate parcel of real property owned by the Unit Owner.[55] As a separately owned parcel of real property, each Unit, together with its Allocated Interest in the Common Elements, must be separately taxed and is entitled to homestead exemption from property taxes in the same manner that an owner of a single-family dwelling would be.[56] In addition, a Unit's Allocated Interests in the Common Elements are not subject to partition from the Unit, and any purported conveyance, judicial sale, or other voluntary or involuntary transfer of an undivided interest in the Common Elements without the Unit to which that interest is allocated is void.[57] In other words, ownership of the Unit itself cannot be separated from ownership of the Allocated Interest in the Common Elements, and a Unit Owner cannot sell his or her Unit and retain ownership of the Allocated Interest in the Common Elements or vice versa.

Identifying the boundaries of a Unit is extremely important in a Condominium Development, as they serve as the delineation of what is considered to be a separately owned Unit versus what is considered to be a Common Element. Determining what portion of the Condominium Development is a Unit not only determines what is separately owned by each Unit Owner, but also what portion of the Condominium Development must be maintained and repaired by the Unit Owner or the Condominium Association. The boundaries of a Unit are required to be defined by the Condominium Declaration, and thus, it is important to review the applicable provisions of the Condominium Declaration to determine the boundaries of any particular Unit. This is particularly true for "Site-

[55] Tex. Prop. Code § 82.005(a).

[56] Tex. Prop. Code § 82.005(b), (d).

[57] Tex. Prop. Code § 82.057(f); *see also* Tex. Prop. Code § 81.109.

Condominium Developments," where the boundaries of Units are more akin to property lines than vertical walls.

In addition to the defined boundaries of Units specified in a Condominium Declaration, the Texas Uniform Condominium Act also provides certain standards for determining the boundaries of a Unit that apply to all Units, except where the Condominium Declaration or Condominium Plat provides otherwise. Under the Texas Uniform Condominium Act:

(1) if walls, floors, or ceilings are designated as boundaries of a Unit, then all lath, furring, wallboard, plasterboard, plaster, paneling, tiles, wallpaper, paint, finished flooring, and any other materials constituting part of the finished surfaces are a part of the Unit, and all other portions of the walls, floors, or ceilings are a part of the Common Elements;[58]

(2) if any chute, flue, duct, wire, conduit, bearing wall, bearing column, or any other fixture is partially within and partially outside the designated boundaries of a Unit, then the portion serving only that Unit is a Limited Common Element allocated solely to that Unit, and the portion serving more than one Unit or the Common Elements is a part of the General Common Elements;[59]

(3) the spaces, interior partitions, and other fixtures and improvements that are within the boundaries of a Unit are a part of the Unit;[60] and

(4) shutters, awnings, window boxes, doorsteps, stoops, porches, balconies, patios, exterior doors, and windows or other fixtures designed to serve a single Unit, but located outside the Unit's boundaries, are Limited Common Elements allocated exclusively to that Unit.[61]

For those Condominium Developments created prior to January 1, 1994, which are subject to the Texas Condominium Act, the boundaries of an Apartment in such a

58 Tex. Prop. Code § 82.052(1).

59 Tex. Prop. Code § 82.052(2).

60 Tex. Prop. Code § 82.052(3).

61 Tex. Prop. Code § 82.052(4).

Condominium Development are the interior surfaces of the Apartment's perimeter walls, floors, and ceilings, and the exterior surfaces of the Apartment's balconies and terraces.[62] In addition, the portions of the building within such boundaries of an Apartment, including the airspace within those boundaries, are also considered to be part of the Apartment.[63]

2.6 Common Elements, Limited Common Elements, and General Common Elements

In order to determine what parts of a Condominium Development constitute Common Elements, it must first be determined what portion of the Condominium Development constitutes Units or Apartments because Common Elements consist of all of the remaining portions of a Condominium Development other than those portions that constitute Units or Apartments. The location of all Units and Common Elements are generally shown on the Condominium Plan(s) and/or Condominium Plat(s) attached to the Condominium Declaration.

Common Elements can be further categorized as either Limited Common Elements or General Common Elements. The Limited Common Elements of a Condominium Development consist of all portions of the Common Elements that are allocated by the Condominium Declaration as Limited Common Elements.[64] In addition, and unless otherwise specified in the Condominium Declaration or Condominium Plat, the Limited Common Elements allocated to a Unit also include:

(1) the portions of any chute, flue, duct, wire, conduit, bearing wall, bearing column, or any other fixture that is located partially within and partially outside the designated boundaries of such Unit and serves only that Unit;[65] and

---

62 Tex. Prop. Code § 81.105(a).

63 Tex. Prop. Code § 81.105(b).

64 Tex. Prop. Code § 82.003(17).

65 Tex. Prop. Code § 82.052(2). However, the portions of any chute, flue, duct, wire, conduit, bearing wall, bearing column, or any other fixture that is located partially within and partially outside of a Unit's designated

(2) any shutter, awning, window box, doorstep, stoop, porch, balcony, patio, exterior door, window, or other fixture that is located outside the designated boundaries of such Unit and designed to serve only that Unit.[66]

General Common Elements, on the other hand, consist of all portions of the Common Elements that do not constitute Limited Common Elements.[67]

2.7 Allocation of Common Element Interests, Common Expense Liabilities, and Votes

A Condominium Declaration subject to the Texas Uniform Condominium Act is also required to allocate to each Unit: (1) a fraction or percentage of undivided ownership interests in the Common Elements; (2) a share of the liability for Common Expenses of the Condominium Association; and (3) the number of membership votes in the Condominium Association such Unit may exercise, and it must state the formulas used to establish such allocations.[68] These three categories of allocated interests are referred to as a Unit's "Allocated Interests." If the Condominium Declaration allows Units to be added or withdrawn from the Condominium Development, then the Condominium Declaration must also state the formulas to be used to reallocate the Allocated Interests among all Units included in the Condominium Development after the addition or withdrawal of

---

boundaries and serves more than one Unit or the Common Elements are considered to be part of the General Common Elements. Tex. Prop. Code § 82.052(2).

66 Tex. Prop. Code § 82.052(4).

67 Tex. Prop. Code § 82.003(14).

68 Tex. Prop. Code § 82.057(a). Except for minor variations due to rounding, the sums of the undivided interests in the Common Elements and of the Common Expense Liability allocated at any time to all the Units must each equal either the whole number one (1.0), if stated as fractions, or one hundred percent (100%), if stated as percentages. Tex. Prop. Code § 82.057(e). If a discrepancy exists between an Allocated Interest and the result derived from application of the pertinent formula, the stated Allocated Interest prevails. Tex. Prop. Code § 82.057(e). The provisions of the Texas Uniform Condominium Act concerning the allocation of Common Element Interests, votes, and Common Expense Liabilities are not applicable to Condominium Developments created prior to January 1, 1994, that are subject to the Texas Condominium Act, and there are no comparable provisions under the Texas Condominium Act. Tex. Prop. Code § 82.102(c).

Units.[69] In addition, these allocations of Allocated Interests may not discriminate in favor of Units owned by a Declarant.[70]

Irrespective of the allocation of Common Elements and Common Expense Liability, the allocation of membership votes in the Condominium Association does not have to be equal or uniform between Units in the Condominium Development. A Condominium Declaration may provide for different allocations of membership votes to Units on particular matters specified in the Condominium Declaration.[71] A Condominium Declaration may also require class voting on specified issues affecting a class of Unit Owners in a Condominium Development if necessary to protect valid interests of such class.[72]

2.8 Condominium Plats and Plans

Condominium Plats and Plans are a required part of a Condominium Declaration under the Texas Uniform Condominium Act and are necessary for identifying the location of Units and Common Elements.[73] Condominium Plats and Plans may be recorded as a part of the Condominium Declaration or recorded separately.[74] Each Condominium Plat or Plan must be legible and contain a certification that such Plat or Plan contains all

---

69 Tex. Prop. Code § 82.057(b).

70 Tex. Prop. Code § 82.057(a).

71 Tex. Prop. Code § 82.057(c).

72 Tex. Prop. Code § 82.057(c). A class of Units, however, may not be categorized on the basis that such Units are owned by the Declarant. Tex. Prop. Code § 82.057(d). Moreover, a Declarant may not use cumulative or class voting to evade any limitation imposed on a Declarant by the Texas Uniform Condominium Act. Tex. Prop. Code § 82.057(d). In other words, a Declarant cannot structure the allocation of membership votes or the manner in which membership votes are cast in order to avoid obligations imposed upon the Declarant by the Texas Uniform Condominium Act.

73 Tex. Prop. Code § 82.059(a). The provisions of the Texas Uniform Condominium Act concerning Condominium Plats and Plans are not applicable to Condominium Developments created prior to January 1, 1994, that are subject to the Texas Condominium Act, and there are no comparable provisions under the Texas Condominium Act. Tex. Prop. Code § 82.002(c).

74 Tex. Prop. Code § 82.059(a).

information required by Section 82.059 of the Texas Uniform Condominium Act.[75] Section 82.059 of the Texas Uniform Condominium Act requires that a Condominium Plat show:[76]

(1) the name and a survey or general schematic map of the entire Condominium Development;

(2) the location and dimensions of all real property not subject to Development Rights (or subject only to a Development Right to withdraw) and the location and dimensions of all existing improvements within such real property;

(3) a legally sufficient description of any real property subject to Development Rights, labeled to identify the rights applicable to each parcel;

(4) the extent of any encroachments by or on any portion of the Condominium Development;

(5) to the extent feasible, a legally sufficient description of all easements serving or burdening any portion of the Condominium Development and the location of any underground utility lines that are actually known by the Declarant at the time of filing the Condominium Declaration to have been constructed outside a recorded easement;

(6) the location and dimensions of any vertical Unit boundaries not shown or projected on the recorded Condominium Plans and such Unit's Identifying Number;

(7) the location, with reference to established data, of any horizontal Unit boundaries not shown or projected on the recorded Condominium Plans and such Unit's Identifying Number;

(8) a legally sufficient description of any real property that the Unit Owners will only own for a certain time period, which must be labeled as "leasehold real property";

(9) the distance between noncontiguous parcels of real property constituting the Condominium Development;

---

75 Tex. Prop. Code § 82.059(a).

76 Tex. Prop. Code § 82.059(b).

(10) the location and dimensions of Limited Common Elements, other than any chute, flue, duct, wire, conduit, bearing wall, bearing column, or any other fixture that is partially within and partially outside the designated boundaries of a Unit that serves only that Unit, and any shutters, awnings, window boxes, doorsteps, stoops, porches, balconies, patios, exterior doors, and windows or other fixtures designed to serve a single Unit, but located outside the Unit's boundaries;

(11) in the case of real property not subject to Development Rights, all other matters required by law on land surveys; and

(12) the distance and bearings locating each building from all other buildings and from at least one boundary line of the real property constituting the Condominium Development.

A Condominium Plat may also show the intended location and dimensions of a contemplated improvement to be constructed anywhere within the Condominium Development, which must be labeled either "MUST BE BUILT" or "NEED NOT BE BUILT."[77] In addition, at least one Condominium Plat, showing: (1) all perimeter land boundaries of the Condominium Development; and (2) the locations on the ground of all buildings labeled "MUST BE BUILT" in relation to such land boundaries, must be certified by an independent licensed surveyor or engineer.[78]

To the extent not shown on the Condominium Plats, Section 82.059 of the Texas Uniform Condominium Act requires that a Condominium Plan show:[79]

(1) the location and dimensions of the vertical boundaries of each Unit and the Unit's Identifying Number;

(2) the horizontal Unit boundaries, with reference to established data, and the Unit's Identifying Number; and

---

77 Tex. Prop. Code § 82.059(c).

78 Tex. Prop. Code § 82.059(g). The certification of any additional Condominium Plats or Plans required by the Texas Uniform Condominium Act may be made by an independent surveyor or engineer, or alternatively, a licensed architect. Tex. Prop. Code § 82.059(g).

79 Tex. Prop. Code § 82.059(d).

(3) any Units, appropriately identified, in which the Declarant has reserved the right to create additional Units or Common Elements.

Notwithstanding, unless the Condominium Declaration provides otherwise, the horizontal boundaries of a portion of a Unit that is located outside of a building are not required to be depicted on the Condominium Plats and Plans.[80] In addition, interior walls and partitions within a Unit are not required to be included in the Condominium Plats or Plans.[81]

2.9 Alteration of Units, Relocation of Boundaries between Adjoining Units, and Subdivision of Units

From time to time, Unit Owners may want to alter their Units, relocate boundaries between adjoining Units, or even subdivide a single Unit into two or more new Units. The ability and procedures to alter a Unit, relocate the boundaries between Units, and/or subdivide a Unit are governed by both a Condominium Association's Declaration and the Texas Uniform Condominium Act (as applicable).[82]

2.9.1 Alteration of a Unit or Partitions between Two Units

Subject to the provisions of the Condominium Declaration, a Unit Owner in a Condominium Development subject to the Texas Uniform Condominium Act may generally make improvements or alterations to his or her Unit so long as they do not impair the structural integrity or mechanical systems or lessen the support of any portion of the Condominium Development.[83] A Unit Owner, however, may not change the appearance

[80] Tex. Prop. Code § 82.059(e). Unless the Condominium Declaration provides otherwise, the horizontal boundaries of a part of a Unit that is located outside of a building is considered to have the same elevation as the horizontal boundaries of the inside part of the Unit. Tex. Prop. Code § 82.059(e).

[81] Tex. Prop. Code § 82.059(e).

[82] The provisions of the Texas Uniform Condominium Act concerning alteration of Units, relocation of boundaries between adjoining Units, and subdivision of Units are not applicable to Condominium Developments created prior to January 1, 1994, that are subject to the Texas Condominium Act, and there are no comparable provisions under the Texas Condominium Act. Tex. Prop. Code § 82.002(c).

[83] Tex. Prop. Code § 82.061(a)(1).

of the Common Elements or the exterior appearance of a Unit or any other portion of the Condominium Development without prior written permission of the Condominium Association.[84]

In addition, if a Unit Owner acquires an adjoining Unit or an adjoining part of an adjoining Unit, then the Unit Owner may, with the prior written approval of the Condominium Association, remove, alter, and create apertures (openings) in an intervening partition (the common wall between the two adjoining Units), even if such intervening partition, or a portion of such intervening partition, is a Common Element, so long as such acts do not impair the structural integrity or mechanical systems or lessen the support of any portion of the Condominium Development.[85] In such circumstances, the removal of partitions or creation of apertures in such partitions does not constitute an alteration of the Unit's boundaries.[86]

2.9.2 Relocation of Boundaries between Adjoining Units

Subject to the provisions of the applicable Condominium Declaration, Unit Owners in a Condominium Development subject to the Texas Uniform Condominium Act may also relocate the boundaries between adjoining Units.[87] In order to relocate the boundaries between adjoining Units, the Owners of those Units must submit a written application to the Condominium Association for amendment of the Condominium Declaration.[88] If the Owners of such adjoining Units have agreed to the manner in which the Allocated Interests of their respective Units are to be reallocated between their Units following the relocation of the boundaries, then the written application must state the

---

84 Tex. Prop. Code § 82.061(a)(2).

85 Tex. Prop. Code § 82.061(a)(3).

86 Tex. Prop. Code § 82.061(b). In other words, even if a wall that serves as boundary between two adjacent Units is removed, the boundary between such Units remains at the location of such removed wall.

87 Tex. Prop. Code § 82.062.

88 Tex. Prop. Code § 82.062.

proposed reallocation.[89] The Board of Directors for the Condominium Association has thirty (30) days from receipt of such written application to determine if the specified manner of reallocation of the Unit Owners' Allocated Interests is unreasonable.[90] Unless the Board of Directors determines that such reallocation is unreasonable, the Condominium Association is required to prepare and record, at the expense of the applicable Unit Owners, an amendment to the Condominium Declaration that: (1) identifies the Units involved; and (2) states the manner of reallocation.[91]

2.9.3 Subdivision of a Unit

If the Condominium Declaration expressly permits it, a Unit may also be subdivided into two or more Units.[92] Subject to the requirements of the Condominium Declaration, upon written application of a Unit Owner to subdivide a Unit, and after payment by the Unit Owner of the cost of preparing and recording amendments to the Condominium Declaration and Condominium Plats and Plans, the Condominium Association must prepare, execute, and record an amendment to the Condominium Declaration, including the Condominium Plats and Plans, necessary to effect the subdivision of the Unit.[93] The amendment to the Condominium Declaration must: (1) be executed by the Owner of the Unit to be subdivided; (2) assign an Identifying Number to each Unit created by the subdivision; and (3) reallocate the Allocated Interests formerly

---

[89] Tex. Prop. Code § 82.062.

[90] Tex. Prop. Code § 82.062.

[91] Tex. Prop. Code § 82.062. Such amendment to the Condominium Declaration must be executed by the applicable Unit Owners and must contain words of conveyance between them. Tex. Prop. Code § 82.062. The Condominium Association must also prepare and record any amendments to the Condominium Plats or Plans necessary to show the altered boundaries between adjoining Units and the Units' dimensions and Identifying Numbers. Tex. Prop. Code § 82.062.

[92] Tex. Prop. Code § 82.063(a).

[93] Tex. Prop. Code § 82.063(a).

allocated to the subdivided Unit to the new Units in any reasonable manner requested by the Owner of the subdivided Unit.[94]

2.10 Maintenance and Repair of Units and Common Elements

One of the more complicated and sometimes divisive issues that can arise between a Condominium Association and a Unit Owner is whose responsibility it is to maintain and/or repair portions of the Condominium Development.[95] Unless otherwise provided by the Condominium Declaration, the Condominium Association is responsible for maintenance, repair, and replacement of the Common Elements (including both Limited and General Common Elements); meanwhile, each Unit Owner is responsible for maintenance, repair, and replacement of the Owner's Unit.[96] In addition, and except as provided by the Condominium Declaration, each Unit Owner is also responsible for the cost of maintenance, repair, and replacement of windows and doors serving only the Owner's Unit and for the cost of maintenance, repair, and replacement of any utility installation or equipment serving only the Owner's Unit, without regard to whether the installation or equipment is located wholly or partially outside the designated boundaries of such Owner's Unit.[97]

---

94 Tex. Prop. Code § 82.063(b).

95 The provisions of the Texas Uniform Condominium Act concerning duties of maintenance, repair, and replacement of Units and Common Elements are not applicable to Condominium Developments created prior to January 1, 1994, that are subject to the Texas Condominium Act, and the comparable provisions under the Texas Condominium Act differ significantly from their counterparts under the Texas Uniform Condominium Act. Tex. Prop. Code § 82.002(c). The Texas Condominium Act provides only that an Apartment Owner in a Condominium Development is responsible for the Apartment Owner's pro rata share of: (1) the expenses to administer the Condominium Development and to maintain and repair the General Common Elements; (2) in proper cases, the expenses to administer the Limited Common Elements of the buildings in the Condominium Development; and (3) other expenses approved by the Council of Owners. Tex. Prop. Code § 81.204(a).

96 Tex. Prop. Code § 82.107(a).

97 Tex. Prop. Code § 82.107(b), (c). For purposes of Section 82.107(b) of the Texas Uniform Condominium Act, utility installations and equipment include electricity, water, sewage, gas, water heaters, heating and air conditioning equipment, and television antennas. Tex. Prop. Code § 82.107(b).

Each Unit Owner is also required to afford to the Condominium Association and other Unit Owners, as well as their respective agents or employees, access through the Owner's Unit that is reasonably necessary for the Condominium Association or other Unit Owners to perform maintenance, repair, or replacement of the Common Elements or other Units, respectively.[98] If damage is inflicted on the Common Elements or on any Unit through which access is taken, then the Unit Owner responsible for the damage, or the Condominium Association, if it is responsible, is liable for the prompt repair of such damage.[99]

Moreover, unless otherwise provided by the Condominium Declaration, a Condominium Association may enter into a Unit, after giving notice to the owner and/or occupant of the Unit, to: (1) prevent or terminate waste of water purchased by the Condominium Association as a Common Expense; or (2) perform maintenance and repairs of the Condominium Development that, if not performed, may result in increased damage by water to components of the Condominium Development that the Condominium Association maintains.[100] In other words, if there is a leak in a toilet within a Unit that is causing water to seep into a portion of the Common Elements, then the Condominium Association may enter into the Unit to repair the leaking toilet after giving notice to the owner or occupant of the Unit.

2.11 Amendment of a Condominium Development's Governing Documents

As a Condominium Development evolves, it is not uncommon for issues to arise that make it necessary or desirable to amend the Condominium Development's Governing Documents. In general, a Condominium Declaration subject to the Texas Uniform

---

[98] Tex. Prop. Code § 82.107(a). The provisions of the Texas Uniform Condominium Act concerning provision of access to the Condominium Association and other Unit Owners are not applicable to Condominium Developments created prior to January 1, 1994, that are subject to the Texas Condominium Act, and there are no comparable provisions under the Texas Condominium Act. Tex. Prop. Code § 82.002(c).

[99] Tex. Prop. Code § 82.107(a).

[100] Tex. Prop. Code § 82.107(d).

Condominium Act, including the Condominium Plats and Plans attached to it, may only be amended by a vote or agreement of Unit Owners representing at least sixty-seven percent (67%) of the votes allocated in the Condominium Association or any larger percentage of allocated votes specified in the Condominium Declaration for purposes of amendment.[101] If all of the Units are restricted exclusively to nonresidential use (such as an office Condominium Development), the Condominium Declaration may be amended by the percentage of allocated votes specified in the Condominium Declaration for the purposes of amendment, even if such percentage is lower than sixty-seven percent (67%) of the votes allocated in the Condominium Declaration.[102]

There are some limited circumstances, however, where an amendment to the Condominium Declaration does not require any vote or agreement of Unit Owners in the Condominium Association. More specifically, a vote or agreement of Unit Owners is not required when a Declarant: (1) records an amendment to the Condominium Declaration for the purpose of curing a defect with the proper execution of a previously recorded Condominium Declaration; (2) records an amendment to the Condominium Declaration and/or new Condominium Plats and Plans for the purpose of exercising a Development Right; and/or (3) records new Condominium Plats or Plans upon exercising a Development Right to conform such Plats or Plans to the requirements of the Texas Uniform Condominium Act.[103] In addition, a vote or agreement of Unit Owners is also

---

[101] Tex. Prop. Code § 82.067(a). The provisions of the Texas Uniform Condominium Act concerning amendment of a Condominium Declaration are not applicable to Condominium Developments created prior to January 1, 1994, that are subject to the Texas Condominium Act, and the comparable provision under the Texas Condominium Act is significantly more restrictive than its counterpart under the Texas Uniform Condominium Act. Tex. Prop. Code §§ 81.111, 82.002(c). Under the Texas Condominium Act, after a Condominium Declaration is recorded with a county clerk, the Condominium Declaration may not be amended except at a meeting of the Apartment Owners at which the amendment is approved by the holders of at least sixty-seven percent (67%) of the ownership interests in the Condominium Development. Tex. Prop. Code § 81.111. Unlike the Texas Uniform Condominium Act, there are no provisions under the Texas Condominium Act that allow for amendment of the Condominium Declaration in certain limited circumstances without the approval of the Apartment Owners.

[102] Tex. Prop. Code § 82.067(a).

[103] Tex. Prop. Code §§ 82.051(c), 82.059(f), 82.060, 82.067(b)(1).

not required when a Condominium Association records an amendment to the Condominium Declaration to reflect: (1) a reallocation of Allocated Interests upon condemnation of a Unit, part of a Unit, or part of a Common Element by a governmental entity; (2) a reallocation of a Common Element as a Limited Common Element; (3) a relocation of boundaries between adjoining Units and a reallocation of Allocated Interests between such Units; and/or (4) a subdivision of a Unit and a reallocation of Allocated Interests previously allocated to the subdivided Unit to the newly created Units.[104] Finally, if permitted by the Condominium Declaration, the Board of Directors of a Condominium Association (as well as the Declarant, so long as it still owns at least one Unit that has never been occupied) may amend the Condominium Declaration without the vote or agreement of Unit Owners in any manner necessary to meet the requirements of the Federal National Mortgage Association,[105] the Federal Home Loan Mortgage Corporation,[106] the Federal Housing Administration,[107] or the Veterans Administration.[108] Finally, no vote or agreement of Unit Owners is required when certain Unit Owners record

---

[104] Tex. Prop. Code §§ 82.007, 82.056(d), 82.058(c), 82.062, 82.063, 82.067(b)(2).

[105] The Federal National Mortgage Association, more commonly known as "Fannie Mae," is a stockholder-owned corporation chartered by the United States Congress in 1968 as a government-sponsored enterprise to purchase and securitize mortgages in order to ensure that funds are consistently available to the institutions that lend money to home buyers. Fannie Mae buys mortgages on the secondary market, pools them, and sells them as mortgage-backed securities to investors on the open market. This secondary mortgage market increases the supply of money available for mortgages lending and increases the money available for new home purchases.

[106] The Federal Home Loan Mortgage Corporation, more commonly known as "Freddie Mac," is a government-sponsored enterprise that was created in 1970 as competition for Fannie Mae and to further increase the availability of funds to finance mortgages and homeownership. The charter of Freddie Mac was essentially the same as Fannie Mae's charter, which is to expand the secondary market for mortgages and mortgage-backed securities by buying mortgages made by savings and loan associations and other depository institutions.

[107] The Federal Housing Administration (FHA) is a United States government agency created as part of the National Housing Act of 1934. The mission of the FHA is to improve housing standards and conditions; to provide an adequate home financing system through insurance of mortgage loans; and to stabilize the mortgage market.

[108] Tex. Prop. Code § 82.067(f). The Veterans Administration, now known as the "United States Department of Veterans Affairs," but more commonly known as the "VA," is a government-run military veteran benefit system that is responsible for administering programs of veterans' benefits, including home loans for veterans, their families, and survivors.

an amendment to the Condominium Declaration in order to: (1) reallocate Limited Common Elements between their Units; (2) reflect a relocation of boundaries between adjoining Units and a reallocation of Allocated Interests between such Units; and/or (3) reflect a subdivision of a Unit and a reallocation of Allocated Interests previously allocated to the subdivided Unit to the new Units.[109]

An amendment to the Condominium Declaration that does require a vote or agreement of Unit Owners in the Condominium Association may be adopted: (1) by written ballot that states the exact wording or substance of the amendment and that specifies the date by which a ballot must be received to be counted; (2) at a meeting of the members of the Condominium Association after written notice of the meeting has been delivered to an owner of each Unit stating that a purpose of the meeting is to consider an amendment to the Condominium Declaration; or (3) by any method permitted by the Condominium Declaration.[110] A Condominium Association's Board of Directors or Membership may not meet to adopt an amendment or other change to its Condominium Declaration, Articles of Incorporation, Bylaws, or Association Rules unless a document showing the specific amendment or other change that would be made to the Condominium Declaration, Articles of Incorporation, Bylaws, or Association Rules has been given to each Unit Owner at least ten (10) days, but no more than twenty (20) days, before the date of such meeting.[111]

Finally, to be effective, an amendment to the Condominium Declaration must be recorded in the Official Public Records of each county in which any portion of the

---

109 Tex. Prop. Code §§ 82.058(b), 82.062, 82.063(b), 82.067(b)(3), 82.068(b).

110 Tex. Prop. Code § 82.067(a)(1)–(3).

111 Tex. Prop. Code § 82.070(a)–(b). The document showing the specific amendment or other change is considered to have been given to a Unit Owner on the date the document(s) showing such information is personally delivered to the Unit Owner, as shown by a receipt signed by the Unit Owner, or on the date shown by the postmark on the envelope containing such document(s) after it is deposited in the United States mail with a proper address and postage paid. Tex. Prop. Code § 82.070(b).

Condominium Development is located.[112] A lawsuit to challenge the validity of an amendment adopted by the Condominium Association under the procedures set forth under the Texas Uniform Condominium Act must be brought within one (1) year from the date the amendment is recorded in the Official Public Records of the applicable county or counties.[113]

2.12 Termination of a Condominium Development

For various reasons, there may come a time when it is necessary or desirable to terminate all or a portion of a Condominium Development. Such circumstances include instances when a governmental entity condemns all or part of a Condominium Development or when all or part of a Condominium Development is destroyed by fire or a catastrophic weather event. In general, a Condominium Development may only be terminated under the circumstances and procedures set forth in its Condominium Declaration or the Texas Uniform Condominium Act.

2.12.1 Agreement to Terminate a Condominium Development

Pursuant to the Texas Uniform Condominium Act, a Condominium Development may be terminated upon: (1) the condemnation of one hundred percent (100%) of the Units in the Condominium Development by a governmental entity; or (2) the agreement of one hundred percent (100%) of the Unit Owners in the Condominium Development.[114] In addition and subject the requirements of the Texas Condominium Act or the Texas Uniform Condominium Act, a Condominium Development may also be terminated in

---

[112] Tex. Prop. Code §§ 82.067(d); 202.006. In addition, an amendment to a Condominium Declaration must be prepared, executed, recorded, and certified by an Officer of the Condominium Association designated for that purpose or, in the absence of an Officer designated for such specific purpose in the Condominium Association's Governing Documents, by the President of the Condominium Association. Tex. Prop. Code § 82.067(g).

[113] Tex. Prop. Code § 82.067(c).

[114] Tex. Prop. Code §§ 81.110, 82.068(a). If the Condominium Development is subject to the Texas Uniform Condominium Act, each holder of a deed of trust or vendor's lien on a Unit in the Condominium Development must also agree to the termination agreement by the Unit Owners. Tex. Prop. Code § 82.068(a).

whole or in part by the agreement of the requisite percentage of Unit Owners specified in its Condominium Declaration.[115]

To be effective, an agreement of Unit Owners to terminate a Condominium Development must be evidenced by a written termination agreement that is executed or ratified by the requisite number of Unit Owners.[116] If, pursuant to a termination agreement, the real property constituting the Condominium Development is to be sold following termination, the termination agreement must also set forth the terms of the sale.[117] In addition, the termination agreement and all ratifications of such agreement must be recorded in the Official Public Records of each county in which a portion of the Condominium Development is located.[118]

2.12.2 Termination Procedure if the Condominium Development Property Is to Be Sold Following Termination

If the real property constituting the Condominium Development is to be sold following termination, then upon termination of the Condominium Development, title to such real property vests in the Condominium Association as trustee for the holders of all interests in the Units, and the Condominium Association is vested with all powers necessary and appropriate to effect such sale, including the power to convey the interests

[115] Tex. Prop. Code §§ 81.110(a), 82.068(a). If the Condominium Development is subject to the Texas Condominium Act and its Condominium Declaration provides for termination of the Condominium Development by the agreement of the Apartment Owners, then the Condominium Development may be terminated by the agreement of sixty-seven percent (67%) of the Apartment Owners or the percentage of Apartment Owners stated in the Condominium Declaration, whichever is greater. Tex. Prop. Code § 81.110(a). If the Condominium Development is subject to the Texas Uniform Condominium Act, the Condominium Declaration may not allow termination of the Condominium Development by the agreement of less than eighty percent (80%) of the votes in the Condominium Association if any Unit is restricted exclusively to residential uses. Tex. Prop. Code § 82.068(a).

[116] Tex. Prop. Code § 82.068(b).

[117] Tex. Prop. Code § 82.068(b).

[118] Tex. Prop. Code § 82.068(b).

of non-consenting Unit Owners.[119] Until the sale has been concluded and the proceeds distributed, the Condominium Association shall continue to exist and retain the powers it had before termination.[120] Unless the termination agreement specifies differently, as long as the Condominium Association holds title to the real property, each Unit Owner and the Unit Owner's successors in interest have an exclusive right to occupy the portion of the real property that formerly constituted the Unit Owner's Unit.[121] During that period of occupancy, a Unit Owner and the Unit Owner's successors in interest remain liable for all Assessments and other obligations imposed on Unit Owners by the Texas Uniform Condominium Act or the applicable Condominium Declaration.[122]

Proceeds from the sale of the Condominium Development's real property following termination must be distributed to Unit Owners and lienholders, as their interests may appear, in proportion to the respective fair market value of the interests of all Unit Owners.[123] The interest of a Unit Owner is the fair market value of the Unit Owner's Unit, Limited Common Elements, and Common Elements interest immediately before the termination, as determined by one or more independent appraisers selected by the Condominium Association.[124] If a Unit or a Limited Common Element is destroyed or damaged to the extent that an appraisal of the fair market value before the destruction cannot be made, then the interest of a Unit Owner is the Unit Owner's Common Element interest immediately before the termination.[125] The decision of the independent appraisers shall be disseminated to the Unit Owners and becomes final unless disapproved by Unit Owners to which twenty-five percent (25%) of the votes in the Condominium Association

[119] Tex. Prop. Code § 82.068(c).

[120] Tex. Prop. Code § 82.068(c).

[121] Tex. Prop. Code § 82.068(c).

[122] Tex. Prop. Code § 82.068(c).

[123] Tex. Prop. Code § 82.068(c), (f).

[124] Tex. Prop. Code § 82.068(f).

[125] Tex. Prop. Code § 82.068(g).

are allocated no later than thirty (30) days after the date of dissemination of the independent appraiser's decision.[126] The proportion of a Unit Owner's interest to that of all Unit Owners is determined by dividing the fair market value of the Unit Owner's Unit and Common Elements interest by the total fair market value of all the Units and Common Elements.[127]

2.12.3 Termination Procedure if the Condominium Development Property Is not to Be Sold Following Termination

If the real property constituting the Condominium Development is not to be sold following termination, then upon termination of the Condominium Development, title to the real property vests in the Unit Owners as tenants in common in proportion to their respective interests, and liens on the Units shift accordingly.[128] While the tenancy in common exists, a Unit Owner and the Unit Owner's successors in interest have an exclusive right to occupy the portion of the real property that formerly constituted the Unit Owner's Unit.[129]

2.12.4 Post-Termination Distribution of Condominium Association's Assets

Following termination of the Condominium Development, and after payment of or provision for the claims of the Condominium Association's creditors, the assets of the Condominium Association shall be distributed to Unit Owners in proportion to their respective interests.[130] It is important to note that the proceeds from the sale of real property in the Condominium Development, held by the Condominium Association as

---

[126] Tex. Prop. Code § 82.068(f).

[127] Tex. Prop. Code § 82.068(f).

[128] Tex. Prop. Code § 82.068(d). "Tenancy in Common" is a form of real property ownership whereby each tenant (i.e., owner) holds an undivided interest in the real property. *See generally*, *Black's Law Dictionary* 1465 (6th ed. 1990).

[129] Tex. Prop. Code § 82.068(d).

[130] Tex. Prop. Code § 82.068(e).

trustee for the holders of all interests in the Units, are not assets of the Condominium Association.[131]

2.12.5 Rescission of Termination Agreement

If the Unit Owners want to rescind the termination of the Condominium Development following approval of a termination agreement, then the Unit Owners may rescind such termination agreement and reinstate the Condominium Declaration by agreement of the same percentage of Unit Owners that was required to terminate the Condominium Development.[132] A properly approved rescission agreement is considered to be retroactively effective back to the date of the election to terminate the Condominium Development.[133] To be effective, the rescission agreement must be in writing, executed by the Unit Owners who desire to rescind, and recorded in the Official Public Records of each county in which any portion of the Condominium Development is located.[134]

2.13 Foreclosure of a Lien Against All or Part of a Condominium Development

Occasionally, there will be a foreclosure or enforcement of a lien against all or part of the Condominium Development. Foreclosure or enforcement of a lien or encumbrance against the entire Condominium Development does not in and of itself terminate the Condominium Development.[135] In addition, foreclosure or enforcement of a lien or encumbrance against a portion of the Condominium Development's property also does not withdraw that portion of property from the Condominium Development, unless such portion is withdrawable real property or unless the mortgage being foreclosed was

---

[131] Tex. Prop. Code § 82.068(e).

[132] Tex. Prop. Code § 82.068(i).

[133] Tex. Prop. Code § 82.068(i).

[134] Tex. Prop. Code § 82.068(i).

[135] Tex. Prop. Code § 82.068(h). The provisions of the Texas Uniform Condominium Act concerning foreclosure of a lien against the Condominium Development are not applicable to Condominium Developments created prior to January 1, 1994, that are subject to the Texas Condominium Act, and there are no comparable provisions under the Texas Condominium Act. Tex. Prop. Code § 82.002(c).

recorded before the date the Condominium Declaration was recorded and the mortgagee did not consent in writing to the execution and recording of the Condominium Declaration.[136]

2.14 Rights of Secured Lenders

In a number of instances, such as the sale or encumbrance of Common Elements or the termination of a Condominium Development, a lender's security may be dramatically affected by acts of the Condominium Association. For such reasons, a Condominium Declaration may require that all or a specified number or percentage of the mortgagees or beneficiaries of deed of trust liens encumbering the Units in the Condominium Development approve specified actions of the Unit Owners or the Board of Directors as a condition to the effectiveness of those actions.[137] In plain English, this means that a Condominium Declaration may require that certain actions approved by the Unit Owners or the Board of Directors must also be approved by a certain number of secured lenders before the approval of such action is effective.

To the extent a Condominium Declaration requires such approval of mortgagees or beneficiaries of deeds of trust liens, such requirement may not operate to deny or delegate control over the Condominium Association's general administrative affairs.[138] In addition, no procedures for the protection of mortgagees or beneficiaries of deed of trust liens may prevent the Condominium Association or the Board of Directors from commencing, intervening in, or settling any litigation or proceeding or receiving and

---

[136] Tex. Prop. Code § 82.068(h).

[137] Tex. Prop. Code § 82.069. The provisions of the Texas Uniform Condominium Act concerning rights of secured lenders are not applicable to Condominium Developments created prior to January 1, 1994, that are subject to the Texas Condominium Act, and the comparable provisions under the Texas Condominium Act differ significantly from their counterparts under the Texas Uniform Condominium Act. Tex. Prop. Code § 82.002(c). Under the Texas Condominium Act, a Condominium Association may not alter or destroy an Apartment or a Limited Common Element without the consent of all affected Apartment Owners and the first lien mortgagees of all affected Apartment Owners. Tex. Prop. Code § 81.104(e).

[138] Tex. Prop. Code § 82.069(1).

distributing insurance proceeds under Section 82.111 of the Texas Uniform Condominium Act.[139] In other words, any procedures provided for in a Condominium Declaration to protect secured lenders may not be so burdensome or broad that it effectively delegates control over the Condominium Association or any lawsuit by the Condominium Association to the secured lenders.

2.15 Organization and Powers of a Condominium Association

Every Condominium Development subject to the Texas Uniform Condominium Act is required to have a Condominium Association, which must be organized as a Texas for-profit or nonprofit corporation.[140] The Declarant of a Condominium Development subject to the Texas Uniform Condominium Act may not convey a Unit in such Condominium Development until the Texas Secretary of State has issued a certificate of incorporation for the Condominium Association.[141] At all times, the membership of the Condominium Association must consist exclusively of all the Unit Owners in the Condominium Development or, following termination of the Condominium Development, all former Unit Owners entitled to distribution of proceeds (or an applicable Unit Owner's heirs, successors, or assigns).[142]

2.15.1 General Powers of Condominium Associations

In most cases, the Condominium Declaration will specify the powers of the Condominium Association. In addition to those powers specifically granted to the

---

[139] Tex. Prop. Code § 82.069(2).

[140] Tex. Prop. Code § 82.101. The provisions of the Texas Uniform Condominium Act concerning organization of the Condominium Association are not applicable to Condominium Developments created prior to January 1, 1994, that are subject to the Texas Condominium Act, and there are no comparable provisions under the Texas Condominium Act. Tex. Prop. Code § 82.002(c). The Texas Condominium Act provides for management of Condominium Associations by a "Council of Owners," which such Act defines as all the Apartment Owners in a Condominium Development. Tex. Prop. Code §§ 81.002(4), 81.201.

[141] Tex. Prop. Code § 82.101.

[142] Tex. Prop. Code § 82.101.

Condominium Association in the Condominium Declaration, the Texas Uniform Condominium Act vests Condominium Associations with certain inherent powers, unless otherwise provided by the Condominium Declaration.[143] More specifically, unless otherwise provided by its Condominium Declaration, a Condominium Association, acting through its Board of Directors, may:[144]

(1) adopt and amend Bylaws;[145]

(2) adopt and amend budgets for revenues, expenditures, and reserves, and collect Assessments for Common Expenses from Unit Owners;[146]

(3) hire and terminate managing agents and other employees, agents, and independent contractors;[147]

(4) institute, defend, intervene in, settle, or compromise litigation or administrative proceedings in its own name on behalf of itself or two or more Unit Owners on matters affecting the Condominium Development;[148]

(5) make contracts and incur liabilities relating to the operation of the Condominium Development;[149]

(6) regulate the use, maintenance, repair, replacement, modification, and appearance of the Condominium Development;[150]

---

143 Tex. Prop. Code § 82.102.

144 Only certain provisions of the Texas Uniform Condominium Act establishing powers of a Condominium Association are applicable to Condominium Developments created prior to January 1, 1994, that are subject to the Texas Condominium Act. Tex. Prop. Code § 82.002(c). The applicable provisions of the Texas Uniform Condominium Act that apply to the Condominium Associations subject to the Texas Condominium Act are Sections 82.102(a)(1)–(7), (a)(12)–(21) (f), and (g). Tex. Prop. Code §§ 82.002(c), 82.102. By process of elimination, Sections 82.102(a)(8)–(11), (b), (c), (d), and (e) of the Texas Property Code does not apply to Condominiums subject to the Texas Condominium Act. Tex. Prop. Code §§ 82.002(c), 82.102.

145 Tex. Prop. Code § 82.102(a)(1).

146 Tex. Prop. Code § 82.102(a)(2).

147 Tex. Prop. Code § 82.102(a)(3).

148 Tex. Prop. Code § 82.102(a)(4).

149 Tex. Prop. Code § 82.102(a)(5).

150 Tex. Prop. Code § 82.102(a)(6).

(7) adopt and amend Association Rules regulating the use, occupancy, leasing or sale, maintenance, repair, modification, and appearance of Units and Common Elements, to the extent the regulated actions affect Common Elements or other Units;[151]

(8) cause additional improvements to be made as a part of the Common Elements;[152]

(9) acquire, hold, encumber, and convey in its own name any right, title, or interest to real or personal property, except Common Elements of the Condominium Development;[153]

(10) grant easements, leases, licenses, and concessions through or over the Common Elements;[154]

(11) impose and receive payments, fees, or charges for the use, rental, or operation of the Common Elements and for services provided to Unit Owners;[155]

(12) impose interest and late charges for late payments of Assessments, returned check charges, and, if notice and an opportunity to be heard are given, reasonable fines for violations of the Condominium Declaration, Bylaws, and Association Rules of the Condominium Association;[156]

---

[151] Tex. Prop. Code § 82.102(a)(7).

[152] Tex. Prop. Code § 82.102(a)(8). This particular provision is not applicable to Condominium Developments created prior to January 1, 1994, that are subject to the Texas Condominium Act. Tex. Prop. Code § 82.002(c).

[153] Tex. Prop. Code § 82.102(a)(9). This particular provision is not applicable to Condominium Developments created prior to January 1, 1994, that are subject to the Texas Condominium Act. Tex. Prop. Code § 82.002(c).

[154] Tex. Prop. Code § 82.102(a)(10). This particular provision is not applicable to Condominium Developments created prior to January 1, 1994, that are subject to the Texas Condominium Act. Tex. Prop. Code § 82.002(c).

[155] Tex. Prop. Code § 82.102(a)(11). This particular provision is not applicable to Condominium Developments created prior to January 1, 1994, that are subject to the Texas Condominium Act. Tex. Prop. Code § 82.002(c).

[156] Tex. Prop. Code § 82.102(a)(12). The notice and opportunity to be heard must be provided to the Unit Owner in accordance with Section 82.102(d) of the Texas Property Code. Tex. Prop. Code § 82.102(a)(12). Section 82.102(d) of the Texas Property Code requires a Condominium Association, before it may assess a fine against a Unit Owner, to give the Unit Owner written notice that: (1) describes the violation and states the amount of the proposed fine; (2) advises the Unit Owner that he or she has thirty (30) days from the date of the notice to request a hearing before the Condominium Association's Board of Directors for the purpose of contesting the fine or damage charge; and (3) allows the Unit Owner a reasonable time, by a specified date,

(13) adopt and amend Association Rules regulating the collection of delinquent Assessments and the application of payments;[157]

(14) adopt and amend Association Rules regulating the termination of utility service to a Unit if the owner of such Unit is delinquent in the payment of an Assessment that is used, in whole or in part, to pay the cost of such utility service;[158]

(15) impose reasonable charges for preparing, recording, or copying Declaration amendments, Resale Certificates, or statements of unpaid Assessments;[159]

(16) enter a Unit for bona fide emergency purposes when conditions present an imminent risk of harm or damage to the Common Elements, another Unit, or the Unit's occupants;[160]

(17) suspend the voting privileges of or the use of certain General Common Elements by a Unit Owner delinquent for more than thirty (30) days in the payment of Assessments;[161]

(18) purchase insurance and fidelity bonds it considers appropriate or necessary;[162]

(19) exercise any other powers conferred on it by its Condominium Declaration or Bylaws;[163]

(20) exercise any other powers that may be exercised in the State of Texas by a corporation of the same type as the Condominium Association;[164] and

---

to cure the violation and avoid the fine, unless the Unit Owner was given notice and a reasonable opportunity to cure a similar violation within the preceding twelve (12) months. Tex. Prop. Code § 82.102(d).

157 Tex. Prop. Code § 82.102(a)(13).

158 Tex. Prop. Code § 82.102(a)(14).

159 Tex. Prop. Code § 82.102(a)(15).

160 Tex. Prop. Code § 82.102(a)(16).

161 Tex. Prop. Code § 82.102(a)(17).

162 Tex. Prop. Code § 82.102(a)(18).

163 Tex. Prop. Code § 82.102(a)(19).

164 Tex. Prop. Code § 82.102(a)(20).

(21) exercise any other powers necessary and proper for the government and operation of the Condominium Association.[165]

2.15.2 Power of Condominium Associations to Borrow Money and to Assign Their Rights to Future Income and Lien Rights as Collateral for a Loan

In 2013, the Texas Legislature amended the Texas Uniform Condominium Act so as to authorize a Condominium Association to borrow money and assign as collateral for the loan its right to future income and its lien rights.[166] Unless a Condominium Association's Dedicatory Instruments require a vote of Unit Owners in order for the Condominium Association to borrow money or assign its right to future income or its lien rights as collateral for a loan, the Condominium Association (by resolution of its Board of Directors) may: (1) borrow money; and (2) assign as collateral for the loan (so authorized by the resolution) the Condominium Association's right to future income, including the right to receive assessments, and its lien rights.[167]

If a Condominium Association's Dedicatory Instruments require a vote of Unit Owners in order for the Condominium Association to borrow money or to assign its right to future income or its lien rights as collateral for a loan, then the loan and/or assignment of its rights must be approved as provided by the applicable Dedicatory Instrument.[168] Notwithstanding, in the event that a loan and/or an assignment of a Condominium Association's rights as collateral for a loan must be approved by the Unit Owners, the Texas Uniform Condominium Act vests its Board of Directors with the authority to

---

[165] Tex. Prop. Code § 82.102(a)(21).

[166] Tex. Prop. Code § 82.102(f). *See also*, Senate Research Center, Bill Analysis, TEX. H.B. 2075, 83rd Leg., R.S. (2013).

[167] Tex. Prop. Code § 82.012(f)-(g).

[168] Tex. Prop. Code § 82.102(g). A vote of Unit Owners to authorize a Condominium Association to borrow money or to assign its right to future income or its lien rights as collateral for a loan must be approved by the requisite number or percentage of Unit Owners specified in the applicable Dedicatory Instrument or by the consent of Unit Owners holding sixty-seven percent (67%) of all voting interests in the Condominium Association, whichever is lower. Tex. Prop. Code § 82.102(g).

determine the manner in which the Unit Owners vote for or consent to such loan or assignment.[169] More specifically, the Condominium Association's Board of Directors is vested with the authority to determine whether a vote of the Unit Owners for such purpose may be cast: (1) electronically; (2) by absentee ballot; (3) in person or by proxy at a meeting called for such purpose; or (4) by written consent.[170]

2.15.3 Power of Condominium Associations to Evict or Collect Rents from a Unit Owner's Tenants

The Texas Uniform Condominium Act also authorizes a Condominium Association to amend the Condominium Declaration to authorize the Board of Directors to: (1) bring an action to evict a tenant of a Unit Owner for the tenant's violation of the Condominium Declaration or the Condominium Association's Bylaws or Rules; (2) bring an action to evict a tenant of a Unit Owner who fails to pay the Condominium Association for the cost of repairs to Common Elements damaged substantially by the Unit Owner's tenant; or (3) collect rents from a tenant of a Unit Owner who is at least sixty (60) days delinquent in the payment of any amount due to the Condominium Association.[171]

2.15.4 Power of Condominium Associations to Sell Real Property in the Condominium Development

The Texas Uniform Condominium Act also authorizes a Condominium Association, on behalf of the Unit Owners, to contract for the sale of real property in the Condominium Development.[172] Such contract, however, will not be binding on the Unit

---

[169] Tex. Prop. Code § 82.102(g).

[170] Tex. Prop. Code § 82.102(g).

[171] Tex. Prop. Code § 82.067(h). The provisions of the Texas Uniform Condominium Act concerning power of a Condominium Association to amend the Condominium Declaration to authorize the Board of Directors to evict a Unit Owner's tenant or to collect rents from a Unit Owner's tenant are not applicable to Condominium Developments created prior to January 1, 1994, that are subject to the Texas Condominium Act, and there are no comparable provisions under the Texas Condominium Act. Tex. Prop. Code § 82.002(c).

[172] Tex. Prop. Code § 82.068(c). The provisions of the Texas Uniform Condominium Act concerning power of a Condominium Association to sell real property in the Condominium Development are not applicable to

Owners until it is approved by the agreement of the required percentage of votes specified in the Condominium Declaration for termination of the Condominium Development or, if none is specified in the Condominium Declaration, then by the agreement of: (1) one hundred percent (100%) of the votes in the Condominium Association; and (2) each holder of a deed of trust or vendor's lien on a Unit in the Condominium Development.[173] To be effective, such agreement must set forth the terms of the sale and, together with all its requisite ratifications, must be recorded in the Official Public Records of each county in which a portion of the Condominium Development is located.[174]

2.15.5 Power of Condominium Associations to Terminate Certain Contracts without Penalty

The Texas Uniform Condominium Act authorizes a Condominium Association in a residential or recreational Condominium Development to terminate, without penalty, contracts or leases between the Condominium Association and a Declarant or an "Affiliate of a Declarant" if: (1) the contract was entered into by the Condominium Association while it was controlled by the Declarant; (2) the Condominium Association terminates the contract or lease within one (1) year from the date a Board of Directors elected by the Unit Owners takes office; and (3) the Condominium Association gives the other party to the contract or lease at least ninety (90) days notice of its intent to terminate the contract or

---

Condominium Developments created prior to January 1, 1994, that are subject to the Texas Condominium Act, and there are no comparable provisions under the Texas Condominium Act. Tex. Prop. Code § 82.002(c).

[173] Tex. Prop. Code § 82.068(a), (c).

[174] Tex. Prop. Code § 82.068(b), (c).

lease.[175] The Texas Uniform Condominium Act defines an "Affiliate of a Declarant" as any person who controls, is controlled by, or is under common control with a Declarant.[176]

2.15.6 Regulations on the Powers of Condominium Associations

The Texas Uniform Condominium Act also imposes certain regulations on the powers granted to a Condominium Association under a Condominium Declaration and the exercise of such power by the Condominium Association. First, the Condominium Declaration may not impose limitations on the power of the Condominium Association to deal with the Declarant that are more restrictive than the limitations imposed on the power of the Condominium Association to deal with other persons.[177] For example, a Condominium Declaration may not restrict the Condominium Association from enforcing Restrictive Covenants against Units owned by the Declarant.

[175] Tex. Prop. Code § 82.105. The provisions of the Texas Uniform Condominium Act concerning the authority of a Condominium Association to terminate certain contracts without penalty are not applicable to Condominium Developments created prior to January 1, 1994, that are subject to the Texas Condominium Act, and there are no comparable provisions under the Texas Condominium Act. Tex. Prop. Code § 82.002(c).

[176] Tex. Prop. Code § 82.003(a)(1). The Texas Uniform Condominium Act further provides that a person or entity "controls" a Declarant if such person or entity: (1) is a general partner, officer, director, or employer of the Declarant; (2) directly or indirectly or acting in concert with one or more other persons or entities, or through one or more subsidiaries, owns, controls, holds with power to vote, or holds proxies representing more than twenty percent (20%) of the voting interests in the Declarant; (3) determines in any manner the election of a majority of the directors of the Declarant; or (4) has contributed more than twenty percent (20%) of the capital of the Declarant. Tex. Prop. Code § 82.003(a)(1). A person or entity "is controlled by" a Declarant if the Declarant: (1) is a general partner, officer, director, or employer of such person or entity; (2) directly or indirectly or acting in concert with one or more other persons or entities, or through one or more subsidiaries, owns, controls, holds with power to vote, or holds proxies representing more than twenty percent (20%) of the voting interests in such entity; (3) determines in any manner the election of a majority of the directors of such entity; or (4) has contributed more than twenty percent (20%) of the capital of such entity. Tex. Prop. Code § 82.003(a)(1).

[177] Tex. Prop. Code § 82.102(b). The provisions of the Texas Uniform Condominium Act concerning prohibitions on Condominium Declaration provisions that impose limitations on the power of the Condominium Association to deal with the Declarant are not applicable to Condominium Developments created prior to January 1, 1994, that are subject to the Texas Condominium Act, and there are no comparable provisions under the Texas Condominium Act. Tex. Prop. Code § 82.002(c).

Second, a Bylaw or Association Rule of a Condominium Association that is arbitrary or capricious will not be enforceable.[178]

Third, the Texas Uniform Condominium Act imposes certain due process requirements on a Condominium Association before it may charge a Unit Owner for property damage for which the Unit Owner is liable or levy a fine against a Unit Owner for violation of the Condominium Declaration, Bylaws, or Association Rules.[179] More specifically, before it may charge for property damage or levy a fine against a Unit Owner, a Condominium Association must give the Unit Owner a written notice that: (1) describes the violation or property damage and states the amount of the proposed fine or damage charge; (2) advises the Unit Owner that he or she has thirty (30) days from the date of the notice to request a hearing before the Condominium Association's Board of Directors for the purpose of contesting the fine or damage charge; and (3) allows the Unit Owner a reasonable time, by a specified date, to cure the violation and avoid the fine, unless the Unit Owner was given notice and a reasonable opportunity to cure a similar violation within the preceding twelve (12) months.[180] The Condominium Association may deliver such written notice to a Unit Owner by giving a copy of it to any occupant of the Unit.[181] Additionally, if the Condominium Association levies a fine or damage charge, it must give notice of the levied fine or damage charge to the Unit Owner no later than thirty (30) days after the date of levying such fine.[182]

---

178 Tex. Prop. Code § 82.102(c). The provisions of the Texas Uniform Condominium Act concerning enforcement of Bylaws and Association Rules are not applicable to Condominium Developments created prior to January 1, 1994, that are subject to the Texas Condominium Act, and there are no comparable provisions under the Texas Condominium Act. Tex. Prop. Code § 82.002(c).

179 Tex. Prop. Code § 82.102(d).

180 Tex. Prop. Code § 82.102(d).

181 Tex. Prop. Code § 82.102(e).

182 Tex. Prop. Code § 82.102(e). The provision of the Texas Uniform Condominium Act concerning the requirement that a Condominium Association give notice of an assessed fine or damage charge to the Unit Owner is not applicable to Condominium Developments created prior to January 1, 1994, that are subject to

2.16 Directors and Officers of a Condominium Association

Unless otherwise provided by its Condominium Declaration or Bylaws, all acts of the Condominium Association must be by and through the Board of Directors for the Condominium Association.[183] The Board of Directors for a Condominium Association must be made up of at least three Directors and, unless otherwise provided by the Condominium Declaration or Bylaws or by other law, such Directors are not required to be Unit Owners in the Condominium Development.[184]

2.16.1 Transition of Control of Condominium Associations

In most instances, the Condominium Declaration will provide for an initial period of "Declarant-Control" of the Condominium Association, during which the Declarant may appoint the Directors and Officers of the Condominium Association (generally referred to as a Condominium Association's "Declarant-Control Period").[185] Regardless of the duration of the Declarant-Control Period specified in the Condominium Declaration, the Texas Uniform Condominium Act requires that control of the Condominium Association's Board of Directors be gradually transitioned from the Declarant to the Unit Owners, other than the Declarant, upon the occurrence of certain benchmarks.

---

the Texas Condominium Act, and there are no comparable provisions under the Texas Condominium Act. Tex. Prop. Code § 82.002(c).

183 Tex. Prop. Code § 82.103(a). The provisions of the Texas Uniform Condominium Act concerning Directors and Officers are not applicable to Condominium Developments created prior to January 1, 1994, that are subject to the Texas Condominium Act, and there are no comparable provisions under the Texas Condominium Act. Tex. Prop. Code § 82.002(c). Notwithstanding, if a Condominium Association of a Condominium Development created prior to January 1, 1994, that is subject to the Texas Condominium Act is incorporated as a Texas nonprofit corporation, there are many similar provisions under the Texas Nonprofit Corporation Law.

184 Tex. Prop. Code § 82.103(a), (e).

185 Tex. Prop. Code § 82.103(c). The provisions of the Texas Uniform Condominium Act concerning transition of control from the Declarant to the Unit Owners are not applicable to Condominium Developments created prior to January 1, 1994, that are subject to the Texas Condominium Act, and there are no comparable provisions under the Texas Condominium Act. Tex. Prop. Code § 82.002(c).

First, no later than one hundred twenty (120) days after conveyance of fifty percent (50%) of the Units in the Condominium Development to Unit Owners other than a Declarant, at least one-third (1/3) of the members of the Board of Directors must be elected by Unit Owners other than the Declarant.[186]

Thereafter, a Condominium Association's period of Declarant-Control terminates one hundred twenty (120) days after the Declarant conveys seventy-five percent (75%) of the total number of Units in the Condominium Development to a person or entity other than the Declarant.[187] Prior to, and at the very least no later than, the date of termination of the Declarant-Control Period, the members of the Board of Directors must all be elected by Unit Owners.[188] In addition, within thirty (30) days of the termination of the Declarant-Control Period, the Board of Directors elected by the Unit Owners must elect the Officers of the Condominium Association.[189] Persons elected to the Board of Directors or as Officers of the Condominium Association shall take office upon election.[190]

2.16.2 Duty of Care of Directors and Officers of Condominium Associations

Except as provided by a Condominium Association's Declaration or Bylaws, or the Texas Uniform Condominium Act, the Board of Directors is vested with the power to

---

[186] Tex. Prop. Code § 82.103(d).

[187] Tex. Prop. Code § 82.103(c). It is important to note that a transfer of Special Declarant Rights by the Declarant does not terminate the period of Declarant control. Tex. Prop. Code § 82.103(c). In addition, a Declarant may voluntarily surrender the right to appoint and remove officers and members of the Board of Directors before termination of the Declarant-Control Period, and in such event, the Declarant may also require for the duration of the period that the Declarant would otherwise control that specified actions of the Condominium Association or Board of Directors be approved by the Declarant before they become effective. Tex. Prop. Code § 82.103(c).

[188] Tex. Prop. Code § 82.103(e). Unless required by the Condominium Declaration or Bylaws, the persons elected to the Board of Directors by Unit Owners upon the termination of the Declarant-Control Period are not required to be Unit Owners. Tex. Prop. Code § 82.103(e).

[189] Tex. Prop. Code § 82.103(e).

[190] Tex. Prop. Code § 82.103(e).

take action on behalf of the Condominium Association so long as such action, in the good-faith judgment of the Board of Directors, is reasonable.[191] Notwithstanding, the Board of Directors may not unilaterally: (1) amend the Condominium Declaration (except as permitted by the Texas Uniform Condominium Act); (2) terminate the Condominium Development; (3) elect members of the Board of Directors; or (4) determine the qualifications, powers and duties, or terms of office of the members of the Board of Directors.[192]

In addition, each Officer and Director of a Condominium Association is considered to be a fiduciary of the Unit Owners in the commission of acts and omissions in the course and scope of their roles as Officers or Directors of the Condominium Association.[193] Notwithstanding, an Officer or Director of the Condominium Association may not be held liable to the Condominium Association or any Unit Owner for monetary damages for an act or omission occurring in such person's capacity as an Officer or Director unless: (1) the Officer or Director breached a fiduciary duty to the Condominium Association or a Unit Owner; (2) the Officer or Director received an improper benefit; or (3) the act or omission was in bad faith, involved intentional misconduct, or was one for which liability is expressly provided by statutory law.[194]

---

[191] Tex. Prop. Code § 82.103(a). The provisions of the Texas Uniform Condominium Act concerning Directors and Officers are not applicable to Condominium Developments created prior to January 1, 1994, that are subject to the Texas Condominium Act, and there are no comparable provisions under the Texas Condominium Act. Tex. Prop. Code § 82.002(c). Notwithstanding, if a Condominium Association of a Condominium Development created prior to January 1, 1994, that is subject to the Texas Condominium Act is incorporated as a Texas nonprofit corporation, there are many similar provisions under the Texas Nonprofit Corporation Law.

[192] Tex. Prop. Code § 82.103(b). The Board of Directors may, however, fill a vacancy in the Board of Directors for the unexpired portion of the term of office for the vacated position. Tex. Prop. Code § 82.103(b).

[193] Tex. Prop. Code § 82.103(a).

[194] Tex. Prop. Code § 82.103(f). Such statutory provision does not diminish a limitation of liability provided to an Officer or Director of a Condominium Association by the Declaration, Bylaws, and/or Articles of Incorporation of the Condominium Association or by other Texas laws. Tex. Prop. Code § 82.103(g). For more information on other limitations of liabilities afforded Officers and Directors of Texas Nonprofit Corporation HOAs under Texas law, please see Chapter 3 of this book.

2.17 Bylaws of Condominium Associations

The administration and operation of a Condominium Association is governed by the Condominium Association's Bylaws, which must provide for:[195]

(1) the number of members on the Board of Directors and the titles of the Officers of the Condominium Association;[196]

(2) election by the Board of Directors of a President, Treasurer, Secretary, and any other Officers the Bylaws specify;[197]

(3) the qualifications, powers and duties, terms of office, the manner of electing and removing a member of the Board of Directors or an Officer, and the manner in which vacancies will be filled;[198]

(4) the powers, if any, that the Board of Directors or an Officer may delegate to other persons or to a managing agent;[199]

(5) the designation of Officers who are authorized to prepare, execute, certify, and record amendments to the Condominium Declaration on behalf of the Condominium Association;

(6) the method of amending the Bylaws;[200] and

(7) the manner of giving notice of meetings of the Condominium Association to Unit Owners.[201]

---

[195] The provisions of the Texas Uniform Condominium Act concerning Bylaws are not applicable to Condominium Developments created prior to January 1, 1994, that are subject to the Texas Condominium Act, and there are no comparable provisions under the Texas Condominium Act. Tex. Prop. Code § 82.002(c).

[196] Tex. Prop. Code § 82.106(a)(1).

[197] Tex. Prop. Code § 82.106(a)(2).

[198] Tex. Prop. Code § 82.106(a)(3).

[199] Tex. Prop. Code § 82.106(a)(4).

[200] Tex. Prop. Code § 82.106(a)(5).

[201] Tex. Prop. Code § 82.106(a)(6).

Subject to the Condominium Declaration, the Bylaws may also provide for other matters the Condominium Association considers desirable, necessary, or appropriate.[202]

2.18 Meetings, Quorums, Voting, and Proxies

Meetings of the Condominium Association's membership must be held at least once each year.[203] Unless the Condominium Declaration provides otherwise, special meetings of the Condominium Association's membership may be called by the President, a majority of the Board of Directors, or Unit Owners having at least twenty percent (20%) of the votes in the Condominium Association.[204]

2.18.1 Notice of Board of Directors and Membership Meetings

In general, Notice of a Board of Directors meeting must be given to each Director as provided by the Condominium Association's Bylaws.[205] If a Condominium Association's Bylaws do not have provisions concerning the manner in which Directors are to be notified of Board Meetings, then the Texas Uniform Condominium Act requires that notice of a Board of Directors meeting must be given to each Director in the same manner in which notice is given to members of the Board of Directors of a nonprofit corporation under Article 2.19 of the Texas Non-Profit Corporation Act.[206]

---

202 Tex. Prop. Code § 82.106(b).

203 Tex. Prop. Code § 82.108(a).

204 Tex. Prop. Code § 82.108(a).

205 Tex. Prop. Code § 82.108(e).

206 Tex. Prop. Code § 82.108(e). Article 2.19 of the Texas Non-Profit Corporation Act provides that regular meetings of the Board of Directors may be held with or without notice as prescribed in the nonprofit corporation's Bylaws, and special meetings of the Board of Directors shall be held upon such notice as is prescribed in the nonprofit corporation's Bylaws. Tex. Rev. Civ. Stat. Ann. art. 1396-2.19. Interestingly, Article 2.19 fails to provide a method of providing notice of a Board of Directors meeting in the absence of a provision in the Bylaws for providing notice of Board of Directors meeting. Tex. Rev. Civ. Stat. Ann. art. 1396-2.19. Notwithstanding, Section 22.217 of the Texas Nonprofit Corporation Law (which is a recodification of Article 2.19 of the Texas Non-Profit Corporation Act) does include a provision stating that notice of a Board of Directors meeting may be delivered personally or in accordance with Section 6.051(b) of the Texas Business Organizations Code. Tex. Bus. Org. Code § 22.217. Section 6.051(b) of the Texas

Notice of a Board of Directors meeting must also be given to each Unit Owner as provided by the Condominium Association's Bylaws.[207] However, unlike Directors, if a Condominium Association's Bylaws do not have a provision requiring that notice of a Board of Directors meeting be given to Unit Owners, then it is not required to provide notice of such meetings to Unit Owners. Notwithstanding, if a Condominium Association receives a written request from a Unit Owner for information concerning the next regular or special meeting of the Board of Directors, the Condominium Association is required to inform such Unit Owner of the time and place of the next regular or special meeting of the Board of Directors.[208] In addition, if the Condominium Association representative to whom the request is made does not know the time and place of the next regular or special Board of Directors meeting, then the Condominium Association must promptly obtain such information and disclose it to the Unit Owner or inform the Unit Owner where he or she may obtain such information.[209]

Similar to Board Meetings, notice of a meeting of the Condominium Association's membership must be given to Unit Owners as provided by the Condominium Association's Bylaws.[210] If the Condominium Association's Bylaws do not have provisions concerning the manner in which Unit Owners are to be notified of membership meetings, then the Texas Uniform Condominium Act requires that notice of a membership meeting be given to each Unit Owner in the same manner in which a notice

---

Business Organizations Code provides that notice of a meeting that is mailed is considered to be given on the date the notice is deposited in the United States mail, with postage paid, in an envelope addressed to the person at the person's address as it appears on the ownership or membership records of the nonprofit corporation; whereas notice of a meeting that is transmitted by facsimile or email is considered to be given when transmitted to a facsimile number or an email address provided by the person, or to which the person consents, for the purpose of receiving notice from the nonprofit corporation. Tex. Bus. Org. Code § 6.051(b).

207 Tex. Prop. Code § 82.108(e).

208 Tex. Prop. Code § 82.108(f).

209 Tex. Prop. Code § 82.108(f).

210 Tex. Prop. Code § 82.108(d).

of meeting is given to members of a nonprofit corporation under Article 2.11 of the Texas Non-Profit Corporation Act.[211]

2.18.2 Manner of Conducting Meetings

Meetings of a Condominium Association's Board of Directors and membership must be open to Unit Owners.[212] The right of Unit Owners to attend a meeting of the Board of Directors, however, is subject to the right of the Board of Directors to adjourn and reconvene in closed "Executive Session" to consider actions involving personnel, pending litigation, contract negotiations, enforcement actions, matters involving the invasion of privacy of individual Unit Owners, or matters that are to remain confidential by request of the affected parties and agreement of the Board of Directors.[213]

Unless the Condominium Declaration, Bylaws, or Articles of Incorporation of the Condominium Association provide otherwise, a meeting of the Board of Directors may be held by any method of communication, including electronic and telephonic methods, if: (1) proper notice of the meeting has been given to each Director; (2) each Director may

---

[211] Tex. Prop. Code § 82.108(d). Article 2.11 of the Texas Non-Profit Corporation Act provides that a written or printed notice stating the place, day, and hour of the meeting (and in the case of a special meeting, the purpose(s) of the meeting) must be delivered to members of the nonprofit corporation at least ten (10) days before, but no more than sixty (60) days before, the date of the meeting. Tex. Rev. Civ. Stat. Ann. art. 1396-2.11. In addition, a notice of a membership meeting must be given to each member of the nonprofit corporation entitled to vote at such membership meeting either by hand-delivery, by facsimile, or by mail, by or at the direction of the President, Secretary, or other Officers or persons calling the meeting. Tex. Rev. Civ. Stat. Ann. art. 1396-2.11. Article 2.11 of the Texas Non-Profit Corporation Act further provides that, if mailed, such meeting notice shall be deemed to be delivered to the member when deposited in the United States mail addressed to the member at his or her address, as it appears on the records of the nonprofit corporation, with postage paid. Tex. Rev. Civ. Stat. Ann. art. 1396-2.11. If such meeting notice is transmitted by facsimile, the meeting notice is deemed to be delivered to the member upon successful transmission of the facsimile. Tex. Rev. Civ. Stat. Ann. art. 1396-2.11.

[212] Tex. Prop. Code § 82.108(b).

[213] Tex. Prop. Code § 82.108(b). An Executive Session of a Board Meeting is a session closed to the public during which only the Board of Directors and such select persons invited by the Board of Directors are permitted to be present. Before a Condominium Association's Board of Directors can adjourn a Board Meeting for the purpose of reconvening in a closed Executive Session, however, the general nature of any business to be considered in Executive Session must first be announced by the Board of Directors at the open meeting. Tex. Prop. Code § 82.108(b).

hear and be heard by every other Director; and (3) the meeting does not involve voting on a fine or damage assessment against a Unit Owner, a Unit Owner's appeal from a denial of architectural control approval, or suspension of a right of a particular Unit Owner before the subject Unit Owner has an opportunity to attend a Board of Directors meeting to present his or her position, including any defense, on such issue.[214] In addition, and unless the Condominium Declaration, Bylaws, or Articles of Incorporation of the Condominium Association provide otherwise, the Board of Directors may also act by unanimous written consent of all the Directors without a meeting, so long as the Board of Directors' action does not involve voting on a fine or damage assessment against a Unit Owner, a Unit Owner's appeal from a denial of architectural control approval, or suspension of a right of a particular Unit Owner before the subject Unit Owner has an opportunity to attend a Board of Directors meeting to present his or her position, including any defense, on such issue.[215]

2.18.3 Quorum Requirement

Before any action may be taken at a meeting of a Condominium Association's Board of Directors or membership, a quorum must be established. Unless the Bylaws of a Condominium Association specifies a larger percentage, a quorum for a Board of Directors meeting is established and considered present throughout such meeting if persons entitled to cast at least fifty percent (50%) of the votes of the Board of Directors are present at the beginning of such meeting.[216] In addition, and unless the Bylaws of a Condominium Association provide otherwise, a quorum for a meeting of a Condominium

[214] Tex. Prop. Code § 82.108(c)(1).

[215] Tex. Prop. Code § 82.108(c)(2). If a Board of Directors takes an action by unanimous written consent, a record of such action must be filed with the minutes of the Board of Directors meetings. Tex. Prop. Code § 82.108(c)(2).

[216] Tex. Prop. Code § 82.109(b). The provisions of the Texas Uniform Condominium Act concerning quorum requirements are not applicable to Condominium Developments created prior to January 1, 1994, that are subject to the Texas Condominium Act, and there are no comparable provisions under the Texas Condominium Act. Tex. Prop. Code § 82.002(c).

Association's membership is established and considered present throughout such meeting if persons entitled to cast at least twenty percent (20%) of the votes that may be cast for election of the Board of Directors are present in person or by proxy at the beginning of such meeting.[217] The Bylaws of a Condominium Association may provide for a quorum requirement for membership meetings that is higher or lower than twenty percent (20%), but it may not reduce the standard for a quorum to less than ten percent (10%) of the votes that may be cast for election of the Board of Directors.[218]

2.18.4 Voting, Use of Proxies, and Cumulative Voting

Once a quorum is established, the Board of Directors at a Board of Directors meeting or the Unit Owners at a meeting of the Condominium Association's membership may consider and vote on items submitted to a vote during the course of their respective meetings.

Allocating and calculating votes at a Condominium Association's membership meeting can sometimes be complicated when there are multiple owners of a Unit. If there are multiple owners of a Unit and only one of the multiple owners of the Unit is present at a meeting of the Condominium Association membership, then that owner may cast the vote or votes allocated to that Unit.[219] If there are multiple owners of a Unit and more than one of the multiple owners is present, however, the vote or votes allocated to that Unit may be cast only in accordance with the owners' unanimous agreement, unless the Condominium Declaration provides otherwise.[220] Multiple owners of a Unit are considered to be in unanimous agreement if one of the multiple owners casts the votes

---

[217] Tex. Prop. Code § 82.109(a).

[218] Tex. Prop. Code § 82.109(a).

[219] Tex. Prop. Code § 82.110(a). The provisions of the Texas Uniform Condominium Act concerning voting and use of proxies are not applicable to Condominium Developments created prior to January 1, 1994, that are subject to the Texas Condominium Act, and there are no comparable provisions under the Texas Condominium Act. Tex. Prop. Code § 82.002(c).

[220] Tex. Prop. Code § 82.110(a).

allocated to such Unit and none of the other co-owners of such Unit makes a prompt protest to the person presiding over the meeting.[221]

In addition, votes allocated to a Unit may be cast at a meeting of the Condominium Association's membership in person or by written proxy duly executed by a Unit Owner.[222] If a Unit is owned by more than one person, each owner of the Unit may vote or register a protest to the casting of votes by the other owners of the Unit through a proxy duly executed by such Unit Owner.[223] In addition, a Unit Owner may not revoke a proxy given to another person except by giving actual notice of revocation to the person presiding over the meeting of the Condominium Association.[224]

Finally, cumulative voting is not allowed at meetings of the Condominium Association's membership.[225]

2.19 Insurance

The Texas Uniform Condominium Act requires all Texas Condominium Associations to carry "commercial general liability" insurance and "property insurance coverage," to the extent reasonably available, on all of the Common Elements of its Condominium Development.[226] It is important to note, however, that even though a Texas Condominium Association has no discretion as to whether to purchase commercial

---

[221] Tex. Prop. Code § 82.110(a).

[222] Tex. Prop. Code § 82.110(b). It is important to note that a proxy is void if it is not dated or if it purports to be revocable without notice. Tex. Prop. Code § 82.110(b). A proxy also terminates one year after its effective date unless it specifies a shorter or longer time. Tex. Prop. Code § 82.110(b).

[223] Tex. Prop. Code § 82.110(b).

[224] Tex. Prop. Code § 82.110(b).

[225] Tex. Prop. Code § 82.110(c). Cumulative voting is a method for promoting minority representation by allowing voters to cumulate all of their votes in only one or two candidates.

[226] Tex. Prop. Code § 82.111(a). Notwithstanding the statutory insurance requirements, if all of the Units in the Condominium Development are restricted to nonresidential use, the Condominium Declaration may vary from, or even waive, all of the insurance requirements under the Texas Uniform Condominium Act. Tex. Prop. Code § 82.111(m).

general liability insurance and property insurance policies, such policies may provide for a commercially reasonable deductible in an amount determined to be appropriate or necessary by the Condominium Association's Board of Directors.[227]

2.19.1 Commercial General Liability Insurance

A Texas Condominium Association is required to maintain, to the extent reasonably available, commercial general liability insurance, including medical payments insurance, in an amount determined by the Board of Directors for the Condominium Association.[228] The amount of commercial general liability insurance determined by the Board of Directors, however, may not be less than any amount specified by the Condominium Declaration and must be sufficient enough to cover all occurrences commonly insured against for death, bodily injury, and property damage arising out of, or in connection with, the use, ownership, or maintenance of the Common Elements.[229]

2.19.2 Property Insurance

A Texas Condominium Association is also required to maintain, to the extent reasonably available, property insurance on the insurable Common Elements in its Condominium Development, which must insure against all risks of direct physical loss commonly insured against (including fire and extended coverage) in a total amount of at least eighty percent (80%) of the replacement cost or actual cash value of the insured property as of the effective date and at each renewal date of an applicable insurance policy.[230]

---

227 Tex. Prop. Code § 82.111(c).

228 Tex. Prop. Code § 82.111(a)(2). The term "commercial general liability insuruance" refers to a standard insurance policy issued to business organizations to protect them against liability claims for bodily injury and property damage arising out of premises, operations, products, and completed operations; and advertising and personal injury liability.

229 Tex. Prop. Code § 82.111(a)(2).

230 Tex. Prop. Code § 82.111(a)(1). The term "property insurance" generally refers to first-party insurance that indemnifies the owner or user of property for its loss, or the loss of its income-producing ability, when

2.19.2 (A) *Property Insurance Policy Coverage Requirements*

If the Condominium Development includes a building containing Units with a horizontal boundary between them (such as a high-rise Condominium Development), then the coverage of the property insurance policy maintained by the Condominium Association, to the extent reasonably available, must include all Units, but it need not include improvements and betterments installed by Unit Owners to their Units.[231] If such property insurance coverage is not reasonably available, then the Condominium Association must provide notice of such fact to all Unit Owners and lienholders by personal delivery or mail.[232]

In addition, a property insurance policy carried by a Condominium Association must provide that:

(1) each Unit Owner is an insured person under the property insurance policy with respect to liability arising out of the person's ownership of an undivided interest in the Common Elements or membership in the Condominium Association;[233]

(2) the insurer waives its right to subrogation under the property insurance policy against all Unit Owners;[234]

---

the loss or damage is caused by a covered peril, such as fire or explosion. Notwithstanding the statutory obligation of a Texas Condominium Association to insure the Common Elements and, under certain circumstances, the Units within its Condominium Development, the holder of a mortgage on a Unit may still require a Unit Owner to acquire insurance in addition to that provided by the Condominium Association. Tex. Prop. Code § 82.111(b)–(c). Moreover, even if a Condominium Association does obtain an insurance policy that covers the Common Elements and Units within a Condominium Development, Unit Owners are not precluded from obtaining insurance on their own Units for their own benefit. Tex. Prop. Code § 82.111(g).

231 Tex. Prop. Code § 82.111(b). The term "betterments" generally refers to improvements or upgrades made to a Unit by its Owner after the original construction of the Unit.

232 Tex. Prop. Code § 82.111(c).

233 Tex. Prop. Code § 82.111(d)(1).

234 Tex. Prop. Code § 82.111(d)(2). The term "subrogation" generally refers to circumstances in which an insurance company tries to recoup expenses for a damage claim it paid out to the insured party when another party caused the damage and should have been responsible for paying at least a portion of such damage.

(3) no action or omission of a Unit Owner, unless within the scope of the Unit Owner's authority on behalf of the Condominium Association, will void the property insurance policy or be a condition to recovery under the property insurance policy;[235] and

(4) if, at the time of a loss under the property insurance policy, there is other insurance in the name of a Unit Owner covering the same property covered by the Condominium Association's property insurance policy, the Condominium Association's policy provides primary insurance.[236]

2.19.2 (B) *Submission of Property Insurance Claim and Payment of Claim*

If there is an event covered by the Condominium Association's property insurance policy, then a claim for any loss covered by such policy, including losses to a Unit, must be submitted by and adjusted with the Condominium Association, not an individual Unit Owner.[237] In addition, if the Board of Directors for the Condominium Association determines it to be necessary or desirable, then the Board of Directors may designate an insurance trustee (called a "Condominium Insurance Trustee") for the purpose of receiving payment of insurance proceeds for a covered loss under the Condominium Association's property insurance policy.[238] In absence of a designated Condominium Insurance Trustee, the insurance proceeds for a covered loss under the Condominium Association's property insurance policy is required to be paid to the Condominium Association.[239] In no event, however, may insurance proceeds from a covered loss under

[235] Tex. Prop. Code § 82.111(d)(3).

[236] Tex. Prop. Code § 82.111(d)(4).

[237] Tex. Prop. Code § 82.111(e). Notwithstanding, if the cost to repair damage to a Unit or Common Element covered by the Condominium Association's property insurance is less than the amount of the applicable insurance deductible, then the Condominium Association is not required to submit a claim for loss covered by such insurance policy to the insurance carrier and the party who would be responsible for the repair in the absence of insurance must pay the cost for the repair of the applicable Unit or Common Element. Tex. Prop. Code § 82.111(j).

[238] Tex. Prop. Code § 82.111(e).

[239] Tex. Prop. Code § 82.111(e).

a Condominium Association's property insurance policy be paid directly to any Unit Owner or lienholder.[240]

The Condominium Insurance Trustee or the Condominium Association shall hold such insurance proceeds in trust for Unit Owners and lienholders as their interests may appear.[241] Subject to the Condominium Association's obligation to promptly repair or replace portions of the Condominium Development for which insurance is required, the insurance proceeds paid to a Condominium Insurance Trustee or the Condominium Association under a property insurance policy must be used first for the repair or restoration of the damaged Common Elements and Units.[242] The Unit Owners and lienholders are not entitled to receive payment of any portion of such insurance proceeds unless there is a surplus of proceeds after such covered property has been completely repaired or restored or the Condominium Development is terminated.[243]

2.19.2 (C) *Payment of Property Insurance Deductibles*

In 2013, the Texas Legislature amended Section 82.111 of the Texas Property Code so as to authorize a Condominium Association's Board of Directors to obtain property insurance that provides for a commercially reasonable deductible in an amount that it determines to be appropriate or necessary.[244] In addition, such amendment of Section 82.111 also established new laws regarding payment of a Condominium Association's property insurance deductible.

More specifically, if damage to a Unit or Common Element is covered by the Condominium Association's property insurance policy, but the cost to repair the damage

[240] Tex. Prop. Code § 82.111(e).

[241] Tex. Prop. Code § 82.111(f).

[242] Tex. Prop. Code § 82.111(f).

[243] Tex. Prop. Code § 82.111(f).

[244] Tex. Prop. Code § 82.111(c).

to the Unit or Common Element is less than the amount of the applicable insurance deductible, then the Condominium Association is not required to submit a claim for loss covered by such insurance policy to the insurance carrier, and the party who would be responsible for the repair in the absence of insurance must pay the cost for the repair of the applicable Unit or Common Element.[245]

On the other hand, if damage to a Unit or Common Element is covered by the Condominium Association's property insurance policy and the cost to repair the damage to such Unit or Common Element is more than the amount of the applicable insurance deductible, then the payment of such insurance deductible, as well as payment of the costs incurred before insurance proceeds are available, shall be determined in accordance with the provisions of the Condominium Association's Dedicatory Instruments.[246] If a Condominium Association's Dedicatory Instruments do not include a provision that governs the payment of the property insurance deductible or the costs incurred before insurance proceeds are available, then the Condominium Association's Board of Directors is authorized to adopt a resolution that governs the payment of such costs.[247] If, under such circumstances, the Condominium Association's Board of Directors has not previously approved a resolution that governs the payment of the property insurance deductible or the costs incurred before insurance proceeds are available, then such costs shall be treated as a Common Expense of the Condominium Association.[248]

Notwithstanding anything to the contrary, however, if damage to a Unit or the Common Elements is due wholly or partly to an act or omission of any Unit Owner or a guest or invitee of the Unit Owner, then the Condominium Association may assess the

245 Tex. Prop. Code § 82.111(j).

246 Tex. Prop. Code § 82.111(k).

247 Tex. Prop. Code § 82.111(k).

248 Tex. Prop. Code § 82.111(k).

deductible expense and any other expense in excess of insurance proceeds against such Unit Owner and his or her Unit.[249]

2.19.2 (D) *Duty to Repair and Restore Condominium Property*

In general, a Texas Condominium Association is required to promptly repair or replace any portion of the Condominium Development, for which insurance is required, that is damaged or destroyed, unless: (1) the Condominium Development is terminated; (2) repair or replacement would be illegal under any state or local health or safety statute or ordinance; or (3) at least eighty percent (80%) of the Unit Owners vote to not rebuild.[250] In addition, if the insurance proceeds do not fully cover the cost to repair or replace the portions of the Condominium Development that the Condominium Association is required to repair or replace, then the cost of repair or replacement in excess of the insurance proceeds and reserves is considered to be a Common Expense of the Condominium Development.[251]

If the entire Condominium Development is not repaired or replaced, then the insurance proceeds received by the Condominium Insurance Trustee or Condominium Association must be allocated as follows: (1) any insurance proceeds attributable solely to the damaged Common Elements shall be used to restore the damaged area of the Common Elements to a condition compatible with the remainder of the Condominium Development; (2) any insurance proceeds attributable solely to damaged Units and

---

249 Tex. Prop. Code § 82.111(l).

250 Tex. Prop. Code § 82.111(i). Each Unit Owner may participate in a vote to not rebuild damaged portions of a Condominium Development, regardless of whether the owner's Unit or Limited Common Element has been damaged or destroyed. Tex. Prop. Code § 82.111(i). In addition, if a vote as to whether or not to rebuild is conducted at a meeting called for such purpose, Unit Owners may vote in person or by proxy at such meeting. Tex. Prop. Code § 82.111(i). If no meeting is held for the purpose of conducting a vote as to whether or not to rebuild, Unit Owners may cast a vote as to whether to rebuild electronically or by written ballot without calling a meeting. Tex. Prop. Code § 82.111(i). It is also important to note that a vote to not rebuild does not increase an insurer's liability to a loss payment obligation under a property insurance policy, nor does such a vote cause a presumption of total loss. Tex. Prop. Code § 82.111(i).

251 Tex. Prop. Code § 82.111(i).

Limited Common Elements that are not to be rebuilt shall be distributed to the Owners of such Units and the Owners of the Units to which such Limited Common Elements were assigned, or to their mortgagees, as their interests may appear; and (3) the remainder of the insurance proceeds shall be distributed to all the Unit Owners in accordance with each Unit Owner's undivided interest in the Common Elements, unless otherwise provided in the applicable Condominium Declaration.[252]

In addition, if the Unit Owners vote to not rebuild any particular Unit, such Unit's Allocated Interests are to be automatically reallocated as if the Unit had been condemned by a governmental entity, and the Condominium Association shall prepare, execute, and record an amendment to the Condominium Declaration reflecting such reallocation.[253] If the Condominium Development is terminated, then the distribution of insurance proceeds is to be performed in the same manner as sales proceeds following termination of a Condominium Development.[254]

2.19.3 Other Insurance Coverage Required by Declaration or Deemed Appropriate by the Board of Directors

In addition to commercial general liability insurance and property insurance, a Condominium Association must carry any additional insurance coverage required by its Condominium Declaration.[255] Even if a Condominium Association's Declaration does not require it to maintain other types of insurance coverage, the Texas Uniform Condominium Act authorizes a Condominium Association's Board of Directors to carry any other

252 Tex. Prop. Code § 82.111(i).

253 Tex. Prop. Code § 82.111(i).

254 Tex. Prop. Code §§ 82.068, 82.111(i).

255 Tex. Prop. Code § 82.111(c).

insurance the Board of Directors considers appropriate to protect the Condominium Development, the Condominium Association, or the Unit Owners.[256]

2.19.4 Additional Insurance Requirements

Finally, an insurer issuing an insurance policy to a Texas Condominium Association may not cancel or refuse to renew such policy less than thirty (30) days after a written notice of a proposed cancellation or nonrenewal of such policy has been mailed to the Condominium Association.[257] In other words, the insurance policy must provide for at least a thirty-day notice period prior to any cancellation or nonrenewal of such insurance policy by the insurer.

2.20 Authority to Levy Assessments and Establishment of an Assessment Lien

In order to maintain required insurance coverage and maintain and repair Common Elements, as well as pay for all Common Expenses required of it and to build up an appropriate reserve fund,[258] a Condominium Association must have an ability to generate revenue. In most cases, a Condominium Association's revenue is generated through Assessments levied against its Unit Owners to pay for such obligations and Common Expenses.[259]

[256] Tex. Prop. Code § 82.111(c).

[257] Tex. Prop. Code § 82.111(h).

[258] A Condominium Declaration may allow the accumulation of reserve funds for an unspecified period to provide for any anticipated expense of the Condominium Development. Tex. Prop. Code § 82.112(f). The provisions of the Texas Uniform Condominium Act concerning accumulation of reserve funds are not applicable to Condominium Developments created prior to January 1, 1994, that are subject to the Texas Condominium Act, and there are no comparable provisions under the Texas Condominium Act. Tex. Prop. Code § 82.002(c).

[259] Tex. Prop. Code § 82.112. It is also important to note that, except as provided by the Condominium Declaration, a Common Expense for the maintenance, repair, or replacement of a Limited Common Element, other than windows, doors, or utility installations or equipment serving only a Unit, shall be assessed against all the Units as if it were for a General Common Element. Tex. Prop. Code § 82.112(d).

2.20.1 Authority to Levy Assessments

The authority of a Condominium Association to levy Assessments is established by the Condominium Association's Declaration and Texas law. In particular, the Texas Condominium Act provides that an Apartment Owner in a Condominium Development created prior to 1994 is responsible for the Apartment Owner's pro rata share of: (1) the expenses to administer the Condominium Development and to maintain and repair the General Common Elements; (2) in proper cases, the expenses to administer the Limited Common Elements of the buildings in the Condominium Development; and (3) other expenses approved by the Council of Owners.[260] Likewise, the Texas Uniform Condominium Act authorizes applicable Condominium Associations to impose and receive payments, fees, or charges for the use, rental, or operation of the Common Elements and for services provided to Unit Owners.[261]

Assessments must be made by a Condominium Association at least annually and must be based on a budget adopted at least annually by the Condominium Association.[262] If a Condominium Association reallocates Common Expense Liabilities during its fiscal year, then any Common Expense Assessments and/or Assessment installment payments not yet due to the Condominium Association must be recalculated in accordance with the reallocated Common Expense Liabilities.[263] In addition, any unpaid, past due Assessments may bear interest at a lawful rate established by the Condominium Association.[264]

---

260 Tex. Prop. Code § 81.204(a).

261 Tex. Prop. Code § 82.101(a)(11).

262 Tex. Prop. Code § 82.112(a). The provisions of the Texas Uniform Condominium Act imposing procedures on the levy of Assessments are not applicable to Condominium Developments created prior to January 1, 1994, that are subject to the Texas Condominium Act, and there are no comparable provisions under the Texas Condominium Act. Tex. Prop. Code § 82.002(c).

263 Tex. Prop. Code § 82.112(e).

264 Tex. Prop. Code § 82.112(c). Section 82.101(a)(12) authorizes all Condominium Associations to impose interest and late charges for late payments of Assessments, returned check charges, and, if notice and an

2.20.2 Establishment of an Assessment Lien

An Assessment levied by the Condominium Association against a Unit or Unit Owner is a personal obligation of the Unit Owner and is secured by a continuing lien in favor of the Condominium Association on the Unit (called an "Assessment Lien").[265] The Condominium Association's Assessment Lien is automatically created by recordation of the Condominium Declaration, which constitutes record notice and perfection of such lien.[266] Unless the Condominium Declaration provides otherwise, no other recordation of a lien or notice of lien is required to perfect a Condominium Association's Assessment Lien.[267] In addition, a Condominium Association's Assessment Lien has priority over any other lien applicable to a Unit except:

(1) a lien for real property taxes and other governmental assessments or charges against the Unit;[268]

(2) a lien or encumbrance recorded before the Condominium Declaration was recorded;[269]

(3) a first vendor's lien or first Deed of Trust Lien recorded before the date on which the Assessment sought to be enforced becomes delinquent

opportunity to be heard are given, reasonable fines for violations of the Condominium's Declaration, Bylaws, and/or Association Rules. Tex. Prop. Code § 82.101(a)(12).

265 Tex. Prop. Code § 82.113(a). A Condominium Association's Assessment Lien also applies to rents and insurance proceeds that relate to an Owner's Unit. Tex. Prop. Code § 82.113(a). For purposes of the Condominium Association's Assessment Lien, the term "Assessments" includes all regular and special Assessments, dues, fees, charges, interest, late fees, fines, collection costs, attorneys fees, and any other amount due the Condominium Association by the Unit Owner or levied against the Unit by the Condominium Association, all of which are enforceable as Assessments and secured by the Condominium Association's Assessment Lien, unless the Condominium Declaration provides otherwise. Tex. Prop. Code § 82.113(a).

266 Tex. Prop. Code § 82.113(c).

267 Tex. Prop. Code § 82.113(c).

268 Tex. Prop. Code § 82.113(b)(1). It is important to note that under Chapter 32 of the Texas Tax Code, foreclosure of a tax lien attaching against a Unit does not discharge the Condominium Association's Assessment Lien for amounts becoming due to the Condominium Association after the date of foreclosure of the tax lien. Tex. Prop. Code § 82.113(l).

269 Tex. Prop. Code § 82.113(b)(2).

under the Condominium Declaration, Bylaws, or Association Rules;[270] and

(4) unless the Condominium Declaration provides otherwise, a lien for construction of improvements to the Unit or an assignment of the right to insurance proceeds on the Unit if the lien or assignment is recorded or duly perfected before the date on which the Assessment sought to be enforced becomes delinquent under the Condominium Declaration, Bylaws, or Association Rules.[271]

In addition, by acquiring ownership of a Unit, a Unit Owner grants to the Condominium Association a power of sale in connection with the Condominium Association's Assessment Lien.[272] The Board of Directors for a Condominium Association may appoint by written resolution an Officer, agent, trustee, or attorney of the Condominium Association to exercise the power of sale on behalf of the Condominium Association.[273] Unless provided otherwise in the Condominium Declaration, a Condominium Association must exercise its power of sale pursuant to the same procedures required for other contractual liens applicable to real property under Chapter 51 of the Texas Property Code.[274]

Pursuant to the power of sale created by the Texas Uniform Condominium Act and/or a Condominium Association's Declaration, a Condominium Association also has the right to foreclose its Assessment Lien by judicial or non-judicial foreclosure procedures.[275] In addition, all costs of foreclosure incurred by the Condominium

---

270 Tex. Prop. Code § 82.113(b)(3).

271 Tex. Prop. Code § 82.113(b)(4).

272 Tex. Prop. Code § 82.113(d).

273 Tex. Prop. Code § 82.113(d).

274 Tex. Prop. Code § 82.113(d).

275 Tex. Prop. Code § 82.113(e). There are two limited exceptions to the right of a Condominium Association to foreclose its Assessment Lien. First, a Condominium Association may not foreclose its Assessment Lien if the amount owed by the Unit Owner to the Condominium Association consists solely of fines. Tex. Prop. Code § 82.113(e). Second, if, on January 1, 1994, a Unit was and continues to be the homestead of the Unit Owner and is subject to a Condominium Declaration that does not contain a valid Assessment Lien against the Unit, the Assessment Lien created by the Texas Uniform Condominium Act does not attach against the

Association may be added to the amount the Unit Owner owes to the Condominium Association.[276] Notwithstanding, at any time prior to conducting a non-judicial foreclosure sale of a Unit, a Unit Owner may avoid foreclosure by paying all amounts owed to the Condominium Association.[277] A Unit Owner, however, may not petition a court to set aside a non-judicial foreclosure sale solely because the purchase price at the foreclosure sale was insufficient to fully satisfy the Unit Owner's debt to the Condominium Association.[278]

2.20.3 Notification of Unit Owner's Assessment Delinquency to Other Lienholders

If a Unit Owner defaults in his or her monetary obligations to the Condominium Association, the Condominium Association is authorized to notify the delinquent Unit Owner's other lienholders of the default and of the Condominium Association's intent to foreclose its Assessment Lien prior to foreclosing such Lien.[279] In addition, if a Unit Owner is delinquent in payment of Assessments to a Condominium Association, then the Condominium Association may contact the delinquent Unit Owner's lienholders to request information about the Unit Owner's debt that is secured by the holder's lien against the Unit and other relevant information.[280] At the request of a Condominium Association for such information, a holder of a recorded lien against the Unit is authorized

Unit until the Unit ceases to be the homestead of the person who has owned the Unit since before January 1, 1994. Tex. Prop. Code § 82.113(k). In other words, if a Condominium Development is subject to the Texas Condominium Act (which does not create an Assessment Lien in favor of the Condominium Association) and the applicable Condominium Declaration does not create an Assessment Lien in favor of the Condominium Association, then the Assessment Lien created by the Texas Uniform Condominium Act in favor of the Condominium Association in such Condominium Development will not preempt a Unit Owner's homestead right if such Unit Owner has continuously owned the Unit as his or her homestead since before the effective enactment date of the Texas Uniform Condominium Act.

276 Tex. Prop. Code § 82.113(e).

277 Tex. Prop. Code § 82.113(j).

278 Tex. Prop. Code § 82.113(e).

279 Tex. Prop. Code § 82.113(h).

280 Tex. Prop. Code § 82.113(m).

under the Texas Uniform Condominium Act to provide such information to the Condominium Association.[281] Similarly, at the request of a delinquent Unit Owner's lienholder to a Condominium Association, the Condominium Association may furnish such lienholder with information about the Condominium Development and the Unit Owner's obligations to the Condominium Association.[282]

Notwithstanding such permissive authority to notify a delinquent Unit Owner's lienholder about such Unit Owner's default in paying Assessments, a Condominium Association is required to provide written notice of a Unit Owner's default in paying Assessments and of the Condominium Association's intent to foreclose its Assessment Lien to any holder of a recorded lien or duly perfected mechanic's lien against a Unit who has given the Condominium Association a written request for notification of such information before the Condominium Association may initiate foreclosure of its Assessment Lien.[283]

2.20.4 Acceptance of a Deed in Lieu of Foreclosure and Bidding on a Unit at a Foreclosure Sale

A Condominium Association may accept a deed in lieu of foreclosure or in lieu of filing a lawsuit against a delinquent Unit Owner to recover a money judgment for sums that may be secured by the Condominium Association's Assessment Lien.[284] In other words, a Unit Owner may simply convey title of a Unit to the Condominium Association in lieu of the Condominium Association foreclosing its Assessment Lien against such Unit or suing such Unit Owner to recover sums owed to the Condominium Association. In addition, if the Condominium Association does foreclose its Assessment Lien against a

---

281 Tex. Prop. Code § 82.113(m).

282 Tex. Prop. Code § 82.113(m).

283 Tex. Prop. Code § 82.113(h).

284 Tex. Prop. Code § 82.113(i).

Unit, the Condominium Association may bid for and purchase such Unit at the foreclosure sale as a Common Expense.[285]

2.20.5 Redemption of a Unit Following Foreclosure

If a Condominium Association forecloses its Assessment Lien against a Unit, the Unit Owner who owned the Unit just prior to the foreclosure has a right to redeem such Unit from the party that purchased the Unit at the foreclosure sale any time before the expiration of ninety (90) days from the date of the foreclosure sale.[286] In other words, if a Condominium Association forecloses its Assessment Lien against a Unit, then the prior owner of such Unit has a right to reacquire ownership of the Unit during a ninety-day period following the foreclosure sale by complying with certain provisions of the Texas Uniform Condominium Act. During such ninety-day "Redemption Period," the party that purchased the foreclosed Unit may not transfer ownership of such Unit to any person other than the redeeming prior owner of such Unit.[287]

The procedure for redeeming a foreclosed Unit depends on whether the Condominium Association purchased the foreclosed Unit at the foreclosure sale or whether it was purchased by a party other than the Condominium Association. If the Condominium Association is the party that purchased the Unit at the foreclosure sale, then in order to redeem the foreclosed Unit, the prior owner of the Unit must pay to the Condominium Association: (1) all amounts owed to the Condominium Association at the time of the foreclosure sale; (2) interest from the date of the foreclosure sale to the date of redemption at the rate provided by the Condominium Declaration for delinquent

---

[285] Tex. Prop. Code § 82.113(f). The Condominium Association may own, lease, encumber, exchange, sell, or convey the Unit as well. Tex. Prop. Code § 82.113(f).

[286] Tex. Prop. Code § 82.113(g).

[287] Tex. Prop. Code § 82.113(g). "Redemption Period" is a term of art utilized in this book that refers to the specified time period following foreclosure of a Homeowners Association's Assessment Lien during which the owner of the real property that was foreclosed upon may redeem (or reacquire) his or her property from the entity or person that purchased it at the foreclosure sale.

Assessments; (3) reasonable attorneys fees and costs incurred by the Condominium Association in foreclosing its Assessment Lien; (4) any Assessment levied against the Unit by the Condominium Association after the foreclosure sale; and (5) any reasonable cost incurred by the Condominium Association as owner of the Unit, including costs of maintenance and leasing of the Unit during the Redemption Period.[288]

Alternatively, if the foreclosed Unit was purchased by a party other than the Condominium Association, then in order to redeem the foreclosed Unit, the prior owner of the Unit must pay to the party that purchased the foreclosed Unit: (1) an amount equal to the amount bid at the foreclosure sale; (2) interest on the bid amount computed from the date of the foreclosure sale to the date of redemption at the rate of six percent (6%); (3) the amount of any Assessments paid by such party to the Condominium Association after the date of foreclosure; and (4) any reasonable costs incurred by such party as the owner of the Unit, including costs associated with maintenance and leasing of the foreclosed Unit.[289] The prior owner of the Unit must also pay to the Condominium Association all assessments that are due as of the date of the redemption and all reasonable attorneys fees and costs incurred by the Condominium Association in foreclosing its Assessment Lien against the foreclosed Unit.[290]

---

[288] Tex. Prop. Code § 82.113(g). It is important to note that the Condominium Association may lease a foreclosed Unit, or otherwise generate income from the use of the foreclosed Unit, during the ninety-day Redemption Period. Tex. Prop. Code § 82.113(g). In such event, all rents and other income collected from the foreclosed Unit by the Condominium Association between the date of the foreclosure sale and the date of redemption belong to the Condominium Association, but the rents and income shall be credited against the redemption amount to be paid to the Condominium Association by the redeeming Unit Owner. Tex. Prop. Code § 82.113(g).

[289] Tex. Prop. Code § 82.113(g). It is important to note that the party that purchased the foreclosed Unit at the foreclosure sale may lease a foreclosed Unit, or otherwise generate income from the use of the foreclosed Unit, during the ninety-day Redemption Period. Tex. Prop. Code § 82.113(g). In such event, all rents and other income collected from the Unit by the party that purchased the foreclosed Unit between the date of the foreclosure sale and the date of redemption belong to such party, but the rents and income shall be credited against the redemption amount to be paid to such party by the redeeming Unit Owner. Tex. Prop. Code § 82.113(g).

[290] Tex. Prop. Code § 82.113(g).

If the prior owner of the foreclosed Unit pays the Condominium Association (and if applicable, the other party that purchased the foreclosed Unit) all of the amounts required to redeem the foreclosed Unit prior to the expiration of the ninety-day Redemption Period, then the party that purchased the foreclosed Unit at the foreclosure sale must execute a deed (with no warranty of title) that conveys ownership of the foreclosed Unit back to the prior owner of the foreclosed Unit.[291] It is important to note that the exercise of a prior owner's right of redemption is not effective against a subsequent purchaser or lender for value without notice of a redemption of such foreclosed Unit after the ninety-day Redemption Period expires, unless the prior owner of the foreclosed Unit records in the local Official Public Records either a redemption deed from the party that purchased the foreclosed Unit or an affidavit stating that he or she has exercised his or her right of redemption of the foreclosed Unit.[292]

2.21 Procedures for Filing a Lawsuit or Initiating an Arbitration Proceeding Concerning a Construction Defect Claim

In 2015, the Texas Legislature enacted Section 82.119 of the Texas Uniform Condominium Act, which establishes procedures that a Condominium Association, consisting of eight or more Units, must comply with before filing a lawsuit or initiating an arbitration proceeding to resolve a claim pertaining to the construction or design of a Unit or the Common Elements (commonly referred to as a "Construction Defect Claim").[293]

Pursuant to Section 82.119 of the Texas Uniform Condominium Code, before filing a lawsuit or initiating an arbitration proceeding to resolve a Construction Defect

---

291 Tex. Prop. Code § 82.113(g).

292 Tex. Prop. Code § 82.113(g).

293 Tex. Prop. Code § 82.119. It is important to note that Section 82.119 is not applicable to Condominium Developments created prior to January 1, 1994, that are subject to the Texas Condominium Act. Tex. Prop. Code § 82.002(c).

Claim, a Condominium Association must first: (1) obtain an inspection and written independent third-party report from a licensed professional engineer; and (2) obtain approval from Unit Owners holding more than fifty percent (50%) of the total votes allocated to all Unit Owners under the Condominium Declaration at a meeting of the Unit Owners.[294] Although listed as two items, there are really three distinct procedures that must be performed in compliance with the requirements of Section 82.119, each of which is explained separately in the following subchapters.

2.21.1 Conducting an Inspection and Obtaining a Written Report from a Licensed Professional Engineer

To comply with Section 82.119, a Condominium Association must first obtain an inspection of the applicable Units and/or Common Elements by a licensed professional engineer (called a "Construction Defect Inspection"), who must also prepare a written independent third-party report (called a "Construction Defect Report").[295] Before a Condominium Association may conduct the Construction Defect Inspection, the Condominium Association must provide written notice of the Construction Defect Inspection to each party who may be subject to the Construction Defect Claim (generally referred to as the "Construction Defect Respondents") at least ten (10) days before the date of the Construction Defect Inspection.[296] The written notice of the Construction Defect Inspection must:

(1) identify the licensed professional engineer engaged to perform the Construction Defect Inspection and prepare the Construction Defect Report;[297]

---

[294] Tex. Prop. Code § 82.119(b). It is important to note that the procedures required by Section 82.119 are in addition to any procedures or preconditions required by a Condominium Association's Condominium Declaration to be satisfied before the Condominium Association may file a lawsuit or initiate an arbitration proceeding. Tex. Prop. Code § 82.119(b).

[295] Tex. Prop. Code § 82.119(b)(1).

[296] Tex. Prop. Code § 82.119(c).

[297] Tex. Prop. Code § 82.119(c)(1).

(2) identify the specific Units and/or Common Elements to be inspected;[298] and

(3) include the date and time that the Construction Defect Inspection will occur.[299]

In addition, each of the Construction Defect Respondents may attend the Construction Defect Inspection, either personally or through an agent.[300]

After completing the Construction Defect Inspection, the licensed professional engineer that conducted such inspection must prepare a Construction Defect Report.[301] The Construction Defect Report must:

(1) identify the specific Units or Common Elements subject to the Construction Defect Claim;[302]

(2) describe the present physical condition of the Units or Common Elements subject to the Construction Defect Claim;[303] and

(3) describe any modifications, maintenance, or repairs to the Units or Common Elements performed by the Unit Owners or the Condominium Association.[304]

2.21.2 Pre-Meeting Dissemination of the Construction Defect Report and Meeting Notice Requirements

Although the second requirement under Section 82.119 is obtainment of approval from Unit Owners to the filing of a lawsuit or initiation of an arbitration proceeding concerning a Construction Defect Claim, there are two additional steps that the

[298] Tex. Prop. Code § 82.119(c)(2).

[299] Tex. Prop. Code § 82.119(c)(3).

[300] Tex. Prop. Code § 82.119(d).

[301] Tex. Prop. Code § 82.119(b)(1).

[302] Tex. Prop. Code § 82.119(b)(1)(A).

[303] Tex. Prop. Code § 82.119(b)(1)(B).

[304] Tex. Prop. Code § 82.119(b)(1)(C).

Condominium Association must perform before it may conduct a meeting of its Unit Owners to approve the filing of such a lawsuit or initiation of such an arbitration proceeding. First, upon completion of the Construction Defect Report, the Condominium Association must: (1) provide a copy of the completed Construction Defect Report to each Unit Owner and to each Construction Defect Respondent; and (2) allow each Construction Defect Respondent at least ninety (90) days after the date of completion of the Construction Defect Report to inspect and correct any Construction Defects identified in such report.[305]

Following the expiration of the ninety-day period allotted to Construction Defect Respondents to inspect and correct the Construction Defects identified in the Construction Defect Report, the Condominium Association must schedule a meeting of the Unit Owners to vote on whether to approve the filing of a lawsuit or initiation of an arbitration proceeding concerning a Construction Defect Claim (called a "Construction Defect Meeting") and provide written notice of such meeting to each Unit Owner (called a "Construction Defect Meeting Notice").[306]

The Construction Defect Meeting Notice must be provided to each Unit Owner at least thirty (30) days before the date of the Construction Defect Meeting.[307] The Construction Defect Meeting Notice must also specify the date, time, and location of the Construction Defect Meeting and include the following additional information:

(1) a description of the nature of the Construction Defect Claim, the relief sought in the Construction Defect Claim, the anticipated duration of

---

[305] Tex. Prop. Code § 82.119(e).

[306] Tex. Prop. Code § 82.119(e). It is important to note that the Condominium Association may not provide notice of the Construction Defect Meeting to Unit Owners until expiration of the ninety-day period allotted to Construction Defect Respondents to inspect and correct the Construction Defects identified in the Construction Defect Report. Tex. Prop. Code § 82.119(e).

[307] Tex. Prop. Code § 82.119(f).

prosecuting the Construction Defect Claim, and the likelihood of success;[308]

(2) a copy of the Construction Defect Report;[309]

(3) a copy of the contract or proposed contract between the Condominium Association and the attorney selected by the Condominium Association's Board of Directors to assert or provide assistance with the Construction Defect Claim;[310]

(4) a description of the attorneys fees, consultant fees, expert witness fees, and court costs, whether incurred by the Condominium Association directly or for which the Condominium Association may be liable as a result of prosecuting the Construction Defect Claim;[311]

(5) a summary of the steps previously taken by the Condominium Association to resolve the Construction Defect Claim;[312]

(6) a statement that initiating a lawsuit or arbitration proceeding to resolve a Construction Defect Claim may affect the market value, marketability, or refinancing of a Unit while the Construction Defect Claim is being prosecuted;[313] and

(7) a description of the manner in which the Condominium Association proposes to fund the cost of prosecuting the Construction Defect Claim.[314]

In addition, the Construction Defect Meeting Notice must be prepared and signed by a person who is not: (1) the attorney who represents or will represent the Condominium Association in the Construction Defect Claim; (2) a member of the law firm of the attorney who represents or will represent the Condominium Association in the Construction Defect Claim; or (3) employed by or otherwise affiliated with the law firm of the attorney who

---

308 Tex. Prop. Code § 82.119(f)(1).

309 Tex. Prop. Code § 82.119(f)(2).

310 Tex. Prop. Code § 82.119(f)(3).

311 Tex. Prop. Code § 82.119(f)(4).

312 Tex. Prop. Code § 82.119(f)(5).

313 Tex. Prop. Code § 82.119(f)(6).

314 Tex. Prop. Code § 82.119(f)(7).

represents or will represent the Condominium Association in the Construction Defect Claim.[315]

2.21.3 Approval of the Unit Owners to the Filing of a Lawsuit or Initiation of an Arbitration Proceeding Concerning a Construction Defect Claim

Finally, the Condominium Association must obtain the approval of Unit Owners to the filing of a lawsuit or initiation of an arbitration proceeding concerning the Construction Defect Claim. Such approval must be obtained from Unit Owners holding more than fifty percent (50%) of the total votes allocated to all Unit Owners under the Declaration, voting in person or by proxy, at a regular, annual, or special meeting of the Unit Owners called in accordance with the Condominium Declaration or Bylaws, as applicable.[316]

It is important to note that the process of obtaining the approval of Unit Owners to the filing of a lawsuit or initiation of an arbitration proceeding concerning the Construction Defect Claim will take, at a minimum, at least one hundred thirty (130) days from the date the written notice of the Construction Defect Inspection is provided to the Construction Defect Respondents. Because of the time constraints of obtaining approval from its Unit Owners, the "statute of limitations" period for a Construction Defect Claim could potentially expire before a Condominium Association can obtain the requisite approval if the Condominium Association waits until the final year of an applicable statute of limitations period to initiate the procedures under Section 82.119.[317] In anticipation of such issue, Section 82.119 provides that the statute of limitations period for filing of a lawsuit or initiation of an arbitration proceeding concerning the Construction Defect

---

315 Tex. Prop. Code § 82.119(g).

316 Tex. Prop. Code § 82.119(b)(2).

317 The "statute of limitations" period is a statutorily created time period within which a party must file a lawsuit or initiate an arbitration proceeding against another party for an existing cause of action.

Claim is tolled until the first anniversary of the date the procedures under Section 82.119 are initiated by the Condominium Association, provided such procedures are initiated during the final year of the applicable statute of limitations period.[318] In other words, if a Condominium Association initiates the procedures under Section 82.119 during the final year of an applicable statute of limitations period, then such statute of limitations period will be tolled for one (1) year from the date the first written notice of the Construction Defect Inspection is provided to a Construction Defect Respondent.

2.22 Books and Records and Annual Audit Requirements

All Texas Condominium Associations are required to keep certain "Books and Records," to perform an annual audit of its financial records, and to make such Books and Records and annual audit available to Unit Owners for inspection.

2.22.1 Books and Records Required to Be Kept by Condominium Associations

Texas Condominium Associations are required to keep the following Books and Records:

(1) detailed financial records that comply with generally accepted accounting principles and that are sufficiently detailed to enable the Condominium Association to prepare a Resale Certificate required by the Texas Uniform Condominium Act;[319]

(2) the plans and specifications used to construct the Condominium Development, except for buildings originally constructed prior to January 1, 1994;[320]

(3) the Condominium Information Statement and any amendments to it;[321]

---

318 Tex. Prop. Code § 82.119(h).

319 Tex. Prop. Code § 82.114(a)(1).

320 Tex. Prop. Code § 82.114(a)(2).

321 Tex. Prop. Code § 82.114(a)(3).

(4) the name and mailing address of each Unit Owner;[322]

(5) voting records, proxies, and correspondence relating to amendments to the Condominium Declaration;[323] and

(6) minutes of meetings of the Condominium Association's membership and its Board of Directors.[324]

2.22.2 Inspection of Books and Records by Unit Owners

A Condominium Association must also make all financial and other records of the Condominium Association reasonably available for examination by a Unit Owner and/or a Unit Owner's agent at the Condominium Association's registered office or its principal office in the State of Texas.[325] It is important to note that an attorney's files and records relating to the Condominium Association are not records of the Condominium Association and are not subject to inspection by Unit Owners or production in a legal proceeding.[326]

2.22.3 Annual Audit Requirement

In addition, a Condominium Association is required to obtain an independent audit of its financial records on an annual basis, the cost of which is to be treated as a Common Expense.[327] Such audits must be performed by a certified public accountant if required by: (1) the Condominium Association's Bylaws; (2) a vote of the Board of Directors; or (3) a majority vote of the members of the Condominium Association voting at a meeting of the Condominium Association's membership.[328] The Condominium

322 Tex. Prop. Code § 82.114(a)(4).

323 Tex. Prop. Code § 82.114(a)(5).

324 Tex. Prop. Code § 82.114(a)(6).

325 Tex. Prop. Code § 82.114(b).

326 Tex. Prop. Code § 82.114(b).

327 Tex. Prop. Code § 82.114(c).

328 Tex. Prop. Code § 82.114(c).

Association must also make copies of its annual audits available for inspection by its Unit Owners.[329]

2.23 Management Certificates

All Texas Condominium Associations are required to record a Management Certificate in the Official Public Records of each county in which any portion of the Condominium Development is located.[330] A Management Certificate must be signed and acknowledged by an Officer of the Condominium Association, and it must identify the following information:

(1) the name of the Condominium Development;[331]

(2) the name of the Condominium Association;[332]

(3) the location of the Condominium Development;[333]

(4) the recording data for the Condominium Declaration;[334]

(5) the mailing address of the Condominium Association or the name and mailing address of the person or entity managing the Condominium Association;[335] and

(6) any other information the Condominium Association considers appropriate.[336]

In addition, a Condominium Association is required to record a new or updated Management Certificate no later than thirty (30) days after the date the Condominium

329 Tex. Prop. Code § 82.114(c).

330 Tex. Prop. Code § 82.116.

331 Tex. Prop. Code § 82.116(a)(1).

332 Tex. Prop. Code § 82.116(a)(2).

333 Tex. Prop. Code § 82.116(a)(3).

334 Tex. Prop. Code § 82.116(a)(4).

335 Tex. Prop. Code § 82.116(a)(5).

336 Tex. Prop. Code § 82.116(a)(6).

Association has notice of a change in any of the requisite information stated in a previously recorded Management Certificate.[337] If a Condominium Association delays or fails to record a Management Certificate or updated Management Certificate, the Condominium Association and its Officers, Directors, employees, and agents are not subject to liability to any person for such delay or failure, unless such delay or failure to record a Management Certificate or updated Management Certificate is willful or caused by gross negligence.[338]

2.24 Resale Certificates

Under the Texas Uniform Condominium Act, a Unit Owner, other than a Declarant, who intends to sell his or her Unit is required to furnish a prospective purchaser of such Unit with a current copy of the Condominium Declaration, Bylaws, any Association Rules adopted by the Condominium Association, and a Resale Certificate for the Unit before executing a contract of sale or conveying the Unit.[339] The Resale Certificate must be issued by the Condominium Association, must have been prepared no earlier than three (3) months prior to the date it is delivered to the prospective purchaser, and must contain the current operating budget of the Condominium Association and statements identifying the following information:

(1) any right of first refusal or other restraint contained in the Condominium Declaration that restricts the right to transfer a Unit;[340]

(2) the amount of the periodic Common Expense Assessment and any unpaid Common Expenses or special Assessments currently due and payable from the selling Unit Owner;[341]

337 Tex. Prop. Code § 82.116(b).

338 Tex. Prop. Code § 82.116(c).

339 Tex. Prop. Code § 82.157(a).

340 Tex. Prop. Code § 82.157(a)(1).

341 Tex. Prop. Code § 82.157(a)(2).

(3) the amount of any other unpaid fees or amounts currently due and payable to the Condominium Association by the selling Unit Owner;[342]

(4) capital expenditures, if any, approved by the Condominium Association for the next twelve (12) months;[343]

(5) the amount of reserves, if any, for capital expenditures and the amount of any portion of those reserves designated by the Condominium Association for a specified project;[344]

(6) any unsatisfied judgments against the Condominium Association;[345]

(7) the nature of any pending lawsuits against the Condominium Association;[346]

(8) any insurance coverage provided by the Condominium Association for the benefit of Unit Owners;[347]

(9) whether the Board of Directors for the Condominium Association has knowledge that any alterations or improvements to the subject Unit or to the Limited Common Elements assigned to such Unit violate the Condominium Declaration, Bylaws, or Association Rules;[348]

(10) whether the Board of Directors for the Condominium Association has received notice from a governmental authority concerning violations of health or building codes with respect to the subject Unit, the Limited Common Elements assigned to such Unit, or any other portion of the Condominium Development;[349]

---

342 Tex. Prop. Code § 82.157(a)(3).

343 Tex. Prop. Code § 82.157(a)(4).

344 Tex. Prop. Code § 82.157(a)(5).

345 Tex. Prop. Code § 82.157(a)(6).

346 Tex. Prop. Code § 82.157(a)(7).

347 Tex. Prop. Code § 82.157(a)(8).

348 Tex. Prop. Code § 82.157(a)(9).

349 Tex. Prop. Code § 82.157(a)(10).

(11) the remaining term of any leasehold estate that affects the Condominium Development and the provisions governing an extension or renewal of such lease;[350]

(12) the name, mailing address, and telephone number of the Condominium Association's managing agent, if any;[351]

(13) the Condominium Association's current operating budget and balance sheet;[352] and

(14) all fees payable to the Condominium Association or an agent of the Condominium Association that are associated with the transfer of a Unit's ownership, including a description of each fee, to whom the fee is paid, and the amount of the fee.[353]

Within ten (10) days of receiving a written request from a Unit Owner for a Resale Certificate, a Condominium Association must furnish to the selling Unit Owner (or such Unit Owner's agent) a Resale Certificate containing the requisite information that is signed and dated by an Officer or authorized agent of the Condominium Association.[354] If a Condominium Association does not furnish a Resale Certificate within the ten-day period or the Resale Certificate omits one or more of the required items of information, then the Unit Owner may provide the prospective purchaser with a sworn affidavit signed by the Unit Owner in lieu of the Resale Certificate.[355] Such affidavit must state that the Unit Owner requested information from the Condominium Association concerning its financial condition and the Condominium Association did not timely provide a Resale Certificate or the information required of the Resale Certificate.[356] If a Unit Owner has furnished such an affidavit to a prospective purchaser, then the Unit Owner and the

350 Tex. Prop. Code § 82.157(a)(11).

351 Tex. Prop. Code § 82.157(a)(12).

352 Tex. Prop. Code § 82.157(a)(13).

353 Tex. Prop. Code § 82.157(a)(14).

354 Tex. Prop. Code § 82.157(b).

355 Tex. Prop. Code § 82.157(b).

356 Tex. Prop. Code § 82.157(b).

prospective purchaser may agree in writing to waive the requirement to furnish a Resale Certificate.[357]

A selling Unit Owner (or such Unit Owner's agent) is not liable to a prospective purchaser of such Unit for the failure or delay of the Condominium Association to provide the Resale Certificate in a timely manner.[358] In addition, a Condominium Association is not liable to a selling Unit Owner for delay or failure to furnish a Resale Certificate.[359] An Officer or agent of the Condominium Association is also not individually liable for a delay or failure to furnish a Resale Certificate, unless the Officer or agent willfully refuses to furnish the Resale Certificate or is grossly negligent in not furnishing the Resale Certificate.[360]

Finally, it is very important that a Resale Certificate issued by a Condominium Association be accurate. If a properly executed Resale Certificate incorrectly states the total amount of delinquent sums owed by the selling Unit Owner to the Condominium Association, then the purchaser of such Unit is not liable for payment of additional undisclosed delinquencies that are unpaid as of the date the Resale Certificate is prepared that exceed the delinquent amount stated in the Resale Certificate.[361] In other words, if the Resale Certificate incorrectly understates the amount of the delinquent Assessments the selling Unit Owner owes to the Condominium Association, then the purchaser is not liable for the amount of delinquent Assessments that were due and payable as of the date of the Resale Certificate that were not included in the Resale Certificate. In addition, a purchaser, lender, or title insurer who relies on a Resale Certificate is also not liable for any debt or

---

[357] Tex. Prop. Code § 82.157(b).

[358] Tex. Prop. Code § 82.157(c). Additionally, a failure to provide a Resale Certificate does not void a deed to a purchaser. Tex. Prop. Code § 82.157(b).

[359] Tex. Prop. Code § 82.157(b).

[360] Tex. Prop. Code § 82.157(b).

[361] Tex. Prop. Code § 82.157(c).

claim that is not disclosed in the Resale Certificate, and the Condominium Association may not deny the validity of any statement in the Resale Certificate.[362] A Resale Certificate, however, does not affect a Condominium Association's right to recover debts or claims that arise or become due after the date the Resale Certificate is prepared, nor does it affect the enforcement of the Condominium Association's Assessment Lien as to future Assessments.[363]

2.25 Obligations of Unit Owners

The Texas Uniform Condominium Act also imposes certain statutory obligations upon Unit Owners in Texas. First, all Unit Owners are required to provide to their respective Condominium Association within thirty (30) days of acquiring an ownership interest in a Unit the following information:

(1) the Unit Owner's mailing address, telephone number, and driver's license number, if any;[364]

(2) the name and address of the holder of any lien against the Unit and the loan number for any loans related to such liens;[365]

(3) the name and telephone number of any person occupying the Unit other than the Unit Owner;[366] and

(4) the name, address, and telephone number of any person managing the Unit as an agent of the Unit Owner.[367]

---

[362] Tex. Prop. Code § 82.157(e).

[363] Tex. Prop. Code § 82.157(d).

[364] Tex. Prop. Code § 82.114(e)(1).

[365] Tex. Prop. Code § 82.114(e)(2).

[366] Tex. Prop. Code § 82.114(e)(3).

[367] Tex. Prop. Code § 82.114(e)(4).

A Unit Owner must also notify the Condominium Association of any changes in such requisite information within thirty (30) days from the date the Unit Owner becomes aware that such requisite information has changed.[368]

Second, unless otherwise provided by the Declaration, Bylaws, or Association Rules of the Condominium Association, Unit Owners in a Condominium Development subject to the Texas Uniform Condominium Act are required to:[369]

(1) pay Assessments, interest, and other charges properly levied by the Condominium Association against the Unit Owner or the Owner's Unit, and to pay all regular periodic Assessments without demand by the Condominium Association;[370]

(2) comply with the Declaration, Bylaws, and Association Rules of the Condominium Association, including any amendments to such documents;[371] and

(3) pay for damage to the Condominium Development caused by the negligence or willful misconduct of the Unit Owner, an occupant of the Owner's Unit, or any such Unit Owner's or occupant's family, guests, employees, contractors, agents, or invitees.[372]

Finally, the Texas Uniform Condominium Act provides that Unit Owners are liable to the Condominium Association for violations of the Declaration, Bylaws, or Association Rules of the Condominium Association (including any amendments) that are committed by the Unit Owner, an occupant of the Owner's Unit, or any such Unit Owner's

[368] Tex. Prop. Code § 82.114(f). In addition, a Unit Owner must also provide current requisite information to the Condominium Association upon its request. Tex. Prop. Code § 82.114(f).

[369] The provisions of the Texas Uniform Condominium Act imposing an obligation on Unit Owners to pay Assessments, comply with Governing Documents, and pay for damages caused to the Condominium Development are not applicable to Condominium Developments created prior to January 1, 1994, that are subject to the Texas Condominium Act, and there are no comparable provisions under the Texas Condominium Act. Tex. Prop. Code § 82.002(c).

[370] Tex. Prop. Code § 82.117(1).

[371] Tex. Prop. Code § 82.117(2).

[372] Tex. Prop. Code § 82.117(3).

or occupant's family, guests, employees, agents, or invitees.[373] Unit Owners are also liable for any costs incurred by the Condominium Association to obtain compliance by such Unit Owner, occupant, or any such Unit Owner's or occupant's family, guests, employees, agents, or invitees with the Declaration, Bylaws, or Association Rules of the Condominium Association, including attorneys fees incurred by the Condominium Association, whether or not a lawsuit is filed.[374]

2.26 Violation of the Texas Uniform Condominium Act and Enforcement of a Condominium Association's Governing Documents

The Texas Uniform Condominium Act establishes a legal cause of action against a Declarant or any other person subject to the Texas Uniform Condominium Act who violates a provision of the Texas Uniform Condominium Act, a Condominium Declaration, or a Condominium Association's Bylaws.[375] Such cause of action may be asserted by any person or class of persons adversely affected by the violation of the Texas Uniform Condominium Act or a Condominium Association's Governing Documents.[376] The Texas Uniform Condominium Act further provides that the prevailing party in a lawsuit to enforce a Condominium Association's Declaration, Bylaws, or Association Rules is entitled to recover reasonable attorneys fees and costs of litigation incurred by such party from the nonprevailing party.[377]

---

[373] Tex. Prop. Code § 82.117(4).

[374] Tex. Prop. Code § 82.117(4).

[375] Tex. Prop. Code § 82.161(a). The category of persons who can be held liable under Section 82.161(a) for a violation of the Texas Uniform Condominium Act or the Governing Documents of a Condominium Association includes the Condominium Association and Unit Owners.

[376] Tex. Prop. Code § 82.161(a).

[377] Tex. Prop. Code § 82.161(b). It is important to note that a prevailing party's entitlement to an award of attorneys fees under Section 82.161(b) may not apply if the violation is solely related to a violation of the Texas Uniform Condominium Act. At least one Texas Court of Appeals has held in a memorandum opinion that Section 82.161 does not apply to a violation of the Texas Uniform Condominium Act where there was not also a violation of the Association's Declaration, Bylaws, or rules. *West Campus Ramsey Properties, Ltd.*

v. Encinal Condominium Owners' Association, Inc., No. 03-09-00146-CV, 2009 WL 5149935 (Tex. App.—Austin December 30, 2009, pet. denied).

CHAPTER 3 FORMATION AND ADMINISTRATION OF TEXAS HOMEOWNERS ASSOCIATIONS

CHAPTER 3 FORMATION AND ADMINISTRATION OF TEXAS HOMEOWNERS ASSOCIATIONS

3.1 Formation of and Laws Applicable to the Administration of Texas Homeowners Associations

In most instances, Homeowners Associations in Texas are incorporated as nonprofit corporations. This is certainly true for Condominium Associations subject to the Texas Uniform Condominium Act, which are required to be formed as either for-profit or nonprofit corporations.[1] For such reason, this book will primarily focus on Texas laws governing the formation and administration of Texas Homeowners Associations that are incorporated as nonprofit corporations. To distinguish those Homeowners Associations that are not incorporated or not incorporated as a Texas nonprofit corporation, when referring to Texas Homeowners Associations that are incorporated as nonprofit corporations in the context of applicable provisions of the Texas Nonprofit Corporation Law, such Homeowners Associations shall be referred to as "Nonprofit Corporation HOAs." In addition, in order to distinguish those Homeowners who are members of a Homeowners Association that is incorporated as a nonprofit corporation from those who are members of a Homeowners Association that is not incorporated as a nonprofit corporation, when referring to Homeowners that are members of a Homeowners Association that is incorporated as a nonprofit corporation in the context of applicable provisions of the Texas Nonprofit Corporation Law, such Homeowners shall be referred to as "Member-Homeowners."

While most laws governing the formation and administration of a Nonprofit Corporation HOA are found in the Texas Nonprofit Corporation Law, there are several provisions in the Texas Uniform Condominium Act and Chapter 209 of the Texas Property Code that impose additional procedures and requirements upon all incorporated and unincorporated Condominium Associations and Subdivision Associations,

---

1 Tex. Prop. Code § 82.101.

respectively. In many cases, the applicable provisions under the Texas Nonprofit Corporation Law, Texas Uniform Condominium Act, and Chapter 209 of the Texas Property Code are similar, but in several instances they differ significantly from each other. In such instances, the conflicting provisions under the Texas Uniform Condominium Act and Chapter 209 of the Texas Property Code control over those under the Texas Nonprofit Corporation Law.

Because most laws governing the formation and administration of Texas Nonprofit Corporation HOAs are found in the Texas Nonprofit Corporation Law, Chapter 3 of this book will focus primarily on the applicable provisions of such statute. This book will also cite to the relevant provisions of both the Texas Uniform Condominium Act and Chapter 209 of the Texas Property Code where applicable, and where such provisions differ from those under the Texas Nonprofit Corporation Law, this book will explain the differences.

3.1.1 Texas Law Governing Nonprofit Corporation HOAs

All Texas Nonprofit Corporation HOAs are governed by the Texas Nonprofit Corporation Law.[2] In general, state law ranks higher in authority than a Homeowners Association's Governing Documents; and, as a result, the provisions of the Texas Nonprofit Corporation Law will generally control in the event of a conflict between such provisions and a Nonprofit Corporation HOA's Governing Documents. However, there are many provisions of the Texas Nonprofit Corporation Law that apply in addition to the provisions of a Nonprofit Corporation HOA's Governing Documents, as well as other provisions of the Texas Nonprofit Corporation Law that serve as "gap-fillers," or default rules, that apply only in the event a Nonprofit Corporation HOA's Governing Documents fail to address an applicable issue. Consequently, there are many instances in this book where an explanation of a statutory provision of the Texas Nonprofit Corporation Law is

---

2 Tex. Bus. Org. Code § 402.005.

predicated with a statement similar to: "unless otherwise provided in the Nonprofit Corporation HOA's Articles of Incorporation or Bylaws. . . ." In such instances, the particular statutory provision is not applicable if the substance of such provision is already addressed in the Nonprofit Corporation HOA's Governing Documents, in which case the applicable provision of the Governing Documents would take precedence over the statutory provision. Accordingly, it is important to always read and understand both the Texas Nonprofit Corporation Law and a particular Nonprofit Corporation HOA's Governing Documents in order to determine whether a specific statutory law preempts the Nonprofit Corporation HOA's Governing Documents, applies in addition to its Governing Documents, or is subordinate to its Governing Documents.

3.1.2 Texas Law Governing Unincorporated Nonprofit Associations

Although most Homeowners Associations in Texas are incorporated as nonprofit corporations, there are many that are not incorporated at all. The Texas Uniform Unincorporated Nonprofit Association Act provides for some limited statutory law that is applicable to unincorporated nonprofit associations, called "Nonprofit Associations" under such Act.[3] The Texas Uniform Unincorporated Nonprofit Association Act defines a Nonprofit Association as an unincorporated organization, other than one created by a trust, that consists of three or more members joined by mutual consent for a common, nonprofit purpose.[4] Most unincorporated Texas Homeowners Associations will constitute a Nonprofit Association under the Texas Uniform Unincorporated Nonprofit Association Act.[5]

---

3 Tex. Bus. Org. Code §§ 1.008(k), 252.001, *et seq.*

4 Tex. Bus. Org. Code § 252.001(2).

5 In order to distinguish Texas Homeowners Associations that are unincorporated but that constitute a Nonprofit Association under the Texas Uniform Unincorporated Nonprofit Association Act from Homeowners Associations that are incorporated or that do not constitute a Nonprofit Association, such Homeowners Associations that do constitute Nonprofit Associations shall be referred to as "Nonprofit Association HOAs" for the remainder of this book.

A Texas Nonprofit Association HOA is governed primarily by its Governing Documents and, to a limited extent, the provisions of the Texas Uniform Unincorporated Nonprofit Association Act, which vests Nonprofit Associations with certain powers traditionally limited to properly incorporated or registered entities. Such powers include the authority to own real and personal property and enter into contracts in its own name, as well as the ability to insulate its members from liability for claims asserted against the Nonprofit Association HOA.

3.1.2 (A) *Ownership of Real and Personal Property by a Nonprofit Association HOA*

Even though a Texas Nonprofit Association HOA is not an incorporated or registered entity, the Texas Uniform Unincorporated Nonprofit Association Act authorizes it to acquire, hold, encumber, and/or transfer an interest in real or personal property in its own name.[6] In order for a Nonprofit Association HOA to be able to own and/or transfer an interest in real property, it must execute and record a "Statement of Authority to Transfer an Interest in Real Property" in the name of the Nonprofit Association HOA.[7] A Statement of Authority to Transfer an Interest in Real Property is a written document that establishes the authority of a specific person or persons who may execute a deed or other document conveying an ownership interest in real property owned by a Nonprofit Association HOA on its behalf that must be recorded in the Official Public Records of the county in which such real property is located.[8] An interest in real property owned in the name of a Nonprofit Association HOA may be transferred or conveyed by

---

6 Tex. Bus. Org. Code § 252.004(a).

7 Tex. Bus. Org. Code § 252.005(a).

8 Tex. Bus. Org. Code § 252.005. A Statement of Authority to Transfer an Interest in Real Property must contain: (1) the name of the Nonprofit Association HOA; (2) the address of the Nonprofit Association HOA; and (3) the name or title of a person authorized to transfer an estate or interest in real property held in the name of the Nonprofit Association HOA, and it must be executed in the same manner as a deed by someone other than the person who is being authorized to transfer the Nonprofit Association HOA's real property interests. Tex. Bus. Org. Code § 252.005(c)–(d).

any person so authorized in a Statement of Authority to Transfer an Interest in Real Property.[9]

3.1.2 (B) *Enforcement of Rights, Duties, and Liabilities of a Nonprofit Association HOA*

Even though it is not an incorporated or registered entity, a Texas Nonprofit Association HOA is also considered to be a legal entity separate from its members for the purposes of determining and enforcing rights, duties, and liabilities in contract and torts.[10] More specifically, a person may not be held liable for a breach of contract by a Nonprofit Association HOA or for a tortious act or omission for which a Nonprofit Association HOA is liable merely because such person is: (1) a member of the Nonprofit Association HOA or considered to be a member by the Nonprofit Association HOA; or (2) authorized to participate in the management of the affairs of the Nonprofit Association HOA.[11] Moreover, a tortious act or omission committed by a member or other person for which a Nonprofit Association HOA is liable may not also be attributed to another person merely because such person may also be: (1) a member of the Nonprofit Association HOA or considered to be a member by the Nonprofit Association HOA; or (2) authorized to participate in the management of the affairs of the Nonprofit Association HOA.[12] Furthermore, a member of a Nonprofit Association HOA (as well as any person

---

[9] Tex. Bus. Org. Code § 252.005(b). In addition, if the record title to real property is in the name of a Nonprofit Association HOA and a Statement of Authority to Transfer an Interest in Real Property is recorded in the county clerk's office of the county in which a transfer of real property would be recorded, the authority of the person named in such Statement of Authority to Transfer an Interest in Real Property is conclusive in favor of a person who gives value without notice that such person lacks authority. Tex. Bus. Org. Code § 252.005(g).

[10] Tex. Bus. Org. Code § 252.006(a).

[11] Tex. Bus. Org. Code § 252.006(b).

[12] Tex. Bus. Org. Code § 252.006(c). Generally speaking, a tortious act or tort refers to a wrongful act that causes harm to another person or entity for which such actor may be held civilly liable for the damages caused by such act. Some commentators define a tort simply as a personal injury claim or as a civil action other than a breach of contract. The most common type of torts are automobile accidents, defamation, and other types of personal injury claims.

considered to be a member by a Nonprofit Association HOA) may assert a legal claim against the Nonprofit Association HOA and, likewise, a Nonprofit Association HOA may assert a legal claim against a member of the Nonprofit Association HOA (as well as any person considered to be a member by the Nonprofit Association HOA).[13]

In addition, a Texas Nonprofit Association HOA, in its own name, may also institute, defend, intervene, or participate in a judicial, administrative, or other governmental proceeding or in an arbitration, mediation, or any other form of alternative dispute resolution.[14] A Nonprofit Association HOA, in its own name, may also assert a claim in a judicial, administrative, or other governmental proceeding on behalf of members of the Nonprofit Association HOA if: (1) one or more of the Nonprofit Association HOA's members have standing to assert a claim in their own right in such proceeding; (2) the interests the Nonprofit Association HOA seeks to protect are germane to its purposes; and (3) neither the claim asserted nor the relief requested requires the participation of a member of the Nonprofit Association HOA.[15] Finally, a judgment or order rendered against a Nonprofit Association HOA is not by itself a judgment or order against a member of a Nonprofit Association HOA (or any person considered to be a member by the Nonprofit Association HOA).[16]

3.1.2 (C) *Books and Records of a Nonprofit Association HOA*

A Texas Nonprofit Association HOA is required to keep correct and complete "Books and Records" of account for at least three (3) years after the end of each fiscal year; and, it must make such Books and Records available on request to members of the Nonprofit Association HOA for inspection and copying.[17] In addition, the Texas Attorney

---

13 Tex. Bus. Org. Code § 252.006(d).

14 Tex. Bus. Org. Code § 252.007. A judicial proceeding includes a civil lawsuit.

15 Tex. Bus. Org. Code § 252.007.

16 Tex. Bus. Org. Code § 252.008.

17 Tex. Bus. Org. Code § 252.010(a).

General is authorized to inspect, examine, and make copies of a Nonprofit Association HOA's books, records, and any other documents the Attorney General considers necessary and may investigate a Nonprofit Association HOA to determine if a violation of any Texas law has occurred.[18]

3.1.2 (D) *Appointment of a Registered Agent for a Nonprofit Association HOA*

Finally, the Texas Uniform Unincorporated Nonprofit Association Law authorizes a Nonprofit Association HOA to file a statement in the office of the Texas Secretary of State appointing an agent who is authorized to receive service of process on behalf of the Nonprofit Association HOA.[19] A statement appointing an agent on behalf of a Nonprofit Association HOA must contain: (1) the name of the Nonprofit Association HOA; (2) the federal tax identification number of the Nonprofit Association HOA, if applicable; (3) the address of the Nonprofit Association HOA; and (4) the name of the person in Texas authorized to receive service of process on behalf of the Nonprofit Association HOA and such person's address.[20] A statement appointing an agent must be signed by a person authorized to manage the affairs of the Nonprofit Association HOA, as well as the person who is being appointed as the agent for the Nonprofit Association HOA, who by signing such statement accepts the appointment.[21]

3.2 Management of Nonprofit Corporation HOAs by a Board of Directors

Almost all Texas Nonprofit Corporation HOAs are governed by a Board of Directors.[22] The "Board of Directors" means the group of persons vested with the

---

18 Tex. Bus. Org. Code § 252.010(c).

19 Tex. Bus. Org. Code § 252.011(a).

20 Tex. Bus. Org. Code § 252.011(b).

21 Tex. Bus. Org. Code § 252.011(c). The appointed agent may resign as the registered agent for the Nonprofit Association HOA by filing a resignation in the office of the Texas Secretary of State and giving notice to the Nonprofit Association HOA. Tex. Bus. Org. Code § 252.011(c).

22 While the affairs of a Texas Nonprofit Corporation HOA may be managed by the Member-Homeowners of the Nonprofit Corporation HOA, as opposed to a Board of Directors, unless the Articles of Incorporation

management of the affairs of the Nonprofit Corporation HOA on behalf of the Member-Homeowners, regardless of the name used to designate such management group.[23]

The authority of the Board of Directors of a Nonprofit Corporation HOA is derived from and limited to those powers expressly vested in it by its Governing Documents and Texas law. Accordingly, in order to determine the full scope of a particular Nonprofit Corporation HOA's authority and powers, the Declaration, Articles of Incorporation, and Bylaws of the Nonprofit Corporation HOA must be read thoroughly. In general, the Articles of Incorporation and Bylaws of a Nonprofit Corporation HOA will provide the administrative rules and procedures for its operation, while the Declaration will vest the Nonprofit Corporation HOA with certain powers to manage the community. It is not uncommon, however, for there to be an overlap between the different Governing Documents, so all Governing Documents of a Nonprofit Corporation HOA should be reviewed to determine the full scope of its authority and power.[24]

3.3 Transition of Control of a Board of Directors from Declarant to Homeowners

In most cases when a Texas Homeowners Association is created, its Declaration and/or Bylaws will provide for an initial period of "Declarant-Control" of the Homeowners Association, during which the Declarant may unilaterally appoint and/or

---

expressly vest the management of the Nonprofit Corporation HOA in the Member-Homeowners, the management of the Nonprofit Corporation HOA is automatically vested in a Board of Directors. Tex. Bus. Org. Code §§ 22.201, 22.202. Because the management of a Nonprofit Corporation HOA is rarely vested in its Member-Homeowners, this book will primarily focus on the application of the Texas Nonprofit Corporation Law in the context of management of Nonprofit Corporation HOAs by a Board of Directors.

23 Tex. Bus. Org. Code § 22.001.

24 It is also not unheard of for there to be inconsistencies or conflicts between one or more of the Governing Documents. Except in limited circumstances, a provision of the Articles of Incorporation controls over an inconsistent Bylaw provision. Tex. Bus. Org. Code § 22.103(a). One of the limited exceptions to this rule is the number of Directors on the Board of Directors. If the number of Directors is established by the Articles of Incorporation, a Nonprofit Corporation HOA may change the number of Directors by amendment of the Bylaws without actually amending the Articles of Incorporation, unless the Articles of Incorporation provide that a change in the number of Directors may be made only by amendment to the Articles of Incorporation. Tex. Bus. Org. Code § 22.103(b).

remove the Directors and Officers of the Nonprofit Corporation HOA.[25] Such period of time is commonly referred to as a Homeowners Association's "Declarant-Control Period." Regardless of the length of the Declarant-Control Period, it will eventually terminate, and the power to appoint or elect members of the Homeowners Association's Board of Directors will transition to the Homeowners. Following such transition, members of the Homeowners Association's Board of Directors will be elected by the Homeowners.

The timing of the transition of a Homeowners Association from Declarant-Control to "Homeowner-Control" will depend on the express terms of the Homeowners Association's Declaration and/or Bylaws and whether it is a Condominium Association or a Subdivision Association. While the terms for transition of control under a Homeowners Association's Declaration and Bylaws can differ significantly from one Homeowners Association to another, the Texas Uniform Condominium Act and Chapter 209 of the Texas Property Code both impose certain deadlines for partial and/or full transition of control of the Board of Directors from the Declarant to the Homeowners.

3.3.1 (A) *Transition of Control of a Condominium Association's Board of Directors under the Texas Uniform Condominium Act*

In most instances, the Condominium Declaration will provide for an initial period of Declarant-Control of the Condominium Association, during which the Declarant may appoint the Directors and Officers of the Condominium Association. Regardless of the duration of the Declarant-Control Period specified in the Condominium Declaration, the Texas Uniform Condominium Act requires that control of the Condominium Association's Board of Directors be gradually transitioned from the Declarant to the Unit Owners, other than the Declarant, upon the occurrence of certain benchmarks.[26]

---

25 Tex. Prop. Code § 209.00591(c).

26 Tex. Prop. Code § 82.103.

First, no later than one hundred twenty (120) days after conveyance of fifty percent (50%) of the Units in the Condominium Development to Unit Owners other than a Declarant, at least one-third (1/3) of the members of the Board of Directors must be elected by Unit Owners other than the Declarant.[27]

Thereafter, a Condominium Association's period of Declarant-Control terminates one hundred twenty (120) days after the Declarant conveys seventy-five percent (75%) of the total number of Units in the Condominium Development to a person or entity other than the Declarant.[28] Prior to, and at the very least no later than, the date of termination of the Declarant-Control Period, the members of the Board of Directors must all be elected by Unit Owners.[29] In addition, within thirty (30) days of the termination of the Declarant-Control Period, the Board of Directors elected by the Unit Owners must elect the Officers of the Condominium Association.[30] Persons elected to the Board of Directors or as Officers of the Condominium Association shall take office upon election.[31]

3.3.1 (B) *Partial Transition of Control of a Subdivision Association's Board of Directors under Chapter 209 of the Texas Property Code*

Similar to Condominium Associations, the Declaration and/or Bylaws for a Subdivision Association may provide for a period of Declarant-Control of the Board of Directors, during which the Declarant, or persons designated by the Declarant, may appoint and remove Directors and Officers of the Subdivision Association.[32] Regardless of the duration of the period of Declarant-Control specified by the Subdivision Declaration, Chapter 209 of the Texas Property Code requires a partial transition of

---

27 Tex. Prop. Code § 82.103(d).

28 Tex. Prop. Code § 82.103(c).

29 Tex. Prop. Code § 82.103(e).

30 Tex. Prop. Code § 82.103(e).

31 Tex. Prop. Code § 82.103(e).

32 Tex. Prop. Code § 209.00591(c).

control of the Board of Directors from the Declarant to the Lot Owners once the Declarant conveys ownership of seventy-five percent (75%) of the Lots in the Subdivision Development to third parties. More specifically, on or before the 120th day after the date seventy-five percent (75%) of the total number of Lots that may be created and made subject to the Declaration are conveyed to Lot Owners, other than the Declarant or a "Builder," at least one-third (1/3) of the members of the Board of Directors must be elected by Lot Owners, other than the Declarant.[33]

Unlike Condominium Declarations, there is no statutory law that requires a Subdivision Declaration to specify the total number of Lots that may be created and made subject to such Declaration, and in most cases, a Subdivision Declaration will not specify the total number of Lots that may be created and made subject to such Declaration. If a Subdivision Association's Declaration does not specify the number of Lots that may be created and made subject to the Declaration, then at least one-third (1/3) of the members of the Board of Directors must be elected by Lot Owners, other than the Declarant, no later than the tenth (10th) anniversary of the date the Declaration was recorded in the Official Public Records of the county in which the Subdivision Development is located.[34]

3.4 Number of Directors on the Board and Manner of Appointment or Election of Members to the Board of Directors

If a Nonprofit Corporation HOA is to be managed by a Board of Directors, then the Articles of Incorporation must state the names of the members of the initial Board of Directors.[35] The members of the initial Board of Directors shall hold office until the first

---

33 Tex. Prop. Code § 209.00591(c). For purposes of Section 209.00591, the term "Builder" means a person or entity that is in the business of constructing homes who purchased the Lots from the Declarant for the purpose of selling completed homes built on such Lots. Tex. Prop. Code § 209.00591(c). It is important to note that Chapter 209 of the Texas Property Code does not require full transition of control of a Subdivision Association's Board of Directors from the Declarant to the Lot Owners, as the Texas Uniform Condominium Act does for Condominium Associations.

34 Tex. Prop. Code § 209.00591(c).

35 Tex. Bus. Org. Code § 22.205.

annual election of Directors, or for the period of time specified in the Articles of Incorporation or Bylaws of the Nonprofit Corporation HOA.[36] Thereafter, all Directors, other than the initial Directors, are to be elected, appointed, or designated in the manner provided in the Articles of Incorporation or Bylaws of the Nonprofit Corporation HOA, subject to the requirements of Chapter 209 of the Texas Property Code if the Nonprofit Corporation HOA is a Subdivision Association.[37]

3.4.1 Number of Directors on the Board of Directors

The number of Director-positions on the Board of Directors following the replacement of the initial Board of Directors will typically be found in the Articles of Incorporation or Bylaws of the Nonprofit Corporation HOA. If the Nonprofit Corporation HOA's Articles of Incorporation or Bylaws do not specify the number of Directors to comprise the Board of Directors following the replacement of the initial Board of Directors, then the number of Directors shall be the same as the number of initial Directors set by the Articles of Incorporation.[38] The number of initial Directors and/or subsequent Directors, however, may not be less than three.[39]

3.4.2 Manner of Appointment and Election of Directors

The manner in which Directors are appointed or elected to the Board of Directors is primarily dictated by a Nonprofit Corporation HOA's Articles of Incorporation or Bylaws. Pursuant to the Texas Nonprofit Corporation Law, all Directors of a Nonprofit Corporation HOA, other than the initial Directors, are to be elected, appointed, or designated in the manner provided in its Articles of Incorporation or Bylaws.[40]

---

36 Tex. Bus. Org. Code § 22.208.

37 Tex. Bus. Org. Code § 22.206; *but see*, Tex. Prop. Code § 209.00593.

38 Tex. Bus. Org. Code § 22.204.

39 Tex. Bus. Org. Code § 22.204(a).

40 Tex. Bus. Org. Code § 22.206. In the event a Nonprofit Corporation's Articles of Incorporation and Bylaws do not specify the manner in which Directors are to be elected, appointed, or designated, the Texas

Notwithstanding the provisions of a Texas Homeowners Association's Articles of Incorporation or Bylaws concerning the manner of appointment or election of Directors, both the Texas Uniform Condominium Act and Chapter 209 of the Texas Property Code impose restrictions on the election of Directors in a Condominium Association and Subdivision Association, respectively.

3.4.2 (A) *Election of Directors in a Condominium Association under the Texas Uniform Condominium Act*

As noted previously, the Texas Uniform Condominium Act recognizes that a Condominium Association's Declaration may provide for an initial period of Declarant-Control of the Condominium Association, during which the Declarant may appoint the Directors and Officers of the Condominium Association.[41] In such event, during the Declarant-Control Period, the Declarant may appoint the Directors to the Board of Directors.[42] However, within one hundred twenty (120) days after the Declarant conveys fifty percent (50%) of the Units in the Condominium Development to Unit Owners other than the Declarant, at least one-third (1/3) of the members of the Board of Directors must be elected by Unit Owners other than the Declarant; and, within one hundred twenty (120) days after the Declarant conveys seventy-five percent (75%) of the total number of Units in the Condominium Development to Unit Owners other than the Declarant, all of the members of the Board of Directors must be elected by the Unit Owners, including the Declarant if it still owns any Units.[43]

Nonprofit Corporation Law further provides that such Directors are to be elected by the Board of Directors. Tex. Bus. Org. Code § 22.206.

41 Tex. Prop. Code § 82.103(c). The provisions of the Texas Uniform Condominium Act concerning transition of control from the Declarant to the Unit Owners are not applicable to Condominium Developments created prior to January 1, 1994, that are subject to the Texas Condominium Act, and there are no comparable provisions under the Texas Condominium Act. Tex. Prop. Code § 82.002(c).

42 Tex. Prop. Code § 82.103(c).

43 Tex. Prop. Code § 82.103(d)–(e).

3.4.2 (B) *Election of Directors in a Subdivision Association under Chapter 209 of the Texas Property Code*

As also noted previously, the Declaration and/or Bylaws for a Subdivision Association may also provide for a period of Declarant-Control of the Board of Directors, during which the Declarant, or persons designated by the Declarant, may appoint and remove Directors and Officers of the Subdivision Association.[44] While Chapter 209 of the Texas Property Code does not require termination of a Declarant-Control Period or full transition of control of a Board of Directors from the Declarant to the Lot Owners by a certain date, Section 209.00591 does require that within one hundred twenty (120) days after the Declarant conveys seventy-five percent (75%) of the total number of Lots in the Subdivision Development to Lot Owners, other than the Declarant or a builder in the business of constructing homes who purchased the Lots from the Declarant for the purpose of selling completed homes built on the Lots, at least one-third (1/3) of the members of the Board of Directors must be elected by Lot Owners other than the Declarant.[45]

In addition, any member of a Subdivision Association's Board of Directors whose term has expired must be reelected by the Subdivision Association's Lot Owners in order

[44] Tex. Prop. Code § 209.00591(c).

[45] Tex. Prop. Code § 209.00591(c). For purposes of Section 209.00591, the total number of Lots in the Subdivision is calculated as the total number of Lots that may be created and made subject to the Subdivision Declaration as specified by such Declaration. Tex. Prop. Code § 209.00591(c). The language of Section 209.00591 was borrowed from the Texas Uniform Condominium Act, which requires a Condominium Declaration to specify the total number of Units that are to be created. There is no similar requirement for Subdivision Declarations, and most Subdivision Declarations will not specify the total number of Lots that will be created and made subject to such Declaration. In anticipation of such circumstances, Section 209.00591 provides that if a Subdivision Declaration does not specify the number of Lots that may be created and made subject to such Declaration, then at least one-third (1/3) of the members of the Board of Directors must be elected by Lot Owners other than the Declarant no later than the tenth (10th) anniversary of the date the Subdivision Declaration was recorded in the Official Public Records of the county in which the Subdivision Development is located. Tex. Prop. Code § 209.00591(c). It is also important to note that Chapter 209 of the Texas Property Code does not require full transition of control of a Subdivision Association's Board of Directors from the Declarant to the Lot Owners, as the Texas Uniform Condominium Act does for Condominium Associations.

to continue to serve on the Board of Directors.[46] Accordingly, if a Nonprofit Corporation HOA is a Subdivision Association, then the Directors must be reelected, even if its Bylaws state otherwise.

3.5 Eligibility Requirements and Qualifications to Serve as a Director of a Texas Nonprofit Corporation HOA

It is not uncommon for a Homeowners Association to have provisions in its Governing Documents that impose restrictions on who may run for election to or serve on the Board of Directors. Eligibility requirements and qualifications to serve as a Director of a Nonprofit Corporation HOA are governed primarily by a Nonprofit Corporation HOA's Governing Documents, and to the extent a Nonprofit Corporation HOA is a Subdivision Association, also Chapter 209 of the Texas Property Code.

In general, there are no eligibility or qualification requirements to be a Director of a Texas Nonprofit Corporation HOA under the Texas Nonprofit Corporation Law.[47] In addition, unless otherwise required by the Governing Documents of a particular Nonprofit Corporation HOA, a Director is not required to be a resident of the community or even a Member-Homeowner of the Nonprofit Corporation HOA.

Notwithstanding, the Governing Documents of almost all Texas Homeowners Associations will require each Director to at least be a Homeowner in the Homeowners Association following transition of control of the Homeowners Association from the

---

46 Tex. Prop. Code § 209.00593(a). An appointment of a Director to a Subdivision Association's Board of Directors in violation of Section 209.00593 is void. Tex. Prop. Code § 209.00593(c). Section 209.00593, however, does not apply to the appointment of a Director during a Subdivision Association's "Development Period." Tex. Prop. Code § 209.00593(d). For purposes of Section 209.00593, a Subdivision Association's Development Period means a period of time stated in its Declaration during which a Declarant reserves a right to: (1) facilitate the development, construction, and marketing of the Subdivision Development; or (2) direct the size, shape, and composition of the Subdivision Development. Tex. Prop. Code § 209.002(4-a). Section 209.00593 also does not apply to a representative Board of Directors whose members or delegates are elected or appointed by representatives of a Subdivision Association who are elected by the Subdivision Association's Lot Owners. Tex. Prop. Code § 209.00593(e).

47 Tex. Bus. Org. Code § 22.203.

Declarant to the Homeowners. It is also very common for the Governing Documents of a Texas Homeowners Association to require each candidate for election to the Board of Directors to be in good standing, or in other words, to be current or up to date in payment of his or her Assessments. It is also not uncommon for the Governing Documents of a Texas Homeowners Association to provide for disqualification or removal of a Director from the Board of Directors if, during his or her term of service, he or she fails to remain in good standing. To the extent eligibility requirements to run for election to the Board of Directors and/or to continue to serve as a Director, such as those mentioned previously, are contained in a Condominium Association's Governing Documents, such requirements are valid and generally enforceable. The same, however, can no longer be said for Subdivision Associations.

In 2011, the Texas Legislature enacted Section 209.00591 of the Texas Property Code, which applies to all incorporated and unincorporated Subdivision Associations in Texas. Pursuant to Sections 209.00591, any provision in a Subdivision Association's Governing Documents that restricts a Lot Owner's right to run for a position on the Board of Directors of the Subdivision Association is void and unenforceable.[48] In other words, if a Subdivision Association's Bylaws disallow a Lot Owner who is not current in the payment of assessments from running for election to the Board of Directors, such Bylaw provision is no longer enforceable, and such Lot Owner may run for election to the Board of Directors.

Although Section 209.00591 nullifies any eligibility requirement for a Lot Owner to run for election to the Board of Directors, it also establishes a new qualification to serve as a Director of a Texas Subdivision Association. Pursuant to Section 209.00591, any person who was convicted of a felony or a crime involving moral turpitude is disqualified

[48] Tex. Prop. Code § 209.00591(a).

from continued or future service on a Subdivision Association's Board of Directors for twenty (20) years following the date of such conviction.[49]

Such qualification to serve as a Director, however, is not an eligibility requirement to run for the Board of Directors. A Subdivision Association is not required to perform criminal history checks of candidates prior to election to the Board of Directors or even of Directors currently serving on the Board of Directors. But if a Subdivision Association's Board of Directors is presented with a copy of a written record or document from a governmental law enforcement authority (such as a criminal record from the Texas Department of Public Safety) establishing that a currently serving Director has been convicted of a felony or a crime involving moral turpitude within the most recent twenty-year period preceding the date the Board of Directors is presented with such record or document, such Director is: (1) immediately ineligible to serve on the Board of Directors; (2) automatically considered removed from the Board of Directors; and (3) prohibited from future service on the Board of Directors.[50]

3.6 Term of Office for Directors

A Director on the initial Board of Directors of a Texas Nonprofit Corporation HOA holds office either until the first annual election of Directors or for the period of time specified in the Articles of Incorporation or Bylaws for the Nonprofit Corporation HOA, unless he or she resigns or is removed from the Board of Directors prior to such date.[51] Directors, other than the initial Directors of a Texas Nonprofit Corporation HOA,

---

49 Tex. Prop. Code § 209.00591(b). Although "crime involving moral turpitude" is an often-used term of art under Texas law, there exists no statutory definition or definitive standard of what constitutes a "crime involving moral turpitude." Generally speaking, however, a crime of moral turpitude in Texas is a crime that involves dishonesty, fraud, deceit, misrepresentation, or deliberate violence or that reflects adversely on a person's honesty or trustworthiness. *See In re Birdwell*, 20 S.W.3d 685, 687 (Tex. 2000); *In re Humphreys*, 880 S.W.2d 402, 408 (Tex. 1994). The most common example of a misdemeanor (non-felony) crime involving moral turpitude is theft.

50 Tex. Prop. Code § 209.00591(b).

51 Tex. Bus. Org. Code § 22.208.

are elected, appointed, or designated for the terms of office specified by the Articles of Incorporation or Bylaws of the Nonprofit Corporation HOA.[52] In the absence of a provision in a Nonprofit Corporation HOA's Articles of Incorporation or Bylaws specifying the length of the term of office for Directors (other than initial Directors), each such Director shall hold office until the next annual election of Directors, when a successor is elected, appointed, or designated and qualified.[53]

3.7 Resignation or Removal of Directors from the Board

Unless otherwise provided by the Articles of Incorporation or Bylaws, a Director may resign at any time by providing written notice to the Nonprofit Corporation HOA.[54] In addition, a Director of a Nonprofit Corporation HOA may be removed from office under any procedure provided by the Articles of Incorporation or Bylaws.[55]

In the absence of a provision for removal of Directors in the Articles of Incorporation or Bylaws of a Nonprofit Corporation HOA, a Director may be removed from office, with or without cause, by the persons entitled to elect, designate, or appoint the Director to the Board of Directors.[56] Thus, if there is no provision for removal of Directors, and Directors are elected to office, removal of a Director requires an affirmative vote equal to the vote necessary to elect the Director to the Board of Directors.[57] Or said more simply, if there is no procedure for removal of Directors in the Articles of Incorporation or Bylaws of a Texas Nonprofit Corporation HOA, and Directors are elected by a majority vote of the Member-Homeowners, then under such circumstances a Director

[52] Tex. Bus. Org. Code § 22.208.

[53] Tex. Bus. Org. Code § 22.208.

[54] Tex. Bus. Org. Code § 22.211.

[55] Tex. Bus. Org. Code § 22.211.

[56] Tex. Bus. Org. Code § 22.211.

[57] Tex. Bus. Org. Code § 22.211.

may be removed from the Board of Directors by a majority vote of the Member-Homeowners.

3.8 Filling a Vacancy on the Board of Directors

The manner in which a vacancy on the Board of Directors is filled depends on whether the Nonprofit Corporation HOA is a Condominium Association or a Subdivision Association.

3.8.1 Manner of Filling a Vacancy on a Condominium Association's Board of Directors

If a Nonprofit Corporation HOA is a Condominium Association, the manner of filling a vacancy on the Board of Directors is governed by its Governing Documents and the Texas Nonprofit Corporation Law, as the Texas Uniform Condominium Act does not address such issue. Pursuant to the Texas Nonprofit Corporation Law, unless otherwise provided by the Articles of Incorporation or Bylaws of the Condominium Association, a vacancy on the Board of Directors resulting from death, resignation, or removal of a Director shall be filled by the affirmative vote of the majority of the remaining Directors on the Board of Directors, regardless of whether such majority would constitute less than a quorum of the Board of Directors.[58] On the other hand, a vacancy on the Board of Directors occurring because of an increase in the number of Director-positions on the Board of Directors shall be filled by election at an Annual Meeting or at a Special Meeting of the Condominium Association's Unit Owners specifically called for such purpose.[59]

---

58 Tex. Bus. Org. Code § 22.212. A Director elected to fill such a vacancy is elected for the unexpired term of such Director's predecessor in office. Tex. Bus. Org. Code § 22.212.

59 Tex. Bus. Org. Code § 22.212.

3.8.2 Manner of Filling a Vacancy on a Subdivision Association's Board of Directors

If a Nonprofit Corporation HOA is a Subdivision Association, the manner of filling a vacancy on the Board of Directors is governed by its Governing Documents, the Texas Nonprofit Corporation Law, and Chapter 209 of the Texas Property Code. Pursuant to the Texas Nonprofit Corporation Law, unless otherwise provided by the Articles of Incorporation or Bylaws of the Subdivision Association, a vacancy on the Board of Directors resulting from death, resignation, or removal of a Director shall be filled by the affirmative vote of the majority of the remaining Directors on the Board of Directors, regardless of whether such majority would constitute less than a quorum of the Board of Directors.[60] On the other hand, a vacancy on the Board of Directors occurring because of an increase in the number of Director-positions on the Board of Directors shall be filled by election at an Annual Meeting or at a Special Meeting of the Subdivision Association's Lot Owners specifically called for such purpose.[61]

Chapter 209 of the Texas Property Code further provides that a Director appointed to fill a vacancy on the Board of Directors shall serve the unexpired term of such Director's predecessor in office.[62] In addition, any appointment of a person to fill a vacant

---

60 Tex. Bus. Org. Code § 22.212. A Director elected to fill such a vacancy is elected for the unexpired term of such Director's predecessor in office. Tex. Bus. Org. Code § 22.212.

61 Tex. Bus. Org. Code § 22.212. Prior to 2015, Section 209.00593 of the Texas Property Code allowed the Board of Directors of a Subdivision Association to fill a vacancy thereon only if the vacancy was caused by a resignation, death, or disability. In 2015, however, the Texas Legislature removed such restriction and Section 209.00593 now simply states that a Director may be appointed by the Board of Directors to fill a vacancy. Tex. Prop. Code § 209.00593(a).

62 Tex. Prop. Code § 209.00593(a). Section 209.00593, however, does not apply to the appointment of a Director during a Subdivision Association's "Development Period." Tex. Prop. Code § 209.00593(d). For purposes of Section 209.00593, a Subdivision Association's Development Period means a period of time stated in its Declaration during which a Declarant reserves: (1) a right to facilitate the development, construction, and marketing of the Subdivision Development; or (2) a right to direct the size, shape, and composition of the Subdivision Development. Tex. Prop. Code § 209.002(4-a). Section 209.00593 also does not apply to a representative Board of Directors whose members or delegates are elected or appointed by representatives of a Subdivision Association who are elected by the Subdivision Association's Lot Owners. Tex. Prop. Code § 209.00593(e).

position on a Subdivision Association's Board of Directors in violation of the procedures of Chapter 209 is considered void.[63]

3.9 Corporate Officers of a Nonprofit Corporation HOA

In addition to a Board of Directors, a Texas Nonprofit Corporation HOA is also required to have corporate Officers. In general, Officers of a Nonprofit Corporation HOA perform certain duties in the management of the corporation and may have certain powers or authority granted to them by the Governing Documents of the Nonprofit Corporation HOA.[64]

The Governing Documents of a Nonprofit Corporation HOA will generally specify the types, number, and duties or powers of each corporate Officer of the Nonprofit Corporation HOA. Pursuant to the Texas Nonprofit Corporation Law, a Texas Nonprofit Corporation HOA must at least have a President and a Secretary, and may, but is not required to, also have one or more Vice Presidents, a Treasurer, and any other Officers and assistant Officers as are considered necessary by the Nonprofit Corporation HOA.[65]

Most Texas Nonprofit Corporation HOAs have a President, Secretary, and at least a Treasurer, if not also at least one Vice President. The Officer-positions of a Texas Nonprofit Corporation HOA can generally be described as follows:

---

63 Tex. Prop. Code § 209.00593(c). Section 209.00593 controls over any contrary provision in a Subdivision Association's Governing Documents. Tex. Prop. Code § 209.00593(a). Section 209.00593 also authorizes a Subdivision Association's Board of Directors to amend its Bylaws in order to conform such Bylaw provisions to the requirements of Section 209.00593. Tex. Prop. Code § 209.00593(b).

64 Tex. Bus. Org. Code § 3.103.

65 Tex. Bus. Org. Code § 22.231. Any two or more Officer-positions, other than that of President and Secretary, may be held by the same person. Tex. Bus. Org. Code § 22.231. In addition, a properly designated committee may perform the functions of an Officer, and a single committee may perform the functions of any two or more Officers, including the functions of President and Secretary. Tex. Bus. Org. Code § 22.231.

President:

The President of a Nonprofit Corporation HOA is the Officer designated as the "President" under the Nonprofit Corporation HOA's Articles of Incorporation or Bylaws.[66] Where such term is not used in a Nonprofit Corporation HOA's Articles of Incorporation or Bylaws, the Officer or committee of persons authorized to perform the function of the principal executive Officer of the Nonprofit Corporation HOA, regardless of the designated name of such Officer or committee, is considered to be the "President" for purposes of the Nonprofit Corporation Law.[67]

Secretary:

The Secretary of a Nonprofit Corporation HOA is the Officer designated as the "Secretary" under the Nonprofit Corporation HOA's Articles of Incorporation or Bylaws.[68] Where such term is not used in a Nonprofit Corporation HOA's Articles of Incorporation or Bylaws, the Officer or committee of persons authorized to perform the function of Secretary of the Nonprofit Corporation HOA, regardless of the designated name of such Officer or committee, is considered to be the "Secretary" for purposes of the Nonprofit Corporation Law.[69]

Treasurer:

The Treasurer of a Nonprofit Corporation HOA is the Officer designated as the "Treasurer" under the Nonprofit Corporation HOA's Articles of Incorporation or Bylaws.[70] Where such term is not used in a Nonprofit Corporation HOA's Articles of Incorporation or Bylaws, the Officer or committee of persons authorized to perform the

66 Tex. Bus. Org. Code § 1.002(70).

67 Tex. Bus. Org. Code § 1.002(70).

68 Tex. Bus. Org. Code § 1.002(79).

69 Tex. Bus. Org. Code § 1.002(79).

70 Tex. Bus. Org. Code § 1.002(86).

function of Treasurer of the Nonprofit Corporation HOA, regardless of the designated name of such Officer or committee, is considered to be the "Treasurer" for purposes of the Nonprofit Corporation Law.[71]

Vice President:

The Vice President of a Nonprofit Corporation HOA is the Officer designated as the "Vice President" under the Nonprofit Corporation HOA's Articles of Incorporation or Bylaws.[72] Where such term is not used in a Nonprofit Corporation HOA's Articles of Incorporation or Bylaws, the Officer or committee of persons authorized to perform the function of the President of the Nonprofit Corporation HOA on the death, absence, or resignation of the President or on the inability of the President to perform the functions of such office, regardless of the designated name of such Officer or committee, is considered to be the "Vice President" for purposes of the Nonprofit Corporation Law.[73]

The designation of Officer-positions is important because under the Governing Documents of most Texas Homeowners Associations, Officers generally have special rights, duties, and obligations separate and apart from their non-officer co-Directors. More specifically, under most Texas Homeowners Associations' Governing Documents, the President is usually the executive Officer of the Homeowners Association and is responsible for presiding over meetings of its Board of Directors and Homeowners. The President of a Homeowners Association is also generally afforded the power to call special meetings of its Board of Directors and Homeowners. In addition, the Treasurer of a Texas Homeowners Association is generally responsible for keeping the financial books of the

---

[71] Tex. Bus. Org. Code § 1.002(86).

[72] Tex. Bus. Org. Code § 1.002(88).

[73] Tex. Bus. Org. Code § 1.002(88).

Homeowners Association, while the Secretary is generally responsible for keeping the minutes of all meetings of the Homeowners Association's Board of Directors.[74]

In addition to any special powers or duties of corporate officers under a Texas Homeowners Association's Governing Documents, the Texas Nonprofit Corporation Law, Texas Uniform Condominium Act, and Chapter 209 of the Texas Property Code require certain actions of a Homeowners Association be performed by one of its Officers. For instance, any document filed with the Office of the Texas Secretary of State on behalf of a Nonprofit Corporation HOA must be signed by an Officer of the corporation.[75] In addition, both the Texas Uniform Condominium Act and Chapter 209 of the Texas Property Code require Condominium Associations and Subdivision Associations, respectively, to record Management Certificates in the local Official Public Records that are executed by one of its Officers.[76]

3.10 Election or Appointment of Officers

Officers of a Nonprofit Corporation HOA are elected or appointed at the time, in the manner, and for the terms prescribed by the Articles of Incorporation or Bylaws of the Nonprofit Corporation HOA.[77] Notwithstanding, the term of office of an Officer-position may not exceed three (3) years.[78] If the Articles of Incorporation or Bylaws of a Nonprofit Corporation HOA do not include provisions for the election or appointment of Officers,

---

74 In some cases, a Homeowners Association's Governing Documents will also require that certain actions taken by the Board of Directors be memorialized in writing and certified by the Secretary. In most Texas Homeowners Associations, however, the Vice President has no responsibility other than to preside over meetings in the absence of the President.

75 Tex. Bus. Org. Code § 20.001.

76 Tex. Prop. Code §§ 82.116(a), 209.004(a).

77 Tex. Bus. Org. Code § 22.232(a).

78 Tex. Bus. Org. Code § 22.232(a).

then the Officers of the Nonprofit Corporation HOA shall be elected or appointed annually by the Board of Directors.[79]

3.11 Eligibility Requirements and Qualifications to Serve as an Officer

Generally speaking, there are no eligibility or qualification requirements to be an Officer of a Texas Nonprofit Corporation HOA unless expressly provided for in the Nonprofit Corporation HOA's Articles of Incorporation or Bylaws. As a practical note, the Articles of Incorporation and/or Bylaws of most Texas Nonprofit Corporation HOAs often require Officers to be currently serving Directors of the Nonprofit Corporation HOA.

3.12 Removal of Officers

Unless otherwise provided by the Articles of Incorporation or Bylaws of a Nonprofit Corporation HOA, an Officer may be removed, with or without cause, by the Board of Directors or under any other circumstances or procedures set forth in the Articles of Incorporation or Bylaws of the Nonprofit Corporation HOA.[80] It is also important to note that, unless otherwise provided by the Articles of Incorporation or Bylaws of a Nonprofit Corporation HOA, removal of an Officer does not also remove such person from the Board of Directors if he or she is also currently serving as a Director of the Nonprofit Corporation HOA.

3.13 Committees of a Nonprofit Corporation HOA

The Texas Nonprofit Corporation Law authorizes Nonprofit Corporation HOAs to establish two types of committees: "Management Committees" and other "Non-Management Committees." The procedural requirements for establishing a committee,

---

[79] Tex. Bus. Org. Code § 22.232. If the management of a Nonprofit Corporation HOA is vested in the Nonprofit Corporation HOA's Member-Homeowners, then the Officers shall be elected or appointed annually by the Member-Homeowners. Tex. Bus. Org. Code § 22.232.

[80] Tex. Bus. Org. Code § 3.104.

and whether Directors are required to be members of such committee, depend on whether such committee is considered to be a Management Committee or a Non-Management Committee.

It is important to note that an Architectural Committee (or other group of similar designation) is generally not considered to be a "committee" of a Nonprofit Corporation HOA. In most cases, the Architectural Committee is established by the Declaration, not by the Board of Directors of the Nonprofit Corporation HOA. In addition, the Architectural Committee is generally established as a group of individuals separate and apart from the Homeowners Association that has its own exclusive powers and authority to approve proposed construction or modification of improvements upon Lots or Units in the community.[81]

3.13.1 Management Committees

A Management Committee is a committee established by the Board of Directors of a Nonprofit Corporation HOA to exercise the authority of the Board of Directors in the management of the Nonprofit Corporation HOA.[82] If authorized by the Articles of Incorporation or Bylaws, the Board of Directors of a Nonprofit Corporation HOA, by resolution adopted by a majority of the Directors in office, may designate one or more committees to have and exercise the authority of the Board of Directors in the management of the Nonprofit Corporation HOA to the extent authorized by: (1) the resolution; (2) its Articles of Incorporation; or (3) its Bylaws.[83]

The membership of a Management Committee must consist of at least two members, and the majority of the members on the Management Committee must be

81 *See* chapter 8 of this book for a more thorough discussion of Architectural Committees.

82 Tex. Bus. Org. Code § 22.218.

83 Tex. Bus. Org. Code § 22.218(a).

currently serving Directors.[84] If authorized by the Articles of Incorporation or Bylaws of the Nonprofit Corporation HOA, the remaining persons on the Management Committee are not required to be Directors.[85] It is important to note, however, that the designation of a Management Committee and the delegation of authority to it does not operate to relieve the Board of Directors or an individual Director of any responsibility imposed on such Board of Directors or individual Director by Texas law.[86] In addition, a Management Committee member who is not a Director has the same responsibility with respect to the Management Committee as a member who is a Director.[87] In other words, both Director and non-Director members of a Management Committee owe the same fiduciary duties or duties of care owed by Directors serving on a Board of Directors of a Nonprofit Corporation HOA.

3.13.2 Non-Management Committees

Non-Management Committees of a Nonprofit Corporation HOA consist of all other committees established by the Board of Directors that have not been delegated the power to exercise some authority on behalf of the Board of Directors in the management of the Nonprofit Corporation HOA.[88] A Non-Management Committee of a Texas Nonprofit Corporation HOA may be established by a written resolution adopted by the majority of the Board of Directors or unilaterally by the President alone (if authorized to do so by a written resolution of the Board of Directors or by the Nonprofit Corporation HOA's Articles of Incorporation or Bylaws).[89] Unlike a Management Committee, the

---

84 Tex. Bus. Org. Code § 22.218(b).

85 Tex. Bus. Org. Code § 22.218(b).

86 Tex. Bus. Org. Code § 22.218(c).

87 Tex. Bus. Org. Code § 22.218(c).

88 Tex. Bus. Org. Code § 22.219(a).

89 Tex. Bus. Org. Code § 22.219(a).

membership of a Non-Management Committee may be, but is not required to be, limited to currently serving Directors.[90]

3.14 Ex Officio Members of the Board of Directors

The Articles of Incorporation or Bylaws of a Nonprofit Corporation HOA may also provide for "Ex Officio Members" of the Board of Directors.[91] A person designated as an Ex Officio Member of the Board of Directors is entitled to receive notice of and to attend Board of Director meetings, but he or she is not entitled to vote at such meetings unless the Articles of Incorporation or Bylaws of the Nonprofit Corporation HOA authorize Ex Officio Members of the Board of Directors to vote at such meetings.[92]

3.15 Duty of Care of Directors and Officers

Directors and Officers of a Texas Nonprofit Corporation HOA are generally considered to be fiduciaries of such Nonprofit Corporation HOA. This is certainly true for Directors and Officers of a Condominium Association subject to the Texas Uniform Condominium Act, as they are are expressly imposed with fiduciary duties under such law.[93] The imposition of fiduciary duties upon Directors and Officers of Nonprofit Corporations arises under both Texas common law and Texas statutory law, and the scope of such duties and the application of the "Business Judgment Rule" will be determined by the source of such duties.

---

90 Tex. Bus. Org. Code § 22.219(b).

91 Tex. Bus. Org. Code § 22.210. *Black's Law Dictionary* defines the term "ex officio" to mean "by virtue of the office" or "without any warrant or appointment than that resulting from the holding of a particular office." *Black's Law Dictionary* 575 (6th ed. 1990). In the context of Homeowners Associations, some Homeowners Associations' Governing Documents provide that former Officers or Directors may be considered "Ex Officio Members" of the Board of Directors.

92 Tex. Bus. Org. Code § 22.210.

93 Tex. Prop. Code § 82.103(a).

3.15.1 Fiduciary Duty of Directors and Officers and Application of the Business Judgment Rule under Texas Common Law

Under long-established Texas common law, Directors and Officers of a Nonprofit Corporation HOA are considered to be fiduciaries of such corporation.[94] The term "fiduciary" is derived from civil law and generally applies to "any person who occupies a position of peculiar confidence towards another" that imposes upon such person a duty of "integrity and fidelity" and an obligation of "fair dealing and good faith."[95] It is said that a fiduciary owes its principal a high duty of good faith, fair dealing, honest performance, and strict accountability.[96] These "fiduciary duties" are also commonly described as the duties of obedience, loyalty, and due care.[97] The duty of loyalty requires that Directors and Officers must act in good faith and must not allow their personal interest to prevail over the interest of the Nonprofit Corporation HOA. Such duty of loyalty is often described as requiring an extreme measure of candor, unselfishness, and good faith on the part of Directors and Officers.[98]

While Texas statutory law also imposes a duty on corporate Directors and Officers to exercise due care in the management of the corporation's affairs, the common law duty of care that a Director or Officer owes to a corporation has not been precisely defined by Texas courts.[99] Rather, Texas courts have historically applied a flexible standard, generally referred to as the "Business Judgment Rule," in which the court attempts to determine in each case what course of action a reasonable and prudent person

---

94 *Paddock v. Siemoneit*, 218 S.W.2d 428, 431 (Tex. 1949).

95 *Kinzbach Tool Co. v. Corbett-Wallace Corp.*, 160 S.W.2d 509, 512 (Tex. 1942).

96 *Kinzbach Tool Co. v. Corbett-Wallace Corp.*, 160 S.W.2d 509, 512 (Tex. 1942).

97 *Int'l Bankers Life Ins. Co. v. Holloway*, 368 S.W.2d 567, 577 (Tex. 1963).

98 *Int'l Bankers Life Ins. Co. v. Holloway*, 368 S.W.2d 567, 577 (Tex. 1963).

99 *Gearhart Industries, Inc. v. Smith Intern., Inc.*, 741 F.2d 707, 721 (5th Cir. 1984).

under similar circumstances as the applicable Director or Officer would have followed.[100] The Business Judgment Rule applies to the business actions taken by Directors and protects Directors from liability "unless the challenged action is ultra vires or is tainted by fraud."[101]

3.15.2 Duty of Care of Directors under the Texas Nonprofit Corporation Law

The Texas Nonprofit Corporation Law has now codified the duties owed by Directors of a Nonprofit Corporation HOA and adopted a variation of the Business Judgment Rule. Under such law, Directors of a Nonprofit Corporation HOA are required to discharge their duties: (1) in good faith; (2) with ordinary care; and (3) in a manner the Director reasonably believes to be in the best interests of the corporation.[102] This duty also applies to Directors when serving as members of Management and Non-Management Committees established by the Board of Directors, as well as non-Director members of Management Committees.[103]

The Texas Nonprofit Corporation Law also provides that in discharging a duty or exercising a power, a Director may in good faith, and with ordinary care, rely on information, opinions, reports, or statements (including financial statements and other financial data) prepared or presented by: (1) Officers or employees of the Nonprofit Corporation HOA; (2) legal counsel; (3) a certified public accountant; (4) an investment banker; (5) a Management or Non-Management Committee of the Nonprofit Corporation

---

[100] *McCollum v. Dollar*, 213 S.W. 259, 261 (Tex. Comm'n App. 1919, holding approved). In making this determination, courts may consider such relevant factors as the character of the corporation, the condition of its business, and the accepted practices within the corporation.

[101] *Gearhart Industries, Inc. v. Smith Intern., Inc.*, 741 F.2d 707, 721 (5th Cir. 1984). "Ultra vires" is a Latin phrase that means "beyond the powers," and an "ultra vires action" is considered to be an act that is beyond the scope of the powers of a corporation, as defined by its Articles of Incorporation and Bylaws. *See generally*, *Black's Law Dictionary* 1522 (6th ed. 1990).

[102] Tex. Bus. Org. Code § 22.221(a).

[103] Tex. Bus. Org. Code §§ 22.218(c), 22.221(a).

HOA of which the Director is not a member; and/or (6) any other person the Director reasonably believes to possess professional expertise in the matter.[104] However, a Director may not in good faith rely on such information if he or she has knowledge of a matter that makes reliance on such information unwarranted.[105]

3.15.3 Duty of Care of Officers under the Texas Nonprofit Corporation Law

Like Directors, Officers are also considered to be fiduciaries of Texas Nonprofit Corporation HOAs under Texas common law. Unlike Directors, however, the Texas Nonprofit Corporation Law has not expressly codified the fiduciary duties owed by Officers. Accordingly, the fiduciary duty of Officers of a Texas Nonprofit Corporation HOA is still governed primarily by Texas common law.

Notwithstanding, the Texas Nonprofit Corporation Law does provide guidance for the discharge of an Officer's fiduciary duties that are similar to that of Directors. More specifically, the Texas Nonprofit Corporation Law provides that in discharging a duty or exercising a power, an Officer of a Nonprofit Corporation HOA may, in good faith, and with ordinary care, rely on information, opinions, reports, or statements (including financial statements and other financial data) concerning the Nonprofit Corporation HOA or another person that is prepared or presented by: (1) another Officer or an employee of the Nonprofit Corporation HOA; (2) legal counsel; (3) a certified public accountant; (4) an investment banker; and/or (5) a person whom the Officer reasonably believes possesses professional expertise in the matter.[106] Like Directors, Officers also may not in good faith

---

[104] Tex. Bus. Org. Code § 3.102(a).

[105] Tex. Bus. Org. Code § 3.102(b).

[106] Tex. Bus. Org. Code § 3.105.

rely on such information if the Officer has knowledge of a matter that makes such reliance unwarranted.[107]

3.15.4 Application of the Business Judgment Rule under the Texas Nonprofit Corporation Law

The Texas Nonprofit Corporation Law has also codified a variation of the Business Judgment Rule for both Directors and Officers. Under the Texas Nonprofit Corporation Law, a Director of a Nonprofit Corporation HOA may not be held liable to the Nonprofit Corporation HOA, a Member-Homeowner of the Nonprofit Corporation HOA, or another person for an action taken or not taken in his or her capacity as a Director if he or she acted in compliance with the duties imposed by the Texas Nonprofit Corporation Law.[108] In addition, a person seeking to establish personal liability of a Director of a Nonprofit Corporation HOA must prove that the Director did not act: (1) in good faith; (2) with ordinary care; and (3) in a manner the Director reasonably believed to be in the best interest of the Nonprofit Corporation HOA.[109] Similarly, an Officer of a Nonprofit Corporation HOA may not be held liable to the Nonprofit Corporation HOA or any other person for an action taken or omission made by such Officer in his or her capacity as an Officer of the Nonprofit Corporation HOA unless such Officer's conduct was not exercised: (1) in good faith; (2) with ordinary care; and (3) in a manner the Officer reasonably believed to be in the best interest of the Nonprofit Corporation HOA.[110]

---

[107] Tex. Bus. Org. Code § 3.105.

[108] Tex. Bus. Org. Code § 22.221(b).

[109] Tex. Bus. Org. Code § 22.221(b).

[110] Tex. Bus. Org. Code § 22.235.

3.15.5 Duty of Care of Directors and Officers of Condominium Associations under the Texas Uniform Condominium Act

The Texas Uniform Condominium Act also imposes a duty of care upon Directors and Officers of Condominium Associations subject to such Act.[111] More specifically, under the Texas Uniform Condominium Act, each Director and Officer of a Condominium Association is considered to be a fiduciary of the Unit Owners in the commission of acts or omissions as a Director or Officer of the Condominium Association.[112] Notwithstanding, an Officer or Director of the Condominium Association may not be held liable to the Condominium Association or any Unit Owner for monetary damages for an act or omission committed in his or her capacity as a Director or Officer unless: (1) the Director or Officer breached a fiduciary duty to the Condominium Association or a Unit Owner; (2) the Director or Officer received an improper benefit; or (3) such act or omission was committed in bad faith, involved intentional misconduct, or was one for which liability is expressly provided by statutory law.[113]

3.16 Immunity and Indemnity of Directors and Officers of Nonprofit Corporation HOAs

One of the biggest concerns expressed by current and prospective members of Boards of Directors of Homeowners Associations is the potential of personal liability or the fear of being sued for some action or inaction by the Board of Directors. It is not uncommon in our current environment for persons disgruntled by perceived unequal treatment or mistreatment by a Homeowners Association to threaten the Board of Directors, or even individual Directors, with filing a lawsuit against them. While such

---

[111] Tex. Prop. Code § 82.103. The provisions of the Texas Uniform Condominium Act concerning the duty of care of Directors and Officers of a Condominium Association are not applicable to Condominium Developments created prior to January 1, 1994, that are subject to the Texas Condominium Act, and there are no comparable provisions under the Texas Condominium Act. Tex. Prop. Code § 82.002(c).

[112] Tex. Prop. Code § 82.103(a).

[113] Tex. Prop. Code § 82.103(f). Section 82.103(f) does not diminish any limitation of liability provided to a Director or Officer of a Condominium Association by its Declaration, Bylaws, or Articles of Incorporation or under other statutory laws. Tex. Prop. Code § 82.103(g).

threats are rarely followed through, even the potential of being sued or having to pay attorneys fees to defend oneself is enough to discourage most people from wanting to serve on a Board of Directors of a Homeowners Association and has been known to cause some Directors to simply resign. In most cases, however, Directors of Homeowners Associations are immune from personal liability and/or are entitled to be indemnified by the Homeowners Association for any expenses related to the costs of defending a lawsuit and any judgment that may be rendered against them.

3.16.1 Director and Officer Immunity from Liability under the Texas Charitable Immunity and Liability Act of 1987

Texas law provides certain limited immunity from liability for Directors and Officers of Texas Homeowners Associations under Chapter 84 of the Texas Civil Practices and Remedies Code (called the "Charitable Immunity and Liability Act of 1987"). The Texas Charitable Immunity and Liability Act of 1987 was enacted by the Texas Legislature because of the recognized need for "robust, active, bona fide, and well-supported charitable organizations" in Texas and to address the concern for the willingness of volunteers to offer their services if there was a perception of personal liability arising out of their services to these organizations and problems in obtaining affordable liability insurance for such organizations, their employees, and volunteers.[114] Fortunately for Texas Homeowners Associations, the Charitable Immunity and Liability Act of 1987 defines "Charitable Organization" more broadly than the IRS. In addition to income tax exempt organizations, the Texas Charitable Immunity and Liability Act of 1987's definition of Charitable Organization includes "a Homeowners Association as defined by Section 528(c) of the Internal Revenue Code of 1986 or which is exempt from federal income tax under Section 501(a) of the Internal Revenue Code of 1986 by being

[114] Tex. Civ. Prac. & Rem. Code § 84.002.

listed as an exempt organization in Section 501(c)(4) of the code."[115] Such definition of Charitable Organizations will generally include most Texas Homeowners Associations.

Under the Texas Charitable Immunity and Liability Act of 1987, a volunteer of a Charitable Organization (called a "Charitable Volunteer") is immune from civil liability for any act or omission resulting in death, damage, or injury if the Charitable Volunteer was acting in the course and scope of the Charitable Volunteer's duties or functions, including as an Officer, Director, or trustee within the Charitable Organization.[116] Under the Texas Charitable Immunity and Liability Act of 1987, a "Charitable Volunteer" means a person rendering services for or on behalf of a Charitable Organization who does not receive compensation in excess of reimbursement for expenses incurred and includes a person serving as a Director or Officer of the Charitable Organization.[117]

The exemption from liability under the Texas Charitable Immunity and Liability Act of 1987 is only afforded to Charitable Volunteers and not to the Charitable Organization itself.[118] The Texas Charitable Immunity and Liability Act of 1987 does, however, limit the amount of liability a Charitable Organization may incur as a result of

115 Tex. Civ. Prac. & Rem. Code § 84.003(1). Section 528(c) of the Internal Revenue Code of 1986 defines a "Homeowners Association" as a residential Condominium or Subdivision Association that is organized and operated to provide for the acquisition, construction, management, maintenance, and care of the Association's Common Areas or Common Elements and: (1) sixty percent (60%) or more of its gross income for the taxable year consists solely of amounts received as membership dues, fees, or assessments from owners of residential Units or Lots in the Association; (2) ninety percent (90%) or more of its expenditures for the taxable year are for the acquisition, construction, management, maintenance, and care of the Association's Common Areas or Common Elements; (3) no part of its net earnings inures to any private shareholder or individual; and (4) it elects to have Section 528(c) apply to it for the taxable year. 26 U.S.C. § 528(c). Exempt organizations listed under Section 501(c)(4) of the Internal Revenue Code include nonprofit civic leagues or other nonprofit organizations operated exclusively for the promotion of social welfare, the net earnings of which are devoted exclusively to charitable, educational, or recreational purposes and no part of its net earnings inures to the benefit of any private shareholder or individual. 26 U.S.C. § 501(c)(4).

116 Tex. Civ. Prac. & Rem. Code § 84.004(a).

117 Tex. Civ. Prac. & Rem. Code § 84.003(2). Notwithstanding, the Texas Charitable Immunity and Liability Act of 1987 does not limit or modify the duties or liabilities of a Director or Officer to the Member-Homeowners of a Nonprofit Corporation HOA. Tex. Civ. Prac. & Rem. Code § 84.007(b).

118 Tex. Civ. Prac. & Rem. Code § 84.006.

actions by its employees or volunteers if the Charitable Organization maintains certain requisite liability insurance coverage.[119] More specifically, in any civil lawsuit brought against a Charitable Organization that maintains the requisite liability insurance coverage for damages based on an act or omission by its employees or volunteers, liability of the Charitable Organization is limited to monetary damages in a maximum amount of $500,000 for each injured person, $1,000,000 for each single occurrence of bodily injury or death, and $100,000 for each single occurrence for injury or destruction of property.[120] In other words, the amount of liability of the Charitable Organization is limited to the amount of its requisite insurance coverage. Such limitation on liability for a Charitable Organization, however, does not apply to liability resulting from the commission of an act or omission that is intentional, willfully negligent, or done with conscious indifference or reckless disregard for the safety of others.[121]

3.16.2 Contractual Indemnity of Directors and Officers

In addition to the immunity from liability afforded to Directors and Officers of Texas Homeowners Associations under the Texas Charitable Immunity and Liability Act of 1987, in many cases, Directors and Officers of Texas Homeowners Associations are also entitled to indemnification by the Homeowners Association under the Homeowners

---

[119] Tex. Civ. Prac. & Rem. Code § 84.007(g). The Texas Charitable Immunity and Liability Act of 1987 requires a Charitable Organization to maintain insurance coverage that applies to the acts or omissions of the Charitable Organization and its employees and volunteers in the amount of at least $500,000 for each injured person, $1,000,000 for each single occurrence for death or bodily injury, and $100,000 for each single occurrence for injury to or destruction of property. Tex. Civ. Prac. & Rem. Code § 84.007(g). Such insurance coverage may be provided under a contract for insurance, a plan providing for self-insured retention that the Charitable Organization has fully paid or establishes to a court that it is capable of fully and immediately paying, a Lloyd's plan, an indemnity policy to which all requirements for payment have been or will be met, or other plan of insurance authorized by statute and may be satisfied by the purchase of a $1,000,000 bodily injury and property damage combined single limit policy. Tex. Civ. Prac. & Rem. Code § 84.007(g). For the purposes of the Texas Charitable Immunity and Liability Act of 1987, coverage amounts are inclusive of a self-insured retention, a Lloyd's plan, or an indemnity policy to which all requirements for payment have been or will be met. Tex. Civ. Prac. & Rem. Code § 84.007(g).

[120] Tex. Civ. Prac. & Rem. Code § 84.006.

[121] Tex. Civ. Prac. & Rem. Code § 84.007(a).

Association's Governing Documents. Unlike immunity, which exempts Directors and Officers from liability, indemnity consists of an obligation by one person or entity to protect or insure another person or entity against any loss that such person or entity might suffer.[122] In the context of Homeowners Associations, indemnity consists of an obligation by a Homeowners Association to pay for the costs of defense (including attorneys fees) and liability (such as a judgment or fine) incurred by or assessed against a Director or Officer who is named as a defendant in litigation or other proceeding relating to the affairs of such Homeowners Association or acts or omissions committed by such individual in his or her capacity as a Director or Officer of such Homeowners Association.

In general, the Governing Documents for most Homeowners Associations will create a contractual obligation of the Homeowners Association to indemnify its Directors and Officers from liability except under limited circumstances, such as if the Director or Officer acts in bad faith or commits fraud. In most cases, the Governing Documents will require the Homeowners Association to indemnify the Directors and Officers for any fines, judgments, and/or amounts paid in settlement, as well as expenses related to defending such Directors and Officers in a civil lawsuit or criminal prosecution, including their attorneys fees. Because Governing Documents can differ significantly from community to community, each Director and Officer should review the Governing Documents applicable to the Homeowners Association of which he or she serves to determine the existence and scope of any contractual obligation of such Homeowners Association to indemnify him or her and any limits or exceptions to such indemnity obligation.

---

[122] *Black's Law Dictionary* defines "indemnity" as "reimbursement" or "a contractual or equitable right under which the entire loss is shifted from a tortfeasor who is only technically or passively at fault to another who is primarily or actively responsible." *Black's Law Dictionary* 769 (6th ed. 1990).

3.16.3 Statutory Indemnity of Directors and Officers under the Texas Corporation Law

In addition to potential contractual indemnity of Directors and Officers under a Homeowners Association's Governing Documents, the Texas Corporation Law[123] provides for certain circumstances under which a Nonprofit Corporation HOA must indemnify Directors and Officers, called "Mandatory Indemnification," and additional circumstances under which a Nonprofit Corporation HOA may, but is not required to, indemnify Directors and Officers, called "Permissive Indemnification."[124]

The Mandatory Indemnification and Permissive Indemnification provisions arise in circumstances when a current or former "Governing Person" is made a "respondent" in a "proceeding" because such person is or was a Governing Person of a Nonprofit Corporation HOA.[125] The Texas Business Organizations Code defines a Governing Person as a person serving as part of the "Governing Authority" of a corporate entity, and it further defines "Governing Authority" as a person or group of persons who are entitled to manage and direct the affairs of a corporate entity under the Governing Documents of such entity or the Texas Business Organizations Code.[126] Such statutory definition of "Governing Authority" expressly includes the Board of Directors of a nonprofit

[123] The Texas Corporation Law is the short title for Title 1 of the Texas Business Organizations Code, which consists of general provisions that are applicable to all Texas for-profit and nonprofit corporations. Tex. Bus. Org. Code § 1.008.

[124] The Articles of Incorporation of a Nonprofit Corporation HOA may restrict the circumstances under which the Nonprofit Corporation HOA must or may indemnify a person and/or may advance expenses to a person under the Texas Corporation Law. Tex. Bus. Org. Code § 8.003. Accordingly, the statutory authority for Mandatory Indemnification and Permissive Indemnification is subordinate to any restrictions imposed on indemnification of a Director or Officer of the Nonprofit Corporation HOA by its Articles of Incorporation.

[125] Tex. Bus. Org. Code § 8.001, et. seq. The Texas Corporation Law defines "proceeding" as: (1) a threatened, pending, or completed action or other proceeding, whether civil, criminal, administrative, arbitrative, or investigative; (2) an appeal of such action or proceeding; and (3) an inquiry or investigation that could lead to such action or proceeding. Tex. Bus. Org. Code § 8.001(8). The Texas Corporation Law defines "respondent" as a person named as a respondent or defendant in a "proceeding." Tex. Bus. Org. Code § 8.001(10).

[126] Tex. Bus. Org. Code § 1.002(35), (37).

corporation or other persons authorized to perform the functions of the Board of Directors of a nonprofit corporation.[127] In the context of a Nonprofit Corporation HOA managed by a Board of Directors, the term "Governing Person" is synonymous with a Director of the Nonprofit Corporation HOA. The term "Governing Person," however, does not include an Officer of a Texas Nonprofit Corporation HOA who is acting in the capacity of an Officer.[128] Notwithstanding, a Texas Nonprofit Corporation HOA is also required to indemnify an Officer to the same extent that indemnification is required of a Governing Person.[129] Thus, a Texas Nonprofit Corporation HOA's Mandatory Indemnity Obligation extends to current and former Directors, as well as Officers, of the Nonprofit Corporation HOA.

3.16.3 (A) *Mandatory Indemnity of Directors under the Texas Corporation Law*

Under the statutory Mandatory Indemnification provisions, a Nonprofit Corporation HOA is required to indemnify a current or former Director of the Nonprofit Corporation HOA against reasonable "expenses" actually incurred by such person in connection with a proceeding in which such person is a respondent because such person is or was a Director of a Nonprofit Corporation HOA if such person is wholly successful in the defense of such proceeding.[130] It is important to note that the Mandatory Indemnity obligation of a Nonprofit Corporation HOA under the Texas Corporation Law is not invoked until after the current or former Director has successfully defended the

---

127 Tex. Bus. Org. Code § 1.002(35).

128 Tex. Bus. Org. Code § 1.002(35)(B).

129 Tex. Bus. Org. Code § 8.105(b).

130 Tex. Bus. Org. Code § 8.051. The Texas Corporation Law defines "expenses" as court costs, a judgment, a penalty, a settlement, a fine, and an excise or similar tax, as well as reasonable attorneys fees. Tex. Bus. Org. Code § 8.001(3). The Texas Corporation Law further defines "proceeding" as: (1) a threatened, pending, or completed action or other proceeding, whether civil, criminal, administrative, arbitrative, or investigative; (2) an appeal of such action or proceeding; and (3) an inquiry or investigation that could lead to such action or proceeding, and "respondent" as a person named as a respondent or defendant in a "proceeding." Tex. Bus. Org. Code §§ 8.001(8), (10).

proceeding in which he or she is a respondent. In other words, a Texas Nonprofit Corporation HOA does not have to pay the current or former Director's attorneys fees until after the fact, and only if such Director is successful in the defense of such matter.

If a current or former Director is ultimately successful in defense of an applicable matter for which Mandatory Indemnity is invoked, and the Nonprofit Corporation has not reimbursed such Director the reasonable expenses actually incurred by such person in connection with defending such proceeding, then the Director is authorized to enforce the Nonprofit Corporation HOA's Mandatory Indemnity obligation by filing a lawsuit against the Nonprofit Corporation HOA. In such event, if a court determines that such Director is entitled to Mandatory Indemnification, then the court is required to order the Nonprofit Corporation HOA to pay such Director the appropriate amount of reasonable expenses he or she incurred in the former proceeding, as well as to award such Director the expenses he or she incurred in securing the indemnification from the Nonprofit Corporation HOA in such lawsuit.[131]

3.16.3 (B) *Permissive Indemnity of Directors under the Texas Corporation Law*

Under the Permissive Indemnification provisions of the Texas Corporation Law, a Nonprofit Corporation HOA may, but is not required to, indemnify a current or former Director who was, is, or is threatened to be made a respondent in a proceeding under certain conditions.[132] In order for a current or former Director to be eligible for Permissive Indemnity by a Texas Nonprofit Corporation HOA, there must be an affirmative

---

[131] Tex. Bus. Org. Code § 8.051(b).

[132] Tex. Bus. Org. Code § 8.101. The Texas Corporation Law defines "proceeding" as: (1) a threatened, pending, or completed action or other proceeding, whether civil, criminal, administrative, arbitrative, or investigative; (2) an appeal of such action or proceeding; and (3) an inquiry or investigation that could lead to such action or proceeding. Tex. Bus. Org. Code § 8.001(8). The Texas Corporation Law defines "respondent" as a person named as a respondent or defendant in a "proceeding." Tex. Bus. Org. Code § 8.001(10).

determination made concerning such Director's conduct, the reasonableness of the Director's expenses, and whether the indemnification should be paid.[133]

First, concerning a Director's conduct, it must be determined that the current or former Director: (1) acted in good faith; and (2) reasonably believed: (i) in the case of conduct by such Director in his or her "official capacity," that his or her conduct was in the Nonprofit Corporation HOA's best interests; or (ii) in any other case, that his or her conduct was not opposed to the Nonprofit Corporation HOA's best interests.[134] In the case of a criminal proceeding, it must additionally be determined that the current or former Director did not have a reasonable cause to believe his or her conduct was unlawful.[135]

Second, it must be determined with respect to expenses of the current or former Director to be indemnified that the amount of such expenses (other than a judgment) are reasonable.[136]

Finally, it must also be determined that indemnification of the current or former Director's reasonable expenses should be paid.[137]

---

133 Tex. Bus. Org. Code § 8.101.

134 Tex. Bus. Org. Code § 8.101(a)(1)(A), (B). The Texas Corporation Law defines "official capacity" as the office of the Governing Person in the Nonprofit Corporation HOA or the exercise of authority by or on behalf of the person serving in such office under the authority of the Texas Corporation Law or the Nonprofit Corporation HOA's Governing Documents. Tex. Bus. Org. Code § 8.001(6). It is also important to note that a current or former Governing Person does not fail to meet the good faith and reasonable belief requirement solely because of the termination of a proceeding by judgment, order, settlement, conviction, or a plea of nolo contendere or its equivalent. Tex. Bus. Org. Code § 8.101(d). In other words, just because a Director settles a civil lawsuit or agrees to a "no contest" plea bargain agreement on a criminal charge related to his or her conduct as a Director does not alone mean that he or she did not act in good faith or that he or she did not reasonably believe that his or her conduct was in the Nonprofit Corporation HOA's best interest or at least not opposed to its best interest.

135 Tex. Bus. Org. Code § 8.101(a)(1)(C).

136 Tex. Bus. Org. Code § 8.101(a)(2).

137 Tex. Bus. Org. Code § 8.101(a)(3).

In addition, the required determinations for Permissive Indemnification must be made by one of the five methods for determining Permissive Indemnification specified by the Texas Corporation Law, which are as follows:

(1) a majority vote of Directors of the Nonprofit Corporation HOA, who at the time of the vote are "disinterested"[138] and "independent"[139] (regardless of whether such disinterested and independent Directors constitute a quorum of the Board of Directors);[140]

(2) a majority vote of a committee established by the Board of Directors of the Nonprofit Corporation HOA, provided (a) such committee is designated by a majority vote of Directors of the Nonprofit Corporation HOA, who at the time of such vote are disinterested and independent (regardless of whether such disinterested and independent Directors constitute a quorum of the Board of Directors), and (b) such committee is composed solely of one or more disinterested and independent Directors of the Nonprofit Corporation HOA;[141]

(3) special legal counsel selected by either (a) a majority vote of disinterested and independent Directors on the Board of Directors of the Nonprofit Corporation HOA; or (b) a majority vote of a committee that is established by a majority vote of disinterested and independent Directors on the Board of Directors and that is composed solely of one or more

[138] For purposes of the Texas Business Organization Code, a person is considered to be "disinterested" with respect to the approval of a contract, transaction, or other matter, or to the consideration of the disposition of a claim or challenge relating to a contract, transaction, or particular conduct, if such person or his or her associate: (1) is not a party to the contract or transaction or materially involved in the conduct that is the subject of the claim or challenge; and (2) does not have a material financial interest in the outcome of the contract or transaction or the disposition of the claim or challenge. Tex. Bus. Org. Code § 1.003(a).

[139] For purposes of the Texas Business Organization Code, a person is considered to be "independent" with respect to considering the disposition of a claim or challenge regarding a contract or transaction, or particular or alleged conduct, if the person: (1) is disinterested; (2) is not an associate or member of the immediate family of: (a) a party to the contract or transaction; or (b) a person who is alleged to have engaged in the conduct that is the subject of the claim or challenge; (3) does not have a business, financial, or familial relationship with a party to the contract or transaction, or with another person who is alleged to have engaged in the conduct, that is the subject of the claim or challenge that could reasonably be expected to materially and adversely affect the judgment of the person in favor of the party or other person with respect to the consideration of the matter; and (4) is not shown, by a preponderance of the evidence, to be under the controlling influence of a party to the contract or transaction that is the subject of the claim or challenge or of a person who is alleged to have engaged in the conduct that is the subject of the claim or challenge. Tex. Bus. Org. Code § 1.004(a).

[140] Tex. Bus. Org. Code § 8.103(a)(1).

[141] Tex. Bus. Org. Code § 8.103(a)(2).

disinterested and independent Directors of the Nonprofit Corporation HOA;[142]

(4) a majority vote of the Member-Homeowners of the Nonprofit Corporation HOA that excludes the votes of each Governing Person who is not disinterested and independent;[143] or

(5) a unanimous vote of the Member-Homeowners of the Nonprofit Corporation HOA.[144]

If there is a provision contained in either: (1) the Governing Documents of a Nonprofit Corporation HOA; (2) a resolution of Member-Homeowners or the Board of Directors for a Nonprofit Corporation HOA; or (3) an agreement (such as a Declaration) that requires a Nonprofit Corporation to indemnify a person who meets the "good faith and reasonable belief" standard, then such provision constitutes an affirmative determination that the indemnification should be paid, even though such provision may not have been adopted or authorized in the same manner that the requisite Permissive Indemnification determinations are required to be made under the Texas Corporation Law.[145] In such event, however, the determination as to whether the current or former Director meets the "good faith and reasonable belief" standard and whether his or her expenses are reasonable still must be made by one of the five methods specified by the Texas Corporation Law.[146]

---

142 Tex. Bus. Org. Code § 8.103(a)(3). If special legal counsel determines that a person meets the "good faith and reasonable belief" standard for Permissive Indemnification, the special legal counsel shall determine whether the amount of expenses other than a judgment is reasonable, but he or she may not determine whether indemnification should be paid. Tex. Bus. Org. Code § 8.103(b). The determination as to whether indemnification should be paid must be made by one of the other authorized methods for determining Permissive Indemnity (i.e., a majority vote of disinterested and independent Directors of the Nonprofit Corporation HOA). Tex. Bus. Org. Code § 8.103(b).

143 Tex. Bus. Org. Code § 8.103(a)(4).

144 Tex. Bus. Org. Code § 8.103(a)(5).

145 Tex. Bus. Org. Code § 8.103(c).

146 Tex. Bus. Org. Code § 8.103(c).

If a Texas Nonprofit Corporation HOA makes the requisite determination for Permissive Indemnity, then it may indemnify a current or former Director against a judgment rendered against such Director in the applicable proceeding and all reasonable expenses actually incurred by such Director in connection with such proceeding.[147] However, if the current or former Director is found to be liable to the Nonprofit Corporation HOA in such proceeding, or is found to be liable in such proceeding because he or she improperly received a personal benefit, then Permissive Indemnity of such Director by the Nonprofit Corporation HOA is limited to only the reasonable expenses actually incurred by such Director in connection with such proceeding and excludes indemnification of any judgment, penalty, and/or fine assessed against such Director.[148] Moreover, a Nonprofit Corporation HOA may not permissively indemnify a current or former Director for any expense if, in addition to being found liable to the Nonprofit Corporation HOA or liable because of receipt of a personal benefit, such Director is additionally found to be liable in relation thereto for: (1) willful or intentional misconduct in the performance of such Director's duty to the Nonprofit Corporation HOA; (2) breach of such Director's duty of loyalty to the Nonprofit Corporation HOA; or (3) an act or omission not committed in good faith that constitutes a breach of a duty owed by such Director to the Nonprofit Corporation HOA.[149] A current or former Director is considered to have been found liable in relation to a claim, issue, or matter only if the liability is established by an order, including a judgment or decree by a court, and all appeals of such order have been exhausted or foreclosed by law.[150]

---

[147] Tex. Bus. Org. Code § 8.102(a).

[148] Tex. Bus. Org. Code § 8.102(b)(1)–(2).

[149] Tex. Bus. Org. Code § 8.102(a)–(b).

[150] Tex. Bus. Org. Code § 8.102(c).

3.16.3 (C) *Payment or Reimbursement of Reasonable Expenses of a Currently Serving Director Prior to Making Requisite Determination for Permissive Indemnity*

Under certain limited circumstances, a Texas Nonprofit Corporation HOA may pay or reimburse the reasonable expenses incurred by a currently serving Director who was, is, or is threatened to be made a respondent in a proceeding in advance of the final disposition of such proceeding and without first making the determinations required for Permissible Indemnification under the Texas Corporation Law.[151] In order for the Nonprofit Corporation HOA to be authorized to do this, the currently serving Director must first deliver to the Nonprofit Corporation HOA a written statement in which he or she makes an affirmation of good faith belief that he or she has met the standard of conduct necessary for Permissive Indemnification.[152]

In addition, the currently serving Director must also deliver to the Nonprofit Corporation HOA a written undertaking (i.e., promissory note) by or on behalf of such currently serving Director in which the maker of such undertaking promises to repay the amount paid or reimbursed by the Nonprofit Corporation HOA to the currently serving Director if the final determination of such proceeding is that such currently serving Director has not met the requisite standard for Permissible Indemnification or that Permissible Indemnification is prohibited because such currently serving Director is found to be liable for either: (1) willful or intentional misconduct in the performance of such person's duty to the Nonprofit Corporation HOA; (2) breach of such currently serving Director's duty of loyalty to the Nonprofit Corporation HOA; or (3) an act or omission not committed in good faith that constitutes a breach of a duty owed by such currently serving Director to the Nonprofit Corporation HOA.[153] In plain English, a Nonprofit

---

[151] Tex. Bus. Org. Code § 8.104.

[152] Tex. Bus. Org. Code § 8.104(a)(1).

[153] Tex. Bus. Org. Code §§ 8.102, 8.104(a)(2). Such written undertaking must be an unlimited general obligation of the maker of such written undertaking, but it does not need to be secured by any collateral. Tex. Bus. Org. Code § 8.104. In addition, the Nonprofit Corporation HOA may accept the nonsecured written

Corporation HOA can indemnify a currently serving Director for his or her expenses in advance of a final resolution of a proceeding if such Director provides the Nonprofit Corporation HOA:

(1) a written document stating that he or she in good faith believes that he or she has met the standard of conduct necessary for Permissive Indemnification; and

(2) an unsecured promissory note in which the currently serving Director, or other person on behalf of the currently serving Director, promises to pay all of the amounts advanced or reimbursed to such currently serving Director in the event that upon final disposition of the proceeding it is determined that the currently serving Director's conduct did not satisfy the requirements for Permissive Indemnification.

In addition, if a Nonprofit Corporation HOA does indemnify or advance expenses to a currently serving Director prior to final disposition of the proceeding, it must report such indemnification or advancement of expenses to the Member-Homeowners of the Nonprofit Corporation HOA in writing in conjunction with or before the notice (or waiver of notice) of the next meeting of the Member-Homeowners.[154] If for some reason a meeting of the Nonprofit Corporation HOA's Member-Homeowners is not held at least once a year, then, at the very least, the Nonprofit Corporation HOA must provide its Member-Homeowners such written report no later than the first (1st) anniversary of the date of the indemnification or advancement of expenses.[155]

3.16.3 (D) *Permissive Indemnification and Advancement of Expenses to Officers and other Persons under the Texas Corporation Law*

In addition to indemnification of and advancement of expenses to a Director, a Nonprofit Corporation HOA may also permissively indemnify and advance expenses to a

---

undertaking from the maker of such undertaking without regard to such person's actual or perceived ability to make repayment. Tex. Bus. Org. Code § 8.104.

[154] Tex. Bus. Org. Code § 8.152.

[155] Tex. Bus. Org. Code § 8.152.

person who is not a Director, including an Officer, employee, or agent of the Nonprofit Corporation HOA, if authorized by: (1) the Nonprofit Corporation HOA's Articles of Incorporation and/or Bylaws; (2) general or specific action of the Nonprofit Corporation HOA's Board of Directors; (3) resolution of the Nonprofit Corporation HOA's Member-Homeowners; (4) contractual agreement; or (5) common law.[156] In addition, an Officer, employee, or agent of a Nonprofit Corporation HOA may seek indemnification or advancement of expenses from a Nonprofit Corporation HOA to the same extent that a Director may seek indemnification or advancement of expenses under the Texas Corporation Law.[157] A Nonprofit Corporation HOA may also pay or reimburse reasonable expenses incurred by a former managerial official or delegate, as well as a current or former employee or agent of the Nonprofit Corporation HOA who was, is, or is threatened to be made a respondent in an applicable proceeding in advance of the final disposition of such proceeding under any terms the Nonprofit Corporation HOA considers appropriate.[158] In other words, a Nonprofit Corporation HOA may reimburse or pay the reasonable expenses of a former managerial official or delegate or a current or former employee or agent without requiring such person to provide the Nonprofit Corporate HOA a written affirmation of his or her good faith belief that he or she has met the requisite standard of conduct for permissive indemnification or a written undertaking to repay the amount paid or reimbursed if it is later determined that the indemnification was prohibited, so long as the Nonprofit Corporation HOA considers it appropriate to do so.

Finally, a determination made by a Nonprofit Corporation HOA to permissively indemnify a person who is not a Director of the Nonprofit Corporation, including an Officer, employee, or agent of the Nonprofit Corporation, is not required to be made in compliance with the methods specified for Permissive Indemnity of a Director of the

[156] Tex. Bus. Org. Code § 8.105(a).

[157] Tex. Bus. Org. Code § 8.105(c).

[158] Tex. Bus. Org. Code § 8.105(d).

Nonprofit Corporation HOA.[159] In other words, such a determination may be made by a simple majority vote of the Board of Directors.

3.16.3 (E) *Court-Ordered Indemnity of Directors under the Texas Corporation Law*

The Texas Corporation Law also authorizes Texas courts under certain circumstances to order a Nonprofit Corporation HOA to indemnify a current or former Director, even if such person does not satisfy the requirements for Mandatory or Permissive Indemnification.[160] More specifically, upon an application to a court by a current or former Director, and after proper notice has been provided as required by the court, a court may order a Nonprofit Corporation HOA to indemnify such current or former Director to the extent the court determines that such person is fairly and reasonably entitled to indemnification by the Nonprofit Corporation HOA in view of all the relevant circumstances, even if such person fails to satisfy the requirements for Permissive Indemnity because such person has been found liable to the Nonprofit Corporation HOA or because such person improperly received a personal benefit (regardless of whether such benefit resulted from an action taken in such person's official capacity).[161] Court-ordered indemnification of a current or former Director, however, is limited to only reasonable expenses actually incurred by such Director and does not include any judgment, fine, or charge assessed against such Director.[162]

---

[159] Tex. Bus. Org. Code § 8.105(e).

[160] Tex. Bus. Org. Code § 8.052(a).

[161] Tex. Bus. Org. Code § 8.052(b).

[162] Tex. Bus. Org. Code § 8.052(c).

CHAPTER 4 MEETINGS OF THE BOARD OF DIRECTORS

CHAPTER 4 MEETINGS OF THE BOARD OF DIRECTORS

4.1 In General

Almost all Texas Nonprofit Corporation HOAs are managed through the actions taken by the Board of Directors. Except in limited circumstances, actions taken by the Board of Directors will occur at a regular or special meeting of the Board of Directors, commonly referred to as a "Board Meeting."[1] Unlike a meeting of a Homeowners Association's membership, which is discussed in chapter 5 of this book, Board Meetings generally involve only the participation of Directors; though, such meetings are required to be open to Homeowners, and Homeowners may generally attend and observe them.

Board Meeting procedures (including location, scheduling, notice of meetings, etc.) are governed by each Homeowners Association's Governing Documents, as well as the Texas Nonprofit Corporation Law (if it is a Nonprofit Corporation HOA), the Texas Uniform Condominium Act (if it is a Condominium Association), and/or Chapter 209 of the Texas Property Code (if it is a Subdivision Association). While the provisions of the Texas Nonprofit Corporation Law apply equally to both Condominiums Associations and Subdivision Associations that are incorporated as nonprofit corporations, the provisions governing Board Meetings within the Texas Uniform Condominium Act and Chapter 209 of the Texas Property Code differ significantly. As a result, the procedures applicable to a meeting of a Board of Directors will greatly depend on whether it is a Condominium Association or a Subdivision Association. Accordingly, this chapter will primarily focus

---

1 Although there is no formal definition of what constitutes a "meeting" of the Board of Directors under the Texas Nonprofit Corporation Law, Chapter 209 of the Texas Property Code defines a Board Meeting as a deliberation between a quorum of the voting members of a Subdivision Association's Board of Directors, or between a quorum of the voting members of a Subdivision Association's Board of Directors and another person, during which Subdivision Association business is considered and the Board of Directors takes formal action. Tex. Prop. Code § 209.0051(b)(1). A Board Meeting, however, does not include the gathering of a quorum of the members of the Board of Directors at a social function unrelated to the business of the Subdivision Association or the attendance by a quorum of the members of the Board of Directors at a regional, state, or national convention, ceremonial event, or press conference, if formal action is not taken and any discussion of Subdivision Association business is incidental to the social function, convention, ceremonial event, or press conference. Tex. Prop. Code § 209.0051(b)(2).

on the provisions of the Texas Nonprofit Corporation Law, but it will also reference and explain the effect of duplicative and/or contrary provisions under the Texas Uniform Condominium Act and Chapter 209 of the Texas Property Code when applicable.

4.2 Board Meeting Procedures Applicable to Subdivision Associations

In 2011, the Texas Legislature enacted the most significant reforms to the laws governing Texas Homeowners Associations since the enactment of the Texas Uniform Condominium Act in 1993. Most of the reforms consisted of adding new provisions to or modifying existing provisions of Chapter 209 of the Texas Property Code, which applies only to Subdivision Associations.

One of the primary goals of such legislative reform was to impose more transparency in the management of Texas Subdivision Associations, and one of the more significant areas of reform was to the laws governing the meetings and operations of Subdivision Associations' Boards of Directors. Prior to 2011, meetings of a Subdivision Association's Board of Directors were governed primarily by its Governing Documents and the Texas Nonprofit Corporation Law, which generally did not require open Board Meetings or that Lot Owners even be notified of Board Meetings.[2] As a result of the 2011 reforms, in addition to its Governing Documents and the Texas Nonprofit Corporation Law, meetings of Texas Subdivision Associations' Boards of Directors are now also governed by Section 209.0051 of the Texas Property Code.[3] Among other things, Section

---

[2] Unless required by its Governing Documents, the Texas Nonprofit Corporation Law does not require meetings of a Nonprofit Corporation HOA's Boards of Directors to be open, nor does it require a Nonprofit Corporation HOA to provide notice of Board Meetings to its members.

[3] Section 209.0051 defines a "Board Meeting" as a "deliberation between a quorum of the voting board of the [Subdivision Association], or between a quorum of the voting board and another person, during which [Subdivision Association] business is considered and the board takes formal action," but "does not include the gathering of a quorum of the board at a social function unrelated to the business of the [Subdivision Association] or the attendance by a quorum of the board at a regional, state, or national convention, ceremonial event, or press conference, if formal action is not taken and any discussion of association business is incidental to the social function, convention, ceremonial event, or press conference." Tex. Prop. Code § 209.0051(b).

209.0051 requires a Subdivision Association to provide advance notice of all Board Meetings to Lot Owners and that such Board Meetings be open to its Lot Owners.[4]

Section 209.0051, however, does not apply to Subdivision Associations that are already subject to the Texas Open Meetings Act.[5] Nor does Section 209.0051 apply to all meetings of a Subdivision Association's Board of Directors if the Subdivision Development is still in a "Development Period."[6] More specifically, the new procedures imposed by Section 209.0051 do not apply to a Subdivision Association's Board of Directors during the "Development Period" of a Subdivision Development unless the Board Meeting is conducted for the purpose of:

(1) adopting or amending the Subdivision Association's Governing Documents, including Declarations, Bylaws, and Association Rules;[7]

(2) increasing the amount of regular Assessments or adopting or increasing a special Assessment;[8]

(3) electing non-developer members to the Subdivision Association's Board of Directors or establishing a process by which such members are elected;[9] or

(4) changing the voting rights of the Subdivision Association's members.[10]

---

4 Tex. Prop. Code § 209.0051.

5 Tex. Prop. Code § 209.0051(a). Section 551.0015 of the Texas Government Code makes certain limited Subdivision Associations in Harris County and the counties adjacent to Harris County subject to the Texas Open Meetings Act. Tex. Gov't Code § 551.0015. Application of the Texas Open Meetings Act is discussed in more detail in subchapter 4.5 of this book.

6 Tex. Prop. Code § 209.0051(i). Chapter 209 defines "Development Period" as a period of time stated in a Subdivision Association's Declaration during which a Declarant reserves a right to facilitate the development, construction, and marketing of the Subdivision Development, or a right to direct the size, shape, and composition of the Subdivision Development. Tex. Prop. Code § 209.002(4-a).

7 Tex. Prop. Code § 209.0051(i)(1).

8 Tex. Prop. Code § 209.0051(i)(2).

9 Tex. Prop. Code § 209.0051(i)(3).

10 Tex. Prop. Code § 209.0051(i)(4).

4.3 Regular and Special Meetings of the Board of Directors

The Governing Documents for most Texas Homeowners Associations will provide for regular meetings of the Board of Directors (generally once a month, but sometimes less often). These regular Board Meetings are generally for the purpose of the Board of Directors to consider and take action necessary for the normal, ongoing operation of the Homeowners Association. The Governing Documents may also authorize the Board of Directors and/or certain Officers to call special meetings of the Board of Directors for certain special or limited purposes. For example, the Governing Documents of a Homeowners Association may require certain actions by the Board of Directors be taken at a special Board Meeting called for that specific purpose or allow a special Board Meeting to be called when it is necessary for the Board of Directors to take some action before the next regularly scheduled Board Meeting. Because the Governing Documents of each Homeowners Association will differ, it is important to review a particular Homeowners Association's Governing Documents when calling and conducting a regular or special Board Meeting to ensure that such meeting is called and conducted in compliance with its Governing Documents.

4.4 Open Board Meetings and Executive Session

Although not required by the Texas Nonprofit Corporation Law, both the Texas Uniform Condominium Act and Chapter 209 of the Texas Property Code require Texas Homeowners Associations' Board Meetings to be open to Homeowners subject to the right of the Board of Directors to meet in "Executive Session."[11] In addition, pursuant to a 2007 amendment to the Texas Open Meetings Act, certain limited Homeowners Associations in Harris County and counties adjacent to Harris County are subject to the

---

[11] Tex. Prop. Code §§ 82.108(b); 209.0051(c). An "Executive Session" of a Board Meeting is a session closed to the public during which only the Board of Directors and such select persons invited by the Board of Directors are permitted to be present. *Black's Law Dictionary* 570 (6th ed. 1990).

Texas Open Meetings Act, which requires every regular, special, or called meeting to be open to the general public.

4.4.1 Open Board Meetings of a Condominium Association's Board of Directors under the Texas Uniform Condominium Act

Under the Texas Uniform Condominium Act, all meetings of a Condominium Association's Board of Directors must be open to Unit Owners, subject to the right of the Board of Directors to adjourn the Board Meeting and reconvene in closed Executive Session to consider actions involving:

(1) personnel;

(2) pending litigation;

(3) contract negotiations;

(4) enforcement actions;

(5) matters involving the invasion of privacy of individual Unit Owners; or

(6) matters that are to remain confidential by request of the affected parties and agreement of the Board of Directors.[12]

Prior to adjourning a Board Meeting for purposes of reconvening in executive session, the general nature of any business to be considered in Executive Session must first be announced at the open Board Meeting.[13]

4.4.2 Open Board Meetings of a Subdivision Association's Board of Directors under Chapter 209 of the Texas Property Code

Under Chapter 209 of the Texas Property Code, all meetings of a Subdivision Association's Board of Directors must be open to Lot Owners, subject to the right of the

12 Tex. Prop. Code § 82.108(b).

13 Tex. Prop. Code § 82.108(b).

Board of Directors to adjourn the Board Meeting and reconvene in closed Executive Session to consider actions involving:

(1) personnel;

(2) pending or threatened litigation;

(3) contract negotiations;

(4) enforcement actions;

(5) confidential communications with the Subdivision Association's attorney;

(6) matters involving the invasion of privacy of individual owners; or

(7) matters that are to remain confidential by request of the affected parties and agreement of the Board of Directors. [14]

Unlike a Condominium Association, the general nature of the business to be considered by a Subdivision Association's Board of Directors in Executive Session is not required to be announced at the open Board Meeting prior to adjourning the Board Meeting and reconvening in Executive Session. Notwithstanding, following an Executive Session by a Subdivision Association's Board of Directors, any decision made in the Executive Session must be summarized orally upon reconvening the open Board Meeting and placed in the minutes for such meeting.[15] The oral summary must be in general terms, without breaching the privacy of any individual Homeowners, violating any privilege, or

---

[14] Tex. Prop. Code § 209.0051(c). Section 209.0051 does not, however, apply to a Subdivision Association that is subject to the Texas Open Meetings Act. Tex. Prop. Code § 209.0051(a). Section 209.0051 also does not apply to a Subdivision Association's Board of Directors during the "Development Period" of a Subdivision Development unless the Board Meeting is conducted for the purpose of: (1) adopting or amending the governing documents, including declarations, bylaws, rules, and regulations of the association; (2) increasing the amount of regular assessments of the association or adopting or increasing a special assessment; (3) electing non-developer board members of the association or establishing a process by which those members are elected; or (4) changing the voting rights of members of the association. Tex. Prop. Code § 209.0051(i). For purposes of Section 209.0051, a Subdivision Association's "Development Period" means a period of time stated in its Declaration during which a Declarant reserves a right to facilitate the development, construction, and marketing of the Subdivision Development, or a right to direct the size, shape, and composition of the Subdivision Development. Tex. Prop. Code § 209.002(4-a).

[15] Tex. Prop. Code § 209.0051(c).

disclosing information that was to remain confidential at the request of the affected parties.[16] In addition, the oral summary must include a general explanation of all expenditures approved in Executive Session.[17]

4.4.3 Meeting in Executive Session

An Executive Session of a Board Meeting is a session closed to the public during which only the Board of Directors and such select persons invited by the Board of Directors are permitted to be present. As noted previously, a Homeowners Association's Board of Directors must conduct their meetings in the open and may only meet in Executive Session as needed for the purpose of considering actions or discussion involving personnel or employee issues, pending litigation, contract negotiations, enforcement actions, matters involving the invasion of privacy of individual property owners, or matters that are to remain confidential by request of an affected party and the agreement of the Board of Directors. In addition, any meetings between the Board of Directors and its legal counsel for purposes of receiving legal advice should also be conducted in Executive Session, as well, so as to preserve the attorney-client privilege of the communications by and between the Board of Directors and its legal counsel.

In general, no action should be taken by the Board of Directors in Executive Session, which should only be used for purposes of discussion between the Board of Directors and any additional persons invited to participate in the Executive Session. If actions to be taken are agreed to by the Board of Directors in the Executive Session, then the Board should wait until it has adjourned its Executive Session and reconvened its open Board Meeting before transacting the applicable business. In order to preserve the confidences of the Executive Session, discussions conducted in the Executive Session

16 Tex. Prop. Code § 209.0051(c).

17 Tex. Prop. Code § 209.0051(c).

should not be recorded, nor should any of the communications made in the Executive Session be reflected in the minutes of the Board Meeting.

Finally, while Directors and other participants are not required by law to keep the matters discussed in Executive Session confidential, *Robert's Rules of Order* provides that anybody permitted to be in attendance at an Executive Session is honor-bound not to divulge anything that occurred.[18] In general, Directors should adhere to this rule for two reasons. First, if attendees of the Executive Session subsequently divulge the substance of the discussions, it essentially defeats the purposes for which the Board of Directors discussed such matters in Executive Session (i.e., maintaining confidentiality). Second, if the matters discussed in Executive Session involve legal advice or communications between the Board of Directors and the Homeowners Association's legal counsel relating to a pending legal matter, then any voluntary disclosure of such information can potentially cause such advice or communications to lose the cloak of attorney-client privilege, which otherwise shields such communication from involuntary disclosure in a lawsuit.

4.5 Homeowners Associations Subject to the Texas Open Meetings Act

The Texas Open Meetings Act is a statute that requires governmental bodies to call and conduct their meetings in an open and public manner, so as to safeguard the public's interest in knowing the workings of its governmental bodies. In general, the Texas Open Meetings Act, except for certain limited exceptions, requires: (1) every regular, special, or called meeting of a governmental body to be open to the public;[19] (2) the governmental body to post written notice of the date, hour, place, and subject of each meeting in a place readily accessible to the general public at least seventy-two (72) hours

[18] *Robert's Rules of Order* (10th Ed.) § 9.

[19] Tex. Gov't Code § 551.002.

before the scheduled time of such meeting;[20] and (3) the governmental body to prepare and keep minutes or make a tape recording of each open meeting of the governmental body as public information.[21] In addition, an action taken by a governmental body in violation of the Texas Open Meetings Act is void and could subject any members of such governmental body who knowingly participated in such violation to criminal and civil liability.[22]

In 2007, the Texas Legislature amended the Texas Open Meetings Act to make such Act applicable to certain limited Homeowners Associations in Harris County and counties adjacent to Harris County.[23] The amendment was for the purpose of addressing certain perceived misconduct by particular Homeowners Associations in the Clear Lake area of Harris County, including the failure to respond to Homeowners' information requests and the closing of formerly public meetings to prevent Homeowners from contributing to meetings.[24] Pursuant to such 2007 amendment, the Texas Open Meetings Act is now applicable to a Homeowners Association in the same manner as a governmental body if: (1) membership in the Homeowners Association is mandatory for owners or for a defined class of owners of private real property in a defined geographic area in a county with a population of 2.8 million or more or in a county adjacent to a county with a population of 2.8 million or more;[25] (2) the Homeowners Association has the power to make mandatory special Assessments for capital improvements or mandatory

---

20 Tex. Gov't Code §§ 551.041, 551.043.

21 Tex. Gov't Code §§ 551.021–551.022.

22 Tex. Gov't Code §§ 551.141–551.146.

23 Senate Research Center, Bill Analysis, Tex. H.B. 3674, 80th Leg., R.S. (2007). Any Subdivision Association that is subject to the Texas Open Meetings Act is excluded from the application of Chapter 209's Board Meeting procedures. Tex. Prop. Code § 209.0051(a).

24 Senate Research Center, Bill Analysis, Tex. H.B. 3674, 80th Leg., R.S. (2007).

25 Tex. Gov't Code §§ 551.0015(a)(1)(A), 552.0036(1)(A). The only Texas county with a population of 2.8 million or more is Harris County, and the counties adjacent to Harris County are Brazoria, Chambers, Fort Bend, Liberty, Montgomery, San Jacinto, and Waller Counties. Source: United States Census Bureau, 2010.

regular Assessments;[26] and (3) the amount of the mandatory special or regular Assessments is or has ever been based in whole or in part on the value at which the state or a local governmental body assesses the Homeowners' property for purposes of ad valorem taxation under Section 20, Article VIII, Texas Constitution.[27] In addition, a Homeowners Association is also subject to the Texas Open Meetings Act in the same manner as a governmental body if the Homeowners Association: (1) provides maintenance, preservation, and architectural control of residential and commercial property within a defined geographic area in a county with a population of 2.8 million or more or in a county adjacent to a county with a population of 2.8 million or more;[28] and (2) is a corporation that: (a) is governed by a board of trustees that may employ a general manager to execute the Homeowners Association's Bylaws and administer the business of the corporation; (b) does not require membership in the corporation by the owners of the property within the defined area; and (c) was incorporated before January 1, 2006.[29]

If a Homeowners Association meets either of these criteria, then the Board of Directors, any committee established by the Board of Directors, as well as the individual members of the Board of Directors or of any such committees, must comply with the terms of the Open Meetings Act. Due to the complex nature of the duties, exceptions, and procedures provided for under the Open Meetings Act, as well as the accompanying potential civil and criminal liability for any violations of such Act, any Homeowners Association subject to the Open Meetings Act needs to seek consultation from competent legal counsel as to the full scope of the requirements under such Act so as to ensure that

---

[26] Tex. Gov't Code §§ 551.0015(a)(1)(B), 552.0036(1)(B).

[27] Tex. Gov't Code §§ 551.0015(a)(1)(C), 552.0036(1)(C).

[28] Tex. Gov't Code §§ 551.0015(a)(2)(A), 552.0036(2)(A). The only Texas county with a population of 2.8 million or more is Harris County, and the counties adjacent to Harris County are Brazoria, Chambers, Fort Bend, Liberty, Montgomery, San Jacinto, and Waller Counties. Source: United States Census Bureau, 2010.

[29] Tex. Gov't Code §§ 551.0015(a)(2)(B), 552.0036(2)(B).

it has adopted appropriate procedures in order to fully comply with the applicable requirements of such Act.

4.6 Location of Board Meetings

The location of Board Meetings will depend on whether the Homeowners Association is a Condominium Association or a Subdivision Association. In general, there are no limitations on where meetings of a Condominium Association's Board of Directors are held. The Texas Uniform Condominium Act does not address the location of Board Meetings, and the Texas Nonprofit Corporation Law simply provides that the Board of Directors may hold meetings in or outside the State of Texas as provided by or fixed in accordance with the Articles of Incorporation or Bylaws of the Nonprofit Corporation HOA or as agreed to by all persons entitled to notice of such meeting.[30]

Boards of Directors of Subdivision Associations, on the other hand, are restricted as to the location of Board Meetings. Chapter 209 of the Texas Property Code requires meetings of a Subdivision Association's Board of Directors to be held in a county in which all or part of the Subdivision Development is located or in a county adjacent to such a county.[31]

4.7 Notice of a Board Meeting to Directors

The requirements for providing notice of a Board Meeting to Directors will depend on whether the meeting is a regular or special Board Meeting. There are, however, some general rules that apply to meeting notices for both regular and special Board Meetings.

---

30 Tex. Bus. Org. Code § 6.001(c).

31 Tex. Prop. Code § 209.0051(c-1). It is important to note that the location requirement does not apply to a meeting of a Subdivision Association's Board of Directors that is held by electronic or telephonic means pursuant to Section 209.0051(c-2). Tex. Prop. Code § 209.0051(c-1).

4.7.1 General Requirements Concerning Notice of a Board Meeting

First, subject to the provisions of the Texas Nonprofit Corporation Law and a Nonprofit Corporation HOA's Governing Documents, notice of Board Meetings must be given in the manner determined by the Board of Directors, and such meeting notice must state: (1) the date and time of the meeting; and (2) the physical location of the meeting and/or the form of communications system to be used for the meeting and the means of accessing it (if the meeting is to held solely or in part by using a conference telephone or other communications system).[32]

4.7.2 Notice of a Regular Board Meeting to Directors

Unless otherwise required by a Nonprofit Corporation HOA's Bylaws, regular meetings of the Board of Directors of a Nonprofit Corporation HOA may be held with or without advance notice to each Director.[33] In addition, and unless required by a Nonprofit Corporation HOA's Bylaws, the business to be transacted at a regular meeting of the Board of Directors is not required to be specified in the notice of the meeting.[34]

If the Homeowners Association is a Condominium Association, however, notice of a meeting of the Board of Directors must be given to each Director in the manner provided by its Bylaws.[35] If the Bylaws of the Condominium Association do not specify a method of giving notice of Board Meetings to Directors, then notice of a Board Meeting must be given to each Director in the manner specified for providing notice of a Board

[32] Tex. Bus. Org. Code § 6.051(a).

[33] Tex. Bus. Org. Code § 22.217(a).

[34] Tex. Bus. Org. Code § 22.217(c).

[35] Tex. Prop. Code § 82.108(e).

Meeting to a Director of a nonprofit corporation under Section B, Article 2.19, Texas Non-Profit Corporation Act.[36]

4.7.3 Notice of a Special Board Meeting to Directors

Unlike notices of regular Board Meetings, notice of a special meeting of a Nonprofit Corporation HOA's Board of Directors must be given to each Director in the manner specified by the Nonprofit Corporation HOA's Bylaws.[37] However, unless required by the Bylaws of a Nonprofit Corporation HOA, the business to be transacted at, or the purpose of, a special Board Meeting is not required to be specified in the notice of a special Board Meeting given to Directors.[38]

4.7.4 Delivery of a Meeting Notice to Directors

If the Texas Nonprofit Corporation Law or the Nonprofit Corporation HOA's Governing Documents require that Directors be provided notice of a Board Meeting, then meeting notices may be delivered to Directors by personal service, mail, facsimile, or email.[39] A meeting notice that is mailed is considered to be given to the Director on the date it is deposited in the United States mail, with postage paid, in an envelope addressed to the Director at his or her address as it appears on the ownership or membership records of the Nonprofit Corporation HOA.[40] A notice transmitted to a Director by facsimile or email is considered to be given when it has been transmitted to a facsimile number or an

---

36 Tex. Prop. Code § 82.108(e). Even though the Texas Non-Profit Corporation Act is no longer in effect, the Texas Uniform Condominium Act still refers to it. Notwithstanding, Article 2.19 of the Texas Non-Profit Corporation Act has been recodified at Section 22.217 of the Texas Nonprofit Corporation Law and remains substantially the same. Tex. Bus. Org. Code § 22.217. Section 22.217 of the Texas Nonprofit Corporation Law provides that regular Board Meetings may be held with or without notice as prescribed by the nonprofit corporation's bylaws and special Board Meetings must be held with notice as prescribed by the nonprofit corporation's bylaws. Tex. Bus. Org. Code § 22.217.

37 Tex. Bus. Org. Code § 22.217(b).

38 Tex. Bus. Org. Code § 22.217(c).

39 Tex. Bus. Org. Code §§ 6.051(b), 22.217(b).

40 Tex. Bus. Org. Code § 6.051(b).

email address provided by the Director, or to which he or she has consented to, for the purpose of receiving notices from the Nonprofit Corporation HOA.[41]

4.7.5 Waiver of Meeting Notice

A notice of a Board Meeting is not required to be given to a Director of a Nonprofit Corporation HOA, who is otherwise entitled to such notice under the Texas Nonprofit Corporation Law or the Nonprofit Corporation HOA's Governing Documents, if the Director signs a written waiver of notice of the meeting, regardless of whether the waiver is signed before or after the time of such meeting.[42] In addition, if a Director who is entitled to but was not provided proper notice of a Board Meeting actually participates in or attends such Board Meeting, then such Director's participation or attendance at such Board Meeting constitutes a waiver of the omitted meeting notice unless he or she participates in or attends such meeting solely to object to the transaction of business at the Board Meeting on the grounds that the meeting was not lawfully called or convened.[43]

4.8 Notice of a Board Meeting to Members of a Homeowners Association

As a result of the enactment of Section 209.0051 of the Texas Property Code by the Texas Legislature in 2011, the requirements for providing notice of Board Meetings to Homeowners differ significantly between Condominium and Subdivision Associations.

4.8.1 Notice of a Board Meeting to Unit Owners by a Condominium Association

The requirements for providing notice of Board Meetings to Unit Owners is governed by a Condominium Association's Governing Documents, the Texas Nonprofit

---

[41] Tex. Bus. Org. Code § 6.051(b).

[42] Tex. Bus. Org. Code § 6.052(a). Unless required by the a Nonprofit Corporation HOA's Articles of Incorporation or its Governing Documents, the business to be transacted at a Board Meeting is not required to be specified in a written waiver of notice of such meeting. Tex. Bus. Org. Code §§ 6.052(c), 22.217(c).

[43] Tex. Bus. Org. Code § 6.052(b).

Corporation Law, and the Texas Uniform Condominium Act. In general, unless required by its Governing Documents, a Condominium Association is not required under Texas statutory law to provide notice of Board Meetings to Unit Owners.[44]

If, however, a Condominium Association's Board of Directors is meeting for the purpose of adopting an amendment or modification to its Declaration, Articles of Incorporation, Bylaws, or Association Rules, then the Board of Directors must give each Unit Owner a document showing the specific amendment or other change(s) that would be made to the Declaration, Articles of Incorporation, Bylaws, or Association Rules no earlier than twenty (20) days, nor later than ten (10) days, before the date of such Board Meeting.[45] Written notice of a proposed amendment of or modification to a Condominium Association's Governing Documents is considered to have been given to a Unit Owner on the earlier of: (1) the date such information is personally delivered to the Unit Owner, as shown by a receipt signed by such Unit Owner; or (2) on the date evidenced by the postmark on an envelope containing such information that is deposited in the United States mail with a proper address and paid postage.[46]

---

44 Tex. Prop. Code § 82.108(e); Tex. Bus. Org. Code § 22.217. Section 82.108(e) requires notice of Board Meetings be given as provided by the Condominium Association's Bylaws, or, if the Bylaws do not provide for notice of Board Meetings, then notice of a Board Meeting must be given to each Director of the Condominium Association in the same manner in which notice is given to the members of the Board of Directors of a nonprofit corporation under Section B of Article 2.19 of the former Texas Non-Profit Corporation Act. Tex. Prop. Code § 82.108(e). Section 82.108, however, does not require that a notice of a Board Meeting be given to Unit Owners in the event that a Condominium Association's Bylaws do not provide for such notice. It is also important to note that Article 2.19 of the Texas Non-Profit Corporation Act has been recodified at Section 22.217 of the Texas Nonprofit Corporation Law and remains substantially the same. Tex. Bus. Org. Code § 22.217. Section 22.217 of the Texas Nonprofit Corporation Law provides that a regular Board Meeting of a Nonprofit Corporation HOA may be held with or without providing notice of such meeting to Directors and Member-Homeowners, as prescribed by the Nonprofit Corporation HOA's Bylaws, but that special Board Meeting must be held with notice as prescribed by the Nonprofit Corporation HOA's Bylaws. Tex. Bus. Org. Code § 22.217.

45 Tex. Prop. Code § 82.070.

46 Tex. Prop. Code § 82.070(b).

Notwithstanding, if a Condominium Association receives a written request from a Unit Owner regarding the time and location of the next regular or special Board Meeting, then it must inform such Unit Owner of the time and place of the next scheduled regular or special meeting of the Board of Directors.[47] If the Condominium Association representative who receives the written request does not know the time and place of the next scheduled regular or special Board Meeting, then the Condominium Association must promptly obtain such information and disclose it to the Unit Owner or inform the Unit Owner where such information may be obtained.[48]

4.8.2 Notice of a Board Meeting to Lot Owners by a Subdivision Association

The requirements for providing notice of Board Meetings to Lot Owners is governed by a Subdivision Association's Governing Documents and Chapter 209 of the Texas Property Code.[49] In addition to complying with any applicable notice requirements under a Subdivision Association's Governing Documents, it must also comply with Section 209.0051 of the Texas Property Code, which requires a Subdivision Association to give its Lot Owners notice of the date, hour, place, and general subject of each regular or special Board Meeting, including a general description of any matter to be brought up for deliberation in executive session at such meeting.[50]

4.8.2 (A) *Notification of the General Subject of a Board Meeting*

Although Section 209.0051 does not specify or establish guidelines for identifying the "general subject" of each regular or special Board Meeting, such

---

47 Tex. Prop. Code § 82.108(f).

48 Tex. Prop. Code § 82.108(f).

49 While meetings of Subdivision Associations' Board of Directors are also governed by the Texas Nonprofit Corporation Law, it requires only that notices of Board Meetings be given as prescribed by the nonprofit corporation's Bylaws. Tex. Bus. Org. Code § 22.217.

50 Tex. Prop. Code § 209.0051(e).

requirement is substantially similar to the meeting notice requirements under the Texas Open Meetings Act, which also requires "written notice of the date, hour, place, and subject of each meeting held by the governmental body."[51] The Texas Supreme Court has held that notice of the subject of a meeting is sufficient under the Texas Open Meetings Act when it alerts a reader that some action will be taken relative to a topic, but the notice need not state all of the possible consequences resulting from consideration of such topic.[52] In other words, to comply with the meeting notice requirements under Section 209.0051, a Subdivision Association should include within each meeting notice an agenda that identifies or describes each item or topic that the Board of Directors may consider or take action on at such meeting.

4.8.2 (B) *Methods for Providing Notice of a Board Meeting to Lot Owners*

Section 209.0051 authorizes two methods for providing notice of Board Meetings to Lot Owners. First, a Subdivision Association may provide notice of a Board Meeting to Lot Owners by mailing a written notice of such meeting to each Lot Owner at least ten (10) days before, but no more than sixty (60) days before, the date of such meeting.[53]

As an alternative to mailing a written notice of a Board Meeting to each Lot Owner, Section 209.0051 authorizes a Subdivision Association to provide notice of a Board Meeting instead by posting and emailing a copy of the meeting notice to Lot Owners.[54] If a Subdivision Association elects to provide notice of a Board Meeting by posting and emailing, then at least seventy-two (72) hours prior to the start of the Board

---

51 Tex. Gov't Code § 551.0041.

52 *See Lower Colorado River Auth. v. City of San Marcos*, 523 S.W.2d 641, 646 (Tex. 1975); *Texas Turnpike Auth. v. City of Fort Worth*, 554 S.W.2d 675, 676 (Tex. 1977).

53 Tex. Prop. Code § 209.0051(e)(1). For example, if a Board Meeting was to be conducted on September 1, notice of such meeting must be mailed to each Lot Owner by no later than August 22, but it may not be mailed to Lot Owners earlier than July 3.

54 Tex. Prop. Code § 209.0051(e)(2).

Meeting, the Subdivision Association must post a notice of the Board Meeting in a conspicuous manner reasonably designed to provide notice to its Lot Owners, either:

(1) in a place located on the Subdivision Association's Common Area property or on other conspicuously located privately owned property within the Subdivision Development (so long as the owner of such privately owned property has consented thereto);[55] or

(2) on any internet website maintained by the Subdivision Association or other internet media.[56]

In addition to posting such meeting notice, at least seventy-two (72) hours prior to the start of the Board Meeting, the Subdivision Association must also send a copy of the meeting notice by email to each Lot Owner who has registered an email address with the Subdivision Association.[57]

4.9 Establishment of a Quorum

Before the Board of Directors may effectively take any action at a Board Meeting, a quorum of Directors must be present at such meeting.[58] The number of Directors that must be present at a Board Meeting in order to establish a quorum is governed by a Homeowners Association's Governing Documents and the Texas Nonprofit Corporation Law, and if it is a Condominium Association, then also the Texas Uniform Condominium Act.

---

[55] Tex. Prop. Code § 209.0051(e)(2)(A)(i).

[56] Tex. Prop. Code § 209.0051(e)(2)(A)(ii).

[57] Tex. Prop. Code § 209.0051(e)(2)(B). A Subdivision Association is not required to proactively solicit email addresses from Lot Owners to utilize the post and email method of providing notice of Board Meetings to Lot Owners. It is the duty of Lot Owners to register an email address with the Subdivision Association and to keep his or her email address updated. Tex. Prop. Code § 209.0051(f). However, the Subdivision Association must establish an email registry and method for Lot Owners to register their email addresses.

[58] A "quorum" is the number of members who must be present in a deliberative body before business may be transacted. *Black's Law Dictionary* 1255 (6th ed. 1990).

The Texas Nonprofit Corporation Law, which applies to all Texas Nonprofit Corporation HOAs, provides that the number of Directors required to be present in order to establish a quorum at a Board Meeting is the lesser of: (1) the majority of the number of Directors set by the Nonprofit Corporation HOA's Bylaws (or in the absence of a Bylaw provision setting the number of Directors, then a majority of the number of Directors specified in the Articles of Incorporation); or (2) the number of Directors specified as a quorum by the Nonprofit Corporation HOA's Articles of Incorporation or Bylaws, so long as such number is not less than three (3) Directors.[59] If, for example, a Nonprofit Corporation HOA's Articles of Incorporation provides for seven Directors and the Bylaws specify that a quorum for purposes of transacting business at a Board Meeting is five Directors, then the Texas Nonprofit Corporation Law only requires the presence of four Directors at a Board Meeting to effectively establish a quorum because a majority of seven Directors is only four Directors, which is the lesser of the majority of Directors specified in the Articles of Incorporation and the number of Directors specified as a quorum in the Bylaws.

To make matters a little more confusing for Condominium Associations subject to the Texas Uniform Condominium Act, such Act provides that unless the Condominium Association's Bylaws specify a larger percentage, a quorum of Directors is established at a Board Meeting by the presence of at least fifty percent (50%) of the Directors entitled to vote at the beginning of the Board Meeting.[60] Under the same prior hypothetical, the number of Directors of a Condominium Association that must be present to establish a quorum would be five, not four, even though the Nonprofit Corporation Law only requires the lesser of the majority of Directors specified in the Articles of Incorporation and the

---

59 Tex. Bus. Org. Code § 22.213(a).

60 Tex. Prop. Code § 82.109. The provisions of the Texas Uniform Condominium Act concerning quorum requirements are not applicable to Condominium Developments created prior to January 1, 1994, that are subject to the Texas Condominium Act, and there are no comparable provisions under the Texas Condominium Act. Tex. Prop. Code § 82.002(c).

number of Directors specified as a quorum in the Articles of Incorporation or Bylaws. This is because, under the Texas Uniform Condominium Act, the number of Directors specified in the Bylaws to establish a quorum takes precedent if the number is higher than fifty percent (50%).[61] Out of an abundance of caution, if a Board of Directors for a Condominium Association subject to the Texas Uniform Condominium Act is in doubt as to whether to use a majority of the number of Directors or the number specified by the Articles of Incorporation or Bylaws that must be present to establish a quorum at a Board Meeting, it should use the higher number so as to avoid the possibility of transacting business without first having established a requisite quorum.

It is also important to note that when counting Directors present at a meeting of a Nonprofit Corporation HOA's Board of Directors for purposes of establishing a quorum, only Directors actually present at the meeting may be counted toward the quorum.[62] In other words, a Director present only by proxy at a Board Meeting may not be counted toward the quorum requirement.[63] Notwithstanding, because Directors of Nonprofit Corporation HOAs may hold Board Meetings by using a conference telephone or similar communications equipment, a Director present by telephone or similar communications equipment is considered to be present and may be counted toward the quorum requirement.[64]

4.10 Voting and Proxies

Once a quorum has been established at a Board Meeting, the Board of Directors may transact business at its meeting. The Board of Directors acts by approving a motion

---

[61] Tex. Prop. Code § 82.109(b).

[62] In addition, a Director participating in a Board Meeting is considered to be present at such meeting, unless the participation is for the express purpose of objecting to the transaction of business at the meeting on the ground that the meeting has not been lawfully called or convened. Tex. Bus. Org. Code § 6.003.

[63] Tex. Bus. Org. Code § 22.213(b).

[64] Tex. Bus. Org. Code § 6.002.

to take some action presented by a Director at a Board Meeting. Unless the Articles of Incorporation or Bylaws of a Nonprofit Corporation HOA require approval by a greater number, an act approved by the majority of the Directors present in person or by proxy at a meeting of the Board of Directors constitutes an act of the Board of Directors.[65]

A Director of a Nonprofit Corporation HOA may vote at a Board Meeting in person or, if specifically authorized by the Articles of Incorporation or Bylaws of the Nonprofit Corporation HOA, by proxy executed in writing by the Director.[66] If a Director of a Nonprofit Corporation HOA is authorized to vote by proxy at a Board Meeting, then the proxy must be in writing and signed by the Director.[67] A written proxy on behalf of a Director expires three (3) months after the date such proxy is executed by the Director, and it is considered to be revocable unless otherwise provided by the proxy or made irrevocable by law.[68]

4.11 Conducting a Board Meeting by Electronic or Telephonic Means

While Directors should generally attend Board Meetings in person at the same physical location, the Texas Nonprofit Corporation Law, Texas Uniform Condominium Act, and Chapter 209 of the Texas Property Code authorize Board Meetings to be conducted by electronic or telephonic means, though the procedure for conducting a Board Meeting by electronic or telephonic means applicable to a Subdivision Association differs significantly from those applicable to Condominium Associations.

---

65 Tex. Bus. Org. Code § 22.214.

66 Tex. Bus. Org. Code § 22.215.

67 Tex. Bus. Org. Code § 22.215. Although a written proxy by a Director is not required to be dated to be valid, as a general rule, a Director executing a proxy should indicate the date of execution on the proxy.

68 Tex. Bus. Org. Code § 22.216.

4.11.1 General Authority of a Nonprofit Corporation HOA to Conduct a Board Meeting by Alternative Methods of Communication under the Texas Nonprofit Corporation Law

In general, the Texas Nonprofit Corporation Law authorizes Directors of a Nonprofit Corporation HOA to hold meetings by using a conference telephone (or similar communications equipment) or other suitable electronic communications system (including video-conferencing technology or the internet) or any combination thereof, so long as the telephone or other equipment or system permits each person participating in the meeting to communicate with all other persons participating in the meeting.[69] In addition, if voting is to take place at a Board Meeting where one or more Directors is attending by telephone or other equipment or system, then the Texas Nonprofit Corporation Law requires the Nonprofit Corporation HOA to implement reasonable measures to verify that every person voting at the meeting by means of remote communications is sufficiently identified and to keep a record of any vote or other action taken.[70]

4.11.2 Specific Authority of a Condominium Association to Conduct a Board Meeting by Alternative Methods of Communication under the Texas Uniform Condominium Act

In addition to such authority under the Texas Nonprofit Corporation Law,[71] the Texas Uniform Condominium Act also authorizes the Board of Directors of a Texas Condominium Association, unless provided otherwise by its Governing Documents, to hold meetings by any method of communication, including electronic and telephonic, if: (1) notice of the meeting has been given to each Director in accordance with the

---

69 Tex. Bus. Org. Code § 6.002(a).

70 Tex. Bus. Org. Code § 6.002(b).

71 It is important to note that if a Texas Condominium Association is incorporated as a nonprofit corporation, it must comply with both the Texas Nonprofit Corporation Law and the Texas Uniform Condominium Act when holding a Board Meeting by electronic or telephonic means.

Condominium Association's Bylaws;[72] (2) each Director may hear and be heard by every other Director at the meeting;[73] and (3) the meeting does not involve voting on a fine, damage assessment, appeal from a denial of architectural control approval, or suspension of a right of a particular Unit Owner before such Unit Owner has an opportunity to attend a Board Meeting to present the Unit Owner's position, including any defense, on the issue.[74]

4.11.3 Specific Authority of a Subdivision Association to Conduct a Board Meeting by Electronic or Telephonic Means under Chapter 209 of the Texas Property Code

In addition to the authority under the Texas Nonprofit Corporation Law,[75] Chapter 209 of the Texas Property Code also authorizes the Board of Directors of a Texas Subdivision Association to hold a Board Meeting by electronic or telephonic means provided that:

(1) each Director may hear and be heard by every other Director;[76]

(2) except for any portion of the meeting conducted in executive session: (a) all Lot Owners in attendance at the meeting may hear all Directors; and (b) Lot Owners are allowed to listen using any electronic or telephonic

---

72 Tex. Prop. Code § 82.108(c)(1). In the absence of a Bylaw provision providing for notice of such meetings to Directors, notice of such meeting must be given to each Director in the manner specified for providing notice of a Board Meeting to a Director of a nonprofit corporation under Article 2.19 of the Texas Non-Profit Corporation Act. Tex. Prop. Code § 82.108(c)(1), (e). Even though the Texas Non-Profit Corporation Act is no longer in effect, the Texas Uniform Condominium Act still refers to it. Notwithstanding, Article 2.19 of the Texas Non-Profit Corporation Act has been recodified at Section 22.217 of the Texas Nonprofit Corporation Law and remains substantially the same. Tex. Bus. Org. Code § 22.217. Section 22.217 of the Texas Nonprofit Corporation Law provides that regular Board Meetings may be held with or without notice as prescribed by the nonprofit corporation's bylaws and special Board Meetings must be held with notice as prescribed by the nonprofit corporation's bylaws. Tex. Bus. Org. Code § 22.217.

73 Tex. Prop. Code § 82.108(c)(2).

74 Tex. Prop. Code § 82.108(c)(3).

75 It is important to note that if a Texas Subdivision Association is incorporated as a nonprofit corporation, it must comply with both the Texas Nonprofit Corporation Law and Chapter 209 of the Texas Property Code when holding a Board Meeting by electronic or telephonic means.

76 Tex. Prop. Code § 209.0051(c-2)(1).

communication method used or expected to be used by a Director to participate in the meeting;[77] and

(3) the notice of the Board Meeting includes instructions for Lot Owners to access any electronic or telephonic communication method required to listen to the meeting.[78]

4.12 Taking Actions without Conducting a Board Meeting

In addition to being authorized to conduct Board Meetings by alternative methods of communication, the Texas Nonprofit Corporation Law, Texas Uniform Condominium Act, and Chapter 209 of the Texas Property Code also authorize Boards of Directors to take action without actually conducting a Board Meeting, though the Texas Uniform Condominium Act and Chapter 209 limit the scope of actions that may be taken by a Board of Directors of a Condominium Association or Subdivision Association under such circumstances.

4.12.1 Taking Actions by Written Consent

In general, the Texas Nonprofit Corporation Law authorizes a Board of Directors of any nonprofit corporation, including a Nonprofit Corporation HOA, to take actions without holding a meeting, providing notice, or even taking a vote if one hundred percent (100%) of the Directors sign a written consent agreeing to such action.[79] A written consent signed by one hundred percent (100%) of the Directors of a Nonprofit Corporation HOA has the same effect and is considered to be the same as a unanimous vote of Directors at a meeting of the Board of Directors.[80]

In addition to approving actions by unanimous written consent, if expressly authorized by its Articles of Incorporation or Bylaws, a Nonprofit Corporation HOA's

---

77 Tex. Prop. Code § 209.0051(c-2)(2).

78 Tex. Prop. Code § 209.0051(c-2)(3).

79 Tex. Bus. Org. Code § 6.201(b).

80 Tex. Bus. Org. Code § 6.201(c).

Board of Directors may take action by written consent signed by less than a unanimity of Directors if a written consent stating the action to be taken is signed by the number of Directors necessary to take such action at a Board Meeting at which all of the Directors are present and voting.[81] In other words, if a Nonprofit Corporation HOA's Articles of Incorporation or Bylaws authorize the Board of Directors to take action by written consent signed by less than a unanimity of Directors and the Board of Directors consists of seven Directors, then an action may be approved without conducting a Board Meeting by a written consent signed by as few as four of the Directors.

Notwithstanding the general authority of a Nonprofit Corporation HOA to take action by unanimous written consent or non-unanimous written consent (if expressly authorized), both the Uniform Condominium Act and Chapter 209 of the Texas Property Code impose restrictions on the actions that may be taken by written consent of a Board of Directors in lieu of conducting a Board Meeting. Such restrictions are discussed in further detail in the following subchapters.

4.12.1 (A) *Actions by Unanimous Written Consent of a Condominium Association's Board of Directors*

Under the Texas Uniform Condominium Act, unless a Condominium Association's Declaration, Articles of Incorporation, or Bylaws provides otherwise, its Board of Directors may take an action by unanimous written consent of all the Directors, without a meeting, so long as such action does not involve voting on: (1) a fine; (2) a damage assessment; (3) an appeal from a denial of architectural control approval; or (4) a suspension of a right of a particular Unit Owner before the Unit Owner has had an opportunity to attend a Board Meeting to present the Unit Owner's position, including any

---

81 Tex. Bus. Org. Code § 22.220(a). To be effective, such non-unanimous written consent must include the date each Director signed the consent. Tex. Bus. Org. Code § 22.220(a). In addition, the Nonprofit Corporation HOA is required to give each Director who did not sign such written consent prompt notice of the action that was approved by the non-unanimous written consent. Tex. Bus. Org. Code § 22.220(b).

defense, on the issue.[82] In addition, if a Condominium Association's Board of Directors approves an action by unanimous written consent of all Directors, then a written record of such approval must be filed with the Condominium Association's records of Board Meeting minutes.[83]

4.12.1 (B) *Actions by Unanimous Written Consent of a Subdivision Association's Board of Directors*

In 2011, the Texas Legislature enacted Section 209.0051(h) of the Texas Property Code, which provided that the Board of Directors of a Subdivision Association could take an action by unanimous written consent of all the Directors, without a meeting, only if the action item: (1) was considered to be a routine and administrative matter; or (2) involved a reasonably unforeseen emergency or urgent necessity that required immediate action by the Board of Directors.[84] Such statutory provision significantly limited the types of actions that the Board of Directors of a Subdivision Association could take by written consent.

In 2015, however, the Texas Legislature amended Section 209.0051(h) by deleting such limitation on the ability of the Board of Directors to take action by unanimous written consent. As modified by the 2015 Texas Legislature, Section 209.0051 now provides that the Board of Directors of a Subdivision Association may take action outside of a Board Meeting, including voting by electronic or telephonic means, without prior notice to Lot Owners, if each Director is given a reasonable opportunity to express the Director's opinion to all other Directors and to vote.[85] The effect of such modification

---

[82] Tex. Prop. Code § 82.108(c)(2).

[83] Tex. Prop. Code § 82.108(c)(2).

[84] Tex. Prop. Code § 209.0051(h).

[85] Tex. Prop. Code § 209.0051(h). If a Subdivision Association's Board of Directors does take an action without conducting a Board Meeting, such action must be summarized orally (including an explanation of any known actual or estimated expenditures that were approved by the Board of Directors) at the next regular or special meeting of the Board of Directors and documented in the minutes of such meeting. Tex. Prop. Code § 209.0051(h).

is to restore the ability of a Subdivision Association to take action by unanimous written consent of the Directors.

Notwithstanding such general authority to take action outside of a Board Meeting, a Subdivision Association's Board of Directors may not consider or vote on any of the following matters unless done so in an open Board Meeting for which notice was provided to Lot Owners:

(1) fines;[86]

(2) damage assessments;[87]

(3) initiation of a foreclosure action;[88]

(4) initiation of an enforcement action against a Lot Owner, unless the enforcement matter involves a violation constituting a threat to health or safety or the initiation of a legal proceeding seeking a temporary restraining order;[89]

(5) increases in assessments;[90]

(6) levying of a special assessment; [91]

(7) an appeal from a denial of architectural control approval;[92]

(8) a suspension of a right of a particular Lot Owner before the Lot Owner has had an opportunity to attend a Board Meeting to present the Lot Owner's position, including any defense, on the issue; [93]

---

[86] Tex. Prop. Code § 209.0051(h)(1).

[87] Tex. Prop. Code § 209.0051(h)(2).

[88] Tex. Prop. Code § 209.0051(h)(3).

[89] Tex. Prop. Code § 209.0051(h)(4).

[90] Tex. Prop. Code § 209.0051(h)(5).

[91] Tex. Prop. Code § 209.0051(h)(6).

[92] Tex. Prop. Code § 209.0051(h)(7).

[93] Tex. Prop. Code § 209.0051(h)(8).

(9) lending or borrowing money;[94]

(10) the adoption or amendment of a Dedicatory Instrument;[95]

(11) the approval of an annual budget or the approval of an amendment of an annual budget that increases the budget by more than 10 percent;[96]

(12) the sale or purchase of real property;[97]

(13) the filling of a vacancy on the Board of Directors;[98]

(14) the construction of capital improvements other than the repair, replacement, or enhancement of existing capital improvements;[99] or

(15) the election of an Officer.[100]

Accordingly, under the amended version of Section 209.0051, a Subdivision Association's Board of Directors may now approve the taking of an action by written consent, without conducting a Board Meeting, so long as the action to be taken is not one of the fifteen types of actions listed above, which may only be approved at a Board Meeting.

4.12.2 Execution of a Written Consent in Lieu of a Board Meeting

To be effective, a Director's consent to the taking of an action must be in writing and signed by such Director.[101] Unless prohibited by a Nonprofit Corporation HOA's Articles of Incorporation or Bylaws, an emailed consent by a Director to the taking of an action by the Nonprofit Corporation HOA is considered to be a signed writing if the email

94 Tex. Prop. Code § 209.0051(h)(9).

95 Tex. Prop. Code § 209.0051(h)(10).

96 Tex. Prop. Code § 209.0051(h)(11).

97 Tex. Prop. Code § 209.0051(h)(12).

98 Tex. Prop. Code § 209.0051(h)(13).

99 Tex. Prop. Code § 209.0051(h)(14).

100 Tex. Prop. Code § 209.0051(h)(15).

101 Tex. Bus. Org. Code § 6.201(b).

contains, or is accompanied by, information from which it can be determined that it was transmitted by such Director and the date on which such Director transmitted it.[102] In addition, any photographic, photostatic, facsimile, or similarly reliable reproduction of a written consent signed by a Director may be substituted or used instead of the original written consent signed by such Director for any purpose for which the original written consent could be used, as long as it is a complete reproduction of the entire original written consent.[103]

4.12.3 Taking Actions by Electronic or Telephonic Vote of a Subdivision Association's Board of Directors without Conducting a Board Meeting

When the 2015 Texas Legislature amended Section 209.0051 of the Texas Property Code, it not only restored the general ability of a Subdivision Association's Board of Directors to take action outside of a meeting by signed written consent of the Directors, but it appears to have also authorized the Board of Directors of a Subdivision Association to take certain types of actions outside of a Board Meeting without any signed written consent. More specifically, Section 209.0051(h) now purports to authorize the Board of Directors of a Subdivision Association to take action outside of a meeting, including voting by electronic or telephonic means, without prior notice to Lot Owners, provided: (1) each Director is given a reasonable opportunity to express the Director's opinion to all other Directors and to vote; and (2) the action does not involve one of the fifteen types of actions that may only be considered or voted on at an open Board Meeting.[104]

---

[102] Tex. Bus. Org. Code § 6.205(b). Unless the emailed consent is otherwise dated, the date of the electronic transmission is the date on which the consent is considered signed. Tex. Bus. Org. Code § 6.205(c).

[103] Tex. Bus. Org. Code § 6.205(a).

[104] Tex. Prop. Code § 209.0051(h). *See* subchapter 4.12.1(B) of this book for a list of the fifteen matters that may only be considered or voted on by a Subdivision Association's Board of Directors at an open Board Meeting.

Notwithstanding such apparent authority, if a Subdivision Association is incorporated as a nonprofit corporation, then it may not be able to take full advantage of Section 209.0051. This is because a Subdivision Association that is incorporated as a nonprofit corporation must comply with both Chapter 209 of the Texas Property Code and the Texas Nonprofit Corporation Law, and the Nonprofit Corporation Law requires the Board of Directors of all nonprofit corporations, including Subdivision Associations that are incorporated as nonprofit corporations, to approve the taking of an action either: (1) at a Board Meeting at which a quorum of Directors is present; or (2) outside of a Board Meeting, by either unanimous written consent of the Directors or non-unanimous written consent of the Directors (if so authorized by its Articles of Incorporation or Bylaws). Moreover, there is not a provision within Section 209.0051 that states that Section 209.0051 controls over any other statutory law not specifically applicable to Subdivision Associations.[105] Accordingly, despite the apparent authority of Section 209.0051(h), if a Subdivision Association is incorporated as a nonprofit corporation, then the Board of Directors should not take any action outside of a Board Meeting except by unanimous written consent of the Directors or non-unanimous written consent of the Directors (if so authorized by its Articles of Incorporation or Bylaws).

4.13 Agenda and Order of Business at a Board Meeting

The agenda of a meeting generally refers to the schedule of items or topics to be addressed and potential action to be taken at the meeting. The agenda is generally prepared in advance of the meeting by the presiding officer or person calling the meeting and is approved by a majority vote of the participants at the commencement of such meeting.[106] It is not uncommon for an agenda to be circulated in advance of a meeting, and in such

---

[105] By way of example, Section 209.005 of the Texas Property Code, which governs the procedures for Lot Owners to request inspection or copies of a Subdivision Association's records, provides that Section 209.005 "applies to all [Subdivision Associations] and controls over other law not specifically applicable to a [Subdivision Association]." Tex. Prop. Code § 209.005(a).

[106] *Robert's Rules of Order* (10th Ed.) § 41.

cases, the agenda is generally considered to be a proposed agenda, as opposed to an approved agenda, until it is adopted by a majority vote of the participants at the commencement of the meeting.[107] Once approved, the meeting agenda should not be amended absent a two-thirds (2/3) vote of the participants at the meeting.[108]

The order of business generally refers to the established sequence in which business is taken up at a meeting and is usually set out in the agenda for the meeting. The order of business for a Board Meeting may be, but is rarely, specified in a Homeowners Association's Governing Documents. In cases where there is no required order of business, the standard order of business for groups that hold regular meetings is as follows:[109]

(1) reading and approval of the minutes from the previous meeting;

(2) approval of agenda for meeting;

(3) reports of Officers and standing committees;

(4) reports of special or ad-hoc committees;

(5) unfinished business; and

(6) new business.

4.14 Conducting a Board Meeting and Decorum

One of the most difficult responsibilities the President or other person presiding over a Board of Directors meeting can face is conducting an orderly and efficient meeting.

---

107 *Robert's Rules of Order* (10th Ed.) § 41.

108 *Robert's Rules of Order* (10th Ed.) § 41. As noted earlier, a notice of meeting for a meeting of a Subdivision Association's Board of Directors must advise Lot Owners of the general subject of the Board Meeting and it must be given to Lot Owners at least seventy-two (72) hours in advance of such meeting. Tex. Prop. Code § 209.0051(e)(2). As a result, an agenda for a meeting of a Subdivision Association's Board of Directors may be amended at the meeting for the purpose of removing an item from the agenda, but it may not be amended at the meeting for the purpose of adding an item to the agenda unless such item was identified in the notice for such meeting.

109 *Robert's Rules of Order* (10th Ed.) § 41.

Meetings of the Board of Directors of Homeowners Associations are notorious for running long and, in some cases, running amok. It is not uncommon for Homeowners to attend Board Meetings to voice concerns or complaints over actions taken or proposed to be taken by the Board of Directors. In many cases, there is a perceived lack of formality by such Homeowners attending Board Meetings, and they will frequently interject their comments, opinions, and questions while the Board of Directors is trying to conduct its meeting. Tempers can flare between Directors and Homeowners, or even between Directors themselves, and meetings can dissolve into unbridled debates or shouting matches.

In order to prevent such events, it is helpful to conduct meetings pursuant to some form of parliamentary procedure. The most commonly used parliamentary procedure is Robert's Rules of Order.[110] While it is rare that the Governing Documents of a Homeowners Association will obligate the Homeowners Association to conduct its meetings under Robert's Rules of Order, in reality, most Homeowners Associations tend to follow Robert's Rules of Order or a variation of such rules on an informal basis.

In truth, Robert's Rules of Order can be very helpful at Homeowners Association meetings to control the participants and/or attendees, help move things along, and help accomplish the Homeowners Association's business more efficiently. If a Homeowners Association is not already using parliamentary procedures to conduct its Board Meetings, it should consider using Roberts Rules of Order or some other form of parliamentary procedures.[111] This is particularly true for large meetings, such as meetings of members of the Homeowners Association or any meeting that the presiding officer anticipates will be acrimonious. In addition, if significant controversy is anticipated or the need to maintain order is paramount (including those instances where the presiding officer is

[110] A brief summary of *Robert's Rules of Order* can be found in appendix J at the end of this book.

[111] A good source of parliamentary procedures is the National Association of Parliamentarians, whose website is http://parliamentarians.org/.

historically unable to maintain order and move the meeting to a successful conclusion), it may even be advisable to locate a parliamentarian and retain his or her services to assist at the meeting.

Whether or not Robert's Rules of Order or another type of parliamentary procedure is followed, the chairperson of any Homeowners Association meeting should be mindful of the following basic principles in conducting a meeting: (1) courtesy and equal treatment of all participants and attendees; (2) consideration of one matter at a time; and (3) the will of the majority prevails.

4.15 Participation of Non-Directors at a Board Meeting

It is important to note that Board Meetings are meetings of the Board of Directors, not the members of the Homeowners Association. While Homeowners are generally allowed to attend Board Meetings (except while the Board of Directors is meeting in Executive Session), they are not entitled to participate in the Board Meeting and should only be allowed to do so if recognized by the presiding officer during the course of the meeting.[112]

Notwithstanding, Boards of Directors for many Homeowners Associations do set aside a portion of each Board Meeting to accommodate questions or comments from Homeowners in attendance. Such a practice provides an opportunity for those Homeowners who are concerned enough to attend the Board Meeting to address the Board of Directors regarding the matters of concern to them. In general, this is a recommended practice that Homeowners Associations should follow, so long as the amount of time allotted for such practice is limited to a couple of minutes for each Homeowner and such

---

112 If a person intentionally disrupts a meeting of the Board of Directors, it may constitute a criminal offense. Under Section 42.05 of the Texas Penal Code, a person commits a Class B misdemeanor criminal offense if, with intent to prevent or disrupt a lawful meeting, procession, or gathering, he or she obstructs or interferes with the meeting, procession, or gathering by physical action or verbal utterance. Tex. Pen. Code § 42.05. A Class B misdemeanor criminal offense is punishable by a fine not to exceed $2,000 and/or confinement in jail for a term not to exceed 180 days. Tex. Pen. Code § 12.22.

practice does not otherwise unreasonably interfere with the Board of Directors' ability to accomplish the necessary business scheduled for such meeting.

4.16 Recording and Taping of a Board Meeting

Although not common, on occasion someone attending or participating in a Board Meeting may record or tape the meeting with or without the knowledge of the other individuals also in attendance.[113] Texas has no law prohibiting a person from openly, or even surreptitiously, recording verbal statements made in such person's presence. Accordingly, it is not unlawful for a person attending or participating in a meeting of the Board of Directors to record or tape such meeting with or without the knowledge of the other attendees or participants.

4.17 Minutes of a Board Meeting

The Texas Nonprofit Corporation Law, Texas Uniform Condominium Act, and Chapter 209 of the Texas Property Code all require Texas Homeowners Associations to keep minutes of all proceedings or meetings of their Board of Directors and any committees established by their Board of Directors.[114] In general, the term "minutes" refers to the record of the proceeding or meeting of a deliberative assembly and are generally kept by the Secretary or other person performing the duties of Secretary for such group.[115] The minutes should contain mainly a record of what was done at the meeting, as opposed to what was said at the meeting by attendees or participants.[116]

---

[113] In addition, Chapter 209 expressly authorizes a Lot Owner and/or a Subdivision Association to make an audio recording of a Chapter 209 Hearing. Tex. Prop. Code § 209.007(c).

[114] Tex. Bus. Org. Code § 3.151(a); Tex. Prop. Code § 82.114; Tex. Prop. Code § 209.0051(d).

[115] Robert's Rules of Order (10th Ed.) § 48.

[116] Robert's Rules of Order (10th Ed.) § 48.

In general, there are no strict rules or procedures for creating minutes of a meeting. At a minimum, the minutes should contain the following information:

(1) the identity of the assembly (i.e., the name of the Homeowners Association and whether it is a meeting of the Board of Directors or a committee of the Board of Directors);

(2) the kind of meeting (i.e., whether it is a regular, special, adjourned regular, or adjourned special meeting);

(3) the date and time of the meeting, as well as the location of the meeting, if it is not always held at the same location;

(4) if it is a Board Meeting, the identity of all Directors present in person, and if so authorized, all Directors present by proxy;

(5) the fact that the regular presiding Officer and Secretary were present, or in their absence, the names of the persons who substituted for them;

(6) the fact that a quorum was established;

(7) whether the minutes of the previous meeting were read and approved (as read, or if applicable, as corrected) and the date of such previous meeting;

(8) all main motions made before the assembly (except any that were withdrawn), stating:

   (a) the identity of the person making such motion and of the person who seconded such motion;

   (b) the specific wording of each motion that is put to the assembly or otherwise disposed of (i.e., each motion that is proposed, seconded, and voted on);

   (c) the disposition of each such motion (i.e., whether or not it was approved by the applicable voting requirement);

   (d) the number of votes for and against each such motion if the vote is not unanimous; and

   (e) the identity of any participants who affirmatively abstained from voting on each such motion, if applicable; and

(9) the time of adjournment of the meeting.

CHAPTER 5 MEETINGS OF A HOMEOWNERS ASSOCIATION'S MEMBERSHIP

CHAPTER 5 MEETINGS OF A HOMEOWNERS ASSOCIATION'S MEMBERSHIP

5.1 In General

There are certain actions of a Homeowners Association that may only be approved by Homeowners at a meeting of the Homeowners Association's Homeowners or its "Membership" (called a "Membership Meeting"), as opposed to by Directors at a Board Meeting.[1] The most important of these actions is the election of Directors, which usually occurs at an annual meeting of the Homeowners Association's Membership. In addition, there are other matters that may also require the approval of a Homeowners Association's Membership under its Governing Documents or because such matter is considered to be a "fundamental action" under the Texas Nonprofit Corporation Law, which must be approved by a Nonprofit Corporation HOA's Member-Homeowners.

As with Board Meetings, the procedures for calling and conducting a Membership Meeting are primarily governed by each Homeowners Association's Governing Documents.[2] In addition to the Homeowners Association's Governing Documents, the Texas Nonprofit Corporation Law also provides certain procedural requirements for

[1] The Texas Nonprofit Corporation Law uses the term "Member" to refer to a person who has membership rights in a nonprofit corporation under its Certificate of Formation (or Articles of Incorporation) or Bylaws, and as a result, most Texas Homeowners Associations' Certificate of Formation (or Articles of Incorporation) and Bylaws generally utilize the term "Member" in reference to Homeowners who are members of the Homeowners Association within the context of such corporate documents. Because the procedures for calling and conducting a meeting of a Homeowners Association's Homeowners is primarily governed by its corporate Bylaws and the Texas Nonprofit Corporation Law, chapter 5 will use the term "Membership" to refer collectively to all of the property owners who are the members of a particular Homeowners Association and the term "Membership Meeting" to refer to a meeting of a Homeowners Association's Membership when no distinction is to be made between a Condominium Association or Subdivision Association. However, where necessary to distinguish between these two types of Homeowners Associations, chapter 5 will refer to Homeowners in a Subdivision Association as its "Lot Owners" and Homeowners in a Condominium Association as its "Unit Owners."

[2] Such procedural requirements will almost always be found in the Homeowners Association's Bylaws; however, they may sometimes be found in its Articles of Incorporation and/or the Declaration as well. Accordingly, all of a Homeowners Association's Governing Documents should be reviewed carefully before calling or conducting a Membership Meeting.

calling and conducting a meeting of a Nonprofit Corporation HOA's Member-Homeowners, as do the Texas Uniform Condominium Act (if it is a Condominium Association) and Chapter 209 of the Texas Property Code (if it is a Subdivision Association) to a limited extent.[3] Chapter 5 will primarily focus on the provisions of the Texas Nonprofit Corporation Law governing meetings of a Nonprofit Corporation HOA's Member-Homeowners, but it will also reference provisions of the Texas Uniform Condominium Act and Chapter 209 of the Texas Property Code, when applicable.

5.2 Actions that Require Approval of a Homeowners Association's Membership

The Governing Documents for each Homeowners Association will specify certain actions that must be approved by the Homeowners Association's Membership, as opposed to its Board of Directors. In most cases, the most important action required by a Homeowners Association's Governing Documents to be taken by the Homeowners Association's Membership is the election of Directors. In addition to election of Directors, it is very common for the Governing Documents of a Homeowners Association to specify certain additional matters that may, but are not required to, be approved by the Homeowners Association's Membership, as well as certain actions that the Board of Directors may take, but only if first approved by a vote of the Homeowners Association's Membership (such as a levy of special Assessments). It is also very common for a Homeowners Association's Governing Documents to specify certain special actions that may only be taken by the Homeowners Association's Membership at a special Membership Meeting called for that specific purpose (such as removal of a Director from the Board of Directors).

---

[3] In other words, if a Condominium Association is incorporated as a nonprofit corporation, the procedures for calling and conducting a meeting of its Unit Owners are governed by its Governing Documents and the applicable provisions of both the Texas Nonprofit Corporation Law and the Texas Uniform Condominium Act. Similarly, if a Subdivision Association is incorporated as a nonprofit corporation, the procedures for calling and conducting a meeting of its Lot Owners are governed by its Governing Documents and the applicable provisions of both the Texas Nonprofit Corporation Law and Chapter 209 of the Texas Property Code.

In addition to actions requiring the vote of a Homeowners Association's Membership under its Governing Documents, the Texas Nonprofit Corporation Law, Texas Uniform Condominium Act, and Chapter 209 of the Texas Property Code also require that certain actions be approved by the vote of a Texas Homeowners Association's Membership. For instance, the Texas Nonprofit Corporation Law requires that certain "Fundamental Actions" of a Nonprofit Corporation HOA be approved by its Member-Homeowners. Fundamental Actions of a Nonprofit Corporation HOA include:

(1) an amendment of the Nonprofit Corporation HOA's Articles of Incorporation;[4]

(2) a voluntary winding up of the Nonprofit Corporation HOA;[5]

(3) a revocation of a voluntary decision to wind up the Nonprofit Corporation HOA;[6]

(4) a cancellation of an event requiring winding up the Nonprofit Corporation HOA;[7]

(5) a reinstatement of the Nonprofit Corporation HOA;[8]

(6) a distribution plan for the distribution of corporate property upon winding up the Nonprofit Corporation HOA;[9]

(7) a plan of merger for merging the Nonprofit Corporation HOA with another entity;[10]

(8) a sale of all or substantially all of the assets of the Nonprofit Corporation HOA;[11]

---

4 Tex. Bus. Org. Code § 22.164(1).

5 Tex. Bus. Org. Code § 22.164(2).

6 Tex. Bus. Org. Code § 22.164(3).

7 Tex. Bus. Org. Code § 22.164(4).

8 Tex. Bus. Org. Code § 22.164(5).

9 Tex. Bus. Org. Code § 22.164(6).

10 Tex. Bus. Org. Code § 22.164(7).

11 Tex. Bus. Org. Code § 22.164(8).

(9) a plan of conversion to convert the Nonprofit Corporation HOA into another type of entity;[12] and

(10) a plan of exchange of interest.[13]

5.3 Taking Actions by Consent without a Membership Meeting

While most actions requiring the approval of a Homeowners Association's Membership must be voted on at a Membership Meeting, the Texas Nonprofit Corporation Law authorizes the Membership of a Nonprofit Corporation HOA to take certain actions by written consent without a meeting.

5.3.1 Actions by Unanimous Written Consent

The Texas Nonprofit Corporation Law authorizes the Membership of a Nonprofit Corporation HOA to take any action required or authorized under the Texas Nonprofit Corporation Law or the Nonprofit Corporation HOA's Articles of Incorporation or Bylaws without actually holding a meeting, providing notice, or even taking a vote if one hundred percent (100%) of the Member-Homeowners entitled to vote on such action sign a written consent or consents stating the action to be taken.[14] A written consent signed by one hundred percent (100%) of the Member-Homeowners of a Nonprofit Corporation HOA entitled to vote has the same effect as a unanimous vote taken at a Membership Meeting.[15]

5.3.2 Actions by Less than Unanimous Written Consent

In addition to approving actions by unanimous written consent, if expressly authorized by its Articles of Incorporation, the Member-Homeowners of a Texas

[12] Tex. Bus. Org. Code § 22.164(9).

[13] Tex. Bus. Org. Code § 22.164(10).

[14] Tex. Bus. Org. Code § 6.201(a)–(b). Any advance notice required by the Texas Business Organization Code for an action to be taken at a Membership Meeting is not required to be given in order to take an action by written consent. Tex. Bus. Org. Code § 6.204.

[15] Tex. Bus. Org. Code § 6.201(c).

Nonprofit Corporation HOA may also take an action by written consent signed by less than a unanimity of Member-Homeowners if a written consent stating the action to be taken is signed by Member-Homeowners having at least the minimum number of votes that would be necessary to take such action at a Membership Meeting at which all Member-Homeowners are present and voting.[16] To be effective, such non-unanimous written consent or consents must include the date each Member-Homeowner signed the consent and must be delivered to the Nonprofit Corporation HOA within sixty (60) days from the date of the earliest dated signature.[17] Upon receipt of a non-unanimous written consent, a Nonprofit Corporation HOA is required to promptly notify each Member-Homeowner who did not sign such written consent of the action that is the subject of the non-unanimous written consent.[18]

5.3.3 Execution of a Written Consent in Lieu of a Membership Meeting

To be effective, a Member-Homeowner's consent to the taking of an action must be in writing and signed by such Member-Homeowner. Unless prohibited by the Nonprofit Corporation HOA's Articles of Incorporation or Bylaws, an emailed consent by a Member-Homeowner to the taking of an action by the Membership of the Nonprofit Corporation HOA is considered to be a signed writing if the transmission contains, or is accompanied by, information from which it can be determined that the email was sent by

---

16 Tex. Bus. Org. Code § 6.202(b).

17 Tex. Bus. Org. Code § 6.202(c). In addition, if a non-unanimous consent action is not solicited on behalf of the Nonprofit Corporation HOA or its Board of Directors, then such non-unanimous written consent(s) must be delivered to the Nonprofit Corporation HOA by: (1) hand-delivery; (2) certified or registered mail, return receipt requested; or (3) any other means specified in the Nonprofit Corporation HOA's Articles of Incorporation or Bylaws. Tex. Bus. Org. Code § 6.203(a). Such non-unanimous written consent(s) must be delivered to the Nonprofit Corporation HOA at either: (1) its registered office, principal executive office, or place of business; or (2) the managerial official or agent of the Nonprofit Corporation HOA having custody of the Nonprofit Corporation HOA's records of Membership Meetings. Tex. Bus. Org. Code § 6.203(a). If the written consent(s) is to be delivered to the Nonprofit Corporation HOA's principal executive office or place of business, it must be addressed to the chief managerial official of the Nonprofit Corporation HOA or, if the Nonprofit Corporation HOA does not have a chief managerial official, then to its Board of Directors. Tex. Bus. Org. Code § 6.203(b).

18 Tex. Bus. Org. Code § 6.202(d).

such Member-Homeowner and the date on which it was sent.[19] In addition, any photographic, photostatic, facsimile, or similarly reliable reproduction of a written consent signed by a Member-Homeowner may be substituted or used instead of the original written consent signed by the Member-Homeowner for any purpose for which the original written consent could be used, if the reproduction is a complete reproduction of the entire original written consent.[20]

5.4 Location of Membership Meetings

In general, there are no limitations on where Membership Meetings are held. The Texas Corporation Law authorizes a Nonprofit Corporation HOA to hold Membership Meetings in or outside the state as provided by or fixed in accordance with the Articles of Incorporation or Bylaws of the Nonprofit Corporation HOA or as agreed to by all persons entitled to notice of such meeting.[21] In the event the location of Membership Meetings is not established by a Nonprofit Corporation HOA's Articles of Incorporation or Bylaws, and no agreement on the location of the meeting can be reached by all persons entitled to notice of such meeting, then the Membership Meeting may only be held at the registered office of such Nonprofit Corporation HOA.[22]

In addition, while almost all Homeowners will attend Membership Meetings of a Homeowners Association either in person or by proxy, the Texas Corporation Law authorizes Nonprofit Corporation HOAs to hold Membership Meetings by using a conference telephone or similar communications equipment, or other suitable electronic communications system (including videoconferencing technology or the internet or any combination thereof), so long as the telephone or other equipment or system permits each

---

[19] Tex. Bus. Org. Code § 6.205(b). Unless the emailed consent is otherwise dated, the date of the electronic transmission is the date on which the consent is considered signed. Tex. Bus. Org. Code § 6.205(c).

[20] Tex. Bus. Org. Code § 6.205(a).

[21] Tex. Bus. Org. Code § 6.001(c).

[22] Tex. Bus. Org. Code § 6.001(b).

person participating in the meeting to communicate with all other persons participating in the meeting.[23] If voting is to take place at a Membership Meeting where one or more Member-Homeowners is attending by telephone or other equipment or system, the Nonprofit Corporation HOA must implement reasonable measures to verify that every person voting at the Membership Meeting by means of remote communications is sufficiently identified and to keep a record of any vote or other action taken at such meeting.[24]

5.5 Annual Meetings of a Homeowners Association's Membership

The Governing Documents of most Homeowners Associations will require the Homeowners Association to conduct an annual meeting of its Membership, generally at around the same time each year, for the purpose of electing new Directors to the Board of Directors and taking other actions required by the Governing Documents. In addition, both the Texas Nonprofit Corporation Law and Chapter 209 of the Texas Property Code require Nonprofit Corporation HOAs and Subdivision Associations, respectively, to hold annual meetings of their Membership and establish remedies if an annual meeting is not called by the Board of Directors.

5.5.1 Annual Membership Meeting Requirement of Nonprofit Corporation HOAs under the Texas Nonprofit Corporation Law

All Texas Nonprofit Corporation HOAs are required to hold an annual meeting of their Membership at the time stated in or determined in accordance with their Bylaws, unless their Bylaws provide for more than one regular meeting of Member-Homeowners each year.[25] In such event, an annual Membership Meeting is not required, and Director

---

23 Tex. Bus. Org. Code § 6.002(a).

24 Tex. Bus. Org. Code § 6.002(b).

25 Tex. Bus. Org. Code § 22.153(a). As most Homeowners Associations are incorporated as nonprofit corporations, the requirement to call an annual meeting under the Texas Nonprofit Corporation Law will apply to most Homeowners Associations.

elections may be conducted at any of the regular Membership Meetings as provided by the Bylaws.[26]

If the Board of Directors of a Nonprofit Corporation HOA fails to call an annual Membership Meeting when required to do so, a Member-Homeowner of the Nonprofit Corporation HOA may demand that the meeting be held within a reasonable time period.[27] The demand must be made in writing and sent to an Officer of the Nonprofit Corporation HOA by registered mail.[28] If a required annual Membership Meeting is not called by the Nonprofit Corporation HOA before the sixty-first (61st) day after the date of a Member-Homeowner's written demand, the Member-Homeowner may compel the Nonprofit Corporation HOA to hold an annual Membership Meeting by filing a lawsuit against the Board of Directors of the Nonprofit Corporation HOA and seeking an injunction from a court of law ordering the Board of Directors to call an annual Membership Meeting.[29] Notwithstanding, the failure of a Nonprofit Corporation HOA to hold a required annual Membership Meeting at the designated time does not result in the winding up and termination of a Texas Nonprofit Corporation HOA.[30]

5.5.2 Annual Membership Meeting Requirement of Subdivision Associations under Chapter 209 of the Texas Property Code

Chapter 209 of the Texas Property Code requires all Texas Subdivision Associations to call an annual meeting of their Membership.[31] Such statutory requirement

26 Tex. Bus. Org. Code § 22.153(a).

27 Tex. Bus. Org. Code § 22.154(a).

28 Tex. Bus. Org. Code § 22.154(a).

29 Tex. Bus. Org. Code § 22.154(b).

30 Tex. Bus. Org. Code § 22.154(c).

31 Tex. Prop. Code § 209.014(a).

is in addition to the same requirement of Nonprofit Corporation HOAs under the Texas Nonprofit Corporation Law.

Despite the similar nature of the annual meeting requirements under Chapter 209 of the Texas Property Code and the Texas Nonprofit Corporation Law, the statutory provisions differ in two important ways. First, the annual Membership Meeting requirement under Chapter 209 of the Texas Property Code does not provide for an exception if a Subdivision Association's Bylaws provide for more than one regular meeting of its Membership. Consequently, even if a Subdivision Association is incorporated as a nonprofit corporation and its Bylaws provide for more than one regular Membership Meeting each year, it must still hold an annual Membership Meeting each year.

Second, Chapter 209 of the Texas Property Code establishes a different remedy if a Subdivision Association's Board of Directors fails to call an annual Membership Meeting. If a Subdivision Association's Board of Directors does not call an annual meeting of the Subdivision Association's Membership, a Lot Owner may demand that a meeting of the Membership be called by the Board of Directors no later than thirty (30) days from the date of such Lot Owner's demand.[32] To be effective, the Lot Owner's demand must be made in writing and sent by certified mail, return receipt requested, to the registered agent of the Subdivision Association and to the Subdivision Association at the address for the Subdivision Association according to the most recently recorded Management Certificate.[33] In addition, a copy of the written demand to call a Membership Meeting must also be sent to each Lot Owner who is a member of the Subdivision Association.[34]

---

32 Tex. Prop. Code § 209.014(b).

33 Tex. Prop. Code § 209.014(b).

34 Tex. Prop. Code § 209.014(b).

If a Subdivision Association's Board of Directors does not call a meeting of its Membership on or before the thirtieth (30th) day after the date of a demand to call a Membership Meeting, then three or more of the Subdivision Association's Lot Owners may form an election committee for the purpose of calling a Membership Meeting to elect Board Members (called a "Chapter 209 Election Committee").[35] To form a Chapter 209 Election Committee, the Lot Owners forming such committee must file a written notice of the committee's formation with the county clerk of each county in which the Subdivision Development is located.[36] A written notice of the formation of a Chapter 209 Election Committee must contain:

(1) a statement that a Chapter 209 Election Committee has been formed to call a meeting of the Subdivision Association's Lot Owners for the sole purpose of electing Board Members;[37]

(2) the name and residential address of each member of the Chapter 209 Election Committee;[38] and

(3) the name of the Subdivision Development over which the Subdivision Association has jurisdiction under a Dedicatory Instrument.[39]

---

35 Tex. Prop. Code § 209.014(c), (h). If a Subdivision Association is incorporated as a nonprofit corporation and its Board of Directors fails to call an annual meeting, Lot Owners may pursue either or both of the remedies provided under the Texas Nonprofit Corporation Law and Chapter 209 of the Texas Property Code.

36 Tex. Prop. Code § 209.014(c). Upon filing the notice of formation of a Chapter 209 Election Committee, the county clerk is required to enter on such notice of formation the date it is filed and to record a copy of such notice of formation in such county's Official Public Records. Tex. Prop. Code § 209.014(f). Only one Chapter 209 Election Committee may operate in a Subdivision Development at the same time. Tex. Prop. Code § 209.014(g). If more than one committee of Lot Owners in a Subdivision Development files a notice of formation of a Chapter 209 Election Committee with the county clerk, the first committee that files a notice of formation of a Chapter 209 Election Committee in full compliance with the requirements of Section 209.014 of the Texas Property Code constitutes the Chapter 209 Election Committee with the power to call a Membership Meeting for the purpose of electing Board Members. Tex. Prop. Code § 209.014(g).

37 Tex. Prop. Code § 209.014(d)(1).

38 Tex. Prop. Code § 209.014(d)(2).

39 Tex. Prop. Code § 209.014(d)(3).

In addition, each member of the Chapter 209 Election Committee must sign and acknowledge the notice of formation before a notary or other official authorized to take acknowledgments.[40]

Once a Chapter 209 Election Committee has been formed, it may call meetings of the Subdivision Association's Lot Owners for the sole purpose of electing Board Members.[41] All notice, quorum, and voting provisions contained in the Bylaws of the Subdivision Association apply to any Membership Meeting called by the Chapter 209 Election Committee.[42] If a Chapter 209 Election Committee does not hold or conduct a successful election of Board Members within four (4) months after the date the notice for formation of a Chapter 209 Election Committee is filed with the county clerk, then such Chapter 209 Election Committee is automatically dissolved by operation of law.[43]

5.6 Special Meetings of a Homeowners Association's Membership

As with Board Meetings, a Homeowners Association may also need to call a special Membership Meeting when it is necessary for the Homeowners to take some action before the next regularly scheduled Membership Meeting or when the Governing Documents of a Homeowners Association require that certain actions be approved at a special Membership Meeting called for that specific purpose.

The authority to call a special meeting of a Homeowners Association's Membership is governed by its Governing Documents, as well as the Texas Nonprofit Corporation Law, Texas Uniform Condominium Act, and Chapter 209 of the Texas Property Code. In addition to any procedures provided by a Homeowners Association's

---

[40] Tex. Prop. Code § 209.014(e).

[41] Tex. Prop. Code § 209.014(h).

[42] Tex. Prop. Code § 209.014(h).

[43] Tex. Prop. Code § 209.014(g). Any election held or conducted by a Chapter 209 Election Committee after it has dissolved is invalid and ineffective for any purpose. Tex. Prop. Code § 209.014(g).

Governing Documents, under the Texas Nonprofit Corporation Law, a special Membership Meeting may be called by either: (1) the President; (2) a majority of the Board of Directors; (3) Member-Homeowners having not less than one-tenth (1/10) of the votes entitled to be cast at a Membership Meeting; or (4) any other Officers or persons authorized by the Articles of Incorporation or Bylaws of the Nonprofit Corporation HOA.[44]

If a Homeowners Association is a Condominium Association, the Texas Uniform Condominium Act provides that a Special Meeting of Unit Owners may be called by either: (1) the President; (2) a majority of the Board of Directors; or (3) Unit Owners having at least twenty percent (20%) of the votes in the Condominium Association.[45] For those Condominium Associations that are incorporated as nonprofit corporations, the Texas Nonprofit Corporation Law and Texas Uniform Condominium Act create somewhat of a conflict as to what percentage of Member-Homeowners or Unit Owners is sufficient to call a special Membership Meeting: ten percent (10%) or twenty percent (20%)? No Texas court has addressed this issue; however, based on the language of the Texas Nonprofit Corporation Law, which provides for mutually exclusive methods for calling a special Membership Meeting, a special Membership Meeting of a Condominium Association incorporated as a nonprofit corporation could be called by either percentage, or, in other words, by only ten percent (10%) of the Member-Homeowners.

In addition to the applicable procedures under the Texas Nonprofit Corporation Law for calling a special Membership Meeting, Chapter 209 of the Texas Property Code provides for two additional circumstances in which a special meeting of a Subdivision Association's Membership may be called. First, if a Subdivision Association's Board of

[44] Tex. Bus. Org. Code § 22.155. Such procedures apply to all Texas Condominium and Subdivision Associations that are incorporated as nonprofit corporations and are in addition to applicable provisions under the Texas Uniform Condominium Act and Chapter 209 of the Texas Property Code.

[45] Tex. Prop. Code § 82.108(a).

Directors fails to call an annual Membership Meeting, Chapter 209 authorizes its Lot Owners to form a committee for the purpose of calling a special Membership Meeting to elect new Board Members.[46] In addition, upon receipt of a petition executed by Lot Owners holding at least ten percent (10%) of all voting interests in the Subdivision Association, a Subdivision Association's Board of Directors must call a special Membership Meeting for the specific purpose of voting on whether to add or remove (as applicable) a provision in the Subdivision Association's Governing Documents granting the Subdivision Association the right to foreclose an assessment lien.[47]

5.7 Notice of a Membership Meeting

The procedures and requirements for providing notice of a Membership Meeting are governed by a Homeowners Association's Governing Documents, as well as the Texas Nonprofit Corporation Law, the Texas Uniform Condominium Act, and Chapter 209 of the Texas Property Code.

5.7.1 General Requirements Concerning Notice of a Membership Meeting

Subject to the provisions of the Nonprofit Corporation Law and a Nonprofit Corporation HOA's Governing Documents, notice of a Membership Meeting must be given to Member-Homeowners in the manner determined by the Board of Directors.[48] Notwithstanding, at a minimum, a Membership Meeting notice must state: (1) the date and time of the meeting; and (2) the location of the meeting (if the meeting is not held solely by using a conference telephone or other communications system) and/or the form of communications system to be used for the meeting and the means of accessing it (if the meeting is held solely or in part by using a conference telephone or other communications

---

46 Tex. Prop. Code § 209.014.

47 Tex. Prop. Code § 209.0093.

48 Tex. Bus. Org. Code § 6.051(a).

system).[49] In addition, if the meeting is a special Membership Meeting, then the Membership Meeting notice must also state the purpose(s) for which such special Membership Meeting is being called.[50]

The Membership Meeting notice must be delivered to each Member-Homeowner entitled to vote at the Membership Meeting no earlier than sixty (60) days, nor later than ten (10) days, before the date of the Membership Meeting.[51] A notice of Membership Meeting may be delivered to Member-Homeowners by personal delivery, mail, facsimile, or email.[52] If the Membership Meeting notice is given to a Member-Homeowner by mail, then notice is considered to be given on the date it is deposited in the United States mail, with postage paid, in an envelope addressed to the Member-Homeowner at his or her address as it appears on the ownership or membership records of the Nonprofit Corporation HOA.[53] If notice of the Membership Meeting is given to a Member-Homeowner by facsimile or email, then notice is considered to be given when it is transmitted to a facsimile number or email address provided by the Member-Homeowner, or to which the Member-Homeowner consents, for the purpose of receiving meeting notices.[54]

5.7.2 Specific Requirements of Condominium Associations Concerning Notice of a Membership Meeting

In addition to the general requirements concerning notice of Membership Meetings imposed by the Texas Nonprofit Corporation Law, if a Nonprofit Corporation HOA is also a Condominium Association and the Membership Meeting is for the purpose

---

[49] Tex. Bus. Org. Code § 6.051(a).

[50] Tex. Bus. Org. Code § 22.156(a).

[51] Tex. Bus. Org. Code § 22.156(a).

[52] Tex. Bus. Org. Code §§ 6.051(b), 22.156(a).

[53] Tex. Bus. Org. Code § 6.051(b)(1).

[54] Tex. Bus. Org. Code § 6.051(b)(2).

of adopting an amendment or modification to its Declaration, Articles of Incorporation, Bylaws, or Associations Rules, then the Condominium Association must give each Unit Owner a document showing the specific amendment or other change that would be made to the Declaration, Articles of Incorporation, Bylaws, or Association Rules no earlier than twenty (20) days, nor later than ten (10) days, before the date of the Membership Meeting.[55] Written notice of a proposed amendment of, or modification to, a Condominium Association's Governing Documents is considered to have been given to a Unit Owner on the date such information is personally delivered to the Unit Owner, as shown by a receipt signed by such Unit Owner, or on the date mailed to the Unit Owner, as evidenced by the postmark on an envelope containing such information that is deposited in the United States mail with a proper address and paid postage.[56]

5.7.3 Specific Requirements of Subdivision Associations Concerning Notice of a Membership Meeting

In addition to the general requirements concerning notice of a Membership Meeting imposed by the Texas Nonprofit Corporation Law, if a Nonprofit Corporation HOA is a Subdivision Association, then it is also governed by the Membership Meeting notice requirements under Chapter 209 of the Texas Property Code. In general, Chapter 209 of the Texas Property Code requires a Subdivision Association to provide advance notice of an election or vote to all of its Lot Owners who are entitled to vote in such election or vote.[57] The notice requirements under Chapter 209, however, vary depending

---

55 Tex. Prop. Code § 82.070.

56 Tex. Prop. Code § 82.070(b).

57 Tex. Prop. Code § 209.0056. It is important to note that the written notice of election or vote requirement under Section 209.0056 applies generally to all Texas Subdivision Associations, including unincorporated Subdivision Associations, and that Section 209.0056 supersedes any contrary requirements in a Subdivision Association's Governing Documents. Tex. Prop. Code § 209.0056. Section 209.0056, however, does not apply to a Subdivision Association that is subject to Chapter 552 of the Texas Government Code (formally known as the "Texas Public Information Act," but more commonly referred to as the "Texas Open Records Act"). Tex. Prop. Code § 209.0056(c). A Subdivision Association is subject to Chapter 552 of the Texas Government Code if: (1) membership in the Subdivision Association is mandatory for Lot Owners or a defined class of property owners in a defined geographic area in a county with a population of 2.8 million or more (Harris County) or in a county adjacent to a county with a population of 2.8 million or more (Brazoria,

on whether the election or vote is to be conducted at a Membership Meeting (i.e., the election or vote is to be conducted by ballots cast in person or by proxy at the Membership Meeting) or conducted outside of a Membership Meeting (i.e., the election or vote is to be conducted by absentee ballots, electronic ballots, and/or any other method of representative voting or delegated voting authorized by a Subdivision Association's Dedicatory Instruments that occurs outside of a meeting).[58]

If an association-wide election or vote is to be conducted by ballots cast in person or by proxy at a Membership Meeting, a Subdivision Association is required to give written notice of the election or vote to all of its Lot Owners no earlier than sixty (60) days, nor later than ten (10) days, before the date of the Membership Meeting.[59] Such notice requirement is consistent with the Membership Meeting notice requirement applicable to Nonprofit Corporation HOAs under the Texas Nonprofit Corporation Law.[60]

Chambers, Fort Bend, Liberty, Montgomery, San Jacinto, and Waller Counties); the Subdivision Association has the power to make mandatory special assessments for capital improvements or mandatory regular assessments; and the amount of the mandatory special or regular assessments is or has ever been based in whole or in part on the market value of Lot Owners' Lots or property as assessed by the State of Texas or a local governmental entity for purposes of ad valorem taxation; or (2) the Subdivision Association provides maintenance, preservation, and architectural control of residential and commercial property within a defined geographic area in a county with a population of 2.8 million or more (Harris County) or in a county adjacent to a county with a population of 2.8 million or more (Brazoria, Chambers, Fort Bend, Liberty, Montgomery, San Jacinto, and Waller Counties); and the Subdivision Association is a corporation that is governed by a board of trustees who may employ a general manager to execute the Subdivision Association's Bylaws and administer the business of the corporation; does not require membership in the corporation by the Lot Owners within the defined area; and was incorporated before January 1, 2006. Tex. Gov't Code § 552.0036.

58 Tex. Prop. Code § 209.0056. It is important to note that if a Subdivision Association is a Nonprofit Corporation HOA, and is authorized by its Articles of Incorporation or Bylaws to do so, then an election or vote of the Subdivision Association's membership may be conducted by mail, facsimile, email, or any combination of those methods. Tex. Bus. Org. Code § 22.160(d). It is also important to note that if a Subdivision Association is conducting a representative election for purposes of electing representatives who are then vested with the authority to elect or appoint the members of the Subdivision Association's Board of Directors, the Subdivision Association is only required to provide written notice of such representative election to the Lot Owners entitled under its Governing Documents to vote in that particular representative election. Tex. Prop. Code § 209.0056(a)(2).

59 Tex. Prop. Code § 209.0056(a)(1). If the election or vote is to be conducted at a Membership Meeting, the notice of an election or vote can and should be incorporated into the notice of the Membership Meeting.

60 Tex. Bus. Org. Code § 22.156(a).

If the election or vote is to be conducted by absentee ballots, electronic ballots, and/or any other authorized method of voting that occurs outside of a Membership Meeting, then the Subdivision Association is required to give notice of the election or vote to all Lot Owners entitled to vote on any matter under consideration no later than twenty (20) days before the latest date on which a ballot may be submitted to the Subdivision Association in order to be counted.[61] In other words, a Subdivision Association must provide Lot Owners a time period of at least twenty (20) days in which to cast ballots that are submitted to the Subdivision Association outside of a Membership Meeting.[62]

5.7.4 Exceptions to and Waiver of a Membership Meeting Notice

There are a couple exceptions under the Texas Nonprofit Corporation Law to the general requirements concerning Membership Meeting notices.[63] First, a Texas Nonprofit

---

61 Tex. Prop. Code § 209.0056(a-1). It is important to note that while Section 209.0056(a) expressly requires that a notice of election or vote that is to be conducted at a Membership Meeting be in writing, Section 209.0056(a-1) does not explicitly require that the notice of election or vote that is to be conducted outside of a Membership Meeting be in writing. Tex. Prop. Code § 209.0056(a-1). Because of a lack of such requirement under Section 209.0056(a-1), it appears that a notice of election or vote that is to be conducted outside of a Membership Meeting may be provided to Lot Owners verbally instead of in writing. Nevertheless, it is still recommended that such notice of election or vote be provided to Lot Owners in writing so that there is written documentation of the Subdivision Association's compliance with Section 209.0056(a-1).

62 If a Subdivision Association intends to utilize a combination of ballots that will be cast both at and outside of a Membership Meeting, the Subdivision Association can either provide Lot Owners separate notices for the ballots to be cast at the Membership Meeting and the ballots to be cast outside of the Membership Meeting, or the Subdivision Association can provide Lot Owners a consolidated notice that complies with the notice requirements for both types of ballots. If a Subdivision Association intends to utilize a combination of ballots for a Membership Meeting and to provide Lot Owners a consolidated notice, the notice of election or vote must be in writing and given to all Lot Owners no earlier than sixty (60) days, nor later than ten (10) days, before the date of the Membership Meeting, and at least twenty (20) days before the latest date on which a ballot may be submitted to the Subdivision Association in order to be counted. If the deadline to submit a ballot in order to be counted is the date of the Membership Meeting, then the consolidated written notice of an election or vote must be given to Lot Owners at least twenty (20) days before the date of the Membership Meeting, instead of only ten (10) days.

63 It is important to note that to the extent an exception to a Membership Meeting notice requirement under the Texas Nonprofit Corporation Law conflicts with a Membership Meeting notice requirement established by Chapter 209 of the Texas Property Code, the exception will not apply to a Subdivision Association. In other words, an exception to the notice requirements under the Texas Nonprofit Corporation Law will not execuse a Subdivision Association's compliance with the notice requirements under Chapter 209 of the Texas Property Code.

Corporation HOA does not have to provide notice of regular or annual Membership Meetings to Member-Homeowners if its Bylaws provide that none is required.[64]

In addition, a notice of a Membership Meeting is not required to be given to a Member-Homeowner of a Nonprofit Corporation HOA who is otherwise entitled to such notice under the Texas Nonprofit Corporation Law or the Nonprofit Corporation HOA's Governing Documents if the Member-Homeowner signs a written waiver of meeting notice, regardless of whether the waiver is signed before or after the time of such meeting.[65]

Finally, if a Member-Homeowner who is entitled to but was not provided proper notice of a Membership Meeting actually participates in or attends such Membership Meeting, then such Member-Homeowner's participation or attendance at such Membership Meeting constitutes a waiver of a meeting notice unless he or she participates in or attends such meeting solely to object to the transaction of business at the Membership Meeting on the grounds that the meeting was not lawfully called or convened.[66]

5.8 Pre-Membership Meeting Procedures: Setting a Record Date for Determination of Membership and Preparing a Membership Voting List

Prior to sending a Membership Meeting notice to Homeowners, a Homeowners Association must determine who the current members of the Homeowners Association are for purposes of establishing who is entitled to notice of the Membership Meeting

64 Tex. Bus. Org. Code § 22.157(a). It is important to note that this statutory exception has very limited applicability in the context of Homeowners Association Membership Meetings. First, it does not apply to a special Membership Meeting. It also does not apply to a regular or annual meeting of a Subdivision Association's Membership, even if it is incorporated as a nonprofit corporation. Tex. Prop. Code § 209.0056(a). Nor does such exception apply to a meeting of a Condominium Association's Membership if the meeting is for the purpose of voting on an amendment to its Declaration, Articles of Incorporation, Bylaws, and/or Associations Rules. Tex. Prop. Code § 82.070.

65 Tex. Bus. Org. Code § 6.052(a). Unless required by a Nonprofit Corporation HOA's Articles of Incorporation or its Governing Documents, the business to be transacted at a Membership Meeting is not required to be specified in a written waiver of notice of such meeting. Tex. Bus. Org. Code § 6.052(c).

66 Tex. Bus. Org. Code § 6.052(b).

and/or to vote at such meeting. This can sometimes be difficult because a Homeowners Association may not know immediately when a Lot or Unit is sold, or even the identity of the new owner, for several weeks following the closing on such Lot or Unit. In recognition of the potential problems in the timing of identifying members of a nonprofit corporation in advance of a Membership Meeting, the Texas Nonprofit Corporation Law authorizes nonprofit corporations, including Nonprofit Corporation HOAs, under certain conditions to set a specific date in advance of the Membership Meeting as the "Record Date" for purposes of determining the identity of the Member-Homeowners of the Nonprofit Corporation HOA that are entitled to receive notice of the Membership Meeting and to vote at such meeting.[67]

5.8.1 Establishing a Record Date for Determination of Membership

If the Articles of Incorporation of a Nonprofit Corporation HOA establish or provide a manner for establishing a "Record Date" for determining the identity of Member-Homeowners entitled to receive notice of and/or vote at a Membership Meeting, the Board of Directors may set a Record Date at any point in advance of a Membership Meeting so long as the Record Date is no earlier than sixty (60) days before the date scheduled for such Membership Meeting.[68] In addition, if so authorized by the Articles of Incorporation, the Board of Directors may also close the transfer of the Nonprofit Corporation HOA's Membership records for a period of time, not to exceed sixty (60) days, in advance of a Membership Meeting for the purpose of determining the identity of Member-Homeowners who are entitled to receive notice of a Membership Meeting and/or

---

67 Tex. Bus. Org. Code § 22.163(a).

68 Tex. Bus. Org. Code § 6.101(a)–(b). The Record Date for the determination of Member-Homeowners entitled to notice of or to vote at a Membership Meeting is effective for an adjournment of such meeting as well, unless: (1) the Member-Homeowners entitled to vote are determined by closing the transfer of Membership records and the period during which the transfer of records is closed expires; or (2) the Board of Directors of the Nonprofit Corporation HOA sets a new Record Date for determining the right to notice of or to vote at the adjournment of such meeting. Tex. Bus. Org. Code § 6.101(e).

vote at such meeting.[69] In other words, a Nonprofit Corporation HOA can freeze its membership records for up to sixty (60) days while it determines who its Member-Homeowners are. This may be necessary where there is a significant number of Member-Homeowners and Lots or Units are sold often.

If the identity of Member-Homeowners of a Nonprofit Corporation HOA are not otherwise determined using one of the aforementioned methods, then the Record Date for determining the identity of Member-Homeowners of a Nonprofit Corporation HOA who are entitled to notice of a Membership Meeting is considered to be the date that notice of the Membership Meeting is given to the Member-Homeowners entitled to notice of such meeting.[70] In other words, if a Record Date for determining the identity of a Nonprofit Corporation HOA's Membership is not set by the Board of Directors for a date in advance of a Membership Meeting, then the Nonprofit Corporation HOA must provide notice of a Membership Meeting to all persons who are considered to be Member-Homeowners of the Nonprofit Corporation HOA as of the close of business on the business day preceding the date such meeting notice is given to Member-Homeowners by the Nonprofit Corporation HOA.[71]

In addition, if no Record Date is established in advance of a Membership Meeting for determining the identity of Member-Homeowners entitled to vote at such meeting, then all persons who are considered to be Member-Homeowners of the Nonprofit Corporation HOA as of the date of the Membership Meeting, who are otherwise eligible to vote, are entitled to vote at such Membership Meeting.[72]

---

69 Tex. Bus. Org. Code § 6.101(c).

70 Tex. Bus. Org. Code § 6.101(d).

71 Tex. Bus. Org. Code § 22.163(b).

72 Tex. Bus. Org. Code § 22.163(b).

5.8.2 Preparation of a Membership Voting List

After the Board of Directors sets a Record Date for determining the identity of Member-Homeowners entitled to notice of a Membership Meeting, or otherwise mails the notice of the Membership Meeting to its Member-Homeowners, the Nonprofit Corporation HOA must prepare an alphabetical list of the names of all its voting Member-Homeowners, called a "Membership Voting List."[73] The Membership Voting List must identify: (1) the Member-Homeowners of the Nonprofit Corporation HOA who are entitled to notice of such Membership Meeting; (2) the Member-Homeowners of the Nonprofit Corporation HOA who are not entitled to notice of such Membership Meeting; (3) the address of each voting Member-Homeowner; and (4) the number of votes each voting Member-Homeowner is entitled to cast at such Membership Meeting.[74]

No later than the second (2nd) business day after the date notice of a Membership Meeting is given to Member-Homeowners of a Nonprofit Corporation HOA, the Nonprofit Corporation HOA must make the Membership Voting List for such Membership Meeting available at the Nonprofit Corporation HOA's principal office or at a reasonable place in the municipality in which such Membership Meeting will be held (as identified in the Membership Meeting notice) for inspection by Member-Homeowners entitled to vote at such Membership Meeting for the purpose of communication with other Member-Homeowners concerning the Membership Meeting; and, it must continue to make such Membership Voting List available for inspection at its principle office or other reasonable place until the applicable Membership Meeting has occurred.[75] In addition, the

---

[73] Tex. Bus. Org. Code § 22.158(a).

[74] Tex. Bus. Org. Code § 22.158(a).

[75] Tex. Bus. Org. Code § 22.158(b)–(c). A voting Member-Homeowner (or his or her agent or attorney) is entitled upon written demand stating a proper purpose to inspect and copy (at the Member-Homeowner's expense) the Membership Voting List at a reasonable time during the period such list is available for inspection. Tex. Bus. Org. Code §§ 22.158(c), 22.351. Such right to inspect and copy the Membership Voting List is in addition to the general rights of Unit Owners and Lot Owners to inspect and copy the records of Condominium Associations and Subdivision Associations, respectively, under the Texas Uniform Condominium Act and Chapter 209 of the Texas Property Code.

Nonprofit Corporation HOA must also make the Membership Voting List available for inspection by any voting Member-Homeowner (and/or a voting Member-Homeowner's agent or attorney) at all times during the actual Membership Meeting and at any adjournment of such meeting.[76]

5.9 Agenda and Order of Business at a Membership Meeting

The same guidelines for agendas and order of business for Board Meetings apply to Membership Meetings. An agenda is generally prepared in advance of a Membership Meeting by the presiding officer or person calling the meeting, and it is approved by a majority vote of the participants at the commencement of the Membership Meeting.[77] Once approved, the agenda should not be amended absent a two-thirds (2/3) vote of the participants at such meeting.[78] It is not uncommon for an agenda to be circulated in advance of a Membership Meeting, and in such cases, the agenda is generally considered to be a proposed agenda, as opposed to an approved agenda, until it is adopted by a majority vote of the participants at the commencement of such Membership Meeting.[79]

The "order of business" generally refers to the established sequence in which business is taken up at a meeting and is usually set out in the agenda for the meeting. The order of business for a Membership Meeting may be, but is rarely, specified in a Homeowners Association's Governing Documents. In cases where there is no required order of business, the standard order of business for an annual meeting of a Homeowners Association's Membership is as follows:

(1) reading and approval of minutes from the last annual Membership Meeting;

---

[76] Tex. Bus. Org. Code § 22.158(d).

[77] Robert's Rules of Order (10th Ed.) § 41.

[78] Robert's Rules of Order (10th Ed.) § 41.

[79] Robert's Rules of Order (10th Ed.) § 41.

(2) approval of agenda for the Membership Meeting;

(3) reports of Officers and standing committees;

(4) reports of special or ad hoc committees;

(5) unfinished business from the last annual Membership Meeting, if any;

(6) election of Directors and other positions that are filled by the vote of the Membership;

(7) any other new business; and

(8) adjournment.

A standard order of business for a special meeting of a Homeowners Association's Membership, on the other hand, is as follows:

(1) approval of agenda for the special Membership Meeting;

(2) consideration of proposed motions related to the specific purpose for calling the special meeting and/or specific items identified in the special meeting notice; and

(3) adjournment.

5.10 Conducting a Membership Meeting and Decorum

As with Board Meetings, conducting a Membership Meeting of a Homeowners Association can be a difficult task. This is particularly true of Membership Meetings, which generally involve the attendance and/or participation of significantly more persons than at a Board Meeting. As a result, the need to conduct a Membership Meeting in an orderly and efficient manner is even more paramount, and it is strongly advised that Membership Meetings be conducted using some form of parliamentary procedure.

The most commonly used parliamentary procedure is Robert's Rules of Order.[80] While it is rare that the Governing Documents of a Homeowners Association will obligate

80 A brief summary of Robert's Rules of Order can be found in appendix J at the end of this book.

a Homeowners Association to conduct its meetings under Robert's Rules of Order, in reality, most Homeowners Associations tend to follow Robert's Rules of Order, or a variation of such rules, on an informal basis. Use of parliamentary procedure can be very helpful at a Homeowners Association's Membership Meeting to control the participants and/or attendees, help move things along, and help accomplish the Homeowners Association's business more efficiently. If a Homeowners Association is not already using some type of parliamentary procedures to conduct its Membership Meetings, then it should consider using Roberts Rules of Order or some other form of parliamentary procedure.[81] This is particularly true for large meetings, such as Membership Meetings or any meeting that the presiding officer of the meeting anticipates will be acrimonious. In addition, if significant controversy is anticipated or the need to maintain order is paramount (including those instances where the presiding officer is historically unable to maintain order and move the meeting to a successful conclusion), it may even be advisable to locate a parliamentarian and retain his or her services to assist at the meeting.

Whether or not Robert's Rules of Order or another type of parliamentary procedure is followed, the presiding officer or chairperson of any Homeowners Association meeting should be mindful of the following basic principles in conducting a meeting: (1) courtesy and equal treatment of all participants and attendees; (2) consideration of one matter at a time; and (3) the will of the majority prevails.

5.11 Establishment of a Quorum at a Membership Meeting

Before a Homeowners Association's Membership may effectively take any action at a Membership Meeting, a quorum of Members must be present in person or by proxy at such meeting.[82] The number of Members that must be present in person or by proxy at

---

[81] A good source of parliamentary procedures is the National Association of Parliamentarians, the website for which is http://parliamentarians.org/.

[82] A "quorum" is the number of members who must be present in a deliberative body before business may be transacted. *Black's Law Dictionary* 1255 (6th ed. 1990).

a Membership Meeting in order to establish a quorum is governed by a Homeowners Association's Governing Documents, or in the absence of an applicable provision in its Governing Documents, by the Texas Uniform Condominium Act (if it is a Condominium Association subject to such Act) or the Texas Nonprofit Corporation Law (if it is a Condominium Association subject to the Texas Condominium Act or a Subdivision Association that is incorporated as a nonprofit corporation).[83]

More specifically, if a Homeowners Association is a Condominium Association subject to the Texas Uniform Condominium Act, and unless the Bylaws provide otherwise, a quorum of Unit Owners is considered present throughout any meeting of such Condominium Association's Membership if, at the beginning of the Membership Meeting, persons entitled to cast at least twenty percent (20%) of the votes that may be cast for election of Directors to the Board of Directors are present in person or by proxy at such meeting.[84] On the other hand, if a Homeowners Association is a Condominium Association subject to the Texas Condominium Act or a Subdivision Association that is incorporated as a nonprofit corporation, then in the absence of a provision specifying the requirements for establishing a quorum at a Membership Meeting in its Articles of Incorporation or Bylaws, a quorum is established by the presence of Member-

---

[83] The Membership Meeting quorum requirement provisions under the Texas Uniform Condominium Act conflict with the corresponding provisions under the Texas Nonprofit Corporation Law. In addition, the provisions of the Texas Uniform Condominium Act concerning quorum requirements are not applicable to Condominium Developments created prior to January 1, 1994, that are subject to the Texas Condominium Act, and there are no comparable provisions under the Texas Condominium Act. Tex. Prop. Code § 82.002(c). As a result, in the absence of a provision specifying the Membership Meeting quorum requirements in the Governing Documents of a Homeowners Association, the applicable provisions of the Texas Uniform Condominium Act will apply to Condominium Associations created on or after January 1, 1994, while the applicable provisions of the Texas Nonprofit Corporation Law will apply to Condominium Associations created prior to January 1, 1994, and Subdivision Associations that are incorporated as a nonprofit corporations.

[84] Tex. Prop. Code § 82.109(a). The Bylaws of a Condominium Association subject to the Texas Uniform Condominium Act may also provide for a quorum requirement of less than twenty percent (20%), but it may not establish a quorum requirement of less than ten percent (10%) of the votes that may be cast for election of Directors to the Board of Directors. Tex. Prop. Code § 82.109(a).

Homeowners, in person or by proxy, holding at least ten percent (10%) of the votes entitled to be cast at such Membership Meeting.[85]

It is also important to note that if a Homeowners Association is a Subdivision Association, it is authorized by Chapter 209 of the Texas Property Code to conduct Membership voting by absentee and electronic ballots, in addition to voting in person or by proxy.[86] In such event, a properly cast absentee or electronic ballot by a Lot Owner may be counted as a Lot Owner being present and voting for the purpose of establishing a quorum for items appearing on the absentee or electronic ballot.[87]

---

85 Tex. Bus. Org. Code § 22.159(a).

86 Tex. Prop. Code § 209.00592(a). Section 209.00592 supersedes any contrary provision in a Subdivision Association's Governing Documents; however, it does not apply to a Subdivision Association that is subject to Chapter 552 of the Texas Government Code (formally known as the "Texas Public Information Act," but more commonly referred to as the "Texas Open Records Act"). Tex. Prop. Code § 209.00592(f)–(g). A Subdivision Association is subject to Chapter 552 of the Texas Government Code if: (1) membership in the Subdivision Association is mandatory for Lot Owners or a defined class of property owners in a defined geographic area in a county with a population of 2.8 million or more (Harris County) or in a county adjacent to a county with a population of 2.8 million or more (Brazoria, Chambers, Fort Bend, Liberty, Montgomery, San Jacinto, and Waller Counties); the Subdivision Association has the power to make mandatory special assessments for capital improvements or mandatory regular assessments; and the amount of the mandatory special or regular assessments is or has ever been based in whole or in part on the market value of Lot Owners' Lots or property as assessed by the State of Texas or a local governmental entity for purposes of ad valorem taxation; or (2) the Subdivision Association provides maintenance, preservation, and architectural control of residential and commercial property within a defined geographic area in a county with a population of 2.8 million or more (Harris County) or in a county adjacent to a county with a population of 2.8 million or more (Brazoria, Chambers, Fort Bend, Liberty, Montgomery, San Jacinto, and Waller Counties); and the Subdivision Association is a corporation that is governed by a board of trustees who may employ a general manager to execute the Subdivision Association's Bylaws and administer the business of the corporation; does not require membership in the corporation by the Lot Owners within the defined area; and was incorporated before January 1, 2006. Tex. Gov't Code § 552.0036.

87 Tex. Prop. Code § 209.00592(b)(1). An absentee or electronic ballot, however, may not be counted towards a meeting quorum requirement if the Lot Owner attends the Membership Meeting to vote in person. Tex. Prop. Code § 209.00592(b)(2). Nor may an absentee or electronic ballot be counted toward a meeting quorum for an item appearing on the absentee or electronic ballot if the motion or proposal concerning such item is amended at the Membership Meeting in such a manner that it renders the terms of such motion or proposal different from the exact terms of such motion or proposal as stated on the absentee or electronic ballot. Tex. Prop. Code § 209.00592(b)(3). Notwithstanding, if an absentee ballot or electronic ballot is used for a Director election, a nomination for candidacy taken from the floor of the Membership Meeting is not considered an amendment to the proposal for the election and will not invalidate any absentee ballots or electronic ballots cast by Lot Owners for the election prior to the Membership Meeting. Tex. Prop. Code § 209.00592(b-1).

5.12 Voting of Members at a Membership Meeting

Generally, a Homeowners Association's Governing Documents will establish the voting rights of Homeowners, the manner in which votes are to be allocated between Homeowners and/or classes of Homeowners, and the procedures for casting votes. Notwithstanding the provisions of a Homeowners Association's Governing Documents, there are many statutory laws that may also apply to a Homeowners Association if it is incorporated as a nonprofit corporation and/or is a Subdivision Association.

5.12.1 Allocation of Membership Votes

If a Homeowners Association is a nonprofit corporation, the Texas Nonprofit Corporation Law provides that each Member-Homeowner of a Nonprofit Corporation HOA, regardless of class, is entitled to one vote on each matter submitted to a vote of a Nonprofit Corporation HOA's Membership, except to the extent that the voting rights of a defined class of Member-Homeowners are limited, enlarged, or denied by the Nonprofit Corporation HOA's Articles of Incorporation or Bylaws.[88] Accordingly, if a Homeowners Association is a Nonprofit Corporation HOA, it is important to review its Articles of Incorporation and Bylaws to determine the number and manner of allocating votes between its Member-Homeowners and whether any of its Governing Documents modify the standard rule of one vote for each Member-Homeowner.

5.12.2 Disqualification of a Member's Right to Vote

It is not uncommon for a Texas Homeowners Association to have a provision in one of its Governing Documents that limits or restricts the right of a Homeowner to vote if such Homeowner is not current in the payment of his or her Assessments or is the subject

---

88 Tex. Bus. Org. Code § 22.160(a).

of a lawsuit by the Homeowners Association.[89] Neither the Texas Nonprofit Corporation Law nor the Texas Uniform Condominium Act restrict the enforceability of voting disqualification provisions, and any such voting disqualification provisions will generally be enforced unless the Homeowners Association is a Subdivision Association.

There are a couple of statutory provisions under the Texas Property Code that govern a Lot Owner's right to vote in a Subdivision Association election or vote. First, Section 209.0059 of the Texas Property Code provides that any provision in a Subdivision Association's Governing Documents that would disqualify a Lot Owner from voting in an election of Directors or on any matter concerning the rights or responsibilities of the Lot Owner is void and unenforceable.[90] Accordingly, a Subdivision Association may not enforce a voting disqualification provision contained in its Dedicatory Instruments.

In addition, if a Subdivision Association is located in Harris County or a county adjacent to Harris County and: (1) provides maintenance, preservation, and architectural

---

[89] In fact, Section 82.102(a)(17) of the Texas Uniform Condominium Act expressly authorizes a Condominium Association to suspend the voting privileges of a Unit Owner who is more than thirty (30) days delinquent in the payment of Assessments. Tex. Prop. Code § 82.102(a)(17).

[90] Tex. Prop. Code § 209.0059(a). Section 209.0059, however, does not apply to a Subdivision Association that is subject to Chapter 552 of the Texas Government Code (formally known as the "Texas Public Information Act," but more commonly referred to as the "Texas Open Records Act"). Tex. Prop. Code § 209.0059(b). A Subdivision Association is subject to Chapter 552 of the Texas Government Code if: (1) membership in the Subdivision Association is mandatory for Lot Owners or a defined class of property owners in a defined geographic area in a county with a population of 2.8 million or more (Harris County) or in a county adjacent to a county with a population of 2.8 million or more (Brazoria, Chambers, Fort Bend, Liberty, Montgomery, San Jacinto, and Waller Counties); the Subdivision Association has the power to make mandatory special assessments for capital improvements or mandatory regular assessments; and the amount of the mandatory special or regular assessments is or has ever been based in whole or in part on the market value of Lot Owners' Lots or property as assessed by the State of Texas or a local governmental entity for purposes of ad valorem taxation; or (2) the Subdivision Association provides maintenance, preservation, and architectural control of residential and commercial property within a defined geographic area in a county with a population of 2.8 million or more (Harris County) or in a county adjacent to a county with a population of 2.8 million or more (Brazoria, Chambers, Fort Bend, Liberty, Montgomery, San Jacinto, and Waller Counties); and the Subdivision Association is a corporation that is governed by a board of trustees who may employ a general manager to execute the Subdivision Association's Bylaws and administer the business of the corporation; does not require membership in the corporation by the Lot Owners within the defined area; and was incorporated before January 1, 2006. Tex. Gov't Code § 552.0036.

control of residential or commercial Subdivision Development; (2) is a corporation governed by a board of trustees who are allowed to employ a general manager to execute the Subdivision Association's Bylaws and administer the business of the corporation; (3) the corporation does not require membership in the corporation by the owners of such residential or commercial properties; and (4) the corporation was incorporated before January 1, 2006, then such Subdivision Association is also precluded from restricting a Lot Owner from voting in an election based solely on the fact that there is a pending enforcement action by the Subdivision Association against such Lot Owner or such Lot Owner owes the Subdivision Association any delinquent Assessments, fees, or fines.[91]

Finally, in 2015, the Texas legislature amended Section 209.0058 of the Texas Property Code to provide that if a Subdivision Association administers a Subdivision Development consisting of ten or fewer Lots for which the Declaration was recorded prior to January 1, 2015, a person may not vote in an election conducted by such Subdivision Association unless he or she is subject to a Dedicatory Instrument governing the Subdivision Association through which the Subdivision Association exercises its authority.[92]

5.12.3 Membership Voting Approval Requirements

Unless a higher percent is required by Texas law or a Nonprofit Corporation HOA's Governing Documents, a majority vote of the ballots entitled to be cast by the Member-Homeowners present or represented by proxy at a meeting at which a quorum is present constitutes an act of a Nonprofit Corporation HOA's Membership.[93] In other

---

91 Tex. Prop. Code § 209.0055. Section 209.0055 only applies to Subdivision Associations located in a county with a population of 2.8 million or more or in a county adjacent to a county with a population of 2.8 million or more. Tex. Prop. Code § 209.0055(a). The only county in Texas with a population of 2.8 million or more is Harris County, and the counties adjacent to Harris County are Brazoria, Chambers, Fort Bend, Galveston, Liberty, Montgomery, and Waller Counties. Source: United States Census Bureau, 2010 Census.

92 Tex. Prop. Code § 209.0058(c).

93 Tex. Bus. Org. Code § 22.159(b). In the event a Nonprofit Corporation HOA's Articles of Incorporation or Bylaws require the vote or concurrence of a greater proportion of its Member-Homeowners than is required

words, unless a particular action is required by law or a Homeowners Association's Governing Documents to be approved by an affirmative vote greater than a simple majority, then an affirmative vote of a majority of the ballots cast by the Homeowners Association's Membership at a Membership Meeting is all that is necessary to approve a proposed action.[94]

In most cases, matters submitted to and voted on by Homeowners at a Membership Meeting need only be approved by a simple majority of the votes cast at such meeting. However, there are several types of actions under the Texas Nonprofit Corporation Law, Texas Uniform Condominium Act, and Chapter 209 of the Texas Property Code that are required to be approved by an affirmative vote of Homeowners that is greater than just a simple majority. By way of example, the vote required to approve any action considered to be a "Fundamental Action" under the Texas Nonprofit Corporation Law is at least two-thirds (2/3) of the votes of Member-Homeowners present in person or by proxy at a Membership Meeting at which the Fundamental Action is submitted for a vote.[95]

---

by the Texas Nonprofit Corporation Law with respect to an action to be taken by its Member-Homeowners, the Articles of Incorporation or Bylaws control. Tex. Bus. Org. Code §§ 22.159(b), 22.162.

94 In general, the majority vote of the votes entitled to be cast by the Member-Homeowners present or represented by proxy at a meeting at which a quorum is present constitutes an act of a Nonprofit Corporation HOA's Membership. Tex. Bus. Org. Code § 22.159(b). In the event a Nonprofit Corporation HOA's Articles of Incorporation or Bylaws requires the vote or concurrence of a greater proportion of its Member-Homeowners than is required by the Texas Nonprofit Corporation Law with respect to an action to be taken by its Member-Homeowners, the Articles of Incorporation or Bylaws control. Tex. Bus. Org. Code §§ 22.159(b), 22.162.

95 Tex. Bus. Org. Code §§ 22.105(c), 22.162, 22.164(a)(1), (b)(1). Fundamental Actions of a Nonprofit Corporation HOA include: (1) an amendment of the Nonprofit Corporation HOA's Articles of Incorporation; (2) a voluntary winding up of the Nonprofit Corporation HOA; (3) a revocation of a voluntary decision to wind up the Nonprofit Corporation HOA; (4) a cancellation of an event requiring winding up the Nonprofit Corporation HOA; (5) a reinstatement of the Nonprofit Corporation HOA; (6) a distribution plan for the distribution of corporate property upon winding up the Nonprofit Corporation HOA; (7) a plan of merger for merging the Nonprofit Corporation HOA with another entity, (8) a sale of all or substantially all of the assets of the Nonprofit Corporation HOA; (9) a plan of conversion to convert the Nonprofit Corporation HOA into another type of entity; and (10) a plan of exchange of interest. Tex. Bus. Org. Code § 22.164. The two-thirds (2/3) minimum approval requirement for approval of a Fundamental Action trumps any provision in a Nonprofit Corporation HOA's Articles of Incorporation or Bylaws that authorizes the approval of a

5.12.4 Methods for Casting Ballots in a Membership Vote

The methods that may be utilized for casting ballots in an election or vote of a Homeowners Association's Membership depend on the methods authorized by its Articles of Incorporation or Bylaws and whether it is a Subdivision Association. In general, most elections or votes of a Homeowners Association's Membership are conducted at a Membership Meeting, at which its Homeowners will typically cast a ballot in person or by proxy.[96] In addition to casting a ballot in person or by proxy at a Membership Meeting, if a Homeowners Association is a Nonprofit Corporation HOA, and is authorized by its Articles of Incorporation or Bylaws to do so, an election or vote of the Nonprofit Corporation HOA's Membership on any matter may also be conducted by mail, facsimile, email, or any combination of those methods.[97] Finally, if a Homeowners Association is a Subdivision Association, Chapter 209 of the Texas Property Code also authorizes the use of absentee or electronic ballots. Each of these methods for casting ballots is discussed in greater detail in the following subchapters.

5.12.4 (A) *Voting in Person at a Membership Meeting*

Voting in person at a Membership Meeting is the most common way Homeowners cast a ballot in an election or vote. In addition, if a Homeowners Association is a Nonprofit Corporation HOA, the Texas Nonprofit Corporation Law expressly

Fundamental Action by a vote of less than two-thirds (2/3) of such Member-Homeowners' votes. If, however, the Articles of Incorporation of a Nonprofit Corporation HOA require that a Fundamental Action be approved by a vote or concurrence of Member-Homeowners that is greater than two-thirds (2/3) of the votes of such Member-Homeowners, then a Fundamental Action must be approved by the greater number of votes specified by the Articles of Incorporation. Tex. Bus. Org. Code § 22.164(b)(1).

96 Nearly every Texas Homeowners Association allows its Homeowners to cast ballots in an election or vote in person or by proxy at a Membership Meeting. In addition, if a Homeowners Association is incorporated as a nonprofit corporation, the Texas Nonprofit Corporation Law expressly authorizes its Member-Homeowners to vote in person and by proxy, unless proxy voting is prohibited by its Articles of Incorporation or Bylaws. Tex. Bus. Org. Code § 22.160(b).

97 Tex. Bus. Org. Code § 22.160(d).

authorizes its Member-Homeowners to cast their votes in an election or vote in person at a Membership Meeting.[98]

5.12.4 (B) *Voting by Proxy at a Membership Meeting*

Proxy voting is a procedure by which one member of a voting body delegates to another member of such voting body the delegating-member's power to vote in his or her absence.[99] Unless otherwise prohibited by the Articles of Incorporation or Bylaws of a Nonprofit Corporation HOA, the Texas Nonprofit Corporation Law authorizes a Member-Homeowner to vote by proxy at a Membership Meeting.[100] To be effective, a Membership voting proxy must be in writing and executed by the delegating Member-Homeowner or the delegating Member-Homeowner's "attorney-in-fact."[101] Unless a proxy document states that it is irrevocable, a proxy may be revoked by the delegating Member-Homeowner at any time before it is voted.[102] In addition, unless a proxy document states that it shall remain in effect for a period of time in excess of eleven (11) months, it automatically expires eleven (11) months after the date of its execution.[103]

In addition to the Texas Nonprofit Corporation Law, the Texas Uniform Condominium Act also authorizes Unit Owners in a Condominium Association subject to

---

98 Tex. Bus. Org. Code § 22.160(b).

99 *Black's Law Dictionary* defines a "proxy" as a "person who is substituted or deputed by another to represent him and act for him, particularly in some meeting or public body." *Black's Law Dictionary* 1226 (6th ed. 1990). The term "proxy" may also refer to the written document delegating authority by one person to another to act on his behalf. *Id.*

100 Tex. Bus. Org. Code § 22.160(b).

101 Tex. Bus. Org. Code § 22.160(b). "Attorney-in-fact" is a technical term meaning a person having durable power of attorney for another person.

102 Tex. Bus. Org. Code § 22.160(c).

103 Tex. Bus. Org. Code § 22.160(c). It is important to note that if a proxy document states that it is irrevocable, it may not be irrevocable for a period of time longer than eleven (11) months. Tex. Bus. Org. Code § 22.160(c).

such Act to vote by proxy.[104] Pursuant to the Texas Uniform Condominium Act, votes allocated to a Unit may be cast under a written proxy duly executed by a Unit Owner.[105] A Unit Owner may not revoke a written proxy given to another person except by giving actual notice of revocation to the person presiding over the Membership Meeting.[106] In addition, a Unit Owner's voting proxy is considered to be void if it is not dated or if it purports to be revocable without notice.[107] Finally, a Unit Owner's voting proxy automatically terminates one year after the date of its execution, unless it specifies a shorter or longer time period.[108]

5.12.4 (C) *Absentee and Electronic Voting by Lot Owners at a Membership Meeting of a Subdivision Association*

In addition to casting ballots in person or by proxy at a Membership Meeting, Section 209.0041 of the Texas Property Code authorizes Subdivision Associations to conduct Membership voting by absentee ballots and/or electronic ballots.[109] Section

[104] Tex. Prop. Code § 82.110. The provisions of the Texas Uniform Condominium Act concerning voting by proxy are not applicable to Condominium Developments created prior to January 1, 1994, that are subject to the Texas Condominium Act, and there are no comparable provisions under the Texas Condominium Act. Tex. Prop. Code § 82.002(c).

[105] Tex. Prop. Code § 82.110(b). If a Unit is owned by more than one person, each Owner of the Unit may vote or register a protest to the casting of votes by the other co-Owners of such Unit through a proxy duly executed by such Unit Owner. Tex. Prop. Code § 82.110(b).

[106] Tex. Prop. Code § 82.110(b).

[107] Tex. Prop. Code § 82.110(b).

[108] Tex. Prop. Code § 82.110(b).

[109] Tex. Prop. Code § 209.00592(a). Section 209.00592 supersedes any contrary provision in a Subdivision Association's Governing Documents; however, it does not apply to a Subdivision Association that is subject to Chapter 552 of the Texas Government Code (formally known as the "Texas Public Information Act," but more commonly referred to as the "Texas Open Records Act"). Tex. Prop. Code § 209.00592(f)–(g). A Subdivision Association is subject to Chapter 552 of the Texas Government Code if: (1) membership in the Subdivision Association is mandatory for Lot Owners or a defined class of property owners in a defined geographic area in a county with a population of 2.8 million or more (Harris County) or in a county adjacent to a county with a population of 2.8 million or more (Brazoria, Chambers, Fort Bend, Liberty, Montgomery, San Jacinto, and Waller Counties); the Subdivision Association has the power to make mandatory special assessments for capital improvements or mandatory regular assessments; and the amount of the mandatory special or regular assessments is or has ever been based in whole or in part on the market value of Lot Owners' Lots or property as assessed by the State of Texas or a local governmental entity for purposes of ad valorem taxation; or (2) the Subdivision Association provides maintenance, preservation, and architectural control of

209.0041, however, does not require a Subdivision Association to allow its Lot Owners to vote by absentee ballots or electronic ballots.[110] More specifically, Section 209.0041 provides that, unless a Subdivision Association's Dedicatory Instrument provides otherwise, a Subdivision Association is not required to provide a Lot Owner with more than one voting method; but, at a minimum, a Lot Owner must be allowed to vote by either absentee ballot or by proxy.[111]

If a Subdivision Association elects to use absentee ballots, a solicitation for votes by absentee ballot from the Subdivision Association to Lot Owners must include: (1) an absentee ballot form that provides a Lot Owner an opportunity to vote for or against each proposed action to be voted on at the Membership Meeting; and (2) instructions for delivering the completed absentee ballot back to the Subdivision Association, including the delivery location.[112] In addition, the solicitation for votes by absentee ballot must include the following advisory:[113]

residential and commercial property within a defined geographic area in a county with a population of 2.8 million or more (Harris County) or in a county adjacent to a county with a population of 2.8 million or more (Brazoria, Chambers, Fort Bend, Liberty, Montgomery, San Jacinto, and Waller Counties); and the Subdivision Association is a corporation that is governed by a board of trustees who may employ a general manager to execute the Subdivision Association's Bylaws and administer the business of the corporation; does not require membership in the corporation by the Lot Owners within the defined area; and was incorporated before January 1, 2006. Tex. Gov't Code § 552.0036.

110 Tex. Prop. Code § 209.00592(a-1).

111 Tex. Prop. Code § 209.00592(a-1). It is important to note that if a Subdivision Association is incorporated as a nonprofit corporation, it must still allow its Member-Homeowners to vote in person at a Membership Meeting, and unless otherwise provided by its Articles of Incorporation or Bylaws, it must still allow its Member-Homeowners to vote by proxy. Tex. Bus. Org. Code § 22.160(b).

112 Tex. Prop. Code § 209.00592(c)(1)–(2). If an absentee ballot is used for election of Directors, then the ballot should identify each candidate that may be voted for.

113 Tex. Prop. Code § 209.00592(c)(3). Such advisory may be included in the solicitation for votes by absentee ballot or on the absentee ballot itself.

> "By casting your vote via absentee ballot you will forgo the opportunity to consider and vote on any action from the floor on these proposals, if a meeting is held. This means that if there are amendments to these proposals your votes will not be counted on the final vote on these measures. If you desire to retain this ability, please attend any meeting in person. You may submit an absentee ballot and later choose to attend any meeting in person, in which case any in-person vote will prevail."

An electronic ballot means a ballot that is cast by Lot Owners by email, facsimile, or posting on an internet website.[114] To be valid, the method of casting an electronic ballot must be sufficient to confirm the identity of the Lot Owner submitting the ballot and allow the Lot Owner to receive a receipt of the electronic transmission and receipt of his or her ballot.[115] If a Subdivision Association intends to allow Lot Owners to cast an electronic ballot posted on an internet website, then a notice of the posting must be sent to each Lot Owner that contains instructions on obtaining access to the posting on the website.[116]

It is important to note that even though voting by absentee or electronic ballot occurs outside of a meeting, an absentee or electronic ballot cast by a Lot Owner may be counted as such Lot Owner being present and voting at a Membership Meeting for the purpose of establishing a meeting quorum, but only for the items appearing on the ballot.[117] Thus, if there are four items that will be voted on at a Membership Meeting, but only two of the items are listed on an absentee or electronic ballot, then each absentee or electronic ballot cast by a Lot Owner would count as such Lot Owner being present at the Membership Meeting for quorum purposes as to only the two items listed on the absentee or electronic ballot, but not the two items omitted from the absentee or electronic ballot.

---

114 Tex. Prop. Code § 209.00592(d)(1).

115 Tex. Prop. Code § 209.00592(d)(2)–(3).

116 Tex. Prop. Code § 209.00592(e).

117 Tex. Prop. Code § 209.00592(b)(1).

Notwithstanding, if after casting a vote by absentee or electronic ballot a Lot Owner attends the Membership Meeting to vote in person, then such Lot Owner's absentee or electronic ballot may no longer be counted for any purposes, and any ballot cast by such Lot Owner at the Membership Meeting will supersede any previously submitted absentee or electronic ballot for the applicable proposal.[118] Accordingly, if a Lot Owner casts an absentee or electronic ballot prior to a Membership Meeting, but changes his or her mind, such Lot Owner may attend the Membership Meeting in person or by proxy and cast a new ballot, which will supersede the earlier absentee or electronic ballot.

Finally, an absentee or electronic ballot may not be counted toward the final vote on an item appearing on the absentee or electronic ballot if the motion or proposal concerning such item is amended at the Membership Meeting in such a manner that it renders the terms of such motion or proposal different from the exact terms of such motion or proposal as stated on the absentee or electronic ballot.[119] In other words, if an absentee or electronic ballot asks Lot Owners to vote on an amendment to the Subdivision Association's Bylaws and at the Membership Meeting a motion is made and approved to modify the language of the proposed amendment, then all of the absentee and electronic ballots previously submitted will be rendered invalid because they no longer apply to the actual proposal being voted on at the Membership Meeting.

5.13 Election of Directors

In general, the most important matter conducted at an annual Membership Meeting of Homeowners is the election of Directors to the Board of Directors. The manner

---

[118] Tex. Prop. Code § 209.00592(b)(2). Tex. Prop. Code § 209.00592(b)(2).

[119] Tex. Prop. Code § 209.00592(b)(3). If an absentee ballot or electronic ballot is used for a Director election, a nomination for candidacy taken from the floor of the Membership Meeting is not considered an amendment to the proposal for the election and will not invalidate any absentee ballots or electronic ballots cast by Lot Owners for the election prior to the Membership Meeting. Tex. Prop. Code § 209.00592(b-1).

in which Directors are elected to the Board of Directors is typically specified in the Homeowners Association's Governing Documents, but it is also governed by the Texas Nonprofit Corporation Law (if the Homeowners Association is incorporated as a nonprofit corporation) and Chapter 209 of the Texas Property Code (if the Homeowners Association is a Subdivision Association).

5.13.1 Election Voting Systems in General

In general, there are two main types of voting systems: a majority voting system and a plurality voting system; however, there is an almost infinite number of variations and hybrids of these two systems. In a majority voting system, the candidate receiving a majority vote wins. A "majority vote" is a "[v]ote by more than half of voters for candidates or other matter on a ballot."[120] When there are only two candidates, the person who receives the greater number of the votes cast is said to have the majority vote. When there are more than two candidates for the same office, the person who receives the greatest number of votes has a plurality vote, but he or she will not have the majority vote unless he or she receives a greater number of votes than that cast for all of his or her opponents combined. In a majority voting system, if there are more than two candidates for a specific position and none receives more than 50 percent of the votes cast, a run-off election will be held between the two candidates receiving the highest number of votes, with the candidate receiving the greater number of votes cast in the run-off election being considered to have been elected by a majority vote. Majority voting systems are traditionally used in situations where there is only one elected position or the positions are to a specific post, such as a single-member district position on a municipality's governing council where only one person is elected to represent a single district.

A plurality voting system, on the other hand, is traditionally used in situations where multiple candidates are running for election to multiple nonspecific positions or

---

120 *Black's Law Dictionary* 955 (6th ed. 1990).

posts at one time, such as at-large multimember positions on a municipality's governing council. Under a traditional plurality voting system, votes are tabulated and candidates are ranked based on the number of votes each receives, from highest to lowest. The candidates receiving the highest number of votes, up to the total number of open positions, are elected to fill such positions, even if the number of votes a particular candidate received is less than a majority of the votes cast.[121] Today, plurality voting is by far the predominant voting system among US public companies.[122] In fact, Section 21.359 of the Texas For-Profit Corporation Law requires that Directors of a for-profit corporation be elected by a plurality of the votes cast by the shareholders entitled to vote in the election of Directors.[123]

5.13.2 Election Voting under the Texas Nonprofit Corporation Law

While the Texas For-Profit Corporation Law requires Texas for-profit corporations to use a plurality voting system, the Texas Nonprofit Corporation Law does not specifically require Texas Nonprofit Corporation HOAs to do so. Instead, the Texas Nonprofit Corporation Law provides simply that a Member-Homeowner of a Nonprofit Corporation HOA, who is entitled to vote at an election of Directors, is entitled to vote, in person or by proxy, for as many persons as there are Directors to be elected and for whose election the Member-Homeowner has a right to vote.[124] And while the Texas Nonprofit Corporation Law does not require Nonprofit Corporation HOAs to use plurality voting

---

[121] There are also various hybrid forms of plurality and majority voting systems that can require both a majority vote and, in the event of multiple candidates, a plurality vote. In addition, plurality voting systems can vary in relation to specific post requirements and whether vote cumulating and/or vote transferring is allowed.

[122] Practicing Law Institute, Corporate Law and Practice Course Handbook Series, February, 2006, BAKER BOTTS, L.L.P. MEMORANDUM, MAJORITY VOTING IN ELECTION OF DIRECTORS, submitted by James R. Doty.

[123] Tex. Bus. Org. Code § 21.359. While Section 21.359 requires plurality voting, it does allow a for-profit corporation to impose additional "majority vote" requirements in its Articles of Incorporation or Bylaws that would require a director-candidate to also receive the vote of the holders of a specified portion, but not less than a majority, of the shares entitled to vote in order to be elected. Tex. Bus. Org. Code § 21.359.

[124] Tex. Bus. Org. Code § 22.161(a).

systems, the election procedures provided for in most Homeowners Associations' Governing Documents provide for some variation or hybrid form of a plurality voting system, where multiple candidates run for election for multiple open positions on the Board of Directors and the candidates receiving the highest number of votes are elected to fill such positions.

5.13.3 Cumulative Voting

Where plurality election procedures vary, it most likely will be whether cumulative voting is allowed and whether candidates must also receive a majority vote in addition to a plurality vote. In a traditional plurality voting system, each voter is allowed to cast as many votes as there are open positions to be filled. For example, if there are three open positions for which candidates are being elected, then each voter can cast up to three votes. Cumulative voting is a method for promoting minority representation by allowing voters to cumulate all of their votes in only one or two candidates. If cumulative voting is allowed, then each voter may cast each of their votes for a separate candidate or lump some or all of their votes together and cast them in a "cumulative" manner for one or more candidates. If cumulative voting is not allowed, then a voter may cast no more than one vote for any one candidate.

Under the Texas Nonprofit Corporation Law, each Member-Homeowner of a Nonprofit Corporation HOA is allocated one vote for as many Directors as there are to be elected.[125] Generally speaking, a Member-Homeowner may not cast his or her votes in a cumulative manner unless cumulative voting is expressly authorized by the Articles of Incorporation.[126] If a Member-Homeowner of a Nonprofit Corporation HOA is authorized to and intends to cumulate his or her election votes, such Member-Homeowner is required

125 Tex. Bus. Org. Code § 22.161(a).

126 Tex. Bus. Org. Code § 22.161(b). If the Articles of Incorporation of a Nonprofit Corporation HOA do not expressly authorize cumulative voting, then cumulative voting is disallowed.

to give written notice of his or her intention to do so to the Secretary of the Nonprofit Corporation HOA no later than the day before the date of the election.[127]

If a Homeowners Association is a Condominium Association subject to the Texas Uniform Condominium Act, however, its Unit Owners are expressly prohibited from cumulative voting.[128] Such prohibition against cumulative voting applies even if the Articles of Incorporation for such a Condominium Association authorizes cumulative voting. Accordingly, even if such a Condominium Association is incorporated as a nonprofit corporation and its Articles of Incorporation expressly authorize cumulative voting, Unit Owners in such Condominium Association are still prohibited from casting their votes in a cumulative manner.

5.13.4 Deadlines for Partial and/or Full Transition of Authority to Elect Directors from the Declarant to the Homeowners

In most cases when a Texas Homeowners Association is created, its Declaration and/or Bylaws will provide for an initial period of "Declarant-Control" of the Homeowners Association, during which the Declarant may unilaterally appoint and/or remove the Directors and Officers of the Nonprofit Corporation HOA.[129] Such period of time is commonly referred to as a Homeowners Association's "Declarant-Control Period." Regardless of the length of the Declarant-Control Period, it will eventually terminate, and the power to appoint or elect members of the Homeowners Association's Board of Directors will transition to the Homeowners. Following such transition,

---

[127] Tex. Bus. Org. Code § 22.161(c).

[128] Tex. Prop. Code § 82.110(c). The provisions of the Texas Uniform Condominium Act concerning cumulative voting are not applicable to Condominium Developments created prior to January 1, 1994, that are subject to the Texas Condominium Act, and there are no comparable provisions under the Texas Condominium Act. Tex. Prop. Code § 82.002(c).

[129] Tex. Prop. Code § 209.00591(c).

members of the Homeowners Association's Board of Directors will be elected by the Homeowners.

The timing of the transition of a Homeowners Association from Declarant-Control to "Homeowner-Control" will depend on the express terms of the Homeowners Association's Declaration and/or Bylaws and whether it is a Condominium Association or a Subdivision Association. While the terms for transition of control under a Homeowners Association's Declaration and Bylaws can differ significantly from one Homeowners Association to another, the Texas Uniform Condominium Act and Chapter 209 of the Texas Property Code both impose certain deadlines for partial and/or full transition of control of the Board of Directors from the Declarant to the Homeowners.

5.13.4 (A) *Transition of Control of a Condominium Association's Board of Directors under the Texas Uniform Condominium Act*

In most instances, the Condominium Declaration will provide for an initial period of Declarant-Control of the Condominium Association, during which the Declarant may appoint the Directors and Officers of the Condominium Association. Regardless of the duration of the Declarant-Control Period specified in the Condominium Declaration, the Texas Uniform Condominium Act requires that control of the Condominium Association's Board of Directors be gradually transitioned from the Declarant to the Unit Owners, other than the Declarant, upon the occurrence of certain benchmarks.

First, no later than one hundred twenty (120) days after conveyance of fifty percent (50%) of the Units in the Condominium Development to Unit Owners other than a Declarant, at least one-third (1/3) of the members of the Board of Directors must be elected by Unit Owners other than the Declarant.[130]

[130] Tex. Prop. Code § 82.103(d).

Thereafter, a Condominium Association's period of Declarant-Control terminates one hundred twenty (120) days after the Declarant conveys seventy-five percent (75%) of the total number of Units in the Condominium Development to a person or entity other than the Declarant. Prior to, and at the very least no later than, the date of termination of the Declarant-Control Period, the members of the Board of Directors must all be elected by Unit Owners.[131] In addition, within thirty (30) days of the termination of the Declarant-Control Period, the Board of Directors elected by the Unit Owners must elect the Officers of the Condominium Association. Persons elected to the Board of Directors or as Officers of the Condominium Association shall take office upon such election.[132]

5.13.4 (B) *Partial Transition of Control of a Subdivision Association's Board of Directors under Chapter 209 of the Texas Property Code*

Similar to Condominium Associations, the Declaration and/or Bylaws for a Subdivision Association may provide for a period of Declarant-Control of the Board of Directors, during which the Declarant, or persons designated by the Declarant, may appoint and remove Directors and Officers of the Subdivision Association.[133] Regardless of the period of Declarant-Control provided by the Subdivision Declaration and/or Bylaws, on or before the 120th day after the date seventy-five percent (75%) of the total number of Lots that may be created and made subject to the Declaration are conveyed to Lot Owners, other than the Declarant or a builder in the business of constructing homes who purchased the Lots from the Declarant for the purpose of selling completed homes built on the Lots, at least one-third (1/3) of the members of the Board of Directors must be elected by Lot Owners, other than the Declarant.[134] If a Subdivision Association's

---

131 Tex. Prop. Code § 82.103(c).

132 Tex. Prop. Code § 82.103(e).

133 Tex. Prop. Code § 209.00591(c).

134 Tex. Prop. Code § 209.00591(c). It is important to note that Chapter 209 of the Texas Property Code does not require full transition of control of a Subdivision Association's Board of Directors from the Declarant to the Lot Owners, as the Texas Uniform Condominium Act does for Condominium Associations.

Declaration does not specify the number of Lots that may be created and made subject to the Declaration, then at least one-third (1/3) of the members of the Board of Directors must be elected by Lot Owners, other than the Declarant, no later than the tenth (10th) anniversary of the date the Declaration was recorded in the Official Public Records of the county in which the Subdivision Development is located.[135]

5.13.5 Solicitation of Interested Directorial Candidates by Subdivision Associations

In 2015, the Texas Legislature amended Section 209.00593 of the Texas Property Code to establish a new procedure for soliciting interested candidates in advance of a Director election that is applicable to all Texas Subdivision Associations that administer a Subdivision Development that consists of more than one hundred Lots.[136] Under such new procedure, at least ten (10) days before the date an applicable Subdivision Association disseminates absentee ballots or other ballots to its Members for purposes of voting in a Director election, the Subdivision Association must provide notice to its Lot Owners that informs them of the upcoming Director election and solicits candidates interested in running for a position on the Board of Directors (commonly referred to as a "Candidacy-Solicitation Notice").[137]

The Candidacy-Solicitation Notice must contain instructions for an eligible candidate to notify the Subdivision Association of his or her request to be placed on the ballot and the deadline by which such request must be submitted to the Subdivision

135 Tex. Prop. Code § 209.00591(c).

136 Tex. Prop. Code § 209.00593. Accordingly, the new procedure for soliciting interested candidates is inapplicable to Subdivision Associations that administer a Subdivision Development consisting of 100 or fewer Lots.

137 Tex. Prop. Code § 209.00593(a-1).

Association, which may not be earlier than the tenth (10th) day after the date the Subdivision Association provides the Candidacy-Solicitation Notice to its Lot Owners.[138]

An applicable Subdivision Association must provide the Candidacy-Solicitation Notice to its Lot Owners in a manner similar to notices of a Board Meeting. More specifically, an applicable Subdivision Association may either mail the Candidacy-Solicitation Notice to each Lot Owner or post the Candidacy-Solicitation Notice in a conspicuous manner reasonably designed to provide notice to the Subdivision Association's Lot Owners, either:

(1) in a place located on the Subdivision Association's Common Area property or on other conspicuously located privately owned property within the Subdivision Development (so long as the owner of such privately owned property has consented thereto); or

(2) on any internet website maintained by the Subdivision Association or other internet media.[139]

In addition to posting such Candidacy-Solicitation Notice, the Subdivision Association must also email a copy of the Candidacy-Solicitation Notice to each Lot Owner who has registered an email address with the Subdivision Association.[140]

Finally, the Subdivision Association must include on each absentee ballot or other ballot used for the Director election the name of each eligible candidate from whom the Subdivision Association received a timely request to be placed on the ballot.[141]

---

[138] Tex. Prop. Code § 209.00593(a-1).

[139] Tex. Prop. Code § 209.00593(a-2).

[140] Tex. Prop. Code § 209.00593(a-2).

[141] Tex. Prop. Code § 209.00593(a-3).

5.14 Statutory Requirements and Procedures for Casting, Tabulating, and Recounting Membership Ballots Applicable to Subdivision Associations

Chapter 209 of the Texas Property Code imposes upon Texas Subdivision Associations certain requirements and procedures for casting, tabulating, and recounting ballots cast by Lot Owners in an election or vote. In 2015, the Texas Legislature significantly modified such requirements and procedures, which are described in greater detail in the following subchapters.

5.14.1 Use of Written and Secret Ballots

Prior to 2015, Section 209.0058 of the Texas Property Code required any votes cast by a Subdivision Association's Lot Owners to be cast by a signed written ballot. In 2015, the Texas Legislature enacted Senate Bills 864 and 1168, both of which modify Section 209.0058 so as to effectively allow a Subdivision Association to use secret ballots in lieu of a written signed ballot.[142] The language of such bills, however, is somewhat conflicting in nature in two regards and requires additional explanation.

Senate Bill 864 is the more simple and straightforward of the two bills. Under Senate Bill 864, the modified version of Section 209.0058 of the Texas Property Code still requires all votes cast by a Subdivision Association's Lot Owners to be cast by a signed written ballot unless the vote is cast by secret ballot pursuant to rules adopted by the Subdivision Association that are designed to reasonably ensure that: (1) a Lot Owner cannot cast more votes than the Lot Owner is eligible to cast in an election or vote; and (2) the Subdivision Association counts each vote cast by a Lot Owner that the Lot Owner is eligible to cast.[143] Accordingly, under Senate Bill 864's modified version of Section

---

142 *See* Tex. S.B. 864, 84th Leg., R.S. (2015); Tex. S.B. 1168, 84th Leg., R.S. (2015).

143 Tex. Prop. Code § 209.0058(a), (d) (*as modified by Senate Bill 864*). Senate Bill 864's modified version of Section 209.0058(a) states "[e]xcept as provided by Subsection (d), any vote cast in an election or vote by a member of a property owners' association must be in writing and signed by the member." Tex. Prop. Code § 209.0058(a) (*as modified by Senate Bill 864*). The new subsection (d) under Section 209.0058 added by Senate Bill 864 provides that a Subdivision Association may adopt rules to allow voting by secret ballot by Lot Owners, which must "take measures to reasonably ensure that: (1) a member cannot cast more votes than

209.0058, all votes cast by a Lot Owner would have to be cast either by signed written ballot or by secret ballot that conforms to the statutorily required rules adopted by the Subdivision Association.

Under Senate Bill 1168, the modified Section 209.0058 now permits a Subdivision Association to allow Lot Owners to vote verbally at a Membership Meeting on certain matters. More specifically, under Senate Bill 1168's modified version of Section 209.0058, a vote cast by a Lot Owner must be cast by a signed written ballot (or by secret ballot) if his or her vote is cast outside of a Membership Meeting (i.e., by absentee or electronic ballot, and/or any other method of representative voting or delegated voting authorized by a Subdivision Association's Dedicatory Instruments that occurs outside of a meeting) [144] or is cast:

(1) in an election to fill a position on the Board of Directors;[145]

(2) on a proposed adoption or amendment of a Dedicatory Instrument;[146]

(3) on a proposed increase in the amount of a regular assessment or the proposed adoption of a special assessment;[147] or

(4) on the proposed removal of a Director from the Board of Directors.[148]

---

the member is eligible to cast in an election or vote; and (2) the association counts every vote cast by a member that is eligible to cast a vote." Tex. Prop. Code § 209.0058(d) (*as modified by Senate Bill 864*).

144 Tex. Prop. Code § 209.0058(a)(1) (*as modified by Senate Bill 1168*). It is important to note that if a Subdivision Association is a Nonprofit Corporation HOA, and it is further authorized by its Articles of Incorporation or Bylaws to do so, then the Subdivision Association may conduct an election or vote of its membership by mail, facsimile, email, or any combination of those methods. Tex. Bus. Org. Code § 22.160(d).

145 Tex. Prop. Code § 209.0058(a)(2) (*as modified by Senate Bill 1168*). Notwithstanding, written and signed ballots are not required if the Director election is an uncontested race. Tex. Prop. Code § 209.0058(c). An election is considered an uncontested race if the number of candidates is equal to or less than the number of open positions on the Board of Directors to be filled by the election.

146 Tex. Prop. Code § 209.0058(a)(3) (*as modified by Senate Bill 1168*).

147 Tex. Prop. Code § 209.0058(a)(4) (*as modified by Senate Bill 1168*).

148 Tex. Prop. Code § 209.0058(a)(5) (*as modified by Senate Bill 1168*).

Senate Bill 1168's modified version of Section 209.0058 further provides that if a vote of Lot Owners is to be cast in person or by proxy at a Membership Meeting and the vote does not involve: (1) an election or removal of a Director; (2) an adoption or amendment of a Dedicatory Instrument; or (3) an increase of a regular assessment or adoption of a special assessment, then a Subdivision Association may, but is not required to, conduct such vote by signed written ballots or secret ballots.[149] In other words, Senate Bill 1168's modified version of Section 209.0058 now allows a Subdivision Association to conduct verbal votes on administrative or procedural matters at a Membership Meeting, such as a motion to approve the minutes from a prior Membership Meeting or a motion to adjourn the Membership Meeting.[150]

While Senate Bill 1168's modified version of Section 209.0058 also authorizes a Subdivision Association to allow Lot Owners to cast votes by secret ballot (in lieu of signed written ballots) pursuant to rules adopted by the Subdivision Association, the required rules for conducting a vote by secret ballot differ from the rules required by Senate Bill 864's modified version of Section 209.0058. More specifically, Senate Bill 1168's modified version of Section 209.0058 requires the rules adopted by a Subdivision Association for conducting a vote by secret ballot be designed to reasonably ensure that: (1) a Lot Owner cannot cast more votes than the Lot Owner is eligible to cast in an election or vote; and (2) the Subdivision Association counts each vote cast by a Lot Owner that

---

149 Tex. Prop. Code § 209.0058(a-1) (*as modified by Senate Bill 1168*). Under Senate Bill 1168's modified version of Section 209.0058, if a Subdivision Association does elect to use a ballot under such optional circumstances, then the ballot must be either: (1) in writing and signed by the Lot Owner; or (2) cast by secret ballot in accordance with rules adopted by the Subdivision Association for voting by secret ballot under Section 209.0058. Tex. Prop. Code § 209.0058(a-1) (*as modified by Senate Bill 1168*).

150 It is important to note, however, Senate Bill 1168's modified version of Section 209.0058 does not expressly grant a Subdivision Association the right to conduct a verbal vote. Instead, Senate Bill 1168's modified version of Section 209.0058 simply creates an exception to the statutory requirement that a Subdivision Association conduct membership elections and votes by signed written ballots (or secret ballots). If a Subdivision Association's Dedicatory Instruments require a vote to be cast by a written and signed ballot, then the Subdivision Association is still required to use signed written ballots even if the subject matter of the vote does not require the use of signed written ballots (or secret ballots) under Senate Bill 1168's modified version of Section 209.0058.

the Lot Owner is eligible to cast; but unlike Senate Bill 864's modified version of Section 209.0058, Senate Bill 1168's modified version of Section 209.0058 also requires that if the vote involves the election of a person to the Board of Directors, the rules must allow each candidate in such election to designate a person to observe the counting of the ballots.[151]

Thus, as written, Senate Bill 864's modified version of Section 209.0058 requires a Subdivision Association's Lot Owners to cast a vote by either a signed written or secret ballot on all votes, while Senate Bill 1164's modified version of Section 209.0058 only requires a Subdivision Association's Lot Owners to cast a vote by either a signed written or secret ballot if the vote is to be cast outside of a meeting or the vote involves an election or removal of a Director, an adoption or amendment of a Dedicatory Instrument, or an increase of a regular assessment or adoption of a special assessment. In addition, while Senate Bill 1168's modified version of Section 209.0058 requires the rules adopted by a Subdivision Association for conducting a vote by secret ballot to allow candidates to designate an individual to observe the counting of the ballots, Senate Bill 864's modified version of Section 209.0058 omits any such requirement. Until the conflicting language between Senate Bills 864 and 1168 is corrected by the Texas Legislature in a future session, a Subdivision Association should comply with both modified versions of Section 209.0058 by requiring all votes cast by its Lot Owners be either by signed written ballot or by secret ballot that conforms to rules adopted by the Subdivision Association, which should include a rule permitting each candidate in a directorial election of which secret ballots are to be used to designate a person to observe the counting of the ballots.

[151] Tex. Prop. Code § 209.0058(d) (*as modified by Senate Bill 1168*). Notwithstanding, a designated observer is not entitled to see the name of the person who casts a ballot, and any designated observer who is disruptive may be removed. Tex. Prop. Code § 209.0058(d)(3) (*as modified by Senate Bill 1168*).

5.14.2 Tabulation of and Access to Ballots

Section 209.00594 of the Texas Property Code imposes restrictions on who may tabulate or be given access to ballots cast in an election or vote by a Subdivision Association's Lot Owners. More specifically, a person who is a candidate in a Subdivision Association election or who is otherwise the subject of a vote by a Subdivision Association's Lot Owners may not tabulate or otherwise be given access to the ballots cast in such election or vote.[152] In addition, any person who is related within the third degree by consanguinity or affinity to a person who is a candidate in a Subdivision Association election or is the subject of a vote by a Subdivision Association's Lot Owners is also prohibited from tabulating or otherwise being given access to the ballots cast in such election or vote.[153] Summarized in plain English, neither a candidate, nor any relative or in-law of a candidate, may tabulate or be given access to applicable ballots.

It is important to note that only the people who are to tabulate the ballots cast in an election or vote by a Subdivision Association's Lot Owners may be given access to such ballots.[154] In addition, the people who tabulate the ballots cast in an election or vote

---

152 Tex. Prop. Code § 209.00594(a).

153 Tex. Prop. Code § 209.00594(a). Two individuals are considered to be related to each other by consanguinity if one is a descendant of the other or they share a common ancestor. Tex. Gov't Code § 573.022(a). An individual's relatives within the third degree by consanguinity include such individual's: (1) parents and children (relatives in the first degree); (2) brothers, sisters, grandparents, and grandchildren (relatives in the second degree); and (3) great-grandparents, great-grandchildren, aunts who are a sister of a parent of the individual, uncles who are a brother of a parent of the individual, nephews who are a child of a brother or sister of the individual, and nieces who are a child of a brother or sister of the individual (relatives in the third degree). Tex. Gov't Code § 573.023(c). Two individuals are considered to be related to each other by affinity if they are married to each other or the spouse of one of the individuals is related by consanguinity to the other individual. Tex. Gov't Code § 573.024(a). An individual's relatives within the third degree by affinity include: (1) such individual's spouse; (2) anyone related within the third degree by consanguinity to such individual's spouse; and (3) the spouse of anyone related to such individual within the third degree by consanguinity. Tex. Gov't Code § 573.025(a).

154 Tex. Prop. Code § 209.00594(c). Except for those persons who tabulate the ballots cast in a Membership election or vote, no other person may be given access to the ballots cast in a Membership election or vote unless it is pursuant to a recount process authorized by law. Tex. Prop. Code § 209.00594(c).

by a Subdivision Association's Lot Owners are expressly prohibited from disclosing to any other person how any particular individual voted.[155]

5.14.3 Recount of Ballots

Section 209.0057 of the Texas Property Code establishes procedures for a Lot Owner to compel a recount of ballots cast at a meeting of a Subdivision Association's Lot Owners.[156] In order to compel a recount of ballots, a Lot Owner must submit a written demand for a recount to the Subdivision Association within fifteen (15) days from the later of: (1) the date of the Membership Meeting at which the applicable election or vote is held; or (2) the date the result of the applicable election or vote is announced.[157] The written demand for a recount must be submitted to the Subdivision Association either:

(1) by verified mail or by delivery by the United States Postal Service with signature confirmation service to the Subdivision Association at the

[155] Tex. Prop. Code § 209.00594(b-1).

[156] Tex. Prop. Code § 209.0057. Section 209.0057, however, does not apply to a Subdivision Association that is subject to Chapter 552 of the Texas Government Code (formally known as the "Texas Public Information Act," but more commonly referred to as the "Texas Open Records Act"). Tex. Prop. Code § 209.0057(a). A Subdivision Association is subject to Chapter 552 of the Texas Government Code if: (1) membership in the Subdivision Association is mandatory for Lot Owners or a defined class of property owners in a defined geographic area in a county with a population of 2.8 million or more (Harris County) or in a county adjacent to a county with a population of 2.8 million or more (Brazoria, Chambers, Fort Bend, Liberty, Montgomery, San Jacinto, and Waller Counties); the Subdivision Association has the power to make mandatory special assessments for capital improvements or mandatory regular assessments; and the amount of the mandatory special or regular assessments is or has ever been based in whole or in part on the market value of Lot Owners' Lots or property as assessed by the State of Texas or a local governmental entity for purposes of ad valorem taxation; or (2) the Subdivision Association provides maintenance, preservation, and architectural control of residential and commercial property within a defined geographic area in a county with a population of 2.8 million or more (Harris County) or in a county adjacent to a county with a population of 2.8 million or more (Brazoria, Chambers, Fort Bend, Liberty, Montgomery, San Jacinto, and Waller Counties); and the Subdivision Association is a corporation that is governed by a board of trustees who may employ a general manager to execute the Subdivision Association's Bylaws and administer the business of the corporation; does not require membership in the corporation by the Lot Owners within the defined area; and was incorporated before January 1, 2006. Tex. Gov't Code § 552.0036.

[157] Tex. Prop. Code § 209.0057(b).

mailing address reflected on its most recently recorded Management Certificate;[158] or

(2) in person to the Subdivision Association's managing agent as reflected on its most recently recorded Management Certificate or to the address at which absentee and proxy ballots are mailed.[159]

If a Lot Owner timely submits a written demand for a recount to a Subdivision Association, then within twenty (20) days from the date the Subdivision Association receives the written demand for a recount, the Subdivision Association is required to estimate the cost for performance of the ballot recount by a person qualified to tabulate votes and must send an invoice for such estimated costs to the requesting Lot Owner at his or her last known address according to the Subdivision Association's records.[160] Within thirty (30) days from the date the invoice for the estimated cost of performing the ballot recount is sent to the requesting Lot Owner, the requesting Lot Owner must pay the invoice in full.[161] If the requesting Lot Owner fails to timely pay such invoice in full, the requesting Lot Owner's demand for a recount is considered withdrawn and the Subdivision Association is no longer required to perform the ballot recount.[162]

---

158 Tex. Prop. Code § 209.0057(b)(1). Chapter 209 defines verified mail as any method of mailing for which evidence of mailing is provided by the United States Postal Service or a common carrier. Tex. Prop. Code § 209.002(13).

159 Tex. Prop. Code § 209.0057(b)(2).

160 Tex. Prop. Code § 209.0057(b-1).

161 Tex. Prop. Code § 209.0057(b-2). If it turns out that the estimated cost to perform the ballot recount is lesser or greater than the actual costs, then within thirty (30) business days from the date the result of the ballot recount is provided to the requesting Lot Owner, the Subdivision Association must send a final invoice to the requesting Lot Owner. Tex. Prop. Code § 209.0057(b-4). If the actual cost of performing the ballot recount exceeds the estimated costs, the additional cost must be paid by the requesting Lot Owner to the Subdivision Association within thirty (30) business days from the date the final invoice is sent to the requesting Lot Owner. Tex. Prop. Code § 209.0057(b-4). If the requesting Lot Owner fails to timely pay the additional cost to the Subdivision Association, such additional cost may be added to the requesting Lot Owner's account as an assessment. Tex. Prop. Code § 209.0057(b-4). If the estimated cost of performing the ballot recount exceeds the actual cost, the requesting Lot Owner is entitled to a refund of the overpaid amount, which must be paid to the requesting Lot Owner by the Subdivision Association at the time the final invoice is sent to the requesting Lot Owner. Tex. Prop. Code § 209.0057(b-4).

162 Tex. Prop. Code § 209.0057(b-3). It is important to note that the Subdivision Association is not required to send the invoice for the estimated costs of performing the ballot recount by any particular method, but the

Upon timely receipt of payment of the estimated cost of performing the ballot recount, a Subdivision Association is required, at the expense of the requesting Lot Owner, to retain and enter into a contract with an independent and qualified person to perform the recount of ballots.[163] To be considered independent, a person may not be a Lot Owner in the Subdivision Association or be related within the third degree by consanguinity or affinity to a Director on the Subdivision Association's Board of Directors.[164] To be qualified to conduct a recount of ballots, such independent person must also be either:

(1) a current or former county judge; county elections administrator; justice of the peace; or county voter registrar;[165] or

(2) a person agreed on by the Subdivision Association and each person requesting the recount.[166]

It is important to note that only the person who is to perform the ballot recount may be given access to the ballots during the recount process.[167] In addition, such person

---

requesting Lot Owner is required to pay such invoice within thirty (30) days from the date such invoice is sent by the Subdivision Association, not the date the requesting Lot Owner receives such invoice.

163 Tex. Prop. Code §§ 209.0057(c)–(d). A Subdivision Association is not required to enter into a contract with an independent and qualified person to perform the recount of ballots until it has received payment for such costs from the requesting Lot Owner. Tex. Prop. Code § 209.0057(d).

164 Tex. Prop. Code § 209.0057(c). Two individuals are considered to be related to each other by consanguinity if one is a descendant of the other or they share a common ancestor. Tex. Gov't Code § 573.022(a). An individual's relatives within the third degree by consanguinity include such individual's: (1) parents and children (relatives in the first degree); (2) brothers, sisters, grandparents, and grandchildren (relatives in the second degree); and (3) great-grandparents, great-grandchildren, aunts who are a sister of a parent of the individual, uncles who are a brother of a parent of the individual, nephews who are a child of a brother or sister of the individual, and nieces who are a child of a brother or sister of the individual (relatives in the third degree). Tex. Gov't Code § 573.023(c). Two individuals are considered to be related to each other by affinity if they are married to each other or the spouse of one of the individuals is related by consanguinity to the other individual. Tex. Gov't Code § 573.024(a). An individual's relatives within the third degree by affinity include: (1) such individual's spouse; (2) anyone related within the third degree by consanguinity to such individual's spouse; and (3) the spouse of anyone related to such individual within the third degree by consanguinity. Tex. Gov't Code § 573.025(a).

165 Tex. Prop. Code § 209.0057(c)(2)(A).

166 Tex. Prop. Code § 209.0057(c)(2)(B).

167 Tex. Prop. Code § 209.00594(c).

is expressly prohibited from disclosing to any other person how any particular individual voted.[168]

A Subdivision Association must complete a ballot recount and provide the result of the ballot recount to each Lot Owner who requested the ballot recount within thirty (30) days from the date the Subdivision Association received payment of the estimated cost of performing the ballot recount.[169] In addition, if the ballot recount changes the result of the Membership election or vote, then the Subdivision Association must reimburse the requesting Lot Owner for the cost of the ballot recount within thirty (30) days from the date the result of the ballot recount is provided to the requesting Lot Owner.[170]

Finally, Section 209.0057 also includes a safe harbor provision for any actions taken by the Board of Directors prior to a ballot recount that changes the results of the election. More specifically, any action taken by the Board of Directors during the period between the initial election vote tally and the completion of the ballot recount is not affected by the ballot recount, even if the ballot recount changes the results of the election.[171] In other words, any action taken by the Board of Directors prior to the completion of the ballot recount will remain valid even if the result of the ballot recount changes the outcome of a director-election.

5.15 Recording and Taping of a Membership Meeting

As with Board Meetings, it is not unlawful for a person attending or participating in a meeting of the Homeowners Association's Membership to record or tape such

168 Tex. Prop. Code § 209.00594(b-1). Notwithstanding, Section 209.00594 may not be construed to affect a person's obligation to comply with a court order for the release of ballots or other voting records. Tex. Prop. Code § 209.00594(d).

169 Tex. Prop. Code § 209.0057(d).

170 Tex. Prop. Code § 209.0057(d). If the recount does not change the results of the election or vote, the Subdivision Association is not required to reimburse the recount costs to the requesting Lot Owner.

171 Tex. Prop. Code § 209.0057(d).

meeting. There is no law in Texas that prohibits a person from openly, or even surreptitiously, recording verbal statements made in such person's presence. Accordingly, it is not unlawful for a person attending or participating in a Membership Meeting to record or tape such meeting with or without the knowledge of the other attendees or participants.

5.16 Minutes of a Membership Meeting

Texas Nonprofit Corporation HOAs and Texas Condominium Associations are required to keep minutes of the proceedings of its Membership.[172] In general, the term "minutes" refers to a record of the proceedings or meetings of a deliberative assembly, which is generally kept by the Secretary or other person performing the duties of Secretary for the assembly.[173] The minutes should contain mainly a record of what was done at the meeting, as opposed to what was said at the meeting by participants.[174]

There are no strict rules or procedures for creating minutes of a meeting. At a minimum, the minutes of a Membership Meeting should generally contain the following information:

(1) the identity of the assembly (i.e., the name of the Homeowners Association and whether it is a meeting of the Board of Directors or the Homeowners Association's Membership);

(2) the kind of meeting (i.e., whether it is an annual meeting, special meeting, or an adjournment of an annual or special meeting);

(3) the date and time of the meeting, and the location of the meeting if it is not always held at the same location;

(4) the fact that the regular presiding officer and Secretary were present, or in their absence, the names of the persons who substituted for them;

---

172 Tex. Bus. Org. Code § 3.151(a); Tex. Prop. Code § 82.114.

173 Robert's Rules of Order (10th Ed.) § 48.

174 Robert's Rules of Order (10th Ed.) § 48.

(5) the fact that a quorum was established;

(6) whether the minutes of the previous meeting were read and approved (as read, or as corrected) and the date of such previous meeting;

(7) all motions made before the assembly (except any that were withdrawn), stating:

(a) the identity of the person making such motion and of the person who seconded such motion;

(b) the specific wording of each motion that is put to the assembly or otherwise disposed of (i.e., each motion that is proposed, seconded, and voted on);

(c) the disposition of the motion (i.e., whether it was approved by the applicable voting requirement);

(d) the number of votes for and against such motion if the vote is not unanimous; and

(e) the identity of any participants who affirmatively abstained from voting, if applicable;

(8) in the case of an annual meeting of a Homeowners Association's Membership, the results from any election of Directors or other applicable positions; and

(9) the time of adjournment of the meeting.

CHAPTER 6 DUTIES AND OPERATION OF TEXAS HOMEOWNERS ASSOCIATIONS

CHAPTER 6 DUTIES AND OPERATION OF TEXAS HOMEOWNERS ASSOCIATIONS

6.1 Source and Scope of a Homeowners Association's Power and Authority

A Texas Homeowners Association is a creation of its Declaration, which in its simplest form constitutes a private contractual agreement establishing an organization of Homeowners to govern over their common-interest community and themselves. Homeowners Associations, unlike governmental entities, have no inherent authority to act or govern. Instead, a Texas Homeowners Association derives its power and authority from primarily its Declaration, which vests it with certain powers to manage the community, and also its Articles of Incorporation and Bylaws, which govern the manner in which it operates.

There is no standard-form Declaration for Texas Homeowners Associations, and the provisions of a Declaration will vary greatly from community to community. The scope of a Homeowners Association's power and authority can be very broad or very limited, or somewhere in between, but it will ultimately depend on the express provisions of the Homeowners Association's Governing Documents. Examples of powers generally granted to Texas Homeowners Associations by their Governing Documents include: the authority to enforce the Governing Documents; the power to levy and collect Assessments; the authority to maintain Common Areas or Common Elements; and the authority to purchase adequate insurance for the Common Areas or Common Elements.

In addition to a Homeowners Association's Governing Documents, Subdivision Associations in Harris, Galveston, and Montgomery counties and all Texas Condominium Associations are also vested with certain statutory powers by virtue of Chapter 204 of the Texas Property Code and the Texas Uniform Condominium Act. Such statutory powers are described in greater detail in the following subchapters.

6.1.1 Additional Powers and Authority Granted to Certain Subdivision Associations in Harris, Galveston, and Montgomery Counties under Chapter 204 of the Texas Property Code

Chapter 204 of the Texas Property Code vests certain enumerated powers in certain residential Subdivision Associations in Harris, Galveston, and Montgomery Counties, in addition to any other powers granted to such Subdivision Associations by their Governing Documents.[1] By its express terms, Chapter 204 applies only to a Subdivision Association that is incorporated as a nonprofit corporation and governs a residential Subdivision Development[2] that is located in whole or in part: (1) in a county with a population of 3.3 million or more (Harris County);[3] (2) in a county with a population of not less than 285,000 and not more than 300,000 that is adjacent to the Gulf of Mexico and that is adjacent to a county having a population of 3.3 million or more (Galveston County);[4] or (3) in a county with a population of 275,000 or more that is adjacent to a county with a population of 3.3 million or more and contains part of a national forest (Montgomery County).[5]

---

[1] *See* Senate Research Center, Bill Analysis, Tex. H.B. 2152, 74th Leg., R.S. (1995); Senate Research Center, Bill Analysis, Tex. H.B. 1632, 79th Leg., R.S. (2005) (amending Chapter 204 so as to extend its application to Subdivision Associations in Montgomery County).

[2] Tex. Prop. Code §§ 204.002(a); 204.003(a). Chapter 204 only applies to the residential portions of a Subdivision Development, and it expressly excludes application of its provisions to any portions of a Subdivision Development that are zoned for or that contain a commercial structure, an industrial structure, an apartment complex, or a Condominium Development. Tex. Prop. Code § 204.002(c).

[3] Tex. Prop. Code § 204.002(a)(1). The only Texas county with a population of 3.3 million or more is Harris County. Source: United States Census Bureau, 2010.

[4] Tex. Prop. Code § 204.002(a)(2). The only Texas county with a population of not less than 285,000 and not more than 300,000 that is adjacent to the Gulf of Mexico and a county with a population of 3.3 million or more is Galveston County. Prior to 2011, Section 204.002(a)(2) applied to counties with a population of 250,000 or more that that were adjacent to the Gulf of Mexico and a county having a population of 2.8 million or more, which included both Brazoria and Galveston Counties. Section 204.002(a)(2) was amended by the Texas Legislature in 2011 to make it applicable to only counties with a population between 285,000 and 300,000, which now excludes Brazoria County (pop. 313,166) from its application. Source: United States Census Bureau, 2010.

[5] Tex. Prop. Code § 204.002(a)(3). The only Texas county with a population of 275,000 or more that is adjacent to a county with a population of 3.3 million or more and contains part of a national forest is Montgomery County (Sam Houston National Forest). Source: United States Census Bureau, 2010.

For those residential Subdivision Associations located in Harris, Galveston, and/or Montgomery Counties that are nonprofit corporations, Chapter 204 of the Texas Property Code vests such Subdivision Associations with certain enumerated powers in addition to any other powers granted under their Governing Documents.[6] Pursuant to Chapter 204, and unless otherwise provided by such Subdivision Associations' Declaration, Articles of Incorporation, or Bylaws, such Subdivision Associations, acting through their Board of Directors or trustees, are vested with the authority to perform the following actions:

(1) adopt and amend Bylaws;[7]

(2) adopt and amend budgets for revenues, expenditures, and reserves and collect regular Assessments or special Assessments for Common Expenses from Lot Owners;[8]

(3) hire and terminate managing agents and other employees, agents, and independent contractors;[9]

(4) institute, defend, intervene in, settle, or compromise litigation or administrative proceedings on matters affecting the Subdivision Development;[10]

(5) make contracts and incur liabilities relating to the operation of the Subdivision Development and the Subdivision Association;[11]

(6) regulate the use, maintenance, repair, replacement, modification, and appearance of the Subdivision Development;[12]

---

6 Tex. Prop. Code § 204.010(b).

7 Tex. Prop. Code § 204.010(a)(1).

8 Tex. Prop. Code § 204.010(a)(2).

9 Tex. Prop. Code § 204.010(a)(3).

10 Tex. Prop. Code § 204.010(a)(4).

11 Tex. Prop. Code § 204.010(a)(5).

12 Tex. Prop. Code § 204.010(a)(6).

(7) make additional improvements to be included as a part of the Common Area in the Subdivision Development;[13]

(8) grant easements, leases, licenses, and concessions through or over the Common Areas in the Subdivision Development;[14]

(9) impose and receive payments, fees, or charges for the use, rental, or operation of the Common Areas in the Subdivision Development and for services provided to the Lot Owners;[15]

(10) impose interest, late charges, and, if applicable, returned check charges for late payments of regular Assessments or special Assessments;[16]

(11) if a notice and an opportunity to be heard are given to an applicable Lot Owner, the Subdivision Association may collect reimbursement of actual attorneys fees and other reasonable costs incurred by the Subdivision Association relating to violations of the Subdivision Development's Declaration or its Bylaws and Rules by such Lot Owner;[17]

(12) charge costs to a Lot Owner's Assessment account and collect the costs in any manner provided in the Declaration for the Subdivision Development for the collection of Assessments;[18]

(13) adopt and amend rules regulating the collection of delinquent Assessments and the application of payments;[19]

(14) impose reasonable charges for preparing, recording, or copying amendments to the Declaration, Resale Certificates, or statements of unpaid Assessments;[20]

---

[13] Tex. Prop. Code § 204.010(a)(7).

[14] Tex. Prop. Code § 204.010(a)(8).

[15] Tex. Prop. Code § 204.010(a)(9).

[16] Tex. Prop. Code § 204.010(a)(10).

[17] Tex. Prop. Code § 204.010(a)(11).

[18] Tex. Prop. Code § 204.010(a)(12).

[19] Tex. Prop. Code § 204.010(a)(13).

[20] Tex. Prop. Code § 204.010(a)(14).

(15) purchase insurance and fidelity bonds, including Directors and Officers' liability insurance, that the Board of Directors considers appropriate or necessary;[21]

(16) if the Declaration allows for an annual increase in the maximum regular Assessment without a vote of the Subdivision Association's Membership, then the Subdivision Association may assess such increase in the amount of regular Assessments annually or may accumulate such increases over a period of years without raising the amount of regular Assessments and then assess the accumulated increase in the amount of regular Assessments after a number of years at one time;[22]

(17) subject to the requirements of the Texas Nonprofit Corporation Law, by majority vote of its Board of Directors, a Subdivision Association may indemnify a Director or Officer of such Subdivision Association who was, is, or may be made a named defendant or respondent in a proceeding because the person is or was a Director;[23]

(18) exercise all other powers conferred on the Subdivision Association by its Declaration, Articles of Incorporation, or Bylaws;[24]

(19) exercise all other powers that may be exercised by a Texas nonprofit corporation;[25]

(20) exercise any other powers necessary and proper for the governance and operation of the Subdivision Association;[26] and

(21) if the Declaration vests architectural control authority in a residential Subdivision Association located in Harris, Galveston, and/or Montgomery Counties, or if such authority is vested in such a Subdivision Association pursuant to Chapter 204 of the Texas Property Code, then the Subdivision Association may also implement written architectural control guidelines for its own use or record such guidelines in the Official Public Records of the applicable county in which it is located, and it may

---

21 Tex. Prop. Code § 204.010(a)(15).

22 Tex. Prop. Code § 204.010(a)(16).

23 Tex. Prop. Code § 204.010(a)(17).

24 Tex. Prop. Code § 204.010(a)(19).

25 Tex. Prop. Code § 204.010(a)(20).

26 Tex. Prop. Code § 204.010(a)(21).

modify such guidelines as the needs of the Subdivision Development change.[27]

6.1.2 Additional Powers and Authority Granted to Condominium Associations under the Texas Uniform Condominium Act

In most cases, the Condominium Declaration will specify the powers of the Condominium Association. In addition to the powers and authority granted to a Condominium Association by its Condominium Declaration and/or other Governing Documents, Texas Condominium Associations are also vested with certain statutory powers by the Texas Uniform Condominium Act. The scope of such powers, however, depends on whether the Condominium Development is subject to the Texas Uniform Condominium Act or its predecessor, the Texas Condominium Act.[28]

[27] Tex. Prop. Code § 204.010(a)(18). Under Section 204.011 of the Texas Property Code, unless the Declaration applicable to a residential Subdivision Development in Harris, Galveston, or Montgomery Counties vests the architectural control authority for the Subdivision Development in the Subdivision Association before the occurrence of any of the following events, such architectural control authority automatically vests in the Subdivision Association upon the earliest occurrence of any one of such events: (1) the term of the architectural control authority expires pursuant to the terms of the Declaration; (2) a residence on the last available building site is completed and sold; (3) the person or entity designated as the architectural control in the Declaration assigns, in writing, the architectural control authority to the Subdivision Association; or (4) an assignee of the original holder abandons its architectural control authority for more than one year. Tex. Prop. Code § 204.011(b). In the event the architectural control authority is transferred to the Subdivision Association, such authority shall remain vested in the Subdivision Association until: (1) the Declaration is modified to reflect otherwise; (2) the Declaration is terminated; or (3) the Subdivision Association ceases to exist. Tex. Prop. Code § 204.011(c).

[28] In general, the Texas Condominium Act only applies to Condominium Developments created prior to January 1, 1994; while, the Texas Uniform Condominium Act applies to Condominium Developments created on or after January 1, 1994. Tex. Prop. Code §§ 81.0011; 82.002. In addition, the Texas Uniform Condominium Act also applies to a Condominium Development created prior to January 1, 1994 (instead of the Texas Condominium Act), if its Condominium Declaration states or has been amended to state that it is to be governed by the Texas Uniform Condominium Act. Tex. Prop. Code § 82.002(a). Notwithstanding, there are certain provisions of the Texas Uniform Condominium Act that apply to a Condominium Development created prior to January 1, 1994, that is governed by the Texas Condominium Act, so long as such applicable provisions of the Texas Uniform Condominium Act do not invalidate existing provisions of the Condominium Development's pre-1994 Condominium Declaration, Bylaws, or Plats and Plans. Tex. Prop. Code § 82.002(c).

6.1.2 (A) *General Powers of a Condominium Association*

In addition to those powers specifically granted to the Condominium Association in its Condominium Declaration, the Texas Uniform Condominium Act vests a Condominium Association with certain inherent powers, unless otherwise provided by its Condominium Declaration.[29] More specifically, unless otherwise provided by its Condominium Declaration, a Condominium Association, acting through its Board of Directors, may:[30]

(1) adopt and amend Bylaws;[31]

(2) adopt and amend budgets for revenues, expenditures, and reserves, and collect Assessments for Common Expenses from Unit Owners;[32]

(3) hire and terminate managing agents and other employees, agents, and independent contractors;[33]

(4) institute, defend, intervene in, settle, or compromise litigation or administrative proceedings in its own name on behalf of itself or two or more Unit Owners on matters affecting the Condominium Development;[34]

(5) make contracts and incur liabilities relating to the operation of the Condominium Development;[35]

---

29 Tex. Prop. Code § 82.102.

30 Only certain provisions of the Texas Uniform Condominium Act statute that establishes the powers of a Condominium Association (Section 82.102) are applicable to Condominium Developments created prior to January 1, 1994, that are subject to the Texas Condominium Act. Tex. Prop. Code § 82.002(c). The applicable provisions of Section 82.102 that apply to Condominium Associations subject to the Texas Condominium Act are Sections 82.102(a)(1)–(7), (a)(12)–(21) (f), and (g). Tex. Prop. Code §§ 82.002(c), 82.102. By process of elimination, Sections 82.102(a)(8)–(11), (b), (c), (d), and (e) of the Texas Property Code do not apply to Condominium Association subject to the Texas Condominium Act. Tex. Prop. Code §§ 82.002(c), 82.102.

31 Tex. Prop. Code § 82.102(a)(1).

32 Tex. Prop. Code § 82.102(a)(2).

33 Tex. Prop. Code § 82.102(a)(3).

34 Tex. Prop. Code § 82.102(a)(4).

35 Tex. Prop. Code § 82.102(a)(5).

(6) regulate the use, maintenance, repair, replacement, modification, and appearance of the Condominium Development;[36]

(7) adopt and amend Association Rules regulating the use, occupancy, leasing or sale, maintenance, repair, modification, and appearance of Units and Common Elements, to the extent the regulated actions affect Common Elements or other Units;[37]

(8) cause additional improvements to be made as a part of the Common Elements;[38]

(9) acquire, hold, encumber, and convey in its own name any right, title, or interest to real or personal property, except Common Elements of the Condominium Development;[39]

(10) grant easements, leases, licenses, and concessions through or over the Common Elements;[40]

(11) impose and receive payments, fees, or charges for the use, rental, or operation of the Common Elements and for services provided to Unit Owners;[41]

(12) impose interest and late charges for late payments of Assessments, returned check charges, and, if notice and an opportunity to be heard are given, reasonable fines for violations of the Condominium Declaration, Bylaws, and Association Rules of the Condominium Association;[42]

---

[36] Tex. Prop. Code § 82.102(a)(6).

[37] Tex. Prop. Code § 82.102(a)(7).

[38] Tex. Prop. Code § 82.102(a)(8). This particular provision is not applicable to Condominium Developments created prior to January 1, 1994, that are subject to the Texas Condominium Act. Tex. Prop. Code § 82.002(c).

[39] Tex. Prop. Code § 82.102(a)(9). This particular provision is not applicable to Condominium Developments created prior to January 1, 1994, that are subject to the Texas Condominium Act. Tex. Prop. Code § 82.002(c).

[40] Tex. Prop. Code § 82.102(a)(10). This particular provision is not applicable to Condominium Developments created prior to January 1, 1994, that are subject to the Texas Condominium Act. Tex. Prop. Code § 82.002(c).

[41] Tex. Prop. Code § 82.102(a)(11). This particular provision is not applicable to Condominium Developments created prior to January 1, 1994, that are subject to the Texas Condominium Act. Tex. Prop. Code § 82.002(c).

[42] Tex. Prop. Code § 82.102(a)(12). The notice and opportunity to be heard that must be given to a Unit Owner before imposing a fine must be provided to the Unit Owner in accordance with Section 82.102(d) of the Texas Property Code. Tex. Prop. Code § 82.102(a)(12). Section 82.102(d) of the Texas Property Code

(13) adopt and amend Association Rules regulating the collection of delinquent Assessments and the application of payments;[43]

(14) adopt and amend Association Rules regulating the termination of utility service to a Unit if the owner of such Unit is delinquent in the payment of an Assessment that is used, in whole or in part, to pay the cost of such utility service;[44]

(15) impose reasonable charges for preparing, recording, or copying Declaration amendments, Resale Certificates, or statements of unpaid Assessments;[45]

(16) enter a Unit for bona fide emergency purposes when conditions present an imminent risk of harm or damage to the Common Elements, another Unit, or the Unit's occupants;[46]

(17) suspend the voting privileges of or the use of certain General Common Elements by a Unit Owner delinquent for more than thirty (30) days in the payment of Assessments;[47]

(18) purchase insurance and fidelity bonds it considers appropriate or necessary;[48]

(19) exercise any other powers conferred on it by its Condominium Declaration or Bylaws;[49]

---

requires a Condominium Association, before it may assess a fine against a Unit Owner, to give the Unit Owner written notice that: (1) describes the violation and states the amount of the proposed fine; (2) advises the Unit Owner that he or she has thirty (30) days from the date of the notice to request a hearing before the Condominium Association's Board of Directors for the purpose of contesting the fine or damage charge; and (3) allows the Unit Owner a reasonable time, by a specified date, to cure the violation and avoid the fine, unless the Unit Owner was given notice and a reasonable opportunity to cure a similar violation within the preceding twelve (12) months. Tex. Prop. Code § 82.102(d).

[43] Tex. Prop. Code § 82.102(a)(13).

[44] Tex. Prop. Code § 82.102(a)(14).

[45] Tex. Prop. Code § 82.102(a)(15).

[46] Tex. Prop. Code § 82.102(a)(16).

[47] Tex. Prop. Code § 82.102(a)(17).

[48] Tex. Prop. Code § 82.102(a)(18).

[49] Tex. Prop. Code § 82.102(a)(19).

(20) exercise any other powers that may be exercised in the State of Texas by a corporation of the same type as the Condominium Association;[50] and

(21) exercise any other powers necessary and proper for the government and operation of the Condominium Association.[51]

6.1.2 (B) *Power of a Condominium Association to Borrow Money and to Assign Its Rights to Future Income and Lien Rights as Collateral for a Loan*

In 2013, the Texas Legislature amended the Texas Uniform Condominium Act so as to authorize a Condominium Association to borrow money and assign as collateral for the loan its right to future income and its lien rights.[52] In addition, unless a Condominium Association's Dedicatory Instruments require a vote of Unit Owners in order for the Condominium Association to borrow money or assign its right to future income or its lien rights as collateral for a loan, the Condominium Association (by resolution of its Board of Directors) may: (1) borrow money; and (2) assign as collateral for such loan the Condominium Association's right to future income, including the right to receive assessments, and its lien rights.[53]

If a Condominium Association's Dedicatory Instruments require a vote of Unit Owners in order for the Condominium Association to borrow money or to assign its right to future income or its lien rights as collateral for a loan, then the loan and/or assignment of its rights must be approved as provided by the applicable Dedicatory Instrument.[54]

---

50 Tex. Prop. Code § 82.102(a)(20).

51 Tex. Prop. Code § 82.102(a)(21).

52 Tex. Prop. Code § 82.102(f). *See also*, Senate Research Center, Bill Analysis, Tex. H.B. 2075, 83rd Leg., R.S. (2013).

53 Tex. Prop. Code § 82.102(f)-(g).

54 Tex. Prop. Code § 82.102(g). A vote of Unit Owners to authorize a Condominium Association to borrow money or to assign its right to future income or its lien rights as collateral for a loan must be approved by the requisite number or percentage of Unit Owners specified in the applicable Dedicatory Instrument or by the consent of Unit Owners holding sixty-seven percent (67%) of all voting interests in the Condominium Association, whichever is lower. Tex. Prop. Code § 82.102(g)

Notwithstanding, in the event that a loan and/or an assignment of a Condominium Association's rights as collateral for a loan must be approved by the Unit Owners, the Texas Uniform Condominium Act vests its Board of Directors with the authority to obtain such approval by a vote of the Unit Owners cast electronically, by absentee ballot, in person or by proxy at a meeting called for such purpose, or by written consent.[55]

6.1.2 (C) *Power of a Condominium Association to Evict or Collect Rents from a Unit Owner's Tenants*

The Texas Uniform Condominium Act also authorizes a Condominium Association to amend its Condominium Declaration to authorize the Board of Directors to: (1) bring an action to evict a tenant of a Unit Owner for the tenant's violation of the Condominium Declaration or the Condominium Association's Bylaws or Rules; (2) bring an action to evict a tenant of a Unit Owner who fails to pay the Condominium Association for the cost of repairs to Common Elements damaged substantially by the Unit Owner's tenant; or (3) collect rents from a tenant of a Unit Owner who is at least sixty (60) days delinquent in the payment of any amount due to the Condominium Association.[56]

6.1.2 (D) *Power of a Condominium Association to Sell Real Property in the Condominium Development*

The Texas Uniform Condominium Act also authorizes a Condominium Association, on behalf of the Unit Owners, to contract for the sale of real property in the Condominium Development.[57] Such contract, however, will not be binding on the Unit

---

[55] Tex. Prop. Code § 82.102(g).

[56] Tex. Prop. Code § 82.067(h). The provisions of the Texas Uniform Condominium Act concerning power of a Condominium Association to amend the Condominium Declaration to authorize the Board of Directors to evict a Unit Owner's tenant or to collect rents from a Unit Owner's tenant are not applicable to Condominium Developments created prior to January 1, 1994, that are subject to the Texas Condominium Act, and there are no comparable provisions under the Texas Condominium Act. Tex. Prop. Code § 82.002(c).

[57] Tex. Prop. Code § 82.068(c). The provisions of the Texas Uniform Condominium Act concerning power of a Condominium Association to sell real property in the Condominium Development are not applicable to Condominium Developments created prior to January 1, 1994, that are subject to the Texas Condominium Act, and there are no comparable provisions under the Texas Condominium Act. Tex. Prop. Code § 82.002(c).

Owners until it is approved by the agreement of the required percentage of votes specified in the Condominium Declaration for termination of the Condominium Development; or, if no such percentage of votes is specified in the Condominium Declaration, then by the agreement of: (1) one hundred percent (100%) of the Unit Owners to whom votes in the Condominium Association have been allocated; and (2) each holder of a deed of trust or vendor's lien on a Unit in the Condominium Development.[58] To be effective, such agreement must set forth the terms of the sale and, together with all the requisite ratifications, must be recorded in the Official Public Records of each county in which a portion of the Condominium Development is located.[59]

6.1.2 (E) *Power of a Condominium Association to Terminate Certain Contracts Without Penalty*

The Texas Uniform Condominium Act authorizes a Condominium Association in a residential or recreational Condominium Development to terminate, without penalty, contracts or leases between the Condominium Association and a Declarant or an "Affiliate of a Declarant" if: (1) the contract was entered into by the Condominium Association while it was controlled by the Declarant; (2) the Condominium Association terminates the contract or lease within one year from the date a Board of Directors elected by the Unit Owners takes office; and (3) the Condominium Association gives the other party to the contract or lease at least ninety (90) days notice of its intent to terminate the contract or lease.[60] The Texas Uniform Condominium Act defines an "Affiliate of a Declarant" as any person who controls, is controlled by, or is under common control with a Declarant.[61]

---

[58] Tex. Prop. Code § 82.068(a), (c).

[59] Tex. Prop. Code § 82.068(b), (c).

[60] Tex. Prop. Code § 82.105. The provisions of the Texas Uniform Condominium Act concerning the authority of a Condominium Association to terminate certain contracts without penalty are not applicable to Condominium Developments created prior to January 1, 1994, that are subject to the Texas Condominium Act, and there are no comparable provisions under the Texas Condominium Act. Tex. Prop. Code § 82.002(c).

[61] Tex. Prop. Code § 82.003(a)(1). The Texas Uniform Condominium Act further provides that a person or entity "controls" a Declarant if such person or entity: (1) is a general partner, officer, director, or employer of

6.1.3 Regulations on the Powers of a Condominium Association

The Texas Uniform Condominium Act also imposes certain regulations on the powers granted to a Condominium Association under a Condominium Declaration and the exercise of such power by the Condominium Association. First, the Condominium Declaration may not impose limitations on the power of the Condominium Association to deal with the Declarant that are more restrictive than the limitations imposed on the power of the Condominium Association to deal with other persons.[62] For example, a Condominium Declaration may not restrict the Condominium Association from enforcing Restrictive Covenants against Units owned by the Declarant.

Second, a Bylaw or Association Rule of a Condominium Association that is arbitrary or capricious is not enforceable.[63]

Third, the Texas Uniform Condominium Act imposes certain due process requirements on a Condominium Association before it may charge a Unit Owner for property damage for which the Unit Owner is liable or levy a fine against a Unit Owner

---

the Declarant; (2) directly or indirectly or acting in concert with one or more other persons or entities, or through one or more subsidiaries, owns, controls, holds with power to vote, or holds proxies representing more than twenty percent (20%) of the voting interests in the Declarant; (3) determines in any manner the election of a majority of the directors of the Declarant; or (4) has contributed more than twenty percent (20%) of the capital of the Declarant. Tex. Prop. Code § 82.003(a)(1). A person or entity "is controlled by" a Declarant if the Declarant: (1) is a general partner, officer, director, or employer of such person or entity; (2) directly or indirectly or acting in concert with one or more other persons or entities, or through one or more subsidiaries, owns, controls, holds with power to vote, or holds proxies representing more than twenty percent (20%) of the voting interests in such entity; (3) determines in any manner the election of a majority of the directors of such entity; or (4) has contributed more than twenty percent (20%) of the capital of such entity. Tex. Prop. Code § 82.003(a)(1).

62 Tex. Prop. Code § 82.102(b). The provisions of the Texas Uniform Condominium Act concerning prohibitions on Condominium Declaration provisions that impose limitations on the power of the Condominium Association to deal with the Declarant are not applicable to Condominium Developments created prior to January 1, 1994, that are subject to the Texas Condominium Act, and there are no comparable provisions under the Texas Condominium Act. Tex. Prop. Code § 82.002(c).

63 Tex. Prop. Code § 82.102(c). The provisions of the Texas Uniform Condominium Act concerning enforcement of Bylaws and Association Rules are not applicable to Condominium Developments created prior to January 1, 1994, that are subject to the Texas Condominium Act, and there are no comparable provisions under the Texas Condominium Act. Tex. Prop. Code § 82.002(c).

for violation of the Condominium Declaration, Bylaws, or Association Rules.[64] More specifically, before it may charge a Unit Owner for property damage or levy a fine against a Unit Owner, a Condominium Association must give the Unit Owner a written notice that: (1) describes the violation or property damage and states the amount of the proposed fine or damage charge; (2) advises the Unit Owner that he or she has thirty (30) days from the date of the notice to request a hearing before the Condominium Association's Board of Directors for the purpose of contesting the fine or damage charge; and (3) allows the Unit Owner a reasonable time, by a specified date, to cure the violation and avoid the fine, unless the Unit Owner was given notice and a reasonable opportunity to cure a similar violation within the preceding twelve (12) months.[65] The Condominium Association may deliver such written notice to a Unit Owner by giving a copy of it to any occupant of the Unit.[66] Additionally, if the Condominium Association levies a fine or damage charge, it must give notice of the levied fine or damage charge to the Unit Owner no later than thirty (30) days after the date of levying such fine.[67]

6.1.4 Limitations on a Subdivision Association's Ability to Transfer an Interest in its Accounts Receivables

In 2011, the Texas Legislature enacted Section 209.0064 of the Texas Property Code, which, among other things, prohibits a Texas Subdivision Association from selling or otherwise transferring any interest in its accounts receivables for a purpose other than as collateral for a loan.[68] In other words, irrespective of any power granted to it under its

---

64 Tex. Prop. Code § 82.102(d).

65 Tex. Prop. Code § 82.102(d).

66 Tex. Prop. Code § 82.102(e).

67 Tex. Prop. Code § 82.102(e). The provision of the Texas Uniform Condominium Act concerning the requirement that a Condominium Association give notice of an assessed fine or damage charge to the Unit Owner is not applicable to Condominium Developments created prior to January 1, 1994, that are subject to the Texas Condominium Act, and there are no comparable provisions under the Texas Condominium Act. Tex. Prop. Code § 82.002(c).

68 Tex. Prop. Code § 209.0064(e).

Governing Documents, a Subdivision Association may not sell a Lot Owner's delinquent Assessment account to a third party.[69]

6.2 Management of Homeowners Associations

The management of a Texas Homeowners Association is almost always vested in a Board of Directors. In addition to setting the policies of the Homeowners Association, the management duties of the Board of Directors include the management of the day-to-day operations of the Homeowners Association. In the case of a large community with substantial Common Areas or Common Elements, amenities, and capital improvements, such duties can be comparable to managing a small business. While a Board of Directors may not delegate its authority to make policy decisions concerning the Homeowners Association, it may, and often does, delegate the responsibility for management of day-to-day operations. The manner in which the management of day-to-day operations is delegated and/or carried out can generally be categorized as one of three types of management systems, although it is not uncommon for there to be some hybrid version of two or more of these forms of management.

6.2.1 Self-Management by the Board of Directors

One of the most common forms of management systems for Homeowners Associations is "self-management" by volunteer Homeowners serving on the Board of Directors or committees established by the Board of Directors. This type of management system is generally used by most small Homeowners Associations who either cannot afford to or simply prefer not to hire a professional management company. In a self-managed Homeowners Association, the volunteer Homeowners perform all of the tasks associated with the day-to-day operations of the Homeowners Association, including keeping the books and records of the Homeowners Association, sending invoices for

69 Texas Condominium Associations, on the other hand, are expressly authorized by the Texas Uniform Condominium Act to borrow money and assign their right to future income and lien rights as collateral for a loan. Tex. Prop. Code § 82.102(a)(17).

Assessments and meeting notices to Homeowners, contracting with service providers (such as landscapers, pool cleaners, etc.), and producing Resale Certificates, among other things.

The primary advantage to this "volunteer" form of self-management is the elimination of the costs of a professional management company or manager and/or salaries of supervisory staff. In addition, volunteer Homeowners are more knowledgeable about the needs and priorities of the community and will generally provide a higher level of personable management.

The major disadvantage to this form of management is the heavy demand placed on the time of volunteer Homeowners. In addition, inexperienced volunteers can potentially cause a Homeowners Association to incur monetary losses by failing to implement essential maintenance and accounting procedures that may have been second nature to a professional manager. Another issue that makes self-management sometimes less preferable is that it is sometimes necessary for a Homeowners Association to engage in collection efforts against Homeowners who have not paid their Assessments, which can put volunteers in the uncomfortable role of being a debt collector to their neighbors or make them targets of abusive conduct by such persons. Use of a professional management company offers a buffer between delinquent or offending Homeowners and the Board of Directors.

6.2.2 Self-Managed by an Employed Manager

In a "self-management by an employed manager" system, a property manager, who may be either a full-time resident or nonresident, is employed and paid by the Homeowners Association to implement Board policy and oversee the day-to-day operation of the Homeowners Association. The primary advantage of this alternative form of management is that it affords the Board of Directors some of the cost savings of volunteer management while providing a full-time employee who is responsible to the Board of Directors for the day-to-day implementation of the Board's policies.

The primary disadvantage is that a single employee generally lacks the full array of knowledge, skills, or experience to oversee all aspects of the operation of a Homeowners Association, and the manager may lack sufficient time to perform all of the supervisory functions for which he or she was hired. In addition, the Board of Directors takes on the additional duties associated with hiring and supervising an employee or employees, including all federal and state laws imposed on employers.

6.2.3 Management by an Independent Management Company

With a "management by an independent management company" system, the Board of Directors enters into a contract with an independent professional management organization to perform full management services for the Homeowners Association. Professional management companies usually employ a trained staff skilled in Association-Governed Community management, and most offer a broad range of management services, from bookkeeping to property maintenance to preparation of a proposed annual budget. This system of management is most common among large Homeowners Associations.

The primary advantages of a professional management company are that the management company's staff is usually very experienced in Association-Governed Community matters and it has the staff and resources to oversee all aspects of management on behalf of the Homeowners Association. In addition, a management company can often marshal the economies of scale to provide common services to all of the Homeowners Associations it manages at costs lower than what a single Homeowners Association could obtain on its own.

The major disadvantage of a professional management company is that it is typically the most expensive of the three management systems, although the additional costs associated with retaining a professional management company are sometimes mitigated by the savings resulting from more effective and efficient operations. In addition, property management companies generally do not provide the same level of individual attention to a Homeowners Association that would be paid by an employed manager who works solely for the Homeowners Association or Homeowners who self-manage their Homeowners Association.

6.3 Emergency Governance of Texas Nonprofit Corporation HOAs

In 2009, the Texas Legislature established certain procedures that a Nonprofit Corporation HOA may adopt so as to provide for its governance during an emergency.[70] More specifically, except as otherwise provided by its Articles of Incorporation and Bylaws, the Board of Directors or Membership of a Nonprofit Corporation HOA may adopt provisions in the Nonprofit Corporation HOA's Articles of Incorporation or Bylaws regarding the management of the Nonprofit Corporation HOA during an emergency, including provisions that: (1) prescribe procedures for calling a meeting of the Board of Directors; (2) establish minimum requirements for participation at the Board Meeting; and (3) designate additional or substitute Directors.[71] To the extent such emergency governance provisions are adopted, they will take effect only in the event of an emergency and will terminate once the emergency ends.[72] In addition, all other provisions of a Nonprofit Corporation HOA's Articles of Incorporation and Bylaws that are consistent with the emergency governance provisions remain in effect during the emergency.[73]

---

[70] Tex. Bus. Org. Code § 3.252. For purposes of such statute, an "emergency" exists if a majority of the Nonprofit Corporation HOA's Board of Directors cannot readily participate in a Board Meeting because of the occurrence of a catastrophic event. Tex. Bus. Org. Code § 3.251.

[71] Tex. Bus. Org. Code § 3.252(a).

[72] Tex. Bus. Org. Code § 3.253.

[73] Tex. Bus. Org. Code § 3.254.

Any such emergency governance provisions must be adopted in accordance with the requirements of the Nonprofit Corporation HOA's Articles of Incorporation or Bylaws and any other applicable provisions of the Texas Nonprofit Corporation Law.[74] In addition, any actions taken by a Nonprofit Corporation HOA in good faith and in accordance with the emergency governance provisions in its Articles of Incorporation or Bylaws are binding upon the Nonprofit Corporation HOA and may not be used to impose liability on a managerial official, employee, or agent of the Nonprofit Corporation HOA.[75]

6.4 Management Certificates

Regardless of the type of management system that is employed, all Texas Homeowners Associations are required to record a Management Certificate in the Official Public Records of each county in which any portion of its residential Development is located.[76] The Management Certificate must be signed and acknowledged by an Officer of the Homeowners Association (or if it is a Subdivision Association, either an Officer or a managing agent) and must identify the following information:

(1) the name of the Subdivision or Condominium Development;[77]

(2) the name of the Subdivision or Condominium Association;[78]

(3) if it is a Subdivision Development, the recording data for the Subdivision Plat creating the Subdivision Development;[79]

(4) the recording data for the Declaration applicable to the Subdivision or Condominium Development;[80]

---

74 Tex. Bus. Org. Code § 3.252(b).

75 Tex. Bus. Org. Code § 3.255.

76 Tex. Prop. Code §§ 82.116(a), 209.004(a).

77 Tex. Prop. Code §§ 82.116(a)(1), 209.004(a)(1).

78 Tex. Prop. Code §§ 82.116(a)(2), 209.004(a)(2).

79 Tex. Prop. Code §§ 82.116(a)(3), 209.004(a)(3).

80 Tex. Prop. Code §§ 82.116(a)(4), 209.004(a)(4).

(5) the name and mailing address of the Subdivision or Condominium Association;[81]

(6) the name and mailing address of the person managing the Subdivision or Condominium Association or its designated representative;[82] and

(7) any other information the Subdivision or Condominium Association considers appropriate.[83]

In addition, all Texas Homeowners Associations must also record an amended Management Certificate within thirty (30) days from the date the Homeowners Association has notice of a change in any information stated in a previously recorded Management Certificate.[84] If a Homeowners Association fails to timely file an amended Management Certificate, so long as the delay or failure to record such amended Management Certificate was not willful or caused by gross negligence, the Homeowners Association and its Officers, Directors, employees, and agents are not subject to liability to any person for such delay or omission.[85]

The failure to file a Management Certificate may, however, affect a Subdivision Association's ability to collect delinquent Assessments owed by a Lot Owner. Section 209.004 of the Texas Property Code imposes certain limitations on the ability of a Subdivision Association to collect unpaid Assessments from a delinquent Lot Owner when he or she goes to sell his or her Lot or to enforce a pre-sale claim against the new owner of a Lot for unpaid Assessments if the Subdivision Association has not recorded a Management Certificate or a requisite amended Management Certificate.[86] Pursuant to

---

[81] Tex. Prop. Code §§ 82.116(a)(5), 209.004(a)(5).

[82] Tex. Prop. Code §§ 82.116(a)(5), 209.004(a)(6).

[83] Tex. Prop. Code §§ 82.116(a)(6), 209.004(a)(7).

[84] Tex. Prop. Code §§ 82.116(b), 209.004(b).

[85] Tex. Prop. Code §§ 82.116(c), 209.004(c).

[86] *See* Tex. Prop. Code § 209.004(d)–(e). Sections 209.004(d) and 209.004(e) of the Texas Property Code were enacted by the Texas Legislature in 2009 and apply to any conveyance of a Lot after September 1, 2009.

Section 209.004, if a Subdivision Association has not recorded a Management Certificate or a requisite amended Management Certificate, and a Lot for which Assessments have not been paid is being purchased by a "bona fide purchaser," then neither such purchaser, his or her lender, nor the title insurance company involved in such purchase is liable to the Subdivision Association for any amount due the Subdivision Association by the prior owner of such Lot as of the date ownership of such Lot is transferred to the purchaser.[87] In addition, neither such bona fide purchaser, his or her lender, and/or the title insurance company is liable for any debt to or claim of the Subdivision Association regarding such Lot that accrued before the date ownership of such Lot is transferred to the bona fide purchaser.[88]

6.5 Recording and Online Publication of Dedicatory Instruments

Chapter 202 of the Texas Property Code, which applies to both Subdivision and Condominium Associations, requires a Homeowners Association to record all "Dedicatory Instruments" applicable to it in the Official Public Records of each county in which a portion of its Development is located.[89] Chapter 202 defines the term "Dedicatory Instrument" as any document governing the establishment, maintenance, or operation of a residential Subdivision Development, Condominium Development, or any similar planned development, including a Declaration or similar written instrument subjecting

---

87 Tex. Prop. Code § 209.004(d)(1). In such event, the Subdivision Association's Assessment Lien is also unenforceable against the transferred Lot for any amount owed to the Subdivision Association by the prior Lot Owner as of the date ownership is transferred to such bona fide purchaser. Tex. Prop. Code § 209.004(e). For purposes of Sections 209.004(d) and 209.004(e), a "bona fide purchaser" means: (1) a person who pays valuable consideration for the Lot, has no notice of the outstanding rights of others, and is acting in good faith; or (2) a third-party lender who acquired a security interest in the Lot under a Deed of Trust Lien. Tex. Prop. Code § 209.004(f).

88 Tex. Prop. Code § 209.004(d)(2). Section 209.004(d)(2) expressly waives any "claims" of a Subdivision Association that fails to record a Management Certificate or amended Management Certificate that accrued prior to the date ownership of the Lot transferred to a bona fide purchaser. Tex. Prop. Code § 209.004(d)(2). Such language could be interpreted by a court to include claims for restrictive covenant violations that preexisted the transfer of ownership of such Lot.

89 Tex. Prop. Code §§ 202.001, 202.006.

real property to Restrictive Covenants, Bylaws, Association Rules, or similar instrument governing the administration or operation of a Homeowners Association, as well as all lawful amendments to such documents.[90] In addition, pursuant to a 2011 amendment to Section 202.006 of the Texas Property Code, a Dedicatory Instrument has no effect and is considered unenforceable until a copy of it is recorded in the Official Public Records of each applicable county.[91] In other words, a Homeowners Association cannot enforce the provisions of any Dedicatory Instrument that has not been recorded in the local Official Public Records.

In addition to recording a copy of all Dedicatory Instruments, Section 207.006 of the Texas Property Code requires all Texas Subdivision Associations to also make copies of their recorded Dedicatory Instruments available on a website if the Subdivision Association has, or a management company on behalf of the Subdivision Association maintains, a publicly accessible website.[92] Thus, in addition to recording copies of its Dedicatory Instruments, a Subdivision Association must also publish copies of its recorded Dedicatory Instruments online if it, or a management company on its behalf, maintains an internet website that is accessible by the public.[93]

6.6 Adoption and Recording of a Payment Plan Guidelines Policy by Subdivision Associations

In 2011, the Texas Legislature enacted Section 209.0062 of the Texas Property Code, which requires the Board of Directors of every Texas Subdivision Association composed of at least fifteen lots to adopt a "Payment Plan Guidelines Policy" that

---

[90] Tex. Prop. Code § 202.001(1). It is important to note, while the term "Dedicatory Instrument" includes a Declaration or other written instrument that makes a Subdivision or Condominium Development subject to a Homeowners Association's Bylaws, a 2014 Texas appellate case law opinion concluded that such term may not include the Bylaws itself. *See Storck v. Tres Lagos Property Owners Ass'n, Inc.*, 442 S.W.3d 730, 738 (Tex. App.—Texarkana 2014, pet. Denied).

[91] Tex. Prop. Code § 202.006.

[92] Tex. Prop. Code § 202.006.

[93] Tex. Prop. Code § 207.006.

establishes an alternative payment schedule by which a Lot Owner may make partial payments to the Subdivision Association for delinquent regular or special Assessments or any other amount owed to the Subdivision Association without accruing additional monetary penalties.[94] A Payment Plan Guidelines Policy is considered to be a Dedicatory Instrument and must be recorded in the Official Public Records of each county in which the applicable Subdivision Development is located.[95]

A Subdivision Association's Payment Plan Guidelines Policy may establish one or more payment plans, but the minimum term for a payment plan established by a Subdivision Association's Payment Plan Guidelines Policy may not be less than three (3) months.[96] In addition, a Subdivision Association is not required to allow a payment plan for any amount that extends more than eighteen (18) months from the date of the Lot Owner's request for a payment plan.[97]

Notwithstanding, a Subdivision Association is not required to make a payment plan available to a Lot Owner if the Lot Owner fails to request a payment plan before the expiration of the cure period specified in a written notice under Section 209.0064(b) of the Texas Property Code.[98] In addition, a Subdivision Association is not required to allow

---

94 Tex. Prop. Code § 209.0062(a). For purposes of Section 209.0062, monetary penalties do not include reasonable costs associated with administering a payment plan or interest. Tex. Prop. Code § 209.0062(a). Section 209.0062 does not apply to Condominium Associations. Tex. Prop. Code § 209.003(d).

95 Tex. Prop. Code § 209.0062(d). A Subdivision Association's failure to record a Payment Plan Guidelines Policy does not prohibit it from entering into a payment plan with a Lot Owner for payment of delinquent regular or special assessments or any other amount owed to the Subdivision Association without accruing additional monetary penalties. Tex. Prop. Code § 209.0062(e).

96 Tex. Prop. Code § 209.0062(b).

97 Tex. Prop. Code § 209.0062(c).

98 Tex. Prop. Code § 209.0062(c). Before a Subdivision Association may hold a delinquent Lot Owner liable for the fees of a Collection Agent, Section 209.0064(b) of the Texas Property Code requires the Subdivision Association to give the Lot Owner a written notice by certified mail that: (1) specifies each delinquent amount owed by the Lot Owner and the total amount of the payment required by the Lot Owner to make his or her account current; (2) describes the options the Lot Owner has to avoid having the account turned over to a Collection Agent, including information regarding availability of a payment plan under the Subdivision Association's Payment Plan Guidelines Policy, if applicable; and (3) provides the Lot Owner a period of at

a Lot Owner to enter into a payment plan more than once in any twelve-month period.[99] Finally, a Subdivision Association is not required to enter into a payment plan with a Lot Owner who failed to honor the terms of a previous payment plan during the two (2) years following the Lot Owner's default under such previous payment plan.[100]

6.7 Adoption and Recording of a Records Production and Copying Policy by Subdivision Associations

In 2011, the Texas Legislature enacted extensive amendments to Section 209.005 of the Texas Property Code, which governs the rights of Lot Owners to inspect and copy the records of a Subdivision Association. Such amendments to Section 209.005 established new procedures for Lot Owners to request inspection and/or copies of a Subdivision Association's records and that require the Subdivision Association to make copies of and deliver such records to a requesting Lot Owner.[101]

The 2011 amendments to Section 209.005 also authorize Texas Subdivision Associations to charge a requesting Lot Owner or other designated representative for the costs of compilation, production, and reproduction of requested information and records and require all Texas Subdivision Associations to adopt a "Records Production and Copying Policy" that prescribes the costs that each such Subdivision Association will charge for the compilation, production, and reproduction of requested information and records.[102] A Records Production and Copying Policy is considered to be a Dedicatory Instrument and must be recorded in the Official Public Records of each county in which

---

least thirty (30) days to cure the delinquency before further collection action may be taken by the Subdivision Association or a Collection Agent retained by it. Tex. Prop. Code § 209.0064(b).

[99] Tex. Prop. Code § 209.0062(c).

[100] Tex. Prop. Code § 209.0062(c). In other words, if a Lot Owner fails to comply with the terms of a payment plan, he or she is not entitled to another payment plan to pay off delinquent Assessments for two (2) years following such Lot Owner's default of the payment plan.

[101] Tex. Prop. Code § 209.005.

[102] Tex. Prop. Code § 209.005(i).

the applicable Subdivision Development is located.[103] In addition, a Subdivision Association may not charge a Lot Owner for the cost of compilation, production, or reproduction of requested information and records under the procedures set forth under Section 209.005 of the Texas Property Code until a Records Production and Copying Policy prescribing such costs has been recorded in the local Official Public Records.[104]

The prescribed charges under a Records Production and Copying Policy may include all reasonable costs of materials, labor, and overhead incurred in the compilation, production, or reproduction of requested information and records, but such costs may not exceed the maximum amount allowed for such item under Texas Administrative Code Title 1, Section 70.3.[105] A sampling of the maximum amounts allowed by Texas Administrative Code Title 1, Section 70.3 for compilation, production, and reproduction of requested information and records (as of January 1, 2012) is as follows:

Standard Paper Copy Charges:

Standard paper copy charges consist of the charges for reproducing requested information and records on standard size paper by means of an office machine copier or a computer printer.[106] The maximum amount that a Subdivision Association may charge a requesting party for standard paper copies of requested information and records is ten

103 Tex. Prop. Code §§ 202.006, 209.005(i).

104 Tex. Prop. Code § 209.005(i).

105 Tex. Prop. Code § 209.005(i). Texas Administrative Code Title 1, Section 70.3 sets forth the maximum amounts a governmental entity in Texas may charge for providing copies of public information to a requesting party and is based on the estimated average costs to governmental entities across Texas associated with providing copies of public information. 1 T.A.C. Section 70.3(a). Such charges are subject to periodic reevaluation and update. 1 T.A.C. Section 70.3(m). Texas Administrative Code Title 1, Section 70.3 was last amended on February 22, 2007. 1 T.A.C. Section 70.3.

106 1 T.A.C. Section 70.3(b)(1).

cents (10¢) per page or part of a page. In addition, each side of a document that has recorded information is considered to be a separate page.[107]

Nonstandard Copy Charges:

Nonstandard copy charges consist of charges for the costs of materials, other than standard size paper, onto which requested information and records are copied.[108] The maximum amount that a Subdivision Association may charge a requesting party for nonstandard copies (excluding any applicable additional charges that may be associated with a particular request, such as labor or overhead charges) are:[109]

(1)	diskette:	$1.00;
(2)	magnetic tape:	actual cost;
(3)	data cartridge:	actual cost;
(4)	tape cartridge:	actual cost;
(5)	CD:	$1.00;
(6)	DVD:	$3.00;
(7)	JAZ drive:	actual cost;
(8)	other electronic media:	actual cost;
(9)	VHS video cassette:	$2.50;
(10)	audio cassette:	$1.00;
(11)	oversize paper copy:	$.50; and
(12)	specialty paper:	actual cost.

[107] 1 T.A.C. Section 70.3(b)(1).

[108] 1 T.A.C. Section 70.3(b)(2).

[109] 1 T.A.C. Section 70.3(b)(2).

Labor Charges:

Labor charges consist of the labor costs incurred in processing a request for information or records. Such labor costs may include the actual time to locate, compile, manipulate data, and reproduce the requested information or record.[110] The maximum amount that a Subdivision Association may charge a requesting party for labor charges is fifteen dollars ($15.00) per hour.[111]

Overhead Charges:

Whenever a labor charge is incurred in processing a request for information or records, a Subdivision Association may also charge a requesting party for any other direct and indirect costs incurred in processing a request for information, including an overhead charge to cover such costs as depreciation of capital assets, rent, maintenance and repair, utilities, and administrative overhead.[112] An overhead charge is computed at twenty percent (20%) of the labor charge made to cover any labor costs associated with a particular request.[113] By way of example, if one hour of labor is expended in processing a particular request for information, then the overhead charge would be $3.00 ($15.00 for one hour of labor multiplied by 20% or .20).

Miscellaneous Supplies Charges:

A Subdivision Association may also charge a requesting party for the actual cost of miscellaneous supplies, such as labels, boxes, and other supplies, used to produce the requested information to such party.[114]

---

110 1 T.A.C. Section 70.3(d).

111 1 T.A.C. Section 70.3(d).

112 1 T.A.C. Section 70.3(e). Overhead charges are in addition to the specific labor charge. 1 T.A.C. Section 70.3(e).

113 1 T.A.C. Section 70.3(e).

114 1 T.A.C. Section 70.3(i).

Postal and Shipping Charges:

A Subdivision Association may also charge a requesting party for any related postal or shipping expenses that are necessary to transmit the reproduced information to such party.[115]

6.8 Adoption and Recording of a Document Retention Policy by Subdivision Associations

In 2011, the Texas Legislature enacted Section 209.005(m) of the Texas Property Code, which requires Texas Subdivision Associations composed of at least fifteen Lots to adopt and comply with a "Document Retention Policy."[116] A Document Retention Policy adopted by a Subdivision Association in compliance with Section 209.005(m) is considered to be a Dedicatory Instrument and must be recorded in the Official Public Records of each county in which its Subdivision Development is located.[117]

At a minimum, a Subdivision Association's Document Retention Policy must comply with the following retention requirements:

(1) a Subdivision Association's Certificate of Formation (formerly called Articles of Incorporation), Bylaws, Declarations (and all other restrictive covenants), and all amendments to the Certificates of Formation, Bylaws, and Declarations must be retained permanently;[118]

(2) a Subdivision Association's financial books and records must be retained for at least seven (7) years;[119]

---

115 1 T.A.C. Section 70.3(j).

116 Tex. Prop. Code § 209.005(m). A Document Retention Policy is an internal policy that outlines the length of time for which an organization will keep certain documents and records, after which such documents may be destroyed or discarded.

117 Tex. Prop. Code § 202.006.

118 Tex. Prop. Code § 209.005(m)(1).

119 Tex. Prop. Code § 209.005(m)(2).

(3) a Subdivision Association's account records of current Lot Owners must be retained for at least five (5) years;[120]

(4) copies of all contracts entered into by a Subdivision Association with a term of one year or more must be retained for at least four (4) years after the expiration of the applicable contract term;[121]

(5) minutes from all meetings of a Subdivision Association's Board of Directors and Membership must be retained for at least seven (7) years;[122] and

(6) a Subdivision Association's tax returns and audit records must be retained for at least seven (7) years.[123]

6.9 Contracts Between a Subdivision Association and a Current Director, Relative of a Current Director, or Company Owned by a Current Director

Chapter 209 of the Texas Property Code imposes certain procedural due process requirements that must be complied with before a Texas Subdivision Association may enter into a contract with a current Director, a person "related to" a current Director, or a company "owned by" a current Director or by a person related to a current Director.[124]

---

120 Tex. Prop. Code § 209.005(m)(3).

121 Tex. Prop. Code § 209.005(m)(4).

122 Tex. Prop. Code § 209.005(m)(5). Though the minutes from meetings of a Subdivision Association's Board of Directors and Membership must only be retained for seven (7) years, it is recommended that such minutes be retained permanently because the minutes serve as a record of all official actions taken by the Board of Directors and Membership and may be necessary to confirm that certain actions were properly approved years after the fact.

123 Tex. Prop. Code § 209.005(m)(6).

124 Tex. Prop. Code § 209.0052. For purposes of Section 209.0052 of the Texas Property Code, a person is considered "related to" a current Director if he or she is related to a current Director within the third degree by consanguinity or affinity, as determined under Chapter 573 of the Texas Government Code. Tex. Prop. Code § 209.0052(b). Two individuals are considered to be related to each other by consanguinity if one is a descendant of the other or they share a common ancestor. Tex. Gov't Code § 573.022(a). An individual's relatives within the third degree by consanguinity include such individual's: (1) parents and children (relatives in the first degree); (2) brothers, sisters, grandparents, and grandchildren (relatives in the second degree); and (3) great-grandparents, great-grandchildren, aunts who are a sister of a parent of the individual, uncles who are a brother of a parent of the individual, nephews who are a child of a brother or sister of the individual, and nieces who are a child of a brother or sister of the individual (relatives in the third degree). Tex. Gov't Code § 573.023(c). Two individuals are considered to be related to each other by affinity if they are married to each other or the spouse of one of the individuals is related by consanguinity to the other individual. Tex. Gov't Code § 573.024(a). An individual's relatives within the third degree by affinity include: (1) such individual's spouse; (2) anyone related within the third degree by consanguinity to such individual's spouse; and (3) the

More specifically, Section 209.0052 of the Texas Property Code provides that a Subdivision Association may enter into an enforceable contract with such an interested Director, relative, or company only if the following conditions are satisfied:[125]

(1) the interested Director, relative, or company bids on the proposed contract and the Subdivision Association has received at least two other bids for the contract from persons not associated with the interested Director, relative, or company, if reasonably available in the community;[126]

(2) the interested Director:

  (a) is not given access to the other bids;

  (b) does not participate in any discussion by the Board of Directors regarding the contract; and

  (c) does not vote on the award of the contract;[127]

(3) the material facts regarding the relationship or interest with respect to the proposed contract are disclosed to or known by the Board of Directors, and the Board of Directors, in good faith and with ordinary care, authorizes the contract by an affirmative vote of the majority of the non-interested Directors;[128] and

---

spouse of anyone related to such individual within the third degree by consanguinity. Tex. Gov't Code § 573.025(a). For purposes of Section 209.0052 of the Texas Property Code, a company is considered "owned by" a current Director or a person related to a current Director, if a current Director or a person related to a current Director within the third degree by consanguinity or affinity has a financial interest in at least fifty-one percent (51%) of the company's profits. Tex. Prop. Code § 209.0052(b).

[125] It is important to note that Section 209.0052 of the Texas Property Code does not apply to a contract entered into by a Subdivision Association during an applicable Subdivision Development's "Development Period." Tex. Prop. Code § 209.0052(a). Chapter 209 of the Texas Property Code defines "Development Period" as a period of time stated in a Subdivision Association's Declaration during which a Declarant reserves a right to facilitate the development, construction, and marketing of the Subdivision Development, or a right to direct the size, shape, and composition of the Subdivision Development. Tex. Prop. Code § 209.002(4-a). In addition, Section 209.0052 only applies to contacts entered into by a Subdivision Association on or after September 1, 2013. *See* Tex. H.B. 503, 83rd Leg., R.S. (2013).

[126] Tex. Prop. Code § 209.0052(b)(1).

[127] Tex. Prop. Code § 209.0052(b)(2).

[128] Tex. Prop. Code § 209.0052(b)(3).

(4) the Board of Directors certifies (by a resolution approved by an affirmative vote of the majority of the non-interested Directors) that the other requirements of Section 209.0052 have been satisfied.[129]

6.10 Resale Certificates

All Texas Homeowners Associations are required to issue a Resale Certificate upon request by a Lot or Unit Owner for the purpose of selling such owner's Lot or Unit.[130] The requisite procedures for promulgating a Resale Certificate and the information required to be included in a Resale Certificate, however, differ significantly between Subdivision and Condominium Associations.[131] Such procedures are described in greater detail in the following subchapters.

6.10.1 Production of Subdivision Information and Resale Certificates by a Subdivision Association

Within ten (10) business days from the date a Subdivision Association receives a written request for "Subdivision Information" from a Lot Owner, a Lot Owner's agent, a potential purchaser of a Lot in the Subdivision Development or such purchaser's agent, or a title insurance company acting on behalf of a Lot Owner or purported purchaser, the Subdivision Association must deliver to such requesting party the following documents and information: (1) a current copy of all Declarations and Restrictive Covenants

---

[129] Tex. Prop. Code § 209.0052(b)(4). In other words, the resolution must certify that: (1) the Subdivision Association received at least two other bids for the contract from persons not associated with the interested Director, relative, or company, or state that two other bids from non-interested parties were not reasonably available in the community; (2) the interested Director was not given access to the other bids (if any), did not participate in any discussion by the Board of Directors regarding the contract, and did not vote on the award of the contract; and (3) the material facts regarding the relationship or interest with respect to the proposed contract was disclosed to or known by the Board of Directors, and the Board of Directors, in good faith and with ordinary care, approved the awarding of the contract to the interested Director, relative, or company by an affirmative vote of the majority of the non-interested Directors.

[130] Tex. Prop. Code §§ 82.157, 207.003. Section 82.157 of the Texas Uniform Condominium Act applies to all Condominium Developments, regardless of when they were created. Tex. Prop. Code § 82.002(c). Chapter 207 of the Texas Property Code applies to all residential Subdivision Developments with a Subdivision Association that is entitled to levy regular or special Assessments. Tex. Prop. Code § 207.002.

[131] Sample Resale Certificates forms for use by both Subdivision Associations and Condominium Associations can be found in the appendix.

applicable to the Subdivision Development; (2) a current copy of the Bylaws and Association Rules of the Subdivision Association; and (3) a Resale Certificate for the requesting owner's Lot or the Lot to be purchased, which must be prepared no earlier than sixty (60) days prior to the date such Resale Certificate is delivered to the requesting party.[132]

6.10.1 (A) *Requisite Contents of a Subdivision Resale Certificate*

Under Chapter 207 of the Texas Property Code, a "Resale Certificate" means a written statement issued, signed, and dated by an Officer or authorized agent of a Subdivision Association that contains the following information: [133]

(1) a statement of any right of first refusal, other than a right of first refusal that is prohibited by statute, and any other restraint contained in the Declaration or Restrictive Covenants that restricts the selling Lot Owner's right to transfer his or her Lot;[134]

(2) the frequency and amount of any regular Assessments;[135]

(3) the purpose and amount of any special Assessment that was previously approved by the Subdivision Association, but that will not be due and payable until after the Resale Certificate is delivered to the requesting party;[136]

---

[132] Tex. Prop. Code § 207.003(a). If the request for Subdivision Information is from a potential purchaser of a Lot or such purchaser's agent, the Subdivision Association may require from such purchaser or purchaser's agent both a written request for Subdivision Information and reasonable evidence verifying that such purchaser has a contractual or other right to acquire a Lot in the Subdivision Development before it begins the process of preparing or delivers the Subdivision Information to such purchaser or purchaser's agent. Tex. Prop. Code § 207.003(a-1). In such event, the Subdivision Association is not required to deliver the requested Subdivision Information to such purchaser or purchaser's agent until ten (10) business days from the date the written request and evidence of the requestor's authority to order a resale certificate is received and verified by the Subdivision Association. Tex. Prop. Code § 207.003(a)–(a-1).

[133] Tex. Prop. Code §§ 207.001(5), 207.003(b).

[134] Tex. Prop. Code § 207.003(b)(1).

[135] Tex. Prop. Code § 207.003(b)(2).

[136] Tex. Prop. Code § 207.003(b)(3).

(4) the total of all amounts due and unpaid to the Subdivision Association that are attributable to the selling Owner's Lot;[137]

(5) capital expenditures, if any, approved by the Subdivision Association for its current fiscal year;[138]

(6) the amount of reserves, if any, for capital expenditures;[139]

(7) the Subdivision Association's current operating budget and balance sheet;[140]

(8) the total of any unsatisfied judgments against the Subdivision Association;[141]

(9) the style and cause number of any pending lawsuit in which the Subdivision Association is a party, other than a lawsuit relating to unpaid ad valorem taxes of an individual member of the Association;[142]

(10) a copy of a certificate of insurance showing the Subdivision Association's property and liability insurance relating to the Common Areas and common facilities;[143]

(11) a description of any condition of the selling Owner's Lot that the Subdivision Association's Board of Directors has actual knowledge is in violation of the Declaration applicable to the Subdivision Development or the Bylaws or Association Rules of the Subdivision Association;[144]

(12) a summary or copy of notices received by the Subdivision Association from any governmental authority regarding health or housing code violations existing on the date the Resale Certificate is prepared relating

---

137 Tex. Prop. Code § 207.003(b)(4).

138 Tex. Prop. Code § 207.003(b)(5).

139 Tex. Prop. Code § 207.003(b)(6).

140 Tex. Prop. Code § 207.003(b)(7).

141 Tex. Prop. Code § 207.003(b)(8).

142 Tex. Prop. Code § 207.003(b)(9).

143 Tex. Prop. Code § 207.003(b)(10).

144 Tex. Prop. Code § 207.003(b)(11).

to the selling Owner's Lot, any Common Areas, or common facilities owned or leased by the Subdivision Association;[145]

(13) the amount of any administrative transfer fee charged by the Subdivision Association for a change of ownership of property in the Subdivision Development;[146]

(14) the name, mailing address, and telephone number of the Subdivision Association's managing agent, if any;[147]

(15) a statement indicating whether the Declaration authorizes the Subdivision Association to foreclose an Assessment Lien on the selling Owner's Lot for failure to pay Assessments;[148] and

(16) a statement of all fees associated with the transfer of ownership, including a description of each fee, to whom each fee is paid, and the amount of each fee.[149]

In addition, if the same party who requested a Resale Certificate requests an updated Resale Certificate within 180 days from the date the original Resale Certificate was issued, then the Subdivision Association must deliver an updated Resale Certificate to such requesting party within seven (7) business days after the date the Subdivision Association receives the written request for an update to the original Resale Certificate.[150] The updated Resale Certificate must contain the following information: (1) if a right of first refusal or other restraint on sale is contained in the Declaration, a statement as to whether the Subdivision Association waives the restraint on sale; (2) the status of any unpaid special Assessments, dues, or other payments attributable to the selling Owner's Lot; and (3) any changes to the information provided in the original Resale Certificate

---

[145] Tex. Prop. Code § 207.003(b)(12).

[146] Tex. Prop. Code § 207.003(b)(13).

[147] Tex. Prop. Code § 207.003(b)(14).

[148] Tex. Prop. Code § 207.003(b)(15).

[149] Tex. Prop. Code § 207.003(b)(16).

[150] Tex. Prop. Code § 207.003(f)–(g).

issued by the Subdivision Association.[151] Unless required by the Declaration, neither the Subdivision Association nor its agent is required to inspect a selling Owner's Lot before issuing a Resale Certificate or an updated Resale Certificate for such Lot.[152]

6.10.1 (B) *Delivery of Subdivision Information and Resale Certificate*

A Subdivision Association is required to deliver the requisite Subdivision Information and an original and any updated Resale Certificate to the person specified in the written request for such Subdivision Information and/or Resale Certificate.[153] The requested Subdivision Information, original Resale Certificate, and/or updated Resale Certificate may be delivered to such person designated by mail, hand-delivery, or any alternative delivery means specified by the requesting party in such written request.[154]

6.10.1 (C) *Allowable Charges for Production and Delivery of Subdivision Information and Resale Certificate*

A Subdivision Association may charge a requesting party a reasonable fee to assemble, prepare, copy, and deliver requested Subdivision Information and an original Resale Certificate, as well as to prepare and deliver an updated Resale Certificate, so long as such Resale Certificates are timely prepared and delivered to the requesting party.[155] In addition, a Subdivision Association may also require advance payment of such charges from the requesting party prior to beginning the process of producing a Resale Certificate,

---

151 Tex. Prop. Code § 207.003(f)–(g).

152 Tex. Prop. Code § 207.003(e).

153 Tex. Prop. Code § 207.003(d). A written request that does not specify the name and location to send such information is not effective and the Subdivision Association need not respond to it. Tex. Prop. Code § 207.003(d).

154 Tex. Prop. Code § 207.003(d).

155 Tex. Prop. Code § 207.003(c). A Subdivision Association, however, may not charge a fee for preparation and delivery of the Subdivision Information and original Resale Certificate if such Resale Certificate is not delivered timely to the requesting party. Tex. Prop. Code § 207.003(c-1). Similarly, a Subdivision Association may not charge a fee for preparation and delivery of an updated Resale Certificate if such updated Resale Certificate is not timely delivered to the requesting party. Tex. Prop. Code § 207.003(c-1).

but it may not process such advance payment for such Resale Certificate until the Resale Certificate is available for delivery.[156] In other words, a Subdivision Association may require the requesting party to deliver a check to it for the costs to produce a Resale Certificate in advance of producing the Resale Certificate, but it may not cash or deposit such check into its account until the Resale Certificate is ready to be picked up by or delivered to the requesting party.

6.10.1 (D) *Remedies of a Selling Lot Owner for Failure of a Subdivision Association to Timely Deliver Requested Subdivision Information or Resale Certificate*

If a Subdivision Association does not timely deliver the requested Subdivision Information, original Resale Certificate, or updated Resale Certificate after receipt of a proper written request, the requesting party may submit a second request for such information to the Subdivision Association, which must be sent to the Subdivision Association by certified mail, return receipt requested, or by hand-delivery.[157] If a Subdivision Association fails to deliver the requested Subdivision Information, original Resale Certificate, or updated Resale Certificate to the requesting party within seven (7) days after a second request for such information was mailed by certified mail, return receipt requested, or hand-delivered (as evidenced by written receipt) to the Subdivision Association, the selling Lot Owner may file a lawsuit against the Subdivision Association and seek one or any combination of two or more of the following remedies:[158]

---

[156] Tex. Prop. Code § 207.003(c-1).

[157] Tex. Prop. Code § 207.004(a).

[158] Tex. Prop. Code § 207.004(b)(1). Notwithstanding, an officer or agent of the Subdivision Association cannot be held liable for a delay or failure to furnish a Resale Certificate. Tex. Prop. Code § 207.005(d). Except for the remedies provided by Section 207.004(b)(1), a Subdivision Association may not be held liable to a selling Lot Owner for damages because of a delay or failure to deliver requested Subdivision Information, an original Resale Certificate, or an updated Resale Certificate. Tex. Prop. Code § 207.005(d).

(1) a court order directing the Subdivision Association to furnish the required Subdivision Information, original Resale Certificate, or updated Resale Certificate;

(2) a judgment against the Subdivision Association for not more than five hundred dollars ($500.00);

(3) a judgment against the Subdivision Association for the Lot Owner's court costs and attorneys fees; and/or

(4) a judgment authorizing the Lot Owner or the Lot Owner's assignee to deduct the amounts awarded to the Lot Owner in such lawsuit from any future regular or special Assessments payable to the Subdivision Association.

Under such circumstances, a selling Lot Owner may also provide a purchaser under contract to buy such Owner's Lot an affidavit that states that the selling Lot Owner, his or her agent, or title insurance company acting on behalf of the selling Lot Owner made two written requests to the Subdivision Association for the required Subdivision Information, original Resale Certificate, and/or updated Resale Certificate in accordance with Chapter 207 of the Texas Property Code and that the Subdivision Association did not timely provide the requested information.[159] If the selling Lot Owner provides such an affidavit to a purchaser under contract to buy such Owner's Lot, then neither such purchaser, purchaser's lender, or the title insurance company is liable to the Subdivision Association for any money that is due and owed to the Subdivision Association by the selling Lot Owner as of the date the affidavit was prepared.[160] In addition, the Subdivision Association's Assessment Lien is unenforceable against the selling Owner's Lot for any

159 Tex. Prop. Code § 207.004(b)(2). In such event, neither the selling Lot Owner's agent or the title insurance company may be held liable to a purchaser for any delay or failure by a Subdivision Association to deliver the requested Subdivision Information, original Resale Certificate, or updated Resale Certificate. Tex. Prop. Code § 207.005(c).

160 Tex. Prop. Code § 207.004(c)(1). In addition, neither such purchaser, purchaser's lender, nor the title insurance company is liable for any debt owed by the selling Lot Owner to the Subdivision Association or any claim by the Subdivision Association that accrued before the date such affidavit was prepared. Tex. Prop. Code § 207.004(c)(1).

amounts owed by the selling Lot Owner to the Subdivision Association as of the date such affidavit was prepared.[161]

6.10.1 (E) *Effect of Erroneous or Omitted Information in a Subdivision Resale Certificate*

Not only is it important that a Subdivision Association timely delivers requested Subdivision Information and Resale Certificates to a requesting party, it is equally important that a Subdivision Association ensures that the information it provides in a Resale Certificate is accurate because a Subdivision Association may not later deny the validity of any statement in a Resale Certificate issued by it.[162] In addition, neither a purchaser, purchaser's agent, purchaser's lender, nor the title insurance company may be held liable to a Subdivision Association for any debt or claim existing as of the date a Resale Certificate was prepared that was not disclosed in the Resale Certificate.[163] Notwithstanding, an erroneous Resale Certificate does not affect the right of a Subdivision Association to recover debts or claims that arise or become due after the date the Resale Certificate is prepared, nor does it affect the enforceability of the Subdivision Association's Assessment Lien as to such Lot for purposes of securing payment of future Assessments that become due after the date the Resale Certificate is prepared.[164]

6.10.2 Production of Condominium Information and Resale Certificates by a Condominium Association

The Texas Uniform Condominium Act requires all Unit Owners, other than a Declarant, who intend to sell their Unit to furnish a purchaser with a current copy of the

[161] Tex. Prop. Code § 207.004(c)(2).

[162] Tex. Prop. Code § 207.005(a).

[163] Tex. Prop. Code § 207.005(a). Moreover, if a Resale Certificate fails to disclose all, or a portion, of any amount of money a selling Lot Owner owes to the Subdivision Association, the Subdivision Association's Assessment Lien automatically terminates as to any such undisclosed amounts that were otherwise due the Subdivision Association on the date the original or updated Resale Certificate (as applicable) is prepared. Tex. Prop. Code § 207.005(a).

[164] Tex. Prop. Code § 207.005(b).

Condominium Declaration, Bylaws, Association Rules, and a Resale Certificate for the Unit before executing a contract of sale or conveying the Unit.[165] The Resale Certificate must be issued by the Condominium Association, must have been prepared no earlier than three (3) months prior to the date it is delivered to the purchaser, and must contain the current operating budget of the Condominium Association and statements identifying the following information:

(1) any right of first refusal or other restraint contained in the Condominium Declaration that restricts the right to transfer a Unit;[166]

(2) the amount of the periodic Common Expense Assessment and the amount of any unpaid Common Expenses or special Assessments currently due and payable to the Condominium Association by the selling Unit Owner;[167]

(3) other unpaid fees or amounts currently due and payable to the Condominium Association by the selling Unit Owner;[168]

(4) capital expenditures, if any, approved by the Condominium Association for the next twelve (12) months;[169]

(5) the amount of reserves, if any, for capital expenditures and the amount of any portion of such reserves that is designated by the Condominium Association for a specified project;[170]

(6) any unsatisfied judgments against the Condominium Association;[171]

(7) the nature of any pending lawsuits against the Condominium Association;[172]

---

165 Tex. Prop. Code § 82.157(a).

166 Tex. Prop. Code § 82.157(a)(1).

167 Tex. Prop. Code § 82.157(a)(2).

168 Tex. Prop. Code § 82.157(a)(3).

169 Tex. Prop. Code § 82.157(a)(4).

170 Tex. Prop. Code § 82.157(a)(5).

171 Tex. Prop. Code § 82.157(a)(6).

172 Tex. Prop. Code § 82.157(a)(7).

(8) insurance coverage provided for the benefit of Unit Owners;[173]

(9) whether the Board of Directors for the Condominium Association has knowledge that any alterations or improvements to the Unit to be sold or to the Limited Common Elements assigned to such Unit violate the Condominium Declaration, Bylaws, or Association Rules;[174]

(10) whether the Board of Directors for the Condominium Association has received notice from a governmental authority concerning violations of health or building codes with respect to the Unit to be sold, the Limited Common Elements assigned to such Unit, or any other portion of the Condominium Development;[175]

(11) the remaining term of any leasehold estate that affects the Condominium Development and the provisions governing an extension or renewal of such lease;[176]

(12) the name, mailing address, and telephone number of the Condominium Association's managing agent, if any;[177]

(13) the Condominium Association's current operating budget and balance sheet;[178] and

(14) all fees payable to the Condominium Association or an agent of the Condominium Association that are associated with the transfer of a Unit's ownership, including a description of each fee, to whom the fee is paid, and the amount of the fee.[179]

To obtain a Resale Certificate, a Unit Owner must deliver a written request to the Condominium Association. Within ten (10) days of receiving a written request for a Resale Certificate from a selling Unit Owner, a Condominium Association must furnish to the selling Unit Owner, or such selling Unit Owner's agent, a Resale Certificate signed

[173] Tex. Prop. Code § 82.157(a)(8).

[174] Tex. Prop. Code § 82.157(a)(9).

[175] Tex. Prop. Code § 82.157(a)(10).

[176] Tex. Prop. Code § 82.157(a)(11).

[177] Tex. Prop. Code § 82.157(a)(12).

[178] Tex. Prop. Code § 82.157(a)(13).

[179] Tex. Prop. Code § 82.157(a)(14).

and dated by an Officer or authorized agent of the Condominium Association containing the requisite information.[180] If a Condominium Association does not furnish a Resale Certificate or any information required in the Resale Certificate within such ten-day period, then the selling Unit Owner may provide the purchaser with a sworn affidavit signed by such selling Unit Owner in lieu of the Resale Certificate.[181] Such affidavit must state that the selling Unit Owner requested information from the Condominium Association concerning its financial condition, as required by Section 82.157 of the Texas Uniform Condominium Act, and that the Condominium Association did not timely provide a Resale Certificate or the information required to be in the Resale Certificate.[182] If a selling Unit Owner furnishes such an affidavit to a purchaser, the Unit Owner and the purchaser may agree in writing to waive the requirement to furnish a Resale Certificate.[183]

Notwithstanding, a Condominium Association may not be held liable to a selling Unit Owner for a delay or failure to furnish a Resale Certificate; and, an Officer or agent of the Condominium Association is not liable for a delay or failure to furnish a Resale Certificate, unless the Officer or agent willfully refuses to furnish the Resale Certificate or is grossly negligent in not furnishing the Resale Certificate.[184] In addition, a selling Unit Owner and/or such Unit Owner's agent also may not be held liable to a purchaser for the failure or delay of a Condominium Association to provide a Resale Certificate in a timely manner.[185]

---

[180] Tex. Prop. Code § 82.157(b).

[181] Tex. Prop. Code § 82.157(b).

[182] Tex. Prop. Code § 82.157(b).

[183] Tex. Prop. Code § 82.157(b).

[184] Tex. Prop. Code § 82.157(b).

[185] Tex. Prop. Code § 82.157(c). Additionally, a failure to provide a Resale Certificate does not void a deed to a purchaser of a Unit. Tex. Prop. Code § 82.157(b).

Finally, if a properly executed Resale Certificate incorrectly states the total amount of delinquent sums the selling Unit Owner owes to the Condominium Association, then the purchaser is not liable for payment of any undisclosed amounts that were otherwise owed to the Condominium Association as of the date the Resale Certificate was prepared that were omitted by the Condominium Association from the delinquent sum stated in the Resale Certificate.[186] In addition, a purchaser, lender, or title insurance company that relies on a Resale Certificate is not liable for any debt or claim that is not disclosed in the Resale Certificate, and the Condominium Association may not deny the validity of any statements in the Resale Certificate.[187] A Resale Certificate, however, does not affect a Condominium Association's right to recover debts or claims that arise or become due after the date the Resale Certificate is prepared, and it does not affect the enforceability of a Condominium Association's Assessment Lien against a Unit for non-payment of Assessments levied after the date the Resale Certificate was prepared.[188]

6.11 Maintenance of Common Areas and Common Elements

The ownership of Common Areas in a Subdivision Development and Common Elements in a Condominium Development differ significantly in many regards, as do the laws regarding the responsibility for their maintenance. Common Areas in a Subdivision Development are owned by the Subdivision Association. As the "owner" of the Common Areas, the Subdivision Association is imposed with all of the duties and obligations normally associated with ownership of real property, including the duty to comply with any local or state statutes or ordinances requiring maintenance or upkeep of real property and structural buildings located thereon. There are no specific Texas laws applicable to Subdivision Associations that regulate a Subdivision Association's ownership of Common Areas or that require it to maintain the Common Areas in a Subdivision

---

[186] Tex. Prop. Code § 82.157(c).

[187] Tex. Prop. Code § 82.157(e).

[188] Tex. Prop. Code § 82.157(d).

Development. Notwithstanding, in almost all Subdivision Associations' Governing Documents, there are provisions that impose contractual obligations upon the Subdivision Association to maintain the Common Areas.

Common Elements, on the other hand, are not owned by the Condominium Association, but instead are owned in-common by all of the Unit Owners.[189] Notwithstanding, a Condominium Association still has an obligation and duty to maintain the Common Elements of the Condominium Development on behalf of the Unit Owners, which stems directly from its Condominium Declaration and either the Texas Condominium Act or the Texas Uniform Condominium Act. Under the Texas Condominium Act (applicable to Condominium Developments created prior to January 1, 1994), the Condominium Association is not directly imposed with the obligation to maintain the Common Elements. Instead, Unit Owners in such a Condominium Development are responsible for their pro rata share of the expenses to administer the Condominium Development and to maintain and repair the General Common Elements and, in some circumstances, the expenses to administer the Limited Common Elements of the buildings in the Condominium Development, as well.[190] Under the Texas Uniform Condominium Act (applicable to Condominium Developments created after January 1, 1994), and except as provided by the Condominium Declaration, the Condominium Association, as opposed to the Unit Owners, is directly responsible for the maintenance, repair, and replacement of the Common Elements in the Condominium Development.[191]

---

[189] *See Dutcher v. Owens*, 647 S.W.2d 948, 949–50 (Tex. 1983) ("In essence, condominium ownership is the merger of two estates in land into one: the fee simple ownership of an apartment or unit in a condominium project and a tenancy in common with other co-owners in the common elements.").

[190] Tex. Prop. Code § 81.204(a).

[191] Tex. Prop. Code § 82.107(a).

6.12 Limitation of Liability of a Texas Homeowners Association under the Texas Charitable Immunity and Liability Act of 1987

Chapter 84 of the Texas Civil Practices and Remedies Code (called the "Charitable Immunity and Liability Act of 1987") establishes certain limitations on the civil liability of Texas "Charitable Organizations." In addition to income tax exempt organizations, the Texas Charitable Immunity and Liability Act of 1987's definition of Charitable Organization includes "a Homeowners Association as defined by Section 528(c) of the Internal Revenue Code of 1986 or which is exempt from federal income tax under Section 501(a) of the Internal Revenue Code of 1986 by being listed as an exempt organization in Section 501(c)(4) of the code."[192] Such definition of Charitable Organizations will generally include most Texas Homeowners Associations.

Under the Texas Charitable Immunity and Liability Act of 1987, if a Charitable Organization maintains certain requisite liability insurance coverage, then the amount of civil liability a Charitable Organization may incur as a result of acts or omissions committed by its employees or volunteers is limited to the coverage limits of such insurance policy.[193] To qualify for such limitation of liability under the Texas Charitable Immunity and Liability Act of 1987, a Charitable Organization must maintain insurance coverage that applies to the acts or omissions of the Charitable Organization and its employees and volunteers in the amount of at least $500,000 for each injured person,

---

[192] Tex. Civ. Prac. & Rem. Code § 84.003(1). Section 528(c) of the Internal Revenue Code of 1986 defines a "Homeowners Association" as a residential Condominium or Subdivision Association that is organized and operated to provide for the acquisition, construction, management, maintenance, and care of the Association's Common Areas or Common Elements and: (1) sixty percent (60%) or more of its gross income for the taxable year consists solely of amounts received as membership dues, fees, or assessments from owners of residential Units or Lots in the Association; (2) ninety percent (90%) or more of its expenditures for the taxable year are for the acquisition, construction, management, maintenance, and care of the Association's Common Areas or Common Elements; (3) no part of its net earnings inures to any private shareholder or individual; and (4) it elects to have Section 528(c) apply to it for the taxable year. 26 U.S.C. § 528(c). Exempt organizations listed under Section 501(c)(4) of the Internal Revenue Code include nonprofit civic leagues or other nonprofit organizations operated exclusively for the promotion of social welfare, the net earnings of which are devoted exclusively to charitable, educational, or recreational purposes and no part of its net earnings inures to the benefit of any private shareholder or individual. 26 U.S.C. § 501(c)(4).

[193] Tex. Civ. Prac. & Rem. Code § 84.007(g).

$1,000,000 for each single occurrence for death or bodily injury, and $100,000 for each single occurrence for injury to or destruction of property.[194] If a Charitable Organization maintains the requisite liability insurance coverage, the maximum amount that it may be held liable for in a civil lawsuit brought against it for damages based on an act or omission by its employees or volunteers is limited to monetary damages in a maximum amount of $500,000 for each injured person, $1,000,000 for each single occurrence of bodily injury or death, and $100,000 for each single occurrence for injury or destruction of property.[195] In other words, the amount of liability of the Charitable Organization is limited to the amount of its requisite insurance coverage. Such limitation on the civil liability of a Charitable Organization, however, does not apply to damages resulting from an act or omission that is intentional, willfully negligent, or done with conscious indifference or reckless disregard for the safety of others.[196]

6.13 Limitation of Liability of a Texas Homeowners Association That Allows Use of Its Property as a Community Garden

In 2015, the Texas Legislature enacted Section 75.0025 of the Texas Civil Practice and Remedies Code, which limits the liability of a Texas Homeowners Association that allows its Common Area or Common Element land to be used as a "community garden."[197] More specifically, Section 75.0025 provides that an owner of

194 Tex. Civ. Prac. & Rem. Code § 84.007(g). Such insurance coverage may be provided under a contract of insurance or other plan of insurance authorized by statute and may be satisfied by the purchase of a $1,000,000 bodily injury and property damage combined single limit policy. Tex. Civ. Prac. & Rem. Code § 84.007(g).

195 Tex. Civ. Prac. & Rem. Code § 84.006.

196 Tex. Civ. Prac. & Rem. Code § 84.007(a).

197 Tex. Civ. Prac. & Rem. Code § 75.0025. Section 75.0025 defines "community garden" as "premises used for recreational gardening by a group of people residing in a neighborhood or community for the purpose of providing fresh produce for the benefit of the residents of the neighborhood or community." Tex. Civ. Prac. & Rem. Code § 75.0025(a). Section 75.0025 of the Texas Civil Practice and Remedies Code is not a statute that is applicable only to Texas Homeowners Associations, rather it applies to any owner, lessee, or occupant of land that gives permission to another person to enter and use the land as a community garden. Tex. Civ. Prac. & Rem. Code § 75.0025(a). Even though a Condominium Association does not own or lease Common Element land, it does occupy and control the use of Common Element land. Accordingly, Section 75.0025 should apply to both Common Area land owned by a Subdivision Association that is used as a community

land that gives permission to another person to enter and use such land as a community garden does not by giving such permission ensure that the premises are safe or assume responsibility or incur any liability for:

(1) damages arising from or related to any bodily or other personal injury to or death of any person who enters the premises for a purpose related to a community garden;

(2) property damage sustained by any person who enters the premises for a purpose related to a community garden; or

(3) an act of a third party that occurs on the premises.[198]

In order to make certain that individuals entering into a community garden are aware of the landowner's limited liability, Section 75.0025 requires the landowner to post and maintain a clearly readable sign in a clearly visible location on or near the community garden that contains the following warning language:[199]

WARNING
TEXAS LAW (CHAPTER 75, CIVIL PRACTICE AND REMEDIES CODE) LIMITS THE LIABILITY OF THE LANDOWNER, LESSEE, OR OCCUPANT FOR DAMAGES ARISING FROM THE USE OF THIS PROPERTY AS A COMMUNITY GARDEN.

6.14 Filing Periodic Reports with the Texas Secretary of State

Most Texas Homeowners Associations are incorporated as nonprofit corporations and must comply with certain statutory provisions under the Texas Nonprofit Corporation

garden and Common Element land controlled by a Condominium Association that is used as a community garden.

[198] Tex. Civ. Prac. & Rem. Code § 75.0025(b). In addition, Section 75.0025 makes clear that the doctrine of attractive nuisance does not apply to a claim for bodily injury or property damages by a person who enters a community garden. Tex. Civ. Prac. & Rem. Code § 75.0025(c). Section 75.0025, however, does not limit the liability of a land owner for an injury caused by willful or wanton acts or gross negligence by such land owner. Tex. Civ. Prac. & Rem. Code § 75.0025(d).

[199] Tex. Civ. Prac. & Rem. Code § 75.0025(e).

Law concerning the reporting of public information. More specifically, upon request by the Texas Secretary of State, a Texas Nonprofit Corporation HOA is required to file a public information report (commonly called a "Periodic Report") at the Office of the Texas Secretary of State.[200] A request for a Periodic Report by the Texas Secretary of State must be in writing and mailed to the Nonprofit Corporation HOA at either: (1) the address of its registered agent; (2) the last known address of the Nonprofit Corporation HOA as it appears in the Secretary of State's records; or (3) the address of any other known place of business of the Nonprofit Corporation HOA.[201]

Within thirty (30) days of receiving a written request for a Periodic Report, a Nonprofit Corporation HOA must submit a written report to the Texas Secretary of State that is signed by an Officer of the Nonprofit Corporation HOA[202] and identifies the following information:

(1) the name of the Nonprofit Corporation HOA;[203]

(2) the state or country under the laws of which the Nonprofit Corporation HOA is incorporated;[204]

(3) the address of the registered office of the Nonprofit Corporation HOA in the State of Texas and the name of the registered agent at such address;[205] and

(4) the names and addresses of the Directors and Officers of the Nonprofit Corporation HOA.[206]

---

200 Tex. Bus. Org. Code § 22.357(a). The Texas Secretary of State may request a Periodic Report on a periodic basis, but he or she may not request such report more often than once every four years. Tex. Bus. Org. Code § 22.357(a).

201 Tex. Bus. Org. Code § 22.358(a).

202 Tex. Bus. Org. Code §§ 22.357(b); 22.359.

203 Tex. Bus. Org. Code § 22.357(a)(1).

204 Tex. Bus. Org. Code § 22.357(a)(2).

205 Tex. Bus. Org. Code § 22.357(a)(3).

206 Tex. Bus. Org. Code § 22.357(a)(5).

In addition, a Nonprofit Corporation HOA must use the Periodic Report form promulgated by the Texas Secretary of State to report such requisite information, and such form should be completed with responsive information that is accurate as of the date the Periodic Report is executed by the Officer of the Nonprofit Corporation HOA.[207]

If a Nonprofit Corporation HOA fails to file the Periodic Report within thirty (30) days from the date the Secretary of State sends a written request, the Nonprofit Corporation HOA's right to transact business in Texas will be forfeited.[208] In such event, the Texas Secretary of State will mail a notice of forfeiture to the Nonprofit Corporation HOA's registered agent or to the Nonprofit Corporation at: (1) the address of its principal place of business as it appears in its Articles of Incorporation; (2) the last known address of the Nonprofit Corporation HOA as it appears in the Secretary of State's records; or (3) the address of any other known place of business of the Nonprofit Corporation HOA.[209]

If a Nonprofit Corporation HOA's right to transact business is forfeited for failure to file a Periodic Report, the Nonprofit Corporation HOA may be revived from forfeiture by filing the required Periodic Report, accompanied by the requisite revival fee, no later

---

207 Tex. Bus. Org. Code § 22.357(b). If a Nonprofit Corporation HOA has previously filed a Periodic Report, the request for a Periodic Report from the Texas Secretary of State will normally include a Periodic Report form that is preprinted with the same information that was previously reported by the Nonprofit Corporation HOA. Tex. Bus. Org. Code § 22.358(b). If the information preprinted on the form is still accurate, an Officer of the Nonprofit Corporation HOA can simply sign and date the preprinted form and send it back to the Secretary of State. If changes need to be made to the preprinted form concerning the identity of a Nonprofit Corporation HOA's Directors and/or registered agent, it can change such information by simply crossing it out and filling in the correct information before sending it back to the Secretary of State. A Nonprofit Corporation HOA may not, however, change the corporation's name simply by crossing it out and filling in the new name; instead, the Nonprofit Corporation HOA must file Articles of Amendment (to its Articles of Incorporation) or a Certificate of Amendment (to its Certificate of Formation) in order to change its corporate name.

208 Tex. Bus. Org. Code § 22.360. A Nonprofit Corporation HOA whose right to transact business has been forfeited cannot maintain any action, suit, or proceeding in any Texas court or amend its Articles of Incorporation. Tex. Bus. Org. Code § 22.362(a). The forfeiture of a Nonprofit Corporation HOA's right to transact business, however, does not: (1) impair the validity of a contract or other act of the Nonprofit Corporation HOA taken prior to the forfeiture; or (2) prevent the Nonprofit Corporation HOA from defending an action, suit, or proceeding in a Texas court. Tex. Bus. Org. Code § 22.362(c).

209 Tex. Bus. Org. Code § 22.361.

than the one hundred twentieth (120th) day after the date the notice of forfeiture was mailed to the Nonprofit Corporation HOA.[210] If a Nonprofit Corporation complies with the requirements for reviving its right to transact business, the Texas Secretary of State is required to revive the right of the Nonprofit Corporation HOA to conduct affairs in Texas, cancel the words regarding the forfeiture on the record of the Nonprofit Corporation HOA, and endorse on the Nonprofit Corporation HOA's record the word "revived" and the date of revival.[211]

If the Nonprofit Corporation HOA does not timely file the Periodic Report and pay the revival fee within the 120-day revival period, the Secretary of State will involuntarily terminate the Nonprofit Corporation HOA.[212] If a Nonprofit Corporation HOA is involuntarily terminated, it can be reinstated at any time by filing the required Periodic Report and paying the requisite filing fee.[213] The Nonprofit Corporation HOA must also pay all fees, taxes, penalties, and interest that were due prior to the termination of the Nonprofit Corporation HOA, as well as an amount equal to the total amount of taxes that the Nonprofit Corporation HOA would have owed during the period of termination if it had not been terminated to begin with.[214]

6.15 Keeping Books and Records

Almost all Texas Homeowners Associations are required to keep certain books and records of account and other information concerning their operations (commonly referred to simply as its "Books and Records").[215] In addition to any obligation to keep

---

210 Tex. Bus. Org. Code § 22.363(a).

211 Tex. Bus. Org. Code § 22.363(b).

212 Tex. Bus. Org. Code § 22.364(a).

213 Tex. Bus. Org. Code § 22.365(a).

214 Tex. Bus. Org. Code § 22.365(a).

215 Although the term "books and records of account" is referenced by the Texas Business Organizations Code and the Texas Uniform Unincorporated Nonprofit Association Act, such statutory term is not defined by such laws. *See* Tex. Bus. Org. Code §§ 3.151; 252.010. *Black's Law Dictionary* defines "books of account"

certain Books and Records mandated by a Homeowners Association's Governing Documents, the Texas Nonprofit Corporation Law and Texas Uniform Unincorporated Nonprofit Association Act require certain Books and Records to be kept by Nonprofit Corporation HOAs and Nonprofit Association HOAs, respectively, as does the Texas Uniform Condominium Act and Chapter 209 of the Texas Property Code, which requires the same of Condominium Associations and Subdivision Associations, respectively. A Texas Homeowners Association will generally be subject to one or more of these statutes, depending on whether the Homeowners Association is incorporated or unincorporated and whether it is a Condominium Association or a Subdivision Association.[216]

More specifically, if a Homeowners Association is incorporated as a nonprofit corporation, then it is required under the Texas Nonprofit Corporation Law to keep: (1) Books and Records of account; (2) minutes of the proceedings of the Board of Directors, committees established by the Board of Directors, and its Membership; (3) a current record of the name and mailing address of each Member-Homeowner of the Nonprofit Corporation HOA; and (4) other books and records as required by the Texas Nonprofit Corporation Law.[217] If, on the other hand, a Homeowners Association is not incorporated, but constitutes a Nonprofit Association HOA under the Texas Uniform Unincorporated

---

as "books in which merchants, traders, and businessmen generally keep their accounts; including journals, ledgers, and other accounting records. *Black's Law Dictionary* 183 (6th ed. 1990).

[216] For example, if a Condominium Association is incorporated as a nonprofit corporation, then it is subject to and must comply with the provisions of both the Texas Nonprofit Corporation Law and the Texas Uniform Condominium Act. On the other hand, if a Subdivision Association is not incorporated, but constitutes a Nonprofit Association HOA, then it is subject to and must comply with the provisions of both the Texas Uniform Unincorporated Nonprofit Association Act and Chapter 209 of the Texas Property Code.

[217] Tex. Bus. Org. Code § 3.151(a). The books of accounts, records, minutes, and membership records of a Texas nonprofit corporation, including a Nonprofit Corporation HOA, may be kept in written paper form or another form capable of being converted into written paper form within a reasonable time (such as an electronic document kept on a computer disc or hard drive). Tex. Bus. Org. Code § 3.151(b). In addition, the current record of the names and addresses for Member-Homeowners must be kept at the Nonprofit Corporation HOA's registered office or principal place of business. Tex. Bus. Org. Code § 3.151(a)(3).

Nonprofit Association Act, then it is simply required to keep correct and complete Books and Records of account for at least three (3) years after the end of each fiscal year.[218]

In addition to any requirements under the Texas Nonprofit Corporation Law or Texas Uniform Unincorporated Nonprofit Association Act (as applicable), Condominium Associations are required under the Texas Uniform Condominium Act, to keep the following Books and Records:

(1) detailed financial records that comply with generally accepted accounting principles and that are sufficiently detailed to enable the Condominium Association to prepare a Resale Certificate (under Section 82.157 of the Texas Uniform Condominium Act);[219]

(2) the plans and specifications used to construct the Condominium Development, except for buildings originally constructed prior to January 1, 1994;[220]

(3) a Condominium Information Statement prepared under Section 82.152 of the Texas Uniform Condominium Act and any amendments to it;[221]

(4) the name and mailing address of each Unit Owner;[222]

(5) voting records, proxies, and correspondence relating to amendments to the Condominium Declaration;[223] and

(6) minutes of meetings of the Condominium Association's Membership and Board of Directors.[224]

---

218 Tex. Bus. Org. Code § 252.010(a). A Nonprofit Association HOA must also make such Books and Records available upon request to its members for inspection and copying. Tex. Bus. Org. Code § 252.010(a).

219 Tex. Prop. Code § 82.114(a)(1).

220 Tex. Prop. Code § 82.114(a)(2).

221 Tex. Prop. Code § 82.114(a)(3).

222 Tex. Prop. Code § 82.114(a)(4).

223 Tex. Prop. Code § 82.114(a)(5).

224 Tex. Prop. Code § 82.114(a)(6).

Similar to Condominium Associations, in addition to any Books and Records required to be kept by the Texas Nonprofit Corporation Law or Texas Uniform Unincorporated Nonprofit Association Act (as applicable), a Subdivision Association must also keep certain Books and Records specified by Chapter 209 of the Texas Property. Unlike the Texas Uniform Condominium Act, however, Chapter 209 does not contain an express laundry list of records that a Subdivision Association must keep. The only provision of Chapter 209 that expressly requires a Subdivision Association to keep a particular record is Section 209.0051, which requires a Subdivision Association to keep a record of each regular or special Board meeting in the form of written minutes of such meeting.[225]

Notwithstanding, Section 209.005(m) requires Texas Subdivision Associations that are composed of at least fifteen Lots to adopt and comply with a "Document Retention Policy" that at a minimum must provide for the retention (for various time periods) of:

(1) a Subdivision Association's Certificate of Formation (formerly called Articles of Incorporation), Bylaws, Declarations (and all other restrictive covenants), and all amendments to the Certificates of Formation, Bylaws, and Declarations;[226]

(2) a Subdivision Association's financial books and records;[227]

(3) a Subdivision Association's account records of current Lot Owners;[228]

(4) copies of all contracts entered into by a Subdivision Association with a term of one year or more;[229]

---

225 Tex. Prop. Code § 209.0051(d).

226 Tex. Prop. Code § 209.005(m)(1).

227 Tex. Prop. Code § 209.005(m)(2).

228 Tex. Prop. Code § 209.005(m)(3).

229 Tex. Prop. Code § 209.005(m)(4).

(5) minutes from all meetings of a Subdivision Association's Board of Directors and Membership;[230] and

(6) a Subdivision Association's tax returns and audit records.[231]

6.16 Inspection of a Homeowners Association's Books and Records by a Director

The right of a Director to inspect the Books and Records of a Homeowners Association is governed by the Homeowners Association's Governing Documents, as well as the Texas Nonprofit Corporation Law if it is incorporated as a nonprofit corporation. Under the Texas Nonprofit Corporation Law, each Director of a Texas Nonprofit Corporation HOA may examine all of the Nonprofit Corporation HOA's Books and Records for any purpose reasonably related to the Director's service on the Board of Directors.[232]

In addition, if a Nonprofit Corporation HOA refuses to allow inspection of its Books and Records by a current Director after receiving a request to do so, the Director may file a lawsuit against the Nonprofit Corporation HOA to force it to allow inspection of the requested Books and Records.[233] If a Director files such a lawsuit against the Nonprofit Corporation HOA and the court determines that: (1) the Director's demand to inspect the Nonprofit Corporation HOA's Books and Records was reasonably related to his or her service on the Board of Directors; and (2) the Nonprofit Corporation HOA refused a good faith request by such Director, then the court may order the Nonprofit Corporation HOA to open its Books and Records so as to permit the Director to inspect, make copies of, and/or take extracts from such requested Books and Records.[234] In such event, the court may also award such Director the attorneys fees he or she incurred in

[230] Tex. Prop. Code § 209.005(m)(5).

[231] Tex. Prop. Code § 209.005(m)(6).

[232] Tex. Bus. Org. Code § 3.152(a).

[233] Tex. Bus. Org. Code § 3.152(b)–(c).

[234] Tex. Bus. Org. Code § 3.152(b).

filing and prosecuting such lawsuit and any other proper relief necessary to compel the Nonprofit Corporation HOA to open its Books and Records to such Director.[235]

6.17 Inspection of a Homeowners Association's Books and Records by a Homeowner

In addition to any rights of a Homeowner to inspect the Books and Records of his or her Homeowners Association under its Governing Documents, Texas Homeowners have a statutory right to inspect the Books and Records of a Homeowners Association under one or more Texas statutes, including the Texas Nonprofit Corporation Law, the Texas Uniform Unincorporated Nonprofit Association Act, the Texas Uniform Condominium Act, and/or Chapter 209 of the Texas Property Code, depending on whether the Homeowners Association is incorporated or unincorporated and whether it is a Condominium Association or a Subdivision Association.[236] The provisions of each such statute differ greatly from each other and are explained in greater detail in the following subchapters.

6.17.1 Member-Homeowner's Right to Inspect Books and Records of a Nonprofit Corporation HOA under the Texas Nonprofit Corporation Law

Under the Texas Nonprofit Corporation Law, Member-Homeowners of a Texas Nonprofit Corporation HOA have a right to inspect and copy the Books and Records of such Nonprofit Corporation HOA.[237] In order to inspect the Books and Records of a

---

[235] Tex. Bus. Org. Code § 3.152(c).

[236] For example, if a Condominium Association is incorporated as a nonprofit corporation, then it is subject to and must comply with the provisions of both the Texas Nonprofit Corporation Law and the Texas Uniform Condominium Act. On the other hand, if a Subdivision Association is not incorporated, but constitutes a Nonprofit Association HOA, then it is subject to and must comply with the provisions of both the Texas Uniform Unincorporated Nonprofit Association Act and Chapter 209 of the Texas Property Code.

[237] Tex. Bus. Org. Code § 22.351. A Texas Nonprofit Corporation HOA is required to keep: (1) books and records of accounts; (2) minutes of the proceedings of its Board of Directors, committees established by its Board of Directors, and its Membership; (3) a current record of the name and mailing address of each Member-Homeowner of the Nonprofit Corporation HOA; and (4) other books and records as required by the Texas Nonprofit Corporation Law. Tex. Bus. Org. Code § 3.151(a).

Nonprofit Corporation HOA, the Member-Homeowner must present the Nonprofit Corporation HOA with a written request stating the scope of the documents requested and the purpose for such request.[238] So long as the request is for a proper purpose, the Member-Homeowner is entitled to examine and copy, at the Member-Homeowner's expense, the Books and Records of the Nonprofit Corporation HOA relevant to the purpose stated in the Member-Homeowner's request.[239] The Member-Homeowner may examine the requested Books and Records at any reasonable time specified by the Member-Homeowner, and the examination may be performed by the Member-Homeowner and/or his or her agent, accountant, or attorney.[240]

6.17.2 Member's Right to Inspect Books and Records of a Nonprofit Association under the Texas Uniform Unincorporated Nonprofit Association Act

Under the Texas Uniform Unincorporated Nonprofit Association Act, a Texas Homeowners Association that constitutes an unincorporated "Nonprofit Association" is required to keep correct and complete Books and Records of account for at least three (3) years after the end of each fiscal year and must make such Books and Records available on request to its members for inspection and copying.[241]

6.17.3 Unit Owner's Right to Inspect Books and Records of a Condominium Association under the Texas Uniform Condominium Act

Under the Texas Uniform Condominium Act, all financial and other records of a Texas Condominium Association must be made reasonably available at its registered

---

238 Tex. Bus. Org. Code § 22.351.

239 Tex. Bus. Org. Code § 22.351.

240 Tex. Bus. Org. Code § 22.351.

241 Tex. Bus. Org. Code § 252.010(a). The Texas Uniform Unincorporated Nonprofit Association Act defines a Nonprofit Association as an unincorporated organization, other than one created by a trust, consisting of three or more members joined by mutual consent for a common, nonprofit purpose. Tex. Bus. Org. Code § 252.010(c).

office or its principal office in Texas for examination by Unit Owners or their agents.[242] Unlike the Texas Nonprofit Corporation Law, there is no similar requirement that the Unit Owner make the request in writing or that the Unit Owner state the purpose for the request.

It is important to note that a Condominium Association that is incorporated as a nonprofit corporation is subject to the statutory requirements for inspection of Books and Records under both the Texas Uniform Condominium Act and the Texas Nonprofit Corporation Law, and in most cases, such a Condominium Association's Books and Records will constitute Books and Records under both statutes. To the extent a file or record kept by an applicable Condominium Association falls into one of the categories of Books and Records required to be kept by the Condominium Association under the Texas Uniform Condominium Act, a Unit Owner should be afforded the right to inspect such file or record without having to request it in writing or to state a purpose for the request. However, to the extent a file or record kept by an applicable Condominium Association falls outside the categories of Books and Records required to be kept by the Condominium Association under the Texas Uniform Condominium Act, a Unit Owner should comply with the requirements for inspection of Books and Records under the Texas Nonprofit Corporation Law, which requires the request to be in writing and that the Unit Owner state a proper purpose for such request.

6.17.4 Lot Owner's Right to Inspect Books and Records of a Subdivision Association under Chapter 209 of the Texas Property Code

Prior to 2011, Chapter 209 of the Texas Property Code required Subdivision Associations to make their Books and Records, including financial records, reasonably available to Lot Owners in accordance with the same procedures for inspection of Books and Records under the Texas Non-Profit Corporation Act, regardless of whether the

[242] Tex. Prop. Code § 82.114(b). An attorney's files and records related to the Condominium Association are not considered to be records of the Condominium Association and are not subject to inspection by Unit Owners. Tex. Prop. Code § 82.114(b).

Subdivision Association was incorporated as a nonprofit corporation. In 2011, however, the Texas Legislature significantly revised Section 209.005 of the Texas Property Code for the purpose of establishing comprehensive procedures for requesting, inspecting, and copying Books and Records of a Subdivision Association that differ significantly from those that previously applied.[243] To the extent a Subdivision Association is incorporated as a nonprofit corporation and is governed by both Chapter 209 and the Texas Nonprofit Corporation Law, the new procedures for requesting, inspecting, and copying Books and Records of a Subdivision Association under Chapter 209 control over the procedures set forth in the Nonprofit Corporation Law.[244]

6.17.4 (A) *Procedures for Requesting Inspection and/or Copies of a Subdivision Association's Books and Records*

Pursuant to Section 209.005 of the Texas Property Code, a Subdivision Association is required to make its Books and Records, including financial records, open

243 House Comm. on Judicial Affairs, Bill Analysis, Tex. H.B. 356, 70th Leg., R.S. (1987).

244 Tex. Prop. Code § 209.005(a). The procedures for requesting, inspecting, and copying Books and Records of a Subdivision Association under Chapter 209, however, do not apply to a Subdivision Association that is subject to Chapter 552 of the Texas Government Code (formally known as the "Texas Public Information Act," but more commonly referred to as the "Texas Open Records Act"). Tex. Prop. Code § 209.005(b). A Subdivision Association is subject to Chapter 552 of the Texas Government Code if: (1) membership in the Subdivision Association is mandatory for Lot Owners or a defined class of property owners in a defined geographic area in a county with a population of 2.8 million or more (Harris County) or in a county adjacent to a county with a population of 2.8 million or more (Brazoria, Chambers, Fort Bend, Liberty, Montgomery, San Jacinto, and Waller Counties); the Subdivision Association has the power to make mandatory special assessments for capital improvements or mandatory regular assessments; and the amount of the mandatory special or regular assessments is or has ever been based in whole or in part on the market value of Lot Owners' Lots or property as assessed by the State of Texas or a local governmental entity for purposes of ad valorem taxation; or (2) the Subdivision Association provides maintenance, preservation, and architectural control of residential and commercial property within a defined geographic area in a county with a population of 2.8 million or more (Harris County) or in a county adjacent to a county with a population of 2.8 million or more (Brazoria, Chambers, Fort Bend, Liberty, Montgomery, San Jacinto, and Waller Counties); and the Subdivision Association is a corporation that is governed by a board of trustees who may employ a general manager to execute the Subdivision Association's Bylaws and administer the business of the corporation; does not require membership in the corporation by the Lot Owners within the defined area; and was incorporated before January 1, 2006. Tex. Gov't Code § 552.0036. The only Texas county with a population of 2.8 million or more is Harris County, and the counties adjacent to Harris County are Brazoria, Chambers, Fort Bend, Liberty, Montgomery, San Jacinto, and Waller Counties. Source: United States Census Bureau, 2010.

to and reasonably available for examination by a Lot Owner or any other person designated as a Lot Owner's agent, attorney, or certified public accountant in a writing signed by such Lot Owner.[245] In addition, a Lot Owner and/or such other designated representative is also entitled to obtain copies of such Books and Records from the Subdivision Association.[246]

To inspect and/or obtain copies of a Subdivision Association's Books and Records, a Lot Owner or a Lot Owner's designated representative must submit a written request for information by certified mail to the Subdivision Association at its, or its designated representative's, mailing address as reflected on the most recently recorded Management Certificate for the Association.[247] The written request for information must describe with sufficient detail the Subdivision Association's Books and Records being requested and contain an election to either: (1) inspect such Books and Records before obtaining copies of them; or (2) have the Subdivision Association forward copies of the requested Books and Records without any advance inspection.[248]

6.17.4 (B) *Advance Inspection of a Subdivision Association's Books and Records*

If an advance inspection of a Subdivision Association's Books and Records is requested, then within ten (10) business days from the date the Subdivision Association receives the written request to inspect such Books and Records, it must send to the requesting party an initial written notice specifying the location and alternative dates that

245 Tex. Prop. Code § 209.005(c).

246 Tex. Prop. Code § 209.005(c).

247 Tex. Prop. Code § 209.005(e).

248 Tex. Prop. Code § 209.005(e).

such requesting party may inspect the requested Books and Records, to the extent such Books and Records are in the possession, custody, or control of the Association.[249]

A Subdivision Association should endeavor to make copies of the requested Books and Records available for inspection within ten (10) business days from the date it receives a request for information. However, if a Subdivision Association is unable to produce copies of the requested Books and Records and/or make them available for inspection within ten (10) business days from receipt of the request for information, then the Subdivision Association must state in the initial written notice to the requesting party that the Subdivision Association is unable to produce the requested information within ten (10) business days from the date it received the request for information and must specify an alternative date by which such requested Books and Records will be made available for inspection.[250]

One reason a requesting party may elect to inspect a Subdivision Association's Books and Records in lieu of or before requesting copies of such information and records is to determine if he or she wants to go to the expense of obtaining copies of such information and records or to limit the scope of the information and records that he or she wants to obtain copies of. If a requesting party elects to obtain copies of any of the Books and Records that he or she reviewed during the inspection, at the inspection the requesting party must identify the specific Books and Records that he or she wants the Association to copy and forward to him or her.[251] If copies of identified Books and Records of a Subdivision Association are requested at an inspection of such Books and Records, within

---

249 Tex. Prop. Code § 209.005(e)(1). For the purposes of Section 209.005, "business day" means a day other than Saturday, Sunday, or a state or federal holiday. Tex. Prop. Code § 209.005(q). If an inspection is requested or required, the inspection of the requested Books and Records shall take place at a mutually agreed upon time during normal business hours. Tex. Prop. Code § 209.005(g).

250 Tex. Prop. Code § 209.005(f)(1)–(2). The alternative date set for inspection of such requested Books and Records must be a date that is within fifteen (15) business days from the date of such initial written notice by the Subdivision Association to the requesting party. Tex. Prop. Code § 209.005(f)(2).

251 Tex. Prop. Code § 209.005(g).

ten (10) business days from the date of such inspection, the Subdivision must produce copies of such Books and Records to the requesting party.[252] A Subdivision Association may produce copies of the requested Books and Records to a requesting party in hard copy, electronic form, or any other format reasonably available to it.[253]

6.17.4 (C) *Copying of a Subdivision Association's Books and Records:*

If copies of identified Books and Records of a Subdivision Association are requested without an advance inspection of such Books and Records, within ten (10) business days from the date the Subdivision Association receives the written request for copies of such Books and Records, the Subdivision Association must produce copies of such requested Books and Records, to the extent such books and records are in its possession, custody, or control, to the requesting party.[254] If a Subdivision Association is unable to produce copies of the requested Books and Records to the requesting party within ten (10) business days from the date the Subdivision Association receives the written request for information, it must send to the requesting party an initial written notice within such deadline that: (1) states that the Subdivision Association is unable to produce the identified Books and Records within ten (10) business days from the date it received the written request for information; and (2) specifies an alternative date by which copies of such Books and Records will be sent to the requesting party.[255] A Subdivision Association may produce copies of requested Books and Records to a requesting party in hard copy, electronic form, or any other format reasonably available to it.[256]

---

[252] Tex. Prop. Code § 209.005(f).

[253] Tex. Prop. Code § 209.005(h).

[254] Tex. Prop. Code § 209.005(f).

[255] Tex. Prop. Code § 209.005(f). The alternative date for production of copies of such requested Books and Records must be a date that is within fifteen (15) business days from the date of such initial written notice by the Subdivision Association to the requesting party. Tex. Prop. Code § 209.005(f)(2).

[256] Tex. Prop. Code § 209.005(h).

6.17.4 (D) *Charging and Payment of Costs for the Compilation, Production, and Reproduction of Information Requested under Chapter 209*

Section 209.005 also authorizes a Subdivision Association to charge a requesting Lot Owner for the costs associated with the compilation, production, and/or reproduction of requested Books and Records. Before a Subdivision Association may charge a requesting Lot Owner for such costs, however, it must adopt and record a "Records Production and Copying Policy" that prescribes the costs that such Subdivision Association will charge a Lot Owner for the compilation, production, and reproduction of requested Books and Records.[257] In addition, a Subdivision Association may require advance payment of the estimated costs of compilation, production, and reproduction of the requested information from a requesting Lot Owner before it produces such information to such Lot Owner or his or her designated representative.[258]

If a Subdivision Association requires a requesting Lot Owner to pay the estimated cost of compilation, production, and reproduction of requested information and records in advance, and the actual cost is more or less than the estimated amount paid by the requesting Lot Owner, then the Subdivision Association must submit a final invoice to the requesting Lot Owner within thirty (30) business days from the date the requested information is delivered to the requesting party.[259] In the event the estimated cost paid by the requesting Lot Owner exceeds the actual cost of compilation, production, and

---

257 Tex. Prop. Code § 209.005(i). A Records Production and Copying Policy is considered to be a Dedicatory Instrument and must be recorded in the Official Public Records of each county in which the applicable Subdivision Development is located. Tex. Prop. Code §§ 202.006, 209.005(i). In addition, a Subdivision Association may not charge a Lot Owner for the cost of compilation, production, or reproduction of information requested under the procedures set for under Section 209.005 of the Texas Property Code unless a Records Production and Copying Policy prescribing such costs has been recorded by the Subdivision Association in the Official Public Records of the county in which its Subdivision Development is located. Tex. Prop. Code § 209.005(i).

258 Tex. Prop. Code § 209.005(i). Such estimated costs of compilation, production, and reproduction must be estimated using amounts prescribed by the Subdivision Association's recorded Records Production and Copying Policy. Tex. Prop. Code § 209.005(j).

259 Tex. Prop. Code § 209.005(i).

reproduction of the requested information and records, as reflected in such final invoice, the Subdivision Association must remit payment of such excess amount back to the requesting Lot Owner within thirty (30) business days from the date the final invoice was sent to the requesting Lot Owner.[260] On the other hand, if the actual cost of compilation, production, and reproduction of the requested information and records, as reflected in such final invoice, exceeds the estimated cost paid by the requesting Lot Owner, the requesting Lot Owner must remit payment of such additional amount to the Subdivision Association within thirty (30) business days from the date the final invoice was sent to the requesting Lot Owner.[261] If the requesting Lot Owner fails to remit payment of such additional amount within such thirty (30) business days, then such additional amount may be added to the Lot Owner's account as an Assessment.[262]

6.17.4 (E) *Conditional Exclusion of a Subdivision Association's Attorney's Files and Records from Inspection or Copying by Lot Owners*

Subject to certain exceptions, the files and records of a Subdivision Association's attorney are not considered to be Books or Records of such Subdivision Association and are not subject to inspection or copying by a Lot Owner or his or her designated representative.[263] The first exception to this rule arises if a Subdivision Association's attorney has possession of files and records relating to the Subdivision Association that would be responsive to a legally authorized request to inspect or copy records by a Lot Owner and the Subdivision Association has failed to maintain its own separate copy of such documents.[264] In such event, the documents responsive to a Lot Owner's request to

---

[260] Tex. Prop. Code § 209.005(i).

[261] Tex. Prop. Code § 209.005(i).

[262] Tex. Prop. Code § 209.005(i).

[263] Tex. Prop. Code § 209.005(d). Subject to such exceptions, Section 209.005 also excludes the files and records of a Subdivision Association's attorney from production in a legal proceeding. Tex. Prop. Code § 209.005(d).

[264] Tex. Prop. Code § 209.005(d).

inspect or copy records must be produced by the Subdivision Association by using copies of such documents from its attorney's files and records.[265]

The second exception to this rule concerns a request from a Lot Owner for a copy of a Subdivision Association's invoices for attorneys fees for which the Subdivision Association seeks reimbursement of from such Lot Owner. Pursuant to Section 209.008 of the Texas Property Code, a Subdivision Association, upon a written request from a Lot Owner charged with reimbursement of the Subdivision Association's attorneys fees, is required to provide such Lot Owner copies of invoices for the attorneys fees and other costs for which the Subdivision Association seeks reimbursement of from such Lot Owner.[266]

6.17.4 (F) *Subdivision Association Records that Are Exempted from Inspection and Copying by Lot Owners*

Section 209.005 of the Texas Property Code exempts certain records of a Subdivision Association concerning individual Lot Owners or employees of the Subdivision Association from inspection and copying by other Lot Owners. Except to the extent such information is stated within the minutes of a Board or Membership Meeting, a Subdivision Association is not required to release or allow inspection of any Books or Records that identify:

(1) an individual Lot Owner's history of violations of the Subdivision Association's Dedicatory Instruments (including the Declaration and Association Rules);[267]

---

265 Tex. Prop. Code § 209.005(d). Notwithstanding, such exception does not require production of a document that constitutes attorney work product or that is privileged as an attorney-client communication. Tex. Prop. Code § 209.005(d).

266 Tex. Prop. Code § 209.008(d).

267 Tex. Prop. Code § 209.005(k).

(2) an individual Lot Owner's personal financial information (including records of payment or nonpayment of Assessments or other amounts due the Subdivision Association);[268]

(3) a Lot Owner's contact information (other than the Lot Owner's address);[269] or

(4) information related to an employee of the Subdivision Association (including personnel files).[270]

A Subdivision Association may, however, release general financial information and information concerning violations of a Subdivision Association's Dedicatory Instruments in an aggregated or summary manner that would not identify an individual Lot Owner.[271] Notwithstanding, a Subdivision Association must release Books and Records concerning an individual Lot Owner or make such records available for inspection if: (1) the Subdivision Association receives express written approval from the Lot Owner whose records are the subject of the request for inspection; or (2) a court orders the release of such Books and Records or orders that such Books and Records be made available for inspection.[272]

6.17.4 (G) *Judicial Enforcement of a Lot Owner's Right to Inspect Books and Records of a Subdivision Association*

In addition to establishing new procedures for the inspection and copying of a Subdivision Association's Books and Records, the 2011 amendment to Section 209.005 of the Texas Property Code also established the authority of a Lot Owner who is denied access to or copies of a Subdivision Association's Books and Records (of which he or she is entitled to inspect and copy) to file a lawsuit against the Subdivision Association to

---

268 Tex. Prop. Code § 209.005(k).

269 Tex. Prop. Code § 209.005(k).

270 Tex. Prop. Code § 209.005(k).

271 Tex. Prop. Code § 209.005(k).

272 Tex. Prop. Code § 209.005(l).

compel it to produce such Books and Records.[273] At least ten (10) business days prior to filing such a lawsuit, the Lot Owner must send a written notice to the Subdivision Association advising it of such Lot Owner's intent to file a lawsuit against the Subdivision Association if the requested Books and Records are not produced to such Lot Owner.[274] Such notice must describe with sufficient detail the Books and Records being requested by the Lot Owner and must be sent to the Subdivision Association at the mailing address of the Subdivision Association or its authorized representative, as reflected on its most recently recorded Management Certificate, by either certified mail, return receipt requested, or United States Postal Service delivery with signature confirmation service.[275]

If a Subdivision Association fails to produce the requested Books and Records within ten (10) business days from the date a notice of intent to file a lawsuit is sent to it by a Lot Owner, such Lot Owner may file a lawsuit against the Subdivision Association in the Justice of the Peace Court of the justice precinct in which all or part of the applicable Subdivision Development is located.[276] If the Justice of the Peace finds that the Lot Owner is entitled to inspect and/or to obtain copies of the requested Books and Records, then the Justice of the Peace may grant one or more of the following remedies to the Lot Owner:

(1) a judgment ordering the Subdivision Association to release or allow access to the requested Books and Records;[277]

(2) a judgment against the Subdivision Association for court costs and attorneys fees incurred in connection with such lawsuit;[278] and/or

(3) a judgment authorizing the Lot Owner or the Lot Owner's assignee to deduct the amount of court costs and attorneys fees awarded to him or her

---

273 Tex. Prop. Code § 209.005(n).

274 Tex. Prop. Code § 209.005(p).

275 Tex. Prop. Code § 209.005(p).

276 Tex. Prop. Code § 209.005(n).

277 Tex. Prop. Code § 209.005(n)(1).

278 Tex. Prop. Code § 209.005(n)(2).

from any future regular or special Assessments payable to the Subdivision Association.[279]

If, however, the Subdivision Association prevails in such lawsuit, the Subdivision Association is entitled to a judgment against the Lot Owner for court costs and attorneys fees incurred by the Subdivision Association in connection with such lawsuit.[280]

6.18 Alternative Methods for Providing Notices to Lot Owners by a Subdivision Association

In 2015, the Texas Legislature enacted Section 209.0042 of the Texas Property Code, which authorizes a Texas Subdivision Association to adopt alternative methods of communication for providing notices from the Subdivision Association to its Lot Owners.[281] If the method of providing notice adopted by a Subdivision Association pursuant to Section 209.0042 is different from a specific method of notice that is required by Texas law, however, the Subdivision Association may use such alternative method of providing notice only if the Lot Owner to whom the notice is directed has affirmatively opted to allow the Subdivision Association to use the alternative method of providing notice under such circumstances.[282] By way of illustration, if a Subdivision Association adopts a policy that allows the Subdivision Association to provide all written notices to its Lot Owners by email, then the Subdivision Association may not provide a Lot Owner written notice of a restrictive covenant violation (which is required to be sent by certified mail under Section 209.006 of the Texas Property Code) by email unless such Lot Owner

---

[279] Tex. Prop. Code § 209.005(n)(3).

[280] Tex. Prop. Code § 209.005(o).

[281] Tex. Prop. Code § 209.0042(a).

[282] Tex. Prop. Code § 209.0042(b). Its important to note that a Subdivision Association may not require a Lot Owner to allow the Subdivision Association to use an alternative method of providing notice when a particular method of providing such type of notice is required by Texas law. Tex. Prop. Code § 209.0042(c). In other words, if a particular type of notice is required by Texas law to be sent to Lot Owners by certified mail, a Subdivision Association cannot require a Lot Owner to allow the Subdivision Association to provide such type of notice to him or her by a different method.

has affirmatively elected to receive notice of restrictive covenant violations by such method.

6.19 Audits of a Homeowners Association's Financial Records

There is no Texas law requiring a Subdivision Association to perform an audit of its financial records. Accordingly, unless the Governing Documents of a Subdivision Association requires the Board of Directors to perform an audit of the Subdivision Association's financial records, a Subdivision Association is not required to perform any audit of its financial records.

Unlike Subdivision Associations, however, the Texas Uniform Condominium Act requires all Texas Condominium Associations to obtain an independent audit of its records on an annual basis, the cost of which is to be treated as a Common Expense.[283] Such annual audit does not need to be performed by a certified public accountant, unless the Condominium Association's Bylaws require it or either the Board of Directors or a majority of the Unit Owners at a meeting of the Condominium Association's Membership votes to have the audit performed by a certified public accountant.[284] In addition, copies of the annual audit must be made available to the Unit Owners upon request.[285]

6.20 Applicability of the Texas Open Meetings Act and Public Information Act to Certain Texas Homeowners Associations

The Texas Open Meetings Act is a statute requiring governmental bodies to call and conduct their meetings in an open and public manner, so as to safeguard the public's interest in knowing the workings of its governmental bodies. In general, the Texas Open Meetings Act, except for certain limited exceptions, requires: (1) every regular, special,

[283] Tex. Prop. Code § 82.114(c).

[284] Tex. Prop. Code § 82.114(c).

[285] Tex. Prop. Code § 82.114(c).

or called meeting of a governmental body to be open to the public;[286] (2) the governmental body to post written notice of the date, hour, place, and subject of each meeting in a place readily accessible to the general public at least seventy-two (72) hours before the scheduled time of such meeting;[287] and (3) the governmental body to prepare and keep minutes or make a tape recording of each open meeting of the governmental body as public information.[288] In addition, an action taken by a governmental body in violation of the Texas Open Meetings Act is void and could subject any members of such governmental body who knowingly participated in such violation to criminal and civil liability.[289]

Governmental bodies in Texas are also subject to the Texas Public Information Act (informally known as the "Open Records Act"), the stated policy of which is "that each person is entitled, unless otherwise expressly provided by law, at all times to complete information about the affairs of government and the official acts of public officials and employees."[290] Subject to numerous exceptions and required procedures, the Open Records Act requires public information officers of governmental bodies to preserve records of public information and to make such records available for public inspection and copying.[291] "Public information" means information that is collected, assembled, or maintained under a law, an ordinance, or in connection with the transaction of official business by a governmental body (or on behalf of a governmental body if the

286 Tex. Gov't Code § 551.002.

287 Tex. Gov't Code §§ 551.041, 551.043.

288 Tex. Gov't Code §§ 551.021, 551.022.

289 Tex. Gov't Code §§ 551.141–551.146.

290 Tex. Gov't Code § 552.001.

291 Tex. Gov't Code § 552.203. The exceptions and procedures applicable under the Open Meetings Act are too numerous and complex to provide a thorough explanation of them within the confines of this book. For a more thorough explanation of the Open Meetings Act, please refer to the *Open Meetings 2008 Handbook* and the *2008 Open Meetings Act Made Easy*, which are both published by the Texas Attorney General's Office and can be viewed at http://www.oag.state.tx.us/open/index.shtml.

governmental body owns the information or has a right of access to it).[292] Similar to the Open Meetings Act, a failure to comply with the requirements of the Texas Open Records Act could subject a governmental body and its members to criminal and civil liability.[293]

In 2007, the Texas Legislature amended the Texas Open Meetings Act and Texas Open Records Act to make such Acts applicable to certain limited Homeowners Associations in Harris County and counties adjacent to Harris County.[294] The amendment was for the purpose of addressing certain perceived misconduct by particular Homeowners Associations in the Clear Lake area of Harris County, including the failure to respond to Homeowners' information requests and the closing of formerly public meetings to prevent Homeowners from contributing to meetings.[295] As a result of such 2007 amendment, the Texas Open Meetings and Open Records Acts are now applicable to a Homeowners Association in the same manner as a governmental body if: (1) membership in the Homeowners Association is mandatory for owners or for a defined class of owners of private real property in a defined geographic area in a county with a population of 2.8 million or more or in a county adjacent to a county with a population of 2.8 million or more;[296] (2) the Homeowners Association has the power to make mandatory special Assessments for capital improvements or mandatory regular Assessments;[297] and (3) the amount of the mandatory special or regular Assessments is or has ever been based in whole or in part on the value at which the state or a local governmental body assesses the Homeowners' property for purposes of ad valorem taxation under Section 20, Article

292 Tex. Gov't Code § 552.002.

293 Tex. Gov't Code §§ 552.321-552.353.

294 Senate Research Center, Bill Analysis, Tex. H.B. 3674, 80th Leg., R.S. (2007).

295 Senate Research Center, Bill Analysis, Tex. H.B. 3674, 80th Leg., R.S. (2007).

296 Tex. Gov't Code §§ 551.0015(a)(1)(A), 552.0036(1)(A). The only Texas county with a population of 2.8 million or more is Harris County, and the counties adjacent to Harris County are Brazoria, Chambers, Fort Bend, Liberty, Montgomery, San Jacinto, and Waller Counties. Source: United States Census Bureau, 2010.

297 Tex. Gov't Code §§ 551.0015(a)(1)(B), 552.0036(1)(B).

VIII, Texas Constitution.[298] In addition, a Homeowners Association is also subject to the Texas Open Meetings and Open Records Acts in the same manner as a governmental body if the Homeowners Association: (1) provides maintenance, preservation, and architectural control of residential and commercial property within a defined geographic area in a county with a population of 2.8 million or more or in a county adjacent to a county with a population of 2.8 million or more;[299] and (2) is a corporation that: (i) is governed by a board of trustees that may employ a general manager to execute the Homeowners Association's Bylaws and administer the business of the corporation; (ii) does not require Membership in the corporation by the owners of the property within the defined area; and (iii) was incorporated before January 1, 2006.[300]

If a Homeowners Association meets either of these criteria, then the Board of Directors and any committees established by the Board of Directors, as well as the individual members of the Board of Directors or of any such committees, must comply with the terms of the Open Meetings and Open Records Acts. Due to the complex nature of the duties, exceptions, and procedures provided for under these statutory schemes, as well as the accompanying potential civil and criminal liability for violations, any Homeowners Association subject to the Open Meetings Act and Open Records Act needs to seek consultation from competent legal counsel as to the full scope of the requirements under such Acts so as to ensure that it has adopted appropriate procedures in order to fully comply with such requirements.

---

298 Tex. Gov't Code §§ 551.0015(a)(1)(C), 552.0036(1)(C).

299 Tex. Gov't Code §§ 551.0015(a)(2)(A), 552.0036 (2)(A). The only Texas county with a population of 2.8 million or more is Harris County, and the counties adjacent to Harris County are Brazoria, Chambers, Fort Bend, Liberty, Montgomery, San Jacinto, and Waller Counties. Source: United States Census Bureau, 2010.

300 Tex. Gov't Code § 551.0015(a)(2)(B), 552.0036(2)(B).

6.21 Installation of Traffic Signs on Streets within a Subdivision Association's Jurisdiction

Section 430.002 of the Texas Transportation Code authorizes certain Subdivision Associations to erect a speed feedback sign[301] and/or a solar-powered light-emitting diode (LED) stop sign on a road, highway, or street within the Subdivision Association's jurisdiction if: (1) the Subdivision Association receives the consent of the governing body of the city or county that maintains the road, highway, or street for the placement of such sign; and (2) the Subdivision Association pays for the installation of the sign.[302] If a Subdivision Association installs a speed feedback sign or a solar-powered light-emitting diode (LED) stop sign pursuant to Section 430.002, then it is responsible for the maintenance of such sign.[303]

---

301 A "speed feedback" sign (also called a radar speed sign, speed display sign, a driver feedback sign, or a "your speed" sign) is an interactive sign, generally constructed of a series of LEDs, that displays vehicle speed as motorists approach the sign.

302 Tex. Transp. Code § 430.002(b). Section 430.002 applies to all "property owners' associations" as described by Section 204.004 of the Texas Property Code. Tex. Transp. Code § 430.002(a). Section 204.004 describes a property owners association as a designated representative of the owners of property in a subdivision development, which: (1) has a membership that consists of the owners of property within such subdivision development; (2) is either an incorporated nonprofit corporation or unincorporated nonprofit association; and (3) has a Board of Directors or Trustees that are elected or appointed in accordance with the applicable provisions of the restrictions and the Subdivision Association's Articles of Incorporation or Bylaws. Tex. Prop. Code § 204.004.

303 Tex. Transp. Code § 430.002(c).

CHAPTER 7 LEVYING AND COLLECTING ASSESSMENTS

CHAPTER 7 LEVYING AND COLLECTING ASSESSMENTS

7.1 In General

Texas Homeowners Associations provide essential services to the residential communities they serve that affect the property values of the individual Lots or Units within such communities. This is particularly true in Condominium Developments subject to the Texas Uniform Condominium Act, where the Condominium Association is directly responsible for maintaining and repairing the Common Elements of the Condominium Development. In order to pay for the costs of such services, almost all Homeowners Associations are authorized by their Governing Documents to levy "Assessments" against the Lots or Units within their development.[1] In addition, the Governing Documents of each such Homeowners Association will also typically provide for an underlying contractual lien against the applicable Lots or Units in favor of the Homeowners Association to secure payment of such Assessments, which is generally referred to as an "Assessment Lien."

Assessments are the lifeblood of Homeowners Associations, without which Homeowners Associations would be unable to fulfill their duties to their community. Inevitably, some Lot or Unit Owners in every Homeowners Association will not pay levied Assessments and, by consequence, the Homeowners Association will be put in the unenviable position of having to engage in collection efforts against such Homeowners. A Homeowners Association's Board of Directors has a duty to act in the best interest of its community and with due care in the management of the Homeowners Association's affairs, which in most cases means that the Board of Directors has an obligation to make an effort to collect such unpaid Assessments and, in appropriate circumstances, to foreclose its Assessment Lien against a delinquent Homeowner.

---

[1] Generally speaking, the term "Assessment" refers to a charge, fee, or dues that each Homeowner is required to pay his or her Homeowners Association pursuant to the Homeowners Association's Dedicatory Instruments or Texas law. *See generally* Tex. Prop. Code §§ 82.113(a); 204.001(3)–(4); 209.002(1).

Perhaps no function of a Homeowners Association has attracted as much public media attention as the collection of Assessments and the exercise of foreclosure rights in connection with such collection efforts. In fact, in response to certain public outcry following the foreclosure of an Assessment Lien by a Homeowners Association in Harris County in 2001, the Texas Legislature enacted the Texas Residential Property Owners Protection Act (which is codified at Chapter 209 of the Texas Property Code and is more commonly referred to as Chapter 209 of the Texas Property Code, or simply "Chapter 209").[2] Chapter 209 of the Texas Property Code, among other things, imposes certain due process requirements on Texas Subdivision Associations before they can assess a fine, file a lawsuit, foreclose an Assessment Lien, and/or seek reimbursement of attorneys fees against a Homeowner.[3]

This chapter will cover basic principles concerning the authority of Homeowners Associations to levy Assessments and the establishment of Assessment Liens, as well as the regulations and procedures that govern foreclosure of Assessment Liens and redemption of a Lot or Unit by its owner following foreclosure of a Homeowners Association's Assessment Lien. This chapter is intended as a guide for educational purposes only, and for several reasons it should not be used as a self-instruction manual by a Homeowners Associations for collection of Assessments. First, collection of Assessments is subject to many federal and state laws, in addition to the Texas Uniform Condominium Act and Chapter 209 of the Texas Property Code, including, but not limited to, the Federal and Texas fair debt collection statutes and the Texas Constitution's protection of a Homeowner's residential homestead. Second, the foreclosure of an Assessment Lien on real property must comply with both the Homeowners Association's

[2] Tex. Prop. Code § 209.001. The enacting legislation notes that it was enacted in honor of Wenonah Blevins, a woman whose home was foreclosed upon by a Homeowners Association in Harris County, and that the Texas Residential Property Owners Protection Act may be unofficially referred to as the "Wenonah Blevins Residential Property Owners Protection Act."

[3] Tex. Prop. Code § 209.006, et. seq.

Governing Documents and all applicable provisions of the Texas Property Code and applicable provisions of the Texas Rules of Civil Procedure. If an Assessment Lien foreclosure is performed improperly, it could subject a Homeowners Association to liability for wrongful foreclosure. Finally, the ability to collect unpaid Assessments or foreclose an Assessment Lien can also be subject to certain prohibitions under the United States Bankruptcy Code if a Homeowner files for bankruptcy protection.

More importantly, foreclosure of a Homeowners Association's Assessment Lien may not be appropriate or in a Homeowners Association's best interest in all circumstances. The advisability of foreclosing an Assessment Lien should be made on a case-by-case basis with due consideration given to the amount of unpaid Assessments owed by the Homeowner and the amount of time such Assessments have been in arrearage; the existence and amounts of any senior liens attached to the delinquent Homeowner's Lot or Unit; whether the Homeowners Association is authorized to conduct non-judicial foreclosure of its Assessment Lien; and the cost of foreclosing the Assessment Lien, among other factors. For such reasons, a Homeowners Association should not engage in collection efforts without retaining, or at least consulting, a professional management company or competent attorney to assist it.

7.2 Source and Scope of a Homeowners Association's Authority to Levy Assessments against Homeowners

The authority of a Texas Homeowners Association to levy Assessments is primarily derived from its Governing Documents. If the Homeowners Association is a Condominium Association, the Texas Uniform Condominium Act also provides authority for all Texas Condominium Associations to levy Assessments against their Unit Owners for Common Expenses of the Condominium Development.[4]

4 Tex. Prop. Code § 82.102(a)(2).

The term "Assessment" refers to the charges that a Homeowners Association assesses against its Homeowners to pay for common expenses associated with the operation of the Homeowners Association and maintenance of the Common Areas or Common Elements in the community. Assessments can take many forms, but they are generally categorized as either Regular Assessments, Special Assessments, or Individual Assessments.

The term "Regular Assessments" (also sometimes called "Annual Assessments") refers to those Assessments that are levied by a Homeowners Association in a uniform manner against all Homeowners in a community on some type of regular basis, such as monthly, quarterly, biannually, or annually.

The term "Special Assessments," on the other hand, refers to Assessments that are levied by a Homeowners Association in a uniform manner against all Homeowners in a community on a one-time basis due to some special circumstance. Under most Declarations, before a Homeowners Association's Board of Directors can levy a Special Assessment against its Homeowners, such Special Assessment must be approved by such Homeowners.

Finally, the term "Individual Assessments" refers to Assessments that are levied by a Homeowners Association against Homeowners on an individual, non-uniform, basis. Two common examples of an Individual Assessment are an Assessment levied by a Subdivision Association against a particular Lot Owner for damage to the Common Areas and an Assessment levied against each particular Unit Owner by a Condominium Association that pays for all water usage by the entire Condominium Development, the amount of which is based on the amount of water usage by each such Unit Owner. Depending on the basis for an Individual Assessment, it may be levied by a Homeowners Association on a regular basis or on a one-time basis due to some special circumstance.

The type of Assessments and the amount of each Assessment that a Homeowners Association may levy against its Homeowners will generally be controlled by the provisions of the Homeowners Association's Governing Documents, and the Board of Directors may not exceed such authority. A Homeowners Association's Declaration will also typically impose certain procedures for the approval of a Special Assessment by its Board of Directors and/or its Membership, as well as establish limitations on the ability of the Homeowners Association to increase the amount of Regular Assessments. Accordingly, the Board of Directors of a Homeowners Association should become familiar with its Governing Documents prior to levying any type of Assessments against its Homeowners.

7.3 Obligation of Homeowners to Pay Assessments

The authority of a Homeowners Association to levy Assessments necessarily includes an obligation of its Homeowners to pay such Assessments. In most cases where the Governing Documents create the authority to levy Assessments, there will also be a provision mandating that the obligation to pay such Assessments is a personal obligation of the Homeowner.[5] Such a provision means that the Homeowner remains obligated to pay all Assessments levied against such Homeowner's Lot or Unit during the time of his or her ownership of such property, regardless of whether such Homeowner subsequently ceases owning such property. In other words, if Assessments levied against a Lot or Unit during the period of a person's ownership are not paid, such person continues to have a personal obligation to pay such unpaid Assessments even after his or her ownership terminates. This is because the obligation to pay the Assessments is personal to the Homeowner, not the Lot or Unit. This is certainly true for Unit Owners, whether so provided in the Condominium Association's Governing Documents or not, because the

[5] Such obligation is contractual in nature and is binding upon a Homeowner who acquires title to an applicable Lot or Unit.

Texas Uniform Condominium Act establishes the personal liability of Unit Owners to pay Assessments levied during their ownership of their Unit.[6]

In some limited instances, a Homeowners Association's Declaration may also provide for the assumption of liability for a prior Homeowner's unpaid Assessments by a new owner acquiring ownership of a Lot or Unit if the new owner had knowledge of such unpaid Assessments at the time of conveyance. In such cases, it is very important that the Homeowners Association specifically identifies the amount of any unpaid Assessments previously levied against the Lot or Unit in any Resale Certificates produced by the Homeowners Association to prospective purchasers of such property.

7.4 Assessment of Late Fees and Interest

If a Homeowner fails to timely pay an Assessment to his or her Homeowners Association, such Homeowners Association may have the authority to assess late fees and/or interest against such Homeowner. The ability of a Homeowners Association to assess late fees or charge interest on unpaid Assessments is primarily governed by the Homeowners Association's Governing Documents, but it also depends on whether the Homeowners Association is a Condominium Association or a Subdivision Association.

If a Homeowners Association is a Condominium Association, the Texas Uniform Condominium Act specifically authorizes a Condominium Association, unless otherwise provided by its Declaration, to: (1) collect Assessments for Common Expenses from Unit Owners; (2) impose interest and late charges for late payments of Assessments and returned check charges; (3) suspend the voting privileges of or the use of certain general Common Elements by an owner delinquent for more than thirty (30) days in the payment of Assessments; (4) impose reasonable charges for preparing and recording statements of

---

6 Tex. Prop. Code § 82.113(a).

unpaid Assessments; and (5) adopt and amend Association Rules regulating the collection of delinquent Assessments and the application of payments.[7]

If a Homeowners Association is a Subdivision Association that is incorporated as a nonprofit corporation and located in Harris, Galveston, or Montgomery County, Chapter 204 of the Texas Property Code[8] specifically authorizes such a Subdivision Association, unless otherwise provided by its Declaration, Articles of Incorporation, or Bylaws, to: (1) collect regular Assessments or special Assessments for Common Expenses from Lot Owners;[9] (2) impose interest, late charges, and, if applicable, returned check charges for late payments of regular Assessments or special Assessments;[10] (3) charge costs to a Lot Owner's Assessment account and collect the costs in any manner provided in the Declaration for the Subdivision Development for the collection of Assessments;[11] and (4) adopt and amend rules regulating the collection of delinquent Assessments and the application of payments.[12]

---

[7] Tex. Prop. Code § 82.102.

[8] By its express terms, Chapter 204 of the Texas Property Code applies only to a Subdivision Association that is incorporated as a nonprofit corporation and governs a residential Subdivision Development that is located in whole or in part: (1) in a county with a population of 3.3 million or more (Harris County); (2) in a county with a population of not less than 285,000 and not more than 300,000 that is adjacent to the Gulf of Mexico and that is adjacent to a county having a population of 3.3 million or more (Galveston County); or (3) in a county with a population of 275,000 or more that is adjacent to a county with a population of 3.3 million or more and contains part of a national forest (Montgomery County). Tex. Prop. Code §§ 204.002(a); 204.003(a). The only Texas county with a population of 3.3 million or more is Harris County. The only Texas county with a population of not less than 285,000 and not more than 300,000 that is adjacent to the Gulf of Mexico and a county with a population of 3.3 million or more is Galveston County. The only Texas county with a population of 275,000 or more that is adjacent to a county with a population of 3.3 million or more and contains part of a national forest is Montgomery County (Sam Houston National Forest). Source: United States Census Bureau, 2010.

[9] Tex. Prop. Code § 204.010(a)(2).

[10] Tex. Prop. Code § 204.010(a)(10).

[11] Tex. Prop. Code § 204.010(a)(12).

[12] Tex. Prop. Code § 204.010(a)(13). Any rules regulating the collection of delinquent Assessments and the application of payments that are adopted by a Subdivision Association subject to Chapter 204 must comply with the provisions of Chapter 209 of the Texas Property Code that govern the collection of Assessments and application of payments.

There is no similar statutory authority to assess late fees or interest that is vested in unincorporated Subdivision Associations located in Harris, Galveston, or Montgomery County, nor is there any such statutory authority that is vested in Subdivision Associations that are located outside of Harris, Galveston, and Montgomery Counties, regardless of whether they are incorporated as nonprofit corporations. As a result, if a Homeowners Association is a Subdivision Association that is either unincorporated or is located in a county other than Harris, Galveston, or Montgomery County, then in order to assess late fees or interest against a Lot Owner who fails to timely pay an Assessment, such Subdivision Association must be expressly authorized to do so by its Governing Documents. In other words, unless the Declaration, Articles of Incorporation, or Bylaws of such a Subdivision Association expressly authorizes it to assess late fees or make Lot Owners liable for interest on past-due Assessments, it may not assess such Lot Owners for late fees or interest on past-due Assessments.

7.5 Payment Plan and Priority of Payment Schedule Requirements Applicable to Subdivision Associations

In 2011, the Texas Legislature enacted the most significant reforms to the laws governing Texas Homeowners Associations since the enactment of the Texas Uniform Condominium Act in 1993. Most of the reforms consisted of adding new provisions to or modifying existing provisions of Chapter 209 of the Texas Property Code, which applies only to Subdivision Associations. Accordingly, the majority of these new laws affect primarily only Subdivision Associations and not Condominium Associations. Among other things, the 2011 Texas Legislature enacted new laws that require certain Subdivision Associations to allow delinquent Lot Owners to pay off outstanding amounts owed to such a Subdivision Association in installments over time and that mandate the manner in which a Lot Owner's payments are applied to his or her delinquent Assessment account.

7.5.1 Payment Plan Requirement Applicable to Subdivision Associations Consisting of Fifteen or More Lots

Section 209.0062 of the Texas Property Code requires all Subdivision Associations consisting of at least fifteen Lots to adopt reasonable payment plan guidelines by which Lot Owners may pay off delinquent regular or special Assessments or any other amounts owed to the Subdivision Association over a period of time without accruing additional monetary penalties (hereinafter referred to as a "Payment Plan Guidelines Policy").[13] In other words, an applicable Texas Subdivision Association must offer its Lot Owners an opportunity to pay their delinquent Assessments under an installment payment plan.[14]

With the exception of one limitation concerning the minimum duration of a payment plan, the terms of an applicable Subdivision Association's Payment Plan Guidelines Policy is left to the discretion of its Board of Directors. The minimum term of a payment plan offered by an applicable Subdivision Association under its Payment Plan Guidelines Policy must be at least three (3) months.[15]

---

[13] Tex. Prop. Code § 209.0062(a). For purposes of Section 209.0062, monetary penalties do not include reasonable costs associated with administering the payment plan or accrued interest. Tex. Prop. Code § 209.0062(a).

[14] An applicable Subdivision Association, however, is not required to allow a Lot Owner to enter into a payment plan more than once in any 12-month period or to enter into a payment plan with a Lot Owner if such Lot Owner failed to honor the terms of a previous payment plan and it has been less than two years since such Lot Owner's default under the previous payment plan. Tex. Prop. Code § 209.0062(c). In addition, a Subdivision Association is not required to make a payment plan available to a Lot Owner if the Lot Owner fails to request a payment plan before the expiration of the cure period specified in a written notice under Section 209.0064(b) of the Texas Property Code. Tex. Prop. Code § 209.0062(c). It is important to note that Section 209.0064(b) of the Texas Property Code requires a Subdivision Association to give a delinquent Lot Owner a written notice by certified mail that describes the options the Lot Owner has to avoid having the account turned over to a Collection Agent, including information regarding availability of a payment plan under the Subdivision Association's Payment Plan Guidelines Policy (if applicable), before the Subdivision Association may hold such delinquent Lot Owner liable for the fees of the Collection Agent. Tex. Prop. Code § 209.0064(b).

[15] Tex. Prop. Code § 209.0062(b). While there is no required maximum duration of a payment plan, Section 209.0062 does provide that a Subdivision Association is not required to allow a payment plan for any amount

In addition, a Payment Plan Guidelines Policy is also considered to be a Dedicatory Instrument, and a copy of such policy must be recorded by the Subdivision Association in the Official Public Records of each county in which all or a portion of its Subdivision Development is located.[16] It is also important to note that even if an applicable Subdivision Association fails to record a Payment Plan Guidelines Policy in the Official Public Records of each county in which it is located, such failure does not excuse a Subdivision Association from its obligation to allow a Lot Owner to pay off delinquent amounts owed to the Subdivision Association in installments over a period of time of at least three (3) without accruing additional monetary penalties.[17]

7.5.2 Priority of Payment Schedule Applicable to All Subdivision Associations

Section 209.0063 of the Texas Property Code establishes a priority of payments schedule that dictates the manner and order in which a Subdivision Association must apply payments from a Lot Owner to outstanding amounts such Lot Owner owes to the Subdivision Association. Pursuant to Section 209.0063, a payment received by a Subdivision Association from a Lot Owner must be applied to such Lot Owner's debt in the following order of priority:

(1) any delinquent Assessments owed by the Lot Owner;[18]

(2) any current Assessment owed by the Lot Owner;[19]

(3) any attorneys fees or third-party collection costs incurred by the Subdivision Association associated solely with collection of Assessments or any other charges that are secured by the Subdivision Association's

that extends more than eighteen (18) months from the date of the Lot Owner's request for a payment plan. Tex. Prop. Code § 209.0062(c)

[16] Tex. Prop. Code §§ 202.006, 209.0062(d).

[17] Tex. Prop. Code § 209.0062(e).

[18] Tex. Prop. Code § 209.0063(a)(1).

[19] Tex. Prop. Code § 209.0063(a)(2).

Assessment Lien or that could provide the basis for foreclosure of its Assessment Lien against the Lot Owner's Lot;[20]

(4) any attorneys fees incurred by the Subdivision Association that could not provide a basis for foreclosure of the Subdivision Association's Assessment Lien against the Lot Owner's Lot;[21]

(5) any fines assessed by the Subdivision Association against the Lot Owner;[22] and

(6) any other amount the Lot Owner owes to the Subdivision Association.[23]

Notwithstanding, a Subdivision Association is not required to apply a Lot Owner's payment in the aforementioned order of priority if at the time the Subdivision Association receives such payment the Lot Owner is in default of his or her payment obligations under a payment plan entered into with the Subdivision Association.[24] In such event, the Subdivision Association may apply the Lot Owner's payment in its normal or customary manner, except that the Subdivision Association still may not apply any portion of the Lot Owner's payment to fines assessed against the Lot Owner before satisfying all delinquent Assessments, incurred attorneys fees and third-party collection costs the Lot Owner owes to the Subdivision Association.[25]

7.6 Reimbursement of Collection Costs and Attorneys Fees Incurred by a Homeowners Association

When a Homeowner fails to pay an Assessment, a Homeowners Association will often attempt to collect such unpaid Assessment from the Homeowner. In such event, the Homeowners Association will generally incur some costs associated with its efforts to

---

20 Tex. Prop. Code § 209.0063(a)(3).

21 Tex. Prop. Code § 209.0063(a)(4).

22 Tex. Prop. Code § 209.0063(a)(5).

23 Tex. Prop. Code § 209.0063(a)(6).

24 Tex. Prop. Code § 209.0063(b)(1).

25 Tex. Prop. Code § 209.0063(b)(2).

collect the unpaid Assessment, which may include attorneys fees. The ability of a Homeowners Association to seek reimbursement of collection costs and/or attorneys fees incurred by the Homeowners Association in its efforts to collect an unpaid Assessment from a Homeowner is controlled by the Homeowners Association's Governing Documents, as well as the Texas Uniform Condominium Act and Chapters 204 and 209 of the Texas Property Code. The provisions of such laws differ significantly and are explained in greater detail in the following subchapters.

7.6.1 Reimbursement of Collection Costs and Attorneys Fees Incurred by a Condominium Association

The ability of a Condominium Association to recover its costs of collection, including attorneys fees, from a delinquent Unit Owner is controlled by its Governing Documents and the Texas Uniform Condominium Act. In addition to any applicable authority granted to a Condominium Association in its Governing Documents, the Texas Uniform Condominium Act expressly authorizes a Condominium Association to charge a delinquent Unit Owner for all costs of collection and attorneys fees incurred by it in the collection of unpaid Assessments, and it makes a delinquent Unit Owner liable to the Condominium Association for such costs of collection and attorneys fees, whether or not a lawsuit is filed.[26] In addition, a Condominium Association is not required to provide a delinquent Unit Owner with any notices prior to assessing a Unit Owner for attorneys fees incurred by the Condominium Association, nor is there any limitation on the amount of attorneys fees that a Condominium Association may seek reimbursement of in a non-judicial foreclosure of its Assessment Lien.[27]

26 Tex. Prop. Code §§ 82.113(a); 82.117(1), (4). It is important to note that the provisions of the Texas Uniform Condominium Act imposing an obligation on Unit Owners to pay Assessments, comply with Governing Documents, and pay for damages caused to the Condominium Development are not applicable to Condominium Developments created prior to January 1, 1994, that are subject to the Texas Condominium Act, and there are no comparable provisions under the Texas Condominium Act. Tex. Prop. Code § 82.002(c).

27 Tex. Prop. Code § 82.113.

7.6.2 Reimbursement of Collection Costs and Attorneys Fees Incurred by a Subdivision Association

With the exception of certain Subdivision Associations located in Harris, Galveston, and Montgomery Counties, the ability of a Texas Subdivision Association to hold a delinquent Lot Owner liable for its costs of collection, including attorneys fees, associated with the collection of delinquent Assessments must be authorized by the Subdivision Association's Governing Documents. If a Subdivision Association is incorporated as a nonprofit corporation and is located in Harris, Galveston, or Montgomery County, however, Chapter 204 of Texas Property Code[28] specifically authorizes such a Subdivision Association, unless otherwise provided by its Declaration, Articles of Incorporation, or Bylaws, to: (1) collect regular Assessments or special Assessments for common expenses from Lot Owners;[29] (2) impose interest, late charges, and, if applicable, returned check charges for late payments of regular Assessments or special Assessments;[30] (3) charge costs to a Lot Owner's Assessment account and collect the costs in any manner provided in the Declaration for the Subdivision Development for

---

[28] By its express terms, Chapter 204 of the Texas Property Code applies only to a Subdivision Association that is incorporated as a nonprofit corporation and governs a residential Subdivision Development that is located in whole or in part: (1) in a county with a population of 3.3 million or more (Harris County); (2) in a county with a population of not less than 285,000 and not more than 300,000 that is adjacent to the Gulf of Mexico and that is adjacent to a county having a population of 3.3 million or more (Galveston County); or (3) in a county with a population of 275,000 or more that is adjacent to a county with a population of 3.3 million or more and contains part of a national forest (Montgomery County). Tex. Prop. Code §§ 204.002(a); 204.003(a). The only Texas county with a population of 3.3 million or more is Harris County. The only Texas county with a population of not less than 285,000 and not more than 300,000 that is adjacent to the Gulf of Mexico and a county with a population of 3.3 million or more is Galveston County. The only Texas county with a population of 275,000 or more that is adjacent to a county with a population of 3.3 million or more and contains part of a national forest is Montgomery County (Sam Houston National Forest). Source: United States Census Bureau, 2010.

[29] Tex. Prop. Code § 204.010(a)(2).

[30] Tex. Prop. Code § 204.010(a)(10).

the collection of Assessments;[31] and (4) adopt and amend rules regulating the collection of delinquent Assessments and the application of payments.[32]

Chapter 204 of the Texas Property Code, however, does not apply to an unincorporated Subdivision Association located in Harris, Galveston, or Montgomery County.[33] In addition, there is no other similar type of statutory authority to charge a Lot Owner for costs that is applicable to Subdivision Associations that are located outside of Harris, Galveston, and Montgomery Counties, regardless of whether the Subdivision Association is incorporated as a nonprofit corporation or not. As a result, if a Homeowners Association is a Subdivision Association that is either unincorporated or is located in a county other than Harris, Galveston, or Montgomery County, in order to assess a delinquent Lot Owner for costs of collection and attorneys fees incurred by it in the collection of unpaid Assessments, such Subdivision Association must be expressly authorized to do so by its Governing Documents. In other words, unless the Declaration, Articles of Incorporation, or Bylaws of such a Subdivision Association makes a Lot Owner liable to the Subdivision Association for its costs of collection and attorneys fees in the event such Lot Owner fails to timely pay his or her Assessments, a delinquent Lot Owner is not liable for, and the Subdivision Association may not require such Lot Owner to reimburse the Subdivision Association for, its costs of collection or attorneys fees without the Subdivision Association filing a lawsuit against the delinquent Lot Owner to collect such unpaid Assessments.[34]

---

31 Tex. Prop. Code § 204.010(a)(12).

32 Tex. Prop. Code § 204.010(a)(13). Any rules regulating the collection of delinquent Assessments and the application of payments that are adopted by a Subdivision Association subject to Chapter 204 must comply with the provisions of Chapter 209 of the Texas Property Code that govern the collection of Assessments and application of payments.

33 Tex. Prop. Code §§ 204.002(a); 204.003(a).

34 There are three Texas statutes that provide for the potential recovery of attorneys fees in a lawsuit to enforce the terms of a Declaration, including the obligation of a Homeowner to pay Assessments authorized by the Declaration. Such statutes include Section 5.006 of the Texas Property Code and Chapters 37 and 38 of the Texas Civil Practice and Remedies Code. Under all such statutes, a court is required or authorized to

In most cases, however, a Subdivision Association's Declaration will include an express provision that makes a Lot Owner who fails to timely pay an Assessment liable for costs of collection, including any attorneys fees, incurred by such Subdivision Association. And, while Chapter 209 of the Texas Property Code does not vest a Subdivision Association with the authority to assess a delinquent Lot Owner for costs of collection and attorneys fees incurred by it in the collection of unpaid Assessments, Chapter 209 does impose several due process requirements and restrictions on the ability of a Subdivision Association to seek reimbursement of costs of collection and attorneys fees incurred in its efforts to collect delinquent Assessments from a Lot Owner, which are discussed in greater detail in the following subchapters.

7.6.2 (A) *Required Written Notice before a Lot Owner May Be Held Liable for Attorneys Fees and/or Collection Agent Fees*

There are two statutory provisions under Chapter 209 that require a Subdivision Association to provide a Lot Owner certain written notice before it may hold such Lot Owner liable for attorneys fees incurred in the collection of unpaid Assessments. The first statute is Section 209.008 of the Texas Property Code, which provides that a Subdivision Association may not collect reimbursement of reasonable attorneys fees and other reasonable costs incurred in collecting amounts due a Subdivision Association for enforcing its Declaration, Bylaws, or Association Rules from a Lot Owner unless such Lot Owner is first provided a written notice that attorneys fees and costs will be charged to the Lot Owner if the delinquency or violation continues after a certain date.[35]

---

award a party who asserts a lawsuit for breach of a Declaration his or her reasonable attorneys fees. *See* Tex. Prop. Code § 5.006 (a court shall allow to a prevailing party, who asserted an action based on breach of a restrictive covenant pertaining to real property, reasonable attorneys fees); Tex. Civ. Prac. & Rem. Code § 37.009 (the court may award costs and reasonable and necessary attorneys fees as are equitable and just); Tex. Civ. Prac. & Rem. Code § 38.001 (a person may recover reasonable attorneys fees from an individual or corporation, in addition to the amount of a valid claim and costs, if the claim is based on a written contract).

35 Tex. Prop. Code § 209.008(a). It is important to note that despite the express language of Section 209.008(a) that requires a Subdivision Association to provide written notice to a Lot Owner stating that he or she will be charged attorneys fees if a "delinquency" continues after a certain date before it can collect

The second statute is Section 209.0064 of the Texas Property Code, which is one of the reforms enacted by the Texas Legislature in 2011. While Section 209.008 applies expressly to attorneys fees, Section 209.0064 applies to fees of a "Collection Agent."[36] The term "Collection Agent" is a new term of art created by Section 209.0064 and is defined as a "debt collector" under the federal Fair Debt Collection Practices Act.[37] In general, an attorney retained by a Subdivision Association to collect unpaid Assessments owed to it by a Lot Owner is considered a "debt collector" under the federal Fair Debt Collection Practices Act.[38] Accordingly, the notice requirement under Section 209.0064, which applies to the collection of a Collection Agent's fees, applies equally to the collection of attorneys fees incurred by a Subdivision Association in the collection of unpaid Assessments.

Section 209.0064 provides that a Subdivision Association may not hold a Lot Owner liable for fees of a Collection Agent retained by the Subdivision Association unless

---

reimbursement of attorneys fees and other costs incurred by the Subdivision Association relating to collecting amounts due the Subdivision Association from the Lot Owner, one Texas Court of Appeals has held that such provision does not apply to attorneys fees incurred by a Subdivision Association merely to collect delinquent Assessments or to enforce its Assessment Lien for nonpayment of Assessments. *See Haas v. Ashford Hollow Cmty. Imprv. Ass'n*, 209 S.W.3d 875, 885 (Tex. App.—Houston [14th Dist.] 2006, no pet.). Neither the Texas Supreme Court, nor any other Texas Courts of Appeals, however, has addressed the applicability of Section 209.008(a) to attorneys fees incurred in the collection of Assessments. For such reason, Texas Subdivision Associations should still adhere to the requirements of Section 209.008(a).

36 Tex. Prop. Code § 209.0064.

37 Tex. Prop. Code § 209.0064(a). The term "debt collector" under the federal Fair Debt Collection Practices Act means "any person who uses any instrumentality of interstate commerce or the mails in any business the principal purpose of which is the collection of any debts, or who regularly collects or attempts to collect, directly or indirectly, debts owed or due or asserted to be owed or due another." 15 U.S.C. § 1692a(6). Such term, however, does not generally apply to a creditor attempting to collect a debt owed to it on its own behalf, nor to any officer or employee of a creditor while, in the name of the creditor, is attempting to collect debts for such creditor. 15 U.S.C. § 1692a(6); *see also Wadlington v. Credit Acceptance Corp.*, 76 F.3d 103, 106 (6th Cir. 1996). The application of the federal Fair Debt Collection Practices Act to Texas Homeowners Associations is discussed in greater detail in subchapter 7.15 of this book.

38 *See Heintz v. Jenkins*, 514 U.S. 291, 298–99 (1995).

the Subdivision Association first provides written notice to the Lot Owner by certified mail that:

(1) specifies each delinquent amount owed by the Lot Owner and the total amount of the payment required by the Lot Owner to make his or her account current;[39]

(2) provides the Lot Owner a period of at least thirty (30) days to cure the delinquency before further collection action may be taken by the Subdivision Association or a Collection Agent retained by it;[40] and

(3) if the Subdivision Association is composed of at least fifteen Lots or its Dedicatory Instruments contain a requirement to offer a payment plan to a delinquent Lot Owner, describes the options the Lot Owner has to avoid having the account turned over to a Collection Agent, including information regarding availability of a payment plan under the Subdivision Association's Payment Plan Guidelines Policy or Dedicatory Instruments.[41]

It is important to note that the notice information required to be given to a Lot Owner by a Subdivision Association under Sections 209.008 and 209.0064 of the Texas Property Code can be consolidated and provided to a Lot Owner in a single letter.

---

39 Tex. Prop. Code § 209.0064(b)(1).

40 Tex. Prop. Code § 209.0064(b)(3).

41 Tex. Prop. Code § 209.0064(b)(2). If a Subdivision Association is composed of fifteen (15) or more Lots, Chapter 209 requires it to record a Payment Plan Guidelines Policy and to allow a Lot Owner to pay off a delinquent account under an installment payment plan. Tex. Prop. Code § 209.0062. If a Subdivision Association is composed of less than fifteen (15) Lots, however, Chapter 209 does not require it to record a Payment Plan Guidelines Policy or to allow a Lot Owner to pay off a delinquent account under an installment payment plan. Tex. Prop. Code § 209.0062. Notwithstanding, if such a Subdivision Association's Dedicatory Instruments require it to offer a payment plan to a delinquent Lot Owner, then it must do so in accordance with the terms of such Dedicatory Instrument and it must describe the options available to the Lot Owner to avoid having the account turned over to a Collection Agent in the written notice required by Section 209.0064(b). Tex. Prop. Code § 209.0064(b)(2).

7.6.2 (B) *Restrictions on Agreements between a Subdivision Association and a Collection Agent (or an Attorney that Provides Collection Services)*

In addition to requiring that a written notice be sent to a delinquent Lot Owner before a Subdivision Association may hold such Lot Owner liable for the fees of a Collection Agent, Section 209.0064 of the Texas Property Code also imposes several restrictions on the contractual terms between a Subdivision Association and a Collection Agent retained by it to collect unpaid Assessments or other amounts owed to the Subdivision Association. It is important to note that such restrictions apply equally to the contractual terms between a Subdivision Association and an attorney that performs collection services for the Subdivision Association.[42]

First, a Lot Owner may not be held liable for the fees of a Collection Agent retained by a Subdivision Association if its obligation to pay the Collection Agent for fees or costs associated with a collection action is in any way dependent or contingent on amounts recovered from a Lot Owner.[43] In other words, if the agreement between the Subdivision Association and its Collection Agent provides that the Subdivision Association is not obligated to pay fees to the Collection Agent for its services unless the Collection Agent successfully recovers money from a delinquent Lot Owner, then the Lot Owner is not liable for the fees charged by the Collection Agent to the Subdivision Association and the Subdivision Association may not seek reimbursement of such fees from the Lot Owner.

Second, a Lot Owner may not be held liable for the fees of a Collection Agent retained by a Subdivision Association if the payment agreement between the Subdivision

---

[42] In general, an attorney retained by a Subdivision Association to collect unpaid Assessments owed to it by a Lot Owner is considered a "debt collector" under the federal Fair Debt Collection Practices Act, and thus constitutes a "Collection Agent" under Section 209.0064 of the Texas Property Code. Tex. Prop. Code § 209.0064(a); *Heintz v. Jenkins*, 514 U.S. 291, 298–99 (1995).

[43] Tex. Prop. Code § 209.0064(c)(1).

Association and the Collection Agent does not require payment by the Subdivision Association of all applicable fees to the Collection Agent for the actions it undertakes to collect unpaid Assessments or other amounts owed to the Subdivision Association by a Lot Owner.[44] In other words, a payment agreement between a Subdivision Association and a Collection Agent must require the Subdivision Association to pay the Collection Agent's applicable fees for all collection actions performed by such Collection Agent, regardless of whether the Collection Agent actually recovers any amounts from a delinquent Lot Owner.

Finally, an agreement between a Subdivision Association and a Collection Agent may not prohibit a delinquent Lot Owner from contacting the Subdivision Association's Board of Directors or its managing agent regarding such Lot Owner's delinquency.[45]

7.6.2 (C) *Restrictions on the Manner of Payment of Attorneys Fees and Other Collection Costs*

Chapter 209 also imposes certain restrictions on the manner of payment of attorneys fees and other amounts collected from a Lot Owner. More specifically, Section 209.008 requires that all attorneys fees, costs, and other amounts collected from a Lot Owner by a Subdivision Association must be deposited into an account maintained at a financial institution in the name of the Subdivision Association or its managing agent, in which the only signatories on such account are the Subdivision Association's Directors, its managing agent, and/or employees of its managing agent.[46] In other words, if a Subdivision Association employs an attorney or Collection Agent to collect its unpaid Assessments (plus any costs of collection and/or attorneys fees incurred by such Subdivision Association), then any payments collected from a delinquent Lot Owner must be made payable to the Subdivision Association, not its attorney or Collection Agent, and

---

44 Tex. Prop. Code § 209.0064(c)(2).

45 Tex. Prop. Code § 209.0064(d).

46 Tex. Prop. Code § 209.008(c).

must be deposited in a bank account maintained by the Subdivision Association or its property manager on its behalf.

7.6.2 (D) *Statutory Limitations on the Amount of Attorneys Fees that May Be Charged to a Lot Owner for Non-Judicial Foreclosure of a Subdivision Association's Assessment Lien*

Finally, in an effort to discourage non-judicial foreclosure of Assessment Liens by Texas Subdivision Associations, Chapter 209 imposes a limit on the amount of attorneys fees a Subdivision Association may seek reimbursement of in a non-judicial foreclosure proceeding. If the Declaration of a Subdivision Association allows for non-judicial foreclosure of its Assessment Lien, the amount of attorneys fees that such Subdivision Association may include with the amount of unpaid Assessments being sought in a non-judicial foreclosure of its Assessment Lien is limited to the greater of: (1) one-third (1/3) of the amount of all unpaid Assessments and actual costs of collection (excluding attorneys fees) owed by the Lot Owner, plus interest and court costs if interest and/or court costs are permitted to be included in the amount secured by the Assessment Lien pursuant to Texas law or the Subdivision Association's Declaration; or (2) $2,500.[47] In short, Chapter 209 caps the amount of reimbursable attorneys fees that can be charged against a delinquent Lot Owner in a non-judicial foreclosure at either one-third (1/3) of the total amount owed to the Subdivision Association that is secured by the Assessment Lien (excluding attorneys fees) or $2,500, whichever amount is greater.

Such restriction on the amount of reimbursable attorneys fees that can be charged against a delinquent Lot Owner, however, only applies if a Subdivision Association forecloses its Assessment Lien by non-judicial foreclosure procedures. It does not prevent a Subdivision Association from recovering or collecting attorneys fees in excess of such limited amount by other collection methods, such as judicial foreclosure of a Subdivision

[47] Tex. Prop. Code § 209.008(f).

Association's Assessment Lien.[48] Thus, if a Subdivision Association were to foreclose its Assessment Lien by a judicial foreclosure lawsuit, the statutory cap on the recovery or collection of attorneys fees would not apply.

7.7 Creation, Scope, and Priority of an Assessment Lien

A lien is a form of security interest granted over an item of property to secure the payment of a debt or performance of some other obligation. In the context of Homeowners Associations, a Homeowner's obligation to pay Assessments levied by a Homeowners Association is typically secured by an "Assessment Lien" in favor of the Homeowners Association that attaches to each Lot or Unit in the applicable development. If a Homeowner fails to pay his or her Assessments, a Homeowners Association with an Assessment Lien may foreclose such lien on the Homeowner's Lot or Unit. In other words, the Homeowners Association may sell a delinquent Homeowner's Lot or Unit at a public auction and use the proceeds from such sale to satisfy the amounts owed by such Homeowner to the Homeowners Association.

7.7.1 Creation and Perfection of an Assessment Lien

An Assessment Lien is essentially a contractual lien in favor of a Homeowners Association that is created by and reserved in the Declaration establishing such Homeowners Association. If the Homeowners Association is a Subdivision Association, the creation and reservation of an Assessment Lien in favor of the Subdivision Association must be expressly specified in the Declaration. If the Homeowners Association is a Condominium Association, however, a lien securing payment of Assessments is

48 Tex. Prop. Code § 209.008(f).

automatically created in favor of the Condominium Association by the filing of its Declaration, whether expressly mentioned in the Declaration or not.[49]

In most situations, a Homeowners Association's Declaration will also provide that the Assessment Lien is evidenced by the recordation of the Declaration alone and that there is no requirement of the Homeowners Association to record additional documents or notices in the Official Public Records of the county in which the Subdivision or Condominium Development is located in order to establish or perfect its lien. This is certainly true for Condominium Associations because the Texas Uniform Condominium Act expressly provides that a Condominium Association's Assessment Lien is created by the recording of its Declaration, which constitutes record notice and perfection of such lien.[50] There is no comparable Texas law concerning establishment of an Assessment Lien in favor of a Subdivision Association, and because Declarations of Texas Homeowners Associations are rarely drafted in the same way, a Subdivision Association's Declaration should be carefully reviewed to ensure that an Assessment Lien in its favor has been properly established and to identify any specific procedural requirements for validly perfecting such Assessment Lien.

Regardless of whether a Homeowners Association is required to record any additional documents or notices in order to perfect its Assessment Lien, many Homeowners Associations still prefer to record a "Notice of the Assessment Lien" in the Official Public Records of the county in which the Homeowners Association is located so as to put third parties, including any potential purchasers or title companies, on notice that

---

[49] Tex. Prop. Code § 82.113(a). There is no comparable Texas law that establishes an Assessment Lien in favor of Subdivision Associations, so the creation of an Assessment Lien in its favor must be expressly set out in the Subdivision Association's Declaration.

[50] Tex. Prop. Code § 82.113(c). The Texas Uniform Condominium Act further provides that unless the Condominium Association's Declaration provides otherwise, no other recordation of a lien or notice of lien is required. Tex. Prop. Code § 82.113(c).

there are unpaid Assessments currently outstanding with respect to a particular Lot or Unit that are secured by an Assessment Lien.

7.7.2 Scope of an Assessment Lien

In most cases, a Homeowners Association's Declaration will provide that an Assessment Lien secures not only payment of unpaid Assessments levied by the Homeowners Association, but also late charges, reasonable costs of collections (including attorneys fees), interest, and in some cases, even fines assessed by the Homeowners Association. The scope of a Condominium Association's Assessment Lien is defined by the Texas Uniform Condominium Act, which provides that such Assessment Lien secures payment of all regular and special Assessments, dues, fees, charges, interest, late fees, fines, collection costs, attorneys fees, and any other amount due to the Condominium Association by a Unit Owner or levied against a Unit by the Condominium Association, unless the Condominium Association's Declaration provides otherwise.[51] There is no similar Texas law that defines the scope of a Subdivision Association's Assessment Lien. Consequently, an Assessment Lien in favor of a Subdivision Association only secures payment of the types of debts specifically identified in the Declaration as being secured by the Assessment Lien.

The defined scope of a Homeowners Association's Assessment Lien is important because a Homeowners Association cannot foreclose its Assessment Lien as a result of non-payment of amounts not expressly secured by the Assessment Lien under its Declaration (or under the Texas Uniform Condominium Act if it is a Condominium Association).[52] In other words, a Subdivision Association may not foreclose its

---

[51] Tex. Prop. Code § 82.113(a).

[52] *See Brooks v. Northglen Assoc.*, 141 S.W.3d 158, 170–71 (Tex. 2004).

Assessment Lien upon a Lot for certain unpaid charges if the Declaration does not expressly state that the Assessment Lien secures payment of such charges.

7.7.3 Priority of an Assessment Lien

The priority of a lien refers to its hierarchal relationship to other liens attached to a Lot or Unit, in which liens of greater priority are superior to liens of lesser priority. In general, and subject to several exceptions, under Texas law, the priority of a lien is established by the date that the document creating the lien is recorded in the Official Public Records of the county in which the real property subject to such lien is located. Liens recorded first in time are considered to be "senior," or of higher priority than all liens recorded later in time. Liens recorded later in time are considered to be "junior," or lower in priority than those liens recorded before it. In simpler terms, every lien is junior to all liens recorded before it and senior to all liens recorded after it. There are, however, some limited exceptions to this rule. A senior lienholder may agree to subrogate (or make subordinate) its lien to another lien that would otherwise be a junior lien. In addition, under the Texas Tax Code, liens that secure the payment of property taxes owed to ad valorem taxing entities take priority over all previously recorded liens, specifically including any Assessment Liens.[53]

The priority of a lien effects its treatment in a foreclosure proceeding. In simple terms, when a lien is foreclosed, the trustee must apply the proceeds from the foreclosure sale of the property first to the debt secured by the lien that was foreclosed and then to the debt secured by any junior liens in order of their priority. In other words, if there are any remaining proceeds left over after satisfying the debt secured by the lien that was foreclosed, then the trustee must apply the remaining proceeds to the debt secured by the

53 Tex. Tax Code § 32.05. Ad valorem taxes are taxes that are based on the value of property, such as real property, and are often referred to as "property taxes." Ad valorem taxing entities consist of governmental entities that are authorized under Texas law to assess ad valorem taxes upon property, such as cities and counties.

next-highest priority lien that is junior to the lien that was foreclosed. If there are still proceeds remaining after satisfying the next-highest priority lien that is junior to the lien that was foreclosed, then the trustee must apply the remaining proceeds to the second-highest priority lien that is junior to the lien that was foreclosed, and so on, until there are no remaining proceeds or no additional junior liens. In the latter scenario, the remaining proceeds would be remitted to the owner of the property that was foreclosed.

Regardless of whether there are any proceeds left over to satisfy the debts secured by junior liens, the foreclosure of a senior lien will extinguish all liens junior to it, and following the foreclosure sale, such junior liens are no longer attached to the property.[54] The trustee conducting the foreclosure sale, however, does not pay any of the proceeds from the foreclosure sale to senior lienholders, and the foreclosure sale does not remove senior liens or otherwise affect the enforceability of such senior liens. Instead, the purchaser of property at the foreclosure sale takes ownership of the foreclosed property free of all junior liens, but still subject to all senior liens, which can still be foreclosed upon on the property in the future.

In most cases, the Assessment Lien created by a Declaration is effective upon the recording of the Declaration, which is almost always recorded by the real estate developer before any applicable property is developed or sold to Homeowners. As a result, Assessment Liens are typically recorded prior to and preexist a Homeowner's purchase of his or her Lot or Unit. Consequently, a Homeowners Association's Assessment Lien is generally recorded prior to and would normally be of higher priority than a mortgage lien (also called a "Deed of Trust Lien") recorded by a lending institution that finances a Homeowner's purchase of a Lot or Unit.[55] In almost all cases, however, the Declaration

---

54 *See Mays v. Bank One, N.A.*, 150 S.W.3d 897, 900 (Tex. App.—Dallas 2004, no pet.).

55 A "Deed of Trust Lien" is a written instrument that is used to secure the repayment of a mortgage by placing conditional legal title to the real property securing such mortgage in a neutral third party (typically called the "trustee"), who may later exercise a power of sale to foreclose such real property in the event the

of a Texas Homeowners Association will provide its Assessment Lien is subordinated in priority to a lender's Deed of Trust Lien.[56] As a result, there is almost always a Deed of Trust Lien that is senior to the Homeowners Association's Assessment Lien. In addition, there could be other potential liens that are given priority over the Homeowners Association's Assessment Lien by the Declaration, so a review of a particular Homeowners Association's Declaration and the local Official Public Records is required to determine the priority of its Assessment Lien.

For Condominium Developments, by virtue of the Texas Uniform Condominium Act, an Assessment Lien in favor of a Condominium Association has priority over any other lien except:

(1) a lien for real property taxes and other governmental assessments or charges against a Unit;[57]

(2) a lien or encumbrance recorded before the Condominium Association's Declaration is recorded;[58]

(3) a first vendor's lien or first Deed of Trust Lien recorded before the date on which the Assessment sought to be enforced becomes delinquent under the Condominium Association's Declaration, Bylaws, or Association Rules;[59] and

---

borrower fails to repay such mortgage. A Deed of Trust Lien is the most common form of lien used to secure a lender who finances a Homeowner's purchase of a Lot or Unit.

56 This is because a lending institution will almost always require that it have the most senior lien on any real property collateralizing a mortgage loan. Since a Homeowners Association's Assessment Lien is generally created before an individual owner purchases his or her Lot or Unit, unless the Homeowners Association's Declaration subordinates the priority of its Assessment Lien under that of the lending institution's lien, most lending institutions would refuse to loan money to a Homeowner to purchase an applicable Lot or Unit for fear that foreclosure of the Homeowners Association's Assessment Lien could wipe out its lien.

57 Tex. Prop. Code § 82.113(b)(1). Foreclosure of a tax lien does not discharge the Condominium Association's Assessment Lien for amounts becoming due after the date of foreclosure of the tax lien. Tex. Prop. Code § 82.113(l).

58 Tex. Prop. Code § 82.113(b)(2).

59 Tex. Prop. Code § 82.113(b)(3).

(4) unless the Declaration provides otherwise, a lien for construction of improvements to a Unit or an assignment of the right to insurance proceeds on the Unit if the lien or assignment is recorded or duly perfected before the date on which the Assessment sought to be enforced becomes delinquent under the Condominium Association's Declaration, Bylaws, or Association Rules.[60]

7.8 Foreclosure of an Assessment Lien

There are two types of procedures for foreclosing an Assessment Lien under Texas law: judicial foreclosure and non-judicial foreclosure. All Texas Homeowners Associations are authorized to foreclose their Assessment Lien by judicial foreclosure procedures, but they may only foreclose their Assessment Lien by non-judicial foreclosure procedures if expressly authorized to do so by their Declaration or Texas law.

The Texas Uniform Condominium Act expressly authorizes all Texas Condominium Associations to foreclose their Assessment Lien by judicial or non-judicial foreclosure procedures.[61] Accordingly, a Condominium Association may foreclose an Assessment Lien by either judicial or non-judicial foreclosure procedures even if its Declaration does not contain a provision expressly authorizing non-judicial foreclosure of its Assessment Lien.

With respect to Subdivision Associations, however, there is no comparable law authorizing Texas Subdivision Associations to conduct non-judicial foreclosure of their Assessment Lien. As a result, a Texas Subdivision Association may only foreclose its Assessment Lien by non-judicial foreclosure procedures if expressly authorized to do so under its Declaration.

Judicial and non-judicial foreclosure procedures differ significantly from each other, as do the non-judicial foreclosure procedures that must be followed by

---

60 Tex. Prop. Code § 82.113(b)(4).

61 Tex. Prop. Code § 82.113(e).

Condominium and Subdivision Associations. Such procedures and differences are explained in more detail in the following subchapters.

7.8.1 Judicial Foreclosure of an Assessment Lien

Judicial foreclosure refers to the process by which the right to foreclose a lien is established by judicial proceeding and then is carried out by order of the court. In order to judicially foreclose an Assessment Lien, a Homeowners Association must file a lawsuit against the delinquent Homeowner (called a "Judicial Foreclosure Lawsuit") and obtain a judgment against such Homeowner that: (1) establishes the amount owed to the Homeowners Association (including the specific amount owed that is secured by the Homeowners Association's Assessment Lien); and (2) orders the Homeowners Association's Assessment Lien be foreclosed on such Homeowner's property to satisfy the amount awarded to the Homeowners Association by the judgment that is secured by its Assessment Lien.

7.8.1 (A) *Burden of Proof in a Judicial Foreclosure Lawsuit*

At a trial on the merits of a Judicial Foreclosure Lawsuit, a Homeowners Association will have to prove: (1) the defendant-Homeowner's Lot or Unit is subject to the applicable Declaration; (2) the Declaration authorizes the Homeowners Association to levy Assessments against the defendant-Homeowner's Lot or Unit; (3) the defendant-Homeowner has not paid the Assessments levied against his or her Lot or Unit; (4) the amount of delinquent Assessments and other amounts owed by the defendant-Homeowner to the Homeowners Associations; (5) the Declaration creates an Assessment Lien in favor of the Homeowners Association that secures payment of delinquent Assessments and other amounts owed by the defendant-Homeowner to the Homeowners Association; and (6) the amount of delinquent Assessments and other amounts owed by the defendant-Homeowner to the Homeowners Associations that are secured by the Homeowners Association's Assessment Lien. Assuming the Homeowners Association prevails at trial in the Judicial Foreclosure Lawsuit, the court will enter judgment in favor of the

Homeowners Association in which it awards the Homeowners Association a monetary award and orders the Homeowners Association's Assessment Lien be foreclosed on the defendant-Homeowner's Lot or Unit to satisfy the portion of the monetary award that is secured by the Homeowners Association's Assessment Lien.

7.8.1 (B) *Conducting a Judicial Foreclosure Sale*

Following the entry of a judgment ordering the foreclosure of the Homeowners Association's Assessment Lien upon the defendant-Homeowner's Lot or Unit, the clerk of the court will prepare an "Order of Sale," which directs the sheriff or constable of the county in which the defendant-Homeowner's Lot or Unit is located to sell such Lot or Unit by public auction and to apply the proceeds from such sale to the secured amount awarded to the Homeowners Association under the judgment. The Order of Sale should describe the Lot or Unit to be sold with legal sufficiency and contain appropriate directions as to the time, place, terms, and conditions of the sale.[62]

Real property to be sold by a sheriff or constable pursuant to an Order of Sale is required to be sold by public auction, at the courthouse door of the county in which the property is located, on the first Tuesday of the month between the hours of 10:00 a.m. and 4:00 p.m.[63] Prior to conducting a sale of real property under an Order of Sale, the sheriff or constable is required to advertise the time and place of sale of such real property by having a notice of sale, specifying such information, published in the English language in a newspaper published in the county in which the defendant-Homeowner's Lot or Unit is located, at least once a week for three consecutive weeks preceding the date of such sale.[64]

---

62 *Allday v. Whittaker*, 1 S.W. 794, 795 (Tex. 1886).

63 Tex. R. Civ. P. 646a. For purposes of a judicial foreclosure, the term "courthouse door" of a county refers to either of the principal entrances to the building provided by the proper authority for the holding of the district court; or, if from any cause there is no such building, then the door of the building where the district court was last held in such county shall be deemed to be the courthouse door. Tex. R. Civ. P. 648.

64 Tex. R. Civ. P. 647. The first of said three publications is required to appear not less than twenty (20) days immediately preceding the date of sale. Tex. R. Civ. P. 647. If there is no newspaper published in the county, or none that will publish the notice of sale for the requisite compensation set by court rule, the sheriff, or

In addition, the sheriff or constable must give the defendant-Homeowner (or his or her attorney) written notice of such sale by either personal-delivery or mail.[65] The notice of sale that is required to be published and given to the defendant-Homeowner must contain a statement of the authority by virtue of which the sale is to be made, the time of levy, the time and place of sale, and a brief description of the property to be sold, as well as give the number of acres, original survey, locality in the county, and the name by which the land is most generally known.[66]

The sheriff or constable must sell the property to the highest bidder at the sale for cash, unless the highest bidder is the judgment creditor. In such event, the judgment creditor is entitled to apply the amount awarded in the judgment against his or her bid amount.[67] The proceeds from the sale will be applied first to the amounts awarded to the judgment creditor, and if there is any remaining surplus proceeds, then to the defendant-Homeowner.

7.8.2 Non-Judicial Foreclosure of an Assessment Lien

Unlike a judicial foreclosure, a non-judicial foreclosure is conducted without court supervision and is not carried out by the county sheriff. Instead, a non-judicial foreclosure sale is performed by a trustee appointed by the Homeowners Association without any prior hearing or judicial determination.

Non-judicial foreclosures of real property in Texas are governed by Chapter 51 of the Texas Property Code, and non-judicial foreclosure of an Assessment Lien by a

---

constable must then post such notice in writing in three public places in the county, one of which shall be at the courthouse door of such county, for at least twenty (20) days successively next before the date of sale. Tex. R. Civ. P. 647.

65 Tex. R. Civ. P. 647.

66 Tex. R. Civ. P. 647.

67 *Blum v. Rogers*, 9 S.W. 595, 597 (Tex. 1888); *Needham v. Cooney,* 173 S.W. 979, 982 (Tex. Civ. App.—El Paso 1915, writ ref'd).

Homeowners Association must be done in compliance with both Chapter 51 and the Homeowners Association's Declaration. The non-judicial foreclosure process essentially consists of three steps: (1) appointment of a trustee; (2) notice of the foreclosure sale; and (3) conducting the foreclosure sale.[68]

7.8.2 (A) *Appointment of a Trustee to Exercise a Power of Sale*

The non-judicial foreclosure process requires the Homeowners Association to first appoint a person to act as a trustee for the purpose of conducting a non-judicial foreclosure sale of the subject property under the provisions of the Declaration.[69] The authority to appoint a trustee to exercise a "power of sale" against another person's property must be granted by contract or law.[70] Under the Texas Uniform Condominium Act, when a Unit Owner acquires ownership of a Unit, the Unit Owner is considered to have automatically granted the Condominium Association a power of sale in connection with the Condominium Association's Assessment Lien.[71] The Texas Uniform Condominium Act further provides that the Board of Directors of a Condominium Association may, by written resolution, appoint an officer, agent, trustee, or attorney of the Condominium Association to exercise such power of sale on behalf of the Condominium Association.[72]

In the case of Texas Subdivision Associations, there is no similar statutory law that provides for the automatic grant of a power of sale on behalf of a Lot Owner in favor

---

68 If a Subdivision Association is foreclosing its Assessment Lien against a delinquent Lot Owner's Lot, however, Chapter 209 of the Texas Property Code requires it to first obtain a court order authorizing the non-judicial foreclosure of its Assessment Lien. Tex. Prop. Code § 209.0092.

69 In most cases, the trustee appointed by the Homeowners Association will be its attorney, but it is not required to be.

70 A "power of sale" refers to the right and power granted to a third party (such as a mortgagee or a trustee) to sell real property at a public auction upon the default in the payment of debt secured by such real property. *See generally*, *Black's Law Dictionary* 1172 (6th ed. 1990).

71 Tex. Prop. Code § 82.113(d).

72 Tex. Prop. Code § 82.113(d).

of his or her Subdivision Association or that authorizes a Subdivision Association's Board of Directors to appoint a trustee to exercise a power of sale on behalf of the Subdivision Association, and any such power of sale must be expressly authorized by the Subdivision Association's Declaration.[73] Generally speaking, however, in almost all cases where a Declaration establishes an Assessment Lien in favor of a Subdivision Association and authorizes it to foreclose such Assessment Lien by non-judicial foreclosure procedures, the Declaration will also include provisions granting the Subdivision Association a power of sale and setting forth procedures for appointing a trustee to conduct a non-judicial foreclosure sale of a delinquent Homeowner's Lot.

7.8.2 (B) *Notice of Non-Judicial Foreclosure Sale*

The second step of the non-judicial foreclosure process consists of providing notice of the foreclosure sale to the delinquent Homeowner and the public. If the delinquent Homeowner's property is used as his or her residence, however, before an

[73] It is important to note that in 2015, the Texas Legislature modified Section 209.0092 of the Texas Property Code to provide that a Subdivision Association whose Dedicatory Instruments grant it a right of foreclosure of an Assessment Lien is considered to have any power of sale required by law as a condition of using the expedited judicial procedure governed Texas Rules of Civil Procedure 735 and 736. Tex. Prop. Code § 209.0092(a). The effect of such 2015 amendment to Section 209.0092, however, is unclear based on the limited scope of its language. More specifically, Section 209.0092 of the Texas Property Code prohibits a Subdivision Association from foreclosing an Assessment Lien by non-judicial foreclosure procedures unless it first obtains a court order through an expedited judicial procedure governed by Texas Rules of Civil Procedure 735 and 736, which may only be utilized by Subdivision Associations that have been granted a power of sale. Tex. R. Civ. P. 735.1. A Subdivision Association must have a power of sale in order to sell a Lot Owner's Lot through a non-judicial foreclosure procedure. Section 209.0092 requires a Subdivision Association to obtain a court order prior to conducting a non-judicial foreclosure sale of a Lot Owner's Lot, which may be obtained through the expedited judicial proceeding, but such expedited judicial proceeding is not a judicial foreclosure procedure and the order issued by a court through an expedited judicial proceeding is not an order of sale. Rather, the expedited judicial foreclosure proceeding is a procedure for obtaining permission to proceed with conducting a non-judicial foreclosure of an Assessment Lien and the order issued by a court in an expedited judicial proceeding simply permits a Subdivision Association to proceed with the foreclosure of its Assessment Lien by non-judicial foreclosure procedures pursuant to a pre-existing power of sale. As modified, Section 209.0092 now provides that a Subdivision Association is considered to have any power of sale required as a condition of using the expedited judicial procedure to obtain a court order permitting it to proceed with non-judicial foreclosure of its Assessment Lien, but Section 209.0092 still does not actually grant a power of sale on behalf of a Lot Owner in favor of his or her Subdivision Association, which a Subdivision Association must have in order to actually conduct the non-judicial foreclosure sale of a Lot Owner's Lot.

appointed trustee may initiate the notice of the foreclosure sale process, the trustee must provide the delinquent Homeowner a written notice, by certified mail, that: (1) states that the Homeowner is in default of such Homeowner's obligation to pay Assessments under the Declaration; (2) identifies the amount of delinquent Assessments and other amounts owed by such Homeowner to the Homeowners Association that is secured by the Homeowners Association's Assessment Lien; and (3) gives such Homeowner at least twenty (20) days to cure the default by paying all outstanding secured amounts owed to the Homeowners Association.[74] Such written notice must also state the name and address of the sender of such notice and include the following advisory statement conspicuously printed in boldface or underlined type:[75]

> **"Assert and protect your rights as a member of the armed forces of the United States. If you are or your spouse is serving on active military duty, including active military duty as a member of the Texas National Guard or the National Guard of another state or as a member of a reserve component of the armed forces of the United States, please send written notice of the active duty military service to the sender of this notice immediately."**

If the delinquent Homeowner does not cure his or her default within twenty (20) days of receipt of such notice, the appointed trustee may then proceed with the non-judicial foreclosure process by providing the delinquent Homeowner and the public with notice of the intended foreclosure sale of the delinquent Homeowner's Lot or Unit.

A "Notice of Foreclosure Sale" must be provided to the Homeowner and the public by the appointed trustee at least twenty-one (21) days before the date of the foreclosure sale by:

---

[74] Tex. Prop. Code § 51.002(d). Service of notice of default on a delinquent Homeowner by certified mail is considered completed when the written notice is deposited in the United States mail, postage prepaid, and addressed to the Homeowner at the Homeowner's last known address. Tex. Prop. Code § 51.002(e).

[75] Tex. Prop. Code § 51.002(i).

(1) posting a copy of the Notice of Foreclosure Sale at the courthouse door of each county in which the Lot or Unit is located;[76]

(2) filing in the office of the county clerk of each county in which the Lot or Unit is located a copy of the Notice of Foreclosure Sale that was posted at the courthouse door;[77] and

(3) serving the delinquent Homeowner with a copy of the Notice of Foreclosure sale by certified mail.[78]

In addition, the Notice of Foreclosure Sale must identify the property to be foreclosed, the date and location at which the sale will take place, and the earliest time at which the sale will begin.[79]

7.8.2 (C) *Conducting a Non-Judicial Foreclosure Sale*

A non-judicial foreclosure sale of real property must be by public auction and may only be held between the hours of 10:00 a.m. and 4:00 p.m. on the first Tuesday of any calendar month.[80] In addition, the foreclosure sale must take place at the area

---

[76] Tex. Prop. Code § 51.002(b)(1). If the Lot or Unit is located in more than one county, a copy of the Notice of Foreclosure Sale must be posted at the courthouse door of each such county and the Notice of Foreclosure Sale must designate the county in which the Lot or Unit will be sold. Tex. Prop. Code § 51.002(b)(1).

[77] Tex. Prop. Code § 51.002(b)(2).

[78] Tex. Prop. Code § 51.002(b)(3). Service of a Notice of Foreclosure Sale on a delinquent Homeowner by certified mail is considered completed when the written Notice of Foreclosure Sale is deposited in the United States mail, postage prepaid, and addressed to the Homeowner at the Homeowner's last known address. Tex. Prop. Code § 51.002(e). In addition, if the delinquent Homeowner's property is not being used as his or her residence and a written notice giving the delinquent Homeowner a twenty-day period to cure the default was not sent to him or her, then the Notice of Foreclosure Sale served on the delinquent Homeowner must state the name and address of the sender of such notice and include the following advisory statement conspicuously printed in boldface or underlined type: "Assert and protect your rights as a member of the armed forces of the United States. If you are or your spouse is serving on active military duty, including active military duty as a member of the Texas National Guard or the National Guard of another state or as a member of a reserve component of the armed forces of the United States, please send written notice of the active duty military service to the sender of this notice immediately." Tex. Prop. Code § 51.002(i).

[79] Tex. Prop. Code § 51.002(b); *see also*, *Myrad Props., Inc. v. LaSalle Bank Nat'l Ass'n*, 252 S.W.3d 605, 615 (Tex. App.—Austin 2008), ref'd on other grounds, 300 S.W.3d 746 (Tex. 2009) ("The notice of foreclosure sale must provide a description or other identification of the property to be sold.").

[80] Tex. Prop. Code § 51.002(a). The Notice of Foreclosure Sale must include a statement of the earliest time at which the sale will begin, and the foreclosure sale must begin no later than three hours after the time stated in the Notice of Foreclosure Sale. Tex. Prop. Code § 51.002(b), (c).

designated for foreclosure sales at the county courthouse in the county in which the Lot or Unit is located; or, if the Lot or Unit is located in more than one county, the sale may be made at the courthouse of any county in which such Lot or Unit is located, so long as it is the county courthouse designated in the Notice of Foreclosure Sale.[81]

On the date of the foreclosure sale, the appointed trustee will appear at the designated area of the courthouse for conducting foreclosure sales and simply read a copy of the Notice of Foreclosure Sale, state the terms of the sale (for example, cash bids only), and open the sale up for bidding. The appointed trustee may set reasonable conditions for conducting the public sale if the conditions are announced before bidding is opened by the appointed trustee.[82]

The Texas Uniform Condominium Act authorizes Condominium Associations to bid for and purchase a Unit at foreclosure as a Common Expense.[83] In addition, almost all Subdivision Associations are authorized by their Governing Documents to purchase a Lot being foreclosed upon. Bids to purchase a Lot or Unit by a Condominium or Subdivision Association at the foreclosure sale may be by credit against the amounts owed to such Homeowners Association by the delinquent Homeowner to the extent such bid amount does not exceed what the Homeowner owes the Homeowners Association. In other words, if the amount owed by the delinquent Homeowner to the Homeowners Association that is secured by the Homeowners Association's Assessment Lien is $1,000, then the Homeowners Association may bid on the subject property by credit up to a bid amount of $1,000. If, however, the Homeowners Association bids an amount in excess of $1,000,

---

81 Tex. Prop. Code § 51.002(a), (b)(1). The commissioners court of each Texas county is required to designate the area at the local courthouse where foreclosure sales are to take place and shall record the designation in the Official Public Records of such county. Tex. Prop. Code § 51.002(a). If no area is designated by the commissioners court, the notice of sale must designate the area where the sale covered by such Notice of Foreclosure Sale is to take place, and the sale must occur in that area. Tex. Prop. Code § 51.002(a).

82 Tex. Prop. Code § 51.0075(a).

83 Tex. Prop. Code § 82.113(f). Texas Condominium Associations are also expressly authorized to own, lease, encumber, exchange, sell, or convey a Unit purchased at foreclosure. Tex. Prop. Code § 82.113(f).

then any amount above $1,000 is considered to be a cash bid, and the Homeowners Association must produce cash in the amount of such cash bid at the foreclosure sale if it is the highest bidder.

At the conclusion of the foreclosure sale, the appointed trustee will collect the purchase price from the highest bidder, if the highest bid is in whole or in part a cash bid, and will execute a trustee's deed conveying the property to such highest bidder.[84] To the extent any part of the purchase price of the foreclosed property consists of cash, the appointed trustee must then disburse the sales proceeds as provided by Texas law.[85]

7.8.2 (D) *Limitation on Amount of Attorneys Fees that May Be Included in a Non-Judicial Foreclosure of an Assessment Lien by a Subdivision Association*

Chapter 209 of the Texas Property Code imposes a limit on the amount of attorneys fees a Subdivision Association may seek reimbursement of in a non-judicial foreclosure proceeding. The amount of attorneys fees that a Subdivision Association may include with the amount of unpaid Assessments being sought in a non-judicial foreclosure of its Assessment Lien is limited to the greater of: (1) one-third (1/3) of the amount of all unpaid Assessments and actual costs of collection (excluding attorneys fees) owed by the Lot Owner, plus interest and court costs if interest and/or court costs are permitted to be included in the amount secured by the Assessment Lien pursuant to Texas law or the Subdivision Association's Declaration; or (2) $2,500.[86] In other words, Chapter 209 caps the amount of reimbursable attorneys fees that can be charged against a delinquent Lot Owner by a Subdivision Association in a non-judicial foreclosure at either one-third (1/3)

---

[84] In addition, if the non-judicial foreclosure sale is on behalf of a Subdivision Association, the appointed trustee must attach a conformed copy of the order granting the Subdivision Association's a Non-Judicial Foreclosure Application to the trustee's deed. Tex. R. Civ. P. 736.12.

[85] Tex. Prop. Code § 51.0075(f).

[86] Tex. Prop. Code § 209.008(f).

of the total amount owed to the Subdivision Association that is secured by the Assessment Lien (excluding attorneys fees) or $2,500, whichever amount is greater.

7.9 Pre-Foreclosure Due Process Procedures Required of Subdivision Associations

Chapter 209 of the Texas Property Code requires Texas Subdivision Associations to comply with certain due process procedures before they may foreclose an Assessment Lien. Such due process procedures require Subdivision Associations to send a written notice of a Lot Owner's delinquent Assessment account to all holders of recorded junior "Deed of Trust Liens" applicable to the Lot to be foreclosed, and if such foreclosure is to be conducted by non-judicial foreclosure procedures, to obtain a court order authorizing the non-judicial foreclosure of its Assessment Lien through an expedited judicial proceeding that is governed by Texas Rules of Civil Procedure 735 and 736.[87]

7.9.1 Required Notice to Holders of a Junior Deed of Trust Lien and Opportunity to Cure the Assessment Delinquency

Section 209.0091 of the Texas Property Code requires a Texas Subdivision Association to provide written notice of a Lot Owner's delinquent Assessment account and an opportunity to cure such delinquent Assessment account to holders of recorded "Deed of Trust Liens" that are inferior in priority to (or otherwise junior to) the Subdivision Association's Assessment Lien before it may foreclose such Assessment Lien.[88] More specifically, such written notice must provide an applicable lienholder notice

---

[87] Tex. Prop. Code §§ 209.0091; 209.0092. A "Deed of Trust Lien" is a written instrument that is used to secure the repayment of a mortgage by placing conditional legal title to the real property securing such mortgage in a neutral third party (typically called the "trustee"), who may later exercise a power of sale to foreclose such real property in the event the borrower fails to repay such mortgage. A Deed of Trust Lien is the most common form of lien used to secure a lender who finances a Homeowner's purchase of a Lot or Unit. Texas Rules of Civil Procedure 735 and 736 also govern expedited judicial proceedings for obtaining required judicial authorization to non-judicially foreclose liens securing a home equity loan, a reverse mortgage, and/or a home equity line of credit. Tex. R. Civ. P. 735, 736.

[88] Tex. Prop. Code § 209.0091(a). A "Deed of Trust Lien" is a written instrument that is used to secure the repayment of a mortgage by placing conditional legal title to the real property securing such mortgage in a neutral third party (typically called the "trustee"), who may later exercise a power of sale to foreclose such

of the total amount of the Lot Owner's delinquent Assessment account that is giving rise to the foreclosure and allow such lienholder a sixty-day period from the date such written notice is mailed to the lienholder to pay such delinquent Assessment account before the Subdivision Association may proceed with foreclosure of its Assessment Lien.[89] In addition, such written notice must be sent by certified mail to the address of an applicable lienholder as shown on the recorded Deed of Trust Lien or other recorded document in the Official Public Records relating to the applicable Lot for which such notice is being given.[90]

7.9.2 Required Court Order Authorizing Non-Judicial Foreclosure of a Subdivision Association's Assessment Lien

Pursuant to Section 209.0092 of the Texas Property Code, before a Subdivision Association may initiate foreclosure of an Assessment Lien by non-judicial foreclosure procedures, it must first obtain a court order authorizing it to proceed with such foreclosure through an expedited judicial proceeding (called an "Expedited Non-Judicial Foreclosure Proceeding") that is governed by Texas Rules of Civil Procedure 735 and 736 and Sections 17.031 and 154.028 of the Texas Civil Practice and Remedies Code.[91] The

---

real property in the event the borrower fails to repay such mortgage. A Deed of Trust Lien is the most common form of lien used to secure a lender who finances a Homeowner's purchase of a Lot or Unit. Notwithstanding any other laws, a Subdivision Association may provide written notice under Section 209.0091 to any holder of a lien recorded against a delinquent Lot Owner's property. Tex. Prop. Code § 209.0091(c). In other words, a Subdivision Association may send a notice of a Lot Owner's delinquent Assessment account to a holder of a Deed of Trust Lien that is superior in priority to (or otherwise senior to) the Subdivision Association's Assessment Lien.

89 Tex. Prop. Code § 209.0091(a).

90 Tex. Prop. Code § 209.0091(b). Prior to 2015, Section 209.0091 required the written notice to be sent to applicable lienholders by certified mail, return receipt requested. In 2015, the Texas Legislature amended Section 209.0091 so to require the written notice to be sent by only certified mail. Tex. Prop. Code § 209.0091(b).

91 Tex. Prop. Code § 209.0092; Tex. Civ. Prac. & Rem. Code §§ 17.031, 154.028; Tex. R. Civ. P. 735.1. Although a Texas Subdivision Association is required to obtain a court order through an expedited judicial proceeding prior to conducting a non-judicial foreclosure of its Assessment Lien, such expedited judicial proceeding is not the equivalent of a Judicial Foreclosure Lawsuit. Tex. R. Civ. P. 735.2. In addition, a Subdivision Association is not relieved of the statutory limitation on the amount of attorneys fees that may be included in a non-judicial foreclosure sale even though it has obtained a court order authorizing the non-

procedures for obtaining a court order through an Expedited Non-Judicial Foreclosure Proceeding is described in more detail in the following subchapters.

7.9.2 (A) *Power of Sale Prerequisite*

Pursuant to Texas Rule of Civil Procedure 735.1, the procedure for obtaining a court order authorizing foreclosure of an Assessment Lien through an Expedited Non-Judicial Foreclosure Proceeding only applies to the foreclosure of an Assessment Lien created by a Declaration that grants the Subdivision Association a "power of sale."[92] In other words, if a Subdivision Association has not been granted a power of sale within the Declaration creating the Assessment Lien, then it cannot utilize the procedure for obtaining a court order authorizing foreclosure of such Assessment Lien through an Expedited Non-Judicial Foreclosure Proceeding.

There is a very logical reason for this requirement. A Subdivision Association is only required to obtain a court order pre-authorizing foreclosure of its Assessment Lien if it elects to foreclose such lien by non-judicial foreclosure procedures.[93] In addition, a court order obtained through an Expedited Non-Judicial Foreclosure Proceeding merely

---

judicial foreclosure through an expedited judicial proceeding established by Texas Rules of Civil Procedure 735 and 736. *See* Tex. Prop. Code § 209.008(f). Notwithstanding, even if an Assessment Lien is eligible to be foreclosed by non-judicial foreclosure procedures, a Subdivision Association can still elect to foreclose its Assessment Lien by judicial foreclosure procedures. Tex. Prop. Code § 209.0092(d); Tex. R. Civ. P. 735.3. In such event, the Subdivision Association is not required to obtain a court order under the expedited procedures established by Texas Rules of Civil Procedure 735 and 736 before initiating a Judicial Foreclosure Lawsuit. *See* Comment to 2011 Change to Texas Rules of Civil Procedure 735 and 736 ("Any lien which can be foreclosed under Rule 736 may also be foreclosed in an action for judicial foreclosure, as Rule 735.3 states, but no lienholder is required to obtain both a Rule 736 order and a judgment for judicial foreclosure.").

92 Tex. R. Civ. P. 735.1; *see also*, Comment to 2011 Change to Texas Rules of Civil Procedure 735 and 736 ("Rule 735.1 makes the expedited procedures of Rule 736 available only when the lienholder has a power of sale but a court order is nevertheless required by law to foreclose the lien."). A "power of sale" refers to the right and power granted to a third-party (such as a mortgagee or a trustee) to sell real property at a public auction upon the default in the payment of debt secured by such real property. *See generally*, *Black's Law Dictionary* 1172 (6th ed. 1990).

93 *See* Comment to 2011 Change to Texas Rules of Civil Procedure 735 and 736. In other words, if a Subdivision Association elects to foreclose its Assessment Lien by filing a Judicial Foreclosure Lawsuit, it does not have to obtain a court order authorizing it to do so through an Expedited Non-Judicial Foreclosure Proceeding before filing the Judicial Foreclosure Lawsuit.

authorizes a Subdivision Association to "proceed with the foreclosure process under applicable law and the terms of the lien sought to be foreclosed."[94] In plain English, this means that the court order obtained through an Expedited Non-Judicial Foreclosure Proceeding merely authorizes a Subdivision Association to proceed with the foreclosure of its Assessment Lien by non-judicial foreclosure procedures in accordance with Texas law and the terms of the Declaration creating such Assessment Lien.

Chapter 51 of the Texas Property Code is the statutory law that governs the process for non-judicially foreclosing a lien against real property.[95] In order to non-judicially foreclose a lien under Chapter 51, a lienholder must have a power of sale.[96] Accordingly, in order to proceed with the foreclosure of its Assessment Lien by non-judicial foreclosure procedures after obtaining a court order through an Expedited Non-Judicial Foreclosure Proceeding, the Subdivision Association must have a power of sale granted by the Declaration creating such Assessment Lien.[97]

In recognition of the limited nature of an order obtained through an Expedited Non-Judicial Foreclosure Proceeding and the need of a Subdivision Association to have a power of sale to conduct a non-judicial foreclosure sale of a delinquent Lot Owner's Lot after obtaining a court order authorizing such foreclosure, the rules of procedure promulgated by the Texas Supreme Court for conducting an Expedited Non-Judicial

---

94 Tex. R. Civ. P. 736.9. *See also*, Order of the Texas Supreme Court granting final approval of forms for expedited foreclosure proceedings, dated February 10, 2014, filed in Misc. Docket No. 14-9047.

95 Tex. Prop. Code § 51.001, et seq.

96 *See* Chapter 51 of the Texas Property Code, which governs the procedures for conducting a non-judicial foreclosure sale of a Lot or Unit pursuant to a power of sale. Tex. Prop. Code § 51.001, et seq. If a lienholder has not been granted a power of sale, the lienholder must foreclose his or her lien by filing a judicial foreclosure lawsuit and obtaining a foreclosure judgment that containing an "order of sale," which authorizes a sheriff or constable to seize and sell the real property subject to the lien at public auction in order to satisfy the amount awarded in such foreclosure judgment. Tex. R. Civ. P. 309.

97 A power of sale to sell a Lot or Unit to satisfy unpaid Assessments may be vested in a Homeowners Association by either statute (as is the case with the Texas Uniform Condominium Act for Condominium Associations) or contract (such as a Declaration, which is often the case with both Condominium and Subdivision Associations). *See generally*, Tex. Prop. Code § 82.113(d).

Foreclosure Proceeding restrict the use of such proceeding to only Subdivision Associations that are foreclosing an Assessment Lien created by a Declaration that grants the Subdivision Association a power of sale.[98]

Prior to 2015, if a Subdivision Association's Declaration did not expressly authorize it to foreclose its Assessment Lien by non-judicial foreclosure procedures and convey a power of sale to the Subdivision Association for such purpose, then such Subdivision Association was not authorized to utilize the procedures for an Expedited Non-Judicial Foreclosure Proceeding under Texas Rules of Civil Procedure 735 and 736, and it could only foreclose its Assessment Lien by filing a Judicial Foreclosure Lawsuit. In 2015, however, the Texas Legislature amended Section 209.0092 of the Texas Property Code to provide that a Subdivision Association whose Dedicatory Instruments grant it a right of foreclosure is considered to have any power of sale required by law as a condition of obtaining a court order through an Expedited Non-Judicial Foreclosure Proceeding.[99] In other words, if a Subdivision Association's Declaration authorizes it to foreclose an Assessment Lien by any method, Section 209.0092 now provides that such Subdivision Association will be considered to have the required power of sale necessary to utilize the procedures for obtaining a court order authorizing foreclosure of an Assessment Lien through an Expedited Non-Judicial Foreclosure Proceeding, even if the Declaration creating the Assessment Lien does not actually grant such Subdivision Association a power of sale. Or said even more simply, the amended version of Section 209.0092 now authorizes all Subdivision Associations to utilize the procedures for obtaining a court order pre-authorizing foreclosure of an Assessment Lien through an Expedited Non-Judicial Foreclosure Proceeding.

---

98 Tex. R. Civ. P. 735.1 ("[Texas Rule of Civil Procedure] 736 provides the procedure for obtaining a court order, when required, to allow foreclosure of a lien containing a power of sale in the security instrument, dedicatory instrument, or declaration creating the lien").

99 Tex. Prop. Code § 209.0092(a).

It is important to note, however, that while the 2015 amendment to Section 209.0092 appears to grant a Subdivision Association a power of sale, the actual effect of such amendment to Section 209.0092 is unclear based on the limited scope of its language. More specifically, as modified, Section 209.0092 now provides that a Subdivision Association is "considered to have any power of sale required by law as a condition of using the procedures described by [Section 209.0092]" to obtain a court order through an Expedited Non-Judicial Foreclosure Proceeding; however, Section 209.0092 does not actually grant a Subdivision Association the power of sale needed in order to foreclose an Assessment Lien under Chapter 51 of the Texas Property Code. Thus, while Section 209.0092 now grants a Subdivision Association a sufficient power of sale for purposes of utilizing an Expedited Non-Judicial Foreclosure Proceeding to obtain a court order permitting it to proceed with non-judicial foreclosure of its Assessment Lien, because of the limited scope of the power of sale granted to Subdivision Associations under Section 209.0092, it is unclear whether such power of sale is sufficient to actually authorize a Subdivision Association to sell a delinquent Lot Owner's Lot under the procedures required by Chapter 51 of the Texas Property Code. As a result of the lack of clarity concerning the effect of the 2015 amendment to Section 209.0092, a Subdivision Association that has not been expressly granted a power of sale in the Declaration creating the Assessment Lien should exercise caution before foreclosing its Assessment Lien by non-judicial foreclosure procedures until a Texas appellate court has determined whether such amendment validly authorizes it do so.

7.9.2 (B) *Filing a Non-Judicial Foreclosure Application by a Subdivision Association*

To initiate an Expedited Non-Judicial Foreclosure Proceeding, a Subdivision Association must file a verified application (called a "Non-Judicial Foreclosure

Application") in a court of competent jurisdiction in the county in which all or part of the Lot to be foreclosed is located.[100] The Non-Judicial Foreclosure Application must:

(1) identify the name and last known address of the Subdivision Association (referred to as the "Petitioner" under Texas Rule of Civil Procedure 736);[101]

(2) identify the name and last known address of each person obligated to pay the unpaid Assessments secured by the Subdivision Association's Assessment Lien who has a current ownership interest in the Lot to be foreclosed (referred to as the "Respondent" under Texas Rule of Civil Procedure 736);[102]

(3) identify the Lot to be foreclosed by its legal description and commonly known street address;[103]

(4) state that the lien to be foreclosed is a "property owners' association assessment lien under Section 29.0092 of the Texas Property Code";[104]

(5) describe the authority of the Subdivision Association to seek foreclosure of the Assessment Lien;[105]

(6) identify, as of a specific date not less than sixty (60) days prior to the date the Non-Judicial Foreclosure Application is filed, the number of unpaid regular and special Assessments owed by the Lot Owner to the Subdivision Association and the amount required to cure such Lot Owner's default;[106]

(7) state that all requisite notices to cure such Lot Owner's delinquent Assessment account have been mailed to each person as required under

100 Tex. R. Civ. P. 736.1(a). A Non-Judicial Foreclosure Application may also be filed in a probate court with jurisdiction over proceedings involving a Lot that is part of a decedent's estate. Tex. R. Civ. P. 736.1(a).

101 Tex. R. Civ. P. 736.1(d)(1)(A).

102 Tex. R. Civ. P. 736.1(d)(1)(B).

103 Tex. R. Civ. P. 736.1(d)(2).

104 Tex. R. Civ. P. 735.1, 736.1(d)(3)(A).

105 Tex. R. Civ. P. 736.1(d)(3)(B). In most cases, such authority will be the Declaration or other Dedicatory Instrument that establishes the Assessment Lien and the Subdivision Association's authority to foreclose such lien by non-judicial foreclosure procedures.

106 Tex. R. Civ. P. 736.1(d)(3)(E).

applicable law and the Declaration and that any applicable opportunities to cure such delinquent Assessment account have expired;[107]

(8) state that before the Non-Judicial Foreclosure Application was filed, any other prior action required to be performed under applicable law and the Declaration was performed;[108] and

(9) conspicuously state: (a) "that legal action is not being sought against the occupant of the property, unless the occupant is also named as a Respondent in the application;" and (b) "that if the Petitioner obtains a court order, the Petitioner will proceed with a foreclosure of the Lot in accordance with applicable law and the terms of the lien sought to be foreclosed."[109]

In addition, the Non-Judicial Foreclosure Application must include an affidavit of material facts signed by a representative of the Subdivision Association describing the basis for foreclosure, and it must include an attached, legible copy of: (1) the Subdivision Association's Declaration or other Dedicatory Instrument establishing its Assessment Lien; and (2) each notice required to be mailed to the Lot Owner before the Non-Judicial Foreclosure Application was filed and proof of mailing of each such notice.[110]

Upon filing the Non-Judicial Foreclosure Application, the court clerk will issue a separate citation for each Lot Owner identified as a "Respondent" and one additional citation for the occupant or occupants of the Lot to be foreclosed.[111] The clerk of the court is required to serve each applicable Lot Owner and the occupant(s) of the Lot to be

---

[107] Tex. R. Civ. P. 736.1(d)(3)(F).

[108] Tex. R. Civ. P. 736.1(d)(3)(G).

[109] Tex. R. Civ. P. 736.1(d)(5). The comments to Texas Rule of Civil Procedure 735.1(d)(5) make reference to Section 1.201(b)(10) of the Texas Business and Commerce Code in regards to the requirement of conspicuousness. Pursuant to Section 1.201(b)(10), to be conspicuously stated, language must be written, displayed, or presented so that a reasonable person against which it is to operate ought to have noticed it. Tex. Bus. & Com. Code § 1.201(b)(10). Statements in the body of a document may be made conspicuous by use of larger type than the surrounding text, or by use of contrasting type, font, or color to the surrounding text of the same size, or by being set off from surrounding text of the same size by symbols or other marks that call attention to the statements. Tex. Bus. & Com. Code § 1.201(b)(10)(B).

[110] Tex. R. Civ. P. 736.1(d)(6).

[111] Tex. R. Civ. P. 736.3(a)(1).

foreclosed with a citation and copy of the Non-Judicial Foreclosure Application in accordance with Rule 736 or 106 of the Texas Rules of Civil Procedure, or in any other manner provided for the service of lawsuit petitions under the Texas Rules of Civil Procedure.[112]

7.9.2 (C) *Responding to a Non-Judicial Foreclosure Application*

A Lot Owner served with a citation and copy of the Non-Judicial Foreclosure Application may contest such application by filing a written response to the Non-Judicial Foreclosure Application by the first (1st) Monday after the expiration of thirty-eight (38) days from the date the Lot owner was served with the citation and copy of the Non-Judicial Foreclosure Application.[113] The response must be signed by the applicable Lot Owner and must affirmatively state or allege (as applicable):

---

112 Tex. Civ. Prac. & Rem. Code §§ 17.031, 154.028. Rule 736 of the Texas Rules of Civil Procedure requires the clerk of the court to serve each applicable Lot Owner and the occupant(s) of the Lot to be foreclosed with a citation and copy of the Non-Judicial Foreclosure Application by both first class mail and certified mail. Tex. R. Civ. P. 736.3(b)(1). A citation directed to an applicable Lot Owner must be mailed to his or her last known address, as identified in the Non-Judicial Foreclosure Application. Tex. R. Civ. P. 736.3(b)(1). A citation directed to an occupant or occupants of the Lot to be foreclosed must be mailed to "Occupant of [Lot's mailing address]" at the address of the Lot to be foreclosed, as identified in the Non-Judicial Foreclosure Application. Tex. R. Civ. P. 736.3(b)(1). If a citation is mailed by the court clerk in accordance with Texas Rule of Civil Procedure 736.3(b)(1), the date of service is the date and time the citation was placed in the custody of the United States Postal Service in a properly addressed, postage prepaid envelope in accordance with the clerk's standard mailing procedures. Tex. R. Civ. P. 736.3(b)(2). Rule 106 of the Texas Rules of Civil Procedure, which governs service of citations and lawsuit petitions in general, requires that a citation be served, by a sheriff, constable or other person authorized by law or by written order of the court, by either: (1) hand-delivery; or (2) registered or certified mail, return receipt requested. Tex. R. Civ. P. 103, 106.

113 Tex. R. Civ. P. 736.5(b). If the Lot Owner was served with citation in accordance with Rule 736 of the Texas Rules of Civil Procedure, the Lot Owner must file the written response by the first (1st) Monday after the expiration of thirty-eight (38) days from the date the citation was placed in the custody of the United States Postal Service, as stated on the citation. Tex. R. Civ. P. 736.5(b). If, on the other hand, the Lot Owner was served with citation in accordance with Rule 106 of the Texas Rules of Civil Procedure, the Lot Owner must file the written response by the first (1st) Monday after the expiration of thirty-eight (38) days from the date the Lot Owner was served with the citation, by a sheriff, constable or other person authorized by law or by written order of the court, by either: (1) hand-delivery; or (2) registered or certified mail, return receipt requested. Tex. Civ. Prac. & Rem. Code §§ 17.031, 154.028(a); Tex. R. Civ. P. 103, 106, 736.5(b).

(1) why the Lot Owner is not obligated for payment of the amounts secured by the Subdivision Association's Assessment Lien;[114]

(2) why the number of months of alleged default or pay off amounts are materially incorrect;[115]

(3) why any document attached to the Non-Judicial Foreclosure Application is not a true and correct copy of the original;[116] or

(4) if the Lot Owner has paid the amounts that the Subdivision Association claims is unpaid, the distinct nature of such payments.[117]

A response filed by a Lot Owner, however, may not state an independent claim for relief, and the court is required, without a hearing, to strike and dismiss any counterclaim, cross-claim, third-party claim, intervention, or cause of action filed by a Lot Owner in an Expedited Non-Judicial Foreclosure Proceeding.[118]

7.9.2 (D) *Ruling on a Non-Judicial Foreclosure Application*

If no response to the Non-Judicial Foreclosure Application is filed by an applicable Lot Owner by the due date, the Subdivision Association may file a motion and proposed order to obtain a default order granting the Non-Judicial Foreclosure Application.[119] In such event, and so long as the Non-Judicial Foreclosure Application complies with the requirements of Texas Rule of Civil Procedure 736 and was properly

---

[114] Tex. R. Civ. P. 736.5(c)(2).

[115] Tex. R. Civ. P. 736.5(c)(3).

[116] Tex. R. Civ. P. 736.5(c)(4).

[117] Tex. R. Civ. P. 736.5(c)(5); *see also* Tex. R. Civ. P. 95.

[118] Tex. R. Civ. P. 736.5(d). Notwithstanding, if an applicable Lot Owner provides proof to the court clerk that he or she filed bankruptcy before an order granting the Non-Judicial Foreclosure Application is signed by the judge, the Expedited Non-Judicial Foreclosure Proceeding must be abated so long as the automatic stay under the Bankruptcy Code is effective. Tex. R. Civ. P. 736.10.

[119] Tex. R. Civ. P. 736.7(a). For the purposes of obtaining a default order granting the Non-Judicial Foreclosure Application, all facts alleged in the Non-Judicial Foreclosure Application that are supported by the included affidavit of material facts constitute prima facie evidence of the truth of the matters alleged. Tex. R. Civ. P. 736.7(a). "Prima facie" is a Latin expression meaning on its first encounter, first blush, or at first sight. In the context of a legal proceeding, "prima facie evidence" refers to evidence that—unless rebutted—would be sufficient to prove a particular proposition or fact.

served on all applicable Lot Owners, the court must grant the Non-Judicial Foreclosure Application by default order no later than thirty (30) days after a motion for default order is filed by the Subdivision Association.[120]

If a response to the Non-Judicial Foreclosure Application is filed by a Lot Owner, then the court must conduct a hearing on the merits of the Non-Judicial Foreclosure Application after providing reasonable notice of the hearing date to the parties.[121] A hearing on a Subdivision Association's Non-Judicial Foreclosure Application must be held by the Court within thirty (30) days of a request for a hearing by any party to the Expedited Non-Judicial Foreclosure Proceeding, but such hearing may not be held during the first twenty (20) days following the date such request for a hearing is filed.[122] In other words, if the Subdivision Association or the Lot Owner requests a hearing on the merits of the Non-Judicial Foreclosure Application, the court must set a hearing date that is no later than thirty (30) days, nor earlier than twenty (20) days, after the date the request for a hearing is filed.

At the hearing on the merits of the Non-Judicial Foreclosure Application, the Subdivision Association has the burden to prove by affidavits on file or evidence presented at the hearing the grounds for granting the order sought in the Non-Judicial Foreclosure Application.[123] If the Subdivision Association establishes the authority and basis for it to foreclose its Assessment Lien by non-judicial foreclosure procedures, the

---

120 Tex. R. Civ. P. 736.7(b).

121 Tex. R. Civ. P. 736.6. A court is prohibited from conducting a hearing on a Non-Judicial Foreclosure Application unless a response is filed by an applicable Lot Owner. Tex. R. Civ. P. 736.6.

122 Tex. R. Civ. P. 736.6. The parties to an Expedited Non-Judicial Foreclosure Proceeding are not permitted to conduct discovery. Tex. R. Civ. P. 736.4. Discovery is the formal process under the Texas Rules of Civil Procedure by which a party to a lawsuit may obtain information and documents relevant to the claims and defenses asserted in the lawsuit from the other parties in the lawsuit. *See generally*, Tex. R. Civ. P. 190–215.

123 Tex. R. Civ. P. 736.6.

court must issue an order granting the Non-Judicial Foreclosure Application; otherwise, the court must deny such application.[124]

An order granting a Subdivision Association's Non-Judicial Foreclosure Application must describe:

(1) the material facts establishing the basis for foreclosure of the Subdivision Association's Assessment Lien;[125]

(2) the Lot to be foreclosed by its legal description and commonly known mailing address;[126]

(3) the name and last known address of each Lot Owner subject to the order;[127] and

(4) the recording or indexing information of the Declaration or other Dedicatory Instrument establishing the Assessment Lien to be foreclosed.[128]

Once the court enters an order granting its Non-Judicial Foreclosure Application, a Subdivision Association may proceed with the foreclosure of its Assessment Lien by non-judicial foreclosure procedures.[129] In addition, upon completion of the non-judicial foreclosure sale of the applicable Lot, a conformed copy of the order granting the Subdivision Association's Non-Judicial Foreclosure Application must be attached to the trustee's or substitute trustee's foreclosure deed.[130]

---

[124] Tex. R. Civ. P. 736.8(a). An order granting or denying a Non-Judicial Foreclosure Application is final and is not subject to a motion for rehearing, new trial, bill of review, or appeal. Tex. R. Civ. P. 736.8(c). Such order, however, is without prejudice and has no res judicata, collateral estoppel, estoppel by judgment, or other effect in any other judicial proceeding. Tex. R. Civ. P. 736.9.

[125] Tex. R. Civ. P. 736.8(b)(1).

[126] Tex. R. Civ. P. 736.8(b)(2).

[127] Tex. R. Civ. P. 736.8(b)(3).

[128] Tex. R. Civ. P. 736.8(b)(4).

[129] Tex. R. Civ. P. 736.9.

[130] Tex. R. Civ. P. 736.12.

7.9.2 (E) *Court-Ordered Mediation of an Expedited Non-Judicial Foreclosure Proceeding*

In 2013, the Texas Legislature enacted a new statutory provision that authorizes a court to order mediation of an Expedited Non-Judicial Foreclosure Proceeding under certain limited circumstances.[131] More specifically, Section 154.028 of the Texas Civil Practice and Remedies Code authorizes a trial court, following the timely filing of a response by the applicable Lot Owner but prior to conducting a hearing on the merits of the Non-Judicial Foreclosure Application, to conduct a hearing to determine whether to order mediation of an Expedited Non-Judicial Foreclosure Proceeding (called a "Mediation Determination Hearing").[132]

Notwithstanding such general authority to conduct a Mediation Determination Hearing, a trial court may not order mediation of the Expedited Non-Judicial Foreclosure Proceeding without conducting a Mediation Determination Hearing and a Mediation Determination Hearing may not be conducted by the court before the expiration of the delinquent Lot Owner's deadline to file a response to the Non-Judicial Foreclosure Application.[133] In addition, a trial court may be further restricted from conducting a Mediation Determination Hearing or ordering mediation of an Expedited Non-Judicial Foreclosure Proceeding, depending on the manner in which the Lot Owner was served

---

131 Tex. Civ. Prac. & Rem. Code § 154.028.

132 Tex. Civ. Prac. & Rem. Code § 154.028(a). It is important to note that the Subdivision Association or the delinquent Lot Owner may request a hearing to determine whether mediation of the Expedited Non-Judicial Foreclosure Proceeding is necessary or whether the Non-Judicial Foreclosure Application is defective. Tex. Civ. Prac. & Rem. Code § 154.028(a).

133 Tex. Civ. Prac. & Rem. Code § 154.028(a)–(b). The court may not conduct a Mediation Determination Hearing or order mediation of an Expedited Non-Judicial Foreclosure Proceeding if the Subdivision Association served the Lot Owner with citation in compliance with Rule 106 of the Texas Rules of Civil Procedure, and a written response to the Non-Judicial Foreclosure Application has not been filed with the court by the first (1st) Monday after the expiration of thirty-eight (38) days from the date the delinquent Lot Owner was served with the citation, by a sheriff, constable, or other person authorized by law or by written order of the court, by either: (1) hand-delivery; or (2) registered or certified mail, return receipt requested. Tex. Civ. Prac. & Rem. Code § 154.028(j); Tex. R. Civ. P. 103, 106, 736.5(b).

with a citation and copy of the Non-Judicial Foreclosure Application and the timeliness of the Lot Owner's filed response thereto.

More specifically, if an applicable Lot Owner was served with a citation and copy of the Non-Judicial Foreclosure Application in accordance with Rule 106 and fails to file a written response by the first (1st) Monday after the expiration of thirty-eight (38) days from the date such Lot Owner was served with the citation and the copy of the Non-Judicial Foreclosure Application, then such response is considered untimely and the court may not conduct a Mediation Determination Hearing, and consequently, it may not order the Expedited Non-Judicial Foreclosure Proceeding to mediation.[134]

Alternatively, if an applicable Lot Owner was served with a citation and copy of the Non-Judicial Foreclosure Application in accordance with Rule 736 (instead of Rule 106), and he or she files a written response any time before the Subdivision Association files a motion to obtain a default order granting the Non-Judicial Foreclosure Application, then the trial court may conduct a Mediation Determination Hearing and order the Expedited Non-Judicial Foreclosure Proceeding to mediation without any limitation.[135] On the other hand, if the applicable Lot Owner was served with a citation and copy of the Non-Judicial Foreclosure Application in accordance with Rule 736 (instead of Rule 106),

[134] Tex. Civ. Prac. & Rem. Code § 154.028(j). If the court cannot conduct a Mediation Determination Hearing, then it also cannot order mediation of the Expedited Non-Judicial Foreclosure Proceeding. Tex. Civ. Prac. & Rem. Code § 154.028(a).

[135] Tex. Civ. Prac. & Rem. Code § 154.028(a), (j)–(k). If a Lot Owner is served with citation in compliance with Rule 736 of the Texas Rules of Civil Procedure, instead of Rule 106, the trial court is not expressly precluded from conducting a Mediation Determination Hearing; however, a court may not conduct a Mediation Determination Hearing until after the Lot Owner files a response to the Non-Judicial Foreclosure Application. Tex. Civ. Prac. & Rem. Code § 154.028(a). In addition, because a court-ordered mediation must be conducted before the expiration of any deadline imposed by Rule 736 and the only deadline imposed by Rule 736 following the expiration of the deadline to file a response to the Non-Judicial Foreclosure Application is the 30-day deadline imposed on the court to grant a motion to obtain a default order under Rule 736.7(b), unless the Subdivision Association files a motion to obtain a default order because the Lot Owner has failed to file a response to the Non-Judicial Foreclosure Application, there are not any other deadlines imposed by Rule 736 that would limited the ability of the trial court to conduct a Mediation Determination Hearing or impose a deadline by which a court-ordered mediation must be conducted. Tex. Civ. Prac. & Rem. Code § 154.028(f), (j), (l); Tex. R. Civ. P. 736.7(b).

and he or she files a written response after the Subdivision Association files a motion to obtain a default order granting the Non-Judicial Foreclosure Application, but before the trial court grants such default order, then the trial court may still conduct a Mediation Determination Hearing and order the Expedited Non-Judicial Foreclosure Proceeding to mediation, provided the mediation is conducted within twenty-nine (29) days from the date the Subdivision Association filed the motion to obtain a default order.[136] Under such circumstances, however, if the applicable Lot Owner fails to attend the Mediation Determination Hearing, then the court may not order mediation of the Expedited Non-Judicial Foreclosure Proceeding and must grant or deny the Subdivision Association's motion to obtain a default order at the Mediation Determination Hearing.[137]

If the court elects to conduct a Mediation Determination Hearing, such hearing may, at the court's discretion, be conducted by telephone.[138] At least ten (10) days before the date of a Mediation Determination Hearing, the court is required to send a notice of the Mediation Determination Hearing to the parties that notifies them as to whether the hearing will be conducted by telephone and, if applicable, instructions for contacting the court and attending the hearing by telephone.[139] If the delinquent Lot Owner is provided notice of a Mediation Determination Hearing by the Court, but the Lot Owner fails to attend such hearing, then the court is prohibited from ordering the Expedited Non-Judicial Foreclosure Proceeding to mediation and must grant the Non-Judicial Foreclosure

---

136 Tex. Civ. Prac. & Rem. Code § 154.028(f), (j), (l); Tex. R. Civ. P. 736.7(b). If a trial court orders an Expedited Non-Judicial Foreclosure Proceeding to mediation, the mediation must take place not later than the 29th day after the date the petitioner filed a motion for default order. Tex. Civ. Prac. & Rem. Code § 154.028(l).

137 Tex. Civ. Prac. & Rem. Code § 154.028(k).

138 Tex. Civ. Prac. & Rem. Code § 154.028(c).

139 Tex. Civ. Prac. & Rem. Code § 154.028(d).

Application by default if it complies with the requirements of Texas Rule of Civil Procedure 736 and was properly served on the delinquent Lot Owners.[140]

At a Mediation Determination Hearing, the court must consider any objections to the referral of the Expedited Non-Judicial Foreclosure Proceeding to mediation.[141] If the court orders the Expedited Non-Judicial Foreclosure Proceeding to mediation, the mediator to be appointed by the court may be selected by the agreement of the Subdivision Association and the delinquent Lot Owner at the Mediation Determination Hearing.[142] If the Subdivision Association and delinquent Lot Owner are unable to agree on the selection of a mediator at the Mediation Determination Hearing, then the court may appoint the mediator instead.[143]

If the court orders the Expedited Non-Judicial Foreclosure Proceeding to mediation, the court-ordered mediation must be conducted before the expiration of any deadline imposed by Rule 736 of the Texas Rules of Civil Procedure.[144] In addition, the

---

140 Tex. Civ. Prac. & Rem. Code § 154.028(k); Tex. R. Civ. P. 736.7.

141 Tex. Civ. Prac. & Rem. Code § 154.028(e). Even if the court orders the Expedited Non-Judicial Foreclosure Proceeding to mediation, the Subdivision Association and the delinquent Lot Owner may agree to waive the mediation process. Tex. Civ. Prac. & Rem. Code § 154.028(i).

142 Tex. Civ. Prac. & Rem. Code § 154.028(g).

143 Tex. Civ. Prac. & Rem. Code § 154.028(g). If a mediator is appointed by the court because the parties are unable to agree on the selection of a mediator, the court must provide the Subdivision Association and the delinquent Lot Owner with the name of the chosen mediator at the mediation hearing. Tex. Civ. Prac. & Rem. Code § 154.028(g).

144 Tex. Civ. Prac. & Rem. Code § 154.028(f). Although a court-ordered mediation of an Expedited Non-Judicial Foreclosure Proceeding must be conducted before the expiration of any deadline imposed by Rule 736 of the Texas Rules of Civil Procedure, if the Lot Owner filed a response to the Non-Judicial Foreclosure Application, there are no additional deadlines imposed by Rule 736 following the filling of such response. Tex. R. Civ. P. 736. Under such circumstance, the only additional time frame referenced by Rule 736 concerns the timing of a hearing on the merits of the Non-Judicial Foreclosure Application, which requires that such hearing be held no later than thirty (30) days, or earlier than twenty (20) days, after a request for such hearing is made by any party. Tex. R. Civ. P. 736.6. On the other hand, if a Lot Owner is served with citation in compliance with Rule 736 of the Texas Rules of Civil Procedure, instead of Rule 106, and fails to file a written response to the Non-Judicial Foreclosure Application, but appears at the Mediation Determination Hearing, and the court orders the Expedited Non-Judicial Foreclosure Proceeding to mediation, then the Subdivision Association may still file a motion and proposed order to obtain a default order granting the Non-Judicial Foreclosure Application. In such event, the court-ordered mediation must be conducted within twenty-nine

mediator's fee must be divided equally between the Subdivision Association and the Lot Owner or Owners.[145]

7.9.2 (F) *Procedures for Legally Challenging a Non-Judicial Foreclosure Proceeding and/or an Order Granting a Non-Judicial Foreclosure Application*

As noted earlier, a Lot Owner may not assert an independent claim for relief (such as a counterclaim or third-party claim) in a response to a Non-Judicial Foreclosure Application, and an order granting a Non-Judicial Foreclosure Application is final and not subject to appeal.[146] In addition, an order granting or denying a Non-Judicial Foreclosure Application is final and is not subject to a motion for rehearing, new trial, bill of review, or appeal.[147]

The only method for a Lot Owner to legally challenge a Non-Judicial Foreclosure Application or an order granting a Non-Judicial Foreclosure Application is to file a separate, independent lawsuit against the Subdivision Association that puts in issue any matter related to the origination, servicing, or enforcement of the Subdivision Association's Assessment Lien.[148] If a Lot Owner files such a lawsuit against the Subdivision Association in a court of competent jurisdiction at any time prior to 5:00 p.m. on the Monday before the scheduled non-judicial foreclosure sale of an applicable Lot, then the Expedited Non-Judicial Foreclosure Proceeding and/or the order granting a Non-

(29) days from the date the Subdivision Association filed its motion for default order. Tex. Civ. Prac. & Rem. Code § 154.028(m).

145 Tex. Civ. Prac. & Rem. Code § 154.028(h).

146 Tex. R. Civ. P. 736.5(d), 736.8(c). Notwithstanding, if an applicable Lot Owner provides proof to the court clerk that he or she filed bankruptcy before an order granting the Non-Judicial Foreclosure Application is signed by the judge, the Expedited Non-Judicial Foreclosure Proceeding must be abated so long as the automatic stay under the Bankruptcy Code is effective. Tex. R. Civ. P. 736.10.

147 Tex. R. Civ. P. 736.8.

148 Tex. R. Civ. P. 736.8(c).

Judicial Foreclosure Application is automatically stayed.[149] In other words, even if a court has already executed an order granting a Subdivision Association's Non-Judicial Foreclosure Application and the applicable Lot has been scheduled for a non-judicial foreclosure sale (which must occur on the first Tuesday of the month), a Lot Owner can still stop the non-judicial foreclosure sale of his or her Lot by filing an independent lawsuit against the Subdivision Association by 5:00 p.m. the day before the scheduled sale. If a non-judicial foreclosure sale of an applicable Lot has already been scheduled, then upon filing the independent lawsuit, the Lot Owner must give prompt notice of the filing of such lawsuit to the Subdivision Association or its attorney, as well as the foreclosure trustee or substitute trustee, by any reasonable means necessary to stop such scheduled foreclosure sale.[150]

In addition, within ten (10) days of filing such independent lawsuit, the Lot Owner must also file a motion in the court in which the Expedited Non-Judicial Foreclosure Proceeding is pending that advises such court that the Lot Owner has filed an original proceeding contesting the right of the Subdivision Association to foreclose its Assessment Lien in a court of competent jurisdiction.[151] If at the time such motion is filed no order granting the Subdivision Association's Non-Judicial Foreclosure Application has already been signed by the judge, then the court must dismiss the pending Expedited Non-Judicial Foreclosure Proceeding.[152] On the other hand, if at the time such motion is filed an order granting the Subdivision Association's Non-Judicial Foreclosure Application has already

[149] Tex. R. Civ. P. 736.11(a).

[150] Tex. R. Civ. P. 736.11(b).

[151] Tex. R. Civ. P. 736.11(c). Such motion must include a proposed order to dismiss or vacate the Expedited Non-Judicial Foreclosure Proceeding. Tex. R. Civ. P. 736.11(c).

[152] Tex. R. Civ. P. 736.11(c).

been signed by the judge, then the court must issue an order vacating its prior order granting the Subdivision Association's Non-Judicial Foreclosure Application.[153]

7.10 Statutory Restrictions on the Rights of Homeowners Associations to Foreclose an Assessment Lien

In addition to any restrictions on a Homeowners Association's right to foreclose its Assessment Lien imposed by its Declaration, there are several statutes that restrict or limit the ability of both Condominium Associations and Subdivision Associations to foreclose their Assessment Lien. More specifically, under the Texas Uniform Condominium Act, a Condominium Association may not foreclose its Assessment Lien against a Unit for unpaid Assessments that consist solely of fines.[154]

In addition, pursuant to Chapter 209 of the Texas Property Code, a Subdivision Association may not foreclose an Assessment Lien if the unpaid amounts owed by the Lot Owner consist solely of: (1) fines assessed by the Subdivision Association;[155] (2) attorneys fees incurred by the Subdivision Association solely associated with fines assessed by the Subdivision Association;[156] (3) costs incurred by the Subdivision Association to compile, produce, and/or reproduce information requested by a Lot Owner that are unpaid and were added to the requesting Lot Owner's Assessment account;[157] and/or (4) additional costs

153 Tex. R. Civ. P. 736.11(c). If a Lot is foreclosed by non-judicial foreclosure sale after the automatic stay is invoked by the timely filing of a separate, independent lawsuit by an applicable Lot Owner, such sale is considered void. Tex. R. Civ. P. 736.11(d). If a voided non-judicial foreclosure sale of a Lot occurs, the foreclosure trustee or substitute trustee that conducted the foreclosure sale must return to the buyer of the foreclosed Lot the purchase price paid by such buyer within ten (10) business days from the date such trustee receives notice that such foreclosure sale is void. Tex. R. Civ. P. 736.11(d).

154 Tex. Prop. Code § 82.113(e).

155 Tex. Prop. Code § 209.009(1).

156 Tex. Prop. Code § 209.009(2).

157 Tex. Prop. Code § 209.009(3). If a Subdivision Association requires a requesting Lot Owner to pay the estimated costs of compilation, production, and reproduction of requested information in advance, and the actual costs are more than the estimated amount paid by the requesting Lot Owner, and the Lot Owner subsequently fails to remit payment of such additional costs to the Subdivision Association within thirty (30)

incurred by the Subdivision Association to perform a ballot recount requested by the Lot Owner that are unpaid and were added to the requesting Lot Owner's Assessment account.[158]

7.11 Texas Constitutional Protection of a Homeowner's Homestead

The Texas Constitution affords to its citizens a certain level of protection by keeping the family homestead safe from foreclosure by creditors who seek to satisfy debts, except for a few specifically enumerated types of liens that may be imposed against a Texan's "Homestead." One of the purposes of this constitutional protection is to prevent impoverished debtors from being unable to provide a home for their families.[159]

7.11.1 Scope of Homestead Property and Invocation of Homestead Protection

Generally, a Texan's Homestead has historically consisted of the dwelling house constituting the family residence, together with the land on which it is situated and the appurtenances connected to such dwelling.[160] The amount of land that may constitute a Texan's Homestead is dictated by the Texas Property Code and depends on whether the property is used for purposes of an urban home or a rural home. If a Homestead is used for the purposes of an urban home (or as both an urban home and a place to exercise a calling or business), the Homestead of a family or a single, adult person is limited to no more than ten acres of land, which may be in one or more contiguous lots, together with

business days from receiving a final invoice for such costs, such additional costs may be added to the Lot Owner's account as an Assessment. Tex. Prop. Code § 209.005(i).

158 Tex. Prop. Code § 209.009(3). If a Subdivision Association performs a ballot recount at the request of a Lot Owner, and the actual costs of performing the ballot recount exceeds the estimated costs paid by the Lot Owner, and the Lot Owner subsequently fails to pay the Subdivision Association such additional costs within thirty (30) business days from the date a final invoice for such additional costs is sent to the Lot Owner, such additional costs may be added to the Lot Owner's account as an Assessment. Tex. Prop. Code § 209.0057(b-4).

159 *Lincoln v. Bennett*, 156 S.W.2d 504, 504 (Tex. 1941).

160 *Gann v. Montgomery*, 210 S.W.2d 255, 258 (Tex. Civ. App.—Fort Worth 1948, writ ref'd n.r.e.).

any improvements located thereon.[161] On the other hand, if a Homestead is used for the purposes of a rural home, a Homestead is limited to no more than 200 acres for a family, or 100 acres for a single, adult person, together with any improvements located thereon.[162]

It is important to note that just because a property owner does not currently live at his or her property does not mean that such property is not his or her Homestead. The determination of whether a particular property constitutes a Homestead is dependent primarily on the intention of the property owner. Homestead protection may even be established upon undeveloped land if the property owner has a present intention to occupy and use the premises as his or her home in a reasonable and definite time in the future and has made some preparations toward actual occupancy and use of such property that "are of such character and have proceeded to such an extent as to manifest beyond doubt the intention to complete the improvements and reside upon the place as a home."[163] In addition, even if a property owner moves from real property that he or she previously resided at as his or her Homestead, such property does not lose its Homestead status unless the property owner moves from the property with the intention not to return and claim such property as his or her Homestead.[164] It is the acquisition of a new Homestead, not merely the acquisition of a new home, that operates as an abandonment of Homestead rights, and even the temporary leasing of a property owner's Homestead to a third party

161 Tex. Prop. Code § 41.002(a). A Homestead is considered to be urban if, at the time the designation is made, the property is: (1) located within the limits of a municipality or its extraterritorial jurisdiction or within a platted subdivision; and (2) served by police protection, paid or volunteer fire protection, and at least three of the following services are provided by a municipality or a third party under contract to a municipality: (A) electric; (B) natural gas; (C) sewer; (D) storm sewer; and (E) water. Tex. Prop. Code § 41.002(c).

162 Tex. Prop. Code § 41.002(b). A Homestead that is used for rural purposes may consist of one or more parcels. Tex. Prop. Code § 41.002(b).

163 *Lilly v. Lewis*, 249 S.W. 1095, 1096 (Tex. Civ. App.—San Antonio 1923, no writ).

164 *Burkhardt v. Lieberman*, 159 S.W.2d 847, 852 (Tex. 1942).

does not constitute abandonment of the Homestead status where no other Homestead has been acquired by the property owner.[165]

7.11.2 Preemption of Homestead Protection by a Preexisting Assessment Lien

Under the Texas Constitution, only specific types of liens enumerated as exceptions to Homestead protection may be foreclosed upon a Texan's Homestead.[166] Such enumerated liens, however, do not include an Assessment Lien in favor of a Homeowners Association.

Notwithstanding, it is well established under Texas law that while the Texas Constitution's protection of Homestead may protect a Homeowner's Lot or Unit from foreclosure by certain creditors, it will not extinguish or subvert a lien that preexists the invocation of the Homeowner's Homestead status to his or her property.[167] On such basis, in 1987, the Texas Supreme Court held in Inwood North Homeowners' Association v. Harris that a preexisting Assessment Lien in favor of a Homeowners Association was superior to the Homeowner's Homestead rights because the Assessment Lien had been in existence prior to the Homeowner's ownership of the subject property, and the invocation of such Homestead status did not extinguish the preexisting Assessment Lien.[168] The controlling and determinative factor in the Texas Supreme Court's holding in Inwood North Homeowners' Association v. Harris was that the Assessment Lien had attached to

---

[165] *Rancho Oil Co. v. Powell*, 175 S.W.2d 960, 963 (Tex. 1943) ("The acquiring of a new home is not always the acquiring of a new homestead, and one does not necessarily abandon a homestead by merely moving his home.").

[166] The Texas Constitution enumerates eight exceptions to Homestead protection from forced sale, including: (1) purchase money security; (2) taxes due on the Homestead; (3) certain owelty on partition; (4) refinancing of certain liens; (5) security for improvements; (6) certain extensions of credit in the nature of an equity loan; (7) reverse mortgages; and (8) special financing concerning manufactured homes. *See* Tex. Const. art. XVI, § 50(a)(1)–(8).

[167] *See Inwood North Homeowners' Association v. Harris*, 736 S.W.2d 632, 634–35 (Tex. 1987).

[168] *Inwood North Homeowners' Association v. Harris*, 736 S.W.2d 632, 635–36 (Tex. 1987).

the Homeowner's property prior to the establishment of the Homeowner's Homestead and, therefore, preempted the subsequent invocation of such Homeowner's Homestead protection.[169] Accordingly, the dispositive issue in determining whether a Homeowners Association's Assessment Lien preempts a Homeowner's Homestead protection on his or her property is whether the Homeowners Association's Assessment Lien attached to the Homeowner's property before he or she established it as his or her Homestead. In other words, a Homeowners Association must determine when its Assessment Lien actually attaches to a Homeowner's Lot or Unit in order to determine whether its Assessment Lien will preempt a Homeowner's invocation of Homestead protection.

This issue is easily determined for Condominium Associations. By virtue of the Texas Uniform Condominium Act, an Assessment Lien in favor of a Condominium Association is created by and attaches to the Units in the applicable Condominium Development upon the recording of the Condominium Declaration.[170] Thus, whether or not it is specifically stated within the Condominium Declaration, a Condominium Association's Assessment Lien attaches immediately to all Units within the Condominium Development upon the recording of the Condominium Declaration and will preempt any subsequent invocation of Homestead protection by a Unit Owner, except in one limited circumstance. If, on January 1, 1994 (the date the Texas Uniform Condominium Act became effective), a Unit was, and has continuously remained, the Homestead of the Unit Owner and such Unit is subject to a Condominium Declaration that does not contain a valid Assessment Lien against such Unit, then the Assessment Lien created by the Texas Uniform Condominium Act does not attach to the Unit until the Unit ceases to be the Homestead of the Unit Owner who has continuously owned such Unit since before

---

169 *Inwood North Homeowners' Association v. Harris*, 736 S.W.2d 632, 635 (Tex. 1987) ("Thus, this case revolves around when the lien attached on the property. If it occurred simultaneously to or after the homeowners took title, there is authority which would deem the homestead right superior.").

170 Tex. Prop. Code § 82.113(c).

January 1, 1994.[171] In other words, if a Condominium Development is subject to the Texas Condominium Act (which does not create an Assessment Lien in favor of the Condominium Association) and the applicable Condominium Declaration does not create an Assessment Lien in favor of such Condominium Association, then the Assessment Lien created by the Texas Uniform Condominium Act in favor of the Condominium Association will not preempt a Unit Owner's Homestead right if such Unit Owner has continuously owned the Unit as his or her Homestead since before the effective enactment date of the Texas Uniform Condominium Act.

There is no similar Texas law applicable to Subdivision Developments. Thus, in order to determine when a Subdivision Association's Assessment Lien attaches to the Lots in its Subdivision Development, the provision in its Declaration that establishes the Assessment Lien must be carefully examined. Not all Declarations are drafted in the same manner, and not all provisions creating an Assessment Lien in favor of a Subdivision Association provide that the Assessment Lien attaches to the subject Lots at the time the Declaration is recorded. When reviewing the language of a Declaration provision that establishes an Assessment Lien, it must be determined whether the lien-creation language contains words of present intent to establish an Assessment Lien or future intent to establish an Assessment Lien. For example, where a Declaration states something to the effect of "by the recording of this Declaration, a lien to secure the payment of assessments is hereby created . . ." such present-tense language clearly indicates that the Assessment Lien is created by the recording of the Declaration and it will preexist the eventual invocation of Homestead protection by the owners of Lots in such Subdivision Development.

On the other hand, a Declaration may state something to the effect of "in the event an owner shall fail to pay assessments, the Association's lien shall become a continuing

[171] Tex. Prop. Code § 82.113(k).

lien on the property. . . ." This is the type of future-tense language that suggests that the Declaration creates an immediate contractual right to place a lien on a subject Lot in the future upon the failure of a Lot Owner to pay his or her Assessments, but it does not create a lien that "attaches" to all of the Lots in the Subdivision Development at the time the Declaration was recorded.[172] In such circumstance, a Texas court may determine that the Subdivision Association's Assessment Lien does not preexist a Homeowner's invocation of Homestead protection, in which event it would be unlawful for the Subdivision Association to foreclose its Assessment Lien on a Homeowner's property if such property is the Homeowner's Homestead.[173]

In general, if it is questionable as to when an Assessment Lien in favor of a Subdivision Association attaches to the Lots in the Subdivision Development, the Subdivision Association should not conduct a non-judicial foreclosure of its Assessment Lien if there is any chance that the subject Lot may be the Homeowner's Homestead.

7.12 Protection of Active Duty Military Servicemembers from Foreclosure

In addition to the constitutional protections from foreclosure afforded to a Texan's Homestead, in 2009, the Texas Legislature enacted certain statutory restrictions against foreclosure of contractual liens on real property owned by a "Military Servicemember" during a period of his or her "Active Duty Military Service" or during the nine (9) months

---

172 *See Red Rock Properties 2005, Ltd. v. Chase Home Finance, L.L.C.*, No. 14-08-00352-CV, 2009 Tex. App. WL 1795037 (Houston [14th Dist.] June 25, 2009, n. pet. h.) (not designated for publication).

173 While there is no Texas appellate case law designated for publication that specifically addresses a distinction between present-tense and future-tense language of a Declaration provision creating an Assessment Lien in regards to controlling the date of "attachment" of the lien, there are several cases concerning other types of contractual liens that do hold it is the attachment and not merely the right to attach a lien in the future that controls in the context of a preexisting lien being superior to a subsequent invocation of Homestead protection. In addition, a 2009 Houston Court of Appeal's opinion (that was not designated for publication) specifically held that a Subdivision Association's Declaration that stated that the Assessment Lien "shall attach from the date of the failure of payment of the assessment" did not create a preexisting lien superior to the Homeowner's invocation of Homestead protection. *Red Rock Properties 2005, Ltd. v. Chase Home Finance, L.L.C.*, No. 14-08-00352-CV, 2009 Tex. App. WL 1795037 (Houston [14th Dist.] June 25, 2009, n. pet. h.) (not designated for publication).

after the date on which such Active Duty Military Service concludes.[174] Such statute only applies to an obligation: (1) that is secured by a contractual lien on real property that includes a dwelling owned by a Military Servicemember; (2) that originated before the date on which the Military Servicemember's Active Duty Military Service commenced; and (3) for which the Military Servicemember is still obligated.[175]

A foreclosure sale of an applicable property owned by a Military Servicemember under a mortgage, deed of trust, or other contractual lien (such as an Assessment Lien) may not be conducted during such Military Servicemember's period of Active Duty Military Service or during the nine (9) months after the date on which such Active Duty Military Service period concludes unless the sale, foreclosure, or seizure is conducted pursuant to either: (1) a court order issued before the sale, foreclosure, or seizure of such property; or (2) a waiver agreement executed by the Military Servicemember.[176] If a

[174] Tex. Prop. Code § 51.015(d). The Texas Property Code defines "Military Servicemember" as: (1) a member of the armed forces of the United States; (2) a member of the Texas National Guard or the National Guard of another state serving on active duty under an order of the President of the United States; or (3) a member of a reserve component of the armed forces of the United States who is on active duty under an order of the President of the United States. Tex. Prop. Code § 51.015(a)(3). The Texas Property Code defines "Active Duty Military Service" as: (1) service as a member of the armed forces of the United States; or (2) with respect to a member of the Texas National Guard or the National Guard of another state or a member of a reserve component of the armed forces of the United States, active duty under an order of the President of the United States. Tex. Prop. Code § 51.015(a)(1). In addition, a dependent of a Military Servicemember may also be entitled to the protections of Section 51.015 of the Texas Property Code if such dependent's ability to comply with an obligation that is secured by a mortgage, deed of trust, or other contract lien on real property is materially affected by such Servicemember's Active Duty Military Service. Tex. Prop. Code § 51.015(g).

[175] Tex. Prop. Code § 51.015(b).

[176] Tex. Prop. Code § 51.015(d). An agreement by a Military Servicemember to waive his or her rights under Section 51.015 of the Texas Property Code must be: (1) in writing in at least twelve-point type; (2) executed as an instrument separate from the obligation to which the waiver applies; and (3) made under a written agreement that is executed during or after the conclusion of such Military Servicemember's period of Active Duty Military Service and specifies the legal instrument to which the waiver applies (and, if the Military Servicemember is not a party to such legal instrument, also specifies the Military Servicemember concerned). Tex. Prop. Code § 51.015(e). If a waiver agreement is executed by a Military Servicemember, or a dependent of such Military Servicemember, who subsequent to executing such waiver agreement enters into Active Duty Military Service, the waiver agreement shall not be valid once the Active Duty Military Services commences unless the waiver agreement was executed by the Military Servicemember or his or her dependent during the applicable period described by 50 U.S.C. App. Section 516, as that section existed on January 1, 2009. Tex. Prop. Code § 51.015(j) (such period of time is described as the period of time commencing on the date the Military Servicemember receives an order to report for Active Duty Military Service and ending on the date

lawsuit to foreclose a lien against applicable property owned by a Military Servicemember is filed during such Military Servicemember's period of Active Duty Military Service or during the nine (9) months after the date on which such Active Duty Military Service period concludes, then upon the application of a Military Servicemember whose ability to comply with the contractual obligations secured by the lien is materially affected by such Servicemember's Active Duty Military, a court must either: (1) stay the proceedings for a period of time as justice and equity require; or (2) adjust the obligations of the contract secured by the lien to preserve the interests of all parties.[177] More importantly, if a person knowingly makes, or causes to be made, a sale, foreclosure, or seizure of applicable property owned by a Military Servicemember during such Military Servicemember's period of Active Duty Military Service or during the nine (9) months after the date on which such Active Duty Military Service period concludes in violation of such statutory restrictions, then he or she commits a Class A misdemeanor criminal offense.[178] An individual adjudged guilty of a Class A misdemeanor may be punished by a fine up to $4,000, confinement in jail for up to one year, or both.[179]

Accordingly, it is very important that a Homeowners Association contemplating initiation of foreclosure procedures on its Assessment Lien perform some reasonable due

---

on which such Military Servicemember reports for Active Duty Military Service or, if such order is revoked before the Military Servicemember so reports, then ending on the date such order is revoked).

[177] Tex. Prop. Code § 51.015(c). Even if a Military Servicemember does not specifically request relief from a court under Section 51.015 of the Texas Property Code, a court may on its own motion, after conducting a hearing on such motion: (1) stay the proceedings for a period of time as justice and equity require; or (2) adjust the obligations of the contract secured by the lien to preserve the interests of all parties. Tex. Prop. Code § 51.015(c). A court that issues a stay or takes any other action under Section 51.015 of the Texas Property Code regarding the enforcement of an obligation that is subject to such statute may grant a similar stay or take similar action with respect to a surety, guarantor, endorser, accommodation maker, co-maker, or other person who is or may be primarily or secondarily subject to such obligation. Tex. Prop. Code § 51.015(h).

[178] Tex. Prop. Code § 51.015(f). For purposes of Section 51.015 of the Texas Property Code, a "person" includes a corporation, organization, government or governmental subdivision or agency, business trust, estate, trust, partnership, association, and any other legal entity. Tex. Prop. Code § 51.015(a)(4); Tex. Gov't Code § 311.005(2).

[179] Tex. Pen. Code § 12.21.

diligence to determine whether the delinquent Homeowner is a Military Servicemember who is in a period of Active Duty Military Service or in the nine-month period following the conclusion of his or her Active Duty Military Service. The most direct way to determine a Homeowner's military status is to request confirmation of such information from the Homeowner him- or herself or from other residents of the property or even the delinquent Homeowner's neighbors. Alternatively, the Servicemembers Civil Relief Act Centralized Verification Service ("SCRACVS") maintains a website, at which a search can be performed to determine if an individual is on active military duty. SCRACVS's website covers Military Servicemembers serving in the army, navy, national guard, air force, marines, public health service and national oceanic and atmospheric administration.[180]

7.13 Post-Foreclosure Notice Requirements of Subdivision Associations

A Subdivision Association that conducts a foreclosure sale of a Homeowner's Lot, whether by judicial or non-judicial foreclosure procedures, must send to the Lot Owner and all "lienholders of record," within thirty (30) days after the date of the foreclosure sale, a written notice stating the date and time the foreclosure sale occurred and informing the Lot Owner and such lienholders of the right of the Lot Owner and/or any such lienholder to redeem the Lot, or in other words, to have the foreclosed Lot conveyed back to the Lot Owner.[181] Such post-foreclosure notice of redemption rights must be sent by certified mail, return receipt requested, to: (1) the Lot Owner at his or her last known mailing address, as reflected in the records of the Subdivision Association;[182] (2) each lienholder of record at the address of such lienholder, as reflected in the most

[180] www.servicememberscivilreliefact.com/scra/defense-manpower-data-center/.

[181] Tex. Prop. Code § 209.010(a), (d). For purposes of sending such post-foreclosure notice of redemption rights to lienholders of record, the term "lienholder of record" means a holder of a lien attached to the subject Lot that may be foreclosed by non-judicial foreclosure, such as a Deed of Trust Lien. *See* Tex. Prop. Code § 209.010(b)(2).

[182] Tex. Prop. Code § 209.010(b)(1).

recent lien recorded by such lienholder in the Official Public Records of the county in which the subject Lot is located;[183] and (3) each assignee of a recorded lienholder who has provided proper notice to the Subdivision Association of such assignment.[184] In addition, within thirty (30) days from the date the Subdivision Association sends such post-foreclosure notice of redemption rights to the Lot Owner and each lienholder of record, the Subdivision Association must record an affidavit in the Official Public Records of the county in which the subject Lot is located that: (1) states the date on which such notices were sent to the Lot Owner and each applicable lienholder; and (2) contains a legal description of the subject Lot.[185]

7.14 Homeowner's Right of Redemption following a Foreclosure Sale

Following a foreclosure sale of a Lot or a Unit, the former owner of the foreclosed Lot or Unit may redeem his or her property from foreclosure under certain limited circumstances. In other words, the former Lot or Unit Owner may be able to get their home conveyed back to them from whoever purchased it at the foreclosure sale. The procedures for redeeming a foreclosed Lot and Unit differ significantly and are explained separately in the following subchapters.

---

183 Tex. Prop. Code § 209.010(b)(2). If a recorded lien does not include an address for the lienholder, then the Subdivision Association does not have a duty to provide a post-foreclosure notice of redemption rights to such lienholder. Tex. Prop. Code § 209.010(b-1).

184 Tex. Prop. Code § 209.010(b)(3). In order to constitute a proper notice of assignment, the notice of assignment must be in writing, contain the mailing address of the assignee, and be mailed by certified mail, return receipt requested, or by United States mail, with signature confirmation, to the Subdivision Association at the mailing address specified in the most recent Management Certificate filed of record in the Official Public Records of the county in which the Subdivision Development is located. Tex. Prop. Code § 209.010(b)(3). In addition, for purposes of providing notice to the lienholders of record, the Lot Owner is deemed by law to have given approval to the Subdivision Association to notify such lienholders of the foreclosure and their post-foreclosure redemption rights. Tex. Prop. Code § 209.010(b-2).

185 Tex. Prop. Code § 209.010(c).

7.14.1 Redemption of a Lot Foreclosed by a Subdivision Association

If a Subdivision Association forecloses its Assessment Lien against a Lot that is located in a residential Subdivision Development, the former Lot Owner or a lienholder of record can redeem such foreclosed Lot from the person or entity that purchased it at the foreclosure sale any time within 180 days from the date the Subdivision Association mails the required post-foreclosure notice of redemption rights to the subject Lot Owner and applicable lienholders of record.[186] During this 180-day Redemption Period, a person or entity that purchases the Lot at the foreclosure sale may not transfer ownership of such Lot to a person or entity other than a redeeming Lot Owner.[187]

The procedures for redemption of a foreclosed Lot by the former Lot Owner or a lienholder will depend on whether the foreclosed Lot was purchased at the foreclosure sale by the Subdivision Association or by a person or entity other than the Subdivision Association.

---

[186] Tex. Prop. Code § 209.011(b). The term "lienholder of record" means a holder of a lien attached to the subject Lot that may be foreclosed by non-judicial foreclosure, such as a Deed of Trust Lien. *See* Tex. Prop. Code § 209.010(b)(2). A lienholder of record, however, may not redeem an applicable Lot within the first ninety (90) days of such 180-day Redemption Period and may only redeem such Lot if the Lot Owner has not already redeemed it. Tex. Prop. Code § 209.011(b). It is also important to note that if a redeeming Lot Owner or lienholder sends a written request to redeem an applicable Lot by certified mail, return receipt requested, to the person or entity that purchased the Lot at the foreclosure sale on or before the last day of the 180-day Redemption Period, the Lot Owner's or lienholder's right of redemption is extended until the tenth (10th) day after the date the Subdivision Association or other person or entity that purchased the foreclosed Lot provides written notice to such Lot Owner or lienholder that specifies the amounts that must be paid to redeem the Lot. Tex. Prop. Code § 209.011(m).

[187] Tex. Prop. Code § 209.011(c). The person or entity that purchases the Lot at the foreclosure sale can, however, take possession of and occupy the Lot during the 180-day Redemption Period, and can even lease the foreclosed Lot to a third-person and collect rents during such time period. Notwithstanding, unless the occupants of a foreclosed Lot voluntarily vacate such Lot, the purchaser of an occupied Lot at a foreclosure sale of a Subdivision Association's Assessment Lien must commence and prosecute an eviction lawsuit against the occupants of such Lot in order to recover possession of such Lot from such occupants. Tex. Prop. Code § 209.011(a). In addition, any lease of a foreclosed Lot during the 180-day Redemption Period is subject to the right of redemption by the Lot Owner or an applicable lienholder and the redeeming Lot Owner's right to reoccupy the Lot immediately after the Lot has been properly redeemed. Tex. Prop. Code § 209.011(k).

7.14.1 (A) *Redemption Procedures if a Foreclosed Lot Is Purchased at the Foreclosure Sale by the Subdivision Association*

If the Subdivision Association purchases the Lot at the foreclosure sale, then in order to redeem the foreclosed Lot, a redeeming Lot Owner or lienholder must pay the Subdivision Association:

(1) all amounts owed to the Subdivision Association at the time of the foreclosure sale;[188]

(2) accrued interest on all such amounts owed to the Subdivision Association, from the date of the foreclosure sale through the date of redemption, at the interest rate stated in the Subdivision Association's Declaration for delinquent Assessments or, if no interest rate is stated, at an annual interest rate of ten percent (10%);[189]

(3) all costs incurred by the Subdivision Association to foreclose its Assessment Lien and any additional costs that will be incurred to convey the foreclosed Lot back to the Lot Owner upon redemption, including reasonable attorneys fees;[190]

(4) any Assessments levied against the foreclosed Lot by the Subdivision Association after the date of the foreclosure sale;[191]

(5) any reasonable costs incurred by the Subdivision Association during its ownership of such foreclosed Lot, including mortgage payments, costs of repair and maintenance of such Lot, and any costs incurred in leasing such foreclosed Lot;[192] and

(6) the purchase price paid by the Subdivision Association at the foreclosure sale, less any amounts due the Subdivision Association at the time of the foreclosure sale that were satisfied out of the foreclosure sale proceeds.[193]

---

188 Tex. Prop. Code § 209.011(d)(1).

189 Tex. Prop. Code § 209.011(d)(2).

190 Tex. Prop. Code § 209.011(d)(3).

191 Tex. Prop. Code § 209.011(d)(4).

192 Tex. Prop. Code § 209.011(d)(5).

193 Tex. Prop. Code § 209.011(d)(6).

If the Subdivision Association leases the foreclosed Lot, or otherwise generates income from the use of the foreclosed Lot, during the Redemption Period and the foreclosed Lot is subsequently redeemed, then all rents and other income collected by the Subdivision Association from the date of the foreclosure sale until the date of redemption belong to the Subdivision Association.[194] In such event, the amount of such rents and income collected by the Subdivision Association must be credited against the amounts that must be paid to the Subdivision Association in order to redeem the foreclosed Lot.[195] In addition, if the former Lot Owner makes any partial payment(s) of the amounts owed to the Subdivision Association at any time prior to the expiration of the 180-day Redemption Period, but fails to pay all amounts necessary to redeem the foreclosed Lot before the 180-day Redemption Period expires, then the Subdivision Association must refund any partial payments back to the former Lot Owner.[196]

If a redeeming Lot Owner or lienholder pays the Subdivision Association all of the amounts required to redeem the foreclosed Lot prior to the expiration of the 180-day Redemption Period, the Subdivision Association must immediately execute and deliver to the redeeming party a deed transferring ownership of the foreclosed Lot back to the former Lot Owner.[197] If the Subdivision Association fails to do so, then the redeeming Lot Owner or lienholder may file a lawsuit against the Subdivision Association to compel the Subdivision Association to covey the foreclosed Lot back to the former Lot Owner.[198] In such event, if the redeeming Lot Owner or lienholder is the prevailing party in such

---

[194] Tex. Prop. Code § 209.011(i).

[195] Tex. Prop. Code § 209.011(i). In addition, if there is any remaining amount of rent or other income after applying it to the amounts to be paid the Subdivision Association, such surplus must be refunded to the Lot Owner. Tex. Prop. Code § 209.011(i).

[196] Tex. Prop. Code § 209.011(l). The refunded partial payments must be mailed to the Lot Owner at his or her last known address as shown in the Subdivision Association's records within thirty (30) days of the expiration date of the 180-day Redemption Period. Tex. Prop. Code § 209.011(l).

[197] Tex. Prop. Code § 209.011(f). Even if the foreclosed Lot is redeemed by a lienholder, the foreclosed Lot must be conveyed back to the former Lot Owner, not the redeeming lienholder. Tex. Prop. Code § 209.011(f).

[198] Tex. Prop. Code § 209.011(f).

lawsuit, he or she may also recover his or her reasonable attorneys fees from the Subdivision Association.[199]

If the former Lot Owner and applicable lienholders fail to redeem the foreclosed Lot within the 180-day Redemption Period, or before any extended Redemption Period expires, the Subdivision Association must record an affidavit in the Official Public Records of the county in which the foreclosed Lot is located stating that the former Lot Owner and applicable lienholders, if any, did not redeem the foreclosed Lot during the Redemption Period or any extended Redemption Period.[200] A Subdivision Association that purchases a Lot at the foreclosure sale (and any person or entity that subsequently purchases the foreclosed Lot from the Subdivision Association) may presume conclusively that the former Lot Owner and all applicable lienholders did not redeem the foreclosed Lot unless the former Lot Owner and/or any applicable lienholder files in the Official Public Records of the county in which the foreclosed Lot is located either: (1) a deed from the Subdivision Association conveying ownership of the foreclosed Lot back to the redeeming Lot Owner; or (2) an affidavit that: (a) states that the foreclosed Lot has been redeemed; (b) contains a legal description of the foreclosed Lot; and (c) includes the name and mailing address of the person who redeemed the foreclosed Lot.[201] If the former Lot Owner and all applicable lienholders fail to either record a redemption deed from the Subdivision Association or an affidavit stating that the foreclosed Lot has been redeemed before the expiration of the 180-day Redemption Period, then the former Lot Owner's and lienholders' right of redemption as against a subsequent purchaser or lender expires after the expiration of such 180-day Redemption Period.[202]

---

199 Tex. Prop. Code § 209.011(f).

200 Tex. Prop. Code § 209.011(n).

201 Tex. Prop. Code § 209.011(h).

202 Tex. Prop. Code § 209.011(g).

7.14.1 (B) *Redemption Procedures if a Foreclosed Lot Is Purchased at the Foreclosure Sale by a Person or Entity other than the Subdivision Association*

If a Lot is purchased at the foreclosure sale by a person or entity other than the Subdivision Association, the redemption requirements of a redeeming Lot Owner or lienholder differ slightly. In order to redeem a foreclosed Lot purchased by a person or entity other than the Subdivision Association, the former Lot Owner or lienholder must still pay the Subdivision Association:

(1) all amounts owed to the Subdivision Association at the time of the foreclosure sale, less the foreclosure sales price received by the Subdivision Association from the person or entity that purchased the foreclosed Lot;[203]

(2) accrued interest on all amounts owed to the Subdivision Association, from the date of the foreclosure sale through the date of redemption, at the interest rate stated in the Declaration for delinquent Assessments or, if no rate is stated in the Declaration, at an annual interest rate of ten percent (10%);[204]

(3) all costs incurred by the Subdivision Association to foreclose its Assessment Lien and any additional costs that will be incurred to convey the foreclosed Lot back to the redeeming Lot Owner, including reasonable attorneys fees;[205]

(4) any unpaid Assessments levied by the Subdivision Association against the foreclosed Lot after the date of the foreclosure sale;[206] and

(5) any taxable court costs incurred in an eviction proceeding brought by the Subdivision Association to acquire possession of the foreclosed Lot prior to its redemption.[207]

---

[203] Tex. Prop. Code § 209.011(e)(1)(A).

[204] Tex. Prop. Code § 209.011(e)(1)(B).

[205] Tex. Prop. Code § 209.011(e)(1)(C).

[206] Tex. Prop. Code § 209.011(e)(1)(D).

[207] Tex. Prop. Code § 209.011(e)(1)(E).

In addition, the Lot Owner must also pay to the person or entity that purchased the foreclosed Lot at the foreclosure sale:

(1) any Assessments levied by the Subdivision Association against the foreclosed Lot after the date of the foreclosure sale that were paid to the Subdivision Association by such person or entity;[208]

(2) the purchase price of the foreclosed Lot paid by such person or entity at the foreclosure sale;[209]

(3) the amount of any fees that will be incurred by such person or entity upon redemption of the foreclosed Lot to record a deed conveying ownership of the foreclosed Lot back to the former Lot Owner;[210]

(4) the amount of any ad valorem property taxes, penalties, and interest paid by such person or entity on the foreclosed Lot after the date of the foreclosure sale;[211] and

(5) any taxable court costs incurred in an eviction proceeding brought by such person or entity to acquire possession of the foreclosed Lot prior to its redemption.[212]

Similar to Subdivision Associations, if the person or entity that purchased the foreclosed Lot leases it, or otherwise generates income from the use of the foreclosed Lot, during the Redemption Period and the foreclosed Lot is subsequently redeemed, then all rents and other income collected by such person or entity from the date of the foreclosure sale until the date of redemption belong to such person or entity, but the amount of such rents and income must be credited against the amounts that must be paid to such person or entity in order to redeem the foreclosed Lot.[213] Unlike Subdivision Associations,

---

208 Tex. Prop. Code § 209.011(e)(2)(A).

209 Tex. Prop. Code § 209.011(e)(2)(B).

210 Tex. Prop. Code § 209.011(e)(2)(C).

211 Tex. Prop. Code § 209.011(e)(2)(D).

212 Tex. Prop. Code § 209.011(e)(2)(E).

213 Tex. Prop. Code § 209.011(i). If the amount of rent and income collected by the person or entity that purchased the foreclosed Lot exceeds the amount required to be paid to such person or entity in order to

however, if the person or entity who purchased the foreclosed Lot receives any partial payments of the amount required to redeem the foreclosed Lot from the former Lot Owner prior to the expiration of the 180-day Redemption Period, but does not receive all amounts necessary to redeem the foreclosed Lot before the 180-day Redemption Period expires, such person or entity has no duty to refund the partial payments it received back to the former Lot Owner.[214]

If a redeeming Lot Owner or lienholder pays the Subdivision Association and the person or entity that purchased the foreclosed Lot all of the amounts required to redeem the foreclosed Lot prior to the expiration of the 180-day Redemption Period, such person or entity that purchased the foreclosed Lot must immediately execute and deliver to the redeeming party a deed transferring ownership of the foreclosed Lot back to the former Lot Owner.[215] If the person or entity that purchased the foreclosed Lot fails to immediately execute and deliver to the redeeming party a deed transferring ownership of the foreclosed Lot back to the former Lot Owner upon completion of the redemption requirements, the redeeming Lot Owner or lienholder may file a lawsuit against such person or entity to

---

redeem the foreclosed Lot, upon redemption of the foreclosed Lot, any excess amount of rent and income collected by such person or entity must be refunded to the former Lot Owner. Tex. Prop. Code § 209.011(i).

214 Tex. Prop. Code § 209.011(l). On the other hand, if a Subdivision Association receives any partial payments from a redeeming Lot Owner prior to the expiration of the 180-day Redemption Period, but he or she fails to pay all amounts necessary to redeem the Lot before the 180-day Redemption Period expires, the Subdivision Association must refund any partial payments it received back to the Lot Owner. Tex. Prop. Code § 209.011(l).

215 Tex. Prop. Code § 209.011(f). Before executing a deed transferring the foreclosed Lot back to the Lot Owner, the person or entity that purchased the foreclosed Lot is required to obtain an affidavit from the Subdivision Association or its authorized agent that states that all amounts owed to the Subdivision Association that must be paid by the redeeming Lot Owner or lienholder to redeem the Lot have been paid. Tex. Prop. Code § 209.011(j). The failure of the person or entity that purchased the Lot to comply with this requirement will not affect the validity of a foreclosed Lot's redemption. Tex. Prop. Code § 209.011(j). In addition, if all amounts owed to a Subdivision Association in order to redeem a foreclosed Lot have been paid, the Subdivision Association is required to provide the person or entity that purchased the foreclosed Lot with an affidavit stating that such amounts have been paid no later than the tenth (10th) day after the date the Subdivision Association receives all such amounts from the redeeming Lot Owner or lienholder. Tex. Prop. Code § 209.011(j).

compel such person or entity to covey the foreclosed Lot back to the former Lot Owner.[216] In such event, if the redeeming Lot Owner or lienholder is the prevailing party in such lawsuit, he or she may also recover his or her reasonable attorneys fees from such person or entity.[217]

If the former Lot Owner and all applicable lienholders fail to redeem the foreclosed Lot within the 180-day Redemption Period or before any extended Redemption Period expires, the person or entity that purchased the Lot at the foreclosure sale must record an affidavit in the Official Public Records of the county in which the foreclosed Lot is located stating that the former Lot Owner and applicable lienholders, if any, did not redeem the foreclosed Lot during the Redemption Period or any extended Redemption Period.[218] The person or entity that purchased the Lot at the foreclosure sale (and any person or entity that subsequently purchases the foreclosed Lot from such person or entity) may presume conclusively that the former Lot Owner and lienholders did not redeem the foreclosed Lot unless the former Lot Owner or redeeming lienholder files in the Official Public Records of the county in which the Lot is located either: (1) a deed from the person or entity that purchased the foreclosed Lot at the foreclosure sale conveying ownership of the foreclosed Lot back to the former Lot Owner; or (2) an affidavit that: (a) states the foreclosed Lot has been redeemed; (b) contains a legal description of the foreclosed Lot; (c) and includes the name and mailing address of the person who redeemed the foreclosed Lot.[219] If the redeeming Lot Owner and all lienholders fail to record either the redemption deed from the person or entity that purchased the foreclosed Lot or an affidavit stating that the foreclosed Lot has been redeemed before the expiration of the 180-day Redemption Period, then the former Lot Owner's and lienholders' right of redemption as

---

216 Tex. Prop. Code § 209.011(f).

217 Tex. Prop. Code § 209.011(f).

218 Tex. Prop. Code § 209.011(n).

219 Tex. Prop. Code § 209.011(h).

against a subsequent purchaser or lender expires after the expiration of such 180-day Redemption Period.[220]

7.14.2 Redemption of a Unit Foreclosed by a Condominium Association

The redemption procedures for a foreclosed Unit differ slightly from that of a foreclosed Lot.[221] If a Condominium Association forecloses its Assessment Lien against a Unit, the prior Unit Owner has a right to redeem such Unit from the party that purchased the Unit at the foreclosure sale any time before the expiration of ninety (90) days from the date of the foreclosure sale.[222] During such ninety-day Redemption Period, the party that purchased the foreclosed Unit may not transfer ownership of such Unit to any person other than the redeeming prior owner of such Unit.[223]

If a Condominium Association forecloses its Assessment Lien against a Unit, the Unit Owner who owned the Unit just prior to the foreclosure has a right to redeem such Unit from the party that purchased the Unit at the foreclosure sale any time before the expiration of ninety (90) days from the date of the foreclosure sale.[224] In other words, if a Condominium Association forecloses its Assessment Lien against a Unit, then the prior owner of such Unit has a right to reacquire ownership of the Unit during a ninety-day period following the foreclosure sale by complying with certain provisions of the Texas Uniform Condominium Act. During such ninety-day "Redemption Period," the party that

---

[220] Tex. Prop. Code § 209.011(g).

[221] Among other things, the right of redemption is only ninety (90) days (as opposed to one hundred eighty (180) days) and the right of redemption of a foreclosed Unit may only be exercised by the former Unit Owner, not lienholders. Tex. Prop. Code § 82.113(g). In addition, a Condominium Association is not required to send a Unit Owner a post-foreclosure notice advising such Unit Owner of his or her redemption rights. Tex. Prop. Code § 82.113(g).

[222] Tex. Prop. Code § 82.113(g).

[223] Tex. Prop. Code § 82.113(g).

[224] Tex. Prop. Code § 82.113(g).

purchased the foreclosed Unit may not transfer ownership of such Unit to any person other than the redeeming prior owner of such Unit.[225]

The procedure for redeeming a foreclosed Unit depends on whether the Condominium Association purchased the foreclosed Unit at the foreclosure sale or whether it was purchased by a party other than the Condominium Association. If the Condominium Association is the party that purchased the Unit at the foreclosure sale, then in order to redeem the foreclosed Unit, the prior owner of the Unit must pay to the Condominium Association: (1) all amounts owed to the Condominium Association at the time of the foreclosure sale; (2) interest from the date of the foreclosure sale to the date of redemption at the rate provided by the Condominium Declaration for delinquent Assessments; (3) reasonable attorneys fees and costs incurred by the Condominium Association in foreclosing its Assessment Lien; (4) any Assessment levied against the Unit by the Condominium Association after the foreclosure sale; and (5) any reasonable cost incurred by the Condominium Association as owner of the Unit, including costs of maintenance and leasing of the Unit during the Redemption Period.[226]

Alternatively, if the foreclosed Unit was purchased by a party other than the Condominium Association, then in order to redeem the foreclosed Unit, the prior owner of the Unit must pay to the party that purchased the foreclosed Unit: (1) an amount equal to the amount bid at the foreclosure sale; (2) interest on the bid amount computed from

---

225 Tex. Prop. Code § 82.113(g). "Redemption Period" is a term of art utilized in this book that refers to the specified time period following foreclosure of a Homeowners Association's Assessment Lien during which the owner of the real property that was foreclosed upon may redeem (or reacquire) his or her property from the entity or person that purchased it at the foreclosure sale.

226 Tex. Prop. Code § 82.113(g). It is important to note that the Condominium Association may lease a foreclosed Unit, or otherwise generate income from the use of the foreclosed Unit, during the ninety-day Redemption Period. Tex. Prop. Code § 82.113(g). In such event, all rents and other income collected from the foreclosed Unit by the Condominium Association between the date of the foreclosure sale and the date of redemption belong to the Condominium Association, but the rents and income shall be credited against the redemption amount to be paid to the Condominium Association by the redeeming Unit Owner. Tex. Prop. Code § 82.113(g).

the date of the foreclosure sale to the date of redemption at the rate of six percent (6%); (3) the amount of any Assessments paid by such party to the Condominium Association after the date of foreclosure; and (4) any reasonable costs incurred by such party as the owner of the Unit, including costs associated with maintenance and leasing of the foreclosed Unit.[227] The prior owner of the Unit must also pay to the Condominium Association all assessments that are due as of the date of the redemption and all reasonable attorneys fees and costs incurred by the Condominium Association in foreclosing its Assessment Lien against the foreclosed Unit.[228]

If the prior owner of the foreclosed Unit pays the Condominium Association (and if applicable, the other party that purchased the foreclosed Unit) all of the amounts required to redeem the foreclosed Unit prior to the expiration of the ninety-day Redemption Period, then the party that purchased the foreclosed Unit at the foreclosure sale must execute a deed (with no warranty of title) that conveys ownership of the foreclosed Unit back to the prior owner of the foreclosed Unit.[229] It is important to note that the exercise of a prior owner's right of redemption is not effective against a subsequent purchaser or lender for value without notice of a redemption of such foreclosed Unit after the ninety-day Redemption Period expires, unless the prior owner of the foreclosed Unit records in the local Official Public Records either a redemption deed from

[227] Tex. Prop. Code § 82.113(g). It is important to note that the party that purchased the foreclosed Unit at the foreclosure sale may lease a foreclosed Unit, or otherwise generate income from the use of the foreclosed Unit, during the ninety-day Redemption Period. Tex. Prop. Code § 82.113(g). In such event, all rents and other income collected from the Unit by the party that purchased the foreclosed Unit between the date of the foreclosure sale and the date of redemption belong to such party, but the rents and income shall be credited against the redemption amount to be paid to such party by the redeeming Unit Owner. Tex. Prop. Code § 82.113(g).

[228] Tex. Prop. Code § 82.113(g).

[229] Tex. Prop. Code § 82.113(g).

the party that purchased the foreclosed Unit or an affidavit stating that he or she has exercised his or her right of redemption of the foreclosed Unit.[230]

7.15 The Federal Fair Debt Collection Practices Act and the Texas Debt Collection Practices Act

The collection of delinquent Assessments from Homeowners constitutes "debt collection" under both the Federal Fair Debt Collection Practices Act and the Texas Debt Collection Practices Act, and any actions to collect delinquent Assessments must conform to the requirements of such Acts. The Federal and Texas versions of such Act, however, differ in their application to Texas Homeowners Associations. For such reason, the Federal Fair Debt Collection Practices Act and the Texas Debt Collection Practices Act are explained separately in the following subchapters.

7.15.1 Application of the Federal Fair Debt Collection Practices Act

The Federal Fair Debt Collection Practices Act was passed by Congress in 1977 for the purpose of protecting "consumers" from abusive, deceptive, and unfair debt collections practices.[231] The Federal Fair Debt Collection Practices Act imposes certain regulations on the activities of "Debt Collectors," which the Federal Fair Debt Collection Practices Act defines as any person who uses any instrumentality of interstate commerce or the mails in any business the principal purpose of which is the collection of any debts, or who regularly collects or attempts to collect, directly or indirectly, debts owed or due

---

230 Tex. Prop. Code § 82.113(g).

231 *See* 15 U.S.C. § 1692, *et seq*. The Federal Fair Debt Collection Practices Act only applies to the collection of "consumer debts," which the Federal Fair Debt Collection Practices Act defines as "any obligation or alleged obligation of a consumer to pay money arising out of a transaction in which the money, property, insurance, or services which are the subject of the transaction are primarily for personal, family, or household purposes, whether or not such obligation has been reduced to judgment." 15 U.S.C. § 1692a(5). Assessments by Homeowners Associations generally constitute a consumer debt under the Federal Fair Debt Collection Practices Act. *See Ladick v. Van Gemert*, 146 F.3d 1205, 1206–07 (10th Cir. 1998), *cert. denied*, 119 S. Ct. 511, 142 L. Ed. 2d 424 (U.S. 1998); *Newman v. Boehm, Pearlstein & Bright, Ltd.*, 119 F.3d 477, 481 (7th Cir. 1997).

or asserted to be owed or due another.[232] In other words, a "Debt Collector" under the Federal Fair Debt Collection Practices Act is any person or entity that engages in efforts to collect a debt owing to another person or entity on their behalf.

The Federal Fair Debt Collection Practices Act, however, does not generally apply to a creditor attempting to collect a debt owed to it on its own behalf.[233] Nor does the Federal Fair Debt Collection Practices Act apply to the Officers or employees of a creditor who attempts to collect a debt owed to such creditor on its behalf.[234] Thus, the Federal Fair Debt Collection Practices Act is generally inapplicable to a Texas Homeowners Association, as well as its Officers and employees, when it is attempting to collect unpaid Assessments and other amounts owed to such Homeowners Association on its own behalf.[235] In addition, while a third-party management company or attorney who is engaged to collect delinquent Assessments on behalf of a Homeowners Association may be considered a Debt Collector under the Federal Fair Debt Collection Practices Act (and must comply with its provisions), a Homeowners Association is not generally liable for violations of the Federal Fair Debt Collection Practices Act committed by a third-party management company or attorney attempting to collect a debt on behalf of the Homeowners Association.[236]

---

[232] 15 U.S.C. § 1692a(6).

[233] *See Wadlington v. Credit Acceptance Corp.*, 76 F.3d 103, 106 (6th Cir. 1996).

[234] 15 U.S.C. § 1692a(6).

[235] *See Davis Lake Community Ass'n, Inc. v. Feldmann*, 530 S.E.2d 865, 868 (2000) (holding that a homeowners association collecting past-due assessments was not a debt collector under the Fair Debt Collection Practices Act and that such Act only applies to those who regularly collect debts on behalf of others and does not apply to creditors trying to collect their own debts.).

[236] *See Police v. National Tax Funding, L.P.*, 225 F.3d 379, 403 (3rd Cir. 2000) ("Creditors—as opposed to 'debt collectors'—are generally not subject to the [Federal Fair Debt Collection Practices Act]."); *Russell-Allgood v. Resurgent Capital Services, L.P.*, 515 F. Supp.2d 1307, 1310 (N.D. Ga. 2007) ("[A creditor] is not a 'debt collector' under the Fair Debt Collection Practices Act and therefore cannot be liable under the act.").

7.15.2 Application of the Texas Debt Collection Practices Act

The State of Texas has also enacted statutory laws to protect Texas consumers from abusive, deceptive, and unfair debt collection practices, known as the "Texas Debt Collection Practices Act."[237] Unlike the Federal Fair Debt Collection Practices Act, the Texas Debt Collection Practices Act applies not only to third parties attempting to collect a debt on behalf of another person, but also to creditors who are attempting to collect their own debts on behalf of themselves.[238] Thus, unlike the Federal Fair Debt Collection Practices Act, a Texas Homeowners Association is considered a "Debt Collector" under the Texas Debt Collection Practices Act, and it must refrain from engaging in debt collection practices that are prohibited by such Act when attempting to collect unpaid Assessments from its Homeowners. Such illegal debt collection practices are described in greater detail in the following subchapters.

7.15.2 (A) *Prohibited Debt Collection Practices*

The Texas Debt Collection Practices Act prohibits Debt Collectors from engaging in certain prohibited practices in attempting to collect a debt, including: (1) use of threats or coercion; (2) oppression, harassment, or abuse of a person; (3) use of unfair or unconscionable means; and (4) use of fraudulent, deceptive, or misleading representations.

---

[237] *See* Tex. Fin. Code § 392.001, *et seq*. Similar to the Federal Fair Debt Collection Practices Act, the Texas Debt Collection Practices Act only applies to consumer debts, which the Texas Debt Collection Practices Act defines as an obligation or alleged obligation primarily for personal, family, or household purposes, arising from a transaction or alleged transaction. Tex. Fin. Code § 392.001(2).

[238] Tex. Fin. Code § 392.001(3), (5), (6). Under the Texas Debt Collection Practices Act, the term "Debt Collector" means "a person who directly or indirectly engages in debt collection" and includes a creditor collecting its own debt. Tex. Fin. Code § 392.001(6). The Texas Debt Collection Practices Act also imposes additional obligations upon "Third-Party Debt Collectors," which the Texas Debt Collection Practices Act defines as a person or entity that would constitute a "Debt Collector" under the Federal Fair Debt Collection Practices Act, but such term does not include an attorney collecting a debt as an attorney on behalf of and in the name of a client, unless such attorney has non-attorney employees who are regularly engaged to solicit debts for collection or who regularly make contact with debtors for the purpose of collection or adjustment of debts. Tex. Fin. Code § 392.001(6).

Use of Threats or Coercion:

Under the Texas Debt Collection Practices Act, a Debt Collector may not use threats, coercion, or attempts to coerce that employ any of the following practices:[239]

(1) using, or threatening to use, violence or other criminal means to cause harm to a person or property of a person;

(2) falsely accusing, or threatening to falsely accuse, a person of fraud or any other crime;

(3) representing, or threatening to represent, to any person other than the consumer that a consumer is willfully refusing to pay a non-disputed consumer debt when the debt is in dispute and the consumer has notified the debt collector in writing of the dispute;

(4) threatening to sell or assign to another the underlying obligation of the consumer and falsely representing that the result of such sale or assignment would be that the consumer would lose a defense to the consumer debt or would be subject to illegal collection attempts;

(5) threatening that the debtor will be arrested for nonpayment of a consumer debt without proper court proceedings;

(6) threatening to file a charge, complaint, or criminal action against a debtor when the debtor has not violated a criminal law;

(7) threatening that nonpayment of a consumer debt will result in the seizure, repossession, or sale of the person's property without proper court proceedings; or

(8) threatening to take an action prohibited by law.

Notwithstanding, the Texas Debt Collection Practices Act does not prevent a Debt Collector from: (1) informing a debtor that the debtor may be arrested after proper court proceedings if the debtor has violated a criminal law of the State of Texas; (2) threatening to institute civil lawsuits or other judicial proceedings to collect a consumer debt, such as a Judicial Foreclosure Lawsuit to foreclose a Homeowners Association's Assessment

[239] Tex. Fin. Code § 392.301(a).

Lien; or (3) exercising, or threatening to exercise, a statutory or contractual right of seizure, repossession, or sale that does not require court proceedings, such as a non-judicial foreclosure of a Homeowners Association's Assessment Lien.[240]

Oppression, Harassment, or Abuse of a Person:

Pursuant to the Texas Debt Collection Practices Act, a Debt Collector also may not oppress, harass, or abuse a person by: (1) using profane or obscene language or language intended to abuse unreasonably the hearer or reader; (2) placing telephone calls without disclosing the name of the individual making the call and with the intent to annoy, harass, or threaten a person at the called number; (3) causing a person to incur a long distance telephone toll, telegram fee, or other charge by a medium of communication without first disclosing the name of the person making the communication; or (4) causing a telephone to ring repeatedly or continuously, or making repeated or continuous telephone calls, with the intent to harass a person at the called number.[241]

Use of Unfair or Unconscionable Means:

A Debt Collector is also prohibited under the Texas Debt Collection Practices Act from using unfair or unconscionable means to collect a debt that employ any one of the following practices:

(1) seeking or obtaining a written statement or acknowledgment in any form that specifies that a consumer's obligation is one incurred for necessaries of life if the obligation was not incurred for those necessaries;[242]

(2) collecting, or attempting to collect, interest or a charge, fee, or expense incidental to the obligation, unless the interest or incidental charge, fee,

[240] Tex. Fin. Code § 392.301(b).

[241] Tex. Fin. Code § 392.302.

[242] Tex. Fin. Code § 392.303(a)(1).

or expense is expressly authorized by the agreement creating the obligation or is legally chargeable to the consumer;[243] or

(3) collecting, or attempting to collect, an obligation under a check, draft, debit payment, or credit card payment, if: (a) the check or draft was dishonored or the debit payment or credit card payment was refused by the bank because the check or draft was not drawn or the payment was not made by a person authorized to use the applicable account; (b) the Debt Collector has received a written notice from a person authorized to use the applicable account that the check, draft, or payment was unauthorized; and/or (c) the person authorized to use the account has filed a report concerning the unauthorized check, draft, or payment with a law enforcement agency and has provided the Debt Collector with a copy of such report.[244]

Use of Fraudulent, Deceptive, or Misleading Representations:

A Debt Collector is additionally prohibited under the Texas Debt Collection Practices Act from using a fraudulent, deceptive, or misleading representation that employs the following practices in order to collect a debt or obtain information about the consumer:

(1) using a name other than the true business or professional name or the true personal or legal name of the Debt Collector while engaged in debt collection;[245]

(2) failing to maintain a list of all business or professional names known to be used, or formerly used, by persons collecting, or attempting to collect, consumer debts for the Debt Collector;[246]

---

243 Tex. Fin. Code § 392.303(a)(2).

244 Tex. Fin. Code § 392.303(a)(3). Notwithstanding, a Debt Collector is not prohibited from collecting or attempting to collect an obligation under a check, draft, debit payment, or credit card payment if the Debt Collector has credible evidence, including a document, video recording, or witness statement, that the report filed with a law enforcement agency is fraudulent and that the check, draft, or payment was authorized. Tex. Fin. Code § 392.303(c).

245 Tex. Fin. Code § 392.304(a)(1).

246 Tex. Fin. Code § 392.304(a)(2).

(3) representing falsely that the Debt Collector has information or something of value for the consumer in order to solicit or discover information about the consumer;[247]

(4) failing to disclose clearly in any communication with the debtor the name of the person to whom the debt has been assigned or is owed when making a demand for money;[248]

(5) using a written communication that fails to indicate clearly the name of the Debt Collector and the Debt Collector's street address or post office box and telephone number if the written notice refers to a delinquent consumer debt;[249]

(6) using a written communication that demands a response to a place other than the Debt Collector's or creditor's street address or post office box;[250]

(7) misrepresenting the character, extent, or amount of a consumer debt, or misrepresenting the consumer debt's status in a judicial or governmental proceeding;[251]

(8) representing falsely that a Debt Collector is vouched for, bonded by, or affiliated with, or is an instrumentality, agent, or official of, this state or an agency of federal, state, or local government;[252]

(9) using, distributing, or selling a written communication that simulates, or is represented falsely to be, a document authorized, issued, or approved by a court, an official, a governmental agency, or any other governmental authority or that creates a false impression about the communication's source, authorization, or approval;[253]

---

247 Tex. Fin. Code § 392.304(a)(3).

248 Tex. Fin. Code § 392.304(a)(4).

249 Tex. Fin. Code § 392.304(a)(6). A Debt Collector is not, however, required to disclose the names and addresses of employees of the Debt Collector. Tex. Fin. Code § 392.304(c).

250 Tex. Fin. Code § 392.304(a)(7). Section 392.304(a)(7) does not, however, require a response to be sent to the address of an employee of a Debt Collector. Tex. Fin. Code § 392.304(d).

251 Tex. Fin. Code § 392.304(a)(8).

252 Tex. Fin. Code § 392.304(a)(9).

253 Tex. Fin. Code § 392.304(a)(10).

(10) using a seal, insignia, or design that simulates that of a governmental agency;[254]

(11) representing that a consumer debt may be increased by the addition of attorneys fees, investigation fees, service fees, or other charges if a written contract or statute does not authorize the additional fees or charges;[255]

(12) representing that a consumer debt will definitely be increased by the addition of attorneys fees, investigation fees, service fees, or other charges if the award of the fees or charges is subject to judicial discretion;[256]

(13) representing falsely the status or nature of the services rendered by the Debt Collector or the Debt Collector's business;[257]

(14) using a written communication that violates the United States postal laws and regulations;[258]

(15) using a communication that purports to be from an attorney or law firm if it is not;[259]

(16) representing that a consumer debt is being collected by an attorney if it is not;[260]

(17) representing that a consumer debt is being collected by an independent, bona fide organization engaged in the business of collecting past due accounts when the debt is being collected by a subterfuge organization under the control and direction of the person who is owed the debt;[261] or

---

[254] Tex. Fin. Code § 392.304(a)(11).

[255] Tex. Fin. Code § 392.304(a)(12).

[256] Tex. Fin. Code § 392.304(a)(13).

[257] Tex. Fin. Code § 392.304(a)(14).

[258] Tex. Fin. Code § 392.304(a)(15).

[259] Tex. Fin. Code § 392.304(a)(16).

[260] Tex. Fin. Code § 392.304(a)(17).

[261] Tex. Fin. Code § 392.304(a)(18).

(18) using any other false representation or deceptive means to collect a debt or obtain information concerning a consumer.[262]

7.15.2 (B) *Use of Independent Third-Party Debt Collectors*

In most circumstances, Texas Homeowners Associations do not engage in debt collection efforts themselves, but rather contract with management companies and/or retain attorneys to perform collection services on their behalf. If a Homeowners Association's management company and/or attorney is considered to be a Third-Party Debt Collector under the Texas Debt Collection Practices Act, then such management company or attorney has additional duties under the Texas Debt Collection Practices Act. For example, a Third-Party Debt Collector or credit bureau may not engage in debt collection unless the Third-Party Debt Collector has obtained a surety bond issued by a surety company authorized to do business in the State of Texas and filed it with the Texas Secretary of State.[263] While use of an independent Third-Party Debt Collector may alleviate some potential liability of a creditor, a creditor may not use an independent Third-Party Debt Collector if the creditor has actual knowledge that the independent Third-Party Debt Collector repeatedly or continuously engages in acts or practices that are prohibited by the Texas Debt Collection Practices Act.[264]

7.15.2 (C) *Liability for Violations of the Texas Debt Collection Practices Act*

If a Debt Collector commits one or more of the enumerated unlawful debt collection practices identified by the Texas Debt Collection Practices Act, then it may be subject to both civil and criminal liability. More specifically, a violation of the Texas Debt

[262] Tex. Fin. Code § 392.304(a)(19).

[263] Tex. Fin. Code § 392.101.

[264] Tex. Fin. Code § 392.306.

Collection Practices Act constitutes a misdemeanor offense, punishable by a fine of not less than $100 or more than $500 for each violation.[265]

In addition, a violation of the Texas Debt Collection Practices Act also constitutes a deceptive trade practice under the Texas Deceptive Trades Practices Act, and any person affected by a violation of the Texas Debt Collection Practices Act may file a lawsuit against the offending Debt Collector for injunctive relief to prevent or restrain the Debt Collector from continuing to commit such violation and to recover actual damages sustained as a result of such violation.[266] Moreover, if the violation of the Texas Debt Collection Practices Act by the Debt Collector involves use of threats or coercion by representing, or threatening to represent, to any person other than the consumer that such consumer is willfully refusing to pay a non-disputed consumer debt when the debt is in dispute and such consumer has notified the Debt Collector in writing of the dispute, the affected person is entitled to not less than $100 for each such violation.[267] If such affected person prevails in the civil lawsuit against the Debt Collector, he or she is also entitled to an award of the amount of reasonable attorneys fees and court costs incurred by him or her in such lawsuit.[268] On the other hand, if the trial court finds that a civil lawsuit was brought by such person in bad faith, or for purposes of harassment, then the court is required to award the Debt Collector its reasonable attorneys fees and court costs against the person who filed the civil lawsuit.[269]

---

[265] Tex. Fin. Code § 392.402(a)–(b). A misdemeanor charge for violation of the Texas Debt Collection Practices Act must be filed against the Debt Collector within one year from the date the alleged violation occurred. Tex. Fin. Code § 392.402(c).

[266] Tex. Fin. Code §§ 392.403(a), 392.404. In addition to a person affected by a violation of the Texas Debt Collection Practices Act, if the Texas Attorney General reasonably believes that a Debt Collector is violating, or is about to violate, the Texas Debt Collection Practices Act, the Attorney General may file a lawsuit in the name of the State of Texas against the Debt Collector to restrain or enjoin it from continuing to commit such violation. Tex. Fin. Code § 392.403(d).

[267] Tex. Fin. Code § 392.403(e).

[268] Tex. Fin. Code § 392.403(b).

[269] Tex. Fin. Code § 392.403(c).

7.15.2 (D) *Violations Resulting from Bona Fide Errors*

The Texas Debt Collection Practices Act does provide a defense from liability for a good faith accidental violation of the prohibited collection practices. More specifically, a Debt Collector will not be considered to have violated the Texas Debt Collection Practices Act if the action complained of resulted from a "bona fide error" that occurred notwithstanding the use of reasonable procedures adopted to avoid such error.[270] A "bona fide error" is an error made by a Debt Collector in the course of a good faith attempt at compliance with the statutory requirements of the Texas Debt Collection Practices Act.[271] However, in order to use this defense, the Debt Collector must show that he or she used reasonable procedures to prevent the error that caused the violation in question.[272] In the absence of such a showing, a Debt Collector may not be entitled to the bona fide error defense.[273]

7.15.2 (E) *Violations of the Texas Debt Collection Practices Act by Homeowners Associations*

Although Texas Homeowners Associations are subject to all of the prohibited debt collection practices enumerated under the Texas Debt Collection Practices Act, there are a few that tend to arise more often than the others in the context of Assessment collection by a Texas Homeowners Association. First, it is a violation of the Texas Debt Collection Practices Act for a Homeowners Association to represent to a Homeowner that the amount of the Homeowner's delinquent Assessments, or other amount owed to the Homeowners Association, may be increased by the addition of attorneys fees,

---

270 Tex. Fin. Code § 392.401(a)(3).

271 *See CA Partners v. Spears*, 274 S.W.3d 51, 71 (Tex. App.—Houston [14th Dist.] 2008, pet. denied).

272 *See CA Partners v. Spears*, 274 S.W.3d 51, 71 (Tex. App.—Houston [14th Dist.] 2008, pet. denied); *Cent. Adjustment Bureau, Inc. v. Gonzales*, 528 S.W.2d 314, 316 (Tex. Civ. App.—San Antonio 1975, no writ) (interpreting former version of Texas Debt Collection Practices Act).

273 *See CA Partners v. Spears*, 274 S.W.3d 51, 71 (Tex. App.—Houston [14th Dist.] 2008, pet. denied); *Cent. Adjustment Bureau, Inc. v. Gonzales*, 528 S.W.2d 314, 316 (Tex. Civ. App.—San Antonio 1975, no writ).

investigation fees, service fees, or other charges, if the Declaration applicable to such Homeowners Association does not authorize the Homeowners Association to charge its Homeowners for such additional fees or charges.[274] Similarly, it is also a violation for a Texas Homeowners Association to collect or attempt to collect from a Homeowner interest or a charge, fee, or expense incidental to the Homeowner's obligation to pay Assessments, such as a late charge or collection fee, unless the interest or incidental charge, fee, or expense is expressly authorized by its Declaration or is legally chargeable to the Homeowner.[275] It is not uncommon for Homeowners Associations to charge delinquent Homeowners late charges, interest, collection fees, and attorneys fees; however, a Homeowners Association may only assess such charges or fees to a Homeowner if its Declaration expressly provides for it or it is authorized to do so by statute (such as the Texas Uniform Condominium Act).

Second, it is a violation of the Texas Debt Collection Practices Act for a Texas Homeowners Association to misrepresent to a Homeowner the character, extent, or amount of a consumer debt.[276] Accordingly, it is very important that a Homeowners Association keep accurate accounting records of its delinquent accounts.

Finally, it is also a violation of the Texas Debt Collection Practices Act for a Texas Homeowners Association to represent, or threaten to represent, to any person other than the delinquent Homeowner himself or herself that such Homeowner is willfully refusing to pay a non-disputed debt when the obligation to pay the debt or amount of the debt is in dispute and the Homeowner has notified the Homeowners Association in writing of his or her dispute concerning the debt owed to the Homeowners Association.[277] This issue tends to arise when a Homeowners Association wants to publish in its newsletter or

---

[274] Tex. Fin. Code § 392.304(a)(12).

[275] Tex. Fin. Code § 392.302(a)(2).

[276] Tex. Fin. Code § 392.304(a)(8).

[277] Tex. Fin. Code § 392.301(a)(3).

on its community website a list of delinquent Homeowners who have not paid their Assessments. If a Homeowner has notified the Homeowners Association in writing of his or her dispute concerning the amounts owed to the Homeowners Association, then it may be a violation of the Texas Debt Collection Practices Act to include such Homeowner's identity on such list or to threaten to include such Homeowner's identity on any such list.

7.16 Filing of Bankruptcy by a Homeowner

The filing of bankruptcy by a Homeowner can have significant effect on a Homeowners Association's right to collect past due Assessments, and possibly future Assessments as well, from such Homeowner. The term "bankruptcy" comes from the Italian word for broken bench, "banca rotta," and refers to the ancient practice of destroying a businessman's trading bench when he was unable to pay his debts. The United States first empowered Congress to pass uniform laws on the subject of bankruptcy at the Constitutional Convention; however, the power went largely unexercised for many years.[278] Federal bankruptcy law existed periodically from 1800 to 1802, 1841 to 1843, and 1867 to 1878, but it was not until 1898 that permanent bankruptcy law was enacted, which remained in effect for eighty years until it was replaced by the Bankruptcy Reform Act of 1978.[279] There have been a number of amendments to the bankruptcy law since 1978, the most recent being the Bankruptcy Abuse Prevention and Consumer Protection Act of 2005, which President George W. Bush signed into law on April 20, 2005.

The Bankruptcy Code, as the bankruptcy law is known, is codified at Title 11 of the United States Code and is the uniform federal law that governs all bankruptcy cases. The bankruptcy process is further governed by the Federal Rules of Bankruptcy Procedure and by the local rules of each bankruptcy court. The laws and procedures governing

[278] Charles Jordan Tabb, The History of Bankruptcy Laws in the United States, 3 Am. Bankr. Inst. L. Rev. 5, 2 (Spring, 1995).

[279] Charles Jordan Tabb, The History of Bankruptcy Laws in the United States, 3 Am. Bankr. Inst. L. Rev. 5, 2 (Spring, 1995).

bankruptcy are too vast and complex to be explained in any summarized or brief manner within the confines of this book; however, it is important to understand the basic issues that arise when a Homeowner files for bankruptcy protection.

7.16.1 Types of Bankruptcies

There are six types of bankruptcy cases that may be filed under the Bankruptcy Code. Homeowners Associations, however, are only likely to encounter bankruptcy cases filed by individuals under either Chapters 7 or 13 of the Bankruptcy Code, which are the two bankruptcy procedures that apply to individuals who file bankruptcy (who are commonly referred to as "Bankruptcy Debtors").

A Chapter 7 bankruptcy case involves the liquidation of the Bankruptcy Debtor's "non-exempt" assets.[280] In a Chapter 7 case, a bankruptcy trustee, appointed by the Bankruptcy Court, gathers all of the Bankruptcy Debtor's non-exempt assets, if any, sells them, and uses the proceeds from the sale of such non-exempt assets to pay creditors' claims in accordance with bankruptcy law.[281] At the conclusion of a successful Chapter 7 proceeding, the Bankruptcy Debtor will receive a discharge that legally relieves him or her of the obligation to pay certain dischargeable debts.[282]

A Chapter 13 bankruptcy case, on the other hand, does not involve the liquidation of the Bankruptcy Debtor's non-exempt assets. Instead, under a Chapter 13 bankruptcy, an individual Bankruptcy Debtor who meets certain income requirements is allowed to develop a plan to repay all or part of their debts to their creditors over a specified period of time (called a "Reorganization Plan").[283] Under Chapter 13, the Bankruptcy Debtor

---

280 The Bankruptcy Code allows Bankruptcy Debtors to keep certain "exempt" property that is not subject to liquidation by the bankruptcy trustee. *See* 11 U.S.C. § 522.

281 *See* 11 U.S.C. § 701, *et seq.*

282 *See* 11 U.S.C. § 727.

283 *See* 11 U.S.C. § 1301, *et seq.*

proposes a Reorganization Plan, under which the disposable income of the Bankruptcy Debtor will be used to repay his or her creditors a portion of the amounts owed to them through monthly installment payments over a three- or five-year period.[284] If the Bankruptcy Debtor's current monthly income is less than the median income level for the State of Texas, then the Reorganization Plan will be for three (3) years, unless the Bankruptcy Court approves a longer period "for cause."[285] If the Bankruptcy Debtor's current monthly income is greater than the median income level for the State of Texas, the Reorganization Plan generally must be for five (5) years.[286] In no case, however, may a Chapter 13 Reorganization Plan provide for installment payments by the Bankruptcy Debtor over a period longer than five (5) years.[287] At the conclusion of a successful Chapter 13 Reorganization Plan, the Bankruptcy Debtor will have repaid certain debts, will receive a discharge from other obligations, and will be able to retain certain non-exempt assets.[288] Any portion of the dischargeable debts still owed to creditors by the Bankruptcy Debtor at the conclusion of the Reorganization Plan may no longer be enforced against the Bankruptcy Debtor.[289]

7.16.2 Automatic Stay against Further Collection Efforts

A bankruptcy case is initiated by the filing of a petition for bankruptcy protection by the Bankruptcy Debtor (or the Bankruptcy Debtor's bankruptcy attorney).[290] Upon the filing of a bankruptcy petition, the Bankruptcy Debtor is automatically under the

---

284 *See* 11 U.S.C. § 1325. For purposes of a Chapter 13 Reorganization Plan, "disposable income" means current monthly income received by the Bankruptcy Debtor (other than child support payments, foster care payments, or certain disability payments for a dependent child), minus any amounts reasonably necessary for the Bankruptcy Debtor's living expenses, subject to certain guidelines and rules. 11 U.S.C. § 1325.

285 *See* 11 U.S.C. § 1325.

286 *See* 11 U.S.C. § 1325.

287 *See* 11 U.S.C. § 1325.

288 *See* 11 U.S.C. § 1328.

289 *See* 11 U.S.C. § 1328.

290 *See* 11 U.S.C. § 301.

protection of an automatic stay.[291] The automatic stay protects the Bankruptcy Debtor and his or her assets by preventing creditors from taking any new action or continuing any prior action against the Bankruptcy Debtor to collect the outstanding debt owed by the Bankruptcy Debtor outside of the bankruptcy case.[292] The automatic stay covers numerous actions, but in general, creditors must immediately halt any debt collection efforts, repossessions, foreclosures, and lawsuits against the Bankruptcy Debtor until appropriate approval is granted by the Bankruptcy Court or the bankruptcy case is either concluded or dismissed.[293]

The penalties for violations of the automatic stay are severe, and Homeowners Associations should be careful to avoid any further collection efforts once it becomes aware of the filing of a bankruptcy petition by a Homeowner.[294] Any collection action taken by a Homeowners Association that is deemed a willful violation of the automatic stay may entitle the bankrupt-Homeowner to actual damages, attorneys fees, and even punitive damages.[295]

7.16.3 Pre-Petition and Post-Petition Debt

The date the bankruptcy petition is filed is very important because it will determine what amounts owed to a Homeowners Association by a bankrupt-Homeowner are considered Pre-Petition Debts versus Post-Petition Debts. All amounts that are due and owing by a bankrupt-Homeowner to a Homeowners Association at the time the bankruptcy petition is filed are considered Pre-Petition Debts. All amounts that become due and owing to the Homeowners Association by the bankrupt-Homeowner after the bankruptcy petition is filed are considered Post-Petition Debts. In general, a bankruptcy

---

291 *See* 11 U.S.C. § 362.

292 *See* 11 U.S.C. § 362.

293 *See* 11 U.S.C. § 362.

294 *See* 11 U.S.C. § 362(k).

295 *See* 11 U.S.C. § 362(k).

will only discharge a bankrupt-Homeowner's Pre-Petition Debts and will not affect or discharge the bankrupt-Homeowner's Post-Petition Debts, such as Assessments levied after the bankruptcy petition is filed and other amounts that come due during the pendency of the bankruptcy case.[296]

7.16.4 Filing a Proof of Claim

When a Bankruptcy Debtor files for bankruptcy protection, he or she is required to provide a list of all of his or her creditors to the Bankruptcy Court, which will then send each such creditor a notice of the Bankruptcy Debtor's bankruptcy filing (generally referred to as a "Notice of Bankruptcy"). The Notice of Bankruptcy sets out important dates and deadlines for creditors, including the date the bankruptcy petition was filed and the deadline to file a "Proof of Claim." A Proof of Claim is a written statement by a creditor describing the amount of debt owed by the Bankruptcy Debtor to the creditor and the basis for such debt.[297] A timely filed Proof of Claim constitutes prima facie evidence of the validity and amount of a creditor's claim against the Bankruptcy Debtor.[298]

If a creditor does not timely file a Proof of Claim, then the creditor's claim will not be included within the debts to be paid, in whole or in part, by the bankruptcy trustee in a Chapter 7 bankruptcy case or under the Reorganization Plan in a Chapter 13 bankruptcy case. Thus, regardless of what type of bankruptcy case a bankrupt-Homeowner files, the Homeowners Association should file a Proof of Claim in the

---

[296] As a practical note, in order to avoid confusion or mistakes, once a Homeowners Association becomes aware of a Homeowner's bankruptcy, the Homeowners Association should start a new account ledger for all Assessments and other amounts that become due by the bankrupt-Homeowner after the date the bankruptcy petition was filed, so as to have two different account ledgers—one for Pre-Petition Debt and one for Post-Petition Debt.

[297] Fed. R. Bankr. P. 3001(a). There is an official bankruptcy form published by the Judicial Conference for filing Proofs of Claims. *See* Official Bankruptcy Form No. 9.

[298] Fed. R. Bankr. P. 3001(f). "Prima facie" is a Latin expression meaning on its first encounter, first blush, or at first sight. In the context of a legal proceeding, "prima facie evidence" refers to evidence that—unless rebutted—would be sufficient to prove a particular proposition or fact.

Homeowner's bankruptcy case in order to preserve its claim for unpaid Assessments and other amounts owed to it and must do so by the deadline established by the Bankruptcy Court for creditors to file Proofs of Claims.

7.16.5 Secured versus Unsecured Debt

One of the issues that must be determined in order to complete a Proof of Claim is whether the debt owed to the Homeowners Association is a secured or unsecured debt of the bankrupt-Homeowner. Secured debt can generally be described as any debt that is backed by a mortgage, pledge of collateral, or other lien or security interest, such as a mortgage lien on a house.[299] An unsecured debt, on the other hand, is generally described as a debt that is backed by nothing more than the Bankruptcy Debtor's promise to pay.

In determining whether a particular debt constitutes a secured debt, Texas Bankruptcy Courts are guided by Texas law.[300] Under Texas law, amounts owed by a Homeowner to a Homeowners Association that are secured by a contractual Assessment Lien are generally considered to be secured debts. Thus, all amounts owed by a bankrupt-Homeowner to the Homeowners Association that are secured by its Assessment Lien are considered to be secured debts, and any other amounts owed by the bankrupt-Homeowner to the Homeowners Association that are not secured by its Assessment Lien are considered to be unsecured debts. For Condominium Associations, the Texas Uniform Condominium Act provides that an Assessment Lien for a Condominium Association secures payment for all regular and special Assessments, dues, fees, charges, interest, late fees, fines, collection costs, attorneys fees, and any other amount due to the Condominium Association by the Unit Owner or levied against the Unit by the Condominium

---

[299] A "security interest" is defined by the Bankruptcy Code as a lien created by agreement. 11 U.S.C. § 101(51). The Bankruptcy code further defines a "lien" as a charge against or interest in property to secure payment of a debt or performance of an obligation. 11 U.S.C. § 101(37).

[300] *See In re Peacock*, 6 B.R. 922, 924 (Bankr. N.D. Texas 1980).

Association, unless the Condominium Association's Declaration provides otherwise.[301] There is no similar statutory provision for Subdivision Associations. Consequently, a Subdivision Association's Assessment Lien only secures the types of debts specifically identified in the Declaration as being secured by its Assessment Lien. By way of illustration, if a bankrupt-Lot Owner owes a Subdivision Association $500 in unpaid Assessments and $200 in fines at the time the bankruptcy petition is filed, and the Assessment Lien created by the Subdivision Association's Declaration provides that it only secures payment of unpaid Assessments and costs of collection (and omits any mention of fines), then the Subdivision Association would have a claim against the bankrupt-Lot Owner for $700, $500 of which is a secured debt and $200 of which is an unsecured debt.

It is also important to note that a debt secured by a lien is only a secured debt to the extent of the value of such creditor's interest in the collateral.[302] In other words, when a Homeowner files for bankruptcy protection, the debt owed to the Homeowners Association by such bankrupt-Homeowner is only secured to the extent there is value in such bankrupt-Homeowner's Unit or Lot that would be subject to the Homeowners Association's Assessment Lien. If the market value of the Unit or Lot is less than the total amounts owed by the bankrupt-Homeowner to superior lienholders, such as the first mortgage lienholder, then the otherwise secured amounts owed to a Homeowners Association may later be declared as unsecured debt because there is not enough value in the Lot or Unit to secure the amounts owed to the Homeowners Association.[303] In cases where the value of the Unit or Lot exceeds the total amount of the superior liens, but is still not enough to cover the full amount of the secured amount owed to the Homeowners Association, only the portion of the otherwise secured amount owed to the Homeowners

---

301 Tex. Prop. Code § 82.113(a).

302 11 U.S.C. § 506(a).

303 11 U.S.C. § 506(a); *See Bartee v. Tara Colony Homeowners Ass'n*, 212 F.3d 277, 280 (5th Cir. 2000).

Association, for which there is value in the property, will still be considered to be a secured debt, with the remaining amount declared to be unsecured.[304] Notwithstanding, a determination as to whether all or a portion of debt otherwise secured by a lien will lose its status of secured debt due to insufficient value in the collateral will be made by the Bankruptcy Court during the course of the bankruptcy case. For purposes of filing a Proof of Claim, Homeowners Associations need not concern themselves with whether the Bankruptcy Court might later determine that there is insufficient value in the bankrupt-Homeowner's Unit or Lot to fully secure the amounts owed to the Homeowners Association, and it should identify all such amounts that are secured by its Assessment Lien as secured debts and any remaining amounts as unsecured debts.

7.16.6 Discharge of Debt Owed to a Homeowners Association and Payment of Claims

Upon the successful completion of a Chapter 7 or Chapter 13 bankruptcy case, the Bankruptcy Debtor's Pre-Petition "dischargeable debts" are discharged, meaning that the Bankruptcy Debtor is released from any personal liability for payment of such debts and the creditors of such debts are prohibited from taking any future action against the Bankruptcy Debtor to collect such debts.[305] The discharge of Pre-Petition Debts, however, only releases the Bankruptcy Debtor for personal liability for such debts; it does not release the "in rem" liability for a secured debt to the extent of the value of the collateral.[306] In other words, secured Pre-Petition Debts owed by a bankrupt-Homeowner to a Homeowners Association are not discharged to the extent there is still value in the bankrupt-Homeowner's Unit or Lot securing the amounts owed to the Homeowners Association. Or said even simpler, the bankrupt-Homeowner no longer has a personal obligation to pay the Pre-Petition Debt owed to the Homeowners Association, but the

---

304 *See Bartee v. Tara Colony Homeowners Ass'n*, 212 F.3d 277, 280 (5th Cir. 2000).

305 11 U.S.C. §§ 727, 1328. A discharge, however, does not generally affect a Bankruptcy Debtor's liability for Post-Petition Debts.

306 The term "in rem" essentially means "with respect to the thing itself" (i.e., the collateral).

bankrupt-Homeowner's Unit or Lot is still subject to the Homeowners Association's Assessment Lien for such Pre-Petition Debts.

Thus, in both Chapter 7 and Chapter 13 bankruptcy cases, if the bankrupt-Homeowner intends to continue to own the Unit or Lot subject to the Homeowners Association's Assessment Lien following the bankruptcy discharge, then the bankrupt-Homeowner will be required to pay all Pre-Petition Debt secured by the Assessment Lien, as well as Post-Petition Debt owed to the Homeowners Association.[307] If the bankrupt-Homeowner surrenders the Unit or Lot to the bankruptcy trustee or a secured creditor for liquidation, however, the probability of a Homeowners Association recovering any portion of its claim for the Pre-Petition Debt will be determined by the categorization of such debt as being either secured or unsecured.

Under the statutory order of distribution, which governs the order in which creditors are paid, secured claims get paid before unsecured claims to the extent of the value secured. In other words, if the bankrupt-Homeowner abandons the Unit or Lot, the Homeowners Association will only receive payment on its claim of secured debt if there are any proceeds remaining from the sale of such Unit or Lot after satisfaction of all other superior liens on the Unit or Lot. To the extent there is no remaining value or proceeds, or at least not enough to cover the full amount of the Homeowners Association's claim of secured debt, the remaining amount of the Homeowners Association's otherwise secured claim will be considered to be unsecured. Creditors with claims of unsecured debt generally have the lowest probability of recovering any amount of their claims. In general, unsecured creditors get paid last in a Chapter 7 bankruptcy case, and only if there is money still left after paying all the claims of higher priority creditors. Creditors with claims of unsecured debt in a Chapter 13 bankruptcy case must be treated equally as a class of

---

307 11 U.S.C. § 523(A)(16). In a Chapter 13 bankruptcy case, if the bankrupt-Homeowner is going to retain the property, Pre-Petition Debt owed to the Homeowners Association will be paid through the bankrupt-Homeowner's Reorganization Plan, and Post-Petition debt will be paid directly to the Homeowners Association by the bankrupt-Homeowner as it comes due. *See* 11 U.S.C. § 1326.

creditors, and the class of unsecured creditors will typically be allotted some small portion of the amounts to be paid to creditors by the Bankruptcy Debtor out of his or her disposable income over the period of the Reorganization Plan, but which could be as little as zero for all unsecured creditors.[308]

[308] The only safeguard for unsecured creditors in a Chapter 13 bankruptcy case is that the value of the payments to be made on each unsecured claim under the proposed Reorganization Plan may not be less than the amount that would be paid on such claim if the bankruptcy case was a Chapter 7 liquidation case. *See* 11 U.S.C. § 1325(a)(4).

CHAPTER 8 ARCHITECTURAL COMMITTEES

CHAPTER 8 ARCHITECTURAL COMMITTEES

8.1 In General

One of the main purposes of a Common-Interest Development's Declaration is to preserve and protect the value of Lots or Units in the Development by the regulation of architectural design and quality of buildings or other structures (generally referred to as "Improvements") constructed in the Development. This is accomplished through the incorporation of Restrictive Covenants in a Declaration that establish certain architectural and construction specifications for Improvements and the creation of a committee of individuals whose job it is to determine if proposed construction or modification of Improvements on a Homeowner's Lot or Unit comply with such specifications. This committee or group of individuals can go by many synonymous names, such as "Architectural Committee," "Architectural Control Committee," "Architectural Review Committee," and "Design Review Committee" (and are commonly known by related abbreviations, such as "AC," "ACC," "ARC," or "DRC"). While in some cases such architectural control function is performed by the Board of Directors of a Homeowners Association, in most cases such function is performed by a group of individuals separate and apart from the Board of Directors. For simplicity, this book shall refer to all such committees vested with the authority to review and approve proposed construction or modification of Improvements in a Subdivision or Condominium Development, including a Board of Directors acting in such capacity, as simply the "Architectural Committee."

The purpose of the Architectural Committee is to serve as a "gate-keeping" function for maintaining a uniform or harmonious architectural style and attractive appearance of all Improvements that are constructed or erected on a Homeowner's Lot or Unit in the development. In most Declarations, Homeowners are required to submit an application for the construction of new Improvements or the modification of existing Improvements to the Architectural Committee for its review in advance of initiating construction, and the Architectural Committee is vested with exclusive discretion to determine whether such proposed construction of new Improvements or modification of existing Improvements is in compliance with the Restrictive Covenants applicable to the community and is aesthetically attractive and harmonious with the other structures in the community. The authority to review and approve construction of new Improvements and/or modifications to existing Improvements is generally referred to as the "Architectural Control Authority."

8.2 Establishment of an Architectural Committee

One of the biggest misconceptions regarding an Architectural Committee is that it is a committee of a Homeowners Association. It is not. A committee of a Homeowners Association is technically a committee created by a Board of Directors of a Nonprofit Corporation HOA under the statutory authority established by the Texas Nonprofit Corporation Law.[1] An Architectural Committee, on the other hand, is established by a Declaration, not by a Nonprofit Corporation HOA's Board of Directors, and it is generally established as a group separate and independent from the Nonprofit Corporation HOA, with its own exclusive powers and authority to approve proposed construction or modification of Improvements upon Lots and Units. For such reason, the provisions of a Homeowners Association's Articles of Incorporation and Bylaws, and even the Texas Nonprofit Corporation Law, typically do not apply to an Architectural Committee.

And, unlike committees established by the Board of Directors of a Nonprofit Corporation HOA, there is no statutory law governing the formation and organization of Architectural Committees, and the formation and organization of a particular Architectural Committee, as well as the scope of its Architectural Control Authority and the procedures for submitting an application for approval of a proposed Improvement to it, will almost always be dictated exclusively by the provisions of the Declaration that

1 Tex. Bus. Org. Code § 22.218. The authority of Nonprofit Corporation HOAs to establish corporate committees under the Texas Nonprofit Corporation Law is described in more detail in chapter 3 of this book.

establishes such Architectural Committee. Thus, the number of voting and/or non-voting members on an Architectural Committee, qualifications to serve on the Architectural Committee (if any), and procedures for election or appointment of members to the Architectural Committee, as well as procedures for removal of members from the Architectural Committee, will all be dictated by the provisions of the Homeowners Association's Declaration and other Governing Documents. And, while the Governing Documents for each Homeowners Association can differ significantly from community to community, in most cases, the Architectural Committee will be comprised of Homeowners, who are either elected to the Architectural Committee by their fellow Homeowners in the community or appointed to such committee by the Board of Directors of the Homeowners Association.

While there is no specific statutory requirement under Texas law as to who performs such architectural review function or how such group is organized, there are provisions in the Texas Property Code concerning the transfer of Architectural Control Authority to Subdivision Associations in Harris, Galveston, and Montgomery Counties. Chapter 204 of the Texas Property Code, which by its express terms only applies to residential Subdivision Developments that are located in whole or in part in: (1) a county with a population of 3.3 million or more;[2] (2) a county with a population of not less than 285,000 and not more than 300,000 that is adjacent to the Gulf of Mexico and that is adjacent to a county having a population of 3.3 million or more;[3] or (3) a county with a population of 275,000 or more that is adjacent to a county with a population of 3.3 million

2 Tex. Prop. Code § 204.002(a)(1). The only Texas county with a population of 3.3 million or more is Harris County. Source: United States Census Bureau, 2010.

3 Tex. Prop. Code § 204.002(a)(2). The only Texas county with a population of not less than 285,000 and not more than 300,000 that is adjacent to the Gulf of Mexico and a county with a population of 3.3 million or more is Galveston County. Prior to 2011, Section 204.002(a)(2) applied to counties with a population of 250,000 or more that were adjacent to the Gulf of Mexico and a county having a population of 2.8 million or more, which included both Brazoria and Galveston Counties. Section 204.002(a)(2) was amended by the Texas Legislature in 2011 to make it applicable to only counties with a population between 285,000 and 300,000, which now excludes Brazoria County (pop. 313,166) from its application. Source: United States Census Bureau, 2010.

or more and contains part of a national forest,[4] provides that unless the Declaration applicable to such a Subdivision Development vests Architectural Control Authority in the Subdivision Association before the occurrence of any of the following events, such Architectural Control Authority automatically vests in the Subdivision Association upon the earliest occurrence of any one of such events:

(1) the term of the Architectural Control Authority expires pursuant to the terms of the Declaration;[5]

(2) a residence on the last available building site is completed and sold;[6]

(3) the person or entity designated as the Architectural Committee in the Declaration assigns, in writing, the Architectural Control Authority to the Subdivision Association;[7] or

(4) an assignee of the original holder of the Architectural Control Authority abandons such authority for more than one year.[8]

8.3 Promulgation of Architectural Guidelines

In addition to the authority to review and approve or deny proposed construction or modification of Improvements, the Declaration of a Homeowners Association will also often grant the Architectural Committee the authority to create rules or guidelines (typically called "Architectural Guidelines"). The Architectural Guidelines generally consist of a written document that sets forth various standards relating to building materials and construction specifications for Improvements placed or constructed upon any Lot or Unit, and they are intended to serve as a guideline as to what the Architectural Committee has already determined is in compliance with the applicable Declaration's

---

[4] Tex. Prop. Code § 204.002(a)(3). The only Texas county with a population of 275,000 or more that is adjacent to a county with a population of 3.3 million or more and contains part of a national forest is Montgomery County (Sam Houston National Forest). Source: United States Census Bureau, 2010.

[5] Tex. Prop. Code § 204.011(b)(1).

[6] Tex. Prop. Code § 204.011(b)(2).

[7] Tex. Prop. Code § 204.011(b)(3).

[8] Tex. Prop. Code § 204.011(b)(3).

Restrictive Covenants and is harmonious with the community's architecture and appearance.

There is no inherent authority of an Architectural Committee to promulgate Architectural Guidelines. If the Declaration applicable to a Subdivision or Condominium Development does not expressly provide for such authority, then the Architectural Committee does not possess the authority to establish Architectural Guidelines.[9] It is also important to note that Architectural Guidelines are generally considered to be a Dedicatory Instrument under the Texas Uniform Condominium Act and Chapter 202 of the Texas Property Code, and in order to be enforceable, it must be recorded in the Official Public Records of each county in which the development subject to such Architectural Guidelines is located.[10]

8.4 Architectural Review by an Architectural Committee

The scope of an Architectural Committee's review of an application for proposed construction or modification of an Improvement is generally dictated by the express provisions of the Declaration establishing such committee, and an Architectural Committee may not exercise Architectural Control Authority over characteristics of a proposed Improvement that is not expressly within such scope of review. While the scope of an Architectural Committee's Architectural Control Authority can vary from

[9] There is a limited exception to this rule for Subdivision Associations in Harris, Galveston, and Montgomery Counties under Chapter 204 of the Texas Property Code. Under Chapter 204, if the Declaration for a Subdivision Development located, in whole or in part, in one of the applicable counties vests Architectural Control Authority in the Subdivision Association, then the Subdivision Association is authorized to implement written architectural control guidelines for its own use or to record such guidelines in the Official Public Records of the applicable county in which it is located, and it may also modify such guidelines as the needs of the Subdivision Development change. Tex. Prop. Code § 204.010(a)(18).

[10] Tex. Prop. Code §§ 82.003(11-a); 202.001, 202.006. Chapter 202 and the Texas Uniform Condominium Act define the term "Dedicatory Instrument" as any governing instrument covering the establishment, maintenance, and operation of a residential Subdivision Development, Condominium Development, or any similar planned development, including a Declaration or similar instrument subjecting real property to Restrictive Covenants, Bylaws, Association Rules, or similar instrument governing the administration or operation of a Homeowners Association. Tex. Prop. Code §§ 82.003(11-a); 202.001(1).

community to community, in most cases the Declaration will authorize the Architectural Committee to review an application for proposed construction or modification of an Improvement so as to determine whether such proposed construction or modification complies with the Restrictive Covenants contained within such Declaration and to ensure that it will be architecturally harmonious with the other Improvements already constructed in the development. Of these two types of architectural review, determining whether proposed construction or modification of an Improvement complies with applicable Restrictive Covenants is the easier of the two because it is most often an objective task that involves reviewing the plans and specifications submitted by a Homeowner and checking to see if it complies with the Restrictive Covenants concerning construction of Improvements, such as restrictions on height, width, location, and type of construction material, to name a few.

The second type of architectural review, ensuring architectural harmony and compatibility of a proposed Improvement, is one of the most important gatekeeping functions performed by an Architectural Committee because it involves making a very subjective determination that is based solely on the discretion of the Architectural Committee members. Determining whether a proposed Improvement is harmonious and/or compatible with other existing Improvements in a development can give both the Architectural Committee members and Homeowners fits because harmony is difficult to define and is often very subjective. The term "harmony" is defined by *Webster's College Dictionary* as an "agreement; accord; . . . a consistent, orderly, or pleasing arrangement of parts."[11] In the context of Common-Interest Developments, harmony pertains to the characteristics of an Improvement that is to be constructed or modified as compared with the characteristics of existing residential dwellings and other structures, and the overall development of the community. To be in harmony, the Improvement that is to be constructed or modified must be compatible with its surroundings. In this sense, harmony

[11] Random House *Webster's College Dictionary* 611 (1991).

and compatibility of a proposed Improvement involves a determination as to whether it will be consistent with the other preexisting Improvements in the community in its architectural style, mass (size and form), proportion (relationship of height to width), scale (mass and proportion), and complimentary or similar (but not necessarily duplicative) use of materials, color, and design details, as well as the location and impact of the proposed Improvement on adjacent properties if it involves new construction. In many cases, the determination of harmony and/or compatibility is a "you know it when you see it" determination. For example, construction of a Spanish-styled hacienda-type residence in a community of craftsman-styled bungalows or construction of a 10,000-square foot home in a community consisting of homes with no more than 2,500-square foot interior space would not be harmonious or compatible with the other homes in the development.

Not all determinations of harmony and/or compatibility, however, are so simple or obvious. The determination of harmony and compatibility often involves striking a balance between what an applicant-Homeowner wants or thinks is attractive versus what is consistent with the rest of the existing homes or other Improvements in the development. In reviewing plans and specifications for proposed construction or modification of an Improvement, the Architectural Committee should refrain from imposing its subjective opinions as to what is aesthetically attractive onto an applicant-Homeowner. Instead, the Architectural Committee should endeavor to allow an applicant-Homeowner to construct and/or modify an Improvement in any manner such Homeowner believes is attractive and desirable, so long as it is in compliance with the Restrictive Covenants and not incompatible with the existing homes and other Improvements in the development.

8.5 Time Period for Approving or Denying a Proposed Construction Project

In most cases, a Declaration will require Homeowners to obtain the prior written approval of the Architectural Committee in advance of commencing construction or modification of an Improvement on their Lot or Unit. In turn, the Declaration will generally also require the Architectural Committee to approve or deny an application for proposed construction or modification of an Improvement within some delineated time period, typically, thirty (30) days, and provide that if the Architectural Committee fails to timely do so, the proposed construction or remodeling project is considered approved. In such circumstances, it is very important that the Architectural Committee review and rule on a proposed construction or remodeling project in the manner and within the time frame required by the Declaration.

8.6 Authority of an Architectural Committee to Grant a Variance

It is very common for a Declaration to also vest the Architectural Committee with the power to grant a Homeowner a variance from compliance with one or more of the Restrictive Covenants in the Declaration regarding construction or modification of an Improvement. Such authority to grant variances is generally limited to circumstances where the Architectural Committee determines there is good cause or justification for allowing the deviation and such variance will not have an adverse impact on the community. The authority of an Architectural Committee to grant a variance, however, is not inherent. Nor is there any such authority established by Texas statutory law. If a Declaration establishing an Architectural Committee does not expressly vest it with authority to grant variances, then such Architectural Committee has no such authority to do so.[12]

8.7 Limitations on an Architectural Committee's Architectural Control Authority

The authority of the Architectural Committee to approve or deny a Homeowner's application to construct or modify an Improvement is not without limitation. In a 1981 case law opinion, entitled Davis v. Huey, the Texas Supreme Court held that Declaration provisions requiring the submission of plans to and prior consent of an Architectural

[12] *See Johnson v. Dick*, 281 S.W.2d 171, 175 (Tex. Civ. App.—San Antonio 1955, no writ).

Committee before construction of Improvements are valid "insofar as they furnish adequate notice to the homeowners of the specific restriction sought to be enforced" and that an Architectural Committee may not impose building restrictions upon Homeowners that are more stringent than those specifically set out in the Declaration through its discretionary authority to disapprove proposed construction projects.[13] In other words, even if a Declaration vests an Architectural Committee with discretionary approval authority, the Architectural Committee is not permitted to alter or expand the specific building restrictions or to impose limitations on a Homeowner's construction or remodeling project that are more restrictive than the specific restrictions set out elsewhere in the Declaration.[14]

The factual circumstances of the Davis v. Huey case provide a good illustration of the limitation on an Architectural Committee's Architectural Control Authority. In such case, the Architectural Committee of a Subdivision Development in Austin, Texas, disapproved the proposed plans for the construction of an applicant-Homeowner's home on the basis that the proposed placement of the house on the applicant-Homeowner's Lot, which complied with the specific set-back restrictions in the applicable Declaration, would obstruct the view of a Homeowner who had already built a home on a nearby Lot.[15] The Texas Supreme Court held that the Architectural Committee could not impose more restrictive restrictions concerning the placement or location of houses to be built on a Homeowner's Lot than the specific set-back restrictions provided by the applicable Declaration and that the Architectural Committee's refusal to approve the applicant-

---

13 *Davis v. Huey*, 620 S.W.2d 561, 566-67 (Tex. 1981).

14 *See Whiteco Metrocom, Inc. v. Industrial Properties Corp.*, 711 S.W.2d 81, 82 (Tex. App.—Dallas 1986, writ refused n.r.e.); *Catalina Square Improvement Comm. v. Metz*, 630 S.W.2d 324, 327 (Tex. App.—Houston [14th Dist.] 1982, writ ref'd n.r.e.).

15 *Davis v. Huey*, 620 S.W.2d 561, 564 (Tex. 1981).

Homeowner's construction plans on such basis exceeded the Architectural Committee's authority and was void.[16]

8.8 Challenge of an Architectural Committee's Determination

It is not unusual for a Homeowner unsatisfied by the determination of the Architectural Committee to question the basis of its decision or assert that the Architectural Committee's determination was improper. A challenge to an Architectural Committee's determination can take two different forms. First, some Declarations provide for a right of appeal of an Architectural Committee's determination to the Board of Directors for the Homeowners Association. In such event, the Board of Directors is often vested with the authority to reverse or modify the determination of the Architectural Committee. In most cases, however, the Architectural Committee is vested with exclusive and final authority to approve or disapprove a Homeowner's application to construct or modify an Improvement, and the Board of Directors for the Homeowners Association has no authority under the Declaration to review or modify the determination of the Architectural Committee. Under such circumstances, the only form of challenge to an Architectural Committee's determination is by judicial proceeding.

In a judicial proceeding involving a challenge to an Architectural Committee's determination on a proposed construction or remodeling project, Texas courts should uphold the determination of the Architectural Committee so long as its exercise of discretionary authority in making such determination was reasonable. In addition, Chapter 202 of the Texas Property Code creates a rebuttable presumption that the exercise of discretionary authority by a Homeowners Association or other representative group designated by an owner of real property concerning a Restrictive Covenant, such as an Architectural Committee, is reasonable unless a court of law determines that the exercise

[16] *Davis v. Huey*, 620 S.W.2d 561, 566 (Tex. 1981).

of such discretionary authority was arbitrary, capricious, or discriminatory.[17] Under Chapter 202, a Homeowner challenging a determination by an Architectural Committee has the burden to overcome the presumption that the Architectural Committee's exercise of discretionary authority was reasonable by proving that its determination was either arbitrary, capricious, or discriminatory.[18]

There is very little Texas case law as to what actions by a Homeowners Association or an Architectural Committee may or may not be considered arbitrary, capricious, or discriminatory. There is, however, some Texas case law on what is considered arbitrary, capricious, or discriminatory in general that does provide some basic guidance as to the meaning of such terms. Texas courts have defined the term "arbitrary" as the failure to exercise an honest judgment, as well as an act that is "fixed or done capriciously or at pleasure; not founded in the nature of things; non-rational; not done or acting according to reason or judgment; depending on the will alone; tyrannical; despotic."[19] Texas courts have also construed as arbitrary: (1) actions made without fair, solid, and substantial cause or reason; (2) "willful and unreasoning action"; and (3) "action without consideration and in disregard of the facts and circumstances of the case."[20]

---

17 Tex. Prop. Code § 202.004(a). One Texas Court of Appeals, however, has held that unless a Declaration requires the determination of an Architectural Committee to be reasonable, the Architectural Committee's discretionary determination is not challengeable on the basis that it is was arbitrary, capricious, or discriminatory. *La Ventana Ranch Owners' Ass'n v. Davis*, 363 S.W.3d 632 (Tex. App.—Austin, no pet.) (holding "[i]n light of the plain language of the [Declaration] granting the [Architectural Committee's] 'sole and absolute discretion' to determine whether the necessary conditions for granting a variance have been met, we conclude that the arbitrary-and-capricious standard set forth in section 202.004(a) is inapplicable to this determination. . . . [and the jury's finding that the Architectural Committee acted arbitrarily and capriciously] is legally irrelevant to the validity of the variances.").

18 Tex. Prop. Code § 202.004(a).

19 *See Goodrum v. State*, 158 S.W.2d 81, 87 (Tex. Civ. App.—Galveston 1942, writ ref'd w.o.m.); *Corneil v. Swisher County*, 78 S.W.2d 1072, 1074 (Tex. Civ. App.—Amarillo 1935, no writ).

20 *See Mitchell's Inc. v. Nelms*, 454 S.W.2d 809, 814 (Tex. Civ. App.—Dallas 1970, writ ref'd n.r.e.); *Webb v. Dameron*, 219 S.W.2d 581, 584 (Tex. Civ. App.—Amarillo 1949, writ ref'd n.r.e.).

Texas case law often uses the terms "capricious" and "arbitrary" synonymously, and in many respects such words are synonymous.[21] The term "capricious" has been construed by some Texas courts to mean freakish, whimsical, fickle, changeable, unsteady, and arbitrary; meanwhile, other Texas courts have held that an action is not arbitrary or capricious when exercised honestly and upon due consideration, even if an erroneous conclusion was reached.[22] In other words, a determination of arbitrariness is focused on the manner in which the determination was reached, not whether the determination is actually correct. Even if the Architectural Committee's determination is ultimately mistaken or wrong, its determination is not necessarily arbitrary unless there was no basis for its determination.

The meaning of the term "discriminatory" differs significantly from that of "arbitrary" and "capricious." Black's Law Dictionary defines "discriminatory" as "a failure to treat all persons equally where no reasonable distinction can be found between those favored and those not favored."[23] A claim of discriminatory treatment is often based on unequal treatment of an individual or class of individuals on the basis of race, religion, nationality, or sex. However, in the context of a judicial review of an Architectural Committee's determination, discriminatory treatment is not limited to such categories. One such example would be if the Architectural Committee granted variances from compliance with a Restrictive Covenant to Homeowners serving as Directors on the Board of Directors, but refused to grant a variance to other Homeowners under similar circumstances.

If the Architectural Committee's determinations fail to treat all Homeowners uniformly when they are seeking approval to perform the same, or very similar,

---

21 *See Webb v. Dameron*, 219 S.W.2d 581, 584 (Tex. Civ. App.—Amarillo 1949, writ ref'd n.r.e.).

22 *See Webb v. Dameron*, 219 S.W.2d 581, 584 (Tex. Civ. App.—Amarillo 1949, writ ref'd n.r.e.); *Anderson v. Clajon Gas Co.*, 677 S.W.2d 702, 705 (Tex. App.—Houston [1st Dist.] 1984, no writ).

23 *Black's Law Dictionary* 467 (6th ed. 1990).

construction or remodeling projects, and there is no reasonable distinction between the proposed construction or remodeling projects, then it could be found to be discriminatory if the decision is based on treating certain classes of Homeowners differently or found to be arbitrary if there is no reasonable basis for the differential treatment. There is no requirement, however, that an Architectural Committee approve a particular proposed Improvement simply because the same or a similar Improvement was previously approved for a different Lot or Unit. Although proposed construction projects can be very similar, the conditions of Lots (and Site-Condominium Units), including size and topography, are rarely the same or very similar. Every review process by the Architectural Committee should take into consideration the plans and specifications for the proposed construction or remodeling project, conditions of the Lot or Unit for which it is proposed, and the conditions and compatibility of the proposed construction or remodeling project with Lots and Units in close proximity with the Lot or Unit for which it is proposed. An Architectural Committee may properly reach different determinations as to the same or similar proposed construction or remodeling projects so long as there is a distinctive or reasonable basis for doing so.

CHAPTER 9 ENFORCEMENT OF RESTRICTIVE COVENANTS

CHAPTER 9 ENFORCEMENT OF RESTRICTIVE COVENANTS

9.1 In General

While the terms "Declaration" and "Restrictive Covenants" are often used interchangeably by lawyers and laypersons alike, the terms actually refer to two separate things. The term "Declaration" generally refers to the main document governing a Texas Homeowners Association, whereas the term "Restrictive Covenants" generally refers to the individual contractual obligations within the Declaration that regulate the use of the Lots or Units in the development by the Homeowners. The Texas Property Code defines a "Restrictive Covenant" as "any covenant, condition, or restriction contained in a Dedicatory Instrument, whether mandatory, prohibitive, permissive, or administrative." In simpler terms, Restrictive Covenants are the legal obligations imposed on a Lot or Unit that require the Homeowner to do something (such as maintain his or her yard) or to refrain from doing something (such as parking a trailer on the driveway). These land-use restrictions or Restrictive Covenants "run with the land," meaning they attach to a property and each subsequent owner of such property becomes obligated to comply with such Restrictive Covenants upon acquiring ownership of such property, whether or not he or she has actual knowledge of the Restrictive Covenants at the time he or she acquires ownership of such property.

Restrictive Covenants are intended to preserve and protect the property values of Homeowners' Lots and Units in Common-Interest Developments by imposing certain obligations on Homeowners to do, or refrain from doing, certain actions that may affect the value of the Lots or Units in such development or the peaceful enjoyment of other Homeowners living in the development. For example, a Restrictive Covenant may restrict what Homeowners can do on their property (such as prohibiting the parking or storing of a recreational vehicle in the driveway) or may impose certain affirmative duties upon Homeowners to do some act (such as mandating that Homeowners maintain the landscaping in their yard and the exterior appearance of their homes).

Though all Homeowners subject to a Declaration have an equal right to enforce the Restrictive Covenants contained therein against all other Homeowners subject to the same Declaration, Homeowners living in an Association-Governed Community often look to the Homeowners Association to enforce an applicable Restrictive Covenant when a Homeowner, or his or her tenants, fails to comply with it. Enforcement of Restrictive Covenants can be one of the most challenging endeavors faced by a Homeowners Association. Restrictive Covenant enforcement can generate high emotions, and in some cases, it has been known to generate full "neighborhood disputes" or to even lead to physical confrontations between neighbors; after all, it is well-known that emotions run higher and tempers shorter the closer an issue gets to a person's front door. While there are many theories as to why "neighborhood disputes," in general, and enforcement of Restrictive Covenants, in particular, generate so much emotion, in most cases it is rooted in a perception by Homeowners that certain perceived implied property rights are being infringed upon either by a Homeowners Association, which is attempting to enforce a Restrictive Covenant against them, or a neighbor, who is violating a Restrictive Covenant in a manner that affects them or their use of their home. While there are many perceived property rights, there are a certain few that commonly manifest themselves in the context of Restrictive Covenants. These perceived property rights include:[1]

> **A Man's Home Is His Castle:** This perception is based on the English common law principle that one is the king or queen of his or her castle and no one should be able to tell the king or queen what he or she can or can't do there. Many Texans of the redder neck variety have taken this ancient proverb and put a "Don't Mess with Texas" spin on it, resulting in the fundamental belief that no one has the right to tell a Texan what he or she can or can't do with his or her home, especially an un-American factious-run Homeowners Association. God Bless Texas!
>
> **Not in My Backyard:** This perception is actually an expansion of "A Man's Home Is His Castle," where the four corners of one's backyard are

[1] *See Roy D. Hailey*, Practical Tips for Dealing with Property Owners Associations (2005) (presented at the twenty-seventh Annual Texas Advanced Real Estate Law Course). Excerpt adapted and printed with the permission of the author, Roy D. Hailey.

extended to the boundaries of the entire neighborhood and beyond, which ultimately results in the war cry: "You can't do that in my neighborhood. You have no right!" This perception typically manifests when a Homeowner perceives a neighbor's actions as having an effect on his or her property value or peaceful enjoyment of his or her home. When you juxtapose this perception against the previous one, you have the makings of a head-on collision between one Homeowner's backyard and another's castle.

The Largest Financial Investment in Life: In most cases, a person's home represents the largest financial investment he or she will ever make. Of course, everyone wants to protect such investment, whether it is by making improvements to his or her castle or making sure the neighbor's castle does not bring down the value of his or her own castle. This perception is bolstered by the belief that Restrictive Covenants and Homeowners Associations exist to protect property values.

Home Is Where the Heart Is: Lest we forget that we are dealing with a Homeowner's "home," where he or she lives, raises a family, and celebrates life's events. Homeowners often have deep-seated emotions that are attached to their homes that are often predicated on images of Mom, apple pie, Lassie, etc.—and what red-blooded American wouldn't fight for these things? Semper Fi!

Whether one's castle is 600 square feet or 6,000 square feet, all of these perceptions are invoked in some degree when one owns real property. The bottom line is that neighborhood disputes, in general, and enforcement of Restrictive Covenants, in particular, can sometimes engender the extremes in people.

For such reasons, enforcement of Restrictive Covenants can have emotional consequences similar in rank to collection of delinquent Assessments and foreclosure of Assessment Liens. While not for the faint of heart, a Homeowners Association cannot shy away from its duty to enforce its Restrictive Covenants. When a Homeowners Association fails to enforce its Restrictive Covenants, it often leads to more restrictive covenant violations of a similar nature and claims of discrimination or being singled out by other Homeowners against whom the Homeowners Association does enforce Restrictive Covenants. In addition, a lack of enforcement of violations of a Restrictive Covenant over a long period of time can also potentially result in such Restrictive Covenant being deemed waived by a court of law and no longer enforceable. In order to avoid such consequences, it is important that Homeowners Associations consistently and uniformly enforce their applicable Restrictive Covenants.

9.2 Interpretation of Restrictive Covenants

One of the more difficult tasks in enforcing a Restrictive Covenant can be ascertaining its true meaning. Frequently, Homeowners Associations are faced with a Restrictive Covenant that may be written so broadly that it seems to apply to everything or written so narrowly that it is unclear whether the Restrictive Covenant applies to anything that might be slightly different than the specific circumstance expressed in the Restrictive Covenant. Even worse, a Restrictive Covenant may be written in such a vague manner that, depending on how you interpret it, it could mean two very different things. For such reasons, the first step in the enforcement of Restrictive Covenants is determining the meaning or scope of such provisions.

In order to properly determine the meaning or scope of a Restrictive Covenant, one must understand the rules of interpretation utilized by Texas courts, which is ultimately who is charged with interpreting a Restrictive Covenant in any lawsuit to enforce such covenant. Traditionally, Texas courts have utilized the same rules of interpretation normally used in interpreting contracts to interpret Restrictive Covenants. As with interpretation of contracts, a court's primary task in construing the meaning of a Restrictive Covenant is to determine and give effect to the parties' intent as expressed within the "four corners" of the Declaration itself.[2] Texas courts will garner such intent from the language used in the Declaration by: (1) affording words and phrases their plain, ordinary, and generally accepted meanings, unless the Declaration itself assigns specific meanings to such words or phrases; and (2) reading the Declaration as a whole, so as to

---

2 *See Gulf Ins. Co. v. Burns Motors, Inc.*, 22 S.W.3d 417 (Tex. 2000); *Luckel v. White*, 819 S.W.2d 459, 461-63 (Tex. 1991).

ensure that every provision is given effect (and no provision is rendered meaningless).[3] To determine the plain, ordinary, accepted meaning of a word or phrase, one should consult a dictionary, which is the most commonly used source for determining the plain, ordinary, accepted meaning of words and phrases.

The ability to determine the meaning of a word or phrase within a Restrictive Covenant provision will have a direct impact on its enforceability. This is because Texas is a property rights state and Texas law has a well-established tradition of disfavoring any restrictions on the free use of real property by its owner. Texas law, however, also strongly favors the enforceability of contractual obligations, of which Restrictive Covenants are one type. In balancing these important principles, the Texas Supreme Court has consistently held that although Restrictive Covenants restricting the free use of real property are not favored, when Restrictive Covenants are confined to a lawful purpose, are within reasonable bounds, and the language employed is clear and unambiguous, such covenants will be enforced.[4] If there is ambiguity or doubt as to the intended meaning of a Restrictive Covenant, however, the covenant is to be "strictly construed" against the party seeking to enforce it in favor of the free and unrestricted use of the property.[5] In other words, if a Restrictive Covenant is ambiguous because it is subject to more than one reasonable interpretation, Texas courts will interpret the covenant in the least restrictive

---

3 *See Cross Timbers Oil Co. v. Exxon Corp.*, 22 S.W.3d 24, 26-28 (Tex. App.—Amarillo 2000, no pet.).

4 *See Davis v. Huey*, 620 S.W.2d 561 (Tex. 1981). A Restrictive Covenant is considered unambiguous if the language of the applicable Restrictive Covenant can be given a certain or definite meaning. *See Pilarcik v. Emmons*, 966 S.W.2d 474, 478 (Tex. 1998). However, a term is not considered ambiguous because of a simple lack of clarity. *See Universal C.I.T. Credit Corp. v. Daniel*, 243 S.W.2d 154, 157 (Tex. 1951). Nor does an ambiguity arise because of a mere disagreement over the interpretation of a restrictive covenant. *See Air Park-Dallas Zoning Comm. v. Crow-Billingsley Airpark, Ltd.*, 109 S.W.3d 900, 909 (Tex. App.—Dallas 2003, no pet.). An ambiguity arises only if the Restrictive Covenant is susceptible to more than one reasonable interpretation. *See Columbia Gas Transmission Corp. v. New Ulm Gas, Ltd.*, 940 S.W.2d 587, 589 (Tex. 1996).

5 *See Wilmoth v. Wilcox*, 734 S.W.2d 656, 657 (Tex. 1987).

of the reasonable interpretations. This common law "strict-construction" rule for interpretation of Restrictive Covenants has been the law of Texas since at least 1925.[6]

In 1987, however, the Texas Legislature enacted Section 202.003 of the Texas Property Code, which mandates that all Restrictive Covenants, regardless of the date on which the Restrictive Covenant was created, "shall be liberally construed to give effect to its purposes and intent."[7] While the Texas Legislature's stated intent in enacting Section 202.003 of Texas Property Code was to change the manner in which Restrictive Covenants were to be interpreted,[8] Texas appellate courts have been in continuous disagreement since its enactment as to whether Section 202.003 actually does modify the way in which Texas courts are to interpret Restrictive Covenants. Some Texas courts of appeals have followed the statutory liberal construction standard created by Section 202.003,[9] while others have simply continued to follow the common law strict-construction rule.[10] In contrast, other Texas courts of appeals have concluded that there is no discernible conflict between the common law strict-construction rule and Section 202.003's liberal-construction rule;[11] and even one Texas court of appeals has referred to

---

6 *See Settegast v. Foley Brothers Dry Goods Co.*, 270 S.W. 1014, 1016 (Tex. 1925).

7 Tex. Prop. Code § 202.003.

8 *See* House Comm. On Judicial Affairs, Bill Analysis, Tex. H.B. 356, 70th Leg., R.S. (1987); *Benard v. Humble*, 990 S.W.2d 929, 930-31 (Tex. App.—Beaumont 1999, pet. denied).

9 *See Village of Pheasant Run Homeowners Ass'n, Inc. v. Kastor*, 47 S.W.3d 747, 750-51 (Tex. App.—Houston [14th Dist.] 2001, pet. denied) (holding that Restrictive Covenant under review "falls within Section 202.003(a) and is unambiguous, therefore, we construe it liberally"); *Benard v. Humble,* 990 S.W.2d 929, 930-31 (Tex. App.—Beaumont 1999, pet. denied); *Candlelight Hills Civic Ass'n, Inc. v. Goodwin*, 763 S.W.2d 474, 477 (Tex. App.—Houston [14th Dist.] 1988, writ denied); *Dyegard Land P'ship v. Hoover*, 39 S.W.3d 300, 309 (Tex. App.—Fort Worth 2001, no pet.); *see also Herbert v. Polly Ranch Homeowners Ass'n*, 943 S.W.2d 906, 908 n. 2 (Tex. App.—Houston [1st Dist.] 1996, no writ).

10 *See Pebble Beach Prop. Owners' Ass'n v. Sherer*, 2 S.W.3d 283, 288 (Tex. App.—San Antonio 1999, pet. denied).

11 *See Reagan Nat'l Adver. of Austin, Inc. v. Capital Outdoors, Inc.*, 96 S.W.3d 490, 493 n. 2 (Tex. App.—Austin 2002, pet. denied); *Dyegard Land P'ship v. Hoover*, 39 S.W.3d 300, 309 (Tex. App.—Fort Worth 2001, no pet.); *Simon Prop. Group (Tex.) L.P. v. May Dep't Stores Co.*, 943 S.W.2d 64, 71 (Tex. App.—Corpus Christi 1997, no writ); *Ashcreek Homeowner's Ass'n, Inc. v. Smith*, 902 S.W.2d 586, 588-89 (Tex. App.—Houston [1st Dist.] 1995, no writ); *Crispin v. Paragon Homes, Inc.*, 888 S.W.2d 78, 81 n. 1 (Tex. App.—Houston [1st Dist.] 1994, writ denied). Of the courts of appeal who have determined that there is no

both rules together without even discussing whether such rules conflict or are harmonious.[12] Such consternation on this issue has even led one Texas court of appeals to specifically plead with the Texas Supreme Court in a case law opinion to address and resolve this issue.[13] And while the Texas Supreme Court has expressly acknowledged that there are disputes among the Texas appellate courts as to whether there is a discrepancy between the common law "strict-construction" rule and statutory "liberal-construction" rule and which rule now applies, the Texas Supreme Court has yet to resolve the issue.[14]

This issue of interpretation is not simply an academic one. It is not uncommon for a property condition to arise at a Lot or Unit that draws the ire of neighbors either because it is an eyesore or infringes on the neighbors' peaceful enjoyment of their own homes. In most cases, the neighbors will complain to the Homeowners Association and demand that it correct the situation. Sometimes the offending property condition is expressly prohibited under the Declaration. Often, however, such property condition is not expressly prohibited

---

discernible conflict, there is no common agreement in the conclusions to be drawn from such determination. For example, some courts of appeals have simply continued to apply the common law strict-construction rule without a precise explanation of how the statutory and common law construction rules interact without inconsistency. *See Reagan Nat'l Adver. of Austin, Inc. v. Capital Outdoors, Inc.*, 96 S.W.3d 490, 493 n. 2 (Tex. App.—Austin 2002, pet. denied) ; *Dyegard Land P'ship v. Hoover*, 39 S.W.3d 300, 309 (Tex. App.—Fort Worth 2001, no pet.); *Simon Prop. Group (Tex.) L.P. v. May Dep't Stores Co.*, 943 S.W.2d 64, 71 (Tex. App.—Corpus Christi 1997, no writ); *Crispin v. Paragon Homes, Inc.*, 888 S.W.2d 78, 81 n. 1 (Tex. App.—Houston [1st Dist.] 1994, writ denied). Still others of these courts of appeals have held that the common law strict-construction rule applies only when there is an ambiguity concerning the drafter's intent; however, to determine if an ambiguity concerning the drafter's intent exists, these courts of appeals must first apply Section 202.003's liberal-construction mandate. *See Quinn v. Harris*, No. 03-98-00117-CV, 1999 WL 125470 at *2, n. 3 (Tex. App.—Austin March 11, 1999, pet. denied) (not designated for publication); *Hodas v. Scenic Oaks Prop. Ass'n*, 21 S.W.3d 524, 528 (Tex. App.—San Antonio 2000, pet. denied). And one court of appeals has even attempted to harmonize both construction rules by applying the liberal-construction rule but toning the liberality of its construction based on the given facts of the case. *See Benard v. Humble*, 990 S.W.2d 929, 930–31 (Tex. App.—Beaumont 1999, pet. denied).

12 *See Air Park-Dallas Zoning Comm. v. Crow-Billingsley Airpark, Ltd.*, 109 S.W.3d 900, 909 (Tex. App.—Dallas 2003, no pet.).

13 *See City of Pasadena v. Gennedy*, 125 S.W.3d 687, 694 (Tex. App.—Houston [1st Dist.] 2003, pet. denied) ("We respectfully urge the Supreme Court to resolve the differences among the courts of appeals on this issue.").

14 *See Pilarcik v. Emmons*, 966 S.W.2d 474, 478 (Tex. 1998).

under the Declaration because it would be practically impossible to identify every possible action or omission by a Homeowner that could result in a property condition that negatively affects property values or other Homeowners' peaceful enjoyment of their own homes. In such circumstances, and being mindful that the purpose of Restrictive Covenants is to preserve and protect property values, there is a tendency of Homeowners Associations to want to interpret one or more of the Restrictive Covenants in a manner that would apply to such offending property condition.

Under a "strict-construction" standard, words used in a particular Restrictive Covenant provision, and the Declaration as a whole, may not be enlarged, extended, stretched, or changed by interpretation or construction; rather, the words must be given their commonly accepted meaning. If the Restrictive Covenant is susceptible to more than one reasonable interpretation given its plain meaning, then under a "strict-construction" application, the trial court would interpret the Restrictive Covenant in the least restrictive of the reasonable interpretations. In other words, under the strict-construction rule, if an act or omission by a Homeowner is not expressly prohibited by a Restrictive Covenant, then such act or omission is not a violation of such Restrictive Covenant. The practical effect of the strict-construction rule is that it is nearly impossible to enforce Restrictive Covenants against property conditions or actions of a Homeowner that are not expressly prohibited by such Restrictive Covenants.

On the other hand, under the "liberal-construction" rule, the trial court may look beyond the plain meaning of the express language used in the Restrictive Covenant and is authorized to liberally construe the Restrictive Covenant to give effect to its purposes and intent, which is generally to preserve property values in the community and protect Homeowners' peaceful enjoyment of their homes. By application of the liberal-construction rule, a trial court may be authorized to interpret the Restrictive Covenants in any reasonable manner that would preserve property values and other Homeowners' peaceful enjoyment of their homes. In other words, if a Restrictive Covenant is subject to more than one reasonable interpretation, then under the liberal-construction rule, the trial court could interpret the Restrictive Covenant in the most restrictive of the reasonable interpretations.

As of the publishing of the third edition of this book, the Texas Supreme Court has still not resolved the continuing conflict over the proper method of interpreting Restrictive Covenants. Until such time as the Texas Supreme Court reconciles the perceived conflict between the common law "strict-construction" rule and the statutory "liberal-construction" rule, the proper manner as to how to interpret, and ultimately enforce, Restrictive Covenants will remain unclear. This can create potential problems for Homeowners Associations seeking to enforce poorly or narrowly drafted Restrictive Covenants in circumstances where the offending conditions of a Lot or Unit differ slightly from the express language of the Restrictive Covenants. Until the proper standard of construction for Restrictive Covenants is determined, Homeowners Associations would be well advised to continue to apply only the "strict-construction" rule, since there is no dispute as to the enforcement of Restrictive Covenants under such interpretation standard. If a Homeowners Association pursues enforcement of a Restrictive Covenant under the "liberal-construction" rule and files a lawsuit against an offending Homeowner, it could run into a trial court judge who believes that Section 202.003's liberal-construction rule does not supplant the common law strict-construction rule. In such event, the judge may rule that the applicable Restrictive Covenant does not prohibit the offending property condition and render a judgment in favor of the Homeowner.

9.3 Parties Who May Enforce Restrictive Covenants

In general, any Homeowner who is bound by a Restrictive Covenant may also enforce such Restrictive Covenant against the other Homeowners subject to the same Restrictive Covenant.[15] In other words, all of the Lot Owners in a Subdivision

---

[15] *See Ski Masters of Texas, LLC v. Heinemeyer*, 269 S.W.3d 662, 668–69 (Tex. App.—San Antonio 2008, no pet.) ("Where an owner of a tract subdivides and sells the subdivided parcels to separate grantees, imposing

Development that are subject to a Declaration have an equal right to enforce any of the provisions in the Declaration against all of the other Lot Owners in such Subdivision Development. The same is true for Unit Owners in a Condominium Development.

In addition to the applicable Homeowners, the Declaration may also authorize other certain individuals or entities to enforce the Restrictive Covenants. For example, if a Declaration establishes a Homeowners Association that does not own any Common Areas or other real property subject to the Declaration, then such Homeowners Association will almost always be granted express authority to enforce the Restrictive Covenants by the Declaration.

In addition to those parties specifically authorized by a Declaration to enforce the Restrictive Covenants, there are several governmental entities that have statutory authority to enforce Restrictive Covenants. For example, if a Subdivision or Condominium Development is located in the boundaries of a municipal utility district, then Chapter 54 of the Texas Water Code authorizes the municipal utility district to enforce Restrictive Covenants applicable to Condominium and Subdivision Developments located within the municipal utility district's boundary area for the purpose of preserving the property value of the real properties that make up its ad valorem tax base.[16]

Finally, Chapter 203 of the Texas Property Code also authorizes the county attorney of a Texas county with a population of more than 200,000 to enforce certain types

---

restrictions on the use of each parcel pursuant to a general plan or scheme of development, each grantee may enforce the restrictions against each other grantee.").

16 Tex. Water Code § 54.237 ("A district may take all actions necessary to enforce a restriction, including the initiation, defense, or intervention in litigation or an administrative proceeding to enjoin or abate the violation of a restriction when, in the reasonable judgment of the board of directors of the district, enforcement of the restriction is necessary to sustain taxable property values in the district."). Ad valorem taxes are taxes that are based on the value of property, such as real property, and are often referred to as "property taxes."

of Restrictive Covenants affecting Subdivision Developments in such county.[17] The types of Restrictive Covenants that may be enforced by an applicable county attorney are those that: (1) affect the use to which real property may be put; (2) fix the distance at which buildings or other structures must be set back from adjacent property, streets, or Lot lines; (3) affect the size of Lots; or (4) affect the size, type, or number of buildings or other structures that may be built on real property.[18]

9.4 Procedural Due Process Requirements for Enforcement of Restrictive Covenants

Before a Texas Homeowners Association may initiate Restrictive Covenant enforcement procedures, it may be required to first comply with certain prerequisite procedures or to provide its Homeowners certain notices. It is not uncommon for a Declaration to require a Homeowners Association to provide a Homeowner notice of an alleged violation of an applicable Restrictive Covenant and an opportunity to cure such violation before the Homeowners Association may initiate enforcement procedures. In addition to any procedural requirements set forth in a Homeowners Association's Declaration or other Governing Documents, Chapter 209 of the Texas Property Code and the Texas Uniform Condominium Act also impose certain procedural due process requirements upon Subdivision and Condominium Associations, respectively, before they may engage in certain Restrictive Covenant enforcement procedures.

---

17 Tex. Prop. Code §§ 203.001–203.003. The Texas counties having a population of more than 200,000 are Bell, Bexar, Brazoria, Cameron, Collin, Dallas, Denton, El Paso, Fort Bend, Galveston, Harris, Hidalgo, Jefferson, Lubbock, McLennan, Montgomery, Nueces, Smith, Tarrant, Travis, Webb, and Williamson Counties. Source: United States Census Bureau, 2010.

18 Tex. Prop. Code § 203.002.

9.4.1 Procedural Due Process Requirements for Enforcement of Restrictive Covenants by a Subdivision Association under Chapter 209

In 2001, the Texas Legislature enacted the Texas Residential Property Owners Protection Act, which is codified at Chapter 209 of the Texas Property Code ("Chapter 209").[19] Chapter 209 took effect January 1, 2002, and applies to all residential Subdivision Developments that are subject to a Declaration that: (1) require Lot Owners in such Subdivision Development to be mandatory members in a Homeowners Association; and (2) authorize such Homeowners Association to levy regular or special Assessments against such Lot Owners.[20] It does not, however, apply to Condominium Developments.[21]

9.4.1 (A) *Chapter 209 Notice Requirement*

One of the primary purposes of Chapter 209 is to impose certain due process requirements on a Subdivision Association before it can suspend a Lot Owner's rights under the Declaration, file a lawsuit against a Lot Owner, assess a fine against a Lot Owner, charge a Lot Owner for property damage, or seek reimbursement of attorneys fees from a Lot Owner for alleged violations of the Subdivision Association's Dedicatory Instruments.[22] More specifically, Chapter 209 requires a Subdivision Association to give a written notice (generally called a "Chapter 209 Notice") to a Lot Owner before the Subdivision Association may: (1) suspend such Lot Owner's right to use a Common Area; (2) file a lawsuit against a Lot Owner (other than a lawsuit to collect an unpaid regular or special Assessment or to foreclose the Subdivision Association's Assessment Lien); (3)

---

[19] Chapter 209 of the Texas Property Code was enacted as a result of public outcry following the foreclosure of a house valued at $150,000 that was owned by Wenonah Blevins, an eighty-three-year-old widow who owed approximately $800 in delinquent Assessments to her Homeowners Association. In fact, the legislative history of Chapter 209 notes that Chapter 209 was "enacted in honor of Wenonah Blevins and may be unofficially referred to as the Wenonah Blevins Residential Property Owners Protection Act." Tex. S.B. 507, 77th Leg., R.S. (2001).

[20] Tex. Prop. Code § 209.003(a)–(b).

[21] Tex. Prop. Code § 209.003(d).

[22] Tex. Prop. Code § 209.006.

charge a Lot Owner for property damage; or (4) levy a fine against a Lot Owner for a violation of the Subdivision Association's Declaration, Bylaws, or Association Rules.[23]

The Chapter 209 Notice must be sent to the Lot Owner by certified mail,[24] and it must:

(1) describe the violation or property damage that is the basis for the suspension action, charge, or fine and state any amount due the Subdivision Association from the Lot Owner, if any;[25]

(2) inform the Lot Owner that he or she:

(a) may request a hearing before the Board of Directors on or before the thirtieth (30th) day after the date the Chapter 209 Notice was mailed to the Lot Owner;[26] and

(b) may have special rights or relief related to the enforcement action under federal law, including the Servicemembers Civil Relief

---

23 Tex. Prop. Code § 209.006(a). It is important to note that a Subdivision Association is not required to give a Lot Owner a Chapter 209 Notice for a restrictive covenant violation for which the Lot Owner has been previously given a Chapter 209 Notice and the opportunity to exercise any rights available under Section 209.006 of the Texas Property Code in the preceding six months. Tex. Prop. Code § 209.006(a). Accordingly, if a Lot Owner was already given a Chapter 209 Notice for a restrictive covenant violation, the Subdivision Association is not required to send the Lot Owner an additional Chapter 209 Notice before suspending a Lot Owner's rights under the Declaration, assessing a fine against a Lot Owner, or charging a Lot Owner for property damage for a reoccurrence or continuation of the same restrictive covenant violation committed during the six-month period following the date of such prior Chapter 209 Notice.

24 Tex. Prop. Code § 209.006(a). It is important to note that prior to 2015, Section 209.006 of the Texas Property Code required the Chapter 209 Notice to be sent to a Lot Owner by certified mail, return receipt requested. In 2015, the Texas Legislature amended Section 209.006(a) to state that the Chapter 209 Notice must be sent to a Lot Owner by "certified mail" (thereby deleting the requirement that it include a return receipt request), but amended Section 209.006(b) to state that the Chapter 209 Notice must be sent to a Lot Owner by "verified mail." Tex. Prop. Code §§ 209.006(a)–(b). Chapter 209 defines "verified mail" as any method of mailing for which evidence of mailing is provided by the United States Postal Service or a common carrier. Tex. Prop. Code § 209.002(13). Such definition of verified mail would include certified mail, as well as other methods of mailing for which evidence of mailing is provided by the United States Postal Service or a common carrier. Based on the conflicting requirements imposed by the 2015 amendments to Section 209.006, Texas Subdivision Associations should send Chapter 209 Notices to Lot Owners by certified mail, which would satisfy both the certified mail and verified mail requirements under Section 209.006.

25 Tex. Prop. Code § 209.006(b)(1).

26 Tex. Prop. Code § 209.006(b)(2)(B).

Act (50 U.S.C. § 3901 et seq.), if the Lot Owner is serving on active military duty;[27] and

(3) if the restrictive covenant violation is of a "curable nature"[28] and does not pose a "threat to public health or safety,"[29] then the Chapter 209 Notice must also:

(a) inform the Lot Owner that he or she is entitled to a reasonable period to cure the violation and avoid the fine or suspension;[30] and

(b) specify the date by which the Lot Owner must cure the violation in order to avoid the fine.[31]

---

27 Tex. Prop. Code § 209.006(b)(2)(C).

28 Tex. Prop. Code § 209.006(b)(2)(A). Section 209.006 does not expressly define what is considered to be a restrictive covenant violation of a "curable nature," but it does define what is considered a restrictive covenant violation of an "uncurable nature." For purposes of Section 209.006, a restrictive covenant violation is considered uncurable if the violation has occurred but is not a continuous action or a condition capable of being remedied by affirmative action. Tex. Prop. Code § 209.006(g). By deduction, a restrictive covenant violation would be of a curable nature if the violation is a continuous action or a condition capable of being remedied by affirmative action. For illustrative purposes, Section 209.006 identifies the following actions and conditions as examples of actions and conditions that are considered uncurable: (1) shooting fireworks; (2) an act constituting a threat to health or safety; (3) a noise violation that is not ongoing; (4) property damage, including the removal or alteration of landscape; and (5) holding a garage sale or other event prohibited by a Dedicatory Instrument. Tex. Prop. Code § 209.006(h). In addition, Section 209.006 identifies the following actions and conditions as examples of actions and conditions that are considered curable: (1) a parking violation; (2) a maintenance violation; (3) the failure to construct improvements or modifications in accordance with approved plans and specifications; and (4) an ongoing noise violation such as a barking dog. Tex. Prop. Code § 209.006(i). It is also important to note that Section 209.006 expressly states that the nonrepetition of a one-time restrictive covenant violation or other restrictive covenant violation that is not ongoing (i.e., a restrictive covenant violation of a uncurable nature) is not considered an adequate remedy. Tex. Prop. Code § 209.006(g). In other words, simply not repeating a one-time restrictive covenant violation does not cure the violation.

29 Tex. Prop. Code § 209.006(b)(2)(A). For purposes of Section 209.006, a restrictive covenant violation is considered a threat to public health or safety if the violation could materially affect the physical health or safety of an ordinary resident. Tex. Prop. Code § 209.006(f).

30 Tex. Prop. Code § 209.006(b)(2)(A).

31 Tex. Prop. Code § 209.006(b)(3). The cure date specified in the Chapter 209 Notice must provide a reasonable period of time for the Lot Owner to cure the restrictive covenant violation(s) of a curable nature. Tex. Prop. Code § 209.006(c). In addition, if the Lot Owner cures such restrictive covenant violation before the expiration of the cure date specified in the Chapter 209 Notice, a fine may not be assessed for the violation. Tex. Prop. Code § 209.006(e).

9.4.1 (B) *Chapter 209 Hearing Requirement*

As noted in the previous subchapter, a Chapter 209 Notice must inform a Lot Owner that he or she may request a hearing before the Subdivision Association's Board of Directors. The hearing before the Board of Directors that a Lot Owner has a right to request is generally referred to as a "Chapter 209 Hearing," and the purpose of such hearing is to provide an opportunity and a forum for a Lot Owner to meet with the Board of Directors to discuss and verify facts and attempt to amicably resolve the dispute before the Subdivision Association initiates more substantial enforcement procedures.[32] A Chapter 209 Hearing may be held before the Board of Directors or a committee appointed by the Board of Directors for such purpose, but if it is to be held before a designated committee, then the Chapter 209 Notice must also state that the Lot Owner has the right to appeal the decision of the designated committee to the Board of Directors by written notice to the Board of Directors.[33]

If a Chapter 209 Hearing is requested timely by a Lot Owner, then the Subdivision Association must hold a hearing before the Board of Directors, or a designated committee, within thirty (30) days from the date of the Subdivision Association's receipt of the Lot Owner's request.[34] The Subdivision Association must also notify the Lot Owner of the date, time, and place of the hearing at least ten (10) days before the date of the hearing.[35] If a postponement of the original Chapter 209 Hearing date is requested by either the Board of Directors or the Lot Owner, then the hearing date must be rescheduled for a new date within ten (10) days of the original hearing date.[36] Any additional requests for postponement of the Chapter 209 Hearing are not required to be granted, but the parties

32 *See generally*, Tex. Prop. Code §§ 209.006–209.007.

33 Tex. Prop. Code § 209.007(b).

34 Tex. Prop. Code § 209.007(a)–(b).

35 Tex. Prop. Code § 209.007(c).

36 Tex. Prop. Code § 209.007(c).

may reschedule the hearing date if both the Subdivision Association and Lot Owner agree to do so.[37]

The Chapter 209 Hearing should be attended by at least a quorum of the Board of Directors. The Lot Owner and/or the Board of Directors may make an audio recording of a Chapter 209 Hearing.[38] The Lot Owner may also bring legal representation with him or her. The Lot Owner, however, is not required to be present in order to hold a Chapter 209 Hearing. Thus, in the event a Lot Owner requests a Chapter 209 Hearing, but then fails to appear for the hearing, the Board of Directors should conduct the hearing without the Lot Owner's attendance or participation.

9.4.1 (C) *Exceptions to the Chapter 209 Notice and Hearing Requirements*

There are two exceptions to the Chapter 209 Notice and Hearing procedure requirements. First, a Subdivision Association is not required to provide a Lot Owner with a Chapter 209 Notice or conduct a Chapter 209 Hearing prior to filing: (1) a lawsuit against a Lot Owner in which the Subdivision Association is seeking a temporary restraining order or temporary injunction; or (2) a lawsuit to judicially foreclose its Assessment Lien.[39] In both cases, however, following the filing of the lawsuit, the Subdivision Association or the defendant–Lot Owner may file a motion to compel mediation of the lawsuit.[40]

Second, the Chapter 209 Notice and Hearing procedure does not apply to a Homeowners Association's temporary suspension of a Lot Owner's right to use Common Areas if the temporary suspension is the result of a violation that occurred in a Common Area and involved a significant and immediate risk of harm to others in the Subdivision

---

37 Tex. Prop. Code § 209.007(c).

38 Tex. Prop. Code § 209.007(c).

39 Tex. Prop. Code § 209.007(d).

40 Tex. Prop. Code § 209.007(d).

Development.[41] Such temporary suspension, however, is only effective until the Board of Directors makes a final determination on the suspension action after complying with the Chapter 209 Notice and Hearing procedure.[42] In other words, a Subdivision Association may only suspend a Lot Owner's right to use Common Areas under such circumstance until a Chapter 209 Notice is delivered to the Lot Owner and the Board of Directors makes a final determination on such suspension action at or after a Chapter 209 Hearing, if a hearing is timely requested by the Lot Owner.

9.4.2 Procedural Due Process Requirements for Enforcement of Restrictive Covenants by a Condominium Association under the Texas Uniform Condominium Act

Texas Condominium Associations have significantly less procedural due process requirements for enforcement of Restrictive Covenants than do Subdivision Associations. Before a Condominium Association may charge a Unit Owner for property damage for which the Unit Owner is liable or levy a fine against a Unit Owner for violation of the Declaration, Bylaws, or Condominium Association Rules, it must give the Unit Owner a written notice that:

(1) describes the violation or property damage and states the amount of the proposed fine or damage charge;[43]

(2) states that not later than the thirtieth (30th) day after the date of such notice, the Unit Owner may request a hearing before the Board of Directors to contest the fine or damage charge;[44] and

(3) allows the Unit Owner a reasonable time, by a specified date, to cure the violation and avoid the fine unless the Unit Owner was given notice and

---

41 Tex. Prop. Code § 209.007(d).

42 Tex. Prop. Code § 209.007(d).

43 Tex. Prop. Code § 82.102(d) (1).

44 Tex. Prop. Code § 82.102(d) (2).

a reasonable opportunity to cure a similar violation within the preceding twelve (12) months.[45]

In addition, a Condominium Association may send such written notice to a Unit Owner by mail or may deliver such written notice to the Unit Owner by simply giving a copy of such notice to any occupant of such Unit Owner's Unit.[46] Finally, after a Condominium Association assesses a fine or charge for damage against a Unit Owner, it must give such Unit Owner notice of the assessed fine or damage charge no later than the thirtieth (30th) day after the date such fine or damage charge is assessed.[47]

Unlike Subdivision Associations subject to Chapter 209 of the Texas Property Code, Condominium Associations are not required to provide written notice and an opportunity for a hearing to Unit Owners prior to suspending a Unit Owner's right to use Common Element amenities or filing a lawsuit against a Unit Owner to enforce his or her compliance with the applicable Restrictive Covenants. In addition, the Texas Uniform Condominium Act does not impose any due process notice requirement before a Condominium Association may impose liability against a Unit Owner for attorneys fees incurred by a Condominium Association in enforcing a Restrictive Covenant against a Unit Owner. Finally, while the Texas Uniform Condominium Act does require a Condominium Association to provide a Unit Owner written notice and an opportunity for a hearing before charging such Unit Owner for property damage or assessing a fine against such Unit Owner, the Texas Uniform Condominium Act does not impose any requirements on when the hearing must be conducted or require a postponement of a scheduled hearing if a Unit Owner requests one.

---

45 Tex. Prop. Code § 82.102(d) (3).

46 Tex. Prop. Code § 82.102(e).

47 Tex. Prop. Code § 82.102(e).

9.5 Enforcement of Restrictive Covenants by Non-Judicial Procedures: Self-Help Remedies and Assessment of Fines

Although the most common method of Restrictive Covenant enforcement is by judicial proceeding (which is discussed in the next subchapter), two common methods of enforcing Restrictive Covenants without filing a lawsuit may be available to a Homeowners Association under its Declaration. The first method consists of remediation of a restrictive covenant violation through the exercise of "Self-Help Remedies," and the second method involves the assessment of fines against an offending Homeowner.

9.5.1 Remediation of a Restrictive Covenant Violation by Exercise of Self-Help Remedies

"Self-Help Remedies" refer to those provisions within a Declaration that authorize the Homeowners Association to take certain actions to cure an existing violation of a Restrictive Covenant itself if an offending Homeowner refuses to do it. In most cases, the Declaration provision will also authorize the Homeowners Association to assess the costs of curing the violation against the offending Homeowner in the same or a similar manner as Assessments. For example, a Declaration may provide that if a Homeowner fails to maintain his or her property in an attractive and healthy manner, then the Homeowners Association may maintain the Homeowner's property and assess the cost of such maintenance against the Homeowner.

There is no inherent right or ability of a Homeowners Association to exercise Self-Help Remedies to cure a violation of a Restrictive Covenant. Self-Help Remedies must be expressly authorized in the Declaration. In other words, if a Homeowners Association's Declaration does not expressly authorize the Homeowners Association to take a certain action to cure a Homeowner's violation of the Restrictive Covenants, then the Homeowners Association has no authority to take such action.

In addition, the exercise of a Self-Help Remedy must be done in compliance with any procedural requirements or other conditions specified by the Declaration. For example, a Declaration will commonly require some form of notice be given to the Homeowner in advance of exercising a Self-Help Remedy. In such event, it is very important that the Homeowners Association strictly comply with all necessary procedures and notice requirements before exercising the Self-Help Remedy.

Finally, Texas Homeowners Associations should exercise caution in using Self-Help Remedies. There is no inherent right of a Homeowners Association to enter upon a Homeowner's property without such Homeowner's permission, and an unauthorized entry upon another's real property constitutes trespass under Texas law. Under a Declaration that provides for Self-Help Remedies, the existence of a restrictive covenant violation establishes the authority of the Homeowners Association to enter upon the Homeowner's property, without his or her express permission, for the purpose of performing the Self-Help Remedy. Under such circumstances, the Homeowners Association's entry upon the Homeowner's property is not considered to be a trespass because the Homeowner's violation of the Restrictive Covenant triggers the Homeowners Association's contractual authority under the Declaration to enter upon the Homeowner's Lot or Unit for the purpose of curing the violation.

If after the Homeowners Association enters upon the Homeowner's property it is later determined that the Homeowner was not actually in violation of the Restrictive Covenant, then the Homeowners Association's entry upon the Homeowner's property will have been without authority and may constitute trespassing. In such event, not only would the Homeowners Association not be able to assess the costs of curing the purported violation against the Homeowner, but the Homeowners Association may also be liable for trespass and any resulting damages to the Homeowner or his or her property. For such reasons, Self-Help Remedies should only be exercised when the offending property condition is a clear violation of the applicable Restrictive Covenant giving rise to the Self-Help Remedy. If it is uncertain whether the Homeowner's property condition or actions are a clear violation of the Restrictive Covenant, the Homeowners Association should not exercise an applicable Self-Help Remedy.

9.5.2 Assessment of Fines against a Homeowner for Violation of a Restrictive Covenant

Another non-judicial method for enforcement of Restrictive Covenants by a Homeowners Association is the assessment of fines against a Homeowner who refuses to cure or stop repeating a violation of the Homeowners Association's Declaration, Bylaws, or Association Rules. A Texas Homeowners Association, however, does not have an inherent power or authority to fine Homeowners and/or residents for violations of the community's Governing Documents. The power or authority of a Homeowners Association to adopt a fining policy and/or to assess fines must be found in its Governing Documents or state law. In addition, before a Homeowners Association can assess a fine, it must first comply with the applicable due process requirements and restrictions imposed by its Governing Documents and either the Texas Uniform Condominium Act (if it is a Condominium Association) or Chapter 209 of the Texas Property Code (if it is a Subdivision Association), as is applicable.

9.5.2 (A) *Assessment of Fines by a Condominium Association*

In addition to any express authority to assess fines under a Condominium Association's Declaration, the Texas Uniform Condominium Act expressly authorizes all Texas Condominium Associations to assess fines against Unit Owners for violations of the Declaration, Bylaws, or Association Rules.[48] Thus, all Texas Condominium Associations have statutory authority to assess fines against Unit Owners, whether or not it is so stated in their Declaration.

48 Tex. Prop. Code § 82.102(a) (12).

Before a Condominium Association may levy a fine against a Unit Owner for violation of its Declaration, Bylaws, or Association Rules, the Condominium Association must give the Unit Owner a written notice that:

(1) states the amount of the proposed fine;[49]

(2) states that no later than the thirtieth (30th) day after the date of the notice, the Unit Owner may request a hearing before the Board of Directors to contest the fine;[50] and

(3) allows the Unit Owner a reasonable time, by a specified date, to cure the violation and avoid the fine unless the Unit Owner was given notice and a reasonable opportunity to cure a similar violation within the preceding twelve months.[51]

In addition, a Condominium Association must also give a Unit Owner written notice of a levied fine or damage charge to the Unit Owner no later than the thirtieth (30th) day after the date a fine or damage charge is levied against a Unit Owner.[52]

Finally, it is also important to note that the term "Assessment" under the Texas Uniform Condominium Act includes fines, attorneys fees, and any other amount owed to the Condominium Association by the Unit Owner or levied against the Unit by the Condominium Association.[53] As a result, the payment of fines levied by a Condominium Association is secured by its Assessment Lien. A Condominium Association, however, may not foreclose its Assessment Lien against a Unit if the unpaid amounts owed to a Condominium Association by the Unit Owner consist solely of fines.[54]

---

[49] Tex. Prop. Code § 82.102(d) (1).

[50] Tex. Prop. Code § 82.102(d) (2).

[51] Tex. Prop. Code § 82.102(d) (3).

[52] Tex. Prop. Code § 82.102(e).

[53] Tex. Prop. Code § 82.113(a).

[54] Tex. Prop. Code § 82.113(e).

9.5.2 (B) *Assessment of Fines by a Subdivision Association*

Unlike Condominium Associations, Texas Subdivision Associations have no statutory authority to assess fines against Lot Owners for violation of a Declaration, Bylaws, or Association Rules, and any such authority to levy fines must be expressly authorized by its Governing Documents. In addition, if a Subdivision Association is authorized to levy fines against a Lot Owner, then it must comply with the due process procedures mandated by its Governing Documents and Chapter 209 of the Texas Property Code.

Pursuant to Chapter 209, before a Subdivision Association may levy fines against a Lot Owner, the Subdivision Association must send a Chapter 209 Notice to the Lot Owner.[55] The Chapter 209 Notice must be sent to the Lot Owner by certified mail,[56] and it must:

(1) describe the violation or property damage that is the basis for the fine and state any amount due the Subdivision Association from the Lot Owner;[57]

---

[55] Tex. Prop. Code § 209.006(a). It is important to note that a Subdivision Association is not required to give a Lot Owner a Chapter 209 Notice for a restrictive covenant violation for which the Lot Owner has been previously given a Chapter 209 Notice and the opportunity to exercise any rights available under Section 209.006 of the Texas Property Code in the preceding six months. Tex. Prop. Code § 209.006(a). Accordingly, if a Lot Owner was already given a Chapter 209 Notice for a restrictive covenant violation, the Subdivision Association is not required to send the Lot Owner an additional Chapter 209 Notice before assessing a fine for a reoccurrence or continuation of the same restrictive covenant violation committed during the six-month period following the date of such prior Chapter 209 Notice.

[56] Tex. Prop. Code § 209.006(a). It is important to note that prior to 2015, Section 209.006 of the Texas Property Code required the Chapter 209 Notice to be sent to a Lot Owner by certified mail, return receipt requested. In 2015, the Texas Legislature amended Section 209.006(a) to state that the Chapter 209 Notice must be sent to a Lot Owner by "certified mail" (thereby deleting the requirement that it include a return receipt request), but amended Section 209.006(b) to state that the Chapter 209 Notice must be sent to a Lot Owner by "verified mail." Tex. Prop. Code §§ 209.006(a)–(b). Chapter 209 defines "verified mail" as any method of mailing for which evidence of mailing is provided by the United States Postal Service or a common carrier. Tex. Prop. Code § 209.002(13). Such definition of verified mail would include certified mail, as well as other methods of mailing for which evidence of mailing is provided by the United States Postal Service or a common carrier. Based on the conflicting requirements imposed by the 2015 amendments to Section 209.006, Texas Subdivision Associations should send Chapter 209 Notices to Lot Owners by certified mail, which would satisfy both the certified mail and verified mail requirements under Section 209.006.

[57] Tex. Prop. Code § 209.006(b)(1).

(2) inform the Lot Owner that he or she:

(a) may request a hearing before the Board of Directors on or before the thirtieth (30th) day after the date the Chapter 209 Notice was mailed to the Lot Owner;[58] and

(b) may have special rights or relief related to the enforcement action under federal law, including the Servicemembers Civil Relief Act (50 U.S.C. § 3901 et seq.), if the Lot Owner is serving on active military duty;[59] and

(3) if the restrictive covenant violation is of a "curable nature"[60] and does not pose a "threat to public health or safety,"[61] the Chapter 209 Notice must also:

(a) inform the Lot Owner that he or she is entitled to a reasonable period to cure the violation and avoid the fine;[62] and

---

[58] Tex. Prop. Code § 209.006(b)(2)(B).

[59] Tex. Prop. Code § 209.006(b)(2)(C).

[60] Tex. Prop. Code § 209.006(b)(2)(A). Section 209.006 does not expressly define what is considered to be a restrictive covenant violation of a "curable nature," but it does define what is considered a restrictive covenant violation of an "uncurable nature." For purposes of Section 209.006, a restrictive covenant violation is considered uncurable if the violation has occurred but is not a continuous action or a condition capable of being remedied by affirmative action. Tex. Prop. Code § 209.006(g). By deduction, a restrictive covenant violation would be of a curable nature if the violation is a continuous action or a condition capable of being remedied by affirmative action. For illustrative purposes, Section 209.006 identifies the following actions and conditions as examples of actions and conditions that are considered uncurable: (1) shooting fireworks; (2) an act constituting a threat to health or safety; (3) a noise violation that is not ongoing; (4) property damage, including the removal or alteration of landscape; and (5) holding a garage sale or other event prohibited by a Dedicatory Instrument. Tex. Prop. Code § 209.006(h). In addition, Section 209.006 identifies the following actions and conditions as examples of actions and conditions that are considered curable: (1) a parking violation; (2) a maintenance violation; (3) the failure to construct improvements or modifications in accordance with approved plans and specifications; and (4) an ongoing noise violation such as a barking dog. Tex. Prop. Code § 209.006(i). It is also important to note, Section 209.006 expressly states that the nonrepetition of a one-time restrictive covenant violation or other restrictive covenant violation that is not ongoing (i.e., a restrictive covenant violation of a uncurable nature) is not considered an adequate remedy. Tex. Prop. Code § 209.006(g). In other words, simply not repeating a one-time restrictive covenant violation does not cure the violation.

[61] Tex. Prop. Code § 209.006(b)(2)(A). For purposes of Section 209.006, a restrictive covenant violation is considered a threat to public health or safety if the violation could materially affect the physical health or safety of an ordinary resident. Tex. Prop. Code § 209.006(f).

[62] Tex. Prop. Code § 209.006(b)(2)(A).

(b) specify the date by which the Lot Owner must cure the violation in order to avoid the fine.[63]

In addition, unless expressly provided in the Subdivision Association's Declaration, fines assessed by a Subdivision Association are not considered "Assessments" and are not secured by the Subdivision Association's Assessment Lien. Even if the Declaration for a Subdivision Association provides that payment of fines assessed against its Lot Owners are secured by the Subdivision Association's Assessment Lien, Chapter 209 still prohibits a Subdivision Association from foreclosing its Assessment Lien against a Lot if the amount owed to the Subdivision Association by the Lot Owner consists solely of: (1) fines assessed by the Subdivision Association; or (2) attorneys fees incurred by the Subdivision Association solely associated with fines assessed by the Subdivision Association.[64]

9.6 Enforcement of Restrictive Covenants by Judicial Proceeding

The most common method of enforcement of a Restrictive Covenant is by judicial enforcement, in which the Homeowners Association files a civil lawsuit against the offending Homeowner for violation of a Restrictive Covenant. A lawsuit to enforce Restrictive Covenants may be filed in a Texas justice court, county court, or district court in the county in which the Homeowner's property is located.[65] Notwithstanding, most

63 Tex. Prop. Code § 209.006(b)(3). The cure date specified in the Chapter 209 Notice must provide a reasonable period of time for the Lot Owner to cure the restrictive covenant violation(s) of a curable nature. Tex. Prop. Code § 209.006(c). In addition, if the Lot Owner cures such restrictive covenant violation before the expiration of the cure date specified in the Chapter 209 Notice, a fine may not be assessed for the violation. Tex. Prop. Code § 209.006(e).

64 Tex. Prop. Code § 209.009.

65 A Texas justice court, however, has limited jurisdiction regarding Restrictive Covenant enforcement lawsuits. A Texas justice court's subject-matter jurisdiction is restricted to lawsuits concerning enforcement of Restrictive Covenants applicable to a Subdivision Development that do not concern a structural change to a dwelling. Tex. Gov't Code § 27.034(a). The jurisdiction of a justice court in such regard is concurrent with the jurisdiction of a Texas district court. Tex. Gov't Code § 27.034(d).

Restrictive Covenant lawsuits are filed in the district or county court because of the nature of the issues and the relief being sought by the Homeowners Association.[66]

A Restrictive Covenant enforcement lawsuit is prosecuted in a similar manner as a lawsuit to enforce the terms of a contract. Unlike a traditional breach of contract lawsuit, where the plaintiff seeks a recovery of compensable monetary damages caused by the defendant's breach, in a Restrictive Covenant enforcement lawsuit, the Homeowners Association seeks enforcement of the Restrictive Covenant by "specific performance."[67] Specific performance is a form of remedial injunctive relief in which a court orders a party that is in breach of its contractual obligations to perform or comply with such contractual obligations. In the context of a Restrictive Covenant enforcement lawsuit, specific performance takes the form of a permanent injunction rendered by the court in which it orders the defendant-Homeowner to do or cease from doing such acts or omissions that are resulting in such Homeowner's violation of the applicable Restrictive Covenant.[68] Unlike a Restrictive Covenant, an injunction does not "run with the land"; rather, an injunction is personal to the defendant-Homeowner and is typically only enforceable for so long as such Homeowner owns the subject property.

If a Homeowners Association prevails at a trial on the merits of a Restrictive Covenant enforcement lawsuit, then the court should order the defendant-Homeowner permanently enjoined from continuing the conduct or activity complained of. If thereafter the defendant-Homeowner fails to comply with the court's permanent injunction, then such defendant-Homeowner will be considered to be in contempt of a court-ordered

---

[66] While Texas justice courts have limited jurisdiction to hear Restrictive Covenant enforcement lawsuits, they do not have authority to grant a writ of injunction, which is the most common relief sought in a Restrictive Covenant enforcement lawsuit. Tex. Gov't Code § 27.034(j).

[67] "Specific performance" is a breach of contract remedy that requires exact performance of a contract or contractual obligation in the specific form in which it was made, or according to the precise terms agreed upon. *Black's Law Dictionary* 1138 (6th ed. 1990).

[68] An "injunction" is a court order prohibiting someone from doing some specified act or commanding someone to do a specific affirmative act or thing. *Black's Law Dictionary* 784 (6th ed. 1990).

injunction. "Contempt of court," as it is generally called, is a pseudo-criminal offense that can be punished by both civil fines and incarceration.[69]

In addition to injunctive relief, a court may also assess civil damages against a defendant-Homeowner in a Restrictive Covenant enforcement lawsuit. Chapter 202 of the Texas Property Code authorizes a court in a Restrictive Covenant enforcement lawsuit to assess civil damages against a defendant-Homeowner in an amount not to exceed $200 for each day of the violation.[70]

9.7 Affirmative Defenses to Judicial Enforcement of Restrictive Covenants: Statute of Limitations and Abandonment and Waiver

When a Homeowners Association pursues judicial enforcement of a Restrictive Covenant, the offending Homeowner may raise an affirmative defense to the legal ability of the Homeowners Association to enforce the Restrictive Covenant at issue. An "affirmative defense" is a defense that seeks to establish a reason independent of the merits of the plaintiff's claims for why the plaintiff in a lawsuit should not prevail, and it is considered to be a defense of avoidance of liability, rather than a defense in denial of liability.[71] The two most common affirmative defenses that arise in Restrictive Covenant enforcement lawsuits are the statute of limitations and abandonment and waiver.

---

69 *See* Tex. Gov't Code §§ 21.001–21.002.

70 Tex. Prop. Code § 202.004(c). Although called "civil damages" under Chapter 202, such damages are considered to be punitive damages by Texas appellate courts because damages assessed under Chapter 202 are unrelated to the type or extent of any injury or harm caused by the restrictive covenant violation. *See Sanchez v. Southampton Civic Club, Inc.*, 367 S.W.3d 429, 436 (Tex. App.—Houston [14th Dist.] 2012, no pet.); *Uptegraph v. Sandalwood Civic Club*, 312 S.W.3d 918, 937 (Tex. App.—Houston [1st Dist.] 2010, no pet.) (holding that civil damages awarded by a trial court under Chapter 202 are not limited to compensation for actual harm or injury from the violation of a restrictive covenant); *but see*, *KBG Investments, LLC v. Greenspont Property Owners' Ass'n, Inc.*, No. 14–14–00484–CV, slip op. at 4, 2015 WL 5770828, at*9 (Tex. App.—Houston [14th Dist.] October 1, 2015, no. pet. h.) (holding that "civil damages" under Chapter 202 constitute exemplary damages that are subject to the provisions of Chapter 41 of the Texas Civil Practice and Remedies Code and cannot be awarded by a trial court without proof of actual damages).

71 *See In re C.M.*, 996 S.W.2d 269, 270 (Tex. App.—Houston [1st Dist.] 1999, no pet.); *Great Am. Prods. v. Permabond Int'l*, 94 S.W.3d 675, 683 (Tex. App.—Austin 2002, pet. denied).

9.7.1 Statute of Limitations

The "Statute of Limitations" is a statutorily created time period within which a party must bring a lawsuit against another party for an existing cause of action. The Statute of Limitations is designed to encourage a plaintiff to bring a lawsuit within a limited period of time and to timely notify the defendant of the existence of the claim so the defendant may prepare its defense and preserve relevant evidence.[72] To "bring suit" within an applicable Statute of Limitations, the plaintiff must both file suit within the appropriate time period and use due diligence to serve the defendant with process.[73] As a general rule, a cause of action accrues and the Statute of Limitations begins to run when facts come into existence that authorize a party to seek a judicial remedy.[74] In most circumstances, a cause of action accrues when a wrongful act causes a legal injury, regardless of when the plaintiff learns of such injury or whether all resulting damages have yet to have occurred.[75]

The Statute of Limitations period to bring a lawsuit to enforce a Restrictive Covenant is four (4) years from the date the cause of action for breach of the Restrictive Covenant accrues.[76] A cause of action for breach of a Restrictive Covenant accrues upon the actual breach of the Restrictive Covenant by the Homeowner.[77] If a lawsuit to enforce a Restrictive Covenant is not brought within four (4) years of the Homeowner breaching such Restrictive Covenant, then such cause of action will be "time-barred" by the Statute

---

72 *See Broom v. MacMaster*, 992 S.W.2d 659, 664 (Tex. App.—Dallas 1999, no pet.).

73 *See Gant v. DeLeon*, 786 S.W.2d 259, 260 (Tex. 1990).

74 *See Provident Life & Accident Ins. Co. v. Knott*, 128 S.W.3d 211, 221 (Tex. 2003).

75 *See Provident Life & Accident Ins. Co. v. Knott*, 128 S.W.3d 211, 221 (Tex. 2003).

76 *See* Tex. Civ. Prac. & Rem. Code § 16.051; *Buzbee v. Castlewood Civic Club, et al.*, 737 S.W.2d 366, 368 (Tex. App.—Houston [14th Dist.] 1985, no writ).

77 *See Colton v. Silsbee State Bank*, 952 S.W.2d 625, 630 (Tex. App.—Beaumont 1997, no writ).

of Limitations, and the Homeowners Association will not be able to enforce the Restrictive Covenant against such Homeowner as to that specific violation.[78]

If, however, the existence of a restrictive covenant violation is undiscoverable or was fraudulently concealed, then the four-year Statute of Limitations period will not start running until the violation is, or reasonably should have been, discovered.[79] This circumstance is referred to as the "Discovery Rule," and it is applicable in "cases where the nature of the injury incurred is inherently undiscoverable and the evidence of injury is objectively verifiable."[80] An injury is considered to be inherently undiscoverable if, by its nature, it is unlikely to be discovered within the prescribed Statute of Limitations period despite due diligence.[81] In the context of Restrictive Covenant enforcement, the Discovery Rule may become applicable if a restrictive covenant violation is inherently undiscoverable because it is shielded from public view, such as behind a privacy fence. In such circumstances, the accrual of the cause of action for breach of the Restrictive Covenant, which starts the running of the four-year Statute of Limitations period, is deferred until the Homeowners Association knows of, or in the exercise of reasonable diligence should have known of, the restrictive covenant violation.[82] In such event, a lawsuit to enforce the Restrictive Covenant must be brought within four (4) years of the date the Homeowners Association knew of, or should have reasonably known of, such restrictive covenant violation.[83]

---

78 *See Hidden Valley Civic Club v. Brown*, 702 S.W.2d 665, 668 (Tex. App.—Houston [14th Dist.] 1985, no writ); *Schoenhals v. Close*, 451 S.W.2d 597, 599 (Tex. Civ. App.—Amarillo 1970, no writ).

79 *See Park v. Baxter*, 572 S.W.2d 794, 795 (Tex. Civ. App.—Tyler 1978, writ ref'd n.r.e.).

80 *See Computer Assocs. Int'l, Inc. v. Altai, Inc.*, 918 S.W.2d 453, 455–56 (Tex. 1996).

81 *Wagner & Brown, Ltd. v. Horwood*, 58 S.W.3d 732, 734–35 (Tex. 2001).

82 *See Computer Assocs. Int'l, Inc. v. Altai, Inc.*, 918 S.W.2d 453, 455–56 (Tex. 1996); *Salinas v. Gary Pools, Inc.*, 31 S.W.3d 333, 336 (Tex. App.—San Antonio 2000, no pet.).

83 *See Computer Assocs. Int'l, Inc. v. Altai, Inc.*, 918 S.W.2d 453, 455-56 (Tex. 1996); *Salinas v. Gary Pools, Inc.*, 31 S.W.3d 333, 336 (Tex. App.—San Antonio 2000, no pet.).

A second circumstance that delays commencement of the Statute of Limitations period is known as the "Doctrine of Fraudulent Concealment."[84] Similar to the Discovery Rule, the Doctrine of Fraudulent Concealment also defers the accrual of a cause of action until the plaintiff discovers, or should have discovered, the deceitful conduct or facts giving rise to the cause of action.[85] The Fraudulent Concealment Doctrine defers the accrual of a cause of action because "a person cannot be permitted to avoid liability for his actions by deceitfully concealing wrongdoing until limitations have run."[86] For the Doctrine of Fraudulent Concealment to apply, a Homeowners Association must prove that the defendant-Homeowner: (1) had actual knowledge of the restrictive covenant violation; (2) intended to conceal the restrictive covenant violation; and (3) did conceal the restrictive covenant violation from the Homeowners Association and the other Homeowners in the community.[87]

9.7.2 Abandonment and Waiver

The other common affirmative defense raised by Homeowners in Restrictive Covenant enforcement lawsuits is that the applicable Restrictive Covenant has been abandoned and its enforcement waived. The Supreme Court of Texas declared more than fifty years ago that a court may refuse to enforce a Restrictive Covenant "because of the acquiescence of the lot owners in such substantial violations within the restricted area as to amount to an abandonment of the covenant or a waiver of the right to enforce it."[88] In the context of Restrictive Covenants, the concepts of abandonment and waiver go hand in hand, and a finding that a Restrictive Covenant has been abandoned is essentially the

---

[84] Fraudulent concealment is defined as the hiding or suppression of a material fact or circumstance which a party is legally or morally bound to disclose. *Black's Law Dictionary* 662 (6th ed. 1990).

[85] *See Earle v. Ratliff*, 998 S.W.2d 882, 888 (Tex. 1999).

[86] *See S.V. v. R.V.*, 933 S.W.2d 1, 6 (Tex. 1996).

[87] *See Shah v. Moss*, 67 S.W.3d 836, 841 (Tex. 2001).

[88] *Cowling v. Colligan*, 312 S.W.2d 943, 945 (Tex. 1958).

same, and must have the same evidentiary support, as a finding that the right to enforce the Restrictive Covenant has been waived.[89]

9.7.2 (A) *Establishment of Abandonment and Waiver*

In order to establish abandonment or waiver, the offending Homeowner bears the burden of proving that the other Homeowners in the applicable Subdivision or Condominium Development and/or the Homeowners Association have voluntarily and intentionally relinquished their right to enforce the applicable Restrictive Covenant.[90] To satisfy this burden, the offending Homeowner must prove that the violations then existing were so extensive and material as to lead an "average person" to reasonably conclude that the subject Restrictive Covenant had been abandoned.[91] Among the factors to be considered by the "average person" are the number, nature, and severity of the then-existing violations, any prior acts of enforcement of the Restrictive Covenant, and whether it is still possible to realize a substantial degree of the benefits intended through the Restrictive Covenant.[92] The failure of a Homeowners Association or other Homeowners

---

[89] *See, e.g., Jim Rutherford Invs., Inc. v. Terramar Beach Cmty. Ass'n*, 25 S.W.3d 845, 852 (Tex. App.—Houston [14th Dist.] 2000, pet. denied) ("[T]o establish . . . waiver in a deed restriction case, the non-conforming user must prove that the violations then existing are so great as to lead the average man to [reasonably] conclude [that] the restriction in question [has] been abandoned and its enforcement waived."); *Pebble Beach Prop. Owners' Ass'n v. Sherer*, 2 S.W.3d 283, 289–90 (Tex. App.—San Antonio 1999, pet. denied) ("To satisfy [the] burden [for proving waiver], Sherer must prove the violations then existing were so extensive and material as to reasonably lead to the conclusion that the restrictions had been abandoned."); *Traeger v. Lorenz*, 749 S.W.2d 249, 250–51 (Tex. App.—San Antonio 1988, no writ) (holding that a party to the lawsuit was entitled to single jury question on abandonment and waiver).

[90] *See Dempsey v. Apache Shores Prop. Owners Ass'n*, 737 S.W.2d 589, 595 (Tex. App.—Austin 1987, no writ); *Massachusetts Bond. & Ins. Co. v. Orkin Exterm. Co.*, 416 S.W.2d 396, 401 (Tex. 1967).

[91] *Jim Rutherford Invs., Inc. v. Terramar Beach Cmty. Ass'n*, 25 S.W.3d 845, 847, 851 (Tex. App.—Houston [14th Dist.] 2000, pet. denied); *Dempsey v. Apache Shores Prop. Owners Ass'n*, 737 S.W.2d 589, 595 (Tex. App.—Austin 1987, no writ); *Zent v. Murrow*, 476 S.W.2d 875, 880 (Tex. Civ. App.—Austin 1972, no writ); *Moran v. Memorial Point Property Owners Association*, 410 S.W.3d 397, 405-06 (Tex. App.—Houston [14th Dist.] 2013, no pet.) (holding that evidence of restrictive covenant violations that were of a different nature that the subject restrictive covenant is not sufficient to prove that the subject restrictive covenant had been waived or abandoned).

[92] *See Jim Rutherford Invs., Inc. v. Terramar Beach Cmty. Ass'n*, 25 S.W.3d 845, 847, 851 (Tex. App.—Houston [14th Dist.] 2000, pet. denied).

to object to previous trivial violations will generally not amount to an abandonment or waiver of a Restrictive Covenant.[93] On the other hand, a court will sustain findings that a Restrictive Covenant has been abandoned or waived where the Homeowner resisting enforcement of the Restrictive Covenant presents proof that the violations then existing were so extensive and material as to reasonably lead to the conclusion that such Restrictive Covenant had been abandoned or waived.[94]

In analyzing whether there has been an abandonment or waiver of a Restrictive Covenant, courts do not limit their focus to the actions, inactions, or subjective intent of any one party affected by the Restrictive Covenant. Rather, the court should consider the equities of the entire situation,[95] including, but not limited to: (1) the nature and severity of past violations relative to the Restrictive Covenant sought to be enforced;[96] (2) the extent to which the person attempting to enforce the Restrictive Covenant relied on the

---

[93] *See Stewart v. Welsh*, 178 S.W.2d 506, 508 (Tex. 1944) ("[H]e is not precluded from enforcing a restriction against an owner whose violation of it materially affects him, by failing to complain of another's violation which does not materially affect him in the enjoyment of his property or which is merely trivial."); *Sharpstown Civic Ass'n, Inc. v. Pickett*, 679 S.W.2d 956, 958 (Tex. 1984); *Pebble Beach Prop. Owners' Ass'n v. Sherer*, 2 S.W.3d 283, 290 (Tex. App.—San Antonio 1999, pet. denied); *Hicks v. Loveless*, 714 S.W.2d 30, 34-36 (Tex. App.—Dallas 1986, writ ref'd n.r.e.).

[94] *Pebble Beach Prop. Owners' Ass'n v. Sherer*, 2 S.W.3d 283, 290 (Tex. App.—San Antonio 1999, pet. denied); *Dempsey v. Apache Shores Prop. Owners Ass'n*, 737 S.W.2d 589, 594 (Tex. App.—Austin 1987, no writ); *Tanglewood Homes Ass'n, Inc. v. Henke*, 728 S.W.2d 39, 43–44 (Tex. App.—Houston [1st Dist.] 1987, writ ref'd n.r.e.); *Hicks v. Loveless*, 714 S.W.2d 30, 35 (Tex. App.—Dallas 1986, writ ref'd n.r.e.).

[95] *See Cowling v. Colligan*, 312 S.W.2d 943, 946 (Tex. 1958) (stating that in deciding a restrictive covenant case, a court's "judgment must arise out of a balancing of equities or of relative hardships"); *Gigowski v. Russell*, 718 S.W.2d 16, 22 (Tex. App.—Tyler 1986, writ ref'd n.r.e.) ("In determining whether it would be inequitable to enforce a restrictive covenant against a particular lot owner, we must weigh the equities of the owner in violation of the covenant against the equities favoring other lot owners who acquired their property on the strength of the restriction.").

[96] *See Sharpstown Civic Ass'n, Inc. v. Pickett*, 679 S.W.2d 956, 958 (Tex. 1984) (enforcing residential-only restriction when prior violation of small office building was insignificant compared to proposed use of commercial car wash); *Cowling v. Colligan*, 312 S.W.2d 943, 946–47 (Tex. 1958) (enforcing residential-only restriction when only past violation was "advent of churches into the subdivision"); *Hicks v. Loveless*, 714 S.W.2d 30, 34–36 (Tex. App.—Dallas 1986, writ ref'd n.r.e.) (holding that past violations of residential-only restriction were minor when compared to use of property for machine shop).

Restrictive Covenant in purchasing his or her property;[97] and (3) the number of properties subject to the Restrictive Covenant relative to the number of violations.[98]

When analyzing the relativity of violations to the number of properties subject to the Restrictive Covenant, courts often rely upon statistical evidence. In the limited number of Texas appellate cases that have addressed the sufficiency of the evidence concerning the abandonment or waiver of Restrictive Covenants, Texas courts have generally been very reluctant to find the existence of an abandonment or waiver of a Restrictive Covenant where the violation ratio is less than nine percent (9%) of the applicable Lots or Units subject to the Restrictive Covenant.[99]

---

97 *See, e.g., Ski Masters of Texas, LLC v. Heinemeyer*, 269 S.W.3d 662, 672–73 (Tex. App.—San Antonio 2008, no pet.) (affirming the enforcement of a restrictive covenant in part because of evidence that the parties seeking to enforce a residential-only restriction relied on such restriction when purchasing their property); *Simms v. Lakewood Vill. Prop. Owners Ass'n*, 895 S.W.2d 779, 786–87 (Tex. App.—Corpus Christi 1995, no writ) ("To hold [that the restrictions were waived] would be an injustice to the many lot owners who purchased their property in reliance upon the protection afforded by the covenants and are still relying upon that protection.").

98 *See Tanglewood Homes Ass'n, Inc. v. Henke*, 728 S.W.2d 39, 44 (Tex. App.—Houston [1st Dist.] 1987, writ ref'd n.r.e.) (holding that evidence of fifteen violations of a set-back restriction for garages and carports out of fifty-six total properties subject to the set-back restriction was sufficient to support the jury's finding of abandonment of that restriction; but further holding that five minor violations of a set-back restriction applicable to the main residence would not support the jury's waiver finding); *see also Jim Rutherford Invs., Inc. v. Terramar Beach Cmty. Ass'n*, 25 S.W.3d 845, 852 (Tex. App.—Houston [14th Dist.] 2000, pet. denied) (holding that evidence of only one violation of a set-back restriction will not support an abandonment finding); *Pebble Beach Prop. Owners' Ass'n v. Sherer*, 2 S.W.3d 283, 290 (Tex. App.—San Antonio 1999, pet. denied) (holding that evidence of fourteen violations of a restrictive covenant prohibiting trailers and mobile homes out of approximately 800 lots will not support abandonment finding).

99 *See, e.g., Jim Rutherford Invs., Inc. v. Terramar Beach Cmty. Ass'n*, 25 S.W.3d 845, 847, 852 (Tex. App.—Houston [14th Dist.] 2000, pet. denied) (The court held that 1.9 percent violation rate of deed restrictions was "not so great as to lead the mind of the average man to reasonably conclude that the restriction in question had been abandoned and its enforcement waived."); *New Jerusalem Baptist Church, Inc. v. City of Houston*, 598 S.W.2d 666, 669 (Tex. Civ. App.—Houston [14th Dist.] 1980, no writ) (affirming trial court's finding that restriction in question had not been abandoned or its enforcement waived where there was only a 2.4 percent violation rate); *Stephenson v. Perlitz*, 537 S.W.2d 287, 289-90 (Tex. Civ. App.—Beaumont 1976, writ ref'd n.r.e.) (holding that there was no evidence of probative value that established or supported finding that there had been a waiver when at most there was no more than nine violations of a restrictive covenant in the entire subdivision consisting of more than one hundred lots (less than 9 percent violation ratio)); *Dempsey v. Apache Shores Prop. Owners Ass'n*, 737 S.W.2d 589, 595 (Tex. App.—Austin 1987, no writ) ("Allowing non-conforming uses on eleven of 2,460 lots would not, as a matter of law, lead the 'average man' to reasonably conclude the restrictions had been abandoned." (4 percent violation ratio)); *Underwood v. Webb*, 544 S.W.2d 187, 190 (Tex. Civ. App.—Waco 1976, writ ref'd n.r.e.) (holding that the evidence "completely

9.7.2 (B) *Effect of a Non-Waiver Provision on an Abandonment and Waiver Defense*

Often the Declarations applicable to Subdivision and Condominium Developments in Texas include a "non-waiver provision" that states in some manner that a failure by the Homeowners Association or by any Homeowner to enforce a provision of the Declaration will not constitute a waiver of the right to do so thereafter. Non-waiver clauses or provisions in contracts, including non-waiver provisions in Declarations, are generally enforceable in Texas.[100] Non-waiver provisions, however, themselves can be waived.[101] At least one Texas court of appeals has suggested that a Restrictive Covenant can be waived, despite the existence of a non-waiver provision, when there is evidence that the violations of the Restrictive Covenant subvert the general scheme or plan of the development.[102] And at least one other Texas Court of Appeals has held that that a "non-waiver provision would be ineffective if a complete abandonment of the entire set of [Restrictive Covenants] has occurred" and such abandonment occurs at a time when the

---

fails to show the existence of such extensive violations throughout the subdivision as to . . . establish a waiver of the right to enforce [a restrictive covenant]" when a subdivision has only two violations out of 493 lots (.4 percent violation ratio)); *Tanglewood Homes Ass'n, Inc. v. Henke*, 728 S.W.2d 39, 44 (Tex. App.—Houston [1st Dist.] 1987, writ ref'd n.r.e.) (holding that there was "no evidence" to support jury's finding that a restrictive covenant had been abandoned where there were only five violations out of fifty-six properties (8.9 percent violation ratio), but finding sufficient evidence to support a jury's finding that a separate restrictive covenant had also been abandoned where there were fifteen violations out of fifty-six properties (14.28 percent violation ratio)).

[100] *See TX Far West, Ltd. v. Texas Investments Management, Inc.*,127 S.W.3d 295, 306 (Tex. App.—Austin 2004, no pet.) (Citing a non-waiver provision, the Austin court reversed a summary judgment that the covenant had been waived and held that the prior owners' acquiescence in alleged violations of the covenant did not establish waiver as a matter of law.); *Simms v. Lakewood Vill. Prop. Owners Ass'n*, 895 S.W.2d 779, 786-87 (Tex. App.—Corpus Christi 1995, no writ) (Stating that a non-waiver provision in the restrictive covenants "was included in the covenant to protect [against] any claims that the covenant had been waived or abandoned because of a failure to prosecute prior violations."); *Musgrove v. Westridge Street Partners I, LLC*, 2009 WL 976010, *4 (Tex. App.—Fort Worth April 9, 2009, pet. denied); *see, also A.G.E., Inc. v. Buford*, 105 S.W.3d 667, 676 (Tex. App.—Austin 2003, pet. denied); *Straus v. Kirby Court Corp.*, 909 S.W.2d 105, 108 (Tex. App.—Houston [14th Dist.] 1995, writ denied).

[101] *See A.G.E., Inc. v. Buford*, 105 S.W.3d 667, 676 (Tex. App.—Austin 2003, pet. denied); *Straus v. Kirby Court Corp.*, 909 S.W.2d 105, 108 (Tex. App.—Houston [14th Dist.] 1995, writ denied); *Winslow v. Dillard Dep't Stores, Inc.*, 849 S.W.2d 862, 863-64 (Tex. App.—Texarkana 1993, writ denied).

[102] *Simms v. Lakewood Vill. Prop. Owners Ass'n, 895* S.W.2d 779, 786 (Tex. App.—Corpus Christi 1995, no writ).

violations are so pervasive that they have "destroyed the fundamental character of the neighborhood."[103]

9.8 Reimbursement of Attorneys Fees Incurred in Restrictive Covenant Enforcement

Texas follows the "American Rule" when it comes to the assessment of attorneys fees arising out of litigation.[104] Under the American Rule, each party to a lawsuit is responsible for paying his or her own attorneys fees, unless there is specific authority established by either contract or statute that provides for the assessment of attorneys fees incurred by one party against the other party.[105] For most Texas Homeowners Associations, there is both contractual and statutory authority for recovery of attorneys fees incurred in Restrictive Covenant enforcement; however, the circumstances in which such authority is triggered can differ significantly.

The ability of a Texas Homeowners Association to recover attorneys fees incurred in the enforcement of Restrictive Covenants is often more difficult than to recover attorneys fees incurred in the collection of delinquent Assessments. This is because most Declarations provide that a Homeowner is liable for all attorneys fees incurred by a Homeowners Association in the collection of delinquent Assessments from such Homeowner and that the liability for such attorneys fees is secured by the Homeowners Association's Assessment Lien. That is generally not the case for attorneys fees incurred by a Homeowners Association in the enforcement of Restrictive Covenants, and the recovery of such attorneys fees will often depend on several issues, including whether the

---

103 *Musgrove v. Westridge Street Partners I, LLC*, 2009 WL 976010, *4 (Tex. App.—Fort Worth April 9, 2009, pet. denied) (citing *Burke v. Voicestream Wireless Corp. II*, 87 P.3d 81 (Ariz. Ct. App. 2004)).

104 Most countries, other than the United States, operate under a "loser pays" system for assessment of attorneys fees, commonly called the "English Rule." Under the English Rule, the losing party in a lawsuit pays the successful party's attorney fees. The United States is a notable exception, and most states, including Texas, follow what is commonly called the "American Rule," whereby each party bears its own legal expenses in a lawsuit as a general rule, regardless of who prevails.

105 *New Amsterdam Cas. Co. v. Texas Indus., Inc.*, 414 S.W.2d 914, 915 (Tex. 1967).

applicable Declaration expressly provides for a Homeowner's liability for attorneys fees incurred by a Homeowners Association to enforce Restrictive Covenants against him or her, whether the liability for such attorneys fees is secured by the Homeowners Association's Assessment Lien, and, finally, whether the enforcement action taken by the Homeowners Association involves non-judicial enforcement methods or judicial enforcement procedures.

9.8.1 Contractual Authority for Recovery of Attorneys Fees Incurred in Restrictive Covenant Enforcement

The Declaration of a Homeowners Association is essentially a private contractual agreement that becomes binding upon Homeowners when they acquire ownership of their Lot or Unit. In almost all cases, the Homeowners Association will be expressly authorized under the Declaration to enforce the Restrictive Covenants contained therein, and in most cases, the Declaration will also provide for a right of reimbursement of attorneys fees incurred by the Homeowners Association to enforce the Restrictive Covenants from the offending Homeowner. The language utilized in such provision(s), however, has a dramatic effect on the ability of the Homeowners Association to recover its attorney fees without first pursuing judicial enforcement of the Restrictive Covenant.

In most cases where a Declaration authorizes a Homeowners Association to enforce the Restrictive Covenants, it will also provide that the Homeowners Association is entitled to the recovery of its attorneys fees if it prevails in a lawsuit to enforce the Restrictive Covenants.[106] Such a provision provides sufficient authority for a trial court to

[106] Though not as common, in some cases a Declaration may provide that a Homeowner that fails to comply with the applicable Restrictive Covennants shall be liable to the Homeowners Association for all costs, including attorneys fees, incurred by the Homeowners Association to obtain compliance by such Homeowner regardless as to whether or not a lawsuit is filed. In such cases, the Homeowners Association is often vested with authority to levy an Assessment against such Homeowner for such costs of enforcement. Under such circumstances, the Homeowners Association is not required to file a Restrictive Covenant lawsuit or to be a prevailing party in order to recover its attorneys fees, and such attorneys fees may be collected in the same manner as unpaid Assessments would be under its Declaration.

award a Homeowners Association recovery of attorneys fees incurred by it upon successfully prevailing in a lawsuit to enforce the Restrictive Covenants against a Homeowner. A Homeowners Association, however, will not be considered to have prevailed unless and until a final judgment is rendered in its favor, which necessitates not only filing a lawsuit to enforce the Restrictive Covenant against an offending-Homeowner, but litigating such lawsuit to successful conclusion by summary judgment or trial. Under such circumstances, if a Homeowners Association does not prevail in the lawsuit to enforce a Restrictive Covenant or does not even file such a lawsuit, then it will not be considered a prevailing party and it may not assess or charge the offending-Homeowner for attorneys fees incurred by it in relation to the enforcement of such Restrictive Covenant against such Homeowner.

9.8.2 Statutory Authority for Recovery of Attorneys Fees Incurred in Restrictive Covenant Enforcement

For those Texas Homeowners Associations that do not have contractual authority under their Declaration for the reimbursement of attorneys fees incurred in Restrictive Covenant enforcement, there are at least two Texas statutes of general application that provide authority for the potential recovery of attorneys fees incurred by a Texas Homeowners Association in the enforcement of Restrictive Covenants, and one additional statute that also provides for such authority by a Texas Condominium Association. Each of these statutes is discussed in greater detail in the following subchapters.

9.8.2 (A) *Award of Attorneys Fees under Section 5.006 of the Texas Property Code*

The first statute is Section 5.006 of the Texas Property Code, which provides that in a lawsuit based on a breach of a Restrictive Covenant, the trial court is required to award "a prevailing party who asserted the action" reasonable attorneys fees in addition to the party's costs and damages.[107] Section 5.006 is different from the other two attorney fee statutes for two reasons. First, the award of attorneys fees is mandatory, not discretionary.[108] Second, only the party who filed the lawsuit is entitled to a recovery of reasonable attorneys fees.[109] In other words, if a Homeowners Association or other Homeowner files a lawsuit against a Homeowner for violation of a Restrictive Covenant and the Homeowners Association or such other Homeowner who filed the lawsuit wins, then such party is entitled to an award of reasonable attorneys fees against the offending Homeowner. If, however, the alleged offending Homeowner successfully defends a Restrictive Covenant enforcement lawsuit by the Homeowners Association or another Homeowner, then the alleged offending Homeowner is not entitled to a recovery of his or her attorneys fees under Section 5.006(a) because he or she did not assert the Restrictive Covenant enforcement lawsuit.

9.8.2 (B) *Award of Attorneys Fees under Chapter 37 of the Texas Civil Practice and Remedies Code*

The second statute is Chapter 37 of the Texas Civil Practice and Remedies Code, which is called the "Texas Uniform Declaratory Judgment Act."[110] Under Chapter 37, a person interested under a deed, written contract, or other writing constituting a contract, or whose rights, status, or other legal relations are affected by a statute or contract, may

---

[107] Tex. Prop. Code § 5.006(a). Section 5.006 is a statute of general application, meaning it applies to any party who files a lawsuit for a breach of a Restrictive Covenant, including a Homeowner who files a lawsuit against his or her neighbor for breach of a Restrictive Covenant.

[108] *See Gorman v. Countrywood Prop. Owners Ass'n*, 1 S.W.3d 915, 918 (Tex. App.—Beaumont 1999, pet. denied) ("Although the decision to award attorneys fees to the prevailing party under § 5.006 is not discretionary, the amount to be awarded must nonetheless be reasonable.").

[109] *See Anderson v. New Prop. Owners' Ass'n of Newport, Inc.*, 122 S.W.3d 378, 380 (Tex. App.—Texarkana 2003, pet. denied) ("Only a party who successfully prosecutes a claim alleging breach of a restrictive covenant is entitled to recover attorneys fees."). In order to determine reasonable attorneys fees, the trial court must consider: (1) the time and labor required; (2) the novelty and difficulty of the questions; (3) the expertise, reputation, and ability of the attorney; and (4) any other factor. Tex. Prop. Code § 5.006(b).

[110] Tex. Civ. Prac. & Rem. Code § 37.002. Chapter 37 is also a statute of general application, meaning it's application is not limited to a lawsuit for breach of a Restrictive Covenant.

file a lawsuit to have a court resolve any questions concerning interpretation or validity of such contract and to have the trial court make a declaration of rights, status, or other legal relations thereunder.[111] In other words, under certain circumstances, a Homeowners Association or Homeowner may file a lawsuit against one another in order to have a court resolve a disputed issue concerning the interpretation of the Homeowners Association's Governing Documents or a party's status under such documents, such as whether the Declaration in a particular Condominium Development requires a Unit Owner to repair Limited Common Elements.

In addition, Chapter 37 provides that the trial court in a declaratory judgment lawsuit may award costs and reasonable and necessary attorneys fees as are equitable and just.[112] In contrast to Section 5.006 of the Texas Property Code, which requires the trial court to award attorneys fees to the prevailing party, under Chapter 37, a trial court's award of attorneys fees is discretionary, not mandatory, and it may award attorneys fees, if equitable and just to do so, to either party, including the non-prevailing party. Thus, under Chapter 37, the trial court has discretionary authority to award either party some or all of their attorneys fees, or to award neither party any of their attorneys fees, without regard to whom the prevailing party in the lawsuit is.[113]

9.8.2 (C) *Award of Attorneys Fees under the Texas Uniform Condominium Act*

There are two statutory provisions under the Texas Uniform Condominium Act that address recovery of attorneys fees related to the enforcement of a Restrictive Covenant. The first is Section 82.117 of the Texas Uniform Condominium Act, which

---

111 Tex. Civ. Prac. & Rem. Code § 37.004.

112 Tex. Civ. Prac. & Rem. Code § 37.009; *see also, Bocquet v. Herring*, 972 S.W.2d 19, 20 (Tex. 1998).

113 *Scottsdale Ins. Co. v. Travis*, 68 S.W.3d 72, 77 (Tex. App.—Dallas 2001, pet. denied.) (Under Section 37.009, attorneys fees may be even awarded to the non-prevailing party.).

only applies to Condominium Developments created on or after January 1, 1994.[114] Section 82.117 provides that a Unit Owner is liable to an applicable Condominium Association for violation of a Condominium Declaration, Bylaw, or Association Rule committed by the Unit Owner, an occupant of the Owner's Unit, or the Unit Owner or occupant's family, guests, employees, agents, or invitees, and is further liable for costs incurred by the Condominium Association to obtain compliance by such offending party, including attorneys fees whether or not a lawsuit is filed.[115] In other words, Section 82.117 authorizes an applicable Condominium Association to assess a charge against a Unit Owner for attorneys fees incurred by the Condominium Association to enforce a Restrictive Covenant without having to file a lawsuit.

The second statutory provision is Section 82.161 of the Texas Uniform Condominium Act, which provides that the prevailing party in a lawsuit to enforce a Condominium Declaration, Bylaw, or Association Rule is entitled to reasonable attorneys fees and costs of litigation from the non-prevailing party.[116] Section 82.161 is very similar to Section 5.006 of the Texas Property Code in that it provides for a mandatory award of reasonable attorneys fees to the prevailing party. Unlike Section 5.006, however, the trial court must award reasonable attorneys fees to the prevailing party without regard to whether the prevailing party is the party that asserted or filed the Restrictive Covenant enforcement lawsuit. In other words, a Unit Owner who successfully defends a Restrictive Covenant enforcement lawsuit brought by the Condominium Association or other Unit Owner is entitled to an award of attorneys fees incurred in the defense of such lawsuit.

---

[114] Tex. Prop. Code §§ 82.002(c); 82.117). Section 82.117 is not applicable to Condominium Developments created prior to January 1, 1994, that are subject to the Texas Condominium Act, and there are no comparable provisions under the Texas Condominium Act. Tex. Prop. Code § 82.002(c).

[115] Tex. Prop. Code § 82.117(4).

[116] Tex. Prop. Code § 82.161(b). Unlike Section 82.117 of the Texas Uniform Condominium Act, Section 82.161 applies to all Condominium Associations, including Condominium Developments created prior to January 1, 1994, that are subject to the Texas Condominium Act. Tex. Prop. Code § 82.002(c).

9.8.3 Collection of Attorneys Fees Incurred by a Homeowners Association in Restrictive Covenant Enforcement

The collectability of attorneys fees incurred by a Homeowners Association in enforcing Restrictive Covenants against an offending Homeowner will often depend on whether there is a provision in the Homeowners Association's Declaration authorizing the Homeowners Association to treat such attorneys fees as an Assessment against the Homeowner. For example, some Homeowners Associations' Declarations provide that attorneys fees incurred in the enforcement of Restrictive Covenants may be assessed by the Homeowners Association against the offending Homeowner as a special charge or Assessment that is also secured by the Homeowners Association's Assessment Lien. In such circumstances, the Homeowners Association is not required to file a Restrictive Covenant lawsuit or to be a prevailing party in order to recover its attorneys fees, and such attorneys fees may be collected in the same manner as unpaid Assessments would be under its Declaration.

Generally speaking, however, most Homeowners Associations' Declarations do not authorize them to collect attorneys fees incurred in the enforcement of Restrictive Covenants in the same manner as unpaid Assessments. Unless otherwise provided by its Declaration, attorneys fees incurred by a Homeowners Association in Restrictive Covenant enforcement, even if awarded to the Homeowners Association in a judgment, are not secured by its Assessment Lien.

If a Homeowners Association does obtain a judgment in a Restrictive Covenant enforcement lawsuit against a Homeowner in which it is awarded recovery of its attorneys fees, such judgment may be enforced and collected in the same manner as any monetary judgment under Texas law. Under Texas law, a monetary judgment may be "abstracted" by recording a copy of the judgment in the Official Public Records of each Texas county in which the "judgment debtor" owns property, which effectively creates what is commonly called a "Judgment Lien" that attaches to any non-exempt real or personal property owned by the judgment debtor in such county.[117] Unlike preexisting Assessment Liens, however, Judgment Liens do not preexist a Homeowner's invocation of Homestead protection and may not be foreclosed upon a Homeowner's Homestead property.[118]

9.8.4 Procedural Due Process Requirements for Texas Subdivision Associations to Recover Attorneys Fees Incurred in Restrictive Covenant Enforcement

Chapter 209 of the Texas Property Code not only establishes certain due process requirements before a Subdivision Association may suspend a Lot Owner's right to use a Common Area, file a lawsuit against a Lot Owner, charge a Lot Owner for property damage, or assess a fine against a Lot Owner, it also establishes two additional due process requirements before an offending Lot Owner may be held liable for any attorneys fees incurred by the Subdivision Association in the enforcement of a Restrictive Covenant against such Homeowner.

First, a Subdivision Association may not seek reimbursement of attorneys fees incurred by it in the enforcement of Restrictive Covenants from a Lot Owner unless it has previously provided such Lot Owner a written notice stating that attorneys fees and costs will be charged to the Lot Owner if the violation of the Restrictive Covenants continues after a specified date certain.[119] Second, a Lot Owner is not liable for, nor may a Subdivision Association charge a Lot Owner for, attorneys fees relating to a violation of a Restrictive Covenant that are incurred by the Subdivision Association prior to the expiration of the thirty-day time period to request a Chapter 209 Hearing following delivery of a Chapter 209 Notice to a Homeowner, or if a Chapter 209 Hearing is

---

[117] Tex. Prop. Code § 52.001, *et seq*. A "judgment debtor" is a person against whom a judgment has been recovered, and which remains unsatisfied. *Black's Law Dictionary* 845 (6th ed. 1990). "Non-exempt property" refers to property of a Homeowner that would be exempt from forced sale under Chapter 41 of the Texas Property Code and the Texas Constitution (such as Homestead Property), as well as property that would otherwise be considered "exempt" from creditors in a bankruptcy proceeding under the Bankruptcy Code.

[118] Tex. Prop. Code § 52.001, *et seq*.

[119] Tex. Prop. Code § 209.008(a).

requested, prior to the Subdivision Association conducting such hearing.[120] In other words, a Subdivision Association cannot hold a Homeowner liable for attorneys fees associated with Restrictive Covenant enforcement until it gives the Homeowner an opportunity to meet with the Board of Directors, or if so requested by the Homeowner, until after the Board actually meets with the Homeowner.

Finally, Chapter 209 also requires that all attorneys fees, costs, and other amounts collected from a Lot Owner by a Subdivision Association must be deposited into an account maintained at a financial institution in the name of the Subdivision Association or its managing agent, in which the only signatories on such account are members of the Subdivision Association's Board of Directors or its managing agent or employees of its managing agent.[121] In addition, upon written request by a Lot Owner from whom the Subdivision Association has requested reimbursement of attorneys fees, the Subdivision Association must also provide such Lot Owner copies of the invoices for such attorneys fees and other costs relating to the matter for which the Subdivision Association seeks reimbursement of fees and costs from such Lot Owner.[122] In other words, if a Subdivision Association seeks recovery of attorneys fees related to the enforcement of Restrictive Covenants from a Lot Owner, then upon written request from such Lot Owner, the Association must provide him or her with a copy of the invoices for such attorneys fees.

---

[120] Tex. Prop. Code § 209.008(b).

[121] Tex. Prop. Code § 209.008(c).

[122] Tex. Prop. Code § 209.008(d).

CHAPTER 10 FEDERAL AND STATE LAWS THAT LIMIT OR RESTRICT THE ENFORCEMENT OF RESTRICTIVE COVENANTS

CHAPTER 10 FEDERAL AND STATE LAWS THAT LIMIT OR RESTRICT THE ENFORCEMENT OF RESTRICTIVE COVENANTS

10.1 The Federal and Texas Fair Housing Acts

In 1968, the United States Congress enacted the Fair Housing Act, which made certain activities concerning housing illegal if they were undertaken on the basis of race, color, religion, or national origin. In 1974, the Fair Housing Act was amended to also prevent housing discrimination based on sex (i.e., a person's gender). In 1988, the Fair Housing Act was again amended to also make it unlawful to discriminate against a person on the basis of a "handicap" (or "disability") or a person's "familial status."[1] In 1993, the Texas Legislature enacted the Texas Fair Housing Act for the purposes of: (1) providing for fair housing practices in the State of Texas; (2) creating a procedure for investigating and settling complaints of discriminatory housing practices; and (3) providing rights and remedies substantially equivalent to those granted under the Federal Fair Housing Act.[2]

Under the Fair Housing Act, it is unlawful to discriminate against any person in the terms, conditions, or privileges of sale or rental of a dwelling, or in the provision of services or facilities in connection therewith, because of a person's race, color, religion, national origin, sex, handicap, or familial status.[3] The provision of services or facilities includes amenities and services, the enforcement of Restrictive Covenants, as well as the creation and enforcement of Association Rules and policies that regulate use of or access to a Homeowners Association's Common Areas or Common Elements. As such, Homeowners Associations are subject to the Fair Housing Act and may not create or

---

1 42 U.S.C. § 3604(b). Except for perhaps "familial status," these protected categories are self-explanatory. The term "familial status" means a person under the age of eighteen (18) years who lives with a parent, legal guardian, or other person having custody of such person pursuant to the written permission of such person's parent or legal guardian. 42 U.S.C. § 3606(k).

2 Tex. Prop. Code §§ 301.001–301.002.

3 42 U.S.C. § 3604(b).

enforce a Restrictive Covenant, Association Rule, or policy that discriminates against a protected class of Homeowners or that would have a disparate impact on a specific protected class.[4] When a Homeowners Association enforces its Restrictive Covenants, Association Rules, and/or policies against a person in any protected category, the possibility of a Fair Housing complaint exists and such Homeowners Association should be prepared to demonstrate that its enforcement practices and procedures are implemented in a uniform, consistent, and non-discriminatory manner.

The most common scenarios where a Homeowners Association runs afoul of the Fair Housing Act involve housing practices that are discriminatory against a person on the basis of his or her "familial status" or "handicap" or "disability." Such types of discriminatory housing practices are discussed in greater detail in the following subchapters.

10.1.1 Discrimination on the Basis of Familial Status

The protection of a person's "Familial Status" prohibits discrimination against families with children under the age of eighteen. Unless a building or community qualifies as housing for older persons, it may not discriminate against a person on the basis of Familial Status.[5] That is, it may not discriminate against families in which there are one

---

4 Disparate impact occurs when there is a policy or rule that appears to be neutral on its face, but which operates to disproportionately disadvantage a class of people because of their race, color, national origin, religion, sex, handicap, or familial status. A prima facie case of disparate impact may be established by statistical evidence establishing that a facially neutral policy has a disparate impact on a class of people who are protected against discrimination. Under a disparate impact analysis, a policy, standard, practice, or procedure that appears to be neutral in its terms but in operation disproportionately adversely affects a protected class of people may constitute a violation of the Fair Housing Act.

5 The Fair Housing Act exempts "housing for older persons" from its prohibitions against Familial Status discrimination. 42 U.S.C. § 3607(b)(1)–(3). The Fair Housing Act's definition of "housing for older persons" includes three separate categories of housing: (1) housing provided under any state or federal program that the Department of Housing and Urban Development (more commonly known as "HUD") determines is "specifically designed and operated to assist elderly persons;" (2) housing "intended for, and solely occupied by, persons sixty-two (62) years of age or older;" and (3) housing "intended and operated for occupancy by persons fifty-five (55) years of age or older," which is further defined as housing that has at least eighty percent (80%) of its units occupied by at least one person who is at least fifty-five (55) years of age or older, that complies with HUD rules for verification of such occupancy by reliable surveys and affidavits, and that

or more children under the age of eighteen living with either: (1) a parent; (2) a person who has legal custody of the child or children; or (3) the designee of the parent or legal custodian who has the parent or custodian's written permission.[6] Familial Status protection also applies to pregnant women and anyone securing legal custody of a child under the age of eighteen.

There are two common scenarios where potential Familial Status discriminatory practices can arise in the residential Homeowners Association context. The first scenario involves a Homeowners Association's enforcement of a Restrictive Covenant that restricts the number of occupants that may reside in a dwelling unit (commonly referred to as an "occupancy quota"). While the Fair Housing Act does not expressly prohibit enforcement of occupancy quotas, enforcement of occupancy quotas that would adversely affect families with minor children can be considered to be discriminatory on the basis of the children's Familial Status.[7]

The second scenario that can raise potential issues under the Fair Housing Act involves the creation or enforcement of a Restrictive Covenant, Association Rule, or policy that treats children differently from adults, even if it is for the purpose of protecting children. This scenario most often arises when a Homeowners Association limits certain

---

publishes and adheres to policies and procedures that demonstrate an intent to provide housing for persons fifty-five (55) years of age or older. 42 U.S.C. § 3607(b)(2).

6 42 U.S.C. § 3602(k); Tex. Prop. Code § 301.004.

7 *See Housing Opportunities Project For Excellence, Inc. v. Key Colony No. 4 Condominium Assoc., Inc.*, 510 F. Supp.2d 1003, 1009–1013 (S.D. Fla. 2007) (Condominium Unit Owners' allegations that Condominium Association implemented and enforced occupancy restriction of four residents per Unit stated claim of disparate treatment based on Familiar Status in violation of Federal Fair Housing Act.). Pursuant to an internal Department of Housing and Urban Development memorandum dated March 20, 1991, regarding occupancy quotas that became public policy when it was published in the Federal Register on December 22, 1998, the general rule for occupancy standards as applied to protected families may not be more restrictive than two persons per bedroom. See Fair Housing Enforcement—Occupancy Standards; Notice of Statement of Policy, 63 Fed. Reg. 245 (December 22, 1998). However, other factors, such as the size of the bedrooms and dwelling unit, ages of the children, and configuration of the dwelling unit, may have an effect on whether the enforcement of a two-persons-per-bedroom standard is still too restrictive. *See* Fair Housing Enforcement—Occupancy Standards; Notice of Statement of Policy, 63 Fed. Reg. 245 (December 22, 1998).

facilities or activities by age or legal status, such as to adults only or persons above or below a certain age. Restrictions on children, which are discriminatory on their face, may still be enforceable if the rules are motivated by legitimate concerns for the health and safety of residents and are the least discriminatory manner in which to achieve such purpose. For such reasons, a Homeowners Association should carefully consider any Restrictive Covenant or Association Rule that limits certain facilities or activities by age or legal status before enacting it or proceeding with enforcement of it.

10.1.2 Discrimination on the Basis of a Person's Handicap

In 1988, Congress enacted an amendment to the Fair Housing Act to specifically address problems disabled persons were experiencing in obtaining housing.[8] These amendments, and the regulations promulgated for their enforcement by the Department of Housing and Urban Development (more commonly referred to as "HUD"), added a list of prohibited activities designed specifically to eradicate housing discrimination on the basis of a person's "Handicap."[9]

To promote the civil rights of people with a Handicap (referred to here as simply a "Handicapped-Person" or "Handicapped-Persons"), the Fair Housing Act makes it unlawful to "discriminate in the sale or rental, or to otherwise make unavailable or deny, a dwelling to any purchaser or renter because of a Handicap."[10] Such discriminatory

---

8 There are two primary federal laws that prohibit certain actions in the context of residential housing that are discriminatory to handicapped or disabled persons: the Fair Housing Act and the Americans with Disabilities Act. The Fair Housing Act addresses accommodations for handicapped persons in private residential settings, while the Americans with Disabilities Act applies to public accommodations and to private facilities that provide public accommodations.

9 Although the Fair Housing Act uses the term "Handicap" and the Americans with Disabilities Act uses the term "Disability," both terms have the same legal meaning. *See Bragdon v. Abbott*, 524 U.S. 624, 631 (1998) (noting that the definition of "Disability" in the Americans with Disabilities Act is drawn almost verbatim from the definition of "Handicap" contained in the Fair Housing Amendments Act of 1988). For simplicity and to maintain consistency with the applicable statutes, this book shall use the term "Handicap" when discussing the Federal Fair Housing Act and the term "Disability" when discussing the Americans with Disabilities Act.

10 42 U.S.C. § 3604(f)(1).

housing practices include incidents in which a Homeowners Association refuses to allow a Handicapped-Person to make "Reasonable Modifications" to existing premises and/or refuses to make "Reasonable Accommodations" for a Handicapped-Person in regards to its Association Rules, policies, practices, or services.[11]

The Fair Housing Act defines the term Handicap as: "(1) a physical or mental impairment which substantially limits one or more of such person's major life activities; (2) a record of having such impairment; or (3) being regarded as having such an impairment."[12] In other words, the definition of "Handicap" under the Fair Housing Act encompasses anyone who has an actual Handicap, who is classified or labeled as having a Handicap, or who is treated by others as possessing a Handicap.

In addition, the Fair Housing Act also protects a home buyer or renter from discrimination on the basis that a Handicapped-Person resides in, or intends to reside in, such home buyer's or renter's dwelling after it is sold, rented, or made available to such home buyer or renter, as well as protects a home buyer or renter from discrimination on the basis of a Handicapped-Person being associated with such home buyer or renter.[13] Or

---

[11] 42 U.S.C. § 3604(f)(3)(A)–(B) (stating that "discrimination includes . . . a refusal to permit, at the expense of the handicapped person, reasonable modifications of existing premises occupied or to be occupied by such person if such modifications may be necessary to afford such person full enjoyment of the premises [and] a refusal to make reasonable accommodations in rules, policies, practices, or services, when such accommodations may be necessary to afford a handicapped person equal opportunity to use and enjoy a dwelling."); *see also*, Tex. Prop. Code § 301.025(c)(1)–(2).

[12] 42 U.S.C. § 3602(h). The Texas Fair Housing Act utilizes the term "Disability" instead of "Handicap," and it defines "Disability" as "a mental or physical impairment that substantially limits at least one major life activity, a record of the impairment, or being regarded as having the impairment." Tex. Prop. Code § 301.003(6). The term "Handicap" under the Federal Fair Housing Act does not include current illegal use of or addiction to a controlled substance, and the term "Disability" under the Texas Fair Housing Act does not include current illegal use or addiction to any drug or illegal or federally controlled substance, nor does it apply to an individual because of an individual's sexual orientation or because that individual is a transvestite. *See* 42 U.S.C. § 3602(h); Tex. Prop. Code § 301.003(6).

[13] 42 U.S.C. § 3604(f)(1)(A)–(C) (It shall be unlawful "[t]o discriminate in the sale or rental, or to otherwise make unavailable or deny, a dwelling to any buyer or renter because of a handicap of—(A) that buyer or renter; (B) a person residing in or intending to reside in that dwelling after it is so sold, rented, or made available; or (C) any person associated with that buyer or renter.").

said more simply, it is unlawful to discriminate against a person who purchases a Lot or Unit with the intent to use it as a group home for persons considered to be Handicapped under the Federal Fair Housing Act. Thus, the Fair Housing Act protects both home buyers and renters with Handicaps, as well as persons or entities that provide Handicapped-Persons with housing, including group homes and nonprofit corporations that promote the interests of the disabled.[14]

In most cases, Texas Homeowners Associations are not involved in the selling or leasing of real property, but they are involved in the provision of services or facilities in connection with the selling, leasing, occupancy, and use of residential dwellings. Such is the context in which Homeowners Associations tend to run afoul of the Fair Housing Act in regards to housing practices that discriminate against a person on the basis of his or her Handicap. The types of housing practices by a Homeowners Association that potentially discriminate against a Handicapped-Person tend to involve either: (1) a refusal by the Homeowners Association to allow "Reasonable Modifications" of existing premises that are occupied or to be occupied by an individual with a Handicap; or (2) a refusal of a Homeowners Association to make "Reasonable Accommodations" in Association Rules, policies, practices, or services to an individual with a Handicap. A person with a Handicap may need a Reasonable Accommodation or a Reasonable Modification, or both, in order to have an equal opportunity to use and enjoy a dwelling and/or public and common use

---

[14] It is well settled that a group home for recovering substance abusers has standing to bring Fair Housing Act claims individually and on behalf of its current and potential residents. *See Oxford House-C v. City of St. Louis*, 843 F. Supp. 1556, 1572 (E.D. Mo. 1994) (holding that Oxford House had individual standing to bring a Fair Housing Act claim because the zoning laws in dispute "perceptibly impaired" the organization by: (1) jeopardizing its ability to perform its state contract; (2) potentially causing the failure of the group home at issue; and (3) causing a substantial drain on Oxford House's resources in its role as legal advocate for recovering addicts and alcoholics); *Oxford House, Inc. v. City of Albany*, 819 F. Supp. 1168, 1173–74 (N.D. N.Y. 1993) (finding that an Oxford House's function in founding and supervising program houses gives it sufficient interest in litigation as does the possibility of loss of state loans and funding if the housing is closed); *Havens Realty Corp. v. Coleman*, 455 U.S. 363, 376 (1982) (holding that fair housing "testers" have standing to bring a Fair Housing Act claim "[a]s long as respondents have alleged distinct and palpable injuries that are 'fairly traceable' to petitioners' actions"); *Growth Horizons, Inc. v. Delaware County,* 983 F.2d 1277, 1281–82 (3rd Cir. 1993) (holding that a corporation that provided residential placements for mentally retarded persons was "an aggrieved person" for purposes of the Fair Housing Act).

spaces; and, the failure of a Homeowners Association to afford a Handicapped-Person a requested reasonable modification or accommodation can constitute a violation of the Fair Housing Act.

10.1.2 (A) *Requests for a Reasonable Modification*

Under the Fair Housing Act, a Homeowners Association may commit a discriminatory housing practice by refusing to allow Reasonable Modifications of existing premises that are occupied or to be occupied by an individual with a Handicap, at such individual's own expense, if the proposed modifications may be necessary to afford such individual full enjoyment of the premises of a dwelling.[15] A Reasonable Modification is a structural change made to existing premises, occupied or to be occupied by an individual with a Handicap, that may be necessary to afford such individual full enjoyment of the premises of a dwelling, and includes structural changes to interiors and exteriors of dwellings and to common and public use areas.

Under the Fair Housing Act, a Homeowners Association is only required to permit requested modifications that are reasonable and necessary to the Handicapped-Person. To show that a requested modification may be necessary, there must be an identifiable relationship, or "nexus," between the requested modification and the individual's Handicap. If no such nexus exists, then the Homeowners Association may refuse to allow the requested modification. Examples of modifications that typically are reasonable include widening doorways to make rooms more accessible for persons in wheelchairs; adding a ramp to make a primary entrance accessible for persons in wheelchairs; and altering a walkway to provide access to a public or common use area.

A person makes a Reasonable Modification request under the Fair Housing Act whenever he or she makes clear to the Homeowners Association that he or she is

15 42 U.S.C. § 3604(f)(3)(A); Tex. Prop. Code § 301.025(c)(1).

requesting permission to make a structural change to the premises because of a Handicap. The request for modification need not be in writing and need not be made by the person with the Handicap; rather, it can be made by a family member or someone else who is acting on a Handicapped-Person's behalf. The Fair Housing Act also does not require that a request for Reasonable Modifications be made in a particular manner or at a particular time, nor does it require the person to mention the Fair Housing Act or use the words "Reasonable Modification." The person making the request for a Reasonable Modification, however, must make the request in a manner that a reasonable person would understand it to be a request for permission to make a structural change to the premises because of a Handicap.

A Homeowners Association may not ordinarily inquire as to the nature and severity of an individual's Handicap. However, in response to a request for a Reasonable Modification, a Homeowners Association may request reliable Handicap-related information from the requester that: (1) is necessary to verify that the person meets the Fair Housing Act's definition of Handicap; (2) describes the needed modification; and (3) shows the relationship between the person's Handicap and the need for the requested modification. If a requester's Handicap is known or readily apparent to the Homeowners Association, but the need for the modification is not readily apparent or known, then the Homeowners Association may request only information that is necessary to evaluate the Handicap-related need for the modification. If a person's Handicap and need for the requested modification is readily apparent or known by the Homeowners Association, then the Homeowners Association may not request any additional information about the requester's Handicap or the Handicap-related need for the modification.

A person requesting to make a Reasonable Modification must obtain the Homeowners Association's approval before making such modification, and the Homeowners Association has an obligation to promptly respond to a Reasonable Modification request. An undue delay in responding to a Reasonable Modification request may be deemed to be a failure to permit a Reasonable Modification. In addition, the Homeowners Association generally may not insist on an alternative modification or an alternative design of the modification if it is to be made to the interior of a dwelling, but it may do so if: (1) the modification is to be made to the exterior of a dwelling or a Common Area (or Common Element); and (2) the Homeowners Association's proposed design or alternative modification imposes no additional costs on the Handicapped-Person and still meets his or her needs. If a Homeowners Association would like a proposed modification to be made with more costly materials in order to satisfy the Homeowners Association's aesthetic standards, then the Handicapped-Person must agree to such request by the Homeowners Association if the Homeowners Association agrees to pay for the additional costs of such material.

10.1.2 (B) *Requests for a Reasonable Accommodation*

Under the Fair Housing Act, a Homeowners Association may commit a discriminatory housing practice by refusing to make Reasonable Accommodations in its Association Rules, policies, practices, or services when such accommodations may be necessary to afford an individual with a Handicap an equal opportunity to use and enjoy a dwelling unit, including public and common use areas.[16] Since Association Rules, policies, practices, and services may have a different effect on persons with a Handicap than on other persons, treating persons with a Handicap exactly the same as others will sometimes deny them an equal opportunity to use and enjoy a dwelling. A Reasonable Accommodation is a change, exception, or adjustment to an Association Rule, policy, practice, or service that may be necessary to afford a person with a Handicap an equal opportunity to use and enjoy a dwelling, including public and common use spaces. For instance, a Homeowners Association's rules against large dogs must be waived for a large dog that works as a blind resident's service-animal (i.e., a seeing-eye dog). Allowance for or provision of window air conditioners, handicap parking spaces, and sidewalk ramps are

16 42 U.S.C. § 3604(f)(3)(B); Tex. Prop. Code § 301.025(c)(2).

common types of Reasonable Accommodation requests in a Homeowners Association setting.

Under the Fair Housing Act, a Homeowners Association is only required to permit requested accommodations that are reasonable and necessary to the Handicapped-Person. To show that a requested accommodation may be necessary, there must be an identifiable relationship, or "nexus," between the requested accommodation and the individual's Handicap. A Homeowners Association may deny a request for a Reasonable Accommodation if the request was not made by or on behalf of a person with a Handicap or if there is no Handicap-related need for the requested accommodation. In addition, a request for a Reasonable Accommodation may be denied by a Homeowners Association if providing the accommodation is not reasonable because it would impose an undue financial and administrative burden on the Homeowners Association or would fundamentally alter the nature of the Homeowners Association's operations. The determination of undue financial and administrative burden must be made on a case-by-case basis involving various factors, such as the cost of the requested accommodation, the financial resources of the Homeowners Association, the benefits that the accommodation would provide to the requester, and the availability of alternative accommodations that would effectively meet the requester's Handicap-related needs.

A person with a Handicap is not entitled to receive a Reasonable Accommodation unless such person, or someone acting on his or her behalf, requests one. A request for a Reasonable Accommodation is considered to have been made whenever a person makes clear to the Homeowners Association that a request is being made for an exception, change, or adjustment to an Association Rule, policy, practice, or service because of a person's Handicap. Just like requests for Reasonable Modifications, the Fair Housing Act also does not require that a request for Reasonable Accommodation be made in a particular manner or at a particular time, nor does it require the person to mention the Fair Housing Act or use the words "Reasonable Accommodation."

In addition, a request for Reasonable Accommodation need not be in writing and need not be made by the person with the Handicap; rather, it can be made by a family member or someone else who is acting on such Handicapped-Person's behalf. The person making the request for a Reasonable Accommodation, however, must make the request in a manner that a reasonable person would understand it to be a request for an exception, change, or adjustment to an Association Rule, policy, practice, or service because of a person's Handicap. The request should also explain what type of accommodation is being requested, and if the need for the accommodation is not readily apparent, it should explain the relationship between the requested accommodation and the applicable person's Handicap.

A Homeowners Association may not ordinarily inquire as to the nature and severity of an individual's Handicap. However, in response to a request for a Reasonable Accommodation, a Homeowners Association may request reliable Handicap-related information that: (1) is necessary to verify that the person meets the Fair Housing Act's definition of Handicap; (2) describes the needed accommodation; and (3) shows the relationship between the person's Handicap and the need for the requested accommodation. If the requester's Handicap is known or readily apparent to the Homeowners Association, but the need for the accommodation is not readily apparent or known, then the Homeowners Association may request only information that is necessary to evaluate the Handicap-related need for the accommodation. If a person's Handicap is obvious, or otherwise known to the Homeowners Association, and if the need for the requested accommodation is also readily apparent or known, then the Homeowners Association may not request any additional information about the requester's Handicap or Handicap-related need for the accommodation. Finally, any information regarding a person's Handicap must be kept confidential by a Homeowners Association and it must not be shared with other persons unless they need the information to make or assess a decision to grant or deny a Reasonable Accommodation request or unless disclosure is required by law, such as a subpoena requiring the disclosure of such information.

10.1.3 Investigation and Enforcement of an Alleged Fair Housing Act Violation

The Fair Housing Act is administered by the United States Department of Housing and Urban Development (more commonly known as "HUD").[17] Complaints concerning alleged discriminatory housing practices (commonly referred to as "Fair Housing Complaints") can be filed by any entity, including individuals and community groups. In the context of a Fair Housing Complaint, the person or entity that files a Fair Housing Complaint is known as the "Complainant." The Handicapped-Person allegedly discriminated against to whom the Fair Housing Complaint relates is known as the "Aggrieved Person." And the person or entity against whom the Fair Housing Complaint is filed for allegedly committing discriminatory housing practices is called the "Respondent."

After HUD receives the initial information from a Fair Housing Complaint, an intake specialist will contact the Complainant and interview him or her in order to collect facts about the alleged discriminatory housing practice. Initial interviews are normally conducted by telephone. The intake specialist will then review the allegations to determine whether the complained of matter falls within HUD's jurisdiction. In other words, if the Fair Housing Complaint does not allege a discriminatory housing practice, then it does not fall within HUD's jurisdiction, and HUD cannot accept the Fair Housing Complaint. In such event, HUD must close the case. On the other hand, if a Fair Housing Complaint does allege a discriminatory housing practice, then HUD does have the authority to investigate such alleged discriminatory housing practice, and it will file a Fair Housing Complaint against the Respondent.

In addition, if the Fair Housing Complaint alleges a discriminatory housing practice that arose in the jurisdiction of a state or local agency that has been certified by

[17] 42 U.S.C. § 3608.

the Secretary of HUD as a substantially equivalent enforcement agency, then HUD must refer such Fair Housing Complaint to such state or local agency.[18] HUD has certified the Texas Fair Housing Act as providing rights and remedies that are substantially equivalent to those available under the Federal Fair Housing Act.[19] The Texas Fair Housing Act is administered by the Texas Workforce Commission Civil Rights Division (referred to here as simply the "Texas Workforce Commission"), which has also been certified by HUD as an enforcement agency substantially equivalent to HUD.[20] In general, most Fair Housing Complaints filed against Texas Homeowners Associations for violation of the Federal Fair Housing Act are referred to and investigated by the Texas Workforce Commission.[21] However, the Texas Workforce Commission may also defer proceedings under the Texas Fair Housing Act and refer a complaint alleging a discriminatory housing practice to a municipality that has also been certified by HUD as a substantially equivalent fair housing enforcement agency for investigation and enforcement of Fair Housing Complaints.[22]

10.1.3 (A) *Investigation of a Fair Housing Complaint*

The Texas Workforce Commission is required to promptly investigate the allegations set forth in all Fair Housing Complaints that have been filed with the Texas

---

18 24 C.F.R. § 103.100. An agency to which a Fair Housing Complaint is referred must begin to work with the Complainant within thirty (30) days of such referral or HUD can take the Fair Housing Complaint back.

19 *See* Public Notices of Substantial Equivalency of the Fair Housing Laws of Various States and Localities, 61 Fed. Reg. 53380 (October 11, 1996).

20 Tex. Prop. Code § 301.0015. *See* Notice of Certification and Funding of State and Local Fair Housing Enforcement Agencies Under the Fair Housing Assistance Program; Request for Comments, 73 Fed. Reg. 15535 (March 24, 2008).

21 The statutory provisions concerning the investigation and resolution of a Fair Housing Complaint under the Texas Fair Housing Act are substantially equivalent to the same provisions under the Federal Fair Housing Act.

22 Tex. Prop. Code § 301.068. HUD has certified several local agencies in the State of Texas as being substantially equivalent fair housing enforcement agencies, including the Austin Human Rights Commission, City of Dallas, City of Corpus Christi, Fort Worth Human Relations Commission, and Garland Neighborhood Development Department. *See* Notice of Certification and Funding of State and Local Fair Housing Enforcement Agencies Under the Fair Housing Assistance Program; Request for Comments, 73 Fed. Reg. 15535 (March 24, 2008).

Workforce Commission, as well as all such Fair Housing Complaints that HUD has either referred to the Texas Workforce Commission or has deferred jurisdiction over to the Texas Workforce Commission.[23] To constitute a proper Fair Housing Complaint, the Complaint must be in writing, under oath, and in the form prescribed by the Texas Workforce Commission.[24] An Aggrieved Person may file a Fair Housing Complaint with the Texas Workforce Commission alleging a discriminatory housing practice, or the Texas Workforce Commission may file a Fair Housing Complaint itself.[25] The Fair Housing Complaint, however, must be filed within one (1) year from the date the alleged discriminatory housing practice occurred or terminated, whichever is later in time.[26] Finally, a Fair Housing Complaint may be amended at any time.[27]

Upon the filing of a Fair Housing Complaint, the Texas Workforce Commission is required to: (1) give the Aggrieved Person notice that the Fair Housing Complaint has been received; (2) advise the Aggrieved Person of the time limits and choice of forums for adjudication of a Fair Housing Complaint under the Texas Fair Housing Act; and (3) within twenty (20) days from the date of the filing of the Fair Housing Complaint, serve each Respondent with a notice identifying the alleged discriminatory housing practice and advising the Respondent of the procedural rights and obligations of a Respondent under the Texas Fair Housing Act, as well as provide each Respondent a copy of the original Fair Housing Complaint.[28]

Within ten (10) days from receipt of a notice of the filing of a Fair Housing Complaint and copy of such complaint, a Respondent may file an answer to such Fair

---

[23] Tex. Prop. Code §§ 301.081(a), 301.083(a).

[24] Tex. Prop. Code § 301.081(b).

[25] Tex. Prop. Code § 301.081(c).

[26] Tex. Prop. Code § 301.081(d).

[27] Tex. Prop. Code § 301.081(e).

[28] Tex. Prop. Code § 301.081(f).

Housing Complaint with the Texas Workforce Commission.[29] If a Respondent elects to do so, the answer must be: (1) in writing; (2) under oath; and (3) in the form prescribed by the Texas Workforce Commission.[30]

The Texas Workforce Commission is also required to investigate all Fair Housing Complaints and must complete such investigation within one hundred (100) days of the date the Fair Housing Complaint was filed (generally referred to as the "Discrimination Investigation Period").[31] The Texas Workforce Commission may issue subpoenas and conduct discovery during the course of such investigation and any subsequent hearings under the Texas Fair Housing Act.[32] If the Texas Workforce Commission is unable to complete the investigation within such one hundred-day period, it must also notify the Complainant and the Respondent in writing of the reasons for the delay and must dispose of all administrative proceedings related to such investigation on or before the first (1st) anniversary after the date the Fair Housing Complaint was filed.[33]

After completion of the Texas Workforce Commission's investigation of a Fair Housing Complaint, it must prepare a final investigative report that includes:

(1) the names of all witnesses contacted by the Texas Workforce Commission and the dates of such contacts;[34]

---

29 Tex. Prop. Code § 301.082(a).

30 Tex. Prop. Code § 301.082(b). In addition, an answer may be amended at any time. Tex. Prop. Code § 301.082(c).

31 Tex. Prop. Code § 301.083(b). Even if a Respondent files an answer, it does not inhibit the investigation of a Fair Housing Complaint. Tex. Prop. Code § 301.082(d).

32 Tex. Prop. Code § 301.067.

33 Tex. Prop. Code § 301.083(c).

34 Tex. Prop. Code § 301.087(a)(1).

(2) a summary of correspondence and other contacts with the Aggrieved Person and the Respondent showing the date of each correspondence and contact;[35]

(3) a summary description of other pertinent records;[36]

(4) a summary of any witness statements;[37] and

(5) answers to interrogatories.[38]

The final investigative report may be amended by the Texas Workforce Commission if additional evidence is discovered after preparation of such investigative report.[39] In addition, after completion of its investigation, the Texas Workforce Commission is required to also make all information derived from such investigation and the final investigative report relating to such investigation available at any time to the Aggrieved Person and the Respondent.[40]

10.1.3 (B) *Conciliation of a Fair Housing Complaint*

During the course of the Discrimination Investigation Period, the Texas Workforce Commission must, to the extent feasible, engage in conciliation efforts with respect to the Fair Housing Complaint so as to amicably resolve such Fair Housing Complaint between the Complainant and the Respondent (generally called a "Conciliation Agreement").[41] Any Conciliation Agreement between a Respondent and the Complainant

---

35 Tex. Prop. Code § 301.087(a)(2).

36 Tex. Prop. Code § 301.087(a)(3).

37 Tex. Prop. Code § 301.087(a)(4).

38 Tex. Prop. Code § 301.087(a)(5).

39 Tex. Prop. Code § 301.087(b).

40 Tex. Prop. Code § 301.085(f).

41 Tex. Prop. Code § 301.085(a). It is also important to note that a Conciliation Agreement resolving a Housing Discrimination Complaint is considered to be public information, unless the Complainant and Respondent agree that it is not, and the Texas Workforce Commission determines that disclosure is not necessary to further the purposes of the Texas Workforce Commission. Tex. Prop. Code § 301.085(d). In addition, any statements made or actions taken by the Complainant or Respondent in the course of the

must be approved by the Texas Workforce Commission.[42] In addition, a Conciliation Agreement may provide for binding arbitration or another method of dispute resolution, and any dispute resolution that results from a Conciliation Agreement may also authorize appropriate relief to the Complainant, including monetary relief.[43]

10.1.3 (C) *Determination of Reasonable Cause for a Housing Discrimination Charge*

Based on its completed investigation, the Texas Workforce Commission must determine from the facts whether reasonable cause exists to believe that a discriminatory housing practice has occurred or is about to occur.[44] Such reasonable cause determination must be made no later than the one hundredth (100th) day after the date the Fair Housing Complaint was filed unless: (1) making the determination is impracticable; or (2) the Texas Workforce Commission approves a Conciliation Agreement relating to such Fair Housing Complaint.[45] If the Texas Workforce Commission determines that no reasonable cause exists to believe that a discriminatory housing practice that is the subject of the Fair Housing Complaint has occurred or is about to occur, it must promptly dismiss such Fair Housing Complaint.[46] The Texas Workforce Commission is also required to make a public disclosure of each such dismissal.[47]

---

conciliation process may not be made public or used as evidence in a subsequent proceeding under the Texas Fair Housing Act without the written consent of the persons concerned. Tex. Prop. Code § 301.085(e).

42 Tex. Prop. Code § 301.085(b).

43 Tex. Prop. Code § 301.085(c).

44 Tex. Prop. Code § 301.088(a).

45 Tex. Prop. Code § 301.088(b). If making such reasonable cause determination within the requisite 100-day period is impracticable, the Texas Workforce Commission must notify the Complainant and the Respondent of the reasons for the delay in writing. Tex. Prop. Code § 301.088(c).

46 Tex. Prop. Code § 301.091(a).

47 Tex. Prop. Code § 301.091(b).

If, however, the Texas Workforce Commission determines that reasonable cause does exist to believe that a discriminatory housing practice has occurred or is about to occur, then it must immediately issue a "Housing Discrimination Charge" on behalf of the Aggrieved Person.[48] A Housing Discrimination Charge issued by the Texas Workforce Commission: (1) must consist of a short and plain statement of the facts on which the Texas Workforce Commission finds reasonable cause to believe that a discriminatory housing practice has occurred or is about to occur; and (2) must be based on the final investigative report (but is not required to be limited to the facts or grounds alleged in the Fair Housing Complaint).[49]

A Housing Discrimination Charge may be decided by judicial proceeding (called a "Judicial Determination") or administrative hearing before the Texas Workforce Commission (called an "Administrative Determination"). Within twenty (20) days following issuance of the Housing Discrimination Charge, the Texas Workforce Commission must send a copy of the Housing Discrimination Charge along with information concerning the election of a Judicial Determination to each Respondent and each Aggrieved Person on whose behalf the Fair Housing Complaint was filed.[50] The Texas Workforce Commission must also include with the copy of the Housing Discrimination Charge sent to the Respondent a notice informing the Respondent of the opportunity for an Administrative Determination of such Housing Discrimination Charge.[51]

---

48 Tex. Prop. Code § 301.088(d). If, however, the Aggrieved Person has already filed a civil lawsuit against the Respondent under federal or Texas law seeking relief with respect to the alleged discriminatory housing practice and a trial of such lawsuit has already commenced, then the Texas Workforce Commission may not issue a Housing Discrimination Charge with respect to such alleged discriminatory housing practice. Tex. Prop. Code § 301.092.

49 Tex. Prop. Code § 301.089(a).

50 Tex. Prop. Code § 301.089(b).

51 Tex. Prop. Code § 301.089(c).

10.1.3 (D) *Judicial Determination of a Housing Discrimination Charge*

The Complainant, Respondent, and Aggrieved Person on whose behalf a Fair Housing Complaint was filed have the right to have the claims asserted in a Housing Discrimination Charge decided by Judicial Determination. In order to elect Judicial Determination, the Complainant, Respondent, or an Aggrieved Person must file a written election of Judicial Determination within twenty (20) days from the date such person or entity receives service of both the Housing Discrimination Charge and the requisite information concerning the election of Judicial Determination.[52] In addition, if the Complainant, Respondent, or an Aggrieved Person makes an election of Judicial Determination, then such person or entity is also required to give notice of such election of Judicial Determination to the Texas Workforce Commission and to all other Complainants and Respondents to whom the Housing Discrimination Charge relates.[53]

If a timely election of Judicial Determination is made, then the Texas Workforce Commission is required to authorize and request the Texas Attorney General to file a civil lawsuit seeking relief on behalf of the Aggrieved Person against the Respondent (commonly referred to as a "Judicial Determination Lawsuit") in a state district court within thirty (30) days from the date such election is made.[54] In addition, even if no Judicial Determination is requested by the Complainant, Respondent, or Aggrieved Person, the Texas Workforce Commission may still authorize and request the Texas Attorney General to file a Judicial Determination Lawsuit in district court for appropriate relief if the Texas Workforce Commission has reasonable cause to believe that: (1) a person is engaged in a pattern or practice of resistance to the full enjoyment by another

52 Tex. Prop. Code § 301.093(a), (b). The Texas Workforce Commission may also elect that a Housing Discrimination Charge be resolved by Judicial Determination, and in such event, the Texas Workforce Commission must make such election no later than the twentieth (20th) day after the date the Housing Discrimination Charge is issued. Tex. Prop. Code § 301.093(b).

53 Tex. Prop. Code § 301.093(c).

54 Tex. Prop. Code § 301.131(a).

person of a right granted under the Texas Fair Housing Act; or (2) a person has been denied a right granted by the Texas Fair Housing Act and that denial raises an issue of general public importance.[55] Venue for a Judicial Determination Lawsuit is in the county in which the alleged discriminatory housing practice occurred or is about to occur.[56]

If, after a trial on the merits in a Judicial Determination Lawsuit, the court finds that a discriminatory housing practice has occurred or is about to occur, the court may:

(1) award preventive relief, including a permanent or temporary injunction, restraining order, or other order against the Respondent, for a violation of the Texas Fair Housing Act as necessary to ensure the full enjoyment of the rights granted by such Act;[57]

(2) award other appropriate relief, including monetary damages, reasonable attorneys fees, and court costs;[58] and

(3) for the purpose of vindicating public interest, assess a civil penalty against the Respondent in an amount that does not exceed $50,000 for a first violation or $100,000 for a second or subsequent violation.[59]

Under such circumstances, the court may also award to a plaintiff in such Judicial Determination lawsuit: (1) actual and punitive damages; (2) reasonable attorneys fees; (3) court costs; and (4) a permanent or temporary injunction, temporary restraining order, or other order, including an order enjoining the Respondent from engaging in the discriminatory practice in the future.[60]

---

55 Tex. Prop. Code § 301.132(a). An Aggrieved Person may also intervene in a Judicial Determination Lawsuit filed by the Texas Attorney General. Tex. Prop. Code § 301.131(c).

56 Tex. Prop. Code § 301.131(b).

57 Tex. Prop. Code § 301.132(b)(1).

58 Tex. Prop. Code § 301.132(b)(2).

59 Tex. Prop. Code § 301.132(b)(3).

60 Tex. Prop. Code §§ 301.131(d), 301.153. In addition, the court in a Judicial Determination Lawsuit may award reasonable attorneys fees to the prevailing party and assess court costs against the non-prevailing party. Tex. Prop. Code §§ 301.131(d), 301.156. Thus, if the Respondent is the prevailing party, instead of the Texas Attorney General, the court may award the Respondent his or her attorneys fees and may assess such costs

10.1.3 (E) *Administrative Determination of a Housing Discrimination Charge*

If a timely and proper election of Judicial Determination of a Housing Discrimination Charge is not made by the Complainant, Respondent, or Aggrieved Person, the Texas Workforce Commission is required to resolve such Housing Discrimination Charge by "Administrative Determination," or in other words, to provide for an administrative hearing on the Housing Discrimination Charge.[61] If after conducting an Administrative Determination hearing the Texas Workforce Commission determines that a Respondent has engaged in or is about to engage in a discriminatory housing practice, then the Texas Workforce Commission may order appropriate relief, including actual damages, reasonable attorney fees, court costs, and other injunctive or equitable relief.[62]

In addition, on the basis of vindicating public interest, the Texas Workforce Commission may also assess a civil penalty against the Respondent in an amount that does not exceed: (1) $10,000 if the Respondent has been found by order of the Texas Workforce Commission or a court to have committed a prior discriminatory housing practice; or (2) $25,000 if the Respondent has been found by order of the Texas Workforce Commission or a court to have committed a prior discriminatory housing practice during the five-year period preceding the date in which the subject Housing Discrimination Charge was filed;

against the Texas Attorney General and/or any other non-prevailing party that has intervened in such lawsuit, such as an Aggrieved Person. Tex. Prop. Code § 301.131(c).

61 Tex. Prop. Code § 301.111(a). Chapter 2001 of the Texas Government Code governs an administrative hearing determination of a Housing Discrimination Charge and any appeal of such hearing. Tex. Prop. Code § 301.111(b). In addition, an administrative hearing to determine a Housing Discrimination Charge may not continue after the commencement of a trial of a civil lawsuit filed by an Aggrieved Person against the Respondent under federal or Texas law seeking relief with respect to the same alleged discriminatory housing practice. Tex. Prop. Code § 301.111(c).

62 Tex. Prop. Code § 301.112(a). The Texas Workforce Commission in an Administrative Determination of a Housing Discrimination Charge may also award reasonable attorneys fees to the prevailing party and assess court costs against the non-prevailing party. Tex. Prop. Code § 301.156. In other words, if the Respondent is the prevailing party, the Texas Workforce Commission may award the Respondent his or her attorneys fees and may assess such costs against the non-prevailing party.

or (3) $50,000 if the Respondent has been found by the Texas Workforce Commission or a court to have committed two or more prior discriminatory housing practices during the seven-year period preceding the date in which the subject Housing Discrimination Charge was filed.[63] If the acts constituting the discriminatory housing practice that is the basis of the subject Housing Discrimination Charge are committed by the same individual who has previously been found to have committed acts constituting a discriminatory housing practice, then the Texas Workforce Commission may impose the $25,000 civil penalty for commission of a prior discriminatory housing practice or the $50,000 civil penalty for commission of two or more prior discriminatory housing practices without regard to the period of time within which such prior discriminatory housing practices occurred.[64] Finally, if requested by the Texas Workforce Commission, the Texas Attorney General must sue the Respondent to recover any civil penalty assessed by the Texas Workforce Committee against the Respondent arising out of an Administrative Determination of a Housing Discrimination Charge.[65]

10.1.3 (F) *Housing Discrimination Lawsuit Brought by an Aggrieved Person*

Under the Texas Fair Housing Act, an Aggrieved Person may also file a civil lawsuit against a Respondent in a Texas district court to obtain appropriate relief with respect to the commission of discriminatory housing practices or a breach of a Conciliation Agreement (commonly referred to as a "Housing Discrimination Lawsuit").[66] The Aggrieved Person may file the Housing Discrimination Lawsuit against the Respondent even if no Fair Housing Complaint has previously been filed and regardless of the status of any pending Fair Housing Complaint that was filed.[67] If an

---

63 Tex. Prop. Code § 301.112(b).

64 Tex. Prop. Code § 301.112(c).

65 Tex. Prop. Code § 301.112(d).

66 Tex. Prop. Code § 301.151(a).

67 Tex. Prop. Code § 301.151(c).

Aggrieved Person elects to file a Housing Discrimination Lawsuit, such lawsuit must be filed by the Aggrieved Person within two (2) years from the date of the occurrence or the termination of an alleged discriminatory housing practice or the breach of a Conciliation Agreement, whichever occurs last.[68]

If the Texas Workforce Commission has obtained a Conciliation Agreement from the Respondent with the consent of an Aggrieved Person, however, then the Aggrieved Person may not file a Housing Discrimination Lawsuit against the Respondent with respect to the alleged discriminatory housing practice that forms the basis of the Fair Housing Complaint, except to enforce the terms of the Conciliation Agreement.[69] In addition, an Aggrieved Person may not file a Housing Discrimination Lawsuit against a Respondent with respect to an alleged discriminatory housing practice that forms the basis of a Housing Discrimination Charge issued by the Texas Workforce Commission if the Texas Workforce Commission has already begun an Administrative Determination hearing with respect to such Housing Discrimination Charge.[70]

Upon application by an Aggrieved Person or a Respondent in a Housing Discrimination Lawsuit, the court may appoint an attorney for such person.[71] In addition, if the Texas Workforce Commission certifies a Housing Discrimination Lawsuit as one of general public importance, it may request the Texas Attorney General to intervene in such Housing Discrimination Lawsuit.[72] In such event, the Attorney General may obtain the

---

68 Tex. Prop. Code § 301.151(a). Such two-year period does not include any time during which an administrative hearing by the Texas Workforce Commission is pending with respect to a Fair Housing Complaint or Housing Discrimination Charge. Tex. Prop. Code § 301.151(a).

69 Tex. Prop. Code § 301.151(d).

70 Tex. Prop. Code § 301.151(e). If, however, an Aggrieved Person filed a Housing Discrimination Lawsuit against a Respondent before the commencement of an Administrative Determination of a Housing Discrimination Charge, the Administrative Determination hearing must be discontinued once the trial of the Housing Discrimination Lawsuit commences. Tex. Prop. Code § 301.111(c).

71 Tex. Prop. Code § 301.152.

72 Tex. Prop. Code § 301.155(a).

same relief against the Respondent as is available to the Attorney General in a Judicial Determination of a Housing Discrimination Charge.[73]

Following a trial on the merits in a Housing Discrimination Lawsuit, if the court finds that a discriminatory housing practice has occurred or is about to occur, then the court may award to the Aggrieved Person: (1) actual and punitive damages; (2) reasonable attorneys fees; (3) court costs; and (4) a permanent or temporary injunction, or other order enjoining the Respondent from engaging in such discriminatory housing practice or ordering other appropriate affirmative action.[74]

10.2 Americans with Disabilities Act

In addition to both the Federal and Texas Fair Housing Acts, the Americans with Disabilities Act (commonly referred to as the "ADA") also protects disabled persons from discrimination. While the Fair Housing Act addresses accommodations for Handicapped-Persons in private residential settings, the Americans with Disabilities Act applies to "Public Accommodations."[75] Under the Americans with Disabilities Act, a Public Accommodation is a private entity that owns, leases, or operates a "Place of Public Accommodation."[76] The Americans with Disabilities Act further defines "Place of Public Accommodation" as a facility, operated by a private entity, whose operations affect commerce and falls within one or more of twelve categories listed under Section 12181 of the Americans with Disabilities Act.[77]

---

[73] Tex. Prop. Code § 301.155(b).

[74] Tex. Prop. Code § 301.153. In addition, the court in a Housing Discrimination Lawsuit may award reasonable attorneys fees to the prevailing party and assess court costs against the non-prevailing party. Tex. Prop. Code § 301.156.

[75] 42 U.S.C. § 12182.

[76] 28 C.F.R. § 36.104.

[77] The categories of facilities that are identified under Section 12181 of the Americans with Disabilities Act as "Places of Public Accommodations" are: (1) an inn, hotel, motel, or other place of lodging (except for an establishment located within a building that contains not more than five (5) rooms for rent or hire and that is

The Americans with Disabilities Act prohibits discrimination of a person by a Public Accommodation on the basis of such person's "Disability" and requires Places of Public Accommodation to be designed, constructed, and altered in compliance with the accessibility standards set forth by regulation.[78] As a general rule, the Common Area amenities of a Homeowners Association are not considered to be Places of Public Accommodations if their use is restricted to the exclusive use of the Homeowners Association's members and their tenants and guests.[79] A Homeowners Association, however, could potentially bring itself under the auspices of the Americans with Disabilities Act if it invites the public to use its facilities. For example, if the Homeowners Association allows residents of other neighborhoods to purchase "pool memberships," or

---

actually occupied by the proprietor of the establishment as the residence of the proprietor); (2) a restaurant, bar, or other establishment serving food or drink; (3) a motion picture house, theater, concert hall, stadium, or other place of exhibition or entertainment; (4) an auditorium, convention center, lecture hall, or other place of public gathering; (5) a bakery, grocery store, clothing store, hardware store, shopping center, or other sales or rental establishment; (6) a laundromat, dry cleaner, bank, barber shop, beauty shop, travel service, shoe repair service, funeral parlor, gas station, office of an accountant or lawyer, pharmacy, insurance office, professional office of a health care provider, hospital, or other service establishment; (7) a terminal, depot, or other station used for specified public transportation; (8) a museum, library, gallery, or other place of public display or collection; (9) a park, zoo, amusement park, or other place of recreation; (10) a nursery, elementary, secondary, undergraduate, or postgraduate private school, or other place of education; (11) a day care center, senior citizen center, homeless shelter, food bank, adoption agency, or other social service center establishment; and (12) a gymnasium, health spa, bowling alley, golf course, or other place of exercise or recreation. 42 U.S.C. § 12181.

78 *See* 42 U.S.C. § 12181; 28 C.F.R. § 36.101, *et seq.* Although the Fair Housing Act uses the term "Handicap" and the Americans with Disabilities Act uses the term "Disability," both terms have the same legal meaning. *See Bragdon v. Abbott*, 524 U.S. 624, 631 (1998) (Noting that the definition of "Disability" in the Americans with Disabilities Act is drawn almost verbatim from the definition of "Handicap" contained in the Fair Housing Amendments Act of 1988.). For simplicity and to maintain consistency with the applicable statutes, this book shall use the term "Handicap" when discussing the Federal Fair Housing Act and the term "Disability" when discussing the Americans with Disabilities Act.

79 *See Indep. Hous. Servs. of San Francisco v. Fillmore Ctr. Assocs.*, 840 F. Supp. 1328, 1344 (N.D. Cal. 1993) (stating that residential apartments and condominiums do not constitute public accommodations within the meaning of the American with Disabilities Act); *Regents of the Mercerburg Coll. v. Republic Franklin Ins. Co.*, 458 F.3d 159, fn. 8 (3rd Cir. 2006).

if the Homeowners Association invites civic groups to use its clubhouse for meetings unrelated to any membership affiliation in the Homeowners Association.[80]

If a Homeowners Association does constitute a Public Accommodation because it owns, leases, or operates a Place of Public Accommodation, then it must comply with basic nondiscrimination requirements that prohibit exclusion, segregation, and unequal treatment of Disabled Persons, as well as specific requirements related to: (1) compliance with architectural standards for new and altered buildings;[81] (2) making reasonable modifications to policies, practices, and procedures, when the modifications are necessary to afford goods, services, facilities, privileges, advantages, or accommodations to individuals with Disabilities (unless the modifications would fundamentally alter the nature of the goods, services, facilities, privileges, advantages, or accommodations);[82] (3) taking steps to ensure effective communication with people who have hearing, vision, or speech disabilities;[83] and (4) removing architectural barriers in existing buildings when it is easily accomplishable and able to be carried out without much difficulty or expense.[84]

---

80 If a Homeowners Association simply allows one of its Members to use the Homeowners Association clubhouse for a meeting or social gathering, that by itself is not likely to make it a Place of Public Accommodation.

81 *See* 28 C.F.R. §§ 36.401–36.406.

82 *See* 28 C.F.R. § 36.302.

83 *See* 28 C.F.R. § 36.303.

84 28 C.F.R. § 36.304. Examples of steps to remove architectural barriers include, but are not limited to, the following actions: (1) installing ramps; (2) making curb cuts in sidewalks and entrances; (3) repositioning shelves; (4) rearranging tables, chairs, vending machines, display racks, and other furniture; (5) repositioning telephones; (6) adding raised markings on elevator control buttons; (7) installing flashing alarm lights; (8) widening doors; (9) installing offset hinges to widen doorways; (10) eliminating a turnstile or providing an alternative accessible path; (11) installing accessible door hardware; (12) installing grab bars in toilet stalls; (13) rearranging toilet partitions to increase maneuvering space; (14) insulating lavatory pipes under sinks to prevent burns; (15) installing a raised toilet seat; (16) installing a full-length bathroom mirror; (17) repositioning the paper towel dispenser in a bathroom; (18) creating designated accessible parking spaces; (19) installing an accessible paper cup dispenser at an existing inaccessible water fountain; (20) removing high pile, low density carpeting; and/or (21) installing vehicle hand controls.

10.3 The Federal Communications Commission's Over-the-Air Reception Devices Rule ("OTARD Rule")

Homeowners Associations were once free to adopt and enforce restrictions and regulations on the installation and location of satellite dishes and other types of antennas erected on dwellings within their developments. In 1996, however, the Federal Communications Commission adopted the Over-the-Air Reception Devices rule (called the "OTARD Rule") concerning governmental and nongovernmental restrictions on viewers' ability to receive video programming signals from "Direct Broadcast Satellites" ("DBS"), broadband radio service providers (formerly called "Multichannel Multipoint Distribution Service" or "MMDS"), and Television Broadcast Stations ("TVBS"), which preempts all state, local-governmental, and other non-governmental restrictions regulating installation or use of satellites and antennas.[85]

10.3.1 Scope of Antennas Protected by the OTARD Rule

The OTARD Rule prohibits the enforcement of Restrictive Covenants that impair the installation, maintenance, or use of the following types of antennas used to receive video programming (generally referred to as "Protected Antennas"):

(1) antennas that are used to receive Direct Broadcast Satellite service, including direct-to-home satellite service, or to receive or transmit fixed wireless signals via satellite that are one meter (39.37 inches) or less in diameter, or of any size if located in Alaska;[86]

(2) antennas that are used to receive video programming services via Multipoint Distribution Services, including Multichannel Multipoint Distribution Services, instructional television fixed services, and local Multipoint Distribution Services, or to receive or transmit fixed wireless

[85] 47 C.F.R. § 1.4000. *See also*, the FCC Fact Sheet on Placement of Antennas published by the Federal Communications Commission at http://www.fcc.gov/mb/facts/otard.html.

[86] 47 C.F.R. § 1.4000(a)(1)(i).

signals other than via satellite that are one meter (39.37 inches) or less in diameter or diagonal measurement;[87]

(3) antennas of any size that are used to receive television broadcast signals;[88] and

(4) any mast used to support such antennas.[89]

The OTARD Rule also prohibits Restrictive Covenants that: (1) unreasonably delay or prevent installation, maintenance, or use of Protected Antennas; (2) unreasonably increase the cost of installation, maintenance, or use of Protected Antennas; or (3) preclude reception of an acceptable quality signal by a Protected Antenna.[90]

The OTARD Rule applies to individuals who place Protected Antennas on real property that they own or rent (such as individually owned Lots in a Subdivision Development or Units in a Condominium Development) or that is within their "exclusive use or control" (such as Limited Common Elements assigned to a specific Unit).[91] This would include a Unit Owner who installs a Protected Antenna on a balcony or patio outside of the Unit's boundaries if such patio or balcony constitutes Limited Common Element that is restricted to such Unit Owner's exclusive use.

10.3.2 Exceptions to the OTARD Rule

The OTARD Rule, however, does not preclude a Homeowners Association from adopting and/or enforcing Restrictive Covenants that: (1) do not prevent or unreasonably

---

[87] 47 C.F.R. § 1.4000(a)(1)(ii). For purposes of the OTARD Rule, "fixed wireless signals" means any commercial non-broadcast communications signals transmitted via wireless technology to and/or from a fixed customer location. 47 C.F.R. § 1.4000(a)(2). Fixed wireless signals, however, do not include, among other things, AM radio, FM radio, amateur ("HAM") radio, Citizen's Band (CB) radio, and Digital Audio Radio Service (DARS) signals. 47 C.F.R. § 1.4000(a)(2).

[88] 47 C.F.R. § 1.4000(a)(1)(iii).

[89] 47 C.F.R. § 1.4000(a)(1)(iv).

[90] 47 C.F.R. § 1.4000(a)(3).

[91] 47 C.F.R. § 1.4000(a)(1).

delay installation, maintenance, or use of Protected Antennas (as opposed to restrictions that totally prohibit Protected Antennas or create drawn out application and permit processes);[92] (2) do not unreasonably increase the cost of installation, maintenance, or use of Protected Antennas (as opposed to restrictions requiring expensive fencing and landscaping to screen a Protected Antenna);[93] and/or (3) do not preclude reception of an acceptable, quality signal by a Protected Antenna (as opposed to a restriction requiring placement of a Protected Antenna in an area that prevents a Homeowner from receiving a signal of acceptable quality).[94] For example, a Restrictive Covenant that requires Protected Antennas to be placed, to the extent feasible, in a location not visible from the street would be permissible if the placement allows reception of an acceptable, quality signal and does not unreasonably delay or increase the cost of installation, maintenance, or use of a Protected Antenna. But if a Restrictive Covenant requires that an antenna be placed in a position where reception would be impossible, or would be substantially degraded, such Restrictive Covenant would conflict with the OTARD Rule.

In addition, the OTARD Rule allows a Homeowners Association to enforce Restrictive Covenants that do impair the installation, maintenance, or use of a Protected Antenna if it is necessary for a clearly defined safety objective and it does not impose a more burdensome requirement than is needed to ensure such safety objective.[95] In order for the enforcement of a restriction on the installation, maintenance, or use of a Protected Antenna to be permissible under the OTARD Rule on the basis of a safety objective, the safety reason for the restriction must be written in a document that is readily available to antenna users prior to installation, so that a person wanting to install a Protected Antenna

---

92 47 C.F.R. § 1.4000(a)(3)(i).

93 47 C.F.R. § 1.4000(a)(3)(ii).

94 47 C.F.R. § 1.4000(a)(3)(iii). The OTARD Rule, however, does not prohibit enforcement of a Restrictive Covenant that merely affects a Protected Antenna's ability to receive signals so long as the Restrictive Covenant does not impair such ability.

95 47 C.F.R. § 1.4000(b).

knows what restrictions apply.[96] In addition, the restriction must explain the reason for the safety concern and must be applied in a non-discriminatory manner to the extent possible as to other appurtenances or fixtures that are comparable in size and weight to Protected Antennas and pose a similar or greater safety risk as Protected Antennas.[97] Valid safety-based restrictions include restrictions that prevent people from installing Protected Antennas on fire escapes; that restrict installation of a Protected Antenna within a certain distance from a power line; that mandate compliance with electrical code requirements to properly ground a Protected Antenna; and that prohibit installation of a Protected Antenna at a location that will obstruct a driver's view of an intersection or street, to name a few.

In addition, a Homeowners Association may also enforce a Restrictive Covenant that does impair the installation, maintenance, or use of Protected Antennas on the basis of preserving a prehistoric or historic district, site, building, structure, or object included in (or eligible for inclusion in) the National Register of Historic Places.[98] Such a Restrictive Covenant, however, cannot impose greater restrictions on Protected Antennas than are imposed on the installation, maintenance, or use of other modern appurtenances, devices, or fixtures that are comparable in size, weight, and appearance to the Protected Antennas, and it cannot impose a more burdensome requirement than is needed to ensure the historic preservation goal.[99]

10.3.3 Waiver of the OTARD Rule and Petition for Determination by the Federal Communications Commission

A Homeowners Association may apply to the Federal Communications Commission for a waiver from the OTARD Rule if certain exceptional or unusual

96 47 C.F.R. § 1.4000(b)(1), (3).

97 47 C.F.R. § 1.4000(b)(1).

98 47 C.F.R. § 1.4000(b)(2).

99 47 C.F.R. § 1.4000(b)(2)–(3).

circumstances exist.[100] In addition, if a Homeowners Association wants to determine whether the enforcement of a specific restriction is permissible, it may petition the Federal Communications Commission for a declaratory ruling or file a declaratory judgment lawsuit in a local, federal, or state court.[101] Petitioning the Federal Communications Commission for a declaratory ruling requires the petition and all other related pleadings be sent to the Secretary of the Federal Communications Commission in Washington, DC.[102]

10.4 Freedom to Display the American Flag Act

In 2006, the United States Congress enacted the "Freedom to Display the American Flag Act." The Freedom to Display the American Flag Act prohibits Homeowners Associations from adopting and/or enforcing Restrictive Covenants or Association Rules that would unreasonably restrict Homeowners from displaying the flag of the United States at their property.[103] The substantive part of the Freedom to Display the American Flag Act states that "[a] condominium association, cooperative association, or residential real estate management association may not adopt or enforce any policy, or enter into any agreement, that would restrict or prevent a member of the association from displaying the flag of the United States on residential property within the association with respect to which such member has a separate ownership interest or a right to exclusive possession or use."[104] In other words, the Freedom to Display the American Flag Act protects a Homeowner's right to display an American flag on his or her Lot, Unit, or any Limited Common Element assigned to his or her Unit.

---

100 47 C.F.R. § 1.4000(d).

101 47 C.F.R. § 1.4000(e).

102 47 C.F.R. § 1.4000(h).

103 4 U.S.C. § 5, *et seq.*

104 4 U.S.C. § 5, Section 3.

The Freedom to Display the American Flag Act defines a flag of the United States as "any flag, standard, colors, ensign, or any picture or representation of either, or of any part or parts of either, made of any substance or represented on any substance, of any size evidently purporting to be either of said flag, standard, colors, or ensign of the United States of America or a picture or a representation of either, upon which shall be shown the colors, the stars and the stripes, in any number of either thereof, or of any part or parts of either, by which the average person seeing the same without deliberation may believe the same to represent the flag, colors, standard, or ensign of the United States of America."[105] The Freedom to Display the American Flag Act's definition of United States flag includes not just the current American flag with fifty stars and thirteen stripes, but also historical American flags of any reasonable size, with varying number of stars, both with and without gold fringe, but it does not include other types of patriotic flags that Homeowners might want to display. Most notably, the Freedom to Display the American Flag Act's definition of "flag of the United States" does not include the National League of Families' POW/MIA flag[106] or the flags of the United States Marine Corps, Army, Navy, Air Force, or Coast Guard, as they are not generally considered "flags of the United States" depicting the traditional stars and stripes. In addition, the Freedom to Display the American Flag Act also does not protect the right to display state flags, including the flag of the State of Texas.[107]

105 4 U.S.C. § 5, Section 2(1); 4 U.S.C. § 3.

106 On August 10, 1990, the United States Congress recognized the National League of Families' POW/MIA flag and designated it "as the symbol of our Nation's concern and commitment to resolving as fully as possible the fates of Americans still prisoner, missing, and unaccounted for in Southeast Asia, thus ending the uncertainty for their families and the Nation." P.L. 101-355, 104 Stat. 416.

107 There are a number of other flags that Homeowners might also want to display as symbols of their patriotism, affiliations, and beliefs that are equally excluded from the scope of the Freedom to Display the American Flag Act. For example, neither the United Nations flag nor the flags of foreign countries are protected under the Freedom to Display the American Flag Act. Nor does the Freedom to Display the American Flag Act protect the rainbow flag (a multicolored flag consisting of stripes in the colors of the rainbow that is commonly used as a symbol of LGBT pride), the Confederate flag (often considered one of the most controversial symbols in American history), or other flags of important historical significance, such

The application of the Freedom to Display the American Flag Act, however, is not without limitations. First, the Freedom to Display the American Flag Act does not protect the display or use of an American Flag in a manner that is inconsistent with the rules or customs pertaining to the proper display or use of the American Flag as established pursuant to any applicable provision of law.[108] Second, the Freedom to Display the American Flag Act does not prohibit the enforcement of reasonable restrictions pertaining to the time, place, or manner of displaying the American Flag that are necessary to protect a substantial interest of the Homeowners Association.[109]

Notwithstanding the limitations on the application of the Freedom to Display the American Flag Act, the Act's definition of "flag of the United States" fails to place specific limits on the size of the protected American Flags that may be displayed.[110] According to *Guinness Book of World Records*, the world's largest flag is the "Superflag," an American Flag measuring 255 feet by 505 feet, weighing three thousand pounds, and requiring at least six hundred volunteers to unfurl.[111] Although the possibility of a Homeowner wanting to display a flag as large as the Superflag on their property remains unlikely, the Freedom to Display the American Flag Act protects the right to display or fly an American Flag of any dimension and size within reasonable restrictions pertaining to the time, place, or manner of displaying such flag.[112]

---

as the Bunker Hill flag, the Bonnie Blue flag, the Gadsden Don't Tread on Me flag, and the first Navy Jack flag.

[108] 4 U.S.C. § 5, Section 4(1).

[109] 4 U.S.C. § 5, Section 4(2).

[110] Congress also failed to include express language in the Freedom to Display the American Flag Act concerning flag poles, or more specifically, the size of flag poles that Homeowners may use to display a flag of the United States.

[111] *See* http://www.superflag.com/guinessbook.html.

[112] The provisions in the Freedom to Display the American Flag Act allowing for a flag of "any size" but also allowing for "reasonable time, place, or manner" restrictions by Homeowners Associations could be considered inapposite in certain circumstances. For example, if a Homeowners Association adopts an Association Rule prohibiting a Homeowner from flying a flag that obstructs the view of another Homeowner,

10.5 Texas Community Homes for Disabled Persons Location Act

The Texas Community Homes for Disabled Persons Location Act was enacted by the Texas Legislature in 1985. The Texas Community Homes for Disabled Persons Location Act establishes a right of use and operation of a "Community Home" for "Persons with Disabilities" that meets the qualifications under such Act and invalidates any Restrictive Covenant created or amended on or after September 1, 1985, that would prohibit the use of real property as a Community Home.[113] This would include any Restrictive Covenant that limits homes to single-family use or restricts the use of a home for business purposes.

To qualify as a protected Community Home, a residential dwelling must be either a "Community-Based Residential Home"[114] or an "Assisted Living Facility" licensed under Chapter 247 of the Texas Health and Safety Code,[115] and its exterior structure must

---

a court would have to determine whether this is a reasonable place and manner restriction necessary to protect a substantial interest of the Homeowners Association. Whether a particular restriction on the size of the American Flag or other rule on the time, place, or manner of displaying an American Flag is reasonable and necessary to protect a substantial interest will vary according to the facts of each particular circumstance.

[113] Tex. Hum. Res. Code § 123.003. The Texas Community Homes for Disabled Persons Act defines "Person With a Disability" as a person whose ability to care for himself or herself, perform manual tasks, learn, work, walk, see, hear, speak, or breathe is substantially limited because the person has: (1) an orthopedic, visual, speech, or hearing impairment; (2) Alzheimer's disease; (3) pre-senile dementia; (4) cerebral palsy; (5) epilepsy; (6) muscular dystrophy; (7) multiple sclerosis; (8) cancer; (9) heart disease; (10) diabetes; (11) mental retardation; (12) autism; or (13) emotional illness. Tex. Hum. Res. Code § 123.002.

[114] To qualify as a Community-Based Residential Home, it must be operated by either: (1) the Texas Department of Mental Health and Mental Retardation; (2) a "Community Center" that provides services to "Persons with Disabilities" organized under Chapter 534 of the Texas Health and Safety Code; (3) a Texas nonprofit corporation; or (4) an entity certified by the Texas Department of Human Services as a provider under the medical assistance program serving persons in intermediate care facilities for persons with mental retardation. Tex. Hum. Res. Code § 123.004(1).

[115] An "Assisted Living Facility" under Chapter 247 of the Texas Health and Safety Code means an establishment that furnishes, in one or more facilities, food and shelter to four or more persons who are unrelated to the proprietor of the establishment and provides "Personal Care Services." Tex. Health & Safety Code § 247.002(1). "Personal Care Services" means assistance with meals, dressing, movement, bathing, or other personal needs or maintenance; the administration of medication by a person licensed to administer medication or the assistance with or supervision of medication; and/or general supervision or oversight of the physical and mental well-being of a person who needs assistance to maintain a private and independent residence in an Assisted Living Facility or who needs assistance to manage the person's personal life, regardless of whether a guardian has been appointed for the person. Tex. Health & Safety Code § 247.002(5).

retain compatibility with the surrounding residential dwellings.[116] In addition, a protected Community Home under the Texas Community Homes for Disabled Persons Location Act must provide the Persons with Disabilities who reside in such home with: (1) food and shelter; (2) personal guidance; (3) care; (4) habilitation services; and (5) supervision.[117]

Notwithstanding the protections afforded to a Community Home under the Texas Community Homes for Disabled Persons Location Act, a Community Home must still meet all applicable licensing requirements and may not have more than six persons with disabilities and two supervisors residing in the Community Home at the same time.[118] Moreover, the residents of a Community Home may not keep, either on the premises of the Community Home or on a street adjacent to the Community Home, motor vehicles for the use of the residents in numbers that exceed the number of bedrooms in the home.[119] Finally, the Texas Community Homes for Disabled Persons Location Act mandates that a protected Community Home may not be established within one-half mile of another existing protected Community Home.[120]

10.6 Protection of Solid-Waste Composting, Rain Harvesting, Irrigation Systems, Drought-Resistant Landscaping, and Water-Conserving Natural Turf under Section 202.007 of the Texas Property Code

In 2003, the Texas Legislature enacted Section 202.007 of the Texas Property Code in order to restrict the enforcement of Restrictive Covenants that prohibit certain water-conservation actions by Texas Homeowners, which was amended in 2013 in order to extend its protection to drought-resistant landscaping and water-conserving natural

---

116 Tex. Hum. Res. Code § 123.004.

117 Tex. Hum. Res. Code § 123.005.

118 Tex. Hum. Res. Code §§ 123.006–123.007.

119 Tex. Hum. Res. Code § 123.009.

120 Tex. Hum. Res. Code § 123.008.

turf.[121] Pursuant to Section 202.007, a Texas Homeowners Association may not include or enforce a provision in a Dedicatory Instrument that prohibits or restricts a Homeowner from: (1) implementing measures promoting solid-waste composting of vegetation (including grass clippings, leaves, or brush) or leaving grass clippings uncollected on grass; (2) installing rain barrels or a rainwater harvesting system; (3) implementing efficient irrigation systems, including underground drip or other drip systems; or (4) using drought-resistant landscaping or water-conserving natural turf.[122] Any existing Restrictive Covenant that does impose a prohibition or restriction on such water-conservation actions is considered void.[123] Section 202.007, however, does authorize Homeowners Associations to enforce certain permissible limited regulations concerning: composting devices; rain barrels and rain harvesting devices; and irrigation systems and water-conserving landscaping and hardscape, which are described in greater detail in the following subchapters.

10.6.1 Permissible Regulation of Composting Devices

Notwithstanding the invalidation of any provision in a Dedicatory Instrument that would prohibit or restrict a Homeowner from composting, Section 202.007 does not restrict a Homeowners Association from regulating the requirements for or the location of a composting device (including size, type, shielding, and materials of such device or appurtenance), so long as such regulations do not prohibit the economic installation of the composting device on the Homeowner's property where there is reasonably sufficient area

[121] Senate Research Center, Bill Analysis, Tex. H.B. 645, 78th Leg., R.S. (2003); Senate Research Center, Bill Analysis, Tex. S.B. 198, 83rd Leg., R.S. (2013). Section 202.007, however, does not apply to a Homeowners Association that: (1) is located in a municipality with a population of more than 175,000 that is located in a county in which another municipality with a population of more than 1 million is predominantly located; and (2) manages or regulates a development in which at least four thousand acres of the property is subject to a covenant, condition, or restriction designating the property for commercial use, multifamily dwellings, or open space. Tex. Prop. Code § 202.007(e).

[122] Tex. Prop. Code § 202.007(a).

[123] Tex. Prop. Code § 202.007(b).

to install such device.[124] Section 202.007 also does not require a Homeowners Association to allow a composting device owned by a Lot or Unit Owner to be installed in or on Common Areas or Common Elements, or any other property owned by the Homeowners Association or owned in common by the Members of the Homeowners Association.[125] Nor does Section 202.007 require a Homeowners Association to permit such a device in an area of a Unit or Lot other than a fenced yard or patio.[126]

10.6.2 Permissible Regulation of Rain Barrels and Rain Harvesting Systems

Notwithstanding the invalidation of any provision in a Dedicatory Instrument that would prohibit or restrict a Homeowner from installing rain barrels or a rainwater harvesting system, Section 202.007 does not require a Homeowners Association to allow a rain barrel or rainwater harvesting system owned by a Lot or Unit Owner to be installed in or on Common Areas or Common Elements, or any other property owned by the Homeowners Association or owned in common by the Members of the Homeowners Association.[127] Nor does Section 202.007 require a Homeowners Association to allow a rain barrel or rainwater harvesting system to be installed in the front yard of a Homeowner's Lot or Unit.[128] In addition, Section 202.007 does not require a Homeowners Association to allow the installation of a rain barrel or rain harvesting system that: (1) is of a color other than a color consistent with the color scheme of the Lot or Unit Owner's

---

124 Tex. Prop. Code § 202.007(d)(1).

125 Tex. Prop. Code § 202.007(d)(2).

126 Tex. Prop. Code § 202.007(d)(2).

127 Tex. Prop. Code § 202.007(d)(6)(A).

128 Tex. Prop. Code § 202.007(d)(6)(A)(iii). More specifically, a Homeowners Association is not required to permit installation of a rain barrel or rainwater harvesting system at a location on the Homeowner's Lot or Unit between the front of the home or dwelling and an adjoining or adjacent street. Tex. Prop. Code § 202.007(d)(6)(A)(iii).

home; or (2) displays any language or other content that is not typically displayed by such a barrel or system as it is manufactured.[129]

Section 202.007 also permits a Homeowners Association to regulate the size, type, shielding of, and the materials used in the construction of a rain barrel, rain harvesting device, or other appurtenance that is located on the side of a Lot or Unit Owner's house (i.e., side yard) or at any other location on the Lot or Unit that is visible from a street, another lot, or Common Area or Common Elements so long as such regulations do not: (1) prohibit the economic installation of the device or appurtenance on the Homeowner's Lot or Unit; and (2) there is reasonably sufficient area on the Homeowner's Lot or Unit in which to install the device or appurtenance.[130]

10.6.3 Permissible Regulation of the Installation of Irrigation Systems and Water-Conserving Landscaping and Hardscape

Notwithstanding the invalidation of any provision in a Dedicatory Instrument that would prohibit or restrict a Homeowner from implementing efficient irrigation systems, Section 202.007 does not prohibit a Homeowners Association from regulating the installation of efficient irrigation systems, including establishing visibility limitations for aesthetic purposes.[131] Nor does Section 202.007 restrict a Homeowners Association from regulating the installation or use of gravel, rocks, or cacti or from regulating yard and landscape maintenance, so long as such regulations do not restrict or prohibit turf or landscaping design that promotes water conservation.[132]

---

[129] Tex. Prop. Code § 202.007(d)(6)(B).

[130] Tex. Prop. Code § 202.007(d)(7).

[131] Tex. Prop. Code § 202.007(d)(3).

[132] Tex. Prop. Code § 202.007(d)(4), (5).

10.6.4 Permissible Regulation of Drought-Resistant Landscaping and Water-Conserving Natural Turf

Finally, notwithstanding the invalidation of any provision in a Dedicatory Instrument that would prohibit or restrict a Homeowner from using drought-resistant landscaping or water-conserving natural turf, Section 202.007 does not prohibit a Homeowners Association from requiring a Homeowner to submit a detailed description or a plan for the installation of drought-resistant landscaping or water-conserving natural turf for review and approval by Homeowners Association to ensure, to the extent practicable, maximum aesthetic compatibility with other landscaping in the Condominium or Subdivision Development.[133] If a Homeowners Association does require its Homeowners to submit a detailed description or a plan for the installation of drought-resistant landscaping or water-conserving natural turf for review and approval by the Homeowners Association, then it may not unreasonably deny or withhold approval of a proposed installation of drought-resistant landscaping or water-conserving natural turf or unreasonably determine that the proposed installation is aesthetically incompatible with other landscaping in the Condominium or Subdivision Development.[134]

10.7 Use of an Adjacent Lot for Residential Purposes under Section 209.015 of the Texas Property Code

In 2013, the Texas Legislature enacted Section 209.015 of the Texas Property Code in order to clarify the authority of a Subdivision Association to regulate the use of a secondary Lot owned by a Lot Owner that is adjacent to a residential Lot owned by the same Lot Owner.[135] Pursuant to Section 209.015, a Subdivision Association may not adopt or enforce a provision in a Dedicatory Instrument that prohibits or restricts the Owner of

---

[133] Tex. Prop. Code § 202.007(d)(8).

[134] Tex. Prop. Code § 202.007(d-1).

[135] Senate Research Center, Bill Analysis, Tex. H.B. 35, 83rd Leg., R.S. (2013). Section 209.015 of the Texas Property Code does not apply to Condominium Developments. Tex. Prop. Code § 209.003(d).

a Lot on which a residence is located from using for "residential purposes" an "adjacent lot" also owned by such Lot Owner.[136]

Notwithstanding the invalidation of any provisions of a Subdivision Association's Dedicatory Instruments that would prohibit or restrict a Lot Owner from using an applicable adjacent lot for residential purposes, before a Lot Owner constructs, places, or erects a building, structure, or other improvement to be used for a residential purpose on such adjacent lot, the Lot Owner must still obtain approval from the Subdivision Association (or, if applicable, an Architectural Committee established by the Subdivision Association or its Dedicatory Instruments), based on criteria prescribed by the Dedicatory Instruments specific to the proposed residential purpose use of such adjacent lot, including reasonable restrictions regarding size, location, shielding, and aesthetics of the proposed residential purpose use.[137] In other words, if a Lot Owner intends to construct a garage on an applicable adjacent lot to serve the residence constructed on his primary residential Lot, the Lot Owner must still obtain approval from the Subdivision Association (or, if applicable, an Architectural Committee) based on criteria prescribed by the applicable Dedicatory Instruments specific to garages.

If a Lot Owner owns two Lots that are adjacent to each other and elects to use one of the Lots for "residential purposes" pursuant to Section 209.015, the Lot Owner is then

---

136 Tex. Prop. Code § 209.015(b). For purposes of Section 209.015 of the Texas Property Code, the term "adjacent lot" refers to: (1) a Lot that is contiguous to another Lot that fronts on the same street; (2) a Lot that is contiguous to a corner Lot by either a side property line or a back property line; or (3) if permitted by an applicable Dedicatory Instrument, any Lot that is contiguous to another Lot at the back property line. Tex. Prop. Code § 209.015(a)(1). For purposes of Section 209.015 of the Texas Property Code, the term "residential purposes" with respect to the use of an "adjacent lot" means the placement, construction, or erection thereon of any building, structure, or other improvement customarily appurtenant to a residence, as opposed to use for a business or commercial purpose; and includes the placement, construction, or erection thereon of a garage, sidewalk, driveway, parking area, children's swing or playscape, fence, septic system, swimming pool, utility line, or water well and, if otherwise specifically permitted by the applicable Dedicatory Instruments, the parking or storage of a recreational vehicle. Tex. Prop. Code § 209.015(a)(2). A provision in a Dedicatory Instrument that violates Section 209.015 of the Texas Property Code is considered void. Tex. Prop. Code § 209.015(f).

137 Tex. Prop. Code § 209.015(c).

precluded from selling either Lot separately unless the Lot Owner restores the adjacent lot being used for residential purposes to the condition existing prior to its use for residential purposes.[138] More specifically, if a Lot Owner elects to use an applicable adjacent lot for residential purposes, then the Lot Owner may not sell or transfer ownership of the Lot containing the Lot Owner's residence unless the Lot Owner either: (1) includes the adjacent lot in the sales agreement and transfers both the primary residence lot and the adjacent lot to the new owner under the same dedicatory conditions; or (2) restores the adjacent lot to its original condition before the addition of any improvements constructed, placed, or erected thereon for residential purposes to the extent necessary that the adjacent lot would again be suitable for the construction of a separate residence as originally platted and provided for prior to the conveyance of such adjacent lot to the Lot Owner.[139] Similarly, if a Lot Owner elects to use an applicable adjacent lot for residential purposes, then the Lot Owner may not sell or transfer ownership of such adjacent lot (separate from the Lot containing the Lot Owner's residence) unless the adjacent lot has been restored to its original condition before the addition of any improvements constructed, placed, or erected thereon for residential purposes to the extent necessary that the adjacent lot would again be suitable for the construction of a separate residence as originally platted and provided for prior to the conveyance of such adjacent lot to the Lot Owner.[140]

10.8 Display of Political Signs under Section 202.009 of the Texas Property Code

In 2005, the Texas Legislature enacted Section 202.009 of the Texas Property Code to prohibit Texas Homeowners Associations from restricting Homeowners from exercising their free speech rights through the placement of political signs in their

---

[138] Tex. Prop. Code § 209.015(d).

[139] Tex. Prop. Code § 209.015(d).

[140] Tex. Prop. Code § 209.015(e).

windows and on their lawns.[141] Under Section 202.009, a Homeowners Association may not enforce or adopt a Restrictive Covenant that prohibits a Homeowner from displaying on the Homeowner's property one or more signs advertising a political candidate or ballot item for an election during an applicable election period.[142] An applicable election period consists of the time period commencing ninety (90) days before the date of the election to which a sign relates and continuing until the tenth (10th) day after such election date.[143]

Section 202.009 of the Texas Property Code, however, does not prohibit the enforcement or adoption of a Restrictive Covenant that requires a sign to be ground-mounted or that limits a Homeowner to displaying only one sign for each candidate or ballot item.[144] Nor does Section 202.009 prohibit the enforcement or adoption of a Restrictive Covenant that prohibits a sign that:

(1) contains roofing material, siding, paving materials, flora, one or more balloons or lights, or any other similar building, landscaping, or nonstandard decorative component;[145]

(2) is attached in any way to plant material, a traffic-control device, a light, a trailer, a vehicle, or any other existing structure or object;[146]

(3) includes the painting of architectural surfaces;[147]

(4) threatens the public health or safety;[148]

(5) is larger than four feet by six feet;[149]

---

141 Senate Research Center, Bill Analysis, Tex. H.B. 873, 79th Leg., R.S. (2005).

142 Tex. Prop. Code § 202.009(a).

143 Tex. Prop. Code § 202.009(a).

144 Tex. Prop. Code § 202.009(b).

145 Tex. Prop. Code § 202.009(c)(1).

146 Tex. Prop. Code § 202.009(c)(2).

147 Tex. Prop. Code § 202.009(c)(3).

148 Tex. Prop. Code § 202.009(c)(4).

149 Tex. Prop. Code § 202.009(c)(5).

(6) violates a law;[150]

(7) contains language, graphics, or any display that would be offensive to the ordinary person;[151] or

(8) is accompanied by music or other sounds or by streamers or is otherwise distracting to motorists.[152]

In addition, if a Homeowner Association has authority under its Declaration to remove signs prohibited thereunder from a Lot or Unit, then the Homeowners Association may still remove any sign displayed in violation of a Restrictive Covenant that is not protected by Section 202.009.[153]

10.9 Protection of Solar Energy Devices under Section 202.010 of the Texas Property Code

In 2011, the Texas Legislature enacted Section 202.010 of the Texas Property Code in order to establish rules that allow Texas Homeowners to install "Solar Energy Devices" on the roof of their homes or in their backyard with minimal regulation by their Homeowners Association.[154] Except for certain permissible regulations established by Section 202.010, a Texas Homeowners Association may not include or enforce a provision in a Declaration that prohibits or restricts a Homeowner from installing a Solar Energy Device on his or her property.[155] Notwithstanding, Section 202.010 authorizes

---

150 Tex. Prop. Code § 202.009(c)(6).

151 Tex. Prop. Code § 202.009(c)(7).

152 Tex. Prop. Code § 202.009(c)(8).

153 Tex. Prop. Code § 202.009(d).

154 House Comm. on Business and Industry, Bill Analysis, Tex. H.B. 362, 82nd Leg., R.S. (2011). "Solar Energy Devices" is defined as a system or series of mechanisms designed primarily to provide heating or cooling or to produce electrical or mechanical power by collecting and transferring solar-generated energy. Tex. Prop. Code § 202.010(a)(2); Tex. Tax Code § 171.107(a). Such term also includes mechanical or chemical devices that have the ability to store solar-generated energy for use in heating or cooling or in the production of power. Tex. Prop. Code § 202.010(a)(2); Tex. Tax Code § 171.107(a).

155 Tex. Prop. Code § 202.010(b). A provision of a Declaration that violates Section 202.010 is considered to be void and unenforceable.

Texas Homeowners Associations to adopt new provisions and/or to enforce existing provisions in a Dedicatory Instrument that would regulate certain aspects of the installation and appearance of Solar Energy Devices, including certain regulations that limit the location and manner of installation, and the coloring of the frame, support bracket, and visible piping or wiring.[156]

10.9.1 Permissible Installation Regulation of Solar Energy Devices

Pursuant to Section 202.010 of the Texas Property Code, a Texas Homeowners Association may adopt and/or enforce provisions in a Dedicatory Instrument that require Solar Energy Devices be installed in conformity with certain general installation requirements and/or location-specific installation requirements.[157]

10.9.1 (A) *Permissible General Installation Requirements*

A Homeowners Association may adopt and/or enforce Dedicatory Instrument provisions that impose general installation requirements that restrict a Solar Energy Device from:

(1) being installed or located on Common Areas or Common Elements or any other property that is owned or maintained by the Homeowners Association or owned in common by the Members of the Homeowners Association;[158]

(2) being installed in an area on the Homeowner's Lot or Unit other than: (a) on the roof of the home or of another structure allowed on the Lot or Unit under the applicable Declaration; or (b) in a fenced yard or patio owned and maintained by the Homeowner;[159]

156 Tex. Prop. Code § 202.010(d).

157 Tex. Prop. Code § 202.010(d).

158 Tex. Prop. Code § 202.010(d)(2)–(3).

159 Tex. Prop. Code § 202.010(d)(4).

(3) being installed in a manner that voids material warranties;[160] and/or

(4) being installed without the prior approval of the Architectural Committee.[161]

10.9.1 (B) *Permissible Location-Specific Installation Requirements*

In addition to adopting and/or enforcing regulations that require a Solar Energy Device to be installed on the roof of a home (or other permitted structure) or in a fenced yard or patio, a Homeowners Association may also adopt and enforce Dedicatory Instrument provisions that impose installation requirements specific to roof-mounted Solar Energy Devices and ground-mounted Solar Energy Devices. With regard to roof-mounted Solar Energy Devices, a Homeowners Association may adopt and/or enforce Dedicatory Instrument provisions that impose location-specific installation requirements that:

(1) restrict a Solar Energy Device from being installed in a manner that causes the Solar Energy Device to extend higher than or beyond the roofline;[162]

(2) require a Solar Energy Device to be installed in an area on the roof designated by the Homeowners Association, unless an alternate location desired by the Homeowner increases the estimated annual energy production of the Solar Energy Device by more than ten percent (10%) above the energy production of such device if located in the area designated by the Homeowners Association;[163]

(3) require the Solar Energy Device, as installed, to conform to the slope of the roof and its top edge to be parallel to the roofline;[164] and/or

---

160 Tex. Prop. Code § 202.010(7).

161 Tex. Prop. Code § 202.010(8).

162 Tex. Prop. Code § 202.010(d)(5)(A).

163 Tex. Prop. Code § 202.010(d)(5)(B). Any potential increase in the estimated annual energy production of a Solar Energy Device that may result from installation in an alternative area on a roof must be determined by using a publicly available modeling tool provided by the National Renewable Energy Laboratory. Tex. Prop. Code § 202.010(d)(5)(B).

164 Tex. Prop. Code § 202.010(d)(5)(C).

(4) require any frame, support bracket, and/or visible piping or wiring of the Solar Energy Device to be of a silver, bronze, or black tone that is commonly available in the marketplace.[165]

With regard to ground-mounted Solar Energy Devices installed in a fenced yard or patio, a Homeowners Association may adopt and/or enforce Dedicatory Instrument provisions that restrict a Solar Energy Device installed in a fenced yard or patio from being taller than the fence line.[166]

10.9.2 Other Permissible Regulation of Solar Energy Devices

In addition to the permissible installation regulations, a Homeowners Association may also adopt and/or enforce Dedicatory Instrument provisions that prohibit the installation of a Solar Energy Device that has been determined by a court to constitute either: (1) a threat to public health or safety; or (2) a violation of the law.[167]

10.9.3 Approval of a Solar Energy Device by an Architectural Committee

If a Homeowners Association adopts or has an existing Dedicatory Instrument provision that restricts a Solar Energy Device from being installed without the prior approval of an Architectural Committee, then the Architectural Committee may not withhold approval for the installation of a Solar Energy Device if the proposed Solar Energy Device meets or exceeds the general and location-specific installation requirements, unless the Architectural Committee determines in writing that the placement of the Solar Energy Device in the manner proposed by the Homeowner would create a condition that would substantially interfere with the use and enjoyment of land by causing unreasonable discomfort or annoyance to persons of ordinary sensibilities.[168]

---

165 Tex. Prop. Code § 202.010(d)(5)(D).

166 Tex. Prop. Code § 202.010(d)6).

167 Tex. Prop. Code § 202.010(d)(1).

168 Tex. Prop. Code § 202.010(e).

For purposes of making a determination as to whether the proposed placement of a Solar Energy Device will create a condition that substantially interferes with the use and enjoyment of land, the written approval of the proposed Solar Energy Device by all adjacent property owners constitutes prima facie evidence that the proposed placement of such Solar Energy Device does not create a condition that would substantially interfere with the use and enjoyment of land.[169]

10.9.4 Non-Application of Section 202.010 During a Development Period

Notwithstanding the general invalidation of any provision in a Dedicatory Instrument that would prohibit or restrict a Homeowner from installing a Solar Energy Device on his or her property, Section 202.010 does not restrict a Declarant from prohibiting or restricting a Homeowner from installing a Solar Energy Device on his or her property during a "Development Period," provided the development has fewer than fifty-one planned "Residential Units."[170] For purposes of Section 202.010, a "Development Period" is defined as a period of time stated in a Declaration during which a Declarant reserves: (1) a right to facilitate the development, construction, and marketing of the Subdivision Development; and (2) a right to direct the size, shape, and composition of the Subdivision Development; and a "Residential Unit" is defined as a structure or part of a structure intended for use as a single residence and that is either: (1) a single-family house; or (2) a separate living unit in a duplex, a triplex, or a quadplex.[171]

---

169 Tex. Prop. Code § 202.010(e). "Prima facie" is a Latin expression meaning on its first encounter, first blush, or at first sight. In the context of a legal proceeding, "prima facie evidence" refers to evidence that—unless rebutted—would be sufficient to prove a particular proposition or fact.

170 Tex. Prop. Code § 202.010(f).

171 Tex. Prop. Code § 202.010(a)(1), (1-a). The statutory definition of "Development Period" under Section 202.010 differs slightly from the same defined term under Section 209.002(4-a), which uses the conjunction "or" instead of "and" when referring to the different reserved rights. Tex. Prop. Code §§ 202.010(a)(1), 209.002(4-a). In addition, although Section 202.010 applies equally to Condominium and Subdivision Developments, the statutory definition of "Development Period" under Section 202.010 expressly references only "subdivisions," not "condominiums." Tex. Prop. Code § 202.010(a)(1). Finally, the statutory definition of "Residential Unit" is limited to only single-family houses and separate living units in a duplex (which has only two separate living units), a triplex (which has only three separate living units), and a quadplex (which

10.10 Protection of Weather-Resistant and Energy-Conserving Shingles under Chapter 202.011 of the Texas Property Code

In 2011, the Texas Legislature enacted Section 202.011 of the Texas Property Code in order to establish rules that allow Texas Homeowners to install weather-resistant and energy-conservation shingles on the roofs of their homes.[172] Pursuant to Section 202.011, a Texas Homeowners Association may not include or enforce a provision in a Dedicatory Instrument that prohibits or restricts a Homeowner, who is otherwise authorized to install shingles on the roof of his or her home, from installing shingles that are designed primarily to: (1) be wind and hail resistant; (2) provide heating and cooling efficiencies greater than those provided by customary composite shingles; or (3) provide solar generation capabilities, so long as when installed such alternative shingles resemble shingles that are used or otherwise authorized for use in the Subdivision or Condominium Development, are more durable than, and are of equal or superior quality to, such authorized shingles, and match the aesthetics of the Subdivision or Condominium Development.[173]

10.11 Protected Display of the United States, Texas, and Military Service Branch Flags under Section 202.012 of the Texas Property Code

In 2011, the Texas Legislature enacted Section 202.012 of the Texas Property Code to clarify the rights of Texas Homeowners to display the United States flag and certain other flags.[174] Pursuant to Section 202.012, a Homeowners Association may not adopt or enforce a Dedicatory Instrument provision that prohibits, restricts, or has the effect of prohibiting or restricting a Homeowner from displaying: (1) the flag of the United

---

has only four separate living units). Due to such language, it is unclear whether the Texas Legislature intended the "Development Period" exception to Section 202.010 for Declarants to apply to both Subdivision and Condominium Developments, or solely Subdivision Developments.

172 House Comm. on Business and Industry, Bill Analysis, Tex. H.B. 362, 82nd Leg., R.S. (2011).

173 Tex. Prop. Code § 202.011.

174 House Comm. on Business and Industry, Bill Analysis, Tex. H.B. 2779, 82nd Leg., R.S. (2011).

States of America; (2) the flag of the State of Texas; or (3) an official or replica flag of any branch of the United States armed forces (collectively referred to in this book as simply "Protected Flags").[175]

Notwithstanding, a Homeowners Association may adopt or enforce reasonable Dedicatory Instrument provisions that require:

(1) the flag of the United States to be displayed in accordance with Sections 5–10 of Title 4 of the United States Code;[176]

(2) the flag of the State of Texas to be displayed in accordance with Chapter 3100, Government Code;[177]

(3) any flagpole attached to a dwelling or a freestanding flagpole to be constructed of permanent, long-lasting materials, with a finish appropriate to the materials used in the construction of the flagpole and harmonious with the dwelling;[178]

(4) the display of a Protected Flag, or the location and construction of the supporting flagpole, to comply with applicable zoning ordinances, easements, and setbacks of record;[179] and

(5) a displayed Protected Flag and the flagpole on which it is flown to be maintained in good condition and/or any deteriorated flag or deteriorated or structurally unsafe flagpole to be repaired, replaced, or removed.[180]

---

175 Tex. Prop. Code § 202.012(a).

176 Tex. Prop. Code § 202.012(b)(1)(A). Sections 5–10 of Title 4 of the United States Code is a codification of existing rules and customs pertaining to the display and use of the United States flag, including time and occasions for display of the United States flag; position and manner of display of the United States flag; respect for the United States flag; and conduct during hoisting, lowering, or passing of the United States flag. 4 U.S.C. §§ 5–10.

177 Tex. Prop. Code § 202.012(b)(1)(B). Chapter 3100 of the Texas Government Code codifies the rules for display of the Texas flag, including times, location, and orientation for the display of the Texas flag; the display and mounting of the Texas flag on a flagpole or flagstaff (with and without other flags); display of the Texas flag from or in a building; the hoisting and lowering of the Texas flag; and limitations on the display of the Texas flag. Tex. Gov't Code §§ 3100.001–3100.073.

178 Tex. Prop. Code § 202.012(b)(1)(C).

179 Tex. Prop. Code § 202.012(b)(1)(D).

180 Tex. Prop. Code § 202.012(b)(1)(E).

A Homeowners Association may also adopt or enforce reasonable Dedicatory Instrument provisions that:

(1) regulate the size, number, and location of flagpoles on which Protected Flags are displayed;[181]

(2) govern the size of a displayed Protected Flag;[182]

(3) regulate the size, location, and intensity of any lights used to illuminate a displayed Protected Flag;[183]

(4) impose reasonable restrictions to limit or abate potential noise caused by an external halyard of a flagpole;[184] and/or

(5) prohibit a Homeowner from locating a displayed Protected Flag or flagpole on property that is owned or maintained by the Homeowners Association or owned in common by the Members of the Association.[185]

10.12 Protected Display of Certain Religious Items on the Entry to a Home under Section 202.018 of the Texas Property Code

In 2011, the Texas Legislature enacted Section 202.018 of the Texas Property Code to prohibit Texas Homeowners Associations from restricting Homeowners or residents from displaying or affixing on the entry to their homes one or more religious items that are expected to be displayed by a tenet of such Homeowners' or residents'

---

[181] Tex. Prop. Code § 202.012(b)(2). Such regulations, however, may not restrict a Homeowner from installing or erecting at least one flagpole per property that is: (1) no more than twenty feet in height and located in the "front yard" of the property, subject to any applicable zoning ordinances, easements, and setback restrictions of record; or (2) attached to any portion of a residential structure owned by the Homeowner that is not maintained by the Homeowners Association. Tex. Prop. Code § 202.012(b)(2). Chapter 209 of the Texas Property Code defines a "front yard" as a yard within a Lot that has a front building setback line that is at 15 feet from the front property line of the Lot, which extends the full width of the Lot. Tex. Prop. Code § 202.001(5). A Homeowner who has a "front yard" and otherwise complies with the regulations permitted by Section 202.0012 of the Texas Property Code that have been adopted or are enforceable by his or her Homeowners Association may elect to install a flagpole in the "front yard" or attach a flagpole to the residential structure owned by such Homeowner. Tex. Prop. Code § 202.012(c).

[182] Tex. Prop. Code § 202.012(b)(3).

[183] Tex. Prop. Code § 202.012(b)(4).

[184] Tex. Prop. Code § 202.012(b)(5). A halyard is the rope or line used to hoist a flag up a flagpole.

[185] Tex. Prop. Code § 202.012(b)(6).

religion.[186] Pursuant to Section 202.018, a Homeowners Association may not enforce or adopt a Restrictive Covenant that prohibits a Homeowner or resident from displaying or affixing on the entry to his or her dwelling one or more religious items, the display of which is motivated by the Homeowner's or resident's sincere religious belief.[187]

Notwithstanding the broadness of Section 202.018, Section 202.018 does not authorize a Homeowner or resident to make an alteration to the entry door or door frame of his or her dwelling or to use a material or a color for such entry door or door frame that is not authorized by the Restrictive Covenants governing such dwelling.[188] In addition, Section 202.018 does not prohibit a Homeowners Association from adopting a new Restrictive Covenant or enforcing an existing Restrictive Covenant that, to the extent allowed by the United States and Texas Constitutions, would prohibit the display or affixing of a religious item on the entry to the Homeowner's or resident's dwelling that:

(1) threatens public health or safety;[189]

(2) violates a law;[190]

(3) contains language, graphics, or any display that is patently offensive to a passerby;[191]

(4) is in a location other than the entry door or door frame or extends past the outer edge of the door frame of the Homeowner's or resident's dwelling;[192] and/or

---

[186] Senate Research Center, Bill Analysis, Tex. H.B. 1278, 82nd Leg., R.S. (2011).

[187] Tex. Prop. Code § 202.018(a).

[188] Tex. Prop. Code § 202.018(c).

[189] Tex. Prop. Code § 202.018(b) (1).

[190] Tex. Prop. Code § 202.018(b) (2).

[191] Tex. Prop. Code § 202.018(b) (3).

[192] Tex. Prop. Code § 202.018(b) (4).

(5) individually or in combination with other religious items displayed or affixed on the entry door or door frame of a dwelling exceeds twenty-five square inches in total size.[193]

Section 202.018 also expressly authorizes a Homeowners Association to remove an item displayed in violation of a Restrictive Covenant permitted by Section 202.018.[194]

10.13 Protection of Standby Electric Generators under Section 202.019 of the Texas Property Code

In 2015, the Texas Legislature enacted Section 202.019 of the Texas Property Code in order to establish rules that allow Texas Homeowners to install a "Standby Electric Generator" on their property with minimal regulation by their Homeowners Association.[195] Except for certain permissible regulations established by Section 202.019, a Texas Homeowners Association may not adopt or enforce a Dedicatory Instrument provision that prohibits, restricts, or has the effect of prohibiting or restricting a Homeowner from owning, operating, installing, or maintaining a permanently installed Standby Electric Generator on his or her property.[196] Notwithstanding, Section 202.019 authorizes Texas Homeowners Associations to adopt new provisions and/or to enforce existing provisions in a Dedicatory Instrument that would regulate certain limited aspects of the installation and operation of a Standby Electric Generator. The following is a list of the permitted Dedicatory Instrument provisions that a Homeowners Association may adopt and/or enforce:

---

[193] Tex. Prop. Code § 202.018(b) (5).

[194] Tex. Prop. Code § 202.018(d).

[195] House Comm. on Business and Industry, Bill Analysis, Tex. H.B. 939, 84th Leg., R.S. (2015). A "Standby Electric Generator" is defined as a device that converts mechanical energy to electrical energy and is: (1) powered by natural gas, liquefied petroleum gas, diesel fuel, biodiesel fuel, or hydrogen; (2) fully enclosed in an integral manufacturer-supplied sound attenuating enclosure; (3) connected to the main electrical panel of a residence by a manual or automatic transfer switch; and (4) rated for a generating capacity of not less than seven kilowatts. Tex. Prop. Code § 202.019(a).

[196] Tex. Prop. Code § 202.019(b).

(1) a Dedicatory Instrument provision that requires a Standby Electric Generator to be installed and maintained in compliance with: (a) the manufacturer's specifications; and (b) applicable governmental health, safety, electrical, and building codes;[197]

(2) a Dedicatory Instrument provision that requires all electrical, plumbing, and fuel line connections to be installed only by licensed contractors;[198]

(3) a Dedicatory Instrument provision that requires all electrical connections to be installed in accordance with applicable governmental health, safety, electrical, and building codes;[199]

(4) a Dedicatory Instrument provision that requires all natural gas, diesel fuel, biodiesel fuel, or hydrogen fuel line connections to be installed in accordance with applicable governmental health, safety, electrical, and building codes;[200]

(5) a Dedicatory Instrument provision that requires all liquefied petroleum gas fuel line connections to be installed in accordance with rules and standards promulgated and adopted by the Texas Railroad Commission and other applicable governmental health, safety, electrical, and building codes;[201]

(6) a Dedicatory Instrument provision that requires nonintegral Standby Electric Generator fuel tanks to be installed and maintained to comply with applicable municipal zoning ordinances and governmental health, safety, electrical, and building codes;[202]

(7) a Dedicatory Instrument provision that requires the Standby Electric Generator and its electrical lines and fuel lines to be maintained in good condition;[203]

---

197 Tex. Prop. Code § 202.019(c)(1).

198 Tex. Prop. Code § 202.019(c)(2).

199 Tex. Prop. Code § 202.019(c)(3).

200 Tex. Prop. Code § 202.019(c)(4).

201 Tex. Prop. Code § 202.019(c)(5).

202 Tex. Prop. Code § 202.019(c)(6).

203 Tex. Prop. Code § 202.019(c)(7).

(8) a Dedicatory Instrument provision that requires the repair, replacement, or removal of any deteriorated or unsafe component of a Standby Electric Generator, including electrical or fuel lines;[204]

(9) a Dedicatory Instrument provision that requires a Homeowner to screen a Standby Electric Generator if it is: (a) visible from the street faced by the dwelling; (b) located in an unfenced side or rear yard of a residence and is visible either from an adjoining residence or from adjoining property owned by the Homeowners Association; or (c) located in a side or rear yard fenced by a wrought iron or residential aluminum fence and is visible through the fence either from an adjoining residence or from adjoining property owned by the Homeowners Association;[205]

(10) a Dedicatory Instrument provision that sets reasonable times, consistent with the manufacturer's recommendations, for the periodic testing of a Standby Electric Generator;[206]

(11) a Dedicatory Instrument provision that prohibits the use of a Standby Electric Generator to generate all or substantially all of the electrical power to a residence, except when utility-generated electrical power to the residence is not available or is intermittent due to causes other than nonpayment for utility service to the residence;[207]

(12) a Dedicatory Instrument provision that regulates the location of the Standby Electric Generator;[208] or

(13) a Dedicatory Instrument provision that prohibits a Homeowner from locating a Standby Electric Generator on property: (a) owned or maintained by the Homeowners Association; or (b) owned in common by the Homeowners Association's members.[209]

---

204 Tex. Prop. Code § 202.019(c)(8).

205 Tex. Prop. Code § 202.019(c)(9).

206 Tex. Prop. Code § 202.019(c)(10).

207 Tex. Prop. Code § 202.019(c)(11).

208 Tex. Prop. Code § 202.019(c)(12). Notwithstanding, a Dedicatory Instrument provision that regulates the location of a Standby Electric Generator is unenforceable if: (1) it increases the cost of installing the Standby Electric Generator by more than ten percent (10%); or (2) it increases the cost of installing and connecting the electrical and fuel lines for the Standby Electric Generator by more than twenty percent (20%). Tex. Prop. Code § 202.019(e).

209 Tex. Prop. Code § 202.019(c)(13).

In addition, if a Dedicatory Instrument provision requires a Homeowner to submit an application for approval of improvements located exterior to a residence, then Section 202.019 does not negate such requirement, but the information required to be submitted as part of the application for the installation of a Standby Electric Generator may not be greater or more detailed than the application for any other improvement.[210] Moreover, if a Dedicatory Instrument provision requires that the installation of a Standby Electric Generator be approved before installation, then such approval may not be withheld if the proposed installation meets or exceeds all of the aforementioned permitted Dedicatory Instrument provisions that are adopted by the Homeowners Association.[211]

It is important to note that if a Homeowners Association adopts any of the permitted Dedicatory Instrument provisions permitted by Section 202.019, then such provisions must be reasonably applied and enforced.[212] In addition, if a Homeowners Association or other party entitled to enforce a Dedicatory Instrument provision seeks to enforce a Homeowner's compliance with a permitted Dedicatory Instrument provision adopted by the Homeowners Association, in any hearing, action, or proceeding to determine whether a proposed or installed Standby Electric Generator complies with the requirements of such permitted Dedicatory Instrument provision, the party asserting noncompliance bears the burden of proof.[213]

10.14 Restriction on the Enforcement of Certain Leasing Restrictive Covenants by a Subdivision Association under Section 209.016 of the Texas Property Code

In 2015, the Texas Legislature enacted Section 209.016 of the Texas Property Code in order to establish rules limiting the enforcement of a Dedicatory Instrument provision by a Subdivision Association that requires a Lot Owner to obtain approval of a

---

[210] Tex. Prop. Code § 202.019(g).

[211] Tex. Prop. Code § 202.019(f).

[212] Tex. Prop. Code § 202.019(d).

[213] Tex. Prop. Code § 202.019(h).

prospective tenant from his or her Subdivision Association, or that requires a Lot Owner to submit to the Subdivision Association a copy of a prospective or current tenant's credit report or rental application.[214] More specifically, Section 209.016 restricts a Texas Subdivision Association from adopting or enforcing a Dedicatory Instrument provision that: (1) requires a prospective tenant to be submitted to and approved for tenancy by the Subdivision Association; or (2) requires a credit report or a rental application submitted by a prospective or current tenant (or such person's agent) to the leasing Lot Owner (or such Lot Owner's agent) when applying for tenancy to be submitted to a Subdivision Association.[215] In addition, Section 209 further provides that if a Dedicatory Instrument provision requires a Lot Owner to submit a copy of a lease or rental agreement to the Subdivision Association, then the Lot Owner may redact or otherwise make unreadable any "sensitive personal information" of the tenant contained in the lease or rental agreement.[216]

In other words, a Subdivision Association cannot enforce a Dedicatory Instrument provision that gives it the right to determine who may or may not rent a Lot Owner's property, nor can it enforce a provision that requires a Lot Owner to submit a prospective tenant's credit report or rental application to the Subdivision Association. In addition, while a Subdivision Association can still enforce a Dedicatory Instrument provision that requires a Lot Owner who leases his or her property to provide a copy of the lease or rental agreement to the Subdivision Association, the Lot Owner can redact any sensitive personal information of the tenant contained in the lease or rental agreement.

---

[214] Tex. Prop. Code § 209.016.

[215] Tex. Prop. Code § 209.016(b). Notwithstanding, Section 209.016 does not prohibit the adoption or enforcement of a Dedicatory Instrument provision that restricts or regulates occupancy or leasing of a Lot. Tex. Prop. Code § 209.016(d).

[216] Tex. Prop. Code § 209.016(c). Section 209.016 defines "sensitive personal information" as an individual's: (1) social security number; (2) driver's license number; (3) government-issued identification number; or (4) account, credit card, or debit card number. Tex. Prop. Code § 209.016(a).

10.15 Invalidation of Restrictive Covenants that Require Wood Shingles or that Discriminate against a Person on the Basis of His or Her Race, Color, Religion, or National Origin under Chapter 5 of the Texas Property Code

Chapter 5 of the Texas Property Code imposes certain restrictions on the enforceability of two types of Restrictive Covenants. First, to the extent any Restrictive Covenant requires a residential dwelling to have a wood shingle roof, such Restrictive Covenant is void and unenforceable.[217] Second, if a Restrictive Covenant prohibits the use by or the sale, lease, or transfer of a Lot or Unit to a person because of such person's race, color, religion, or national origin, such provision or restriction is void, and a court is required to dismiss a lawsuit brought to enforce such a voided Restrictive Covenant.[218]

217 Tex. Prop. Code § 5.025.

218 Tex. Prop. Code § 5.026.

CHAPTER 11 AMENDMENT OF GOVERNING DOCUMENTS

CHAPTER 11 AMENDMENT OF GOVERNING DOCUMENTS

11.1 In General

From time to time, a Homeowners Association may find it necessary or desirable to amend or modify one or more of its Governing Documents. The procedures for amending a Declaration, Articles of Incorporation, or Bylaws will almost always be found within the respective document itself. Notwithstanding, there are several statutes that supplement, and in some cases override, the amendment procedures stated in the Governing Documents. There is also a series of statutes in the Texas Property Code that applies only to certain types of Homeowners Associations or certain geographically located Homeowners Associations that provides procedures for creating, renewing, and modifying a Subdivision Association's Declaration when there are no procedures for renewing or modifying its Declaration. Such statutes and procedures are explained in greater detail in the following subchapters.

11.2 Procedures for Amendment of Articles of Incorporation under the Texas Nonprofit Corporation Law

When a Texas Nonprofit Corporation HOA amends its Articles of Incorporation, there are two procedures involved. The first procedure involves the approval of an amendment to the Articles of Incorporation, which is governed by the provisions of the Articles of Incorporation itself and the Texas Nonprofit Corporation Law. The second procedure involves the actual amendment of the Articles of Incorporation, which is governed by Chapters 3 and 4 of the Texas Business Organizations Code.

11.2.1 Procedures for Approving an Amendment to the Articles of Incorporation

The procedures for approving an amendment to a Nonprofit Corporation HOA's Articles of Incorporation depend on whether the Nonprofit Corporation HOA is managed by a Board of Directors or by its Member-Homeowners themselves. If the Nonprofit Corporation HOA is managed by a Board of Directors, the applicable procedures further depend on whether the Nonprofit Corporation HOA even has Member-Homeowners and, if so, whether the Member-Homeowners have voting rights. Procedures for each of these scenarios are described in the following subchapters.

11.2.1 (A) *Amendment Procedure if a Nonprofit Corporation HOA Is Managed by a Board of Directors*

If a Nonprofit Corporation HOA is managed by a Board of Directors and its Member-Homeowners do have voting rights (which is the formation of most Texas Homeowners Associations), then in order to approve a proposed amendment to the Articles of Incorporation, the Board of Directors must first adopt a resolution that specifies the proposed amendment and directs that such proposed amendment be submitted to a vote of Member-Homeowners at an annual or special Membership Meeting.[1] The Nonprofit Corporation HOA must then give each Member-Homeowner entitled to vote at the applicable annual or special Membership Meeting a written notice containing the proposed amendment or a summary of the changes to be effected by such amendment.[2] The written notice must also state the place, date, and time of the Membership Meeting and must be given to the Member-Homeowners no earlier than sixty (60) days, nor later than ten (10) days, before the date of such Membership Meeting.[3] The written notice may be delivered to the Member-Homeowners by personal delivery, mail, facsimile, email, or

---

1 Tex. Bus. Org. Code § 22.105(a). There is one exception to this rule. Except as otherwise provided by the Articles of Incorporation, the Board of Directors of a Nonprofit Corporation HOA with Member-Homeowners having voting rights may, without approval of its Membership, adopt amendments to the Articles of Incorporation for the purpose of: (1) extending the duration of the Nonprofit Corporation HOA if the Nonprofit Corporation HOA was incorporated when limited duration was required by law; (2) deleting the names and addresses of the initial Directors; (3) deleting the name and address of the initial registered agent or registered office, if a statement of change is on file with the Texas Secretary of State; or (4) changing the corporate name by either substituting the word "corporation," "incorporated," "company," or "limited," or the abbreviation "corp.," "inc.," "co.," or "ltd.," for a similar word or abbreviation in the name, or adding, deleting, or changing a geographical attribution to the name. Tex. Bus. Org. Code § 22.107(b).

2 Tex. Bus. Org. Code § 22.105(b).

3 Tex. Bus. Org. Code §§ 6.051(a), 22.156(a); Tex. Prop. Code § 209.0056(a).

any other manner authorized by the Nonprofit Corporation HOA's Governing Documents.[4]

In addition, an amendment to a Nonprofit Corporation HOA's Articles of Incorporation is considered to be a "Fundamental Action" under the Texas Nonprofit Corporation Law.[5] As a result, an amendment to a Nonprofit Corporation HOA's Articles of Incorporation must be approved by an affirmative vote of at least two-thirds (2/3) of the votes entitled to be cast by the Member-Homeowners present in person or by proxy at a Membership Meeting in which the proposed amendment to the Articles of Incorporation is submitted for a vote, unless the Articles of Incorporation require an amendment to be approved by a greater proportion of the Member-Homeowners.[6] In the event of the latter, the proposed amendment must be approved by the percentage of Member-Homeowners specified by the Articles of Incorporation.[7] In addition, if any class of Member-Homeowners is entitled to vote on the proposed amendment to the Articles of Incorporation as a class by the terms of the Articles of Incorporation or the Bylaws, the proposed amendment to the Articles of Incorporation must also be approved by at least two-thirds (2/3) of the votes entitled to be cast by the Member-Homeowners of each class.[8]

If a Nonprofit Corporation HOA is managed by a Board of Directors, but has no members or has no members with voting rights, a proposed amendment to the Articles of

---

4 Tex. Bus. Org. Code §§ 6.051(a), 22.156(a). Subject to the Governing Documents of a Nonprofit Corporation HOA, a notice of a Membership Meeting that is mailed to a Member-Homeowner is considered to be given on the date notice is deposited in the United States mail, with postage paid, in an envelope addressed to such Member-Homeowner at his or her address as it appears on the ownership or membership records of the Nonprofit Corporation HOA. Tex. Bus. Org. Code § 6.051(b). Notice that is transmitted to a Member-Homeowner by facsimile or email is considered to be given when transmitted to a facsimile number or an email address provided by such Member-Homeowner, or to which such Member-Homeowner consents, for the purpose of receiving notice. Tex. Bus. Org. Code § 6.051(b).

5 Tex. Bus. Org. Code § 22.164(a)(1).

6 Tex. Bus. Org. Code §§ 22.105(c), 22.162, 22.164(a)(1), (b)(1).

7 Tex. Bus. Org. Code § 22.162.

8 Tex. Bus. Org. Code § 22.164(c).

Incorporation must be adopted at a meeting of the Board of Directors by the affirmative vote of the majority of the Directors in office, unless the Articles of Incorporation require an amendment to be approved by a greater proportion of the Directors.[9] In the event of the latter, the proposed amendment must be approved by the percentage of Directors specified by the Articles of Incorporation.[10]

11.2.1 (B) *Amendment Procedure if a Nonprofit Corporation HOA Is Managed by its Members without a Board of Directors*

If the management of a Nonprofit Corporation HOA is vested in its Member-Homeowners, instead of a Board of Directors, a proposed amendment to the Nonprofit Corporation HOA's Articles of Incorporation must be submitted to a vote of the Member-Homeowners at an annual, regular, or special meeting of the Nonprofit Corporation HOA's Membership.[11] Except as otherwise provided by the Nonprofit Corporation HOA's Articles of Incorporation or Bylaws, a written notice of the Membership Meeting that contains a copy of the proposed amendment or a summary of the changes to be affected by such amendment must be given to the Member-Homeowners.[12] The written notice must also state the place, date, and time of the meeting and must be given to the Member-Homeowners no earlier than sixty (60) days, but no later than ten (10) days, before the date of such Membership Meeting.[13] The written notice may be delivered to the Member-Homeowners by personal delivery, mail, facsimile, email, or any other manner authorized by the Nonprofit Corporation HOA's Governing Documents.[14]

---

9 Tex. Bus. Org. Code §§ 22.107(a), 22.162, 22.164(b)(3).

10 Tex. Bus. Org. Code § 22.162.

11 Tex. Bus. Org. Code § 22.106(a).

12 Tex. Bus. Org. Code § 22.106(b).

13 Tex. Bus. Org. Code §§ 6.051(a), 22.156(a); Tex. Prop. Code § 209.0056(a).

14 Tex. Bus. Org. Code §§ 6.051(a), 22.156(a). Subject to the Governing Documents of a Nonprofit Corporation HOA, a notice of a Membership Meeting that is mailed to a Member-Homeowner is considered to be given on the date notice is deposited in the United States mail, with postage paid, in an envelope addressed to such Member-Homeowner at his or her address as it appears on the ownership or membership

As noted earlier, an amendment of a Nonprofit Corporation HOA's Articles of Incorporation constitutes a "Fundamental Action," and as a result, a proposed amendment to the Articles of Incorporation must be approved by the affirmative vote of at least two-thirds (2/3) of the votes of Member-Homeowners present at a meeting at which the proposed amendment is submitted for a vote, unless the Articles of Incorporation require an amendment to be approved by a greater proportion of the Nonprofit Corporation HOA's Member-Homeowners.[15] In the event of the latter, the proposed amendment must be approved by the percentage of Member-Homeowners specified by the Articles of Incorporation.[16] In addition, if any class of Member-Homeowners is entitled to vote on the proposed amendment to the Articles of Incorporation as a class by the terms of the Articles of Incorporation or the Bylaws, then the proposed amendment to the Articles of Incorporation must also be approved by at least two-thirds (2/3) of the votes entitled to be cast by the Member-Homeowners of each class.[17]

11.2.2 Procedures for Filing an Amendment of the Articles of Incorporation with the Texas Secretary of State

If a proposed amendment of a Nonprofit Corporation HOA's Articles of Incorporation is approved by the requisite number of Member-Homeowners, the Nonprofit Corporation HOA must then amend its Articles of Incorporation. The procedure for amending a Nonprofit Corporation HOA's Articles of Incorporation is governed by Chapters 3 and 4 of the Texas Business Organizations Code.

---

records of the Nonprofit Corporation HOA. Tex. Bus. Org. Code § 6.051(b). Notice transmitted to a Member-Homeowner by facsimile or email is considered to be given when transmitted to a facsimile number or an email address provided by such Member-Homeowner, or to which such Member-Homeowner consents, for the purpose of receiving notice. Tex. Bus. Org. Code § 6.051(b).

15 Tex. Bus. Org. Code §§ 22.162, 22.164(b)(2).

16 Tex. Bus. Org. Code § 22.162.

17 Tex. Bus. Org. Code § 22.164(c).

Pursuant to Chapter 3 of the Texas Business Organizations Code, in order to amend its Articles of Incorporation, a Nonprofit Corporation HOA must sign and file a Certificate of Amendment with the Office of the Texas Secretary of State.[18] The Certificate of Amendment must:

(1) identify the name of the filing entity and state that the entity is a nonprofit corporation;[19]

(2) include an identification, by reference or description, of each provision of the Articles of Incorporation that is added, altered, or deleted, and if a provision is added or altered, a statement of the text of the added or amended provision;[20]

(3) state that the amendment has been approved in the manner required by the Texas Business Organizations Code and the Governing Documents of the entity;[21] and

(4) include any other matter required by the provisions of the Nonprofit Corporation Law to be in the Certificate of Amendment.[22]

It is important to note that an amendment to a Nonprofit Corporation HOA's Articles of Incorporation will not affect an existing claim or cause of action in favor of or against such Nonprofit Corporation HOA or a pending lawsuit in which such Nonprofit Corporation HOA is a party.[23] In addition, if the name of a Nonprofit Corporation HOA is changed by amendment, a lawsuit brought by or against such Nonprofit Corporation HOA in its former name does not have to be abated or refiled because of the name change.[24]

---

[18] Tex. Bus. Org. Code § 3.052(b).

[19] Tex. Bus. Org. Code § 3.053(1)–(2).

[20] Tex. Bus. Org. Code § 3.053(3).

[21] Tex. Bus. Org. Code § 3.053(4).

[22] Tex. Bus. Org. Code § 3.053(5).

[23] Tex. Bus. Org. Code § 3.056(b).

[24] Tex. Bus. Org. Code § 3.056(c).

11.3 Procedures for and Restrictions on the Amendment of Bylaws

There are very limited statutory provisions regarding amendment of a Texas Nonprofit Corporation HOA's Bylaws, and the amendment process will primarily be governed by the procedures set forth in the Bylaws itself. The Texas Nonprofit Corporation Law, however, does generally authorize a Board of Directors of a Texas Nonprofit Corporation HOA to amend or repeal Bylaws, or adopt new Bylaws, except in the following circumstances:

(1) the power to amend or adopt the proposed Bylaw provision is reserved in whole or in part for the Nonprofit Corporation HOA's Membership under either the Texas Nonprofit Corporation Law or the Nonprofit Corporation HOA's Articles of Incorporation;[25]

(2) the management of the Nonprofit Corporation HOA is vested in the Nonprofit Corporation HOA's Membership;[26] or

(3) in amending, repealing, or adopting a Bylaw, the Member-Homeowners of the Nonprofit Corporation HOA expressly provided that the Board of Directors may not amend or repeal such Bylaw.[27]

In addition, Chapter 209 of the Texas Property Code also authorizes a Subdivision Association's Board of Directors to amend its Bylaws to conform such Bylaws to the statutory requirements concerning the election of Directors under Section 209.00593 of the Texas Property Code.[28]

---

25 Tex. Bus. Org. Code § 22.102(c)(1).

26 Tex. Bus. Org. Code § 22.102(c)(2).

27 Tex. Bus. Org. Code § 22.102(c)(3).

28 Tex. Prop. Code § 209.00593(b). Section 209.00593 of the Texas Property Code provides that any vacant position on a Subdivision Association's Board of Directors resulting from the expiration of a term of office must be filled by election by its Lot Owners. Tex. Prop. Code § 209.00593(a). The authority of a Subdivision Association's Board of Directors to amend its Bylaws under Section 209.00593 applies even if such Bylaws expressly require the approval of Lot Owners to amend its provisions. The statutory requirements concerning election of Directors under Section 209.00593 are discussed in greater detail in Chapter 3 of this book.

Finally, Section 209.0041 of the Texas Property Code prohibits a Subdivision Association from amending its Bylaws in any manner that would render such Bylaws in conflict with its Declaration.[29]

11.4 Procedures for Amendment of a Condominium Declaration under the Texas Uniform Condominium Act

Although the procedures for amendment of a Condominium Declaration will primarily be governed by the procedures set forth in the Condominium Declaration itself, the Texas Uniform Condominium Act also establishes very specific procedures and requirements for amending a Condominium Declaration that vary depending upon who is amending it and the purpose of such amendment.

11.4.1 General Requirements for Amendment of a Condominium Declaration

Except for some limited circumstances, a Condominium Declaration, including the Plats and Plans, for a residential Condominium Development may only be amended by a vote or agreement of Unit Owners representing at least sixty-seven percent (67%) of the votes allocated in the Condominium Association or any larger percentage of allocated votes specified in the Condominium Declaration for purposes of amendment.[30] In

[29] Tex. Prop. Code § 209.0041(i).

[30] Tex. Prop. Code § 82.067(a). If all of the Units are restricted exclusively to nonresidential use, however, the Condominium Declaration may be amended by a percentage of allocated votes specified in the Condominium Declaration for the purposes of amendment that is lower than sixty-seven percent (67%) of the allocated votes. Tex. Prop. Code § 82.067(a). In addition, the provisions of the Texas Uniform Condominium Act concerning amendment of a Condominium Declaration are not applicable to Condominium Developments created prior to January 1, 1994, that are subject to the Texas Condominium Act, and the comparable provision under the Texas Condominium Act is significantly more restrictive than its counterpart under the Texas Uniform Condominium Act. Tex. Prop. Code §§ 81.111, 82.002(c). Under the Texas Condominium Act, after a Condominium Declaration is recorded with a county clerk, the Condominium Declaration may not be amended except at a meeting of the Apartment Owners at which the amendment is approved by the holders of at least sixty-seven percent (67%) of the ownership interests in the Condominium Development. Tex. Prop. Code § 81.111. Unlike the Texas Uniform Condominium Act, there are no provisions under the Texas Condominium Act that allow for amendment of the Condominium Declaration in certain limited circumstances without the approval of the Apartment Owners.

addition, an amendment to the Condominium Declaration may not increase or otherwise modify the obligations imposed by the Condominium Declaration on a Declarant, or reduce or otherwise modify the rights granted by a Condominium Declaration to a Declarant, including Special Declarant Rights, unless the Declarant agrees to such amendment.[31]

11.4.2 Voting Requirements for Certain Amendments of a Condominium Declaration

Notwithstanding such general requirements concerning the amendment of a Condominium Declaration, there are some limited circumstances where an amendment to the Condominium Declaration either: (1) does not require any vote or agreement of the Unit Owners in the Condominium Association; or (2) requires approval by one hundred percent (100%) of the Unit Owners in the Condominium Association.

11.4.2 (A) *Amendments to a Condominium Declaration that Require No Vote of Unit Owners*

Pursuant to the Texas Uniform Condominium Act, there are certain amendments to a Condominium Declaration that require no vote or approval of Unit Owners. More specifically, a vote or agreement of Unit Owners is not required when a Declarant: (1) records an amendment to the Condominium Declaration for the purpose of curing a defect with the proper execution of a previously recorded Condominium Declaration; (2) records either new Plats or Plans upon exercising any Development Right to conform them to the requirements of the Texas Uniform Condominium Act; or (3) records an amendment to the Condominium Declaration and new Plats and Plans for the purpose of exercising a Development Right.[32]

---

31 Tex. Prop. Code § 82.067(e).

32 Tex. Prop. Code §§ 82.051(c), 82.059(f), 82.060, 82.067(b)(1).

In addition, no vote or agreement of Unit Owners is required when certain Unit Owners record an amendment to the Condominium Declaration in order to reflect: (1) a reallocation of Limited Common Elements between their Units; (2) a relocation of boundaries between adjoining Units and a reallocation of Allocated Interests between such Units; and/or (3) a subdivision of a Unit and a reallocation of Allocated Interests previously allocated to the subdivided Unit to the newly created Units.[33]

Moreover, a vote or agreement of Unit Owners is also not required when a Condominium Association records an amendment to the Condominium Declaration to reflect: (1) a reallocation of Allocated Interests upon a Unit, part of a Unit, or part of a Common Element being acquired by condemnation of a governmental entity; (2) a reallocation of Allocated Interests upon the expiration or termination of a Leasehold Condominium that decreases the number of Units in a Condominium; (3) a reallocation of a Common Element as a Limited Common Element; (4) a relocation of boundaries between adjoining Units and a reallocation of Allocated Interests between such Units; and/or (5) a subdivision of a Unit and a reallocation of Allocated Interests previously allocated to the subdivided Unit to the newly created Units.[34]

Finally, if permitted by the Condominium Declaration, the Board of Directors of a Condominium Association (as well as the Declarant, so long as it still owns at least one Unit that has never been occupied) may amend the Condominium Declaration in any manner necessary to meet the requirements of the Federal National Mortgage

[33] Tex. Prop. Code §§ 82.058(b), 82.062, 82.063(b), 82.067(b)(3), 82.068(b).

[34] Tex. Prop. Code §§ 82.007, 82.056(d), 82.058(c), 82.062, 82.063, 82.067(b)(2).

Association,[35] the Federal Home Loan Mortgage Corporation,[36] the Federal Housing Administration,[37] or the Veterans Administration[38] without the vote or agreement of Unit Owners.[39]

It is important to note, however, that a Condominium Association's Board of Directors and/or Membership may not meet to adopt an amendment or other change to a Condominium Declaration (or the Articles of Incorporation, Bylaws, or Association Rules of the Condominium Association) unless the Condominium Association has given each Unit Owner a document showing the specific amendment or other change that would be made to the Condominium Declaration, Articles of Incorporation, Bylaws, or Association Rules.[40] The information showing such specific amendment or other change must be given

---

[35] The Federal National Mortgage Association, more commonly known as "Fannie Mae," is a stockholder-owned corporation chartered by the United States Congress in 1968 as a government-sponsored enterprise to purchase and securitize mortgages in order to ensure that funds are consistently available to the institutions that lend money to home buyers. Fannie Mae buys mortgages on the secondary market, pools them, and sells them as mortgage-backed securities to investors on the open market. This secondary mortgage market increases the supply of money available for mortgages lending and increases the money available for new home purchases.

[36] The Federal Home Loan Mortgage Corporation, more commonly known as "Freddie Mac," is a government-sponsored enterprise that was created in 1970 as competition for Fannie Mae and to further increase the availability of funds to finance mortgages and homeownership. The charter of Freddie Mac was essentially the same as Fannie Mae's charter, which is to expand the secondary market for mortgages and mortgage-backed securities by buying mortgages made by savings and loan associations and other depository institutions.

[37] The Federal Housing Administration, more commonly known as the "FHA," is a United States government agency created as part of the National Housing Act of 1934. The mission of the FHA is to improve housing standards and conditions; to provide an adequate home financing system through insurance of mortgage loans; and to stabilize the mortgage market.

[38] The Veterans Administration, now known as the United States Department of Veterans Affairs, but more commonly known as the "VA," is a government-run military veteran benefit system that is responsible for administering veterans' benefits programs for veterans, their families, and survivors, including home loan programs.

[39] Tex. Prop. Code § 82.067(f).

[40] Tex. Prop. Code § 82.070(a).

to each Unit Owner no earlier than twenty (20) days, nor later than ten (10) days, before the date of such meeting.[41]

11.4.2 (B) *Amendments to a Condominium Declaration that Require Approval of 100 Percent of the Unit Owners*

There are also certain types of amendments to a Condominium Declaration that require the approval of one hundred percent (100%) of the Unit Owners in a Condominium Association. More specifically, except as permitted or required by the Texas Uniform Condominium Act, an amendment to a Condominium Declaration (other than those that the Texas Uniform Condominium Act authorizes to be done without a vote of Unit Owners) that: (1) creates or increases Special Declarant Rights; (2) increases the number of Units in the Condominium Development; (3) changes the boundaries of a Unit; (4) alters or destroys a Unit or Limited Common Element; (5) changes a Unit's Allocated Interest; or (6) changes the use restrictions on a Unit, must be approved by one hundred percent (100%) of the votes of Unit Owners in the Condominium Association.[42]

11.4.3 Procedures for Approval of an Amendment to a Condominium Declaration by Unit Owners

An amendment to the Condominium Declaration that does require a vote or agreement of Unit Owners in the Condominium Association may be adopted: (1) by written ballots that state the exact wording or substance of the proposed amendment and that specifies the date by which a ballot must be received by the Condominium Association to be counted; (2) at a meeting of the Condominium Association's Unit Owners after written notice of the meeting has been delivered to an owner of each Unit

---

[41] Tex. Prop. Code § 82.070(b). The information showing the specific amendment or other change is considered to have been given to a Unit Owner on the date the document showing such information is personally delivered to the Unit Owner (as shown by a receipt signed by the Unit Owner) or on the date shown by the postmark on the envelope containing such information after it is deposited in the United States mail with a proper address and postage paid. Tex. Prop. Code § 82.070(b).

[42] Tex. Prop. Code § 82.067(b), (e).

stating that a purpose of the meeting is to consider an amendment to the Condominium Declaration; or (3) by any method permitted by the Condominium Declaration.[43]

11.4.4 Recording of an Amendment to a Condominium Declaration in the Official Public Records

A Condominium Declaration is considered to be a Dedicatory Instrument, as is an amendment to a Condominium Declaration.[44] Under both the Texas Uniform Condominium Act and Chapter 202 of the Texas Property Code, an amendment to a Condominium Declaration has no effect and is considered unenforceable until a copy of it is recorded in the Official Public Records of each county in which a portion of the Condominium Development is located.[45]

11.4.5 Legal Challenge to the Validity of an Amendment to a Condominium Declaration

A lawsuit to challenge the validity of an amendment to a Condominium Declaration adopted by a Condominium Association under the Texas Uniform Condominium Act must be brought within one (1) year from the date such amendment is recorded in the local Official Public Records.[46]

---

43 Tex. Prop. Code § 82.067(a) (1)–(3).

44 Tex. Prop. Code § 202.001. The term "Dedicatory Instrument" is defined as any document governing the establishment, maintenance, or operation of a residential Subdivision Development, Condominium Development, or any similar planned development, including a Declaration or similar instrument subjecting real property to Restrictive Covenants, Bylaws, Association Rules, or similar instrument governing the administration or operation of a Homeowners Association, as well as all lawful amendments to such documents. Tex. Prop. Code §§ 82.003(11-a); 202.001(1).

45 Tex. Prop. Code §§ 82.067(d); 202.006. In addition, any amendment to a Condominium Declaration that is required by the Texas Uniform Condominium Act to be recorded in the local Official Public Records must be prepared, executed, recorded, and certified by an Officer of the Condominium Association designated for that purpose or, in the absence of such designation, by the President of the Condominium Association. Tex. Prop. Code § 82.067(g).

46 Tex. Prop. Code § 82.067(c).

11.5 Procedures for Amendment of a Subdivision Declaration under Chapter 209 of the Texas Property Code

There are very limited statutory provisions regarding amendment of a Texas Subdivision Association's Declaration, and the amendment process will primarily be governed by the procedures set forth in the Declaration itself. Notwithstanding, in 2011, the Texas Legislature enacted two new provisions to Chapter 209 of the Texas Property Code, both of which may reduce the percentage of votes required to amend a Subdivision Development's Declaration.

11.5.1 General Amendments of a Subdivision Declaration under Section 209.0041

Section 209.0041 of the Texas Property Code reduces the percentage of votes necessary to amend a Declaration for certain Subdivision Associations. Pursuant to Section 209.0041, a Subdivision Association's Declaration may be amended by an affirmative vote of sixty-seven percent (67%) of the total votes allocated to Lot Owners entitled to vote on the amendment of the Declaration, unless the Declaration allows the Declaration to be amended by a lower percentage of votes.[47] Notwithstanding, if a state or federal law requires governmental approval of an amendment to a Declaration, such amendment must still be approved by the appropriate governmental entity to be valid.[48]

Section 209.0041, however, does not apply to all Subdivision Associations or all proposed amendments to a Subdivision Association's Declaration. First, Section 209.0041 only applies to residential Subdivision Developments in which Lot Owners are subject to

[47] Tex. Prop. Code § 209.0041(h). If a Declaration allows an amendment to be approved by a percentage of votes that is less than sixty-seven percent (67%), then the Declaration may be amended under the procedures established by Section 209.0041 using the percentage specified in the Declaration. Tex. Prop. Code § 209.0041(h-1). If a Declaration is silent as to voting rights for an amendment, the Declaration may be amended by a vote of owners owning sixty-seven percent (67%) of the Lots subject to the Declaration. Tex. Prop. Code § 209.0041(h-2). Section 209.0041 supersedes any contrary requirement in an applicable Subdivision Association's Declaration, regardless of the date on which the Declaration was created. Tex. Prop. Code § 209.0041(e), (f).

[48] Tex. Prop. Code § 209.0041(h).

mandatory membership in the Subdivision Association.[49] Thus, it does not apply to a voluntary Subdivision Association or a non-residential Subdivision Association.

In addition, Section 209.0041 does not apply to a mandatory residential Subdivision Association that is subject to Chapter 552 of the Texas Government Code (formally known as the "Texas Public Information Act" but more commonly referred to as the "Texas Open Records Act").[50]

Finally, Section 209.0041 also does not apply to an amendment of a Subdivision Declaration during a "Development Period."[51] For purposes of Section 209.0041, Development Period is defined as a period of time stated in a Declaration during which the Declarant reserves a right to: (1) facilitate the development, construction, and marketing of the Subdivision Development; or (2) direct the size, shape, and composition of the Subdivision Development.[52]

---

49 Tex. Prop. Code § 209.0041(b).

50 Tex. Prop. Code § 209.0041(c). A Subdivision Association is subject to Chapter 552 of the Texas Government Code if: (1) membership in the Subdivision Association is mandatory for Lot Owners or a defined class of property owners in a defined geographic area in a county with a population of 2.8 million or more (Harris County) or in a county adjacent to a county with a population of 2.8 million or more (Brazoria, Chambers, Fort Bend, Liberty, Montgomery, San Jacinto, and Waller Counties); the Subdivision Association has the power to make mandatory special assessments for capital improvements or mandatory regular assessments; and the amount of the mandatory special or regular assessments is or has ever been based in whole or in part on the market value of Lot Owners' Lots or property as assessed by the State of Texas or a local governmental entity for purposes of ad valorem taxation; or (2) the Subdivision Association provides maintenance, preservation, and architectural control of residential and commercial property within a defined geographic area in a county with a population of 2.8 million or more (Harris County) or in a county adjacent to a county with a population of 2.8 million or more (Brazoria, Chambers, Fort Bend, Liberty, Montgomery, San Jacinto, and Waller Counties); and the Subdivision Association is a corporation that is governed by a board of trustees who may employ a general manager to execute the Subdivision Association's Bylaws and administer the business of the corporation; does not require membership in the corporation by the Lot Owners within the defined area; and was incorporated before January 1, 2006. Tex. Gov't Code § 552.0036.

51 Tex. Prop. Code § 209.0041(d).

52 Tex. Prop. Code § 209.002(4-a).

11.5.2 Amendment of a Subdivision Declaration to Grant or Remove a Subdivision Association's Authority to Foreclose its Assessment Lien under Section 209.0093

In addition to Section 209.0041, Section 209.0093 of the Texas Property Code provides that a Subdivision Association's Declaration may also be modified to either grant or remove authority of the Subdivision Association to foreclose an Assessment Lien on lots in the Subdivision Development by an affirmative vote of at least sixty-seven percent (67%) of the total votes allocated to Lot Owners in the Subdivision Association.[53]

Moreover, Section 209.0093 also establishes a procedure for Lot Owners to compel a Subdivision Association to call a special meeting for the purpose of voting on a proposed amendment to grant or remove a Subdivision Association's foreclosure authority.[54] If a Subdivision Association is presented with a petition calling for a vote to adopt a Declaration amendment that modifies the Subdivision Association's foreclosure authority that is signed by Lot Owners holding at least ten percent (10%) of all voting interests in the Subdivision Association, the Subdivision Association must call a special meeting of the HOA's Membership for the purpose of voting on such amendment to the Declaration.

While Section 209.0093 may seem duplicative of the general declaration-amendment procedure under the Section 209.0041 because they both reduce the vote required to amend a Subdivision Association's Declaration to no more than sixty-seven percent (67%) of the votes allocated to Lot Owners, there are several important distinctions. First, Section 209.0093 allows a Declaration to be amended by an affirmative vote of at least sixty-seven percent (67%) of the total votes allocated to Lot Owners in the Subdivision Association, while Section 209.0041 allows a Declaration to be amended by an affirmative vote of at least sixty-seven percent (67%) of the total votes allocated to

53 Tex. Prop. Code § 209.0093.

54 Tex. Prop. Code § 209.0093.

only those Lot Owners entitled to vote on the amendment. Second, Section 209.0093 establishes a procedure for Lot Owners to compel a Subdivision Association to call a special Membership Meeting to vote on an applicable amendment to the Declaration, whereas Section 209.0041 does not. Third, unlike Section 209.0041, Section 209.0093 applies to all Subdivision Associations, including nonresidential Subdivision Associations and Subdivision Associations subject to the Texas Open Records Act, both during and after a "Development Period."

11.5.3 Recording of an Amendment to a Subdivision Declaration in the Official Public Records

A Subdivision Declaration is considered to be a Dedicatory Instrument, as is an amendment to a Subdivision Declaration.[55] As a result, an amendment to a Subdivision Declaration has no effect and is considered unenforceable until a copy of it is recorded in the Official Public Records of each county in which a portion of the Subdivision Development is located.[56]

11.6 Procedures for Extending, Creating, or Modifying a Declaration of Certain Residential Subdivision Developments Located in: a City with a Population of More than 100,000; in an Unincorporated Area of Harris County; or in Brazoria, Fort Bend, Galveston, Liberty, Montgomery, or Waller County, under Chapter 201 of the Texas Property Code

Chapter 201 of the Texas Property Code is one of several Texas statutes that establishes procedures for amending a Declaration that only applies to certain Subdivision Developments in limited cities and counties. By its express terms, Chapter 201 applies to

---

55 Tex. Prop. Code § 202.001. The term "Dedicatory Instrument" is defined as any document governing the establishment, maintenance, or operation of a residential Subdivision Development, Condominium Development, or any similar planned development, including a Declaration or similar instrument subjecting real property to Restrictive Covenants, Bylaws, Association Rules, or similar instrument governing the administration or operation of a Homeowners Association, as well as all lawful amendments to such documents. Tex. Prop. Code §§ 82.003(11-a); 202.001(1).

56 Tex. Prop. Code § 202.006.

only "residential real estate subdivision" developments[57] located in whole or in part within: (1) a city that has a population of more than 100,000, or within the extraterritorial jurisdiction of such a city;[58] (2) the unincorporated area of a county having a population of 3.3 million or more (Harris County);[59] or (3) the incorporated or unincorporated area of a county having a population of 40,000 or more that is adjacent to a county having a population of 3.3 million or more (Brazoria, Fort Bend, Galveston, Liberty, Montgomery, and Waller Counties).[60] In addition, a residential Subdivision Development that is or was

[57] The application of Chapter 201 is further limited to only Subdivision Developments that constitute a "residential real estate subdivision" as defined by Chapter 201. Tex. Prop. Code § 201.001(a). Chapter 201 defines a residential real estate subdivision as: (1) all land encompassed within one or more maps or plats of land that is divided into two or more parts if the maps or plats cover land within a city, town, or village, or within the extraterritorial jurisdiction of a city, town, or village and are recorded in the deed, map, or real property records of a county, and the land encompassed within the maps or plats is or was burdened by restrictions limiting all or at least a majority of the land area covered by the map or plat, excluding streets and public areas, to residential use only; or (2) all land located within a city, town, or village, or within the extraterritorial jurisdiction of a city, town, or village that has been divided into two or more parts and that is or was burdened by restrictions limiting at least a majority of the land area burdened by restrictions, excluding streets and public areas, to residential use only, if the instrument or instruments creating the restrictions are recorded in the deed or real property records of a county. Tex. Prop. Code § 201.003(2).

[58] Tex. Prop. Code § 201.001(a)(1). Texas cities with a current population of more than 100,000 are Abilene, Amarillo, Arlington, Austin, Beaumont, Brownsville, Carrollton, Corpus Christi, Dallas, Denton, El Paso, Fort Worth, Frisco, Garland, Grand Prairie, Houston, Irving, Killeen, Laredo, Lubbock, McAllen, McKinney, Mesquite, Midland, Pasadena, Plano, San Antonio, Waco, and Wichita Falls. Source: United States Census Bureau, 2010. Texas cities which may now or soon have populations of more than 100,000 are College Station (2010 pop. 93,857, 2013 est. pop. 96,000), Lewisville (2010 pop. 95,290, 2013 est. pop. 97,462), Odessa (2010 pop. 99,940, 2013 est. pop. 104,223), Richardson (2010 pop. 99,223, 2013 est. pop. 101,528), Round Rock (2010 pop. 99,887, 2013 est. pop. 104,070), and Tyler (2010 pop. 96,900, 2013 est. pop. 98,335). Source: United States Census Bureau, 2010 Census and 2013 population estimate.

[59] Tex. Prop. Code § 201.001(a)(2)(A). The only Texas county with a current population of 3.3 million or more is Harris County. Source: United States Census Bureau, 2010 Census. Although Section 201.001(a)(2)(A) states that Chapter 201 applies to "residential real estate subdivision" developments located in an unincorporated areas of Harris County, because Chapter 201's definition of "residential real estate subdivision" is limited to Subdivision Developments located within a city, town, or village, or within the extraterritorial jurisdiction of a city, town, or village, the Subdivision Development must actually be located in an unincorporated area of Harris County that is still within the extraterritorial jurisdiction of a city, town, or village. Tex. Prop. Code § 201.003(2).

[60] Tex. Prop. Code §§ 201.001(a)(2)(B), (3). Texas counties having a current population of 40,000 or more that are adjacent to a county having a population of 2.4 million or more are Brazoria, Fort Bend, Galveston, Liberty, Montgomery, and Waller Counties. Source: United States Census Bureau, 2010 Census. Although Section 201.001(a)(2)(B) states that Chapter 201 applies to "residential real estate subdivision" developments located in an unincorporated areas of Brazoria, Fort Bend, Galveston, Liberty, Montgomery, or Waller County, because Chapter 201's definition of "residential real estate subdivision" is limited to Subdivision Developments located within a city, town, or village, or within the extraterritorial jurisdiction of a city, town,

subject to Chapter 201 at any time remains subject to such chapter, regardless of a change in circumstances that removes the Subdivision Development from the applicability criteria, such as a reduction in population.[61]

Chapter 201 was enacted by the Texas Legislature in 1985 because of its concern regarding the pending expiration of Restrictive Covenants applicable to Subdivision Developments in incorporated and extraterritorial jurisdiction areas of municipalities where there are no zoning ordinances, which would create uncertainty in living conditions and discourage investments in affected Subdivision Developments in such areas.[62] The purpose of Chapter 201 is to provide a procedure for extending the term of, creation of, and/or modification of Declarations or other Dedicatory Instruments imposing Restrictive Covenants that govern such affected Subdivision Developments.[63]

11.6.1 Applicability of Chapter 201 Procedures

The procedures under Chapter 201 are intended to apply to only those applicable Subdivision Developments that have a Declaration that is valid only for an initial period of time, which does not automatically renew for successive periods of time by its own terms, and/or which has amendment provisions that impose such a high voting requirement that it would be impractical for the Lot Owners to renew or amend such Declaration.[64] For such reasons, the procedures for extending, renewing, or creating a

---

or village, the Subdivision Development must actually be located in an unincorporated area of Brazoria, Fort Bend, Galveston, Liberty, Montgomery, or Waller County that is still within the extraterritorial jurisdiction of a city, town, or village. Tex. Prop. Code § 201.003(2).

61 Tex. Prop. Code § 201.001(d).

62 House Study Group, Bill Analysis, Tex. H.B. 2256, 69th Leg., R.S. (1985); Tex. Prop. Code § 201.002(a)(1).

63 Tex. Prop. Code §§ 5.026, 201.002. The procedures for amending a Declaration under Chapter 201 are cumulative and not in lieu of any other authorized methods of adding to, modifying, creating, or extending an applicable Subdivision Development's Declaration. Tex. Prop. Code § 201.013.

64 Chapter 201 was originally enacted in 1985 for the purpose of establishing a method, or at least an easier method, for Lot Owners in applicable Subdivision Developments to extend or amend their Subdivision Declaration. The procedures under Chapter 201 for extending or modifying a Subdivision Declaration have

Declaration under Chapter 201 do not apply to a Subdivision Development if the express terms of its applicable Declaration provide for either: (1) automatic extensions of the Declaration's term for an indefinite number of successive specified periods of time subject to a right of waiver or termination, in whole or in part, by a specified percentage of Lot Owners that constitute "less than 50 percent plus one of the owners" of the Lots in the Subdivision Development; or (2) an indefinite number of successive extensions of the Declaration's term by written and filed agreement of a specified percentage of Lot owners that constitutes "less than 50 percent plus one of the owners" of the Lots in the Subdivision Development.[65]

In addition, the procedures for extending, renewing, or creating a Declaration under Chapter 201 also do not apply to a Subdivision Development if, by the express terms of its Declaration, such Declaration may be added to or modified by written and filed agreement of a specified percentage of Lot Owners that is less than seventy-five percent (75%) of all Lot Owners in the Subdivision Development, regardless of whether a provision in the Declaration requires the consent of the Developer of the Subdivision Development or an Architectural Committee for adding to or modifying the Declaration.[66] In plain English, if a Declaration of an applicable Subdivision Development provides for amendment of such Declaration by agreement of less than seventy-five percent (75%) of Lot Owners, then Chapter 201 does not apply to such Subdivision Development either.

---

to some degree been rendered irrelevant by the 2011 enactment of Section 209.0041 of the Texas Property Code, which establishes less burdensome procedures for amending a Subdivision Declaration than those under Chapter 201 and which apply to all Subdivision Developments in Texas. The amendment procedures under Section 209.0041 are discussed in greater detail in subchapter 11.5 of this book.

[65] Tex. Prop. Code § 201.001(b). In other words, if the Declaration of a hypothetical Subdivision Development, consisting of one hundred Lots, provides for automatic extensions of the Declaration for an indefinite period of time unless waived or terminated by fifty or fewer Lot Owners (i.e., a non-majority of Lot Owners), then Chapter 201 does not apply to such Subdivision Development. Similarly, if the Declaration of a hypothetical Subdivision Development, consisting of one hundred Lots, provides for an extension of the Declaration by the agreement of fifty or fewer Lot Owners (i.e., a non-majority of Lot Owners), then Chapter 201 does not apply to such Subdivision Development.

[66] Tex. Prop. Code § 201.001(c).

11.6.2 Procedures for Extension, Creation, and/or Modification of a Declaration under Chapter 201

In order to extend, create, and/or modify a Declaration under Chapter 201, a committee of Lot Owners called a "Chapter 201 Petition Committee" must be established for the purpose of circulating a written document proposing the extension, renewal, creation, and/or modification of a Declaration applicable to such Subdivision Development (called a "Chapter 201 Petition") to all other Lot Owners in such Subdivision Development in compliance with the procedures specified by Chapter 201 of the Texas Property Code.[67]

11.6.2 (A) *Creation of a Chapter 201 Petition Committee*

A Chapter 201 Petition Committee must consist of at least three Lot Owners in the Subdivision Development whose Declaration is to be extended or modified, and it is formed by the filing of a written notice of its formation with the county clerk of each county in which the Subdivision Development is located.[68] Only one committee of Lot Owners in a Subdivision Development may file to operate as a Chapter 201 Petition Committee under Chapter 201 at any given time.[69] If more than one committee of Lot Owners in a Subdivision Development files a written notice of formation of a Chapter 201 Petition Committee, then the committee of Lot Owners that files its notice of formation first constitutes the Chapter 201 Petition Committee with the power to act under Chapter 201.[70]

A written notice of formation of a Chapter 201 Petition Committee must contain:

---

[67] Tex. Prop. Code §§ 201.004–201.005.

[68] Tex. Prop. Code § 201.005(a).

[69] Tex. Prop. Code § 201.005(f).

[70] Tex. Prop. Code § 201.005(f).

(1) a statement that a Chapter 201 Petition Committee has been formed for the purpose of: (a) extending the term of; (b) creating; and/or (c) modifying one or more Declarations;[71]

(2) the name and residential address of each member of the Chapter 201 Petition Committee;[72]

(3) the name of the Subdivision Development to which the applicable Declaration applies and a reference to the Official Public Records or map or plat records where the Declaration sought to be extended, added to, or modified is recorded (or, if the creation of a Declaration is proposed, a reference to the place where the map or other document identifying the Subdivision Development, if any, is recorded);[73]

(4) a general statement of the matters to be included in the Chapter 201 Petition;[74]

(5) if the creation of a Declaration for a Subdivision Development is proposed, a copy of the proposed Chapter 201 Petition creating the Declaration must be attached to the written notice of formation of a Chapter 201 Petition Committee;[75] and

(6) if an amendment or modification of a Declaration is proposed, a copy of the proposed instrument creating the amendment or modification must be attached to the written notice of formation of a Chapter 201 Petition Committee.[76]

---

71 Tex. Prop. Code § 201.005(b)(1).

72 Tex. Prop. Code § 201.005(b)(2).

73 Tex. Prop. Code § 201.005(b)(3).

74 Tex. Prop. Code § 201.005(b)(4).

75 Tex. Prop. Code § 201.005(b)(5).

76 Tex. Prop. Code § 201.005(b)(6). If an amendment or modification of a Declaration is proposed, the proposed instrument creating the amendment or modification must also contain a copy of the original Declaration provision(s) that is to be affected and indicate by appropriate deletions and insertions the changes to be made to such provision(s) by the proposed amendment or modification. Tex. Prop. Code § 201.005(b)(6).

In addition, each member of the Chapter 201 Petition Committee must sign and acknowledge the written notice of formation of a Chapter 201 Petition Committee before a notary or other official authorized to take acknowledgments.[77]

If an individual member of the Chapter 201 Petition Committee ceases to own land in the subject Subdivision Development, the individual's membership on the Chapter 201 Petition Committee automatically terminates.[78] If a vacancy on the Chapter 201 Petition Committee occurs, either because a member of such committee ceases to own land in the Subdivision Development or because a member resigns or dies, a majority of the remaining members on the Chapter 201 Petition Committee may appoint as a successor an individual who owns land in the Subdivision Development and who consents to serve as a successor member to the Chapter 201 Petition Committee.[79] If a successor member is appointed to a Chapter 201 Petition Committee, then a written notice of the name and address of such successor committee member must be filed with the county clerk no later than the tenth (10th) day after the date of the appointment of such successor committee member.[80]

11.6.2 (B) *Required Contents of a Chapter 201 Petition*

Once a Chapter 201 Petition Committee has been established, it may submit for approval to Lot Owners in the applicable Subdivision Development a Chapter 201 Petition that proposes the extension, creation, and/or modification of a Declaration applicable to

---

[77] Tex. Prop. Code § 201.005(c).

[78] Tex. Prop. Code § 201.005(e).

[79] Tex. Prop. Code § 201.005(e).

[80] Tex. Prop. Code § 201.005(e).

such Subdivision Development.[81] A Chapter 201 Petition must contain or be supplemented by one or more written instruments containing the following information:

(1) the name of the Subdivision Development;[82]

(2) a reference to the Official Public Records or map or plat records where the Declaration sought to be extended or modified is recorded (or, in the case of the creation of a Declaration, a reference to the place where the map or other document identifying the Subdivision Development is recorded);[83]

(3) a verbatim statement of any provisions for extension of the term of, or addition to, the Declaration;[84]

(4) if a Declaration is being amended or modified, the text of the proposed amendment or modification, together with a comparison of the original Declaration provision that is affected, which must indicate by appropriate deletion and insertion the proposed amendment or modification to such Declaration provision;[85]

(5) if a Declaration is being created, the text of the proposed instrument creating the Declaration;[86]

(6) original acknowledged signatures of the requisite number of Lot Owners in the Subdivision Development;[87]

(7) alternate boxes, clearly identified in a conspicuous manner next to the place for each Lot Owner's signature on the Chapter 201 Petition, that enables each Lot Owner of record to mark an appropriate box to indicate

---

81 A Chapter 201 Petition may be circulated, signed, acknowledged, and filed by, or on behalf of, Lot Owners in an applicable Subdivision Development at any time during the Chapter 201 Petition Committee's existence. Tex. Prop. Code § 201.006(a).

82 Tex. Prop. Code § 201.007(a)(1).

83 Tex. Prop. Code § 201.007(a)(2).

84 Tex. Prop. Code § 201.007(a)(3). If a Chapter 201 Petition contains provisions extending or renewing the term of a Declaration, the Chapter 201 Petition may provide for an initial extension or renewal period of not more than ten (10) years and additional automatic extensions of the term for not more than ten (10) years each. Tex. Prop. Code § 201.004(c).

85 Tex. Prop. Code § 201.007(a)(4).

86 Tex. Prop. Code § 201.007(a)(5).

87 Tex. Prop. Code § 201.007(a)(6).

the exercise of such Lot Owner's option of either including or excluding his or her Lot from being burdened by the Declaration being extended, created, added to, or modified;[88]

(8) a statement advising Lot Owners who do not sign the Chapter 201 Petition that they must file a lawsuit before the 181st day after the date on which a "Certificate of Compliance" under Chapter 201 of the Texas Property Code is filed by the Chapter 201 Petition Committee in order to challenge the procedures followed by the Chapter 201 Petition Committee in extending, creating, adding to, or modifying a Declaration;[89] and

(9) a statement advising Lot Owners who do not sign the Chapter 201 Petition that they may omit or exclude their Lot from the operation of the extended, created, added to, or modified Declaration by filing a "Statement of Exclusion" before the first (1st) anniversary after the date on which the Lot Owner receives actual notice of the filing of the subject Chapter 201 Petition.[90]

Each Chapter 201 Petition must also show the legal description and street address of the Lot of each signing Lot Owner beside or above such Lot Owner's signature and must include an assertion from each signing Lot Owner that he or she owns record title to such Lot.[91] If there is more than one owner of record for a Lot, each Owner of such Lot

---

88 Tex. Prop. Code § 201.007(a)(7).

89 Tex. Prop. Code § 201.007(a)(8). A "Certificate of Compliance" is a written instrument executed by a majority of the members of a Chapter 201 Petition Committee upon compliance with the requisite procedures for providing notice of a filed Chapter 201 Petition to all Lot Owners in a Subdivision Development and publishing the same in a local newspaper that is recorded in the Official Public Records of each county in which the Subdivision Development is located. Tex. Prop. Code § 201.008(e) (f).

90 Tex. Prop. Code § 201.007(a)(9). A "Statement of Exclusion" is an acknowledged and recorded written statement by a Lot Owner who did not sign a Chapter 201 Petition that describes such Owner's Lot by reference to the recorded map or plat of the Subdivision Development and states that the Lot Owner elects to have his or her Lot deleted and excluded from the operation of a Declaration that is extended, modified, changed, or created under the procedures authorized by Chapter 201 of the Texas Property Code. Tex. Prop. Code § 201.009(b)(4).

91 Tex. Prop. Code § 201.007(c).

must sign the Chapter 201 Petition before such Lot may be counted as being a part of the number of Lot Owners required for an approval of a Chapter 201 Petition to be effective.[92]

11.6.2 (C) *Approval of a Chapter 201 Petition by Requisite Number of Lot Owners*

Depending on the purpose of the Chapter 201 Petition, Chapter 201 of the Texas Property Code provides for varying Lot Owner signature requirements. In order to extend or renew an existing Declaration or to create a new Declaration, the Chapter 201 Petition must be signed and acknowledged by Lot Owners who own, in the aggregate, a majority of either: (1) the total number of Lots in the Subdivision Development; (2) the total number of separately owned parcels, tracts, or building sites in the Subdivision Development, regardless of whether such parcels, tracts, or building sites contain part or all of one or more platted Lots or combinations of Lots in the Subdivision Development; or (3) the combined square footage of all Lots in the Subdivision Development, excluding any area dedicated or used exclusively for roadways or public purposes or by utilities.[93]

On the other hand, in order to modify or add to an existing Declaration, the Chapter 201 Petition must be signed and acknowledged by Lot Owners who own, in the aggregate, at least seventy-five percent (75%) of either: (1) the total number of Lots in the Subdivision Development; (2) the total number of separately owned parcels, tracts, or building sites in the Subdivision Development, regardless of whether such parcels, tracts, or building sites contain part or all of one or more platted Lots or combination of Lots in the Subdivision Development; or (3) the combined square footage of all Lots in the Subdivision Development, excluding any area dedicated or used exclusively for roadways or public purposes or by utilities.[94]

---

92 Tex. Prop. Code § 201.007(c).

93 Tex. Prop. Code § 201.006(b)(1)–(3).

94 Tex. Prop. Code § 201.006(b)(4)–(6).

A Chapter 201 Petition is considered to be effective if it is: (1) signed and acknowledged by the requisite percentage of Lot Owners of any one of the applicable classifications of property in the Subdivision Development; and (2) is filed with the county clerk of each county in which the Subdivision Development is located within two (2) years from the date the Chapter 201 Petition Committee files its written notice of formation with the county clerk.[95]

It is important to note that a Chapter 201 Petition is not effective to extend, create, or modify a Declaration unless the Chapter 201 Petition is filed with the county clerk's office in the county where the Subdivision Development is located before the second (2nd) anniversary of the date the Chapter 201 Petition Committee files the written notice of formation of a Chapter 201 Petition Committee.[96] In addition, if a Chapter 201 Petition Committee does not file the Chapter 201 Petition within such two-year time period, such Chapter 201 Petition Committee is automatically dissolved by operation of law and the Chapter 201 Petition previously circulated by such dissolved Chapter 201 Petition Committee is ineffective to extend, renew, create, add to, or modify a Declaration.[97] Except for very limited circumstances, if a Chapter 201 Petition Committee is dissolved by operation of law, a new Chapter 201 Petition Committee for the same Subdivision Development may not be validly created before the fifth (5th) anniversary of the date of dissolution of the previous Chapter 201 Petition Committee.[98] In other words, upon the dissolution of a Chapter 201 Petition Committee, a new Chapter 201 Petition Committee may not be established in the same Subdivision Development for five (5) years following the dissolution date of the previous Chapter 201 Petition Committee.

95 Tex. Prop. Code §§ 201.004(b), 201.006(d), (f). After a Lot Owner signs a Chapter 201 Petition, the fact that such Lot Owner subsequently conveys his or her Lot to someone else does not affect the previous signing of the Chapter 201 Petition. Tex. Prop. Code § 201.006(e).

96 Tex. Prop. Code § 201.004(b).

97 Tex. Prop. Code § 201.005(f).

98 Tex. Prop. Code § 201.005(f).

11.6.2 (D) *Application and Effective Date of a Chapter 201 Petition*

The provisions of a properly approved Chapter 201 Petition that is filed with the county clerk within the required two-year period becomes applicable to and binding upon all of the Lots in the affected Subdivision Development, except those Lots and other land that are excluded from its application under Section 201.009 of the Texas Property Code.[99] In addition, the extension, creation, and/or modification of a Declaration takes effect on the date the Chapter 201 Petition is filed with the county clerk or the date specified in the Chapter 201 Petition, whichever is later.[100]

11.6.2 (E) *Notice of a Filed Chapter 201 Petition and Certificate of Compliance*

Within sixty (60) days from the date on which a Chapter 201 Petition is filed with the county clerk, the Chapter 201 Petition Committee is required to give written notice of the filed Chapter 201 Petition to all persons who are then the owners of record of the Lots in the affected Subdivision Development.[101] A notice of a filed Chapter 201 Petition must contain: (1) the name of the Subdivision Development to which the Chapter 201 Petition applies; (2) a copy of the Chapter 201 Petition; (3) a statement that the proper number of Lot Owners in the Subdivision Development has signed and acknowledged the Chapter 201 Petition; and (4) the date the Chapter 201 Petition was filed with the county clerk.[102] The written notice of a filed Chapter 201 Petition must be sent by certified mail, return receipt requested, to each Lot Owner in the Subdivision Development as of the date such notice is given, excluding the owner of any Lot or land in such Subdivision Development

---

99 Tex. Prop. Code § 201.004(c). The procedures called for under Chapter 201 are considered to be complete and regular in all respects unless challenged by a declaratory judgment lawsuit to challenge the Chapter 201 Petition's compliance with the procedural requirements of Chapter 201. Tex. Prop. Code § 201.009(a). A judicial challenge of a Chapter 201 Petition's compliance with the procedural requirements of Chapter 201 is discussed more thoroughly in subsequent sections of subchapter 11.6 of this book.

100 Tex. Prop. Code § 201.004(c).

101 Tex. Prop. Code § 201.008(a).

102 Tex. Prop. Code § 201.008(a).

that is dedicated for public use or for use by utilities.[103] In addition, a copy of the written notice of a filed Chapter 201 Petition must be published once a week for two consecutive weeks in a newspaper of general circulation in the county or counties where the Subdivision Development is located.[104]

Upon compliance with the requirements for giving notice of a filed Chapter 201 Petition to Lot Owners and publishing the same in a local newspaper, a Certificate of Compliance executed by a majority of the members of the Chapter 201 Petition Committee must be filed with the county clerk of each county in which the Subdivision Development is located.[105] The county clerk of each county that receives an executed Certificate of Compliance is required to record it in the Official Public Records of such county.[106]

11.6.3 Exclusion of Lots from the Application of a Declaration that Is Extended, Created, and/or Modified under Chapter 201

Notwithstanding a Chapter 201 Petition Committee's compliance with the procedures specified by Chapter 201, a Declaration that is extended, created, and/or modified under Chapter 201 of the Texas Property Code does not affect or encumber a Lot in an applicable Subdivision Development if such Lot is:

(1) a Lot exclusively dedicated for use by the public or for use by a utility;[107]

---

103 Tex. Prop. Code § 201.008(b)(2). If the Chapter 201 Petition Committee acts in good faith in determining ownership of Lots and giving requisite notice of a filed Chapter 201 Petition to Lot Owners, the failure to give personal notice of a filed Chapter 201 Petition to a Lot Owner who actually signed the Chapter 201 Petition will not affect the application of the extension, creation, or modification of a Declaration affected by such Chapter 201 Petition as to such Owner's Lot. Tex. Prop. Code § 201.008(c).

104 Tex. Prop. Code § 201.008(b)(1). The written notice of a filed Chapter 201 Petition that is published in a newspaper may contain a general description of the purpose and effect of such Chapter 201 Petition instead of containing a verbatim copy of the actual Chapter 201 Petition. Tex. Prop. Code § 201.008(d).

105 Tex. Prop. Code § 201.008(e).

106 Tex. Prop. Code § 201.008(f).

107 Tex. Prop. Code § 201.009(b)(1).

(2) the Lot of an owner who elected in the Chapter 201 Petition to exclude his or her Lot from the application of the extension, creation, and/or modification of the subject Declaration;[108]

(3) the Lot of an owner who did not sign the Chapter 201 Petition and did not receive actual notice of the filing of the Chapter 201 Petition;[109]

(4) the Lot of an owner who did not sign the Chapter 201 Petition and filed a Statement of Exclusion within one (1) year after the date on which such Lot Owner received actual notice of the filing of the Chapter 201 Petition;[110] and/or

(5) a Lot owned by a minor or a person judicially declared to be incompetent at the time a Certificate of Compliance is filed by the Chapter 201 Petition Committee, unless: (a) actual notice of the filing of the Chapter 201 Petition was given to a guardian of the minor or incompetent person and the guardian has not filed a Statement of Exclusion; (b) a predecessor in title to the minor or incompetent person signed the filed Chapter 201 Petition while the Lot was still owned by such predecessor; or (c) the incompetent person signed the filed Chapter 201 Petition before a judicial declaration of such person's incompetency.[111]

In addition, a holder of a lien that was established against a Lot in the applicable Subdivision Development before the effective date of a Chapter 201 Petition is not bound by the Chapter 201 Petition unless the lienholder signs the Chapter 201 Petition and such

108 Tex. Prop. Code § 201.009(b)(2).

109 Tex. Prop. Code § 201.009(b)(3).

110 Tex. Prop. Code § 201.009(b)(4). A "Statement of Exclusion" is an acknowledged and recorded written statement by a Lot Owner who did not sign a Chapter 201 Petition that describes such Owner's Lot by reference to the recorded map or plat of the Subdivision Development and states that the Lot Owner elects to have his or her Lot deleted and excluded from the operation of a Declaration that is extended, created, and/or modified under the procedures authorized by Chapter 201 of the Texas Property Code. Tex. Prop. Code § 201.009(b)(4). The county clerk is required to file a Statement of Exclusion in the same manner as the Chapter 201 Petition and Certificate of Compliance. Tex. Prop. Code § 201.009(c). Substantial compliance by a Lot Owner with the requirements for a Statement of Exclusion prevents his or her Lot from being burdened by an extended, created, and/or modified Declaration if the Statement of Exclusion is filed within the requisite time period. Tex. Prop. Code § 201.009(c).

111 Tex. Prop. Code § 201.009(b)(5). A Certificate of Compliance is a written instrument executed by a majority of the members of a Chapter 201 Petition Committee upon compliance with the requisite procedures for providing notice of a filed Chapter 201 Petition to all Lot Owners in a Subdivision Development and publishing the same in a local newspaper that is recorded in the Official Public Records of each county in which the Subdivision Development is located. Tex. Prop. Code § 201.008(e)–(f).

Chapter 201 Petition is later filed.[112] If an applicable lienholder that did not sign the Chapter 201 Petition later acquires title to the applicable Lot through foreclosure, such Lot shall be free of and not subject to the Declaration provision(s) that was extended, created, and/or modified by the Chapter 201 Petition.[113] However, if any other person acquires title to such Lot at the foreclosure sale, such person's ownership of the Lot is subject to the Declaration provision(s) that was extended, created, and/or modified by the Chapter 201 Petition, if any prior owner of the foreclosed Lot signed and acknowledged the Chapter 201 Petition.[114] In other words, if a Lot is foreclosed on by a Lot Owner's lender (who's lien preexists the filed Chapter 201 Petition) and such lender purchases the Lot at foreclosure, then such Lot is not subject to the Declaration provision(s) that was extended, created, and/or modified by the Chapter 201 Petition. If, however, a person other than such lender purchases the Lot at the foreclosure sale, then the Lot remains subject to the Declaration provision(s) that was extended, created, and/or modified by the Chapter 201 Petition.

Notwithstanding any other provision of Chapter 201 of the Texas Property Code, a Lot that is excluded in any manner from the application of a Declaration or Declaration provision that was extended, created, and/or modified by a Chapter 201 Petition (unless the Chapter 201 Petition expressly provides otherwise) is still subject to and governed by all Declarations and/or Declaration provisions, if any, affecting the excluded Lot as such Declarations and/or Declaration provisions existed immediately prior to the effective date of the Chapter 201 Petition, and such Declarations and/or Declaration provisions are continued in effect to the extent originally applicable to the excluded Lot.[115] In addition, after the filing of a Chapter 201 Petition, such Declarations and/or Declaration provisions

[112] Tex. Prop. Code § 201.009(d).

[113] Tex. Prop. Code § 201.009(d).

[114] Tex. Prop. Code § 201.009(d).

[115] Tex. Prop. Code § 201.009(e).

may still be extended, created, and/or modified by a specified percentage of Lot Owners in the applicable Subdivision Development in accordance with the procedures set forth in Chapter 201 or any procedures set forth in the Declaration itself as they existed immediately prior to the effective date of the Chapter 201 Petition, if otherwise still applicable.[116] Said more simply, while an excluded Lot is not subject to the Declaration provisions that were extended, created, and/or modified by a Chapter 201 Petition, such Lot remains subject to all Declarations that existed prior to the Chapter 201 Petition, and such Declaration provisions may still be modified in a manner authorized under such Declaration or by another Chapter 201 Petition in the future.

Finally, if a Chapter 201 Petition is approved and filed in compliance with the requisite procedures under Chapter 201, the Lot Owners within a Subdivision Development covered by such Chapter 201 Petition may not raise in any judicial proceeding the issue that the Declaration or Declaration provisions added, modified, created, or extended under Chapter 201 are not enforceable on the grounds that such Declaration or Declaration provisions are not applicable to all of the Lots in the Subdivision Development.[117] In other words, because Chapter 201 anticipates that not all Lots in an applicable Subdivision Development will be subject to the Declaration provisions added, modified, created, or extended by a Chapter 201 Petition, a Lot Owner that is subject to such Declaration provisions cannot challenge the enforceability of such provisions on the basis that such provisions are not applicable to all Lots in the Subdivision Development.

---

[116] Tex. Prop. Code § 201.009(e). Any Chapter 201 Petition that creates or modifies a Declaration may provide for the subsequent addition to or extension, creation, or modification of, the resulting Declaration by a specified percentage of the Lot Owners in the Subdivision Development as set forth in the continued Declaration. Tex. Prop. Code § 201.009(e).

[117] Tex. Prop. Code § 201.011.

11.6.4 Judicial Challenge of a Chapter 201 Petition's Compliance with the Procedural Requirements of Chapter 201 or to Exclude a Lot from the Application of an Extended, Created, and/or Modified Declaration

In addition to any other type of lawsuit available under Texas law to challenge a Declaration that has been extended, modified, added to, or created under the procedures set forth by Chapter 201, Chapter 201 also authorizes a Lot Owner who neither signed the Chapter 201 Petition (or whose predecessor in interest did not sign the Chapter 201 Petition), nor filed a Statement of Exclusion, to file a lawsuit for declaratory relief in a court of competent jurisdiction in order to: (1) challenge the completeness or regularity of the procedures leading to the recordation of a Certificate of Compliance by the Chapter 201 Petition Committee (so long as the lawsuit is filed within 180 days from the date on which the Certificate of Compliance is filed with the county clerk);[118] or (2) seek an exclusion of the Owner's Lot from the application of the extended, modified, added to, or created Declaration.[119] Such lawsuit for declaratory relief must name as defendants the final members of the Chapter 201 Petition Committee who are still owners of Lots in the Subdivision Development at the time of the filing of the lawsuit.[120] In addition, a lawsuit for a declaratory judgment must name all other Lot Owners in the Subdivision Development as defendants, either as individuals or as members of a class.[121]

---

118 Tex. Prop. Code § 201.010(a)(1), (d). The filing of a lawsuit to challenge the completeness or regularity of the procedures leading to the recordation of a Certificate of Compliance by the Chapter 201 Petition Committee does not prevent the extended, modified, added to, or created Declaration from taking effect in accordance with its terms pending a final judgment in the lawsuit. Tex. Prop. Code § 201.010(d).

119 Tex. Prop. Code § 201.010(a)(2), (d). A Lot Owner who files a lawsuit to exclude such Owner's Lot from application of the extended, modified, added to, or created Declaration is entitled to relief from the court only if such Lot Owner pleads and establishes that the conditions of land use within the Subdivision Development at the time the Certificate of Compliance was filed were incompatible with the extended, modified, added to, or created Declaration. Tex. Prop. Code § 201.010(c). In addition, as an alternative to excluding a specific Lot from the application of the extended, modified, added to, or created Declaration, a court may alter the extended, modified, added to, or created Declaration as it applies to such Lot to better conform it to the incompatible conditions of such Lot. Tex. Prop. Code § 201.010(c).

120 Tex. Prop. Code § 201.010(b).

121 Tex. Prop. Code § 201.010(b).

11.7 Procedures for Extending or Modifying a Declaration of a Residential Subdivision Development and/or Establishing a Mandatory-Membership Subdivision Association Located in Harris, Galveston, or Montgomery County under Chapter 204 of the Texas Property Code

In 1995, the Texas Legislature enacted Chapter 204 to establish less burdensome procedures for Lot Owners in certain residential Subdivision Developments in Harris, Galveston, and Montgomery Counties to extend or modify an existing Declaration applicable to their developments and to provide a mechanism for Lot Owners in applicable Subdivision Developments that have no Subdivision Association to establish a Subdivision Association with mandatory membership.[122] By its express terms, Chapter 204 applies only to a residential Subdivision Development that is located in whole or in part: (1) in a county with a population of 3.3 million or more (Harris County);[123] (2) in a county with a population of not less than 285,000 and not more than 300,000 that is adjacent to the Gulf of Mexico and that is adjacent to a county having a population of 3.3 million or more (Galveston County);[124] or (3) in a county with a population of 275,000 or more that is adjacent to a county with a population of 3.3 million or more and contains part of a national forest (Montgomery County).[125] Chapter 204, however, does not apply to portions of a Subdivision Development that are zoned for or that contain a commercial

---

[122] *See* Senate Research Center, Bill Analysis, Tex. H.B. 2152, 74th Leg., R.S. (1995); SENATE RESEARCH CENTER, BILL ANALYSIS, Tex. H.B. 1632, 79th Leg., R.S. (2005) (amending Chapter 204 so as to extend it to Montgomery County). As originally enacted, Chapter 204 applied to Brazoria County as well, but due to a 2011 amendment to Chapter 204, it was rendered no longer applicable to such county.

[123] Tex. Prop. Code § 204.002(a)(1). The only Texas county with a population of 3.3 million or more is Harris County. Source: United States Census Bureau, 2010 Census.

[124] Tex. Prop. Code § 204.002(a)(2). The only Texas county with a population of not less than 285,000 and not more than 300,000 that is adjacent to the Gulf of Mexico and a county with a population of 3.3 million or more is Galveston County. Prior to 2011, Section 204.002(a)(2) applied to counties with a population of 250,000 or more that were adjacent to the Gulf of Mexico and a county having a population of 2.8 million or more, which included both Brazoria and Galveston Counties. Section 204.002(a)(2) was amended by the Texas Legislature in 2011 to make it applicable to only counties with a population between 285,000 and 300,000, which now excludes Brazoria County (pop. 313,166) from its application. Source: United States Census Bureau, 2010 Census.

[125] Tex. Prop. Code § 204.002(a)(3). The only Texas county with a population of 275,000 or more that is adjacent to a county with a population of 3.3 million or more and contains part of a national forest is Montgomery County (Sam Houston National Forest). Source: United States Census Bureau, 2010 Census.

structure, an industrial structure, an apartment complex, or a Condominium Development.[126]

11.7.1 Declarations that May Be Extended or Modified under the Procedures Set Forth by Chapter 204

The main purpose of Chapter 204 is to establish procedures for extending and/or modifying an existing Declaration where the Subdivision Development has no readily available process to do so.[127] The procedures under Chapter 204 also differ from those under Chapter 201 in that the procedures are to be carried out by the Subdivision Association, as opposed to a "Petition Committee" of Lot Owners. The procedures established by Chapter 204 for extending and/or modifying an existing Declaration, however, do not prevail over any express provisions in such Declaration that already provide a procedure for the extension or modification of such Declaration by a designated number of Lot Owners in the Subdivision Development, unless the designated number of Lot Owners required for approval of an extension and/or modification of such Declaration is more than seventy-five percent (75%) or the Declaration prohibits the extension and/or modification of any of its existing Restrictive Covenants for a certain time period and that time period has not yet expired.[128] In other words, the procedures for extending or

---

126 Tex. Prop. Code § 204.002(c).

127 Chapter 204 was originally enacted in 1995 for the purpose of establishing a method, or at least an easier method, for Lot Owners in applicable Subdivision Developments to extend or amend their Subdivision Declaration. The procedures under Chapter 204 for extending or modifying an existing Subdivision Declaration with a Subdivision Association have to some degree been rendered irrelevant by the 2011 enactment of Section 209.0041 of the Texas Property Code, which establishes less burdensome procedures for amending a Subdivision Declaration than those under Chapter 204 and which apply to all Subdivision Developments in Texas. The amendment procedures under Section 209.0041 are discussed in greater detail in subchapter 11.5 of this book.

128 Tex. Prop. Code § 204.003(a)–(b) (as enacted by Acts 2007, 80th Leg., Chapter 767, § 1, effective Sept. 1, 2007, without reference to the conflicting enactment made by Acts 2007, 80th Leg., Chapter 1367, § 5, effective Sept. 1, 2007). There is one exception to this rule. The procedures provided by Chapter 204 do not prevail over any express provisions in an applicable Declaration that provide for the extension and/or modification of such Declaration by a designated number of Lot Owners in the Subdivision Development under any circumstances if such Subdivision Development is a gated community with private streets that is located in Montgomery County. Tex. Prop. Code § 204.003(c).

modifying a Declaration under Chapter 204 do not apply if there is already a provision in the Declaration that provides procedures for extending or modifying the Declaration, unless such provision requires an extension or modification to be approved by more than seventy-five percent (75%) of the Lot Owners in the applicable Subdivision Development and/or such provision does not allow modification of the Declaration for a certain time period, which has still not expired. In addition, if a Declaration has provisions providing for the extension or renewal of the Declaration, but not for modification or amendment of such Declaration, then such Declaration may also be modified by the procedures set forth in Chapter 204, including modification of the provision that provides for extension or renewal of the Declaration.[129]

11.7.2 Procedures for Extending and/or Modifying an Existing Declaration under Chapter 204

There are essentially three steps to extending and/or modifying an existing Declaration under Chapter 204: (1) approval of a Chapter 204 Declaration Petition by the Board of Directors; (2) approval of the Chapter 204 Declaration Petition by Lot Owners; and (3) recording of the approved Chapter 204 Declaration Petition. Each of these three steps is explained in greater detail in the following subchapters.

11.7.2 (A) *Approval and Circulation of a Chapter 204 Declaration Petition by the Board of Directors*

In order to extend and/or modify an existing Declaration under Chapter 204, the Board of Directors for a residential Subdivision Association in an applicable Subdivision Development must first approve and circulate a written petition that specifies the proposed extension and/or modification of the existing Declaration (called a "Chapter 204

[129] Tex. Prop. Code § 204.003(b) (as enacted by Acts 2007, 80th Leg., Chapter 1367, § 5, effective Sept. 1, 2007, without reference to the conflicting enactment made by Acts 2007, 80th Leg., Chapter 767, § 1, effective Sept. 1, 2007).

Declaration Petition") to all Lot Owners of record in such Subdivision Development.[130] The Chapter 204 Declaration Petition may be hand-delivered to Lot Owners at their Lots within the Subdivision Development or sent by regular mail to the Lot Owners at their last known mailing address, as reflected in the ownership records maintained by the Subdivision Association.[131]

11.7.2 (B) *Approval of a Chapter 204 Declaration Petition by Lot Owners*

Once the Chapter 204 Declaration Petition has been circulated to all Lot Owners, it must then be approved by the owners of at least seventy-five percent (75%) of the Lots (excluding lienholders, contract purchasers, and the owners of mineral interests) in the Subdivision Development or a smaller percentage of Lot Owners if the existing Declaration requires a smaller percentage of Lot Owners to extend and/or modify such Declaration.[132] In addition, if a Subdivision Development consists of multiple sections, each with its own Declaration, but that is represented by a single Subdivision Association, then the approval requirement may be satisfied by obtaining approval of at least seventy-five percent (75%) of the Lot Owners on a section-by-section basis or by the approval of Lot Owners representing seventy-five percent (75%) of the total number of Lots in the Subdivision Association's jurisdiction.[133] In other words, if a hypothetical Subdivision

---

130 Tex. Prop. Code § 204.005(a), (e). A Subdivision Association that approves and circulates a Chapter 204 Declaration Petition is not required to comply with the same provisions for circulating and approving a Chapter 201 Petition under Chapter 201 of the Texas Property Code. Tex. Prop. Code § 204.005(a).

131 Tex. Prop. Code § 204.005(e).

132 Tex. Prop. Code § 204.005(b).

133 Tex. Prop. Code § 204.005(c). If a Chapter 204 Declaration Petition is approved on a Subdivision Association–wide basis by Lot Owners representing at least seventy-five percent (75%) of the total number of Lots in the Subdivision Association's jurisdiction, the extension and/or modification of the Declaration proposed by the Chapter 204 Declaration Petition becomes binding on all Lot Owners in the Subdivision Development. Tex. Prop. Code § 204.005(d). If, however, a Chapter 204 Declaration Petition is adopted on a section-by-section basis, the extension and/or modification to the Declaration proposed by the Chapter 204 Declaration Petition becomes binding upon all of the Lot Owners in each section in which at least seventy-five percent (75%) of the Lot Owners in such section approved the Chapter 204 Declaration Petition, but it will not be binding upon the sections in which the Chapter 204 Declaration Petition failed to be approved by seventy-five percent (75%) of the Lot Owners in such section. Tex. Prop. Code § 204.005(d).

Development consists of ten sections, containing one hundred Lots each, that are represented by a single Subdivision Association, then a Chapter 204 Declaration Petition may be approved by either: the owners of seventy-five Lots in each section on a section-by-section basis or by the owners of 750 Lots on a Subdivision Association-wide basis, regardless of whether the Chapter 204 Declaration Petition was actually approved by seventy-five percent (75%) of the Lot Owners in each particular section.

In addition, the adoption or approval of a Chapter 204 Declaration Petition by Lot Owners may be accomplished in one or more of the following methods: (1) by a written ballot stating the substance of the amendment and specifying the date by which a ballot must be received by the Subdivision Association to be counted; (2) at a meeting of the Subdivision Association's Membership if the written notice for such meeting states the purpose of the meeting and is delivered to each Lot Owner in the Subdivision Development; (3) by door-to-door circulation of the Chapter 204 Declaration Petition by the Subdivision Association or a person authorized by the Subdivision Association; (4) by any other method permitted by the existing Declaration; or (5) by a combination of these methods.[134] In addition, if a Lot is owned by more than one person, the approval of multiple owners of a single Lot may be reflected by the signature of a single co-owner, such as the husband or the wife if a Lot is owned by a married couple.[135]

11.7.2 (C) *Recording a Chapter 204 Declaration Petition*

The third and final step to extend and/or modify an existing Declaration under Chapter 204 is to record an approved Chapter 204 Declaration Petition as a written

[134] Tex. Prop. Code § 204.008.

[135] Tex. Prop. Code § 204.005(e).

instrument in the Official Public Records of each county in which the Subdivision Development is located.[136]

11.7.3 Procedures for Creation of a Mandatory-Membership Subdivision Association under Chapter 204

In addition to establishing a procedure for the extension and/or modification of an existing Declaration, Chapter 204 also establishes procedures for creating a Subdivision Association if the existing Declaration of a Subdivision Development does not provide for one. More specifically, if the existing Declaration of a Subdivision Development does not establish a Subdivision Association for such Subdivision Development and such Declaration requires approval of more than sixty percent (60%) of the Lot Owners in such Subdivision Development in order to add to or modify such Declaration, then a committee of Lot Owners (called a "Chapter 204 Subdivision Association Petition Committee") can be formed to create and circulate a petition to add to or modify the existing Declaration for the sole purpose of establishing a Subdivision Association with mandatory membership of Lot Owners in such Subdivision Development (called a "Chapter 204 Subdivision Association Petition").

11.7.3 (A) *Creation of a Chapter 204 Subdivision Association Petition Committee*

A Chapter 204 Subdivision Association Petition Committee is formed in the same manner as a Chapter 201 Petition Committee.[137] A Chapter 204 Subdivision Association Petition Committee must consist of at least three Lot Owners in the Subdivision Development for which a Subdivision Association is to be established and it is formed by

---

136 Tex. Prop. Code § 204.005(b). An approved Chapter 204 Declaration Petition would also be considered a Dedicatory Instrument. Tex. Prop. Code § 202.001. As a result, a Chapter 204 Declaration Petition is also required under Chapter 202 of the Texas Property Code to be recorded in the Official Public Records of each county in which a portion of the Subdivision Development is located in order to be enforceable. Tex. Prop. Code § 202.006.

137 Tex. Prop. Code § 204.006(a)(1).

the filing of a written notice of the formation of a Chapter 204 Subdivision Association Petition Committee with the county clerk of each county in which the Subdivision Development is located.[138] Only one committee of Lot Owners in a Subdivision Development may operate as a Chapter 204 Subdivision Association Petition Committee under Chapter 204 at any given time.[139] If more than one committee of Lot Owners in a Subdivision Development files a written notice of formation of a Chapter 204 Subdivision Association Petition Committee, then the committee of Lot Owners that files its notice of formation first constitutes the Chapter 204 Subdivision Association Petition Committee with the power to act under Chapter 204.[140]

The written notice of formation of a Chapter 204 Subdivision Association Petition Committee must contain:

(1) a statement that a Chapter 204 Subdivision Association Petition Committee has been formed for the purpose of adding to or modifying an existing Declaration of a Subdivision Development for the sole purpose of creating and operating a Subdivision Association that: (a) will require the mandatory membership of Lot Owners in such Subdivision Development; (b) will have the authority to levy mandatory regular or special Assessments upon such Lot Owners; and (c) will provide for equivalent voting rights for each of the Lot Owners in such Subdivision Development;[141]

(2) the name and residential address of each member of the Chapter 204 Subdivision Association Petition Committee;[142]

(3) the name of the Subdivision Development to which the applicable Declaration applies and a reference to the Official Public Records or map

[138] Tex. Prop. Code §§ 201.005(a), 204.006(a)(1).

[139] Tex. Prop. Code §§ 201.005(f), 204.006(a)(1).

[140] Tex. Prop. Code §§ 201.005(f), 204.006(a)(1).

[141] Tex. Prop. Code §§ 201.005(b)(1), 204.006(a)(1).

[142] Tex. Prop. Code §§ 201.005(b)(2), 204.006(a)(1).

or plat records where the Declaration sought to be added to or modified is recorded;[143]

(4) a general statement of the matters to be included in the Chapter 204 Subdivision Association Petition;[144] and

(5) a copy of the proposed Chapter 204 Subdivision Association Petition creating the Subdivision Association must be attached to the written notice of formation of a Chapter 204 Subdivision Association Petition Committee.[145]

In addition, each member of the Chapter 204 Subdivision Association Petition Committee must sign and acknowledge the written notice of formation before a notary or other official authorized to take acknowledgments.[146]

If an individual member of the Chapter 204 Subdivision Association Petition Committee ceases to own land in the subject Subdivision Development, then the individual's membership on the Chapter 204 Subdivision Association Petition Committee automatically terminates.[147] If a vacancy on the Chapter 204 Subdivision Association Petition Committee occurs, either because a member of such committee ceases to own land in the Subdivision Development or because a member resigns or dies, a majority of the remaining members on the Chapter 204 Subdivision Association Petition Committee may appoint as a successor an individual who owns land in the Subdivision Development and who consents to serve as a successor member to the Chapter 204 Subdivision Association Petition Committee.[148] If a successor member is appointed to a Chapter 204 Subdivision Association Petition Committee, a written notice of the name and address of

143 Tex. Prop. Code §§ 201.005(b)(3), 204.006(a)(1).

144 Tex. Prop. Code §§ 201.005(b)(4), 204.006(a)(1).

145 Tex. Prop. Code §§ 201.005(b)(5)–(6), 204.006(a)(1).

146 Tex. Prop. Code §§ 201.005(c), 204.006(a)(1).

147 Tex. Prop. Code § 201.005(e).

148 Tex. Prop. Code § 201.005(e).

such successor committee member must be filed with the county clerk no later than the tenth (10th) day after the date of the appointment of such successor committee member.[149]

11.7.3 (B) *Circulation and Approval of a Chapter 204 Subdivision Association Petition by Lot Owners*

A Chapter 204 Subdivision Association Petition may be circulated and approved in the same manner as a Chapter 204 Declaration Petition, except that a Chapter 204 Subdivision Association Petition is effective if approved by at least sixty percent (60%) of the Lot Owners in the Subdivision Development (excluding lienholders, contract purchasers, and the owners of mineral interests) instead of seventy-five percent (75%) of such Lot Owners.[150] Similar to a Chapter 204 Declaration Petition, if a Chapter 204 Subdivision Association Petition is approved on a Subdivision Association-wide basis by Lot Owners representing at least sixty percent (60%) of the total number of Lots in the Subdivision Association's jurisdiction, it is binding on all Lots Owners in the Subdivision Development.[151] If, however, a Chapter 204 Subdivision Association Petition is adopted on a section-by-section basis, the Chapter 204 Subdivision Association Petition becomes binding upon all of the Lot Owners in each section in which at least sixty percent (60%) of the Lots Owners in such section approved the Chapter 204 Subdivision Association Petition, but it will not be binding upon the sections in which the Chapter 204 Subdivision

---

149 Tex. Prop. Code § 201.005(e).

150 Tex. Prop. Code § 204.006(a)(2)–(3). In other words, if a Subdivision Development consists of multiple sections, each with its own Declaration, but that are represented by a single Subdivision Association, the approval requirement may be satisfied by obtaining approval of at least sixty percent (60%) of the Lot Owners on a section-by-section basis or by the approval of Lot Owners representing sixty percent (60%) of the total number of Lots in the Subdivision Association's jurisdiction. Tex. Prop. Code §§ 204.005(c), 204.006. Thus, if a hypothetical Subdivision Development consists of ten (10) sections, containing one hundred (100) Lots each, that are represented by a single Subdivision Association, a Chapter 204 Subdivision Association Petition may be approved by either: the owners of sixty (60) Lots in each section on a section-by-section basis; or by the owners of six hundred (600) Lots on a Subdivision Association–wide basis, regardless of whether the Chapter 204 Subdivision Association Petition was actually approved by sixty percent (60%) of the Lot Owners in each particular section.

151 Tex. Prop. Code § 204.006(c).

Association Petition failed to be approved by sixty percent (60%) of the Lot Owners in such section.[152]

If a circulated Chapter 204 Subdivision Association Petition is not approved by the required percentage of Lot Owners within one (1) year from the date the written notice of formation of the Chapter 204 Subdivision Association Petition Committee was recorded, the Chapter 204 Subdivision Association Petition Committee is dissolved by operation of law and the Chapter 204 Subdivision Association Petition circulated by it is considered void.[153] In such event, a new Chapter 204 Subdivision Association Petition Committee may be formed to reattempt approval of a Chapter 204 Subdivision Association Petition.[154]

11.7.4 Vesting of Architectural Control Authority in Certain Applicable Subdivision Developments under Chapter 204

If an applicable residential Subdivision Development that is subject to Chapter 204 is governed by a Declaration that provides for the creation and operation of an "Architectural Committee"[155] with the power to approve or deny applications for proposed original construction or modification of buildings, structures, or improvements on Lots in such Subdivision Development, and such Declaration does not vest such "Architectural Control Authority"[156] in the Subdivision Association before: (1) the term of the

---

[152] Tex. Prop. Code § 204.006(c).

[153] Tex. Prop. Code § 204.006(b). In other words, a Chapter 204 Subdivision Association Petition must be approved by the requisite number of Lot Owners within one (1) year from the date the Chapter 204 Subdivision Association Petition Committee is formed.

[154] Tex. Prop. Code § 204.006(b). Unlike a Chapter 201 Petition Committee, there is no statutory waiting period for forming a new Chapter 204 Subdivision Association Petition Committee.

[155] "Architectural Committee" is a term of art utilized in this book that refers to a committee of individuals vested with the authority to review and approve proposed construction or modification of improvements in a Subdivision or Condominium Development under the Declaration applicable to the community.

[156] "Architectural Control Authority" is a term of art utilized in this book that refers to the power to approve or deny applications for proposed original construction of a new building, structure, or Improvement or modification of an existing building, structure, or Improvement on a Lot or Unit.

Architectural Control Authority expires as prescribed by the Declaration; (2) a residence on the last available building site is completed and sold; (3) the person or entity designated as the Architectural Committee in the Declaration assigns, in writing, such authority to the Subdivision Association; or (4) an assignee of the original holder of the Architectural Control Authority abandons its authority for more than one (1) year, then such Architectural Control Authority automatically vests in the Subdivision Association upon the earliest occurrence of any one of such events.[157] If Architectural Control Authority is transferred to the Subdivision Association, such Architectural Control Authority remains vested in the Subdivision Association until the Declaration is modified to reflect otherwise, the Declaration is terminated, or the Subdivision Association ceases to exist.[158]

In addition, if an existing Declaration applicable to a Subdivision Development does not provide for a Subdivision Association and a Subdivision Association has not been formed, Architectural Control Authority over the entire Subdivision Association vests in an applicable civic association other than a Subdivision Association if:

(1) an Architectural Committee created by the Declaration exercised Architectural Control Authority as provided by the Declaration over all the Lots in the Subdivision Development for at least ten (10) years and over a majority of the Lots in the Subdivision Development for at least twenty (20) years;[159]

(2) the Architectural Committee created by the Declaration assigned Architectural Control Authority over a majority of the Lots in the Subdivision Development to the civic association;[160]

(3) the civic association was assigned the Architectural Control Authority over a majority of the Lots in the Subdivision Development and has

157 Tex. Prop. Code § 204.011(a)–(b).

158 Tex. Prop. Code § 204.011(c).

159 Tex. Prop. Code § 204.011(d)(1).

160 Tex. Prop. Code § 204.011(d)(2).

exercised such Architectural Control Authority over all the Lots in such Subdivision Development for at least ten (10) years;[161] and

(4) the Architectural Control Authority has lapsed in the Lots in which the civic association lacks authority, and the lapse is solely the result of: (a) the automatic termination of the Architectural Control Authority; or (b) the death of a member of the Architectural Committee or another cause resulting from the inability to locate a member of the Architectural Committee or such member's assigns.[162]

11.8 Procedures for Amending a Declaration for Certain Limited Purposes by a Board of Directors of a Texas Homeowners Association Located in a Texas County with a Population of 65,000 or More under Chapter 205 of the Texas Property Code

Chapter 205 was enacted by the Texas Legislature in 1995 in conjunction with Chapter 204 and is another statute with limited applicability (albeit very broad applicability in comparison to Chapter 204).[163] Chapter 205 applies to all Homeowners Associations located in Texas counties with a population of 65,000 or more.[164]

Chapter 205 authorizes the Board of Directors of a Homeowners Association in an applicable county to amend its Declaration for the limited purpose of complying with United States Department of Housing and Urban Development's or United States Department of Veterans Affairs' requirements for subdivision property to qualify for

161 Tex. Prop. Code § 204.011(d)(3).

162 Tex. Prop. Code § 204.011(d)(1).

163 Senate Research Center, Bill Analysis, Tex. H.B. 2152, 74th Leg., R.S. (1995).

164 Tex. Prop. Code §§ 202.001, 205.001(2), 205.002. The Texas counties with a population of 65,000 or more are Angelina, Bastrop, Bell, Bexar, Bowie, Brazoria, Brazos, Cameron, Collin, Comal, Coryell, Dallas, Denton, Ector, El Paso, Ellis, Fort Bend, Galveston, Grayson, Gregg, Guadalupe, Harris, Harrison, Hays, Henderson, Hidalgo, Hunt, Jefferson, Johnson, Kaufman, Liberty, Lubbock, McLennan, Midland, Montgomery, Nueces, Orange, Parker, Potter, Randall, Rockwall, Smith, Tarrant, Taylor, Tom Green, Travis, Victoria, Walker, Webb, Wichita, and Williamson Counties. Source: United States Census Bureau, 2010 Census. Texas counties which may now or soon have populations of more than 65,000 are San Patricio County (2010 pop. 64,804, 2014 est. pop. 66,915), Nacogdoches County (2010 pop. 64,524, 2014 est. pop. 65,301), Starr County (2010 pop. 60,968, 2014 est. pop. 62,955), and Wise County (2010 pop. 59,127, 2014 est. pop. 61,638). Source: United States Census Bureau, 2010 Census and 2014 population estimate.

insured or guaranteed mortgage loans.[165] An amendment of an applicable Declaration for such purpose must: (1) indicate that the amendment is adopted under the authority of Chapter 205 by specifically referencing Section 205.004 of the Texas Property Code; (2) be signed by a majority of the Board of Directors of the Subdivision Association; and (3) be filed in the Official Public Records of each county in which the Subdivision Development is located.[166]

In addition, Chapter 205 further provides that if all or part of a Subdivision Development's Subdivision Plat is revised to create a new subdivision of land within a portion of the original Subdivision Development, then any Declaration that was applicable to the original Subdivision Development before the revision of such Subdivision Plat continues to be applicable to the newly created Subdivision Development, as well.[167] In addition, the owners of Lots in the newly created Subdivision Development may utilize the petition procedures for extending and/or modifying an existing Subdivision Declaration under Chapter 204 of the Texas Property Code in order to modify the Declaration that was applicable to the original Subdivision Development before the revision of its Subdivision Plat.[168]

11.9 Procedures for Extending a Declaration Applicable to the Clear Lake City Community Association in Harris County, Texas, under Chapter 206 of the Texas Property Code

Chapter 206 of the Texas Property Code is a statute with very limited applicability that was enacted in 1997 to specifically address the extension of the Declaration applicable to the Clear Lake City Community Association in Harris County, Texas.[169] By its express

[165] Tex. Prop. Code § 205.004(a).

[166] Tex. Prop. Code § 205.004(b).

[167] Tex. Prop. Code § 205.003(a).

[168] Tex. Prop. Code § 205.003(b).

[169] Senate Research Center, Bill Analysis, Tex. H.B. 2339, 75th Leg., R.S. (1997). The Bill Analysis for House Bill 2339 indicates that Chapter 206 of the Texas Property Code is intended to apply specifically to the

terms, Chapter 206 applies to any residential Subdivision Development that: (1) consists of at least 4,600 homes;[170] (2) is located in whole or in part in a municipality with a population of more than 1.6 million located in a county with a population of 2.8 million or more (Houston);[171] and (3) has a Declaration, the terms of which are automatically extended, but which is also subject to an obligation to pay regular Assessments that is established by a separate Dedicatory Instrument that will expire by its own terms without the ability of the Subdivision Association to extend the term of the Assessment obligation contained in such separate Dedicatory Instrument.[172] Chapter 206 also applies to any residential Subdivision Development that: (1) consists of at least 750 homes;[173] (2) is located in two adjacent municipalities within a county consisting of a population of 2.8 million or more;[174] and (3) is subject to Restrictive Covenants, the terms of which are automatically extended, but which is also subject to an obligation to pay regular Assessments that was established by two separate Dedicatory Instruments that will expire by their own terms without the ability of the Subdivision Association to extend the term of the Assessment obligation contained in such separate Dedicatory Instruments.[175]

Under Chapter 206, an applicable Subdivision Association may approve and submit to a vote of the Lot Owners in the Subdivision Development a proposed amendment to extend a Declaration or Dedicatory Instrument that provides for the

---

Clear Lake City Community Association in Harris County, Texas, but other Subdivision Associations may fall within the scope of Chapter 206's application criteria.

170 Tex. Prop. Code § 206.002(1)(A).

171 Tex. Prop. Code § 206.002(1)(B). The only Texas city that has a population of 1.6 million or more that is located in a county with a population of 2.8 million or more is the City of Houston. Source: United States Census Bureau, 2010 Census.

172 Tex. Prop. Code § 206.002(1)(C).

173 Tex. Prop. Code § 206.002(2)(A).

174 Tex. Prop. Code § 206.002(2)(B). The only Texas county with a population of 2.8 million or more is Harris County. Source: United States Census Bureau, 2010 Census.

175 Tex. Prop. Code § 206.002(2)(C).

imposition of regular Assessments.[176] A proposed extension of such a Declaration or Dedicatory Instrument must be approved by Lot Owners either: (1) by a written ballot that states the substance of the proposed amendment extending the Declaration or Dedicatory Instrument and that specifies the date by which the Subdivision Association must receive a ballot from a Lot Owner for such ballot to be counted; or (2) at a meeting of the Lot Owners in the Subdivision Development.[177] Chapter 206 also provides that in conjunction with a vote by ballot or at a meeting of Lot Owners, the Subdivision Association may also provide for circulation of a petition in the Subdivision Development.[178]

The extension of a Declaration or Dedicatory Instrument that imposes a regular Assessment under the procedures established by Chapter 206 is considered to be approved if a majority of the Lot Owners in the Subdivision Development votes in favor of such extension.[179] In such event, a document certifying that a majority of the Lot Owners voting on the issue approved such extension of the Declaration or Dedicatory Instrument must be recorded in the Official Public Records of the county in which the Subdivision Development is located.[180] An extension of a Declaration or Dedicatory Instrument providing for the imposition of regular Assessments that is approved in accordance with

---

[176] Tex. Prop. Code § 206.003(a).

[177] Tex. Prop. Code § 206.004(a). The Subdivision Association must mail to each Lot Owner, as applicable, the requisite written ballot or notice of meeting. Tex. Prop. Code § 206.004(b). If the Subdivision Association intends to submit a proposed amendment extending the Declaration or Dedicatory Instrument to a vote of Lot Owners at a meeting, the notice of meeting provided to Lot Owners must state the purpose of such meeting. Tex. Prop. Code § 206.004(b)(2). In addition, the Subdivision Association is required to record a copy of the ballot or a petition in the Official Public Records of the county in which the Subdivision Development is located prior to submission of the proposed extension to a vote of the Lot Owners. Tex. Prop. Code § 206.004(e).

[178] Tex. Prop. Code § 206.004(c). Chapter 206, however, does not specify any other procedural requirements for circulating a petition to extend a Declaration or Dedicatory Instrument that provides for the imposition of regular Assessments.

[179] Tex. Prop. Code § 206.003(b). If a Lot is owned by more than one owner, the vote of multiple owners of a Lot may be reflected by the signature or vote of only one of the co-owners of such Lot. Tex. Prop. Code § 206.004(d).

[180] Tex. Prop. Code § 206.003(d).

the procedures under Chapter 206 applies to all Lots in the Subdivision Development, including both residential and commercial property.[181]

11.10 Procedures for Amendment and/or Termination of a Declaration in a Historic Neighborhood Located in the Houston Heights Area of the City of Houston under Chapter 208 of the Texas Property Code

Chapter 208 of the Texas Property Code is the most limited of the statutes with limited applicability and was enacted in 1999 to eliminate any technical defenses against the enforcement of certain Declarations applicable to "Historic Neighborhoods" in the Houston Heights area of Houston, Texas.[182]

11.10.1 Applicability of Chapter 208 to Historic Neighborhoods

Chapter 208 applies only to a Historic Neighborhood that is located in whole or in part in a municipality with a population of 1.6 million or more that is located in a county with a population of 2.8 million or more (Houston).[183] Chapter 208, however, is not applicable to property in the area of a Historic Neighborhood that is zoned for, or that contains, a commercial structure, an industrial structure, an apartment complex, or a Condominium Development, unless the owner of such property signed a Declaration or Dedicatory Instrument that imposes Restrictive Covenants upon such property for the purpose of establishing a "common scheme for preservation of historic property" in a Historic Neighborhood (called a "Historic Preservation Declaration") that is enforceable

---

181 Tex. Prop. Code § 206.003(c).

182 Office of House Bill Analysis, Bill Analysis, Tex. H.B. 1956, 76th Leg., R.S. (1999). A "Historic Neighborhood" is defined by Chapter 208 as: (1) an area incorporated as a separate municipality before the year 1900, but which has been subsequently annexed into another municipality; (2) an area described by a municipality map or subdivision plat filed in the Official Public Records of the county in which such area is located before the year 1900; or (3) an area designated as a historic district or similar designation by the municipality in which such area is located, the Texas Historical Commission, or the National Register of Historic Places. Tex. Prop. Code § 208.001(5).

183 Tex. Prop. Code § 208.002(a). The only Texas city that has a population of 1.6 million or more that is located in a county with a population of 2.8 million or more is the City of Houston. Source: United States Census Bureau, 2010 Census.

by a "Historic Neighborhood Preservation Association."[184] A Historic Neighborhood Preservation Association refers to an association of property owners in a Historic Neighborhood established by a Historic Preservation Declaration for the preservation of historic property in such Historic Neighborhood and to enforce the provisions of such Historic Preservation Declaration.[185]

11.10.2 Procedures for Amendment or Termination of a Historic Preservation Declaration

Chapter 208 establishes procedures for amendment or termination of a Historic Preservation Declaration.[186] Under Chapter 208, an amendment or termination of an applicable Historic Preservation Declaration must be approved by members of the Historic Neighborhood Preservation Association, voting either: (1) by a written ballot that states the substance of the amendment or termination of the Historic Preservation Declaration and specifies the date by which the Historic Neighborhood Preservation Association must receive a ballot for the ballot to be counted; (2) at a meeting of the Historic Neighborhood Preservation Association; (3) by circulation of a petition by the Historic Neighborhood

[184] Tex. Prop. Code § 208.002(c). A "common scheme for preservation of historic property" exists in a Historic Neighborhood if a Historic Preservation Declaration was created by individual Dedicatory Instruments signed by an owner of one or more separately owned parcels or tracts in an applicable Historic Neighborhood and the Historic Preservation Declaration authorizes the establishment of a "Historic Neighborhood Preservation Association" to enforce such Historic Preservation Declaration. Tex. Prop. Code § 208.004(a). A "common scheme for preservation of historic property" does not include property that is not subject to the Historic Preservation Declaration. Tex. Prop. Code § 208.004(b).

[185] Tex. Prop. Code § 208.004(a). A Historic Neighborhood Preservation Association is required to: (1) be a Texas nonprofit corporation or limited liability company organized, in part, to encourage the preservation of property in a Historic Neighborhood; and (2) allow membership to all owners of property in the Historic Neighborhood. Tex. Prop. Code § 208.003(a). A Historic Neighborhood Preservation Association may be composed of only a portion of the owners of property in the Historic Neighborhood. Tex. Prop. Code § 208.003(b). A Historic Neighborhood Preservation Association may also be a Homeowners Association or an organization that is qualified as a charitable organization under Section 501(c)(3) of the Internal Revenue Code. Tex. Prop. Code § 208.003(c).

[186] Tex. Prop. Code § 208.005. The amendment or termination procedures provided by Chapter 208, however, may not be used to amend a Historic Preservation Declaration for the purpose of establishing a regular or special Assessment or modifying a building line established by a Declaration, municipal map, or subdivision plat. Tex. Prop. Code §§ 208.007–208.008.

Preservation Association or a person authorized by the Historic Neighborhood Preservation Association; or (4) by any combination of such methods.[187] If a vote to amend or terminate a Historic Preservation Declaration is to occur at a meeting of the Historic Neighborhood Preservation Association's membership, then before such meeting may be held, the Historic Neighborhood Preservation Association must deliver a written meeting notice that states the purpose of such meeting to each owner of property subject to the "common scheme for preservation of historic property," and it must provide each such property owner with the opportunity to appear and vote at such meeting.[188]

Based on the voting procedure or combination of voting procedures to be used by the Historic Neighborhood Preservation Association to approve an amendment or termination of a Historic Preservation Declaration, the Historic Neighborhood Preservation Association must mail to each owner of property subject to the "common scheme for preservation of historic property," as applicable: (1) the written ballot for voting on the proposed amendment or termination; (2) a notice of the meeting of the Historic Neighborhood Preservation Association's membership at which its members may vote on the proposed amendment or termination; and/or (3) the circulated petition concerning the proposed amendment or termination.[189] The Historic Neighborhood Preservation Association is also required to record a copy of the ballot or petition to be used for such proposed amendment or termination, as applicable, in the Official Public Records of the county in which the Historic Neighborhood is located before any vote of the owners of property subject to the "common scheme for preservation of historic property" may be conducted on such proposed amendment or termination.[190]

---

187 Tex. Prop. Code § 208.006(a). If a property subject to a "common scheme for preservation of historic property" is owned by more than one owner, the vote of multiple owners of such property may be reflected by the vote or signature of one co-owner of such property. Tex. Prop. Code § 208.006(d).

188 Tex. Prop. Code § 208.006(b).

189 Tex. Prop. Code § 208.006(c).

190 Tex. Prop. Code § 208.006(e).

11.10.3 Defenses to Enforcement of a Historic Preservation Declaration

Chapter 208 of the Texas Property Code also restricts certain defenses that may be asserted by a property owner in response to judicial enforcement of Restrictive Covenants contained in a Historic Preservation Declaration. More specifically, an owner of property subject to a Historic Preservation Declaration may not assert as a defense to the enforcement of a Restrictive Covenant that is part of a "common scheme for preservation of historic property" that such owner or owner's predecessor in title signed a blank signature page or similar procedural defect if the signature page was attached to the Historic Preservation Declaration or other Dedicatory Instrument adopted by a Historic Neighborhood Preservation Association and: (1) such Historic Preservation Declaration or other Dedicatory Instrument has been recorded in the local Official Public Records for more than two (2) years; or (2) the Restrictive Covenant, or such Historic Preservation Declaration or other Dedicatory Instrument, is referenced in the property owner's title insurance policy that he or she obtained when he or she purchased their property.[191]

11.11 Procedures for Extension or Modification of a Declaration Applicable to a Residential Subdivision Development Located in Smith, Cherokee, Henderson, Rusk, or Van Zandt County by Petition under Chapter 210 of the Texas Property Code

In 2005, the Texas Legislature enacted Chapter 210 of the Texas Property Code in order to establish statutory procedures for the amendment of Declarations applicable to certain Subdivision Developments located in Smith, Cherokee, Henderson, Rusk, and Van Zandt Counties.[192] By its express terms, Chapter 210 only applies to "residential real estate subdivision" developments[193] that are located in: (1) a county with a population of more

---

[191] Tex. Prop. Code § 208.009.

[192] Senate Research Center, Bill Analysis, Tex. S.B. 1018, 79th Leg., R.S. (2005); Tex. Prop. Code § 211.003.

[193] The application of Chapter 210 is further limited to only Subdivision Developments that constitute a "residential real estate subdivision" as defined by Section 201.003. Tex. Prop. Code § 201.001(a). Section 201.003 defines a residential real estate subdivision as: (1) all land encompassed within one or more maps or plats of land that is divided into two or more parts if the maps or plats cover land within a city, town, or village, or within the extraterritorial jurisdiction of a city, town, or village and are recorded in the deed, map,

than 200,000, but less than 220,000 (Smith County);[194] and/or (2) a county with a population of more than 45,000, but less than 80,000, that is adjacent to a county with a population of more than 200,000, but less than 220,000 (Cherokee, Henderson, Rusk, and Van Zandt Counties).[195]

11.11.1 Procedures for Amendment of a Declaration under Chapter 210

Pursuant to Chapter 210, in addition to any procedures provided in an applicable Subdivision Development's Declaration, a Subdivision Association or a petition committee comprised of at least three Lot Owners in such Subdivision Development

---

or real property records of a county, and the land encompassed within the maps or plats is or was burdened by restrictions limiting all or at least a majority of the land area covered by the map or plat, excluding streets and public areas, to residential use only; or (2) all land located within a city, town, or village, or within the extraterritorial jurisdiction of a city, town, or village that has been divided into two or more parts and that is or was burdened by restrictions limiting at least a majority of the land area burdened by restrictions, excluding streets and public areas, to residential use only, if the instrument or instruments creating the restrictions are recorded in the deed or real property records of a county. Tex. Prop. Code § 201.003(2).

[194] Tex. Prop. Code § 210.002(1). As of the 2010 Census, the only Texas county with a population of more than 200,000 and less than 220,000 is Smith County. Source: United States Census Bureau, 2010 Census. However, the United States Census Bureau estimates that as of 2014, Brazos County's 2010 population of 194,851 has increased to 209,152. Source: United States Census Bureau, 2010 Census and 2014 population estimate. It is important to note that while Section 210.002(1) states that Chapter 210 applies to "residential real estate subdivision" developments located in Smith County, because Chapter 201's definition of "residential real estate subdivision" is limited to Subdivision Developments located within a city, town, or village, or within the extraterritorial jurisdiction of a city, town, or village, an applicable Subdivision Development (unless it is a gated community with private streets) must actually be located in an area of Smith County that is still within a city, town, or village, or within the extraterritorial jurisdiction of a city, town, or village. Tex. Prop. Code § 201.003(2). If a Subdivision Development is a gated community with private streets, then Chapter 210 is still applicable to such Subdivision Development even if it is not located within a city, town, or village, or within the extraterritorial jurisdiction of a city, town, or village. Tex. Prop. Code 210.001(4).

[195] Tex. Prop. Code § 210.002(2). The only Texas counties with a population of more than 45,000 and less than 80,000 that are adjacent to a county with a population of more than 200,000 and less than 220,000 are Cherokee, Henderson, Rusk, and Van Zandt Counties. Source: United States Census Bureau, 2010 Census. Even if Brazos County's population is not between 200,000 and 220,000, there are no counties adjacent thereto that have a population of more than 45,000 and less than 80,000. Source: United States Census Bureau, 2010 Census and 2014 population estimate. It is important to note that while Section 210.002(2) states that Chapter 210 applies to "residential real estate subdivision" developments located in Cherokee, Henderson, Rusk, or Van Zandt County, because Chapter 201's definition of "residential real estate subdivision" is limited to Subdivision Developments located within a city, town, or village, or within the extraterritorial jurisdiction of a city, town, or village, the Subdivision Development must actually be located in an area of Cherokee, Henderson, Rusk, or Van Zandt County that is still within a city, town, or village, or within the extraterritorial jurisdiction of a city, town, or village. Tex. Prop. Code § 201.003(2).

(called a "Chapter 210 Petition Committee") may circulate a petition proposing to extend or modify an existing Declaration.[196] In order to extend or modify an existing Declaration under the procedures established by Chapter 210, the Subdivision Association or Chapter 210 Petition Committee must deliver to each Lot Owner of record in the Subdivision Development a petition describing the exact terms of the proposed extension or modification of the existing Declaration (called a "Chapter 210 Petition").[197] The Chapter 210 Petition must be sent by certified mail, return receipt requested, to each Lot Owner in the applicable Subdivision Development at his or her mailing address, as reflected in the appraisal records maintained by the appraisal district for the county in which the Owner's Lot is located.[198] In addition, the Chapter 210 Petition must state the date by which a response must be received by either the Subdivision Association or Chapter 210 Petition Committee, as is applicable, in order to be counted.[199]

A Chapter 210 Petition may allow each Lot Owner to indicate his or her approval or disapproval as to the entire proposed extension or modification of the existing Declaration or to indicate his or her approval or disapproval as to each specific provision of the proposed extension or modification on a provision-by-provision basis.[200] If a Chapter 210 Petition allows Lot Owners to indicate only approval or disapproval of the entire proposed extension or modification to the existing Declaration, then the proposed

---

[196] Tex. Prop. Code § 210.004(a).

[197] Tex. Prop. Code § 210.005(a).

[198] Tex. Prop. Code § 210.005(e). Separate signature pages may be delivered to each Lot Owner if the proposed extension or modification is stated fully or referenced on each signature page. Tex. Prop. Code § 210.005(d). A reference to a proposed extension or modification in the signature pages may be made by the following or substantially similar wording: "We the undersigned owners of property in the __________ Subdivision indicate by our signatures on this document our approval or disapproval of the proposal(s) circulated by __________ on or about [date] to [extend or modify] our Restrictive Covenants. We acknowledge that we have fully reviewed the proposal(s)." Tex. Prop. Code § 210.005(d). In addition, the signature of a Lot Owner on the Chapter 210 Petition conclusively establishes that the Lot Owner received such Petition. Tex. Prop. Code § 210.005(f).

[199] Tex. Prop. Code § 210.005(b).

[200] Tex. Prop. Code § 210.005(c).

extension or modification is adopted if at least sixty-six percent (66%) of the Lot Owners in the Subdivision Development vote in favor of such proposal.[201] Alternatively, if a Chapter 210 Petition allows Lot Owners to indicate approval or disapproval of each specific provision of the proposed extension or modification on a provision-by-provision basis, then only the specific provisions in which at least sixty-six percent (66%) of the Lot Owners in the Subdivision Development voted in favor are adopted.[202]

A Lot Owner is considered to have cast a vote if such Lot Owner signs the Chapter 210 Petition indicating approval or disapproval of the proposal or one or more specific provisions of the proposal.[203] If a Lot is owned by owners who are married, the approval or disapproval may be reflected by the signature of any one of such married co-owners.[204] If there are multiple owners of a Lot, who are not married to each other, then the approval or disapproval of such Lot Owners may be reflected by the signatures of a majority of the co-owners of such Lot.[205] The Subdivision Association or Chapter 210 Petition Committee shall exclude any votes by lienholders, contract purchasers, and owners of mineral interests, and it may only count a Lot Owner's vote if the Subdivision Association or Chapter 210 Petition Committee receives his or her ballot before the deadline stated in the Chapter 210 Petition.[206]

---

201 Tex. Prop. Code § 210.006(a).

202 Tex. Prop. Code § 210.006(a). In addition, if a Subdivision Development consists of multiple sections, each with its own Declaration, but which are represented by a single Subdivision Association, the entire proposal or specific provisions of a proposal to modify an existing Declaration is effectively adopted if at least sixty-six percent (66%) of the total number of Lot Owners in the whole Subdivision Association vote in favor of such entire proposal or each such specific provision of the proposal. Tex. Prop. Code § 210.007.

203 Tex. Prop. Code § 210.006(d).

204 Tex. Prop. Code § 210.006(c).

205 Tex. Prop. Code § 210.006(c). Accordingly, if there are two unmarried co-owners of a Lot, then both co-owners must sign the Chapter 210 Petition in order for such Lot to be counted.

206 Tex. Prop. Code § 210.006(b), (e).

11.11.2 Certification of Results of a Chapter 210 Petition Vote and Binding Effect of an Approved Chapter 210 Petition

The Subdivision Association or Chapter 210 Petition Committee is required to certify the results of a vote conducted under Chapter 210 by a written resolution that is recorded in the Official Public Records of each county in which the Subdivision Development is located (called a "Chapter 210 Resolution").[207] The Chapter 210 Resolution must specify the number of votes for and the number of votes against the proposal (or the number of votes for and against each specific provision of the proposal) and shall also certify that the Chapter 210 Petition was delivered to each Lot Owner of record in the Subdivision Development.[208] The Subdivision Association or Chapter 210 Petition Committee must also attach to the Chapter 210 Resolution a statement of the exact terms of the proposed extension or modification of the existing Declaration and must make the Chapter 210 Resolution, the Chapter 210 Petition, and all signature pages for the Chapter 210 Petition available for inspection by any Lot Owner upon request.[209]

An extension or modification of an existing Declaration that is approved by the requisite number of Lot Owners under the procedures established by Chapter 210 becomes effective and binding upon all Lots in the applicable Subdivision Development when the Chapter 210 Resolution is filed as a Dedicatory Instrument with the county clerk of each county in which the Subdivision Development is located.[210]

---

207 Tex. Prop. Code §§ 210.004, 210.008(a).

208 Tex. Prop. Code § 210.008(a).

209 Tex. Prop. Code § 210.008(b)–(c).

210 Tex. Prop. Code § 210.004(b)–(c).

11.12 Procedures for Amendment or Modification of Certain Limited Declarations Applicable to Certain Residential Subdivision Developments Located in Texas Counties with a Population of Less Than 135,000, or Located in Llano, Polk, San Jacinto, or Trinity County, under Chapter 211 of the Texas Property Code

In 2005, the Texas Legislature enacted Chapter 211 of the Texas Property Code so as to provide procedures for amendment of certain Declarations applicable to Subdivision Developments located in unincorporated areas of Texas counties that are not governed by Chapter 205.[211] Chapter 211 was subsequently amended in 2011, 2013, and 2015 to expand its application to Subdivision Developments located in certain other additional counties. By its express terms, Chapter 211 now applies only to a residential Subdivision Development in which: (1) all or part of the Subdivision Development is located within an unincorporated area of a county with a population of less than 65,000;[212] (2) all of the Subdivision Development is located within the extraterritorial jurisdiction of a municipality located in a county that has a population of at least 65,000 but less than

---

211 Senate Research Center, Bill Analysis, Tex. H.B. 1631, 79th Leg., R.S. (2005).

212 Tex. Prop. Code § 211.002(a)(1). As of 2010, the Texas counties with a population of less than 65,000 are Anderson, Andrews, Aransas, Archer, Armstrong, Atascosa, Austin, Bailey, Bandera, Baylor, Bee, Blanco, Borden, Bosque, Brewster, Briscoe, Brooks, Brown, Burleson, Burnet, Caldwell, Calhoun, Callahan, Camp, Carson, Cass, Castro, Chambers, Cherokee, Childress, Clay, Cochran, Coke, Coleman, Collingsworth, Colorado, Comanche, Concho, Cooke, Cottle, Crane, Crockett, Crosby, Culberson, Dallam, Dawson, De Witt, Deaf Smith, Delta, Dickens, Dimmit, Donley, Duval, Eastland, Edwards, Erath, Falls, Fannin, Fayette, Fisher, Floyd, Foard, Franklin, Freestone, Frio, Gaines, Garza, Gillespie, Glasscock, Goliad, Gonzales, Gray, Grimes, Hale, Hall, Hamilton, Hansford, Hardeman, Hardin, Hartley, Haskell, Hemphill, Hill, Hockley, Hood, Hopkins, Houston, Howard, Hudspeth, Hutchinson, Irion, Jack, Jackson, Jasper, Jeff Davis, Jim Hogg, Jim Wells, Jones, Karnes, Kendall, Kenedy, Kent, Kerr, Kimble, King, Kinney, Kleberg, Knox, La Salle, Lamar, Lamb, Lampasas, Lavaca, Lee, Leon, Limestone, Lipscomb, Live Oak, Llano, Loving, Lynn, Madison, Marion, Martin, Mason, Matagorda, Maverick, McCulloch, McMullen, Medina, Menard, Milam, Mills, Mitchell, Montague, Moore, Morris, Motley, Nacogdoches, Navarro, Newton, Nolan, Ochiltree, Oldham, Palo Pinto, Panola, Parmer, Pecos, Polk, Presidio, Rains, Reagan, Real, Red River, Reeves, Refugio, Roberts, Robertson, Runnels, Rusk, Sabine, San Augustine, San Jacinto, San Patricio, San Saba, Schleicher, Scurry, Shackelford, Shelby, Sherman, Somervell, Starr, Stephens, Sterling, Stonewall, Sutton, Swisher, Terrell, Terry, Throckmorton, Titus, Trinity, Tyler, Upshur, Upton, Uvalde, Val Verde, Van Zandt, Waller, Ward, Washington, Wharton, Wheeler, Wilbarger, Willacy, Wilson, Winkler, Wise, Wood, Yoakum, Young, Zapata, and Zavala Counties. Source: United States Census Bureau, 2010 Census. Based on the United States Census Bureau's 2014 estimated population data, Nacogdoches County (2010 pop. 64,524, 2014 est. pop. 65,301) and San Patricio County (2010 pop. 64,804, 2014 est. pop. 66,915) may now or soon have populations that exceed 65,000. Source: United States Census Bureau, 2010 Census and 2014 population estimate.

135,000;[213] (3) all of the Subdivision Development is located within the extraterritorial jurisdiction of a municipality located in a county that borders Lake Buchanan and has a population of at least 18,500 and less than 19,500;[214] or (4) all or part of the Subdivision Development is located within a county that borders Lake Livingston and has a population of less than 50,000.[215]

In addition to the geographic restriction on the applicability of Chapter 211, the amendment procedures under Chapter 211 only apply to certain Subdivision Declarations. More specifically, the amendment procedures under Chapter 211 may only be used to amend Subdivision Declarations that by their express terms: (1) do not provide a procedure for amendment of such Declaration; or (2) may only be amended by the unanimous consent of all Lot Owners in the Subdivision Development or all owners of any unit or parcel of the Subdivision Development.[216]

Under Chapter 211, upon the affirmative vote of two-thirds (2/3) of its Board of Directors, an applicable Subdivision Association may submit a procedure for amending an applicable Declaration to a vote of the Lot Owners in the Subdivision Development and/or the owners of a unit or parcel of the Subdivision Development governed by such Declaration.[217] An amendment procedure submitted to a vote under Chapter 211 binds all

---

213 Tex. Prop. Code § 211.002(a)(2). The Texas counties with a population of at least 65,000 but less than 135,000 are Angelina, Bastrop, Bowie, Comal, Coryell, Grayson, Gregg, Guadalupe, Harrison, Henderson, Hunt, Kaufman, Liberty, Orange, Parker, Potter, Randall, Rockwall, Taylor, Tom Green, Victoria, and Walker Counties. Source: United States Census Bureau, 2010 Census. Based on the United States Census Bureau's 2014 estimated population data, Nacogdoches County (2010 pop. 64,524, 2014 est. pop. 65,301) and San Patricio County (2010 pop. 64,804, 2014 est. pop. 66,915) may now or soon have populations that exceed 65,000. Source: United States Census Bureau, 2010 Census and 2014 population estimate.

214 Tex. Prop. Code § 211.002(a)(3). The only Texas county that borders Lake Buchanan and has a population of at least 18,500 but less than 19,500 is Llano County. Source: United States Census Bureau, 2010 Census.

215 Tex. Prop. Code § 211.002(a)(4). The Texas counties that border Lake Livingston and have a population of less than 50,000 are Polk, San Jacinto, and Trinity Counties. Source: United States Census Bureau, 2010.

216 Tex. Prop. Code § 211.002(b).

217 Tex. Prop. Code § 211.004(a).

Lot Owners in the Subdivision Development and/or all owners of an applicable unit or parcel of the Subdivision Development to which the amendment procedure applies if more than two-thirds (2/3) of the voting Lot Owners in the Subdivision Development or two-thirds (2/3) of owners of applicable units or parcels in the Subdivision Development, as is applicable, vote in favor of the amendment procedure.[218]

The Subdivision Association must mail a written notice of a vote to be conducted on a proposed amendment procedure, along with a written ballot, to each affected Lot Owner or owner of a unit or parcel at least thirty (30) days before the date a ballot for such vote must be received by the Subdivision Association to be counted.[219] The notice of the vote must include the exact wording of the proposed amendment procedure and must specify the date by which such property owner's ballot must be received by the Subdivision Association to be counted.[220] The Subdivision Association is also required to pay all costs of printing and mailing the required notices and ballots and canvassing, tabulating, and certifying the vote.[221]

In addition, an applicable property owner may not cast more than one ballot in regards to a vote on a proposed amendment procedure, regardless of the number of Lots and/or parcels he or she owns.[222] Moreover, a ballot cast by an applicable property owner under Chapter 211 is to be done by secret vote, and a ballot may not be counted unless it is placed inside an unmarked envelope that is placed inside another envelope that bears the signature and printed name of the property owner casting the enclosed ballot.[223] The

---

218 Tex. Prop. Code § 211.004(b).

219 Tex. Prop. Code § 211.004(c).

220 Tex. Prop. Code § 211.004(c).

221 Tex. Prop. Code § 211.004(d).

222 Tex. Prop. Code § 211.004(e). If more than one person owns an interest in a Lot, the co–Lot Owners may cast only one vote for such Lot. Tex. Prop. Code § 211.004(e). A person may not vote, however, if such person has an interest in a Lot only by virtue of being a lienholder. Tex. Prop. Code § 211.004(e).

223 Tex. Prop. Code § 211.004(f).

presiding officer of the Subdivision Association shall appoint an election canvassing committee and a committee chairperson to canvass and count the ballots and determine the outcome of the vote on the proposed amendment procedure.[224] If the proposed amendment procedure receives the requisite number of votes, then the election canvassing committee chairperson shall certify the result to the presiding officer of the Subdivision Association.[225] The presiding officer shall then file a Dedicatory Instrument that indicates that the proposed amendment procedure was adopted in the Official Public Records of each county in which all or part of the Subdivision Development is located.[226]

If the amendment procedure is not adopted, the Subdivision Association may not submit the same proposed amendment procedure to a vote of property owners under the procedures of Chapter 211 again until after the expiration of at least one (1) year from the date the result of the vote on the previous proposed amendment procedure was certified by the election canvassing committee chairperson.[227]

11.13 Procedures for Adopting an Extension of a Declaration by a Majority Vote of Lot Owners in Certain Subdivision Developments Located in Houston, Texas, under Chapter 212 of the Texas Property Code

In 2011, the Texas Legislature enacted Chapter 212 of the Texas Property Code so as to provide procedures for Lot Owners to extend the application of Declarations applicable to certain Subdivision Developments located in Houston, Texas, that would expire unless extended.[228] By its express terms, Chapter 212 applies only to a residential Subdivision Development that is located wholly or partly in a municipality with a

---

[224] Tex. Prop. Code § 211.004(g).

[225] Tex. Prop. Code § 211.004(h).

[226] Tex. Prop. Code § 211.004(h). An amendment of a Declaration approved by Lot Owners in accordance with an amendment procedure adopted under the procedures established by Chapter 211 is effective upon the filing of a written instrument reflecting such amendment in the Official Public Records of each county in which all or part of the Subdivision Development is located. Tex. Prop. Code § 211.002(d).

[227] Tex. Prop. Code § 211.004(i).

[228] House Comm. On Business and Industry, Bill Analysis, Tex. H.B. 1071, 82th Leg., R.S. (2011).

population of more than two million that is located in a county with a population of 3.3 million or more (Houston, Harris County), and that is subject to a Declaration, the terms of which:[229]

(1) provide for the expiration of such Declaration upon a specific date;[230]

(2) permit such Declaration to be extended after the initial restriction period expires if a majority of the Lot Owners in the Subdivision Development, by written instrument that is acknowledged and filed for record, signify their consent to the extension of such Declaration for a further period, the maximum length of which is specified by such Declaration;[231] and

(3) do not expressly provide for or expressly prohibit successive extensions of such Declaration after the expiration of the initial extension period.[232]

11.13.1 Procedures for Extension of an Applicable Declaration

Under Chapter 212, an applicable Declaration may be extended by the written consent of the owners of a majority of the Lots in an applicable Subdivision Development, without regard to the number of Lots owned by a particular owner and irrespective of whether an existing Subdivision Association governs such Subdivision Development.[233] For purposes of Chapter 212, a written consent may be reflected by a Lot Owner's signature on a petition or written ballot.[234]

---

229 Tex. Prop. Code § 212.002. The only Texas municipality with a population of more than 2 million located in a county with a population of 3.3 million is the city of Houston. Source: United States Census Bureau, 2010.

230 Tex. Prop. Code § 212.002(2)(A).

231 Tex. Prop. Code § 212.002(2)(B).

232 Tex. Prop. Code § 212.002(2)(C).

233 Tex. Prop. Code §§ 212.003(a); 212.005. In other words, a Declaration may be extended under Section 212 without the creation of or any action by a Subdivision Association. Tex. Prop. Code § 212.005.

234 Tex. Prop. Code § 212.003(b). If there are multiple owners of the same Lot, the vote of such co-owners may be reflected by the signature of one of the co-owners of such Lot. Tex. Prop. Code § 212.004(a). In addition, once a Lot Owner signs a petition or ballot under Chapter 212, the Lot Owner's subsequent conveyance of his or her interest in a Lot or unplatted real property in the Subdivision Development does not affect the validity of his or her signature on the petition or ballot. Tex. Prop. Code § 212.004(b).

Petitions or written ballots, or a combination of both petitions and ballots, may be distributed to the Lot Owners in an applicable Subdivision Development by any method, including by door-to-door circulation and/or at a meeting of the Lot Owners called for the purpose of voting on the proposed extension.[235] In addition, the petitions and/or written ballots, as applicable, must be filed in the Official Public Records of the county in which the Subdivision Development is located before the earlier of:

(1) the first (1st) anniversary of the date on which the first signature is obtained;[236] or

(2) the expiration of the extension period of the Declaration during which the signatures are collected.[237]

11.13.2 Effective Date and Length of an Approved Extension Period

If an extension of a Declaration is approved by the requisite number of Lot Owners under the procedures established by Chapter 212, the extension of such Declaration takes effect on the date the requisite number of petitions and/or written ballots sufficient to reflect the consent of a majority of the applicable Lot Owners is filed and recorded in the Official Public Records of the county in which the applicable Subdivision Development is located.[238] Unless terminated earlier by the written consent of a majority of Lot Owners in the Subdivision Development, an extension of a Declaration under Chapter 212 shall be for a period of time equal to the original term of the Declaration or

[235] Tex. Prop. Code § 212.003(c). Chapter 212 and any petition or ballot made or action taken in connection with an attempt to comply with Chapter 212 is to be liberally construed to effectuate the intent of Chapter 212 and such petition, ballot, or action. Tex. Prop. Code § 212.011(a). In addition, a Declaration that is extended under Chapter 212 shall be liberally construed to give effect to its purposes and intent. Tex. Prop. Code § 212.011(b).

[236] Tex. Prop. Code § 212.003(d)(1).

[237] Tex. Prop. Code § 212.003(d)(1). It is important to note that the required signatures of a majority of the Lot Owners must be obtained during the same extension period of the Declaration. Tex. Prop. Code § 212.003(d).

[238] Tex. Prop. Code § 212.006(a).

a shorter period agreed to by the owners of a majority of the Lots in the Subdivision Development, as reflected in the signed petitions, written ballots, or both, as applicable.[239]

11.13.3 Termination of an Extended Declaration

A Declaration that is extended under the procedures authorized by Chapter 212 may be terminated before the expiration date of the extended period if the written consent to terminate the extension of the Declaration as of a specified date is obtained from the owners of a majority of the Lots in the Subdivision Development.[240] Such written consent of termination may be obtained in the same manner that a written consent to extend a Declaration may be obtained under Chapter 212.[241] To be effective, the petitions and/or written ballots reflecting the consent of the requisite number of Lot Owners to terminate an extended Declaration must be filed in the Official Public Records of the county in which the Subdivision Development is located before the earlier of: (1) the first (1st) anniversary of the date on which the first signature consenting to termination is obtained; or (2) a date specified in the recorded petitions and/or written ballots approving the extension of the Declaration, if applicable.[242]

---

239 Tex. Prop. Code § 212.006(b). It is also important to note that there is no limit on the number of times an applicable Declaration may be extended under the procedures established by Chapter 212, but an applicable Declaration may only be extended once under such procedures during each unexpired extension period of such Declaration. Tex. Prop. Code § 212.003(d).

240 Tex. Prop. Code § 212.007.

241 Tex. Prop. Code § 212.007(a)(1).

242 Tex. Prop. Code § 212.007(a)(2)(B). Petitions and written ballots used to extend a Declaration under the procedures authorized by Chapter 212 may provide: (1) that such Declaration may be terminated during such approved period of extension only on one or more specific date(s) that are specified in such petitions and/or written ballots; or (2) that any future petitions and/or written ballots to be used to terminate such approved period of extension must be filed in the Official Public Records of the applicable county prior to a specific date that is specified in such petitions and/or ballots. Tex. Prop. Code § 212.007(b).

11.13.4 Applicability of an Extended Declaration and Exclusion of Unconstitutional Restrictions

A Declaration that is extended pursuant to the procedures under Chapter 212 is binding upon all Lots and all unplatted real property in the Subdivision Development, without regard to whether the owner or owners of any individual Lot or unplatted real property executed a written consent to the extension of such Declaration.[243] A Declaration that is extended under Chapter 212 is also binding upon a lienholder or a person who acquires title to applicable property at a foreclosure sale or by deed from a foreclosing lienholder.[244]

11.13.5 Use of Extension Procedures Set Forth in the Declaration

In addition to the procedures established by Chapter 212 for the extension of an applicable Declaration, any procedure provided by the original Declaration for the initial extension of such document (including a procedure that requires a specified percentage of a specified class of Lot Owners approve the extension, if applicable) may be used to approve successive extensions of the original Declaration, so long as such procedure requires the extension of the Declaration to be approved by at least a majority of the Lot Owners in the Subdivision Development.[245] In other words, if an applicable Declaration provides procedures for approval of only an initial extension of the Declaration, but not

[243] Tex. Prop. Code § 212.008(a). Although other chapters of the Texas Property Code authorize Homeowners to opt out of Declarations that are extended, created, and/or modified under the procedures established by such chapters (such as Chapter 201), Chapter 212 expressly states that any statute authorizing a Homeowner to opt out of the applicability of a Declaration that governs a Homeowner's property does not apply to a Declaration that is extended under the provisions of Chapter 212. Tex. Prop. Code § 212.008(a).

[244] Tex. Prop. Code § 212.008(b). Notwithstanding, if a provision in a Declaration extended under the procedures established by Chapter 212 is considered to be void and unenforceable under the United States Constitution, the Declaration is treated as if such void and unenforceable provision was never contained in the Declaration. Tex. Prop. Code § 212.009.

[245] Tex. Prop. Code § 212.010(a). The procedure established by Chapter 212 for the extension or termination of an applicable Declaration is cumulative of and not in lieu of any other method by which a Declaration of a Subdivision Development to which Chapter 212 applies may be added to, modified, created, extended, or terminated. Tex. Prop. Code § 212.010(c).

any successive extensions of such Declaration, and such procedures require the approval of at least a majority of the Lot Owners, then Chapter 212 authorizes the use of such procedures to approve successive extensions of such Declaration, as well. Such successive extensions of the Declaration shall be for a period of time equal to the original term of the Declaration or any shorter period agreed to by a majority of the Lot Owners in the Subdivision Development.[246]

11.14 Procedure for Modifying or Terminating a Dedicatory Instrument that Restricts Use of Amenity Property to a Golf Course or Country Club under Chapter 213 of the Texas Property Code

In 2015, the Texas Legislature enacted Chapter 213 of the Texas Property Code so as to provide a procedure for the owners of real property in certain limited golf course Developments to modify or terminate a Dedicatory Instrument that restricts use of certain amenity property in such Developments to a golf course or county club.[247] The application of the procedures established by Chapter 213 is discussed in the following subchapters.

It is important to note that Chapter 213 utilizes certain statutorily defined terms that are unique to Chapter 213, as well as other more common terms that have statutorily defined meanings that are unique to Chapter 213. More specifically, Section 213.001 defines the term "amenity property" to mean "real property the use of which is restricted by a dedicatory instrument to use as a golf course or country club;" the term "Dedicatory Instrument" to mean "a governing instrument that: (A) restricts amenity property to use as a golf course or country club; (B) designates real property in the development, other than the amenity property, as a beneficiary of a restriction [that restricts the amenity property to use as a golf course or country club]; and (C) addresses the establishment, maintenance, and operation of the amenity property"; and the term "development" to

---

246 Tex. Prop. Code § 212.010(b).

247 Tex. Prop. Code § 213.001, et seq. It is important to note that Chapter 213 was established for a limited time period of six years, and such statute will automatically expire on September 1, 2021. Tex. Prop. Code § 213.014.

mean "amenity property and all real property designated as beneficiary property in the dedicatory instrument."[248] In simpler terms, under Chapter 213, a "development" consists of: (1) real property restricted to use as a golf course or country club by a Dedicatory Instrument (hereinafter referred to as "Golf Amenity Property"); and (2) additional real property that is designated by the same Dedicatory Instrument as the beneficiary of the golf course / country club–only restriction imposed by such Dedicatory Instrument (hereinafter referred to as the "Golf Beneficiary Property").[249] Because the meaning of "Development" and "Dedicatory Instrument" have unique meanings under Chapter 213, and in order to distinguish such terms when used in the context of Chapter 213, such terms shall be referred to as a "Golf Development" and "Golf Dedicatory Instrument" for the remainder of this subchapter. In addition, a Restrictive Covenant within a Golf Dedicatory Instrument that restricts a Golf Amenity Property to use as a golf course or country club shall be referred to as a "Golf Restriction" for the remainder of this subchapter.[250]

11.14.1 Applicability of Chapter 213 Procedures

The procedure established by Chapter 213 is intended to apply in circumstances where the Golf Amenity Property has ceased operation as a golf course or country club for a continuous period of at least thirty-six (36) months and the Golf Dedicatory Instrument cannot, or cannot easily, be amended to allow the Golf Amenity Property to be used for other purposes.[251] More specifically, the amendment procedure under Chapter 213 does not apply to a Golf Dedicatory Instrument if:

---

[248] Tex. Prop. Code § 213.002.

[249] The "Golf Beneficiary Property" includes all subdivision lots and condominium units in the "Development." Tex. Prop. Code § 213.001(4)–(5).

[250] Chapter 213 defines a "restrictive covenant" as any covenant, condition, or restriction, whether mandatory, prohibitive, permissive, or administrative, contained or incorporated by reference in a properly recorded map, plat, replat, declaration, dedicatory instrument, or other instrument filed in the real property records or map or plat records. Tex. Prop. Code § 213.001(8)–(9).

[251] The amendment procedures under Chapter 213 supersedes any contrary provision in an applicable Golf Dedicatory Instrument. Tex. Prop. Code § 213.009(b).

(1) the Golf Dedicatory Instrument includes a procedure to modify or terminate a Golf Restriction on the use of a Golf Amenity Property by approval of the owners of less than seventy-five percent (75%) of the subdivision lots and condominium units in the Golf Development;[252] or

(2) the Golf Restriction on the use of a Golf Amenity Property may be modified or terminated under the procedures established by Chapter 81, 82, 201, or 209 of the Texas Property Code.[253]

In other words, the amendment procedure under Chapter 213 only applies to a Golf Dedicatory Instrument if the Golf Restriction cannot be modified or terminated using the statutory provisions under Chapter 81, 82, 201, or 209 of the Texas Property Code and the procedure to modify or terminate the Golf Restriction provided in the Golf Dedicatory Instrument (if any) requires approval of seventy-five percent (75%) or more of the owners of subdivision lots and condominium units in the Golf Development.

In addition, even if Chapter 213 is applicable to a Golf Dedicatory Instrument, the amendment procedure under Chapter 213 may not be used to amend the Golf Dedicatory Instrument unless: (1) the Golf Amenity Property has ceased operation as a golf course or country club for a continuous period of at least thirty-six (36) months; and (2) if zoning regulations apply to the Golf Amenity Property, the owner of the Golf Amenity Property has received all required zoning approvals for any proposed redevelopment of the Golf Amenity Property.[254]

11.14.2 Procedures for Modifying or Terminating a Golf Dedicatory Instrument under Chapter 213

In order to modify or terminate a Golf Dedicatory Instrument under Chapter 213, an authorized "Chapter 213 Petitioner Circulator" must circulate a written document proposing a modification or termination of a Golf Dedicatory Instrument (called a

[252] Tex. Prop. Code § 213.003(b)(1).

[253] Tex. Prop. Code § 213.003(b)(2); *see also*, Tex. Prop. Code §§ 81.111; 82.067; 201.001; 209.0041.

[254] Tex. Prop. Code § 213.004.

"Chapter 213 Petition") to all Lot Owners, Unit Owners, Subdivision Associations, and Condominium Associations in the Golf Development in compliance with the procedure specified by Chapter 213 of the Texas Property Code.[255] A Chapter 213 Petition Circulator may be: (1) an owner of the Golf Amenity Property; (2) an owner of a Golf Beneficiary Property; or (3) a Subdivision Association or Condominium Association that owns and manages the Golf Amenity Property.[256]

11.14.2 (A) *Required Contents of a Chapter 213 Petition*

A Chapter 213 Petition must include all relevant information about the proposed modification or termination of the Golf Dedicatory Instrument, including:

(1) the name of the Development, if any;[257]

(2) the name of the Golf Amenity Property, if any;[258]

(3) the recording information of the Golf Restriction to be modified or terminated;[259]

(4) the text of the Golf Restriction subject to modification or termination;[260]

(5) the text of the Golf Restriction as modified or terminated;[261]

(6) a comparison of the original language of the Golf Restriction and the Golf Restriction as modified or terminated, showing any insertion and deletion of language or punctuation;[262]

(7) reasonable times and dates that the Chapter 213 Petition Circulator will be available at a location in the Golf Development to receive a "signed

---

255 Tex. Prop. Code § 213.005.

256 Tex. Prop. Code § 213.005.

257 Tex. Prop. Code § 213.006(a)(1).

258 Tex. Prop. Code § 213.006(a)(2).

259 Tex. Prop. Code § 213.006(a)(3).

260 Tex. Prop. Code § 213.006(a)(4).

261 Tex. Prop. Code § 213.006(a)(5).

262 Tex. Prop. Code § 213.006(a)(6).

statement" voting in favor or against the proposed modification or termination of a Golf Restriction;[263]

(8) a mailing address, email address, and facsimile number to which a "signed statement" voting in favor or against the proposed modification or termination of a Golf Restriction may be delivered;[264] and

(9) the date by which a signed statement voting in favor or against the proposed modification or termination of a Golf Restriction must be received to be counted.[265]

11.14.2 (B) *Circulation of a Chapter 213 Petition*

Under the Chapter 213 amendment procedure, a Chapter 213 Petition Circulator must deliver a copy of the Chapter 213 Petition to: (1) all Lot Owners and Unit Owners in the Golf Development; and (2) each Subdivision Association and Condominium Association in the Development.[266] A copy of the Chapter 213 Petition may be delivered in any reasonable manner, including:

(1) by regular mail or certified mail, return receipt requested, to the last known address of the applicable Lot Owners, Unit Owners, Subdivision Associations, and Condominium Associations;[267]

(2) personal delivery to the applicable Lot Owners, Unit Owners, Subdivision Associations, and Condominium Associations;[268] or

(3) at a regular meeting of an applicable Subdivision Association or Condominium Association.[269]

---

263 Tex. Prop. Code § 213.006(b)(1).

264 Tex. Prop. Code § 213.006(b)(2).

265 Tex. Prop. Code § 213.006(b)(3).

266 Tex. Prop. Code § 213.007(a).

267 Tex. Prop. Code § 213.007(b)(1).

268 Tex. Prop. Code § 213.007(b)(2).

269 Tex. Prop. Code § 213.007(b)(3).

It is important to note that so long as the Chapter 213 Petition Circulator acts in good faith in determining ownership and delivering copies of the Chapter 213 Petition as required by Chapter 213, the failure of an applicable Lot Owner, Unit Owner, Subdivision Association, or Condominium Association to receive a copy of the Chapter 213 Petition will not affect the application of a properly adopted modification or termination of a Golf Restriction to a Golf Amenity Property under Chapter 213.[270]

11.14.2 (C) *Adoption of a Chapter 213 Petition*

In order to properly adopt a proposed modification or termination of a Golf Restriction, the owners of at least seventy-five percent (75%) of the total number of Lots and Units in the Golf Development, including the owner of the Golf Amenity Property, must vote in favor of the proposed modification or termination of the Golf Restriction.[271]

In order to cast a vote in favor of or against the proposed modification or termination of the Golf Restriction, an owner of an applicable Lot or Unit must deliver a signed statement in conformity with the requirements of Chapter 213 to the Chapter 213 Petition Circulator within the deadline specified in the Chapter 213 Petition (called a "Chapter 213 Signed Statement").[272] A Chapter 213 Signed Statement must include:

(1) the Lot or Unit owner's name, the legal description or street address of his or her Lot or Unit, and his or her mailing address;[273]

(2) a statement that the Lot or Unit owner holds record title to the Lot or Unit, as applicable;[274]

---

[270] Tex. Prop. Code § 213.007(c).

[271] Tex. Prop. Code § 213.008(a).

[272] Tex. Prop. Code § 213.008(b), (f). The Chapter 213 Signed Statement of an applicable Lot or Unit Owner conclusively establishes that: (1) the Chapter 213 Petition was received by the Lot or Unit Owner in accordance with Section 213.007 of the Texas Property Code; and (2) the statement accurately reflects the vote of the Lot or Unit Owner. Tex. Prop. Code § 213.008(g).

[273] Tex. Prop. Code § 213.008(b)(1).

[274] Tex. Prop. Code § 213.008(b)(2).

(3) if more than one person owns an interest in the Lot or Unit, the name and mailing address of each co-owner;[275] and

(4) a statement indicating whether the Lot or Unit owner is in favor of or against the modification or termination of the Golf Restriction proposed by the Chapter 213 Petition.[276]

The Chapter 213 Petition Circulator must accept a Chapter 213 Signed Statement from a Lot or Unit Owner that is delivered: (1) in person to the location in the Golf Development during the time and dates specified in the Chapter 213 Petition; (2) by first class mail to an address stated in the Chapter 213 Petition; (3) by email to an address stated in the Chapter 213 Petition; or (4) by facsimile to a facsimile number stated in the Chapter 213 Petition.[277]

11.14.2 (D) *Certification and Notice of the Adoption of a Chapter 213 Petition*

After the deadline specified in the Chapter 213 Petition, the Chapter 213 Petition Circulator must certify the result of the votes by filing an affidavit (called a "Chapter 213 Certification Affidavit") with the county clerk of the county in which the Golf Restriction that is being modified or terminated is recorded.[278] The Chapter 213 Certification Affidavit must state:

---

275 Tex. Prop. Code § 213.008(b)(3). It is important to note that if more than one person owns an interest in a Lot or Unit, the co-owners of such Lot or Unit may cast only a single vote for that Lot or Unit. Tex. Prop. Code § 213.008(d). The vote of multiple co-owners of a Lot or Unit in favor of or against the proposed modification or termination of a Golf Restriction may be reflected by the signatures of a majority of the co-owners of such Lot or Unit on the Chapter 213 Signed Statement. Tex. Prop. Code § 213.008(d). In addition, the vote of co-owners of a Lot or Unit who are married may be reflected by the signature of only one of those co-owners. Tex. Prop. Code § 213.008(d). Finally, a person whose only property interest in a Lot or Unit is that of a contract purchaser, lienholder, or mineral interest holder may not cast a vote in favor of the proposed modification or termination of the Golf Restriction on behalf of such Lot or Unit. Tex. Prop. Code § 213.008(e).

276 Tex. Prop. Code § 213.008(b)(4). A Lot or Unit Owner may vote only in favor of or against the modification or termination of the Golf Restriction as proposed in the Chapter 213 Petition. Tex. Prop. Code § 213.008(c).

277 Tex. Prop. Code § 213.009(a).

278 Tex. Prop. Code § 213.0010(a).

(1) the name of the Golf Development, if any;[279]

(2) the name of the Golf Amenity Property, if any;[280]

(3) the recording information of the Golf Restriction that was modified or terminated;[281]

(4) the text of the Golf Restriction before modification or termination;[282]

(5) the text of the Golf Restriction as modified or terminated;[283]

(6) the number of votes in favor of and against the proposed modification or termination of the Golf Restriction;[284]

(7) the name and address of the Chapter 213 Petition Circulator;[285] and

(8) the name, address, and telephone number of the person maintaining the original Chapter 213 Petition, the Chapter 213 Signed Statements delivered to the Chapter 213 Petition Circulator, and a copy of the Chapter 213 Certification affidavit.[286]

In addition, the Chapter 213 Petition Circulator must affirm in the Chapter 213 Certification Affidavit that the Chapter 213 Petition was delivered in accordance with the procedures set forth under Chapter 213 of the Texas Property Code.[287]

[279] Tex. Prop. Code § 213.0010(b)(1).

[280] Tex. Prop. Code § 213.0010(b)(2).

[281] Tex. Prop. Code § 213.0010(b)(3).

[282] Tex. Prop. Code § 213.0010(b)(4).

[283] Tex. Prop. Code § 213.0010(b)(5).

[284] Tex. Prop. Code § 213.0010(b)(6).

[285] Tex. Prop. Code § 213.0010(b)(7).

[286] Tex. Prop. Code § 213.0010(b)(8). For at least one year following the date the affidavit is filed with the county clerk, the Chapter 213 Petition Circulator must make available for inspection and copying the original Chapter 213 Petition, the Chapter 213 Signed Statements delivered to the Chapter 213 Petition Circulator, and a copy of the Chapter 213 Certification Affidavit. Tex. Prop. Code § 213.0013.

[287] Tex. Prop. Code § 213.0010(c).

The recording of the Chapter 213 Certification Affidavit constitutes notice that the Golf Restriction is modified or terminated.[288] Nevertheless, the Chapter 213 Petition Circulator must also deliver to each person who resides within 200 feet of the boundary of the Golf Amenity Property a copy of the Chapter 213 Certification Affidavit by: (1) regular mail; (2) certified mail, return receipt requested; or (3) personal delivery.[289]

The modification or termination of the Golf Restriction takes effect on the latter of: (1) the date the Chapter 213 Certification Affidavit is filed with the county clerk; or (2) the date, if any, specified as the effective date in the Chapter 213 Petition.[290]

288 Tex. Prop. Code § 213.0011(a).

289 Tex. Prop. Code § 213.0011(b).

290 Tex. Prop. Code § 213.0012.

CHAPTER 12 RIGHTS AND DUTIES OF TEXAS HOMEOWNERS

CHAPTER 12 RIGHTS AND DUTIES OF TEXAS HOMEOWNERS

12.1 In General

In simple terms, a Homeowners Association is a private organization that is created by private agreement, generally referred to as a Declaration of Covenants, Conditions, and Restrictions, or simply the "Declaration," and whose membership is comprised of the Homeowners in the residential community that is subject to such Declaration. The Declaration is generally drafted by the developer of the Subdivision Development or Condominium Development and is recorded in the Official Public Records of the county in which the development is located prior to selling any Lots or Units to home buyers.[1]

The Declaration constitutes a private contractual agreement between the owners of all Lots or Units subject to such Declaration, and it creates the contractual obligations that each such Homeowner is obligated to comply with. This can sometimes become a surprise to Homeowners when they learn that they are subject to a contract that regulates the use of their home, especially since they did not sign such contract and may even have been completely unaware of it when they purchased their home. By virtue of recording the Declaration in the Official Public Records, however, each Homeowner is presumed to have notice of the Declaration applicable to his or her Lot or Unit, and he or she becomes

---

1 The Declaration is considered to be a recorded encumbrance that "runs with the land," which means that it permanently attaches to the applicable Lots or Units within a development, and all subsequent owners of such Lots or Units take ownership of such Lots or Units subject to the Declaration. A copy of a community's Declaration is often provided to a Homeowner at or prior to closing on the purchase of his or her home. If a Homeowner is unsure of which Declaration or other Dedicatory Instruments are applicable to his or her property, the easiest way to identify such applicable documents is to review the Schedule B of the title insurance policy applicable to such Homeowner's Lot or Unit that he or she received at or prior to closing. A title insurance policy is an insurance policy that assures a purchaser that the title to the property being purchased will be vested in that purchaser upon closing and that it is free from all defects, liens, and encumbrances except those that are listed as exceptions in the policy or excluded from the scope of the policy's coverage. Exclusions to a title insurance policy in Texas are typically listed on Schedule B of the policy and will include all encumbrances of record applicable to the property being purchased. Such encumbrances of record would include all Declarations and other Dedicatory Instruments applicable to such property that have been recorded in the Official Public Records prior to the issuance of such title insurance policy.

obligated to comply with the contractual obligations of the Declaration simply upon acquiring ownership of his or her Lot or Unit, whether or not he or she is actually aware of the Declaration.

In practically all cases in which a Declaration establishes a Homeowners Association, it will also impose an obligation of mandatory membership by the Lot or Unit Owners in such Homeowners Association.[2] As a result of such Declaration obligations, Lot and Unit Owners become members of their respective Homeowners Associations automatically upon acquiring ownership of their respective Lot or Unit, whether they are even aware of it or desire it.

In addition, most Texas Homeowners Associations are incorporated as nonprofit corporations, which are created by the filing of a Certificate of Formation (formerly called Articles of Incorporation), and are further governed by such Certificate of Formation (or Articles of Incorporation), as well as their Bylaws. Bylaws are the rules adopted by a nonprofit corporation to provide for its management and administration.[3] In general, Bylaws will contain provisions for the regulation and management of the affairs of the nonprofit corporation that are consistent with Texas law and the nonprofit corporation's Certificate of Formation (or Articles of Incorporation).[4] A Nonprofit Corporation HOA's Articles of Incorporation and Bylaws, together with its Declaration, form the Governing

---

[2] In addition, the Texas Uniform Condominium Act requires all Condominium Developments subject to such Act to be managed by a Unit Owners' association, whose membership must consist of all Unit Owners in the Condominium Development. Tex. Prop. Code § 82.101.

[3] Tex. Bus. Org. Code § 22.001(2). Bylaws are required to be adopted by a nonprofit corporation's Board of Directors or, if the management of the corporation is vested in the nonprofit corporation's members, by the members of the nonprofit corporation. Tex. Bus. Org. Code § 22.102(a).

[4] Tex. Bus. Org. Code § 22.102(b). The contents of a nonprofit corporation's Bylaws can vary, but they typically include: (1) provisions concerning the number of Directors and Officers for the nonprofit corporation and their terms of office; (2) the manner of electing and removing Directors and Officers; (3) any qualifications to serve as a Director or Officer; (4) the time, place, and procedures for calling a meeting of the Board of Directors or members of the nonprofit corporation; and (5) the procedures for amending the Bylaws.

Documents that primarily govern the relationship between Texas Homeowners Associations and their Homeowners.

In addition to the contractual obligations established by a Homeowners Association's Declaration and other Governing Documents, the Texas Nonprofit Corporation Law, the Texas Uniform Condominium Act, and Chapter 209 of the Texas Property also establishes statutory obligations that Texas Homeowners must comply with, as well as vests Texas Homeowners with certain statutory rights as members of a Homeowners Association. Such duties and rights are explained in greater detail in the following subchapters.

12.2 Homeowners' Contractual Duty to Comply with Restrictive Covenants and Pay Assessments

A Homeowners Association's Declaration creates certain contractual covenants or obligations that become binding upon each Homeowner who acquires ownership of a Lot or Unit subject to such applicable Declaration. While the covenants and obligations established by a Homeowners Association's Declaration and other Governing Documents will often vary from development to development, in almost all cases such covenants and obligations will include the duty of Homeowners to comply with the Restrictive Covenants contained in the Declaration and other Governing Documents and to pay Assessments levied by the Homeowners Association.[5]

It is important to note that the contractual covenants and obligations set forth in a Homeowners Association's Declaration and other Governing Documents are independent

[5] The term "Restrictive Covenants" generally refers to the individual contractual obligations within a Declaration that regulate the use of the Lots or Units in the development by the Homeowners. The Texas Property Code defines a "Restrictive Covenant" as "any covenant, condition, or restriction contained in a Dedicatory Instrument, whether mandatory, prohibitive, permissive, or administrative." Tex. Prop. Code § 202.001(4). In simpler terms, Restrictive Covenants are the legal obligations imposed on a Lot or Unit that require the Homeowner to do something (such as maintain his or her yard) or to refrain from doing something (such as parking a trailer on the driveway).

in nature. In other words, the contractual obligation of Lot and Unit Owners to comply with Restrictive Covenants and pay Assessments are mutually exclusive of the contractual obligations of the Homeowners Association to provide services required of it under its Governing Documents, and a Homeowner may not withhold payment of Assessments on the basis of a perceived lack of performance by the Homeowners Association.

12.3 Unit Owners' Statutory Duty to Comply with a Condominium Association's Declaration and Pay Assessments

In addition to the contractual duties of Homeowners that are established by their Homeowners Association's Declaration and other Governing Documents, the Texas Uniform Condominium Act also establishes certain statutory duties of Unit Owners in a Condominium Development.[6] More specifically, unless otherwise provided by the Condominium Declaration, Bylaws, or Association Rules of a Condominium Association, all Unit Owners are required to: (1) pay Assessments, interest, and other charges properly levied by the Condominium Association against the Unit Owner or the Owner's Unit and to pay all regular periodic Assessments without demand or request by the Condominium Association; (2) comply with the Condominium Declaration, Bylaws, and Association Rules of the Condominium Association, including any amendments to such documents; and (3) pay for any damage to the Condominium Development caused by the negligence or willful misconduct of the Unit Owner, an occupant of the Owner's Unit, and/or the Unit Owner or such occupant's family, guests, employees, contractors, agents, or invitees.[7]

The Texas Uniform Condominium Act also provides that Unit Owners are liable to the Condominium Association for violations of its Condominium Declaration, Bylaws,

---

6 There are no similar statutory requirements applicable to Lot Owners in a Subdivision Development.

7 Tex. Prop. Code § 82.117(1)–(3). It is important to note that the provisions of the Texas Uniform Condominium Act imposing an obligation on Unit Owners to pay Assessments, comply with Governing Documents, and pay for damages caused to the Condominium Development are not applicable to Condominium Developments created prior to January 1, 1994, that are subject to the Texas Condominium Act, and there are no comparable provisions under the Texas Condominium Act. Tex. Prop. Code § 82.002(c).

and/or Association Rules (including any amendments to such documents) committed by the Unit Owner, an occupant of the Owner's Unit, or the Unit Owner or occupant's family, guests, employees, agents, or invitees.[8] In addition, Unit Owners are also liable for all costs incurred by a Condominium Association to obtain compliance by a Unit Owner, an occupant of the Owner's Unit, or the Unit Owner or occupant's family, guests, employees, agents, or invitees with the provisions of its Condominium Declaration, Bylaws, and/or Association Rules, including any attorneys fees incurred by the Condominium Association in such regard, regardless of whether a lawsuit is filed.[9]

12.4 Unit Owners' Statutory Duty to Disclose Certain Information to a Condominium Association

Under the Texas Uniform Condominium Act, Unit Owners have an affirmative duty to disclose certain information to their governing Condominium Association.[10] More specifically, within thirty (30) days after acquiring an interest in a Unit, a Unit Owner must provide the Condominium Association with: (1) the Unit Owner's mailing address, telephone number, and driver's license number, if any; (2) the name and address of the holder of any lien against the Unit and the loan number for all loans secured by the Unit Owner's interest in the Unit; (3) the name and telephone number of any person occupying the Unit other than the Unit Owner; and (4) the name, address, and telephone number of any person managing the Unit as an agent of the Unit Owner.[11] A Unit Owner must also provide such information upon request by the Condominium Association, and must notify the Condominium Association of any changes in such information within thirty (30) days of the Unit Owner having notice of a change in any such information.[12]

---

8 Tex. Prop. Code § 82.117(4).

9 Tex. Prop. Code § 82.117(4).

10 There are no similar statutory requirements applicable to Lot Owners in a Subdivision Development.

11 Tex. Prop. Code § 82.114(e).

12 Tex. Prop. Code § 82.114(f).

12.5 Homeowners' Right to Enforce Restrictive Covenants

In addition to becoming obligated to comply with the Restrictive Covenants contained in a Declaration upon acquiring ownership of a Lot or Unit subject to such Declaration, Texas Homeowners also have a right to enforce such Restrictive Covenants against all other Homeowners subject to the same Declaration. Such right of enforcement is established by contract, common law, and/or statute, depending on whether the Declaration governs a Subdivision Development or a Condominium Development.

12.5.1 Homeowners' Contractual Right to Enforce Restrictive Covenants

As noted earlier, the Declaration constitutes a private contractual agreement between the owners of all Lots or Units subject to such Declaration, and it establishes certain contractual obligations that each such Homeowner is obligated to comply with. As parties to a contract, each Homeowner is not only contractually obligated to comply with the Restrictive Covenants contained in the applicable Declaration, but he or she is also often contractually vested with the right to enforce such Restrictive Covenants against all other Homeowners subject to the same Declaration. Such contractual right to enforce the Restrictive Covenants contained in a Declaration by Homeowners subject to such Declaration exists when a Declaration contains a provision that expressly authorizes such Homeowners to enforce its provisions. Most Homeowners Associations' Declarations contain such a provision, but not all do. Thus, each Homeowners Association's Declaration must be carefully reviewed to confirm the existence of a Homeowner's contractual right to enforce the Restrictive Covenants contained in such Declaration against other Homeowners subject to such Declaration.

12.5.2 Lot Owners' Common Law Right to Enforce Restrictive Covenants

In addition to any contractual right to enforce Restrictive Covenants, Texas Lot Owners are also vested with the right to enforce Restrictive Covenants contained in an applicable Declaration against all other Lot Owners subject to the same Declaration under

Texas common law.[13] The seminal case that establishes such right of enforcement is the 1914 Texas appellate case of Hooper v. Lottman, in which the El Paso Court of Appeals held that when a Developer subdivides property into Lots and creates a Subdivision Development according to a general plan or scheme of development, in which the Lots are restricted to the uses to which they may be put, or the character and location of Improvements thereon, that is imposed through covenants inserted in the deeds for such Lots to purchasers and it appears that such covenants are intended for the benefit of all the Lots in the Subdivision Development, each purchaser of such a Lot, and his or her assigns, may enforce such covenants against any other purchaser of such a Lot, and his or her assigns.[14] In other words, where a Developer of a Subdivision Development imposes restrictions on the use of each subdivided Lot in such Subdivision Development pursuant to a general plan or scheme of development, each owner of such a Lot may enforce such applicable restrictions against all other owners of such a Lot.[15]

12.5.3 Unit Owners' Statutory Right to Enforce Restrictive Covenants

In addition to any contractual right to enforce Restrictive Covenants, Texas Unit Owners are also vested with the right to enforce Restrictive Covenants contained in an applicable Declaration against all other Unit Owners subject to the same Declaration under the Texas Uniform Condominium Act.[16] Pursuant to the Texas Uniform Condominium Act, if any person subject to such Act, including a Condominium Association or Unit Owner, violates the Texas Uniform Condominium Act, a provision

---

13 "Common law" refers to the body of law that develops and derives through judicial decisions, as distinguished from legislative enactments. *Black's Law Dictionary* 276 (6th ed. 1990).

14 *Hooper v. Lottman*, 171 S.W. 270, 272 (Tex. Civ. App.—El Paso 1914, no writ); *see also*, *Evans v. Pollock*, 796 S.W.2d 465, 466 (Tex. 1990) (describing *Hooper v. Lottman* as "[t]he leading Texas case" in this area); *Curlee v. Walker*, 244 S.W. 497, 498 (Tex. 1922).

15 *Hourani v. Katzen*, 305 S.W.3d 239, 251 (Tex. App.—Houston [1st Dist.] 2009, pet. denied) ("We recognize that, notwithstanding the status of the Board, any person entitled to benefit under a restrictive covenant is entitled to enforce it."); *Ski Masters of Texas, LLC v. Heinemeyer*, 269 S.W.3d 662, 668 (Tex. App.—San Antonio 2008, no pet.).

16 Tex. Prop. Code § 82.161(a).

of an applicable Condominium Declaration, or a provision of a Condominium Association's Bylaws, any person adversely affected by such violation, including a Unit Owner, has a claim for appropriate relief against the violating party.[17] In addition, the Texas Uniform Condominium Act also provides that the prevailing party in a lawsuit to enforce the provisions of such Act, a Condominium Declaration, and/or a Condominium Association's Bylaws is entitled to recovery of his or her reasonable attorneys fees and court costs from the nonprevailing party.[18]

12.6 Homeowners' Statutory Right to Notice of Meetings of a Homeowners Association's Board of Directors

In addition to any contractual rights to receive notice of a meeting of a Homeowners Association's Board of Directors established by its Governing Documents, both the Texas Uniform Condominium Act and Chapter 209 of the Texas Property Code establish certain statutory rights of Unit Owners and Lot Owners to receive notice of Board Meetings. Such statutory rights, however, differ significantly.

12.6.1 Unit Owners' Right to Notice of Board Meetings

A Unit Owner's right to receive notice of Board Meetings is governed by his or her Condominium Association's Governing Documents, the Texas Nonprofit Corporation Law, and the Texas Uniform Condominium Act. In general, unless required by its Governing Documents, a Condominium Association is not required to provide notice of Board Meetings to Unit Owners.[19]

---

[17] Tex. Prop. Code § 82.161(a).

[18] Tex. Prop. Code § 82.161(b).

[19] Tex. Prop. Code § 82.108(e); Tex. Bus. Org. Code § 22.217. Section 82.108(e) requires notice of Board Meetings be given as provided by the Condominium Association's Bylaws, or, if the Bylaws do not provide for notice of Board Meetings, then notice of a Board Meeting must be given to each Director of the Condominium Association in the same manner in which notice is given to the members of the Board of Directors of a nonprofit corporation under Section B of Article 2.19 of the former Texas Non-Profit Corporation Act. Tex. Prop. Code § 82.108(e). Section 82.108, however, does not require that a notice of a Board Meeting be given to Unit Owners in the event that a Condominium Association's Bylaws do not provide

If, however, a Condominium Association's Board of Directors is meeting for the purpose of adopting an amendment or modification to its Declaration, Articles of Incorporation, Bylaws, or Association Rules, then the Board of Directors must give each Unit Owner a document showing the specific amendment or other change that would be made to the Declaration, Articles of Incorporation, Bylaws, or Association Rules no earlier than twenty (20) days, nor later than ten (10) days, before the date of such Board Meeting.[20] Written notice of a proposed amendment of or modification to a Condominium Association's Governing Documents is considered to have been given to a Unit Owner on the earlier of: (1) the date such information is personally delivered to the Unit Owner, as shown by a receipt signed by such Unit Owner; or (2) on the date evidenced by the postmark on an envelope containing such information that is deposited in the United States mail with a proper address and paid postage.[21]

In addition, if a Condominium Association receives a written request from a Unit Owner regarding the time and location of the next regular or special Board Meeting, then it must inform such Unit Owner of the time and place of the next scheduled regular or special meeting of the Board of Directors.[22] If the Condominium Association representative who receives the written request does not know the time and place of the next scheduled regular or special Board Meeting, then the Condominium Association must promptly obtain such information and disclose it to the Unit Owner or inform the Unit Owner where such information may be obtained.[23]

---

for such notice. It is also important to note that while meetings of a Condominium Association's Board of Directors are also governed by the Texas Nonprofit Corporation Law, such law requires only that notices of Board Meetings be given as prescribed by the Nonprofit Corporation HOA's Bylaws. Tex. Bus. Org. Code § 22.217.

20 Tex. Prop. Code § 82.070.

21 Tex. Prop. Code § 82.070(b).

22 Tex. Prop. Code § 82.108(f).

23 Tex. Prop. Code § 82.108(f).

12.6.2 Lot Owners' Right to Notice of Board Meetings

A Lot Owner's right to receive notice of Board Meetings is governed by a Subdivision Association's Governing Documents and Chapter 209 of the Texas Property Code.[24] In addition to complying with any applicable notice requirements under its Governing Documents, Chapter 209 requires a Subdivision Association to give its Lot Owners notice of the date, hour, place, and general subject of each regular or special Board Meeting, including a general description of any matter to be brought up for deliberation in "Executive Session" by the Board of Directors at such meeting.[25]

Although Section 209.0051 does not specify or establish guidelines for identifying the "general subject" of each regular or special Board Meeting, such requirement is substantially similar to the meeting notice requirements under the Texas Open Meetings Act, which also requires "written notice of the date, hour, place, and subject of each meeting held by the governmental body."[26] The Texas Supreme Court has held that notice of the subject of a meeting is sufficient under the Texas Open Meetings Act when it alerts a reader that some action will be taken relative to a topic, but the notice need not state all of the possible consequences resulting from consideration of such topic.[27] In other words, in order to comply with the meeting notice requirement under Section 209.0051, a Subdivision Association should include within each meeting notice an agenda identifying each item or topic that the Board of Directors may consider or take

---

[24] While meetings of a Subdivision Association's Board of Directors are also governed by the Texas Nonprofit Corporation Law, such law requires only that notices of Board Meetings be given as prescribed by the Nonprofit Corporation HOA's Bylaws. Tex. Bus. Org. Code § 22.217.

[25] Tex. Prop. Code § 209.0051(e). An "Executive Session" of a Board Meeting is a session closed to the public during which only the Board of Directors and such select persons invited by the Board of Directors are permitted to be present. *Black's Law Dictionary* 570 (6th ed. 1990).

[26] Tex. Gov't Code § 551.0041.

[27] *See Lower Colorado River Auth. v. City of San Marcos*, 523 S.W.2d 641, 646 (Tex. 1975); *Texas Turnpike Auth. v. City of Fort Worth*, 554 S.W.2d 675, 676 (Tex. 1977).

action on at such meeting, but such meeting notice need not identify the specific actions to be taken in regard to such item or topic.

12.6.2 (A) *Methods of Providing Notice of a Board Meeting to Lot Owners*

Section 209.0051 authorizes two methods by which a Subdivision Association may provide notice of a Board Meeting to Lot Owners. First, a Subdivision Association may provide notice of a Board Meeting to Lot Owners by mailing a written notice of such meeting to each Lot Owner at least ten (10) days before, but no more than sixty (60) days before, the date of such meeting.[28]

As an alternative to mailing written notice of a Board Meeting to each Lot Owner, Section 209.0051 also authorizes a Subdivision Association to provide notice of a Board Meeting instead by posting and emailing a copy of the meeting notice to Lot Owners.[29] If a Subdivision Association elects to provide notice of a Board Meeting by posting and emailing such notice, at least seventy-two (72) hours prior to the start of the Board Meeting, the Subdivision Association must post a notice of the Board Meeting in a conspicuous manner reasonably designed to provide notice of such meeting to its Lot Owners, either:

(1) in a place located on the Subdivision Association's Common Area property or on other conspicuously located privately owned property within the Subdivision Development (so long as the owner of such privately owned property has consented thereto);[30] or

(2) on any internet website maintained by the Subdivision Association or other internet media.[31]

---

28 Tex. Prop. Code § 209.0051(e) (1). For example, if a Board Meeting was to be conducted on September 1, notice of such meeting must be mailed to each Lot Owner no later than August 22, and no earlier than July 3.

29 Tex. Prop. Code § 209.0051(e) (2).

30 Tex. Prop. Code § 209.0051(e (2)(A)(i).

31 Tex. Prop. Code § 209.0051(e) (2)(A)(ii).

In addition to posting such meeting notice, at least seventy-two (72) hours prior to the start of the Board Meeting, the Subdivision Association must also send a copy of the meeting notice by email to each Lot Owner who has registered an email address with the Subdivision Association.[32]

12.7 Homeowners' Statutory Right to Attend Board Meetings

Although not required by the Texas Nonprofit Corporation Law, both the Texas Uniform Condominium Act and Chapter 209 of the Texas Property Code require Texas Homeowners Associations' Board Meetings to be open to Homeowners, subject to the right of the Board of Directors to meet in Executive Session.[33] In addition, pursuant to a 2007 amendment to the Texas Open Meetings Act, certain limited Homeowners Associations in Harris County and counties adjacent to Harris County are subject to the Texas Open Meetings Act, which requires every regular, special, or called meeting to be open to the general public.[34]

12.7.1 Open Board Meetings of a Condominium Association's Board of Directors under the Texas Uniform Condominium Act

Under the Texas Uniform Condominium Act, all meetings of a Condominium Association's Board of Directors must be open to Unit Owners, subject to the right of the

---

[32] Tex. Prop. Code § 209.0051(e)(2)(B). A Subdivision Association is not required to proactively solicit email addresses from Lot Owners to utilize the post and email method of providing notice of Board Meetings to Lot Owners. It is the duty of Lot Owners to register an email address with the Subdivision Association and to keep his or her email address updated. Tex. Prop. Code § 209.0051(f). However, the Subdivision Association must establish an email registry and method for Lot Owners to register their email addresses.

[33] Tex. Prop. Code §§ 82.108(b); 209.0051(c). An Executive Session of a Board Meeting is a session closed to the public during which only the Board of Directors and such select persons invited by the Board of Directors are permitted to be present.

[34] A more detailed explanation as to the applicability of the Texas Open Meetings Act to Homeowners Associations may be found in subchapter 4.5 of this book.

Board of Directors to adjourn the Board Meeting and reconvene in closed Executive Session to consider actions involving:[35]

(1) personnel;

(2) pending litigation;

(3) contract negotiations;

(4) enforcement actions;

(5) matters involving the invasion of privacy of individual Unit Owners; or

(6) matters that are to remain confidential by request of the affected parties and agreement of the Board of Directors.

Prior to adjourning a Board Meeting for purposes of reconvening in Executive Session, the general nature of any business to be considered in Executive Session must first be announced at the open Board Meeting.[36]

12.7.2 Open Board Meetings of a Subdivision Association's Board of Directors under Chapter 209 of the Texas Property Code

Under Chapter 209 of the Texas Property Code, all meetings of a Subdivision Association's Board of Directors must be open to Lot Owners, subject to the right of the Board of Directors to adjourn the Board Meeting and reconvene in closed Executive Session to consider actions involving:[37]

---

35 Tex. Prop. Code § 82.108(b).

36 Tex. Prop. Code § 82.108(b).

37 Tex. Prop. Code § 209.0051(c). Section 209.0051 does not, however, apply to a Subdivision Association that is subject to the Texas Open Meetings Act. Tex. Prop. Code § 209.0051(a). Section 209.0051 also does not apply to a Subdivision Association's Board of Directors during the "Development Period" of a Subdivision Development unless the Board Meeting is conducted for the purpose of: (1) adopting or amending the Governing Documents, including Declarations, Bylaws, Association Rules, and/or regulations of the Subdivision Association; (2) increasing the amount of regular Assessments of the Subdivision Association or adopting or increasing a special Assessment; (3) electing non-developer members to the Board of Directors of the Subdivision Association or establishing a process by which those members are elected; or (4) changing the voting rights of the Subdivision Association's Membership. Tex. Prop. Code § 209.0051(i). "Development Period" means a period stated in a Subdivision Association's Declaration during which a Declarant reserves

(1) personnel;

(2) pending or threatened litigation;

(3) contract negotiations;

(4) enforcement actions;

(5) confidential communications with the Subdivision Association's attorney;

(6) matters involving the invasion of privacy of individual owners; or

(7) matters that are to remain confidential by request of the affected parties and agreement of the Board of Directors.

Unlike a Condominium Association, the general nature of the business to be considered by a Subdivision Association's Board of Directors in Executive Session is not required to be announced at the open Board Meeting prior to adjourning the Board Meeting and reconvening in Executive Session. But following an Executive Session by a Subdivision Association's Board of Directors, any decision made in the Executive Session must be summarized orally upon reconvening the open Board Meeting and placed in the minutes for such meeting.[38] The oral summary must be in general terms, without breaching the privacy of any individual Homeowner, violating any privilege, or disclosing any information that was to remain confidential at the request of the affected parties.[39] In addition, such oral summary must include a general explanation of all expenditures approved in Executive Session.[40]

a right to facilitate the development, construction, and marketing of the Subdivision Development, or a right to direct the size, shape, and composition of the Subdivision Development. Tex. Prop. Code § 209.002(4-a).

38 Tex. Prop. Code § 209.0051(c).

39 Tex. Prop. Code § 209.0051(c).

40 Tex. Prop. Code § 209.0051(c).

12.8 Homeowners' Statutory Right to Notice of Meetings of a Homeowners Association's Membership

In addition to any contractual rights to receive notice of a meeting of a Homeowners Association's Membership established by its Governing Documents, the Texas Nonprofit Corporation Law, Texas Uniform Condominium Act, and Chapter 209 of the Texas Property Code all establish certain statutory rights of Homeowners to receive notice of Membership Meetings. Such statutory rights are described in greater detail in the following subchapters.

12.8.1 Member-Homeowners' Right to Notice of Membership Meetings

A Homeowners Association that is incorporated as a nonprofit corporation (referred to as a "Nonprofit Corporation HOA") is required to provide written notice of the place, date, and time of a Membership Meeting to the Member-Homeowners of such Nonprofit Corporation HOA.[41] If the meeting is a special Membership Meeting, then the notice of the meeting must also state the purpose or purposes for which such Membership Meeting is being called.[42]

The notice of a Membership Meeting shall be delivered to each Member-Homeowner entitled to vote at such meeting no earlier than sixty (60) days, nor later than ten (10) days, before the date of such Membership Meeting.[43] The notice of meeting may be given by the Nonprofit Corporation HOA to each Member-Homeowner by personal delivery, mail, facsimile, or email.[44] If a notice of meeting is sent by mail, such meeting notice is considered to be given to the Member-Homeowner on the date such meeting notice is deposited in the United States mail, with postage paid, in an envelope addressed

---

41 Tex. Bus. Org. Code § 22.156(a).

42 Tex. Bus. Org. Code § 22.156(a).

43 Tex. Bus. Org. Code § 22.156(a).

44 Tex. Bus. Org. Code §§ 6.051(b), 22.156(a).

to the Member-Homeowner at his or her address, as it appears on the ownership or Membership records of the Nonprofit Corporation HOA.[45] If the notice of meeting is sent by facsimile or email, such meeting notice is considered to be given to the Member-Homeowner when such meeting notice is transmitted to a facsimile number or an email address provided by such Member-Homeowner, or to which such Member-Homeowner consents, for the purpose of receiving notice from the Nonprofit Corporation HOA.[46]

12.8.2 Unit Owners' Right to Notice of Membership Meetings

In addition to the Membership Meeting notice requirements imposed on Texas Nonprofit Corporation HOAs by the Texas Nonprofit Corporation Law, if a Homeowners Association is a Condominium Association and the Membership Meeting is for the purpose of adopting an amendment or modification to its Declaration, Articles of Incorporation, Bylaws, or Associations Rules, the Texas Uniform Condominium Act requires a Condominium Association to give each Unit Owner a document showing the specific amendment or other change that would be made to the Declaration, Articles of Incorporation, Bylaws, or Association Rules no earlier than twenty (20) days, nor later than ten (10) days, before the date of the Membership Meeting.[47] Written notice of a proposed amendment of, or modification to, a Condominium Association's Governing Documents is considered to have been given to a Unit Owner on the date such information is personally delivered to the Unit Owner, as shown by a receipt signed by such Unit Owner, or on the date it is mailed to the Unit Owner, as evidenced by the postmark on an envelope containing such information that is deposited in the United States mail with a proper address and paid postage.[48]

---

45 Tex. Bus. Org. Code § 6.051(b)(1).

46 Tex. Bus. Org. Code § 6.051(b)(2).

47 Tex. Prop. Code § 82.070.

48 Tex. Prop. Code § 82.070(b).

12.8.3 Lot Owners' Right to Notice of Membership Meetings

In addition to the Membership Meeting notice requirements imposed on Texas Nonprofit Corporation HOAs by the Texas Nonprofit Corporation Law, if a Homeowners Association is a Subdivision Association, it is also governed by the Membership Meeting notice requirements under Chapter 209 of the Texas Property Code.[49] Chapter 209 requires a Subdivision Association to give written notice of an association-wide election or vote to all of its Lot Owners no earlier than sixty (60) days, nor later than ten (10) days, before the date of the Membership Meeting.[50]

---

[49] Tex. Prop. Code § 209.0056. Section 209.0056 supersedes any contrary requirements in a Subdivision Association's Governing Documents; however, it does not apply to a Subdivision Association that is subject to Chapter 552 of the Texas Government Code (formally known as the "Texas Public Information Act," but more commonly referred to as the "Texas Open Records Act"). Tex. Prop. Code § 209.0056(c). A Subdivision Association is subject to Chapter 552 of the Texas Government Code if: (1) membership in the Subdivision Association is mandatory for Lot Owners or a defined class of property owners in a defined geographic area in a county with a population of 2.8 million or more (Harris County) or in a county adjacent to a county with a population of 2.8 million or more (Brazoria, Chambers, Fort Bend, Liberty, Montgomery, San Jacinto, and Waller Counties); the Subdivision Association has the power to make mandatory special assessments for capital improvements or mandatory regular assessments; and the amount of the mandatory special or regular assessments is or has ever been based in whole or in part on the market value of Lot Owners' Lots or property as assessed by the State of Texas or a local governmental entity for purposes of ad valorem taxation; or (2) the Subdivision Association provides maintenance, preservation, and architectural control of residential and commercial property within a defined geographic area in a county with a population of 2.8 million or more (Harris County) or in a county adjacent to a county with a population of 2.8 million or more (Brazoria, Chambers, Fort Bend, Liberty, Montgomery, San Jacinto, and Waller Counties); and the Subdivision Association is a corporation that is governed by a board of trustees who may employ a general manager to execute the Subdivision Association's Bylaws and administer the business of the corporation; does not require membership in the corporation by the Lot Owners within the defined area; and was incorporated before January 1, 2006. Tex. Gov't Code § 552.0036.

[50] Tex. Prop. Code § 209.0056(a)(1). Alternatively, if a Subdivision Association is conducting a particular representative election for purposes of electing representatives who are then vested with the authority to elect or appoint the members of the Subdivision Association's Board of Directors, the Subdivision Association is only required to provided written notice of such representative election to the Lot Owners entitled under its Governing Documents to vote in that particular representative election. Tex. Prop. Code § 209.0056(a)(1). It is important to note that the written notice of election or vote requirement under Section 209.0056 applies to all Texas Subdivision Associations, including unincorporated Subdivision Associations that are considered to be a Nonprofit Association HOAs.

12.9 Lot Owners' Statutory Right to Compel a Vote Recount

Section 209.0057 of the Texas Property Code was enacted by the Texas Legislature in 2011, and it establishes procedures for a Lot Owner to compel a recount of ballots cast at a meeting of a Subdivision Association's Lot Owners.[51] In order to compel a recount of ballots, a Lot Owner must submit a written demand for a recount to the Subdivision Association within fifteen (15) days from the latter of: (1) the date of the Membership Meeting at which the applicable election or vote is held; or (2) the date the result of the applicable election or vote is announced.[52] The written demand for a recount must be submitted to the Subdivision Association either:

(1) by verified mail or by delivery by the United States Postal Service with signature confirmation service to the Subdivision Association at the mailing address reflected on its most recently recorded Management Certificate;[53] or

---

[51] Tex. Prop. Code § 209.0057. Section 209.0057, however, does not apply to a Subdivision Association that is subject to Chapter 552 of the Texas Government Code (formally known as the "Texas Public Information Act," but more commonly referred to as the "Texas Open Records Act"). Tex. Prop. Code § 209.0057(a). A Subdivision Association is subject to Chapter 552 of the Texas Government Code if: (1) membership in the Subdivision Association is mandatory for Lot Owners or a defined class of property owners in a defined geographic area in a county with a population of 2.8 million or more (Harris County) or in a county adjacent to a county with a population of 2.8 million or more (Brazoria, Chambers, Fort Bend, Liberty, Montgomery, San Jacinto, and Waller Counties); the Subdivision Association has the power to make mandatory special assessments for capital improvements or mandatory regular assessments; and the amount of the mandatory special or regular assessments is or has ever been based in whole or in part on the market value of Lot Owners' Lots or property as assessed by the State of Texas or a local governmental entity for purposes of ad valorem taxation; or (2) the Subdivision Association provides maintenance, preservation, and architectural control of residential and commercial property within a defined geographic area in a county with a population of 2.8 million or more (Harris County) or in a county adjacent to a county with a population of 2.8 million or more (Brazoria, Chambers, Fort Bend, Liberty, Montgomery, San Jacinto, and Waller Counties); and the Subdivision Association is a corporation that is governed by a board of trustees who may employ a general manager to execute the Subdivision Association's Bylaws and administer the business of the corporation; does not require membership in the corporation by the Lot Owners within the defined area; and was incorporated before January 1, 2006. Tex. Gov't Code § 552.0036.

[52] Tex. Prop. Code § 209.0057(b).

[53] Tex. Prop. Code § 209.0057(b)(1). Chapter 209 defines verified mail as any method of mailing for which evidence of mailing is provided by the United States Postal Service or a common carrier. Tex. Prop. Code § 209.002(13).

(2) in person to the Subdivision Association's managing agent as reflected on its most recently recorded Management Certificate or to the address at which absentee and proxy ballots are mailed.[54]

If a Lot Owner timely submits a written demand for a recount to a Subdivision Association, within twenty (20) days from the date the Subdivision Association receives the written demand for a recount, the Subdivision Association is required to estimate the cost for performance of the ballot recount by a person qualified to tabulate votes and must send an invoice for such estimated costs to the requesting Lot Owner at his or her last known address according to the Subdivision Association's records.[55] Within thirty (30) days from the date the invoice for the estimated cost of performing the ballot recount is sent to the requesting Lot Owner, the requesting Lot Owner must pay the invoice in full.[56] If the requesting Lot Owner fails to timely pay such invoice in full, the requesting Lot Owner's demand for a recount is considered withdrawn and the Subdivision Association is no longer required to perform the ballot recount.[57]

Upon timely receipt of payment of the estimated cost of performing the ballot recount, a Subdivision Association is required, at the expense of the requesting Lot

54 Tex. Prop. Code § 209.0057(b) (2).

55 Tex. Prop. Code § 209.0057(b-1).

56 Tex. Prop. Code § 209.0057(b-2). If it turns out that the estimated cost to perform the ballot recount is lesser or greater than the actual costs, then within thirty (30) business days from the date the result of the ballot recount is provided to the requesting Lot Owner, the Subdivision Association must send a final invoice to the requesting Lot Owner. Tex. Prop. Code § 209.0057(b-4). If the actual cost of performing the ballot recount exceeds the estimated costs, the additional cost must be paid by the requesting Lot Owner to the Subdivision Association within thirty (30) business days from the date the final invoice is sent to the requesting Lot Owner. Tex. Prop. Code § 209.0057(b-4). If the requesting Lot Owner fails to timely pay the additional cost to the Subdivision Association, such additional cost may be added to the requesting Lot Owner's account as an assessment. Tex. Prop. Code § 209.0057(b-4). If the estimated cost of performing the ballot recount exceeds the actual cost, the requesting Lot Owner is entitled to a refund of the overpaid amount, which must be paid to the requesting Lot Owner by the Subdivision Association at the time the final invoice is sent to the requesting Lot Owner. Tex. Prop. Code § 209.0057(b-4).

57 Tex. Prop. Code § 209.0057(b-3). It is important to note that the Subdivision Association is not required to send the invoice for the estimated costs of performing the ballot recount by any particular method, but the requesting Lot Owner is required to pay such invoice within thirty (30) days from the date such invoice is sent by the Subdivision Association, not the date the requesting Lot Owner receives such invoice.

Owner, to retain and enter into a contract with an independent and qualified person to perform the recount of ballots.[58] To be considered independent, a person may not be a Lot Owner in the Subdivision Association or be related within the third degree by consanguinity or affinity to a Director on the Subdivision Association's Board of Directors.[59] To be qualified to conduct a recount of ballots, such independent person must also be either:

(1) a current or former county judge; county elections administrator; justice of the peace; or county voter registrar;[60] or

(2) a person agreed on by the Subdivision Association and each person requesting the recount.[61]

It is important to note that only the person who is to perform the ballot recount may be given access to the ballots during the recount process.[62] In addition, such person

[58] Tex. Prop. Code §§ 209.0057(c)–(d). A Subdivision Association is not required to enter into a contract with an independent and qualified person to perform the recount of ballots until it has received payment for such costs from the requesting Lot Owner. Tex. Prop. Code § 209.0057(d).

[59] Tex. Prop. Code § 209.0057(c). Two individuals are considered to be related to each other by consanguinity if one is a descendant of the other or they share a common ancestor. Tex. Gov't Code § 573.022(a). An individual's relatives within the third degree by consanguinity include such individual's: (1) parents and children (relatives in the first degree); (2) brothers, sisters, grandparents, and grandchildren (relatives in the second degree); and (3) great-grandparents, great-grandchildren, aunts who are a sister of a parent of the individual, uncles who are a brother of a parent of the individual, nephews who are a child of a brother or sister of the individual, and nieces who are a child of a brother or sister of the individual (relatives in the third degree). Tex. Gov't Code § 573.023(c). Two individuals are considered to be related to each other by affinity if they are married to each other or the spouse of one of the individuals is related by consanguinity to the other individual. Tex. Gov't Code § 573.024(a). An individual's relatives within the third degree by affinity include: (1) such individual's spouse; (2) anyone related within the third degree by consanguinity to such individual's spouse; and (3) the spouse of anyone related to such individual within the third degree by consanguinity. Tex. Gov't Code § 573.025(a).

[60] Tex. Prop. Code § 209.0057(c)(2)(A).

[61] Tex. Prop. Code § 209.0057(c)(2)(B).

[62] Tex. Prop. Code § 209.00594(c).

is expressly prohibited from disclosing to any other person how any particular individual voted.[63]

A Subdivision Association must complete a ballot recount and provide the result of the ballot recount to each Lot Owner who requested the ballot recount within thirty (30) days from the date the Subdivision Association received payment of the estimated cost of performing the ballot recount.[64] In addition, if the ballot recount changes the result of the Membership election or vote, then the Subdivision Association must reimburse the requesting Lot Owner for the cost of the ballot recount within thirty (30) days from the date the result of the ballot recount is provided to the requesting Lot Owner.[65]

Finally, Section 209.0057 also includes a safe harbor provision for any actions taken by the Board of Directors prior to a ballot recount that changes the results of the election. More specifically, any action taken by the Board of Directors during the period between the initial election vote tally and the completion of the ballot recount is not affected by the ballot recount, even if the ballot recount changes the results of the election.[66] In other words, any action taken by the Board of Directors prior to the completion of the ballot recount will remain valid, even if the result of the ballot recount changes the outcome of a director-election.

---

63 Tex. Prop. Code § 209.00594(b-1). Notwithstanding, Section 209.00594 may not be construed to affect a person's obligation to comply with a court order for the release of ballots or other voting records. Tex. Prop. Code § 209.00594(d).

64 Tex. Prop. Code § 209.0057(d).

65 Tex. Prop. Code § 209.0057(d). If the recount does not change the results of the election or vote, the Subdivision Association is not required to reimburse the recount costs to the requesting Lot Owner.

66 Tex. Prop. Code § 209.0057(d).

12.10 Homeowners' Statutory Right to Inspect a Homeowner Association's Books and Records

Almost all Texas Homeowners Associations are required to keep certain books and records of account and other information concerning their operations (commonly referred to simply as its "Books and Records").[67] In addition to any rights of a Homeowner to inspect the Books and Records of his or her Homeowners Association under its Governing Documents, Texas Homeowners have a statutory right to inspect the Books and Records of their Homeowners Association under one or more Texas statutes, including the Texas Nonprofit Corporation Law, the Texas Uniform Unincorporated Nonprofit Association Act, the Texas Uniform Condominium Act, and/or Chapter 209 of the Texas Property Code, depending on whether the Homeowners Association is incorporated or unincorporated and whether it is a Condominium Association or a Subdivision Association.[68] The provisions of each such statute differ greatly from each other and are explained in greater detail in the following subchapters.

12.10.1 Member-Homeowners' Right to Inspect Books and Records of a Nonprofit Corporation HOA under the Texas Nonprofit Corporation Law

Under the Texas Nonprofit Corporation Law, Member-Homeowners of a Texas Nonprofit Corporation HOA have a right to inspect and copy the Books and Records of such Nonprofit Corporation HOA.[69] In order to inspect the Books and Records of a

---

[67] Although the term "books and records of account" is referenced by the Texas Business Organizations Code and the Texas Uniform Unincorporated Nonprofit Association Act, such statutory term is not defined by such laws. *See* Tex. Bus. Org. Code §§ 3.151; 252.010. *Black's Law Dictionary* defines "books of account" as "books in which merchants, traders, and businessmen generally keep their accounts; including journals, ledgers, and other accounting records. *Black's Law Dictionary* 183 (6th ed. 1990).

[68] In other words, if a Condominium Association is incorporated as a nonprofit corporation, then it is subject to and must comply with the provisions of both the Texas Nonprofit Corporation Law and the Texas Uniform Condominium Act. On the other hand, if a Subdivision Association is not incorporated, but constitutes a Nonprofit Association HOA, then it is subject to and must comply with the provisions of both the Texas Uniform Unincorporated Nonprofit Association Act and Chapter 209 of the Texas Property Code.

[69] Tex. Bus. Org. Code § 22.351. A Texas Nonprofit Corporation HOA is required to keep: (1) books and records of accounts; (2) minutes of the proceedings of its Board of Directors, committees established by its

Nonprofit Corporation HOA, the Member-Homeowner must present the Nonprofit Corporation HOA with a written request stating the scope of the documents requested and the purpose for the request.[70] So long as the request is for a proper purpose, the Member-Homeowner is entitled to examine and copy, at the Member-Homeowner's expense, the Books and Records of the Nonprofit Corporation HOA relevant to the purpose stated in the Member-Homeowner's request.[71] The Member-Homeowner may examine the requested Books and Records at any reasonable time specified by the Member-Homeowner, and the examination may be performed by the Member-Homeowner and/or his or her agent, accountant, or attorney.[72]

12.10.2 Members' Right to Inspect Books and Records of a Nonprofit Association under the Texas Uniform Unincorporated Nonprofit Association Act

Under the Texas Uniform Unincorporated Nonprofit Association Act, a Texas Homeowners Association that constitutes an unincorporated "Nonprofit Association" (referred to as a "Nonprofit Association HOA") is required to keep correct and complete Books and Records of account for at least three (3) years after the end of each fiscal year and must make such Books and Records available on request to its members for inspection and copying.[73]

Board of Directors, and its Membership; (3) a current record of the name and mailing address of each Member-Homeowner of the Nonprofit Corporation HOA; and (4) other books and records as required by the Texas Nonprofit Corporation Law. Tex. Bus. Org. Code § 3.151(a).

70 Tex. Bus. Org. Code § 22.351.

71 Tex. Bus. Org. Code § 22.351.

72 Tex. Bus. Org. Code § 22.351.

73 Tex. Bus. Org. Code § 252.010(a). The Texas Uniform Unincorporated Nonprofit Association Act defines a Nonprofit Association as an unincorporated organization, other than one created by a trust, consisting of three (3) or more members joined by mutual consent for a common, nonprofit purpose. Tex. Bus. Org. Code § 252.010(c).

12.10.3 Unit Owners' Right to Inspect Books and Records of a Condominium Association under the Texas Uniform Condominium Act

Under the Texas Uniform Condominium Act, all financial and other records of a Texas Condominium Association, including the annual audit of its records, must be made reasonably available at its registered office or its principal office in Texas for examination by Unit Owners or their agents.[74] Unlike the Texas Nonprofit Corporation Law, there is no similar requirement that the Unit Owner make the request in writing or that the Unit Owner state the purpose for the request.

For those Condominium Associations that are incorporated as a nonprofit corporation, they are subject to the statutory requirements for inspection of Books and Records under both the Texas Uniform Condominium Act and the Texas Nonprofit Corporation Law, and in most cases, an applicable Condominium Association's Books and Records will constitute Books and Records under both statutes. To the extent a file or record kept by an applicable Condominium Association falls into one of the categories of Books and Records required to be kept by the Condominium Association under the Texas Uniform Condominium Act, a Unit Owner should be afforded the right to inspect such file or record without having to request it in writing or to state a purpose for the request. However, to the extent a file or record kept by an applicable Condominium Association falls outside the categories of Books and Records required to be kept by the Condominium Association under the Texas Uniform Condominium Act, a Unit Owner should comply with the requirements for inspection of Books and Records under the Texas Nonprofit Corporation Law, which requires the request to be in writing and that the Unit Owner state a proper purpose for the request.

---

[74] Tex. Prop. Code § 82.114(b)–(c). An attorney's files and records related to the Condominium Association are not considered to be records of the Condominium Association and are not subject to inspection by Unit Owners. Tex. Prop. Code § 82.114(b).

12.10.4 Lot Owners' Right to Inspect Books and Records of a Subdivision Association under Chapter 209 of the Texas Property Code

Prior to 2011, Chapter 209 of the Texas Property Code required Texas Subdivision Associations to make their Books and Records, including financial records, reasonably available to Lot Owners in accordance with the same procedures for inspection of Books and Records under the Texas Non-Profit Corporation Act, regardless of whether the Subdivision Association was incorporated as a nonprofit corporation.[75] In 2011, however, the Texas Legislature significantly revised Section 209.005 of the Texas Property Code for the purpose of establishing comprehensive procedures for requesting, inspecting, and copying Books and Records of a Subdivision Association that differ significantly from those that previously applied to Subdivision Associations under the Texas Non-Profit Corporation Act and/or the Texas Nonprofit Corporation Law.[76] To the extent a Subdivision Association is incorporated as a nonprofit corporation and is governed by both Chapter 209 and the Texas Nonprofit Corporation Law, the procedures for requesting, inspecting, and copying Books and Records of a Subdivision Association under Chapter 209 control over the procedures set forth in the Nonprofit Corporation Law.[77]

---

[75] Until 2006, the statutory laws governing nonprofit corporations were codified at Article 1396 of the Texas Revised Civil Statutes and known as the "Texas Non-Profit Corporation Act." In 2005, however, the Texas Legislature enacted the Texas Business Organizations Code and recodified the statutory laws governing nonprofit corporations at Chapter 22 of such Code. Chapter 22 of the Texas Business Organizations Code is known as the "Texas Nonprofit Corporation Law" and became applicable to all Texas nonprofit corporations, regardless of when they were formed, effective January 1, 2010.

[76] House Comm. On Judicial Affairs, Bill Analysis, Tex. H.B. 356, 70th Leg., R.S. (1987).

[77] Tex. Prop. Code § 209.005(a). The procedures for requesting, inspecting, and copying Books and Records of a Subdivision Association under Chapter 209, however, do not apply to a Subdivision Association that is subject to Chapter 552 of the Texas Government Code (formally known as the "Texas Public Information Act" but more commonly referred to as the "Texas Open Records Act"). Tex. Prop. Code § 209.005(b). A Subdivision Association is subject to Chapter 552 of the Texas Government Code if: (1) membership in the Subdivision Association is mandatory for Lot Owners or a defined class of property owners in a defined geographic area in a county with a population of 2.8 million or more (Harris County) or in a county adjacent to a county with a population of 2.8 million or more (Brazoria, Chambers, Fort Bend, Liberty, Montgomery, San Jacinto, and Waller Counties); the Subdivision Association has the power to make mandatory special assessments for capital improvements or mandatory regular assessments; and the amount of the mandatory

12.10.4 (A) *Procedures for Requesting Inspection and/or Copies of a Subdivision Association's Books and Records*

Pursuant to Section 209.005 of the Texas Property Code, a Subdivision Association is required to make its Books and Records, including financial records, open to and reasonably available for examination by a Lot Owner or any other person designated as a Lot Owner's agent, attorney, or certified public accountant in a writing signed by such Lot Owner.[78] In addition, a Lot Owner and/or such other designated representative is also entitled to obtain copies of the information contained in such Books and Records from the Subdivision Association.[79]

To inspect and/or obtain copies of a Subdivision Association's Books and Records, a Lot Owner, or his or her designated representative, must submit a written request for information by certified mail to the Subdivision Association at its or its designated representative's mailing address as reflected on the most recently recorded Management Certificate for the Subdivision Association.[80] The written request for information must describe with sufficient detail the Subdivision Association's Books and Records being requested and contain an election either to inspect such Books and Records before obtaining copies of them or to have the Subdivision Association forward copies of such Books and Records to the requesting party without any advance inspection.

---

special or regular assessments is or has ever been based in whole or in part on the market value of Lot Owners' Lots or property as assessed by the State of Texas or a local governmental entity for purposes of ad valorem taxation; or (2) the Subdivision Association provides maintenance, preservation, and architectural control of residential and commercial property within a defined geographic area in a county with a population of 2.8 million or more (Harris County) or in a county adjacent to a county with a population of 2.8 million or more (Brazoria, Chambers, Fort Bend, Liberty, Montgomery, San Jacinto, and Waller Counties); and the Subdivision Association is a corporation that is governed by a board of trustees who may employ a general manager to execute the Subdivision Association's Bylaws and administer the business of the corporation; does not require membership in the corporation by the Lot Owners within the defined area; and was incorporated before January 1, 2006. Tex. Gov't Code § 552.0036.

78 Tex. Prop. Code § 209.005(c).

79 Tex. Prop. Code § 209.005(c).

80 Tex. Prop. Code § 209.005(e).

12.10.4 (B) *Advance Inspection of a Subdivision Association's Books and Records*

If an advance inspection of a Subdivision Association's Books and Records is requested, within ten (10) business days from the date the Subdivision Association receives such written request for inspection, it must send to the requesting party an initial written notice specifying the location and alternative dates that such requesting party may inspect the requested Books and Records, to the extent such Books and Records are in the possession, custody, or control of the Association.[81]

A Subdivision Association should endeavor to make copies of the requested Books and Records available for inspection within ten (10) business days from the date it receives such written inspection request. However, if a Subdivision Association is unable to produce copies of the requested Books and Records and/or make them available for inspection within ten (10) business days from receipt of the request for information, the Subdivision Association must state in the initial written notice to the requesting party (or a subsequent written notice) that the Subdivision Association is unable to produce the requested information within ten (10) business days from the date it received the written inspection request and must specify an alternative date by which such requested Books and Records will be made available for inspection.[82]

One reason a requesting party may elect to inspect a Subdivision Association's Books and Records in lieu of or before requesting copies of such information and records is to determine if he or she wants to go to the expense of obtaining copies of such information and records or to limit the scope of the information and records that he or she

---

81 Tex. Prop. Code § 209.005(e)(1). For the purposes of Section 209.005, "business day" means a day other than Saturday, Sunday, or a state or federal holiday. Tex. Prop. Code § 209.005(q). If an inspection is requested or required, the inspection of the requested Books and Records shall take place at a mutually agreed upon time during normal business hours. Tex. Prop. Code § 209.005(g).

82 Tex. Prop. Code § 209.005(f)(1)–(2). The alternative date set for inspection of such requested Books and Records must be a date that is within fifteen (15) business days from the date of such initial written notice by the Subdivision Association to the requesting party. Tex. Prop. Code § 209.005(f)(2).

wants to obtain copies of. If a requesting party elects to obtain copies of any of the Books and Records that he or she reviewed during an inspection, then at the inspection the requesting party must identify the specific Books and Records that he or she wants the Subdivision Association to copy and forward to him or her.[83] If copies of identified Books and Records of a Subdivision Association are requested at an inspection of such Books and Records, then within ten (10) business days from the date of such inspection, the Subdivision must produce copies of such Books and Records to the requesting party.[84] A Subdivision Association may produce copies of the requested Books and Records to a requesting party in hard copy, electronic form, or any other format reasonably available to it.[85]

12.10.4 (C) *Copying of a Subdivision Association's Books and Records*

If copies of identified Books and Records of a Subdivision Association are requested without an advance inspection of such Books and Records, then within ten (10) business days from the date the Subdivision Association receives the written request for copies of such Books and Records, the Subdivision must produce copies of such Books and Records, to the extent such books and records are in its possession, custody, or control, to the requesting party.[86] If a Subdivision Association is unable to produce copies of the requested Books and Records to the requesting party within ten (10) business days from such date, within ten (10) business days from the date the Subdivision Association receives the written request for copies of such Books and Records, it must send to the requesting party an initial written notice stating that the Subdivision Association is unable to produce the identified Books and Records within ten (10) business days from the date it received the request for copies of such Books and Records and must specify an

[83] Tex. Prop. Code § 209.005(g).

[84] Tex. Prop. Code § 209.005(f).

[85] Tex. Prop. Code § 209.005(h).

[86] Tex. Prop. Code § 209.005(f).

alternative date by which copies of such Books and Records will be sent to the requesting party.[87] A Subdivision Association may produce copies of requested Books and Records to a requesting party in hard copy, electronic form, or any other format reasonably available to it.[88]

12.10.4 (D) *Charging and Payment of Costs for the Compilation, Production, and Reproduction of Information Requested under Chapter 209*

Section 209.005 also authorizes a Subdivision Association to charge a requesting Lot Owner for the costs associated with the compilation, production, and/or reproduction of requested information and records. Before a Subdivision Association may charge a requesting Lot Owner for such costs, however, it must adopt and record a "Records Production and Copying Policy" that prescribes the costs that such Subdivision Association will charge a Lot Owner for the compilation, production, and reproduction of requested information and records.[89] In addition, a Subdivision Association may require advance payment of the estimated costs of compilation, production, and reproduction of the requested information and records from a requesting Lot Owner before it produces such information and records to such Lot Owner or his or her designated representative.[90]

---

87 Tex. Prop. Code § 209.005(f). The alternative date for production of such requested Books and Records must be a date that is within fifteen (15) business days from the date of such initial written notice by the Subdivision Association to the requesting party. Tex. Prop. Code § 209.005(f)(2).

88 Tex. Prop. Code § 209.005(h).

89 Tex. Prop. Code § 209.005(i). A Records Production and Copying Policy is considered to be a Dedicatory Instrument and must be recorded in the Official Public Records of each county in which the applicable Subdivision Development is located. Tex. Prop. Code §§ 202.006, 209.005(i). In addition, a Subdivision Association may not charge a Lot Owner for the cost of compilation, production, or reproduction of information requested under the procedures set forth under Section 209.005 of the Texas Property Code unless a Records Production and Copying Policy prescribing such costs has been recorded by the Subdivision Association in the Official Public Records of the county in which its Subdivision Development is located. Tex. Prop. Code § 209.005(i).

90 Tex. Prop. Code § 209.005(i). Such estimated costs of compilation, production, and reproduction must be estimated using amounts prescribed by the Subdivision Association's recorded Records Production and Copying Policy. Tex. Prop. Code § 209.005(j).

If a Subdivision Association requires a requesting Lot Owner to pay the estimated costs of compilation, production, and reproduction of requested information and records in advance and the actual costs are more or less than the estimated amount paid by the requesting Lot Owner, then the Subdivision Association must submit a final invoice to the requesting Lot Owner within thirty (30) business days from the date the requested information is delivered to the requesting party.[91] In the event the estimated costs paid by the requesting Lot Owner exceed the actual costs of compilation, production, and reproduction of the requested information and records, as reflected in such final invoice, the Subdivision Association must remit payment of such excess amount back to the Requesting Lot Owner within thirty (30) business days from the date the final invoice was sent to the requesting Lot Owner.[92] On the other hand, if the actual costs of compilation, production, and reproduction of the requested information and records, as reflected in such final invoice, exceed the estimated costs paid by the requesting Lot Owner, the requesting Lot Owner must remit payment of such additional amount to the Subdivision Association within thirty (30) business days from the date the final invoice was sent to the requesting Lot Owner.[93] If the requesting Lot Owner fails to remit payment of such additional amount within such thirty (30) business days, such additional amount may be added to the Lot Owner's account as an Assessment.[94]

12.10.4 (E) *Conditional Exclusion of a Subdivision Association's Attorney's Files and Records from Inspection or Copying by Lot Owners*

Subject to certain exceptions, the files and records of a Subdivision Association's attorney are not considered to be Books or Records of such Subdivision Association and are not subject to inspection or copying by a Lot Owner or his or her designated

---

91 Tex. Prop. Code § 209.005(i).

92 Tex. Prop. Code § 209.005(i).

93 Tex. Prop. Code § 209.005(i).

94 Tex. Prop. Code § 209.005(i).

representative.[95] The first exception to this rule arises if a Subdivision Association's attorney has possession of files and records relating to the Subdivision Association that would be responsive to a legally authorized request to inspect or copy records by a Lot Owner and the Subdivision Association has failed to maintain its own separate copy of such documents.[96] In such event, the documents responsive to a Lot Owner's request to inspect or copy records must be produced by the Subdivision Association by using copies of such documents from its attorney's files and records.[97]

The second exception to this rule concerns a request from a Lot Owner for a copy of a Subdivision Association's invoices for attorneys fees for which the Subdivision Association seeks reimbursement of from such Lot Owner. Pursuant to Section 209.008 of the Texas Property Code, a Subdivision Association, upon a written request from a Lot Owner charged with reimbursement of the Subdivision Association's attorneys fees, is required to provide such Lot Owner copies of invoices for the attorneys fees and other costs for which the Subdivision Association seeks reimbursement of from such Lot Owner.[98]

12.10.4 (F) *Subdivision Association Records that Are Exempted from Inspection and Copying by Lot Owners*

Section 209.005 of the Texas Property Code exempts certain records of a Subdivision Association concerning individual Lot Owners or employees of the Subdivision Association from inspection and copying by other Lot Owners. Except to the extent such information is stated within the minutes of a Board or Membership Meeting,

95 Tex. Prop. Code § 209.005(d). Subject to such exceptions, Section 209.005 also excludes the files and records of a Subdivision Association's attorney from production in a legal proceeding. Tex. Prop. Code § 209.005(d).

96 Tex. Prop. Code § 209.005(d).

97 Tex. Prop. Code § 209.005(d). Notwithstanding, such exception does not require production of a document that constitutes attorney work product or that is privileged as an attorney-client communication. Tex. Prop. Code § 209.005(d).

98 Tex. Prop. Code § 209.008(d).

a Subdivision Association is not required to release or allow inspection of any Books or Records that identify:

(1) an individual Lot Owner's history of violations of the Subdivision Association's Dedicatory Instruments (including the Declaration and Association Rules);[99]

(2) an individual Lot Owner's personal financial information (including records of payment or nonpayment of amounts due the Subdivision Association);[100]

(3) a Lot Owner's contact information (other than the Lot Owner's address);[101] or

(4) information related to an employee of the Subdivision Association (including personnel files).[102]

A Subdivision Association may, however, release general financial information and information concerning violations of a Subdivision Association's Dedicatory Instruments in an aggregated or summary manner that would not identify an individual Lot Owner.[103] In addition, a Subdivision Association must release Books and Records concerning an individual Lot Owner or make such records available for inspection if: (1) the Subdivision Association receives express written approval from the Lot Owner whose records are the subject of the request for inspection; or (2) a court orders the release of such Books and Records or orders that such Books and Records be made available for inspection.[104]

---

[99] Tex. Prop. Code § 209.005(k).

[100] Tex. Prop. Code § 209.005(k).

[101] Tex. Prop. Code § 209.005(k).

[102] Tex. Prop. Code § 209.005(k).

[103] Tex. Prop. Code § 209.005(k).

[104] Tex. Prop. Code § 209.005(l).

12.10.4 (G) *Judicial Enforcement of a Lot Owner's Right to Inspect Books and Records of a Subdivision Association*

In addition to establishing new procedures for the inspection and copying of a Subdivision Association's Books and Records, the 2011 amendments to Section 209.005 of the Texas Property Code also established the authority of a Lot Owner who is denied access to or copies of Books or Records to which he or she is entitled to inspect and copy to file a lawsuit against the Subdivision Association to compel it to produce such Books and Records.[105] At least ten (10) business days prior to filing such a lawsuit, the Lot Owner must send a written notice to the Subdivision Association advising it of such Lot Owner's intent to file a lawsuit against the Subdivision Association if the requested Books and Records are not produced to such Lot Owner.[106] Such notice must describe with sufficient detail the Books and Records the Lot Owner is requesting and must be sent to the Subdivision Association at the mailing address of the Subdivision Association or its authorized representative, as reflected on its most recently recorded Management Certificate, by either certified mail, return receipt requested, or United States Postal Service delivery with signature confirmation service.[107]

If a Subdivision Association has not produced the requested Books and Records within ten (10) business days from the date a notice of intent to file a lawsuit is sent to it by a Lot Owner, such Lot Owner may file a lawsuit against the Subdivision Association in the Justice of the Peace Court of the justice precinct in which all or part of the applicable Subdivision Development is located.[108] If the Justice of the Peace finds that the Lot Owner is entitled to inspect and/or to obtain copies of the requested Books and Records, the Justice of the Peace may grant one or more of the following remedies to the Lot Owner:

---

105 Tex. Prop. Code § 209.005(n).

106 Tex. Prop. Code § 209.005(p).

107 Tex. Prop. Code § 209.005(p).

108 Tex. Prop. Code § 209.005(n).

(1) a judgment ordering the Subdivision Association to release or allow access to the requested Books or Records;[109]

(2) a judgment against the Subdivision Association for court costs and attorneys fees incurred in connection with such lawsuit;[110] and/or

(3) a judgment authorizing the Lot Owner or the Lot Owner's assignee to deduct the amount of court costs and attorneys fees awarded to him or her from any future regular or special Assessments payable to the Subdivision Association.[111]

If, however, the Subdivision Association prevails in such lawsuit, the Subdivision Association is entitled to a judgment against the Lot Owner for court costs and attorneys fees incurred by the Subdivision Association in connection with such lawsuit.[112]

---

109 Tex. Prop. Code § 209.005(n)(1).

110 Tex. Prop. Code § 209.005(n)(2).

111 Tex. Prop. Code § 209.005(n)(3).

112 Tex. Prop. Code § 209.005(o).

APPENDIX

Appendix A: Glossary of Terms

ACC is a commonly used abbreviation for Architectural Control Committee.

ADA is a commonly used abbreviation for the Americans with Disabilities Act.

Affiliate of a Declarant is a defined term under the Texas Uniform Condominium Act that refers to any person who controls, is controlled by, or is under common control with the Declarant.[1]

Aggrieved Person is a defined term under the Texas Fair Housing Act that refers to any person who is alleged to have been injured by a discriminatory housing practice or who allegedly will be injured by a discriminatory housing practice that is about to occur.[2]

Allocated Interests is a defined term under the Texas Uniform Condominium Act that refers to the undivided interest in the Common Elements, the Common Expense Liability, and votes in the Condominium Association allocated to each Unit in a Condominium Development.[3]

Americans with Disabilities Act refers to the federal law that prohibits discrimination on the basis of a "Disability" and requires "Places of Public Accommodation" to be designed, constructed, and altered in compliance with certain accessibility standards set forth by federal regulation.[4]

Annual Assessment is a commonly used term of art that refers to an Assessment that is levied once a year or on an annual basis.

Annual Meeting is a commonly used term of art that refers to a meeting of a Homeowners Association's Membership, conducted once a year, at which the Membership generally elects individuals to the Board of Directors, as well as votes on other items that may be submitted to a Homeowners Association's Membership for approval.

Apartment is a defined term under the Texas Condominium Act that refers to the portion of a Condominium Development that is separately owned and means an enclosed space, regardless of whether it is designed for residential or other use, that consists of one or more rooms in a building and that has a direct exit to a thoroughfare or to a common space

---

1 Tex. Prop. Code § 82.003(a)(1). For purposes of Tex. Prop. Code § 82.003(a)(1), a "person" may be an individual or an entity.

2 Tex. Prop. Code § 301.003(1).

3 Tex. Prop. Code § 82.003(2).

4 42 U.S.C. § 12102, *et seq.*; 28 C.F.R. § 36.101, *et seq.*

that leads to a thoroughfare.[5] In general, such term is synonymous with the term "Unit" under the Texas Uniform Condominium Act in the context of an apartment-style Condominium Development.

Apartment Owner is a term of art utilized in this book that refers to the owner of an Apartment in an apartment-style Condominium Development governed by the Texas Condominium Act. In general, such term is synonymous with the term "Unit Owner" under the Texas Uniform Condominium Act.

Architectural Committee is a term of art utilized in this book that refers to a committee of individuals vested with the authority to review and approve proposed construction or modification of improvements in a Subdivision or Condominium Development under the Declaration applicable to the community. This committee or group of individuals can go by many synonymous names, such as "Architectural Control Committee," "Architectural Review Committee," and "Design Review Committee;" and they are commonly known by related abbreviations, such as: "ACC," "ARC," or "DRC."

Architectural Control Authority is a term of art utilized in this book that refers to the power to approve or deny applications for proposed original construction of a new building, structure, or Improvement or modification of an existing building, structure, or Improvement on a Lot or Unit.

Architectural Guidelines is a commonly used term of art that refers to rules or guidelines promulgated by an Architectural Committee pursuant to the authority granted to it under an applicable Declaration. Architectural Guidelines generally set forth certain construction standards and specifications that the Architectural Committee has already determined to be in compliance with the provisions of such Declaration and harmonious with the community's architecture and appearance.

Articles of Incorporation is a defined term under the Texas Non-Profit Corporation Act that refers to the document required to be filed with the Texas Secretary of State's office to form a nonprofit corporation and includes any restated and amended Articles of Incorporation.[6] Such term is synonymous with the term "Certificate of Formation" under the Texas Nonprofit Corporation Law.[7]

---

5 Tex. Prop. Code § 81.002(1). For purposes of the Texas Condominium Act, the term "building" includes each principal structure on or to be erected on real property dedicated in a Condominium Declaration as a Condominium Development or condominium regime. Tex. Prop. Code § 81.002(2).

6 Tex. Rev. Civ. Stat. Ann. art. 1396-1.02(A)(4).

7 Tex. Bus. Org. Code § 1.002(6).

Assessment is a commonly used term of art that refers to a monetary charge assessed by a Homeowners Association against a Homeowner pursuant to its Declaration or Bylaws to fund the operation of the Homeowners Association and management of the community or other obligations specified by such Governing Documents.[8] Such term includes regular Assessments, special Assessments, individual Assessments, or any other types of charges specified by a Homeowners Association's Governing Documents or Texas law. For purposes of a Condominium Association's Assessment Lien, the term "Assessment" is defined by the Texas Uniform Condominium Act and includes regular Assessments, special Assessments, dues, fees, charges, interest, late fees, fines, collection costs, attorneys fees, and any other amount due a Condominium Association by a Unit Owner.[9]

Assessment Lien is a term of art utilized in this book that refers to a contractual lien created and reserved in a Declaration (and/or by the Texas Uniform Condominium Act) in favor of a Homeowners Association to secure payment of Assessments.[10]

Association-Governed Community is a commonly used term of art that refers generally to any Subdivision Development or Condominium Development governed by an association of property owners, including single-family Subdivision Developments, Condominium Developments, and other types of planned-unit developments.

Association Rules is a term of art utilized in this book that refers to rules adopted and amended from time to time by the Board of Directors of a Homeowners Association pursuant to its authority to do so under its applicable Declaration. Such rules are sometimes also called "rules and regulations" in a Declaration.

Board of Directors is a defined term under the Texas Nonprofit Corporation Law and means the group of persons vested with the management of the affairs of a Nonprofit Corporation HOA, regardless of the name used to designate such group.[11]

Books and Records is a commonly used term that refers to certain books and records kept by Texas Homeowners Associations regarding their operations and accounts.[12] The term "Books and Records" is also commonly used to refer to the books and records of

---

8 *See generally*, Tex. Prop. Code § 209.002(1).

9 Tex. Prop. Code § 82.113(a).

10 *See* Tex. Prop. Code § 82.113.

11 Tex. Bus. Org. Code § 22.001(1); *see also*, Tex. Prop. Code § 82.003(4).

12 Although the term "books and records of account" is referenced by the Texas Business Organizations Code and the Texas Uniform Unincorporated Nonprofit Association Act, such statutory term is not defined by such laws. *See* Tex. Bus. Org. Code §§ 3.151; 252.010. *Black's Law Dictionary* defines "books of account" as "books in which merchants, traders, and businessmen generally keep their accounts; including journals, ledgers, and other accounting records." *Black's Law Dictionary* 183 (6th ed. 1990).

account required to be kept by Texas Homeowners Associations under the Texas Nonprofit Corporation Law, Texas Uniform Unincorporated Nonprofit Association Act, Texas Uniform Condominium Act, and/or Chapter 209 of the Texas Property Code, as applicable.[13]

Bylaws is a defined term under the Texas Nonprofit Corporation Law that refers to the administrative rules adopted by the Board of Directors to regulate or manage a Nonprofit Corporation HOA, regardless of the name used to designate such rules.[14] Such term is also referenced by the Texas Uniform Condominium Act to refer to the Governing Document of a Condominium Association that establishes rules for its administration and operation.[15]

Candidacy-Solicitation Notice is a term of art utilized in this book that refers to a written notice that must be provided to the members of a Subdivision Association that administers a Subdivision Development consisting of more than one hundred Lots at least ten (10) days before disseminating ballots for a Director election, which must include instructions for an eligible candidate who is interested in running for a position on the Subdivision Association's Board of Directors to notify the Subdivision Association of his or her request to be placed on the ballot and the deadline to submit such request.[16]

Certificate of Compliance is a term of art utilized in this book that refers to a written instrument executed by a majority of the members of a Chapter 201 Petition Committee upon compliance with the requisite procedures for providing notice of a filed Chapter 201 Petition to all Lot Owners in a Subdivision Development and publishing the same in a local newspaper that is recorded in the Official Public Records of each county in which the Subdivision Development is located.[17]

Certificate of Formation is a defined term under the Texas Business Organization Code that refers to the document required to be filed with the Texas Secretary of State's office

[13] Tex. Bus. Org. Code §§ 3.151(a), 252.010; Tex. Prop. Code §§ 82.114(a), 209.005(m).

[14] Tex. Bus. Org. Code §§ 22.001(2), 22.102(b). The contents of a Nonprofit Corporation HOA's Bylaws can vary, but they typically include: (1) provisions concerning the number of Directors and Officers for the Nonprofit Corporation HOA and their terms of office; (2) the manner of electing and removing Directors and Officers; (3) any qualifications to serve as a Director or Officer; (4) the time, place, and procedures for calling a meeting of the Board of Directors or members of the nonprofit corporation; and (5) the procedures for amending the Bylaws.

[15] Tex. Prop. Code § 82.106. The provisions of the Texas Uniform Condominium Act concerning Bylaws are not applicable to Condominium Developments created prior to January 1, 1994, that are subject to the Texas Condominium Act, and there are no comparable provisions under the Texas Condominium Act. Tex. Prop. Code § 82.002(c).

[16] Tex. Prop. Code § 209.00593.

[17] Tex. Prop. Code § 201.008(e)–(f).

to form a nonprofit corporation, and it includes any restated and amended Certificates of Formation.[18] Such term is synonymous with the term "Articles of Incorporation" under the Texas Non-Profit Corporation Act.[19]

Chapter 201 Petition is a term of art utilized in this book that refers to one or more written instruments, however designated or entitled, by which a Declaration or other Dedicatory Instrument is sought to be extended, created, or modified pursuant to the provisions of Chapter 201 of the Texas Property Code.[20]

Chapter 201 Petition Committee is a term of art utilized in this book that refers to a group of three or more Lot Owners who file with the county clerk a requisite notice of formation under Chapter 201 of the Texas Property Code for the purpose of preparing and circulating a Chapter 201 Petition.[21]

Chapter 204 Declaration Petition is a term of art utilized in this book that refers to one or more written instruments, however designated or entitled, by which a Declaration or other Dedicatory Instrument is sought to be extended, renewed, created, or modified pursuant to the provisions of Chapter 204 of the Texas Property Code.[22]

Chapter 204 Subdivision Association Petition is a term of art utilized in this book that refers to one or more written instruments, however designated or entitled, by which a Declaration or other Dedicatory Instrument is sought to be modified for the sole purpose of creating and operating a Subdivision Association pursuant to the provisions of Chapter 204 of the Texas Property Code.[23]

Chapter 204 Subdivision Association Petition Committee is a term of art utilized in this book that refers to a group of three or more Lot Owners who file with the county clerk a requisite notice of formation under Chapter 204 of the Texas Property Code for the purpose of preparing and circulating a Chapter 204 Subdivision Association Petition.[24]

Chapter 209 of the Texas Property Code, also known as the Texas Residential Property Owners Protection Act, but more commonly referred to as simply "Chapter 209," refers to the Texas law that imposes certain due process requirements on a Subdivision

[18] Tex. Bus. Org. Code § 1.002(6).

[19] Tex. Rev. Civ. Stat. Ann. art. 1396-1.02(A)(4).

[20] Tex. Prop. Code § 201.007

. Tex. Prop. Code § 201.003(7).

[22] Tex. Prop. Code § 204.005.

[23] Tex. Prop. Code § 204.006.

[24] Tex. Prop. Code § 204.006.

Association before it may suspend a Lot Owner's right to use a Common Area, initiate judicial proceedings to enforce Restrictive Covenants against a Lot Owner, charge a Lot Owner for property damage, assess a fine against a Lot Owner for violation of a Restrictive Covenant, or charge a Lot Owner for attorneys fees incurred by the Subdivision Association, as well as imposes certain requisite procedures on a Subdivision Association prior to and following foreclosure of an Assessment Lien.[25]

Chapter 209 Election Committee is a term of art utilized in this book that refers to a group of three or more Lot Owners who file with the county clerk a requisite notice of formation under Chapter 209 of the Texas Property Code for the purpose of calling a Membership Meeting to elect Board Members.[26]

Chapter 209 Hearing is a term of art utilized in this book that refers to the hearing before the Board of Directors that a Subdivision Association must afford a Homeowner to discuss and verify facts if timely requested by the Lot Owner following receipt of a Chapter 209 Notice.[27]

Chapter 209 Notice is a term of art utilized in this book that refers to the written notice that a Subdivision Association must give to a Lot Owner before it can suspend a Lot Owner's rights under the Declaration, assess a fine against a Lot Owner, file a lawsuit against a Lot Owner, or seek reimbursement of attorneys fees from a Lot Owner for alleged violations of a Restrictive Covenant.[28]

Chapter 210 Petition is a term of art utilized in this book that refers to one or more written instruments, however designated or entitled, by which a Declaration or other Dedicatory Instrument is sought to be extended or modified pursuant to the provisions of Chapter 210 of the Texas Property Code.[29]

Chapter 210 Petition Committee is a term of art utilized in this book that refers to a group of three or more Lot Owners who may prepare and circulate a Chapter 210 Petition.[30]

Chapter 210 Resolution is a term of art utilized in this book that refers to a written resolution recorded in the local Official Public Records by an applicable Subdivision

[25] *See* Chapter 209 of the Texas Property Code.

[26] Tex. Prop. Code § 209.014.

[27] Tex. Prop. Code §§ 209.006–209.007.

[28] Tex. Prop. Code § 209.006.

[29] Tex. Prop. Code § 210.005(a).

[30] Tex. Prop. Code § 210.004(a).

Association or Chapter 210 Petition Committee that certifies the results of a vote on a proposed extension or modification to a Declaration conducted under the procedures established by Chapter 210 of the Texas Property Code.[31]

Chapter 213 Certificate Affidavit is a term of art utilized in this book that refers to a recorded affidavit by a Chapter 213 Petition Circulator certifying the result of the votes in favor of and against a modification or termination of a Golf Dedicatory Instrument proposed by a Chapter 213 Petition.[32]

Chapter 213 Petition is a term of art utilized in this book that refers to a written document proposing a modification or termination of a Golf Dedicatory Instrument that restricts the use of certain real property as a golf course or country club under the procedure specified by Chapter 213 of the Texas Property Code.[33]

Chapter 213 Petition Circulator (called simply a "Petition Circulator" under Chapter 213 of the Texas Property Code) is a defined term under Chapter 213 of the Texas Property Code that refers to a person who is authorized to circulate a Chapter 213 Petition to all Lot Owners, Unit Owners, Subdivision Associations, and Condominium Associations in a Golf Development under the procedures established by Chapter 213 of the Texas Property Code.[34]

Chapter 213 Signed Statement is a term of art utilized in this book that refers to a signed written statement by an owner of a Lot or Unit within a Golf Development voting in favor of or against a modification or termination of a Golf Dedicatory Instrument proposed by a Chapter 213 Petition.[35]

Charitable Organization is a defined term under the Texas Charitable Immunity and Liability Act of 1987 that refers to an income tax-exempt organization, including a Homeowners Association, as defined by Section 528(c) of the Internal Revenue Code of 1986 or which is exempt from federal income tax under Section 501(a) of the Internal Revenue Code of 1986 by being listed as an exempt organization in Section 501(c)(4) of such code.[36] Such definition generally includes most Texas Homeowners Associations.

---

31 Tex. Prop. Code §§ 210.004, 210.008(a).

32 Tex. Prop. Code § 213.010.

33 Tex. Prop. Code §§ 213.003, 213.006.

34 Tex. Prop. Code §§ 213.001(6), 213.005.

35 Tex. Prop. Code § 213.008.

36 Tex. Civ. Prac. & Rem. Code § 84.003(1).

Charitable Volunteer is a defined term under the Texas Charitable Immunity and Liability Act of 1987 that refers to a person who renders services for, or on behalf of, a Charitable Organization who does not receive compensation for such services other than reimbursement of expenses incurred by such person in the performance of such services.[37] Such term includes a person serving as a Director or Officer of the Charitable Organization.

Common Area is a commonly used term of art that refers to real property in a Subdivision Development that is owned by the Subdivision Association for the benefit of the Lot Owners in such Subdivision Development.

Common Elements is a defined term under the Texas Uniform Condominium Act that refers to all portions of a Condominium Development other than the Units and includes both General Common Elements and Limited Common Elements.[38]

Common Expense Liability is a defined term under the Texas Uniform Condominium Act that refers to the liability for Common Expenses allocated to each Unit in a Condominium Development.[39]

Common Expenses is a defined term under the Texas Uniform Condominium Act that refers to expenditures made by or financial liabilities of the Condominium Association, together with any allocations to reserves.[40]

Common-Interest Development is a commonly used term of art that refers to a real estate development in which a certain defined group of property owners have common-ownership interests, such as a Condominium Development, or are members of a Homeowners Association that owns property for the benefit of such property owners. The term includes Subdivision Developments, Condominium Developments, and any other type of planned-unit development.

Community Association is a defined term under Chapter 206 of the Texas Property Code that refers to an incorporated association created to enforce Restrictive Covenants.[41] Such term is commonly used synonymously with the term "Homeowners Association" or "Property Owners Association."

---

[37] Tex. Civ. Prac. & Rem. Code § 84.003(2).

[38] Tex. Prop. Code § 82.003(5).

[39] Tex. Prop. Code § 82.003(6).

[40] Tex. Prop. Code § 82.003(7).

[41] Tex. Prop. Code § 206.001(1).

Community Associations Institute, also commonly referred to by the abbreviation "CAI," is a national educational membership organization composed of various interest groups serving the Association-Governed Community industry, with local chapters throughout the nation, including Texas.

Community-Based Residential Home is a defined term under the Texas Community Homes for Disabled Persons Location Act and means a community-based residential home operated by either: (1) the Texas Department of Mental Health and Mental Retardation; (2) a community center organized under Chapter 534 of the Texas Health and Safety Code that provides services to Persons with Disabilities; (3) a Texas nonprofit corporation; or (4) an entity certified by the Texas Department of Human Services as a provider under the medical assistance program serving persons in intermediate care facilities for persons with mental retardation.[42]

Community Home is a defined term under the Texas Community Homes for Disabled Persons Location Act and means an entity compliant with the provisions of such act that is either a Community-Based Residential Home or an assisted-living facility licensed under Chapter 247 of the Texas Health and Safety Code.[43]

Complainant is a defined term under the Texas Fair Housing Act that refers to a person or entity, including the Civil Rights Division of the Texas Workforce Commission, that files a Fair Housing Complaint.[44]

Conciliation is a defined term under the Texas Fair Housing Act that refers to the informal negotiations between an Aggrieved Person, Respondent, and the Texas Workforce Commission to resolve issues raised by a Fair Housing Complaint or by the investigation of a Fair Housing Complaint.[45]

Conciliation Agreement is a defined term under the Texas Fair Housing Act that refers to a written agreement between an Aggrieved Person, Respondent, and the Texas Workforce Commission that resolves the issues raised by a Fair Housing Complaint or by the investigation of a Fair Housing Complaint.[46]

Condominium Association (called simply an "Association" under the Texas Uniform Condominium Act) is a defined term under the Texas Uniform Condominium Act that

---

[42] Tex. Hum. Res. Code § 123.004.

[43] Tex. Hum. Res. Code § 123.004.

[44] Tex. Prop. Code § 301.003(2).

[45] Tex. Prop. Code § 301.003(4).

[46] Tex. Prop. Code § 301.003(5).

refers to a Homeowners Association, organized as a for-profit or nonprofit corporation, whose membership consists of the owners of all of the Units in a Condominium Development.

Condominium Declaration (called simply a "Declaration" under the Texas Uniform Condominium Act) is a defined term under the Texas Uniform Condominium Act that refers to the written instrument, however denominated, that creates a Condominium Development, and any amendment to such instrument.[47] In plain English, the Condominium Declaration is the document that creates the Condominium Development and is recorded in the Official Public Records of the county in which such Condominium Development is located.

Condominium Development (called simply a "Condominium" under the Texas Uniform Condominium Act) is a defined term under the Texas Uniform Condominium Act that refers to a form of real property ownership created by statute in which portions of a single Lot or tract of land is designated for separate ownership or occupancy (called Units), and the remaining portions of which are designated for common ownership or occupancy solely by the owners of the separately owned portions (called Common Elements).[48] Such term is synonymous with the term "Condominium Regime."

Condominium Insurance Trustee is a term of art utilized in this book that refers to a person or entity designated as an insurance trustee by the Board of Directors of a Condominium Association for purposes of receiving and holding in trust payment of insurance proceeds for a covered loss under a Condominium Association's property insurance policy.[49]

Condominium Plan (called simply a "Plan" under the Texas Uniform Condominium Act) is a defined term under the Texas Uniform Condominium Act that refers to a dimensional drawing that horizontally and vertically identifies or describes Units and Common Elements contained in buildings in a Condominium Development.[50] A Condominium Plan must be recorded in the Official Public Records and is typically attached to or a part of the Condominium Declaration.[51]

---

[47] Tex. Prop. Code § 82.003(11). The Texas Condominium Act defines the term "Declaration" as the instrument that establishes property under a condominium regime. Tex. Prop. Code § 81.002(5).

[48] Tex. Prop. Code § 82.003(8). The Texas Condominium Act defines the term "condominium" as a form of real property ownership that combines separate ownership of individual apartments or units with common ownership of other elements. Tex. Prop. Code § 81.002(3).

[49] Tex. Prop. Code § 82.111(e) & (f).

[50] Tex. Prop. Code §§ 82.003(18), Tex. Prop. Code § 82.059(d).

[51] Tex. Prop. Code § 82.059(a).

Condominium Plat (called simply a "Plat" under the Texas Uniform Condominium Act) is a defined term under the Texas Uniform Condominium Act that refers to a survey that shows a general schematic map of the Condominium Development and the location and dimensions of any vertical and horizontal Unit boundaries and Limited Common Elements, as well as additional information required by the Texas Uniform Condominium Act.[52] A Condominium Plat must be recorded in the Official Public Records and is typically attached to or a part of the Condominium Declaration.[53]

Construction Defect Claim is a term of art utilized in this book that refers to a claim by a Condominium Association, which is governed by the Texas Uniform Condominium Act and consists of eight or more Units, pertaining to the construction or design of a Unit or the Common Elements within its Condominium Development.[54]

Construction Defect Inspection is a term of art utilized in this book that refers to an inspection of the specific Units and/or Common Elements that are the subject of a Construction Defect Claim by a licensed professional engineer who is to prepare a Construction Defect Report.[55]

Construction Defect Meeting is a term of art utilized in this book that refers to a meeting of an applicable Condominium Association's Unit Owners to vote on whether to approve the filing of a lawsuit or initiation of an arbitration proceeding concerning a Construction Defect Claim.[56]

Construction Defect Meeting Notice is a term of art utilized in this book that refers to a written notice of a Construction Defect Meeting that must be provided to each Unit Owner at least thirty (30) days before the date of the Construction Defect Meeting, which must specify the date, time, and location of the meeting and include other information concerning the Construction Defect Claim, as required by Section 82.119 of the Texas Property Code.[57]

---

52 Tex. Prop. Code §§ 82.003(19), 82.059(b)–(c). As used in the Texas Uniform Condominium Act, the term "Plat" does not have the same meaning as "plat" in Chapter 212 or 232 of the Texas Local Government Code, or other statutes dealing with municipal or county regulation of property development. Tex. Prop. Code § 82.003(19).

53 Tex. Prop. Code § 82.059(a).

54 Tex. Prop. Code § 82.119.

55 Tex. Prop. Code § 82.119(b).

56 Tex. Prop. Code § 82.119(b).

57 Tex. Prop. Code § 82.119(f)–(g).

Construction Defect Report is a term of art utilized in this book that refers to a written report prepared by a licensed professional engineer who performed a Construction Defect Inspection, which must identify certain information concerning the specific Units and/or Common Elements that are the subject of a Construction Defect Claim.[58]

Construction Defect Respondents is a term of art utilized in this book that refers to all persons or entities that may be subject to a Construction Defect Claim by an applicable Condominium Association.[59]

Council of Owners is a defined term under the Texas Condominium Act that refers to all owners of Apartments in a Condominium Development subject to the Texas Condominium Act.[60]

Declarant is a defined term under the Texas Uniform Condominium Act that refers to a person or entity, who: (1) as part of a common promotional plan, offers to dispose of the person's interest in a Unit not previously disposed of; or (2) reserves or succeeds to any Special Declarant Right.[61] In plain English, the Declarant is the individual or entity acting as the developer of a Condominium Development.

Declarant-Control Period is a commonly used term of art that refers to the period of time following the creation of a Homeowners Association during which the Declarant may unilaterally appoint and/or remove the Directors and Officers of a Homeowners Association, or otherwise control the Homeowners Association.[62]

Declaration is a commonly used term of art that refers to the written instrument that is recorded in the Official Public Records of a county (commonly entitled "Declaration of Covenants, Conditions, and Restrictions" or a variation thereof) and imposes contractual obligations (known as Restrictive Covenants) upon certain delineated real property that become binding upon any subsequent owner of such real property.[63] Such contractual obligations typically make the owners of such real property mandatory members of a Homeowners Association and impose certain restrictions upon such owners' use of their property. A "Declaration" is also sometimes synonymously referred to as "CCRs," "land-

---

58 Tex. Prop. Code § 82.119(b).

59 Tex. Prop. Code § 82.119(b)–(c).

60 Tex. Prop. Code § 81.002(4).

61 Tex. Prop. Code § 82.003(10).

62 *See generally*, Tex. Prop. Code § 209.00591(c).

63 *See generally*, Tex. Prop. Code § 209.002(3).

use restrictions," "Restrictive Covenants," "Deed Restrictions," or "Dedicatory Instrument."

Dedicatory Instrument is a defined term under the Texas Uniform Condominium Act and Chapter 202 of the Texas Property Code that refers to each written instrument that governs the establishment, maintenance, and/or operation of a Subdivision Development, Condominium Development, or any other similarly planned development.[64] Such term includes a Declaration or similar instrument subjecting real property to Restrictive Covenants, Bylaws, or similar instruments governing the administration or operation of a Homeowners Association, including Association Rules, and all lawful amendments to such documents.[65] Such term is also synonymous with the term "Governing Documents."

Deed of Trust Lien is a commonly used term of art that refers to a lien that is evidenced by a recorded "Deed of Trust." A Deed of Trust is a written instrument that is used to secure the repayment of a mortgage by placing conditional legal title to the real property securing such mortgage in a neutral third party (typically called the "trustee"), who may later exercise a power of sale to foreclose such real property in the event the borrower fails to repay such mortgage. A Deed of Trust Lien is the most common form of lien used to secure a lender who finances a Homeowner's purchase of a Lot or Unit.

Department of Housing and Urban Development, also commonly referred to by the acronym "HUD," is the governmental agency charged with enforcement of the Federal Fair Housing Act.

Development Period is a defined term under Chapter 209 of the Texas Property Code that refers to the period of time stated in a Subdivision Association's Declaration during which a Declarant reserves a right to facilitate the development, construction, and marketing of the Subdivision Development; or a right to direct the size, shape, and composition of the Subdivision Development.[66]

Development Right(s) is a defined term under the Texas Uniform Condominium Act that refers to a right or combination of rights reserved by a Declarant in the Condominium Declaration to: (1) add real property to a Condominium Development; (2) create new Units, Common Elements, or Limited Common Elements within a Condominium

---

64 Tex. Prop. Code §§ 82.003(11-a); 202.001(1).

65 Tex. Prop. Code §§ 82.003(11-a); 202.001(1).

66 Tex. Prop. Code § 209.002(4-a). The term "Development Period" is also defined in Section 202.010 of the Texas Property Code, which applies equally to Condominium and Subdivision Developments, but such statutory definition of "Development Period" under Section 202.010 expressly references only "subdivisions," not "condominiums." Tex. Prop. Code § 202.010(a)(1).

Development; (3) subdivide Units or convert Units into Common Elements; or (4) withdraw real property from a Condominium Development.[67]

Director is a defined term under the Texas Business Organizations Code that refers to an individual who serves on the Board of Directors of a Nonprofit Corporation HOA.[68]

Disability is a defined term under the Americans with Disabilities Act that means, with respect to an individual: (1) a physical or mental impairment that substantially limits one or more major life activities of such individual; (2) a record of such an impairment; and/or (3) being regarded as having such an impairment.[69] The term "Disability" under the Americans with Disabilities Act has the same legal meaning as the term "Handicap" under the Federal Fair Housing Act.[70] The term "Disability" is also a defined term under the Texas Fair Housing Act and has the same legal meaning as the term "Handicap" under the Federal Fair Housing Act, except that under the Texas Fair Housing Act, such term expressly excludes current illegal use or addiction to any drug or illegal or federally controlled substance, as well as expressly excludes the application of such term to an individual because of such individual's sexual orientation or because such individual is a transvestite.[71]

Executive Session is a commonly used term of art recognized under the Texas Uniform Condominium Act and Chapter 209 of the Texas Property Code that refers to a session of a Board of Directors meeting that is closed to the public.[72]

Ex Officio Member of the Board of Directors is a recognized term under the Texas Nonprofit Corporation Law that refers to a person who, despite not being a Director, is designated under the Articles of Incorporation (or Certificate of Formation) or Bylaws of

---

[67] Tex. Prop. Code § 82.003(12).

[68] Tex. Bus. Org. Code § 1.002(16).

[69] 42 U.S.C. § 12102. Major life activities include, but are not limited to, caring for oneself, performing manual tasks, seeing, hearing, eating, sleeping, walking, standing, lifting, bending, speaking, breathing, learning, reading, concentrating, thinking, communicating, and working, as well as the operation of a major bodily function, including, but not limited to, functions of the immune system, normal cell growth, digestive, bowel, bladder, neurological, brain, respiratory, circulatory, endocrine, and reproductive functions. 42 U.S.C. § 12102.

[70] 42 U.S.C. § 3602. *See Bragdon v. Abbott*, 524 U.S. 624, 631 (1998) (Noting that the definition of "Disability" under the Americans with Disabilities Act is drawn almost verbatim from the definition of "Handicap" contained in the Fair Housing Amendments Act of 1988.).

[71] Tex. Prop. Code § 301.003(6).

[72] *See* Tex. Prop. Code §§ 82.108(b), 209.0051(c).

a Nonprofit Corporation HOA as a person who is entitled to receive notice of and to attend meetings of the Board of Directors.[73]

Expedited Non-Judicial Foreclosure Proceeding is a term of art utilized in this book that refers to an expedited judicial proceeding governed by the Texas Rules of Civil Procedure 735 and 736 through which a Subdivision Association may obtain a court order authorizing it to foreclose its Assessment Lien by non-judicial foreclosure procedures, as required by Chapter 209 of the Texas Property Code.[74]

Fair Housing Act refers to the federal law that makes it unlawful to discriminate against any person in terms, conditions, or privileges in the provision of housing services or facilities on the basis of such person's race, color, religion, national origin, sex, Familial Status, or Handicap.[75]

Fair Housing Complaint is a term of art utilized in this book that refers to a complaint of discriminatory housing practices under the Federal and Texas Fair Housing Acts.

Familial Status is a defined term under both the Federal Fair Housing Act and the Texas Fair Housing Act that refers to a class of people protected from discriminatory housing practices that affect children or families with children. The Federal Fair Housing Act defines "Familial Status" as one or more individuals (who have not attained the age of eighteen years) being domiciled with a parent or another person having legal custody of such individual or individuals or the designee of such parent or other person having such custody pursuant to the written permission of such parent or other person.[76] The Texas Fair Housing Act defines "Familial Status" as being a person who is: (1) pregnant; (2) domiciled with an individual younger than eighteen years of age in regard to whom the person is the parent or legal custodian or has the written permission of the parent or legal custodian for domicile with such minor person; or (3) in the process of obtaining legal custody of an individual younger than eighteen years of age.[77]

Family Home is a defined term under Chapter 202 of the Texas Property Code that refers to a residential home that constitutes a Community Home under the Texas Community Homes for Disabled Persons Location Act.[78]

---

73 Tex. Bus. Org. Code § 22.210.

74 Tex. Prop. Code § 209.0092; Tex. R. Civ. P. 735, 736.

75 *See* 42 U.S.C. § 3601, *et seq.*

76 42 U.S.C. § 3602(k).

77 Tex. Prop. Code § 301.004.

78 Tex. Prop. Code § 202.003(b).

Fannie Mae refers to the Federal National Mortgage Association, a stockholder-owned corporation chartered by the United States Congress in 1968 as a government-sponsored enterprise to purchase and securitize mortgages in order to ensure that funds are consistently available to the institutions that lend money to home buyers. Fannie Mae buys mortgages on the secondary market, pools them, and sells them as mortgage-backed securities to investors on the open market. This secondary mortgage market increases the supply of money available for mortgages lending and increases the money available for new home purchases.

Federal Home Loan Mortgage Corporation, more commonly known as "Freddie Mac," is a government-sponsored enterprise that was created in 1970 as competition for Fannie Mae and to further increase the availability of funds to finance mortgages and homeownership. Freddie Mac buys mortgages on the secondary market, pools them, and sells them as mortgage-backed securities to investors on the open market.

Federal Housing Administration, more commonly referred to by the abbreviation "FHA," is a United States government agency created as part of the National Housing Act of 1934. The mission of the FHA is to improve housing standards and conditions, to provide an adequate home financing system through insurance of mortgage loans, and to stabilize the mortgage market.

Federal National Mortgage Association, more commonly known as "Fannie Mae," is a stockholder-owned corporation chartered by the United States Congress in 1968 as a government-sponsored enterprise to purchase and securitize mortgages in order to ensure that funds are consistently available to the institutions that lend money to home buyers. Fannie Mae buys mortgages on the secondary market, pools them, and sells them as mortgage-backed securities to investors on the open market. This secondary mortgage market increases the supply of money available for mortgages lending and increases the money available for new home purchases.

FHA is an abbreviation that refers to the Federal Housing Administration, a United States government agency created as part of the National Housing Act of 1934. The mission of the FHA is to improve housing standards and conditions, to provide an adequate home financing system through insurance of mortgage loans, and to stabilize the mortgage market.

Freddie Mac refers to the Federal Home Loan Mortgage Corporation, a government-sponsored enterprise that was created in 1970 as competition for Fannie Mae and to further increase the availability of funds to finance mortgages and homeownership. Freddie Mac buys mortgages on the secondary market, pools them, and sells them as mortgage-backed securities to investors on the open market.

Freedom to Display the American Flag Act refers to a federal law that prohibits Homeowners Associations from adopting and/or enforcing Restrictive Covenants or Association Rules that would unreasonably restrict a Homeowner from displaying the American flag at his or her property.[79]

General Common Elements is a defined term under the Texas Uniform Condominium Act that refers to all portions of the Common Elements in a Condominium Development that are not designated as Limited Common Elements.[80]

Golf Amenity Property (called simply "Amenity Property" under Chapter 213 of the Texas Property Code) is a defined term under Chapter 213 of the Texas Property Code that refers to real property within a Golf Development, the use of which is restricted by a Golf Dedicatory Instrument to use as a golf course or country club.[81]

Golf Beneficiary Property is a term of art utilized in this book that refers to real property within a Golf Development that is designated by a Golf Dedicatory Instrument as a beneficiary of a Golf Restriction.[82]

Golf Dedicatory Instrument (called simply "Dedicatory Instrument" under Chapter 213 of the Texas Property Code) is a defined term under Chapter 213 of the Texas Property Code that refers to a governing instrument that: (1) restricts Golf Amenity Property to use as a golf course or country club; (2) designates real property in the Golf Development, other than the Golf Amenity Property, as a beneficiary of a Golf Restriction; and (3) addresses the establishment, maintenance, and operation of the Golf Amenity Property.[83]

---

79 *See* 4 U.S.C. § 5.

80 Tex. Prop. Code § 82.003(14). The Texas Condominium Act defines the term "General Common Elements" as the property that is part of a Condominium Regime other than property that is part of or belongs to an Apartment in the regime, including: (A) land on which the building is erected; (B) foundations, bearing walls and columns, roofs, halls, lobbies, stairways, and all entrance, exit, and communication ways; (C) basements, flat roofs, yards, and gardens, except as otherwise provided; (D) premises for the lodging of janitors or persons in charge of the building, except as otherwise provided; (E) compartments or installation of central services such as power, light, gas, water, refrigeration, central heat and air, reservoirs, water tanks and pumps, and swimming pools; and (F) elevators and elevator shafts, garbage incinerators, and all other devices and installations generally existing for common use. Tex. Prop. Code § 81.002(6).

81 Tex. Prop. Code § 213.001(1).

82 Tex. Prop. Code § 213.001(3)–(4).

83 Tex. Prop. Code § 213.001(3).

Golf Development (called simply a "Development" under Chapter 213 of the Texas Property Code) is a defined term under Chapter 213 of the Texas Property Code that refers to Golf Amenity Property and all Golf Beneficiary Property.[84]

Golf Restriction is a term of art utilized in this book that refers to a restrictive covenant within a Golf Dedicatory Instrument that restricts a Golf Amenity Property to use as a golf course or country club.[85]

Governing Authority is a defined term under the Texas Business Organizations Code that means a person or group of persons who are entitled to manage and direct the affairs of an entity under the Governing Documents of such entity or the Texas Business Organizations Code. Such term includes the Board of Directors of a Nonprofit Corporation HOA or other persons authorized to perform the functions of the Board of Directors of a Nonprofit Corporation HOA.[86]

Governing Document(s) is a commonly used term of art that refers, singularly or collectively, to each written instrument that governs the establishment, maintenance, and operation of a Subdivision Development, Condominium Development, or any other similarly planned development. Such term is synonymous with the term Dedicatory Instrument and includes: (1) a Declaration or Dedicatory Instrument subjecting real property to Restrictive Covenants; (2) Certificate of Formation or Articles of Incorporation; (3) Bylaws; (4) Association Rules; and (5) any other similar instruments governing the administration or operation of a Homeowners Association. "Governing Documents" is also a defined term under the Texas Business Organizations Code and means the Articles of Incorporation (or Certificate of Formation) for a Nonprofit Corporation HOA and all other documents or agreements adopted by the Nonprofit Corporation HOA under the Business Organizations Code to govern the formation or the internal affairs of the Nonprofit Corporation HOA, including its Bylaws.[87]

Governing Person is a defined term under the Texas Business Organizations Code that refers to a person serving as part of the Governing Authority of a business entity.[88] In the

84 Tex. Prop. Code § 213.001(4).

85 Tex. Prop. Code § 213.001. Chapter 213 defines a "restrictive covenant" as any covenant, condition, or restriction, whether mandatory, prohibitive, permissive, or administrative, contained or incorporated by reference in a properly recorded map, plat, replat, declaration, dedicatory instrument, or other instrument filed in the real property records or map or plat records. Tex. Prop. Code § 213.001(8)–(9).

86 Tex. Bus. Org. Code § 1.002(35).

87 Tex. Bus. Org. Code § 1.002(36).

88 Tex. Bus. Org. Code § 1.002(37).

context of Nonprofit Corporation HOAs managed by a Board of Directors, the term Governing Person is synonymous with a Director of the Nonprofit Corporation HOA.

Handicap is a defined term under the Federal Fair Housing Act that means, with respect to a person: (1) a physical or mental impairment that substantially limits one or more of such person's major life activities; (2) a record of having such impairment; and/or (3) being regarded as having such an impairment. The term does not include current, illegal use of, or addiction to, a controlled substance.[89] The term "Handicap" under the Federal Fair Housing Act has the same legal meaning as the term "Disability" under the Americans with Disabilities Act.[90]

Historic Neighborhood is a defined term under Chapter 208 of the Texas Property Code that refers to: (1) an area incorporated as a separate municipality before the year 1900, but which has been subsequently annexed into another municipality; (2) an area described by a municipality map or subdivision plat filed in the Official Public Records of the county in which such area is located before the year 1900; or (3) an area designated as a historic district or similar designation by the municipality in which such area is located, the Texas Historical Commission, or the National Register of Historic Places.[91]

Historic Neighborhood Preservation Association is a term of art used in this book that refers to an association of property owners in a Historic Neighborhood established by a Historic Preservation Declaration for the preservation of historic property in such Historic Neighborhood and to enforce the provisions of such Historic Preservation Declaration.[92]

Historic Preservation Declaration is a defined term under Chapter 208 of the Texas Property Code that refers to a Declaration or Dedicatory Instrument that imposes

---

89 42 U.S.C. § 3602(h).

90 42 U.S.C. § 12102. *See Bragdon v. Abbott*, 524 U.S. 624, 631 (1998) (Noting that the definition of "Disability" under the Americans with Disabilities Act is drawn almost verbatim from the definition of "Handicap" contained in the Fair Housing Amendments Act of 1988.).

91 Tex. Prop. Code § 208.001(5).

92 Tex. Prop. Code § 208.004(a). A Historic Neighborhood Preservation Association is required to: (1) be a Texas nonprofit corporation or limited liability company organized, in part, to encourage the preservation of property in a Historic Neighborhood; and (2) allow membership to all owners of property in the Historic Neighborhood. Tex. Prop. Code § 208.003(a). A Historic Neighborhood Preservation Association may be composed of only a portion of the owners of property in the Historic Neighborhood. Tex. Prop. Code § 208.003(b). A Historic Neighborhood Preservation Association may also be a Homeowners Association or an organization that is qualified as a charitable organization under Section 501(c)(3) of the Internal Revenue Code. Tex. Prop. Code § 208.003(c).

Restrictive Covenants upon certain property located in a Historic Neighborhood for the purpose of establishing a common scheme for preservation of historic property.[93]

HOA is the commonly used abbreviation for Homeowners Association.

Homeowner is a term of art utilized in this book that refers generically to an owner of a Lot or Unit in a residential Subdivision or Condominium Development.[94]

Homeowners Association is a commonly used term of art that refers to an incorporated or unincorporated association owned by, or whose members consist primarily of, the owners of the real property covered by a Declaration and through which such owners, or a Board of Directors or similar governing body, manage or regulate a residential Subdivision Development, Condominium Development, or similarly planned development. Such term is often considered synonymous with the terms "Property Owners Association," "Condominium Association," "Subdivision Association," and/or "Community Association."[95]

Homestead is a defined term under the Texas Constitution and Chapter 41 of the Texas Property Code that refers to real property owned and utilized by a Texas citizen as his or her residence, which is afforded certain protection from foreclosure by creditors under the Texas Constitution and Texas Property Code.[96]

Housing Discrimination Charge is a term of art utilized in this book that refers to a formal charge by the Texas Workforce Commission Civil Rights Division of unlawful housing discrimination made against a Respondent upon a determination by the Texas Workforce Commission Civil Rights Division that reasonable cause does exist to believe

[93] *See* Chapter 208 of the Texas Property Code.

[94] For simplicity, this book refers to all owners of residential property as "Homeowners" when no distinction is to be made between owners of Lots in a residential Subdivision Development and owners of Units in a residential Condominium Development. However, where it is necessary to distinguish between these two types of property owners, this book refers to Homeowners who own a Unit in a Condominium Development as "Unit Owners" and Homeowners who own a Lot in a Subdivision Development or similarly planned development in which all of the land has been divided into two or more parts as "Lot Owners."

[95] For simplicity, this book refers to all residential associations of property owners as "Homeowners Associations" when no distinction is to be made between Homeowners Associations overseeing residential Subdivision Developments and Condominium Developments. However, where it is necessary to distinguish between these two types of property owners associations, this book refers to Homeowners Associations overseeing residential Condominium Developments as "Condominium Associations" and Homeowners Associations overseeing residential Subdivision Developments or similarly planned developments in which all of the land has been divided into two or more parts as "Subdivision Associations."

[96] Tex. Const. art. XVI, § 50; Tex. Prop. Code § 41.002.

that a discriminatory housing practice has occurred or is about to occur based on the findings of the final investigative report of a Fair Housing Complaint.[97]

HUD is the commonly used acronym for the United States Department of Housing and Urban Development.

Identifying Number is a defined term under the Texas Uniform Condominium Act that refers to a symbol or address that separately identifies each Unit in a Condominium Development.[98]

Improvement is a term of art commonly used in Declarations and generally refers to all structures and appurtenances of every type, whether temporary or permanent, that are constructed or erected on real property. Such term is usually defined within a Declaration, but such term commonly includes buildings, outbuildings, sheds, patios, tennis courts, swimming pools, sport courts, garages, driveways, storage buildings, sidewalks, gazebos, signs, fences, gates, screening walls, retaining walls, stairs, decks, landscaping, landscape improvements, hardscape, poles, mailboxes, signs, antennae, exterior air-conditioning equipment, and/or fixtures.

Individual Assessment is a commonly used term of art that refers to an Assessment, charge, fee, or due that is assessed in a non-uniform manner by a Homeowners Association against a Lot or Unit Owner in accordance with the terms of the Homeowners Association's Declaration.

Judicial Foreclosure is a commonly used term of art that refers to the process by which the right to foreclose a lien is established by judicial proceeding and then is carried out by order of the court. In the context of Texas Homeowners Associations, such term refers to a foreclosure of a Homeowners Association's Assessment Lien conducted by a county sheriff or constable pursuant to a judgment rendered by a court of law in a Judicial Foreclosure Lawsuit that orders the Lot or Unit subject to such Assessment Lien be sold in order to satisfy the debts secured by such Assessment Lien.

Judicial Foreclosure Lawsuit is a term of art utilized in this book that refers to a lawsuit brought by a Texas Homeowners Association against a Homeowner in order to obtain a judgment that establishes the amount owed to the Homeowners Association by such Homeowner (including the specific amount owed that is secured by the Homeowners Association's Assessment Lien) and orders the Homeowners Association's Assessment

---

97 Tex. Prop. Code § 301.088(d).

98 Tex. Prop. Code § 82.003(15).

Lien be foreclosed on such Homeowner's property to satisfy the amount awarded to the Homeowners Association that is secured by its Assessment Lien.

Leasehold Condominium is a defined term under the Texas Uniform Condominium Act that refers to a Condominium Development in which all or a portion of the real property is subject to a lease, the expiration or termination of which will terminate the Condominium Development or reduce its size.[99]

Limited Common Element is a defined term under the Texas Uniform Condominium Act that refers to the portion of the Common Elements in a Condominium Development allocated by the Condominium Declaration or by operation of Section 82.052 of the Texas Uniform Condominium Act for the exclusive use of one or more, but less than all, of the Units.[100] In plain English, Limited Common Elements are those portions of a Condominium Development that are not part of an Owner's separate Unit, but which are used exclusively by one or only a few of the Unit Owners. The most illustrative example of a Limited Common Element is a balcony on the outside of an apartment-styled Condominium Development that is accessible by only a single Unit and is intended to be used by only such Unit's Owner.

Lot is a commonly used term of art that refers to a parcel of land within a Subdivision Development created by the recording of a Subdivision Plat that is owned in fee simple by its owner.

Lot Owner is a term of art utilized in this book that refers to an owner of a Lot or similarly defined parcel of land in a Subdivision Development.

Management Certificate is a defined term under the Texas Uniform Condominium Act and Chapter 209 of the Texas Property Code that refers to a written statement that identifies certain requisite information concerning a Homeowners Association and its management, which must be signed and acknowledged by an Officer of the Homeowners Association and recorded in the Official Public Records of each county in which a portion of an applicable Subdivision or Condominium Development is located.[101]

---

[99] Tex. Prop. Code § (16).

[100] Tex. Prop. Code § 82.003(17). The Texas Condominium Act defines the term "Limited Common Elements" as a portion of the Common Elements allocated by unanimous agreement of a Council of Owners for the use of one or more, but less than all, of the Apartments, such as special corridors, stairways and elevators, sanitary services common to the Apartments of a particular floor, and similar areas or facilities. Tex. Prop. Code § 81.002(7).

[101] *See* Section 82.116 of the Texas Property Code (for Condominium Associations) and Section 209.004 of the Texas Property Code (for Subdivision Associations).

Management Committee is a term of art utilized in this book that refers to a committee established by a Board of Directors of a Nonprofit Corporation HOA to exercise the authority of the Board of Directors in the management of the Nonprofit Corporation HOA.[102]

Member is a defined term under the Texas Business Organizations Code that refers to a person who has membership rights in a nonprofit corporation under its Governing Documents.[103] Such term is commonly used in a Homeowners Association's Bylaws to refer to the Homeowners who are members of such Homeowners Association.

Member-Homeowner is a term of art utilized in this book that refers to members of a Homeowners Association that is incorporated as a nonprofit corporation (which is referred to in this book as a Nonprofit Corporation HOA).

Membership is a term of art utilized in this book that refers generically, depending upon the context, to all the members of an unincorporated Nonprofit Association HOA or all Lot Owners in a Subdivision Association or all Unit Owners in a Condominium Association or all Member-Homeowners in a Nonprofit Corporation HOA.

Membership Meeting is a term of art utilized in this book that refers generically, depending upon the context, to an annual or special meeting of the Membership of an unincorporated nonprofit association, a Subdivision Association, a Condominium Association, and/or a Nonprofit Corporation HOA.

Membership Voting List is a term of art recognized under the Texas Nonprofit Corporation Law that refers to an alphabetical list of the names of Member-Homeowners entitled to vote at a meeting of a Nonprofit Corporation HOA's Membership, which is required to be prepared by a Nonprofit Corporation HOA after setting a Record Date for determination of the Nonprofit Corporation HOA's Membership and to be made available to its Member-Homeowners.[104]

Minutes is a commonly used term of art that refers to the written record of a proceeding or meeting of a deliberative assembly, such as a Board of Directors, a committee established by a Board of Directors, and/or the Membership of a Subdivision Association, a Condominium Association, and/or a Nonprofit Corporation HOA.[105]

---

102 Tex. Bus. Org. Code § 22.218(a).

103 Tex. Bus. Org. Code § 1.002(53)(b).

104 Tex. Bus. Org. Code § 22.158(a).

105 Tex. Bus. Org. Code § 3.151(a); *see also*, Tex. Prop. Code § 82.114.

Non-Judicial Foreclosure is a commonly used term of art that refers to the process by which a contractual lien is foreclosed against real property to which it is attached under the provisions of Chapter 51 of the Texas Property Code. In the context of Texas Homeowners Associations, such term refers to a foreclosure of a Homeowners Association's Assessment Lien conducted by a trustee appointed by such Homeowners Association pursuant to the terms of a power of sale granted to such Homeowners Association by its governing Declaration or Texas law.

Non-Judicial Foreclosure Application is a term of art utilized in this book that refers to a verified application (or petition) filed by a Subdivision Association in an Expedited Non-Judicial Foreclosure Proceeding governed by Texas Rule of Civil Procedure 736 for purposes of obtaining a court order authorizing it to foreclose its Assessment Lien by Non-Judicial Foreclosure procedures.[106]

Non-Management Committee is a term of art utilized in this book that refers to any committee, other than a Management Committee, established by a Board of Directors of a Nonprofit Corporation HOA.[107]

Nonprofit Association is a defined term under the Texas Uniform Unincorporated Nonprofit Association Act that refers to an unincorporated organization, other than one created by a trust, consisting of three or more members joined by mutual consent for a common, nonprofit purpose.[108] Almost all unincorporated Texas Homeowners Associations will constitute a Nonprofit Association under the Texas Uniform Unincorporated Nonprofit Association Act.

Nonprofit Association HOA is a term of art utilized in this book to refer to a Homeowners Association that is not incorporated but that constitutes a Nonprofit Association under the Texas Uniform Unincorporated Nonprofit Association Act.

Nonprofit Corporation is a defined term under the Texas Nonprofit Corporation Law that refers to a corporation, no part of the income of which is distributable to a Member, Director, or Officer of such corporation.[109]

Nonprofit Corporation HOA is a term of art utilized in this book that refers to a Homeowners Association that is incorporated as a nonprofit corporation.

---

[106] Tex. Prop. Code § 209.0092; Tex. R. Civ. P. 735, 736.

[107] Tex. Bus. Org. Code § 22.218(b).

[108] Tex. Bus. Org. Code § 252.001(2).

[109] Tex. Bus. Org. Code § 22.001(5).

Notice of Assessment Lien is a term of art utilized in this book that refers to a document filed by a Homeowners Association in the Official Public Records of the county in which it is located to validly perfect an Assessment Lien and/or to put third-parties, including any potential purchasers or title companies, on notice that there are unpaid Assessments currently outstanding for a particular Lot or Unit that are secured by an Assessment Lien on such Lot or Unit.

Officer is a defined term under the Texas Business Organizations Code and means an individual elected, appointed, or designated as an Officer of a Nonprofit Corporation HOA by its Governing Authority or under its Governing Documents.[110]

Official Public Records is a defined term under the Texas Local Government Code that refers to the collection of recorded deeds, mortgages, and other instruments that are required or permitted by law to be recorded or kept by the clerk of each county in Texas.[111]

Official Public Records of Real Property (formerly known as the Official Public Records of Deed Records) is a defined term under the Texas Local Government Code that refers to the class of Official Public Records related to real property.[112] Such records have previously been referred to under Texas law as "Property Records" or "Deed Records," and some Texas statutes still use such terms even today.

OTARD Rule is a commonly used acronym for the Over-the-Air Reception Devices Rule promulgated by the Federal Communications Commission.

Over-the-Air Reception Devices Rule refers to the rule promulgated by the Federal Communications Commission concerning governmental and nongovernmental restrictions on viewers' ability to receive video programming signals from direct broadcast satellites, broadband radio service providers, and television broadcast stations.[113]

Payment Plan Guidelines Policy is a term of art utilized in this book that refers to a written policy establishing reasonable payment plan guidelines that Texas Subdivision

---

110 Tex. Bus. Org. Code § 1.002(61).

111 Tex. Loc. Gov't Code §§ 192.001, 193.001, 193.008. The county clerk is required to certify on all recorded documents the specific location in the Official Public Records at which the instrument is recorded.

112 Tex. Loc. Gov't Code § 193.008.

113 47 C.F.R. § 1.4000.

Associations consisting of at least fifteen Lots are required to adopt and record in the local Official Public Records under Chapter 209 of the Texas Property Code.[114]

Periodic Report is a commonly used term of art that refers to the report required to be periodically filed by Texas Nonprofit Corporation HOAs with the Texas Secretary of State's office.[115]

Person with a Disability is a defined term under the Texas Community Homes for Disabled Persons Location Act that means a person whose ability to care for himself or herself, perform manual tasks, learn, work, walk, see, hear, speak, or breathe is substantially limited because the person has: (1) an orthopedic, visual, speech, or hearing impairment; (2) Alzheimer's disease; (3) pre-senile dementia; (4) cerebral palsy; (5) epilepsy; (6) muscular dystrophy; (7) multiple sclerosis; (8) cancer; (9) heart disease; (10) diabetes; (11) mental retardation; (12) autism; or (13) emotional illness.[116]

Place of Public Accommodation is a defined term under the Americans with Disabilities Act that refers to a facility, operated by a private entity, whose operations affect commerce and fall within one or more of the twelve categories of types of facilities listed under Section 12181 of the Americans with Disabilities Act.[117]

Planned Unit Development is a commonly used term of art used by lenders, financial institutions, and title companies to primarily describe developments with individually owned Lots and Common Areas owned by a Homeowners Association and other similar real estate developments other than Condominium Developments. Such term is commonly regarded as being synonymous with "Subdivision Development."

POA is a commonly used abbreviation for Property Owners Association.

President is a defined term under the Texas Business Organizations Code that refers to the individual designated as President of a Nonprofit Corporation HOA under its Governing Documents or the Officer or committee of persons authorized to perform the functions of the principal executive Officer of a Nonprofit Corporation HOA without regard to the designated name of the Officer or committee.[118]

---

[114] Tex. Prop. Code § 209.0062(a).

[115] Tex. Bus. Org. Code § 22.357.

[116] Tex. Hum. Res. Code § 123.002.

[117] 42 U.S.C. § 12181.

[118] Tex. Bus. Org. Code § 1.002(70).

Property Owners Association is a defined term under Chapter 202 of the Texas Property Code that refers to an incorporated or unincorporated association owned by, or whose members consist primarily of, the owners of the property covered by a Declaration or other Dedicatory Instrument and through which the property owners, or the Board of Directors or similar governing body, manage or regulate the Subdivision Development, Condominium Development, or other similarly planned development.[119] Such term is also a commonly used term of art that refers generically to any type of association established by a Declaration and whose membership consists exclusively of the owners of property subject to such Declaration.

Protected Antennas is a term of art utilized in this book that refers to the class or category of antennas protected under the Federal Communications Commission's Over-the-Air Reception Devices Rule from enforcement of Restrictive Covenants that would otherwise impair the installation, maintenance, or use of such antennas to receive video programming.[120]

Proxy is a commonly used term of art that refers to the delegation of one member's power to vote to another member of the same voting body upon the delegating member's absence. In plain English, the term proxy refers to a written document in which a Homeowner assigns or gives his right to cast a ballot at a Membership Meeting to another person who will attend such meeting and cast a ballot on behalf of such Homeowner.

PUD is a commonly used acronym for Planned Unit Development.

Quorum is a defined term under the Texas Business Organizations Code that refers to the number of Directors or Member-Homeowners who must be present at a meeting of a Nonprofit Corporation HOA's Board of Directors or Membership before business may be transacted at such meeting.[121] Such term is also utilized by the Texas Uniform Condominium Act to refer to the number of Directors and Unit Owners of a Condominium Association that must be present at a meeting of the Condominium Association's Board of Directors or Membership before business may be transacted at such meeting.[122]

Reasonable Accommodation is a recognized term of art under the Federal and Texas Fair Housing Acts that refers to a requested change, exception, or adjustment to a rule, policy, practice, or service that may be necessary to afford a person with a Handicap or

---

119 Tex. Prop. Code § 202.001(2).

120 47 C.F.R. § 1.4000(a).

121 *See* Tex. Bus. Org. Code §§ 22.159, 22.213(a).

122 Tex. Prop. Code § 82.109.

Disability an equal opportunity to use and enjoy a dwelling, including associated public and common use areas.[123]

Reasonable Modification is a recognized term of art under the Federal and Texas Fair Housing Acts that refers to a requested structural change to an existing dwelling that is occupied or to be occupied by an individual with a Handicap or Disability, including associated common and public use areas, that may be necessary to afford such individual full enjoyment of such premises.[124]

Record Date is a recognized term of art under the Texas Nonprofit Corporation Law that refers to a specified date in advance of a Membership Meeting in which a Nonprofit Corporation HOA determines the identity of its Member-Homeowners for purposes of providing notice of such meeting to its Member-Homeowners and compiling a Membership List of such Member-Homeowners who are entitled to vote at such meeting.[125]

Redemption Period is a term of art utilized in this book that refers to the specified time period following foreclosure of a Homeowners Association's Assessment Lien during which the owner of the real property that was foreclosed upon may redeem (or reacquire) his or her property from the entity or person that purchased it at the foreclosure sale.[126]

Regular Assessment, sometimes also called an Annual Assessment, is a commonly used term of art that refers to an Assessment, charge, fee, or due that is assessed in a uniform manner by a Homeowners Association against its Lot or Unit Owners on a regular basis (such as monthly, quarterly, or annually) in accordance with the terms of the Homeowners Association's Declaration.[127]

Resale Certificate is a defined term under both the Texas Uniform Condominium Act and Chapter 207 of the Texas Property Code that refers to a written statement containing certain information regarding a Homeowners Association produced by such Homeowners Association upon the request of a selling owner or prospective purchaser of a Lot or Unit.[128]

---

[123] 42 U.S.C. § 3604(f)(3)(B); Tex. Prop. Code § 301.025(c)(2).

[124] 42 U.S.C. § 3604(f)(3)(A); Tex. Prop. Code § 301.025(c)(1).

[125] Tex. Bus. Org. Code § 22.163.

[126] Tex. Prop. Code § 82.113; Tex. Prop. Code § 209.011.

[127] *See generally*, Tex. Prop. Code § 204.001(3).

[128] Tex. Prop. Code § 82.157; Tex. Prop. Code § 207.001(5).

Respondent is a defined term under the Texas Fair Housing Act that refers to a person accused of committing a discriminatory housing practice in violation of the Texas Fair Housing Act.[129]

Restrictive Covenant is a commonly used term of art that refers to any covenant, condition, or restriction contained in a Declaration or other Dedicatory Instrument, whether mandatory, prohibitive, permissive, or administrative, that is binding up real property and governs the ownership or use of such real property.[130] Other common terms of art that are synonymous with Restrictive Covenant include "Deed Restrictions," "Restrictions," "Covenants," and "Land-Use Restrictions."

Robert's Rules of Order is the informal short title of a book containing rules of order intended to be adopted for use by a deliberative assembly and is the most common form of parliamentary procedure used by Homeowners Associations.

Secretary is a defined term under the Texas Business Organizations Code that refers to the individual designated as Secretary of a Nonprofit Corporation HOA under its Governing Documents or the Officer or committee of persons authorized to perform the functions of Secretary of a Nonprofit Corporation HOA, without regard to the designated name of the Officer or committee.[131]

Self-Help Remedies is a term of art utilized in this book that refers to certain remedial actions that a Homeowners Association is authorized under its Declaration to unilaterally take to cure an existing violation of the Declaration by a Lot Owner or Unit Owner on their respective Lot or Unit.

Site-Condominium Development is a term of art utilized in this book that refers to a Condominium Development in which a single tract of land is divided up between Units and Common Elements, in much the same way a Subdivision Development is divided up between Lots and Common Areas. In a Site-Condominium, the defined boundaries of the separately owned Units are described in the Condominium Plat in much the same manner that the physical boundaries of separately owned Lots are described in a Subdivision Plat of a Subdivision Development, and Unit Owners are permitted to build a detached single-family home within the boundaries of their respective Units in the same way Lot Owners would build a detached single-family home within the boundaries of their respective Lots.

Special Assessment is a commonly used term of art that refers to an Assessment, other than a regular Assessment, that is levied in a uniform manner by a Homeowners

---

129 Tex. Prop. Code § 301.003(10).

130 *See generally*, Tex. Prop. Code § 202.001(4).

131 Tex. Bus. Org. Code § 1.002(79).

Association against its Lot or Unit Owners for a specific designated purpose in accordance with the terms of the Homeowners Association's Declaration.[132]

Special Declarant Rights is a defined term under the Texas Uniform Condominium Act that refers to rights reserved for the benefit of a Declarant in a Condominium Declaration to: (1) complete improvements indicated on Plats and Plans filed with the Condominium Declaration; (2) exercise any Development Right; (3) make the Condominium Development part of a larger Condominium Development or a planned community; (4) maintain sales, management, and leasing offices, signs advertising the Condominium Development, and models; (5) use easements through the Common Elements for the purpose of making Improvements within the Condominium Development or within real property that may be added to the Condominium Development; or (6) appoint or remove any Officer or Director of the Condominium Association during any period of Declarant control.[133]

Special Meeting is a commonly used term of art that refers to a meeting of a Homeowners Association's Board of Directors or Membership that is called for a specific purpose and at which only such items that were identified in the notice of such meeting may be considered and voted upon.

Statement of Authority to Transfer an Interest in Real Property is a term of art recognized under the Texas Uniform Unincorporated Nonprofit Association Act that refers to a written document recorded in the Official Public Records of a county in which real property owned by a Nonprofit Association HOA is located that establishes the authority of a specific person or persons who may execute a deed or other document conveying an ownership interest in real property owned by a Nonprofit Association HOA on its behalf.[134]

Statement of Exclusion is a term of art utilized in this book that refers to an acknowledged and recorded statement by a Lot Owner who did not sign a Chapter 201 Petition, in which such Lot Owner elects to have his or her Lot deleted and excluded from

---

132 *See generally*, Tex. Prop. Code § 204.001(4).

133 Tex. Prop. Code § 82.003(12).

134 Tex. Bus. Org. Code § 252.005. A Statement of Authority to Transfer an Interest in Real Property must contain: (1) the name of the Nonprofit Association HOA; (2) the address of the Nonprofit Association HOA; and (3) the name or title of a person authorized to transfer an estate or interest in real property held in the name of the Nonprofit Association HOA, and it must be executed in the same manner as a deed by someone other than the person who is being authorized to transfer the Nonprofit Association HOA's real property interests. Tex. Bus. Org. Code § 252.005(c)–(d).

the application of a Declaration that is extended, created, and/or modified under the procedures authorized by Chapter 201 of the Texas Property Code.[135]

Subdivision Association is a term of art utilized in this book that refers to a Homeowners Association that governs a Subdivision Development, as opposed to a Condominium Development, and whose Membership consists of Lot Owners in such Subdivision Development.

Subdivision Development is a term of art utilized in this book that refers to all land encompassed within one or more recorded maps or plats of land that is divided into two or more parts (called "Lots") and which is collectively subject to a Declaration or other Dedicatory Instrument imposing Restrictive Covenants upon all such land, excluding streets and public areas.

Subdivision Information is a term of art recognized under Chapter 207 of the Texas Property Code that refers to the documents and information that must be produced by a Subdivision Association upon request of a Lot Owner, a Lot Owner's agent, a potential purchaser of a Lot in the Subdivision Development or such purchaser's agent, or a title insurance company acting on behalf of a Lot Owner or purported purchaser, which generally consists of copies of the Subdivision Association's Governing Documents and the information contained in a Resale Certificate.[136]

Subdivision Plat is a commonly used term of art that refers to a map, drawn to scale, showing the division of a piece of land into blocks, which are often further divided into individual Lots, usually for the purpose of selling the described Lots.

Texas Charitable Immunity and Liability Act of 1987 refers to the Texas law that provides limited immunity from civil liability for volunteers of a Charitable Organization, including its Directors and Officers.[137]

Texas Community Homes for Disabled Persons Location Act refers to the Texas law that prohibits the enforcement of a Restrictive Covenant that would prohibit use of a Lot or Unit as a Community Home.[138]

---

135 Tex. Prop. Code § 201.009(b)(4).

136 Tex. Prop. Code § 207.003.

137 *See* Chapter 84 of the Texas Civil Practice and Remedies Code.

138 *See* Chapter 123 of the Texas Human Resources Code.

Texas Condominium Act refers to the Texas law that governs Condominium Developments established prior to January 1, 1994.[139]

Texas Fair Housing Act refers to the Texas law that makes it unlawful to discriminate against any person in the terms, conditions, or privileges in the provision of housing services or facilities on the basis of race, color, religion, national origin, sex, Familial Status, or Disability.[140] The Texas Fair Housing Act has been certified by the United States Department of Housing and Urban Development as being substantially equivalent to the Federal Fair Housing Act.

Texas Non-Profit Corporation Act refers to the Texas law that governed Texas nonprofit corporations incorporated prior to January 1, 2006, which expired on December 31, 2009.[141]

Texas Nonprofit Corporation Law refers to the Texas law that, as of January 1, 2010, governs all Texas Nonprofit Corporations, including Nonprofit Corporation HOAs, regardless of when they were incorporated.[142]

Texas Open Meetings Act refers to the Texas law that requires governmental bodies to call and conduct its meetings in an open and public manner.[143] The Texas Open Meetings Act was amended in 2007 to make it applicable to the governmental body of certain Texas Homeowners Associations in Brazoria, Chambers, Fort Bend, Harris, Liberty, Montgomery, San Jacinto, and Waller Counties.[144]

Texas Open Records Act is the commonly used name for the Texas Public Information Act and refers to the Texas law that requires governmental bodies to preserve records of public information and to make such records available for public inspection and copying.[145] The Texas Open Records Act was also amended in 2007 to make it applicable to the governmental body of certain Texas Homeowners Associations in Brazoria, Chambers, Fort Bend, Harris, Liberty, Montgomery, San Jacinto, and Waller Counties.[146]

---

[139] *See* Chapter 81 of the Texas Property Code.

[140] *See* Chapter 301 of the Texas Property Code.

[141] *See* Article 1396 of the Texas Revised Civil Statutes.

[142] *See* Chapter 22 of the Texas Business Organizations Code.

[143] *See* Chapter 551 of the Texas Government Code.

[144] Tex. Gov't Code § 551.0015(a)(1).

[145] *See* Chapter 552 of the Texas Government Code.

[146] Tex. Gov't Code § 552.0036(2)(A).

Texas Residential Property Owners Protection Act, also commonly referred to as Chapter 209 of the Texas Property Code or simply "Chapter 209," refers to the Texas law that imposes certain due process requirements on a Subdivision Association before it may suspend a Lot Owner's right to use a Common Area, initiate judicial proceedings to enforce Restrictive Covenants against a Lot Owner, charge a Lot Owner for property damage, assess a fine against a Lot Owner for violation of a Restrictive Covenant, or charge a Lot Owner for attorneys fees incurred by the Subdivision Association, as well as imposes certain requisite procedures on a Subdivision Association prior to and following foreclosure of an Assessment Lien.[147]

Texas Uniform Condominium Act refers to the Texas law that governs Condominium Developments established on or after January 1, 1994, as well as Condominium Developments created prior to January 1, 1994, whose Condominium Declaration states that Chapter 82 of the Texas Property Code shall apply to the Condominium Development.[148]

Texas Uniform Unincorporated Nonprofit Association Act refers to the Texas law that governs unincorporated Nonprofit Associations, including Nonprofit Association HOAs.[149]

Texas Workforce Commission Civil Rights Division is a division of the Texas Workforce Commission and is the governmental agency charged with enforcement of the Texas Fair Housing Act.[150]

Townhouse, also sometimes referred to as a Townhome, is a commonly used term of art that generally refers to row houses or dwellings that are attached side by side.[151]

Treasurer is a defined term under the Texas Business Organizations Code that refers to the individual designated as Treasurer of a Nonprofit Corporation HOA under its Governing Documents, or the Officer or committee of persons authorized to perform the

---

147 *See* Chapter 209 of the Texas Property Code.

148 *See* Chapter 82 of the Texas Property Code.

149 Tex. Bus. Org. Code §§ 1.008(k), 252.001, *et seq.*

150 Tex. Prop. Code § 301.0015.

151 It is important to note that a Townhouse is not a recognized form of real estate ownership under Texas law, and regardless of a Common-Interest Development's description of itself as a "Townhouse Development" or similar moniker, a Common-Interest Development in Texas must be either a Condominium Development or a Subdivision Development. While most Common-Interest Developments in Texas that consist of constructed row houses or attached dwellings constitute Condominium Developments, such type of a Common-Interest Development may be either a Subdivision or Condominium Development.

functions of Treasurer of a Nonprofit Corporation HOA, without regard to the designated name of the Officer or committee.[152]

Unit is a defined term under the Texas Uniform Condominium Act that refers to a physical portion of the Condominium Development designated for separate ownership or occupancy, the boundaries of which are described by the Condominium Declaration.[153]

Unit Owner is a defined term under the Texas Uniform Condominium Act that refers to a Declarant or other person who owns a Unit, but it does not include a person having an interest in a Unit solely as security for an obligation, such as a mortgagee.[154]

VA is a commonly used abbreviation that refers to the Veterans Administration (now known as the "United States Department of Veterans Affairs"), a government-run military veteran benefits system that is responsible for administering benefits programs for veterans and their families, including home loan programs.

Variance is a commonly used term of art that refers to permission granted to a Homeowner by an Architectural Committee to construct or modify an Improvement on the Homeowner's Lot or Unit in a manner that would otherwise be in violation of a Restrictive Covenant applicable to such Lot or Unit.

Veterans Administration, now known as the "United States Department of Veterans Affairs," but more commonly referred to by the abbreviation "VA," is a government-run military veteran benefits system that is responsible for administering benefits programs for veterans and their families, including home loan programs.

Vice President is a defined term under the Texas Business Organizations Code that refers to the individual designated as Vice President of a Nonprofit Corporation HOA under its Governing Documents or the Officer or committee of persons authorized to perform the functions of the President of the entity on the death, absence, or resignation of the President or on the inability of the President to perform the functions of office, without regard to the designated name of the Officer or committee.[155]

Waiver is a commonly used term of art that refers to an affirmative defense to judicial enforcement of a Restrictive Covenant on the basis that the enforcement of a Restrictive Covenant has been intentionally relinquished by the prior non-enforcement of such a

---

[152] Tex. Bus. Org. Code § 1.002(86).

[153] Tex. Prop. Code § 82.003(23).

[154] Tex. Prop. Code § 82.003(24).

[155] Tex. Bus. Org. Code § 1.002(88).

significant number of similar violations of the same Restrictive Covenant that a reasonable person would conclude that the Restrictive Covenant has been abandoned.[156]

156 *See Jim Rutherford Invs., Inc. v. Terramar Beach Cmty. Ass'n*, 25 S.W.3d 845, 847, 851 (Tex. App.—Houston [14th Dist.] 2000, pet. denied); *Dempsey v. Apache Shores Prop. Owners Ass'n*, 737 S.W.2d 589, 595 (Tex. App.—Austin 1987, no writ); *Zent v. Murrow*, 476 S.W.2d 875, 880 (Tex. Civ. App.—Austin 1972, no writ).

Appendix B: Index of Authorities

Constitutional Authority

Statutory Authority

Case Law Authority

Other Authority

Appendix C: Sample Board Meeting Notice (for use by Subdivision Associations)

TEJAS ESTATES HOMEOWNERS ASSOCIATION, INC.

NOTICE OF BOARD OF DIRECTORS MEETING

August 1, 2015

Please be advised that the Board of Directors (the "Board") for Tejas Estates Homeowners Association, Inc. (the "Association") intends to conduct a regular Board Meeting at 7:00 p.m. on September 5, 2015, at the Tejas Estates Clubhouse, located at 1825 Old Three Hundred Way, Austin, Texas 78701.

At the September 5, 2015, Board Meeting, the Board may discuss and/or take formal action concerning the following matters:

APPROVAL OF MINUTES

(1) Approval of Minutes from the August 3, 2015, regular Board Meeting.

OLD BUSINESS

(1) Discuss and potentially take action concerning pending restrictive covenant violations in the community.

(2) Discuss and potentially take action concerning existing past-due homeowner assessment accounts.

(3) Review and approval of the revised agreement for landscaping near the front entry of the community on Old Three Hundred Way.

NEW BUSINESS

(1) Review of insurance policy quotes and selection of new insurance carrier for directors and officers liability policy.

EXECUTIVE SESSION

DRAFTER'S DICTUM – This document is a sample form for illustrative purposes and may or may not conform to the specific requirements of a particular Homeowners Association's Governing Documents. In addition, changes in statutory and case law may modify or nullify provisions of this document or its enforcement or may create rights or duties not anticipated by this document. Users of this sample form document are advised to periodically review applicable statutes and court rulings to ensure its compliance with all applicable laws.

All meetings of the Association's Board of Directors are open to members of the Association subject to the right of the Board to adjourn the Board Meeting and reconvene in closed executive session to consider actions involving: (1) personnel; (2) pending or threatened litigation; (3) contract negotiations; (4) enforcement actions; (5) confidential communications with the Association's attorney; (6) matters involving the invasion of privacy of individual owners; and/or (7) matters that are to remain confidential by request of the affected parties and agreement of the Board. Please be advised that the Board of Directors intends to meet in executive session during the Board Meeting to discuss and/or consider actions regarding the following matter(s):

(1) Discussion of pending lawsuit against Antonio Santa Anna with the Association's attorney.

Sincerely,

The Board of Directors

DRAFTER'S DICTUM – This document is a sample form for illustrative purposes and may or may not conform to the specific requirements of a particular Homeowners Association's Governing Documents. In addition, changes in statutory and case law may modify or nullify provisions of this document or its enforcement or may create rights or duties not anticipated by this document. Users of this sample form document are advised to periodically review applicable statutes and court rulings to ensure its compliance with all applicable laws.

Appendix D: Sample Form of Board Meeting Minutes

TEJAS ESTATES HOMEOWNERS ASSOCIATION, INC.

BOARD OF DIRECTORS MEETING MINUTES – SEPTEMBER 5, 2015

The following meeting minutes reflect the actions taken by the Board of Directors (the "Board") of Tejas Estates Homeowners Association, Inc. (the "Association") at the regular meeting of the Board conducted on September 5, 2015, at Northwest Library, 333 Main Street, Austin, Texas 78735 (the "Board Meeting").

I. Meeting Called to Order 7:00 p.m.

Attending: S. Austin (President), J. Bowie, S. Houston (Vice President), W. Travis (Treasurer)

Absent: D. Crockett (Secretary)

II. Approval of Minutes

A. Minutes from the August 3, 2015, regular board meeting – approved as read by consent of the Board.

B. Minutes from the September 1, 2015, special board meeting – motion to approve minutes as corrected.

By: Samuel Houston
2nd: William Travis

Result: Approved (3 votes for – 1 vote against)

III. Prior Action(s) Taken by Unanimous Written Consent

A. Action taken on August 12, 2015 – See attached written consent.

B. Action taken on August 14, 2015 – The Board of Directors approved December 1, 2015, as the date for the next annual membership meeting.

IV. Committee Reports

A. Architectural Committee: none

DRAFTER'S DICTUM – This document is a sample form for illustrative purposes and may or may not conform to the specific requirements of a particular Homeowners Association's Governing Documents. In addition, changes in statutory and case law may modify or nullify provisions of this document or its enforcement or may create rights or duties not anticipated by this document. Users of this sample form document are advised to periodically review applicable statutes and court rulings to ensure its compliance with all applicable laws.

B. Financial Committee:

W. Travis provided Board of Directors with an updated Financial Statement and Budget.

V. Old Business

A. Motion to turn over restrictive covenant violations by Antonio Santa Anna (3016 Alamo Street) to the law firm of Savrick, Schumann, Johnson, McGarr, Kaminski & Shirley, L.L.P. for further enforcement action.

By: W. Travis
2nd: S. Houston

Result: Approved (Unanimous)

B. Motion to file a Notice of Assessment Lien on property owned by Antonio Santa Anna (3016 Alamo Street).

By: W. Travis
2nd: S. Houston

Result: Approved (Unanimous)

VI. New Business

A. Motion to approve selection of directors and officers liability insurance policy from Lone Star Insurance Company.

By: W. Travis
2nd: S. Houston

Result: Tabled until next meeting

VII. Executive Session

The Board made the following decision(s) while meeting in executive session during the Board Meeting:

A. The Board agreed to hire expert witnesses in the lawsuit against Antonio Santa Anna and to pay such expert witnesses a fee of $1,000.

B. The Board agreed to settle the lawsuit against Anastasio Bustamante for payment of $9,500 to the Association.

DRAFTER'S DICTUM – This document is a sample form for illustrative purposes and may or may not conform to the specific requirements of a particular Homeowners Association's Governing Documents. In addition, changes in statutory and case law may modify or nullify provisions of this document or its enforcement or may create rights or duties not anticipated by this document. Users of this sample form document are advised to periodically review applicable statutes and court rulings to ensure its compliance with all applicable laws.

VIII. Additional Items or Information

Jim Bowie volunteered to serve on the nomination committee for the annual Director elections at the annual membership meeting.

IX. Adjourned at 9:15 p.m.

Approved by the Board of Directors: ☐ as prepared or ☐ as corrected.

______________________________ ______________

Officer or other duly authorized representative of Tejas Estates Homeowners Association, Inc. **Date**

DRAFTER'S DICTUM – This document is a sample form for illustrative purposes and may or may not conform to the specific requirements of a particular Homeowners Association's Governing Documents. In addition, changes in statutory and case law may modify or nullify provisions of this document or its enforcement or may create rights or duties not anticipated by this document. Users of this sample form document are advised to periodically review applicable statutes and court rulings to ensure its compliance with all applicable laws.

Appendix E: Sample Annual Membership Meeting Notice

TEJAS ESTATES CONDOMINIUM COMMUNITY, INC.

NOTICE OF ANNUAL MEETING OF MEMBERS

TO BE HELD ON SEPTEMBER 5, 2015

It is our pleasure to give you notice of and invite you to attend the Annual Meeting of the members of Tejas Estates Condominium Community, Inc. (the "Association"), which will be held at 6:00 p.m. on the fifth day of September 2015, at the Tejas Estates Clubhouse, located at 1725 Republic of Texas Parkway, Austin, Texas 78701. This notice is being provided in accordance with Section 4.4 of the Bylaws of the Association.

A proposed agenda and proxy form for the Annual Meeting of Members are enclosed for your consideration and review. The Board of Directors has included such proxy form with this notice in the event you are unable to attend the Annual Meeting and would like to designate an individual to attend the meeting in your place and vote on your behalf. If you choose to use the proxy form included with this notice, a blank line is provided in the proxy form where you may designate the proxy-holder of your choice. In the event you fail to designate a proxy-holder, yet deliver the executed proxy form to the Association prior to the meeting, the President of the Association will be your designated proxy-holder. **To be effective, the proxy form must be signed and dated.**

A signed proxy form can be either mailed, hand-delivered, or faxed to the Association at the address below or presented to the Association's Secretary, Dave Crockett, at the Annual Meeting, but prior to the time the meeting is called to order. If you elect to mail or fax your signed proxy form to the Association, the proxy form must be received by 5:00 p.m. Central Time at least three (3) days prior to the Annual Meeting to be effective. If you elect to have your signed proxy form presented to the Secretary, such proxy form must be received prior to the time the meeting is called to order to be effective. Please note that if you elect to send your signed proxy form to the Association, it is advisable that you sign two proxy forms and provide one of them to your designated proxy-holder. This will enable your designated proxy-holder to present the signed proxy form to the Secretary at the Annual Meeting in the event the signed proxy form mailed to the Association was not received on a timely basis.

A COMPLETED PROXY FORM THAT IS TO BE RETURNED BY EITHER FAX OR MAIL SHOULD BE SENT TO:

DRAFTER'S DICTUM – This document is a sample form for illustrative purposes and may or may not conform to the specific requirements of a particular Homeowners Association's Governing Documents. In addition, changes in statutory and case law may modify or nullify provisions of this document or its enforcement or may create rights or duties not anticipated by this document. Users of this sample form document are advised to periodically review applicable statutes and court rulings to ensure its compliance with all applicable laws.

Tejas Estates Condominium Community, Inc.
1725 Republic of Texas Parkway
Austin, Texas 78701
Facsimile: (512) 555-1234

(We have included a return envelope for your convenience.)

If you elect to mail or fax the completed proxy form, it must be received by 5:00 p.m. Central Time at least three (3) days prior to the Annual Meeting.

Either of the following conditions will result in a voided proxy form:

(1) if the proxy form is not signed

(2) if the proxy form is not dated

We look forward to your presence and input at the Annual Meeting of the Association and thank you for your continuing interest in the Association.

Sincerely,

The Board of Directors

DRAFTER'S DICTUM – This document is a sample form for illustrative purposes and may or may not conform to the specific requirements of a particular Homeowners Association's Governing Documents. In addition, changes in statutory and case law may modify or nullify provisions of this document or its enforcement or may create rights or duties not anticipated by this document. Users of this sample form document are advised to periodically review applicable statutes and court rulings to ensure its compliance with all applicable laws.

Appendix F: Sample Candidacy-Solicitation Notice (for use by Subdivision Associations consisting of more than 100 Lots)

TEJAS ESTATES HOMEOWNERS ASSOCIATION, INC.

SOLICITATION OF INTERESTED CANDIDATES FOR ELECTION TO THE BOARD OF DIRECTORS

The 2015 annual meeting of the members of Tejas Estates Homeowners Association, Inc. (the "Association") is scheduled to be held on September 5, 2015, at the Tejas Estates Clubhouse, located at 1725 Republic of Texas Parkway, Austin, Texas 78701. At such meeting, the Association will conduct an election to fill three (3) positions on the Association's Board of Directors (the "Board").

The Association's Board is vested with the authority to manage the Association on behalf of all of its members and consists of nine (9) Directors who are elected to serve three (3) year terms of office. Such terms of office are staggered so that three positions on the Board are filled by election of members at each annual meeting.

The Association is seeking candidates who are interested in being considered for election to the Board. Serving on the Board is a great way to contribute to our community and get to know your neighbors. If you are interested in serving on the Board and would like to have your name placed on the ballot for the upcoming director election, please notify the Association of the same by sending an email to the Association's Secretary, Jim Bowie, at secretary@tejasestateshoa.com. To be effective, the email must include your name, property address, and be received by the Association no later than 5:00 p.m. on August 1, 2015.

In addition, the Association would like to include a brief bio of each of the candidates in the notice of the annual meeting provided to the Association's members. You are not required to submit a bio to have your name placed on the ballot, but if you would like to have your bio included in the meeting notice, please attach your bio in Word format to the email you send to the Association's Secretary. The bio should be no more than 200 words and should include information about you (such as how long you have lived in the community, prior leadership roles in the Association or other organizations); why you're interested in serving on the Board; and any education, training, or experience that you believe makes you a good candidate.

DRAFTER'S DICTUM – This document is a sample form for illustrative purposes and may or may not conform to the specific requirements of a particular Homeowners Association's Governing Documents. In addition, changes in statutory and case law may modify or nullify provisions of this document or its enforcement or may create rights or duties not anticipated by this document. Users of this sample form document are advised to periodically review applicable statutes and court rulings to ensure its compliance with all applicable laws.

If you have any questions about service on the Board in general, the upcoming director election, or your bio, please contact the Association's property manager, Stephen Austin, at (512) 555-5555.

Thank you for your continuing interest in the Association.

Sincerely,

The Board of Directors

DRAFTER'S DICTUM – This document is a sample form for illustrative purposes and may or may not conform to the specific requirements of a particular Homeowners Association's Governing Documents. In addition, changes in statutory and case law may modify or nullify provisions of this document or its enforcement or may create rights or duties not anticipated by this document. Users of this sample form document are advised to periodically review applicable statutes and court rulings to ensure its compliance with all applicable laws.

Appendix G: Sample Special Membership Meeting Notice

TEJAS ESTATES HOMEOWNERS ASSOCIATION, INC.

NOTICE OF SPECIAL MEETING OF MEMBERS

TO BE HELD SEPTEMBER 5, 2015

A special meeting of the Members of Tejas Estates Homeowners Association, Inc. (the "Association") will be held on September 5, 2015, at the Tejas Estates Clubhouse, located at 1725 Republic of Texas Parkway, Austin, Texas 78701 (the "Special Membership Meeting"). The Special Membership Meeting is scheduled to begin at 6:00 p.m. Please arrive at the meeting at least fifteen (15) minutes early, so that your attendance can be registered before the meeting commences.

The purpose of the Special Membership Meeting is to discuss and/or vote on the following matters:

(1) Motion to approve special assessment of $1,000.00 per lot.

(2) Motion to amend the Bylaws to increase the number of director positions on the Board of Directors.

(3) Election to fill 2 positions on the Board of Directors.

The Board of Directors has enclosed a proxy form with this notice in the event you are unable to attend the Special Membership Meeting and would like to designate an individual to attend such meeting in your place and vote on your behalf. If you choose to use the proxy form enclosed with this notice, a blank line is provided in the proxy form where you may designate the proxy-holder of your choice. **To be effective, the proxy form must be signed and dated, and either returned to the Association at the address provided below by 5:00 p.m. on the last business day immediately preceding the date of the Special Membership Meeting or presented at the Special Membership Meeting prior to such meeting being called to order.**

The Board of Directors has also enclosed an absentee ballot with this notice in the event you are unable to attend the Special Membership Meeting, but would still like to cast a ballot on the matters to be voted on at such meeting. Please be advised, if you cast your vote via absentee ballot instead of attending the Special Membership Meeting, you will forgo the opportunity to consider and vote on any action from the floor concerning the matters to be voted on at the Special Membership Meeting. This means that if there are individuals nominated for election or amendments made to any pending ballot items from the floor, you will not be able to vote for such nominees and/or your ballot will not be counted on the final vote on any such amended ballot items. **To be effective, the absentee ballot must be signed and dated, and returned to the Association at the address provided below by 5:00 p.m. on the last business day immediately preceding the date of the Special Membership Meeting.**

In addition, the Board of Directors has approved the use of electronic ballots for the Special Membership Meeting. Instructions for casting an electronic ballot will be posted at www.TejasEstatesHOA.com.

Please return executed proxy forms and/or absentee ballots to the Association in advance of the special Membership Meeting at the following address:

1725 Republic of Texas Parkway
Austin, Texas 78701

Finally, the Association's attorney will be present at the meeting to update the Members as to the lawsuit against Antonio De Santa Anna.

We look forward to your presence and input at the special meeting of the Association's Membership.

Sincerely,

The Board of Directors

DRAFTER'S DICTUM – This document is a sample form for illustrative purposes and may or may not conform to the specific requirements of a particular Homeowners Association's Governing Documents. In addition, changes in statutory and case law may modify or nullify provisions of this document or its enforcement or may create rights or duties not anticipated by this document. Users of this sample form document are advised to periodically review applicable statutes and court rulings to ensure its compliance with all applicable laws.

Appendix H: Sample Absentee Ballot Form (for use by Subdivision Associations)

TEJAS ESTATES HOMEOWNERS ASSOCIATION, INC.

ABSENTEE BALLOT

ANNUAL MEMBERSHIP MEETING – SEPTEMBER 5, 2015

The undersigned member of the Tejas Estates Homeowners Association, Inc. (the "Association"), being entitled to vote at the Association's Annual Membership Meeting on September 5, 2015, hereby casts my vote(s) as set forth below. No vote shall be cast for any issue(s) not marked below.

NOTICE REQUIRED BY SECTION 209.00592 OF THE TEXAS PROPERTY CODE

By casting your vote via absentee ballot, you will forgo the opportunity to consider and vote on any action from the floor on these proposals, if a meeting is held. This means that if there are amendments to these proposals, your votes will not be counted on the final vote on these measures. If you desire to retain this ability, please attend any meeting in person. You may submit an absentee ballot and later choose to attend any meeting in person, in which case any in-person vote will prevail.

ELECTION OF DIRECTORS

The following individuals have been nominated for election to the Board of Directors. Please cast your vote for up to 3 candidates by marking an "X" next to the name of the appropriate number of candidates. If you cast more than the permitted number of votes for candidates, your ballot will be invalid.

__________ Samuel Houston
__________ David Crockett
__________ Mirabeau Lamar
__________ Susanna Dickinson
__________ William Travis

DRAFTER'S DICTUM – This document is a sample form for illustrative purposes and may or may not conform to the specific requirements of a particular Homeowners Association's Governing Documents. In addition, changes in statutory and case law may modify or nullify provisions of this document or its enforcement or may create rights or duties not anticipated by this document. Users of this sample form document are advised to periodically review applicable statutes and court rulings to ensure its compliance with all applicable laws.

BALLOT ISSUE 1

Motion to approve special assessment of $1,000.00 per lot. (mark only one):

________ I vote for this item.
________ I vote against this item.

***FOR THIS ABSENTEE BALLOT TO BE EFFECTIVE, YOU MUST SIGN BELOW AND, PRIOR TO THE CALL OF THE MEETING, RETURN YOUR COMPLETED, SIGNED ABSENTEE BALLOT TO THE ASSOCIATION AT:

Tejas Estates Homeowners Association, Inc.
1836 San Jacinto Boulevard
Austin, Texas 78701

Please identify the property address, print the name(s) of the owner(s), and sign and date the absentee ballot.

Owner's Property Address: ________________________________

Owner's Printed Name: ________________________________

Date: ________________

Owner's Signature: ________________________________

Proxy-Holder's signature:* ________________________________

* If this absentee ballot is being cast by a proxy-holder on behalf of the Owner(s), please identify the name(s) of the Owner(s) and their property address, sign the ballot on the Proxy-Holder's signature line, and enclose or attach a copy of the proxy signed by the Owner(s). IF THIS ABSENTEE BALLOT IS CAST BY A PROXY-HOLDER ON BEHALF OF THE OWNER(S), THE PROXY SIGNED BY THE OWNER(S) THAT DESIGNATES THE PROXY-HOLDER MUST BE ATTACHED TO OR ENCLOSED WITH THIS ABSENTEE BALLOT FOR THIS ABSENTEE BALLOT TO BE COUNTED.

DRAFTER'S DICTUM – This document is a sample form for illustrative purposes and may or may not conform to the specific requirements of a particular Homeowners Association's Governing Documents. In addition, changes in statutory and case law may modify or nullify provisions of this document or its enforcement or may create rights or duties not anticipated by this document. Users of this sample form document are advised to periodically review applicable statutes and court rulings to ensure its compliance with all applicable laws.

Appendix I: Sample Proxy Form for a Membership Meeting

<u>TEJAS ESTATES HOMEOWNERS ASSOCIATION, INC.</u>

MEMBERSHIP PROXY

By this Proxy, the undersigned owner of the hereinafter identified lot (the "Property"), being a member of Tejas Estates Homeowners Association, Inc. (the "Association"), on behalf of such owner and all other owners of the Property (collectively, the "Owner") hereby appoints ____________________________ as Owner's true and lawful proxy with full powers of substitution for purposes of establishing a quorum and to represent and cast votes on behalf of Owner at the annual/special meeting of the Association's members to be held on September 5, 2015, (the "Membership Meeting"), or any adjournment thereof, for any and all business as may properly come before the members at such Membership Meeting. **If no name is placed in the above blank, Owner's proxy shall be considered given and assigned to whomever is President of the Association at the commencement of the Membership Meeting.**

The proxy-holder designated above ☐ may or ☐ may not (check one) assign this proxy to another person if the proxy holder cannot, for some unexpected reason, attend the Membership Meeting. If no box is checked, by default the proxy-holder shall be allowed to assign this proxy to another person.

This proxy revokes all proxies previously granted by the owner(s) of the Property. This proxy shall be considered automatically terminated and withdrawn if an owner of the Property: (1) signs and delivers to the Association a written notice of revocation of this proxy prior to the Membership Meeting being called to order; (2) actually attends the Membership Meeting; or (3) signs and delivers to the Association a written proxy appointing someone else, dated later than this proxy. **<u>To be valid, a completed proxy or subsequent proxy revocation must be either delivered to the Association at the mailing address provided below by 5:00 p.m. on the last business day immediately preceding the date of the Membership Meeting or presented at the Membership Meeting prior to such meeting being called to order</u>**. If you are mailing the proxy or a subsequent proxy revocation, please deposit it in the mail at least seven (7) days prior to the Membership Meeting to ensure timely receipt by the Association. A completed proxy or proxy revocation may be delivered to the Association in advance of the Membership Meeting at the following mailing address:

Tejas Estates Homeowners Association, Inc.
c/o Lone Star Property Management

DRAFTER'S DICTUM – This document is a sample form for illustrative purposes and may or may not conform to the specific requirements of a particular Homeowners Association's Governing Documents. In addition, changes in statutory and case law may modify or nullify provisions of this document or its enforcement or may create rights or duties not anticipated by this document. Users of this sample form document are advised to periodically review applicable statutes and court rulings to ensure its compliance with all applicable laws.

1725 Republic of Texas Parkway
Austin, Texas 78701

THIS PROXY IS ONLY VALID FOR BUSINESS THAT WILL BE CONDUCTED AT THE MEETING OF THE ASSOCIATION'S MEMBERSHIP TO BE HELD ON SEPTEMBER 5, 2015, AND FOR ANY ADJOURNMENT THEREOF IN ACCORDANCE WITH THE BYLAWS OF THE ASSOCIATION.

Date: ______________________

Owner's Property Address: ____

Owner's Printed Name: ____

Owner's Signature: ____

DRAFTER'S DICTUM – This document is a sample form for illustrative purposes and may or may not conform to the specific requirements of a particular Homeowners Association's Governing Documents. In addition, changes in statutory and case law may modify or nullify provisions of this document or its enforcement or may create rights or duties not anticipated by this document. Users of this sample form document are advised to periodically review applicable statutes and court rulings to ensure its compliance with all applicable laws.

Appendix J: Sample Minutes from an Annual Membership Meeting

TEJAS ESTATES HOMEOWNERS ASSOCIATION, INC.

2015 ANNUAL MEMBERSHIP MEETING MINUTES

The following membership meeting minutes reflect the actions taken by the members (the "Members") of Tejas Estates Homeowners Association, Inc. (the "Association") at the annual meeting of its Members conducted on September 5, 2015 (the "Membership Meeting").

Location: Tejas Estates Clubhouse, 1836 San Jacinto Drive, Austin, Texas 78701

I. **Meeting Called to Order at 7:12 p.m.**

II. **Quorum Established** – A quorum was established by the presence of Members in person or by proxy.

III. **Approval of Minutes** – The following minutes from previous membership meetings were approved by Members at the Membership Meeting:

A. Minutes from the August 3, 2015, annual membership meeting – approved, as read, by consent of the membership.

IV. **Election** – The following election was conducted at the Membership Meeting:

A. Election to fill 2 positions on the Board of Directors.

All absentee and electronic ballots received by the Association prior to the Membership Meeting and all written ballots cast by Members at the Membership Meeting in person or by proxy were tabulated. The results of the election are as follows:

Candidate:	Votes Received:
Samuel Houston	276
David Crockett	198
Mirabeau Lamar	140
Susanna Dickinson	125

DRAFTER'S DICTUM – This document is a sample form for illustrative purposes and may or may not conform to the specific requirements of a particular Homeowners Association's Governing Documents. In addition, changes in statutory and case law may modify or nullify provisions of this document or its enforcement or may create rights or duties not anticipated by this document. Users of this sample form document are advised to periodically review applicable statutes and court rulings to ensure its compliance with all applicable laws.

Based on such results, the following persons were elected to the Board of Directors:

Samuel Houston

David Crockett

V. **Ballot Item** – The following ballot item was voted on at the Membership Meeting:

A. Ballot Item: Approval of Amendment to Section 2.1 of the Bylaws.

All absentee and electronic ballots received by the Association prior to the Membership Meeting and all written ballots cast by Members at the Membership Meeting in person or by proxy were tabulated. The results of the vote on the Ballot Item are as follows:

Ballot Item:	Votes Received:
For	276
Against	198

Based on such results, the Ballot Item passed.

VI. **Additional Items or Information:**

The treasurer announced that the coupon books for assessment payments would be mailed to all owners by February 1, 2016.

VII. **Meeting Adjourned at 8:05 p.m.**

Approved by the Membership:☐ as prepared or☐ as corrected.

______________________________ ______________

Officer or other duly authorized representative of Tejas Estates Homeowners Association, Inc. **Date**

DRAFTER'S DICTUM – This document is a sample form for illustrative purposes and may or may not conform to the specific requirements of a particular Homeowners Association's Governing Documents. In addition, changes in statutory and case law may modify or nullify provisions of this document or its enforcement or may create rights or duties not anticipated by this document. Users of this sample form document are advised to periodically review applicable statutes and court rulings to ensure its compliance with all applicable laws.

Appendix K: Brief Summary of *Robert's Rules of Order* (for use at a regular or special Membership Meeting)

I. Introduction

1. Call the meeting to order.
2. Establish ground rules:
   a. Inform members of the Homeowners Association that the meeting will be conducted in accordance with Robert's Rules of Order with two slight modifications because of time limitations.

   b. During debate of any pending motion, each member will be allowed to speak one time for no more than three minutes. (Under Robert's Rules of Order, each member of the assembly is generally afforded two opportunities to speak on each pending motion for up to ten minutes each time.)

   c. Let the members know a timer will be kept by the Homeowners Association's Secretary and ask that each person please quickly conclude after the timer goes off.
3. If the meeting is a Special Meeting and was called as a result of a petition by members of the Homeowners Association, then:
   a. Read the petition requesting the Special Meeting.

   b. Read the applicable Bylaw or Texas Nonprofit Corporation Law provision that required the Homeowners Association to call a Special Meeting of the Homeowners Association's Membership, if directed to do so by the petition requesting the Special Meeting.
4. If the meeting is a Special Meeting, then:
   a. Read the Notice of Special Meeting and remind the members that no business, except business related to the purpose stated in the notice of the meeting, shall be transacted at the Special Meeting.

b. Provide a brief summary of any background information regarding the purpose of the Special Meeting, if necessary or warranted.

II. Taking Action on Each Purpose Stated in the Notice of Meeting or Meeting Agenda (this should be repeated for each applicable purpose or topic)

1. State the purpose or topic stated in the notice of meeting or meeting agenda.

2. Open the floor for any motions.

3. If a member or members request that he or she be given the floor, the presiding officer must designate who to give the floor to.

4. Once a member has the floor, they may make a motion.

5. If a motion is made, it must be seconded by another member.

6. Once a motion is made and seconded, the presiding officer must "state" the question. In other words, the presiding officer should restate the exact words of the motion that the membership is to consider and vote on.

7. The Secretary should write down the exact words of the motion and record them in the minutes, along with the identity of the member who made the motion and the member who seconded it.

8. After the presiding officer has stated the question, it may be opened to debate among the assembly.

9. The maker of the motion is generally afforded the preference of speaking first.

10. After the maker of the motion has spoken, the presiding officer may designate the next member who shall be afforded the floor for debate. The presiding officer should continue to afford the floor to each member who requests it until all members have had an opportunity to speak regarding the pending motion.

11. After debate has concluded, the presiding officer should put the question. In other words, the presiding officer should restate the question or motion and call the membership to a vote on such motion.

III. Points of Order

1. Any member may call the attention of the presiding officer to a violation of the parliamentary rules of procedures. Generally, this would be limited to a violation of Robert's Rules of Order or other procedural and/or substantive requirements under the Homeowners Association's Articles of Incorporation, Bylaws, and/or the Texas Nonprofit Corporation Law.

2. This is done by standing up, interrupting the presiding officer or a speaker if necessary, and without waiting to be recognized, calling out, "Point of Order!"

3. Anyone speaking should take a seat, and the presiding officer must ask the member to state his or her point of order.

4. The member calling a point of order should state how the rules are being broken.

5. No second is necessary and no vote is taken.

6. The presiding officer should rule on the point of order before debate continues (generally by stating that "the chair rules that the point of order is well taken" or "the chair rules that the point of order is not well taken," but the presiding officer can also simply state "the point of order is sustained" or "the point of order is overruled").

7. The presiding officer should also give a brief explanation for the ruling, which should be recorded in the minutes.

8. The ruling of the presiding officer may be appealed to the membership by the member who called the point of order by stating, "I appeal from the decision of the chair (or presiding officer)."

9. An appeal must be seconded and is subject to debate in a manner similar to that of a motion. The question is stated and put to a vote as, "Shall the decision of the presiding officer be sustained?" A majority vote in the negative is required to overturn the presiding officer's ruling.

10. If a point of order is overruled by a ruling of the presiding officer, or the membership upon a proper appeal, debate shall then continue on the pending motion where it left off.

IV. Conclusion

1. The presiding officer should announce that he or she will entertain a motion to adjourn.

2. The presiding officer should call for a second to the motion to adjourn.

3. A motion to adjourn should be put to a vote of the membership without debate.

DRAFTER'S DICTUM – This document is a sample form for illustrative purposes and may or may not conform to the specific requirements of a particular Homeowners Association's Governing Documents. In addition, changes in statutory and case law may modify or nullify provisions of this document or its enforcement or may create rights or duties not anticipated by this document. Users of this sample form document are advised to periodically review applicable statutes and court rulings to ensure its compliance with all applicable laws.

Appendix L: Sample Management Certificate Form in Accordance with Chapter 82 of the Texas Property Code (for use by Condominium Associations)

MANAGEMENT CERTIFICATE

TEJAS ESTATES CONDOMINIUM ASSOCIATION, INC.

The undersigned, being an Officer of the Tejas Estates Condominium Association, Inc., and in accordance with Section 82.116 of the Texas Uniform Condominium Act, does hereby certify as follows:

1. The name of the condominium development is Tejas Estates Condominiums (the "Condominium Development").

2. The name of the association for the Condominium Development is the Tejas Estates Condominium Association, Inc. (the "Association").

3. The Condominium Development is located at 1836 Come-and-Take-it Avenue, Gonzales, Texas 78629.

4. The recording data for the declarations applicable to the Condominium Development are as follows:

   Declaration of Covenants, Conditions, and Restrictions for Tejas Estates Condominiums, recorded at Volume 33, Page 240, Condominium Records of Travis County, Texas.

   First Amended Declaration of Covenants, Conditions, and Restrictions for Tejas Estates Condominiums, recorded at Document No. 333333333, Official Public Records of Travis County, Texas.

5. The mailing address and contact information for the Association is:

   1838 Star of Texas Avenue
   Austin, Texas 78701
   Telephone – (512) 555-5555
   Facsimile – (512) 555-6666

DRAFTER'S DICTUM – This document is a sample form for illustrative purposes and may or may not conform to the specific requirements of a particular Homeowners Association's Governing Documents. In addition, changes in statutory and case law may modify or nullify provisions of this document or its enforcement or may create rights or duties not anticipated by this document. Users of this sample form document are advised to periodically review applicable statutes and court rulings to ensure its compliance with all applicable laws.

This Certificate is effective as of the ____ day of __________ 2015.

TEJAS ESTATES CONDOMINIUM ASSOCIATION, INC.,
a Texas nonprofit corporation

____

BY: Stephen F. Austin
ITS: President

THE STATE OF TEXAS §
COUNTY OF GONZALES §

This instrument was acknowledged before me on the ____ day of _________, 2015, by Stephen F. Austin, President of Tejas Estates Condominium Association, Inc., a Texas nonprofit corporation, on behalf of said corporation.

[SEAL]

____
Notary Public Signature

AFTER RECORDING RETURN TO:

Stephen F. Austin, President
Tejas Estates Condominium Association, Inc.
P.O. Box 1234
Gonzales, Texas 78629

DRAFTER'S DICTUM – This document is a sample form for illustrative purposes and may or may not conform to the specific requirements of a particular Homeowners Association's Governing Documents. In addition, changes in statutory and case law may modify or nullify provisions of this document or its enforcement or may create rights or duties not anticipated by this document. Users of this sample form document are advised to periodically review applicable statutes and court rulings to ensure its compliance with all applicable laws.

Appendix M: Sample Management Certificate Form in Accordance with Chapter 209 of the Texas Property Code (for use by Subdivision Associations)

MANAGEMENT CERTIFICATE

TEJAS ESTATES HOMEOWNERS ASSOCIATION, INC.

The undersigned, being an Officer of Tejas Estates Homeowners Association, Inc. (the "Association"), and in accordance with Section 209.004 of the Texas Property Code, does hereby certify as follows:

1. The name of the subdivision development is Tejas Estates (the "Subdivision Development").

2. The name of the Association is Tejas Estates Homeowners Association, Inc. (the "Association").

3. The recording data for the Subdivision Development is as follows:

   Tejas Estates Phase 1, a subdivision of record in Travis County, Texas, according to the map or plat thereof, recorded at Volume 33, Page 120, Deed Records of Travis County, Texas;

   Tejas Estates Phase 2, a subdivision of record in Travis County, Texas, according to the map or plat thereof, recorded at Volume 33, Page 120, Real Property Records of Travis County, Texas;

   Tejas Estates on the Lake, a subdivision of record in Travis County, Texas, according to the map or plat thereof, recorded at Volume 33, Page 120, Plat Records of Travis County, Texas;

   The Overlook at Tejas Estates, a subdivision of record in Travis County, Texas, according to the map or plat thereof, recorded at Document No. 1111111111, Official Public Records of Travis County, Texas.

4. The recording data for the declaration(s) applicable to the Subdivision Development is (are) as follows:

   <u>Master Declaration of Covenants, Conditions, and Restrictions for Tejas Estates</u>, recorded at Volume 33, Page 240, Deed Records of Travis County, Texas;

DRAFTER'S DICTUM – This document is a sample form for illustrative purposes and may or may not conform to the specific requirements of a particular Homeowners Association's Governing Documents. In addition, changes in statutory and case law may modify or nullify provisions of this document or its enforcement or may create rights or duties not anticipated by this document. Users of this sample form document are advised to periodically review applicable statutes and court rulings to ensure its compliance with all applicable laws.

First Amended Master Declaration of Covenants, Conditions, and Restrictions for Tejas Estates, recorded at Volume 33, Page 240, Real Property Records of Travis County, Texas;

Amended and Restated Master Declaration of Covenants, Conditions, and Restrictions for Tejas Estates, recorded at Volume 33, Page 240, Real Property Records of Travis County, Texas;

Section Declaration of Covenants, Conditions, and Restrictions for Tejas Estates Phase 1, recorded at Volume 33, Page 240, Official Public Records of Travis County, Texas;

Development Area Declaration of Covenants, Conditions, and Restrictions for Tejas Estates Phase 2, recorded at Document No. 2222222222, Official Public Records of Travis County, Texas;

Declaration of Covenants, Conditions, and Restrictions for Tejas Estates on the Lake, recorded at Volume 33, Page 240, Deed Records of Travis County, Texas;

First Amended Declaration of Covenants, Conditions, and Restrictions for Tejas Estates on the Lake, recorded at Volume 33, Page 240, Deed Records of Travis County, Texas;

Declaration of Covenants, Conditions, and Restrictions for The Overlook at Tejas Estates, recorded at Volume 33, Page 240, Deed Records of Travis County, Texas;

5. The name and mailing address of the Association:

Tejas Estates Homeowners Association, Inc.
1836 San Jacinto Boulevard
Austin, Texas 78701

6. The name and mailing address of the Association's managing agent:

Stephen F. Austin
Republic of Texas Property Management
1838 Star of Texas Avenue
|Austin, Texas 78701

DRAFTER'S DICTUM – This document is a sample form for illustrative purposes and may or may not conform to the specific requirements of a particular Homeowners Association's Governing Documents. In addition, changes in statutory and case law may modify or nullify provisions of this document or its enforcement or may create rights or duties not anticipated by this document. Users of this sample form document are advised to periodically review applicable statutes and court rulings to ensure its compliance with all applicable laws.

This Management Certificate is effective as of the ____ day of ___________, 20__.

TEJAS ESTATES HOMEOWNERS
ASSOCIATION, INC.,
a Texas nonprofit corporation

____

BY: Samuel Houston
ITS: President

THE STATE OF TEXAS §
COUNTY OF TRAVIS §

This instrument was acknowledged before me on ____ day of _________, 20__, by Samuel Houston, President of Tejas Estates Homeowners Association, Inc., a Texas nonprofit corporation, on behalf of said corporation.

[SEAL]

____
Notary Public Signature

AFTER RECORDING RETURN TO:

Tejas Estates Homeowners Association, Inc.
1836 San Jacinto Boulevard
Austin, Texas 78701

DRAFTER'S DICTUM – This document is a sample form for illustrative purposes and may or may not conform to the specific requirements of a particular Homeowners Association's Governing Documents. In addition, changes in statutory and case law may modify or nullify provisions of this document or its enforcement or may create rights or duties not anticipated by this document. Users of this sample form document are advised to periodically review applicable statutes and court rulings to ensure its compliance with all applicable laws.

Appendix N: Sample Resale Certificate Form in Accordance with Chapter 82 of the Texas Property Code (for use by Condominium Associations)

TEJAS ESTATES CONDOMINIUM ASSOCIATION, INC.

CONDOMINIUM RESALE CERTIFICATE

(Texas Property Code Section 82.157)

This is a Condominium Resale Certificate concerning Condominium Unit ____, in Building ______, of the Tejas Estates Condominiums, a condominium project, located at 1836 Gonzales Lane, City of Austin, County of Travis, Texas (the "Unit"), prepared on behalf of the Tejas Estates Condominium Association, Inc. (the "Association") by the Association's governing body (the "Board").

A. The Declaration ☐ does ☐ does not contain a right of first refusal or other restraint that restricts the right to transfer the Unit. If a right of first refusal or other restraint exists, see Section ____ of the Declaration.

B. The periodic common expense assessment for the Unit is $_________ per _______________.

C. There ☐ is ☐ is not a common expense or special assessment currently due and unpaid by the owner of the Unit to the Association. The total unpaid amount is $ ________________ and is for ____________________________________ .

D. Other amounts ☐ are ☐ are not currently due and payable by the owner of the Unit to the Association. The total unpaid amount is $_______________ and is for ____________________________________ .

E. Capital expenditures approved by the Association for the next twelve (12) months are $________________.

F. Reserves for capital expenditures are $_________________; of this amount, $______________ has been designated for ____________________________ .

G. The current operating budget of the Association is attached.

H. The amount of unsatisfied judgments against the Association is $____________.

DRAFTER'S DICTUM – This document is a sample form for illustrative purposes and may or may not conform to the specific requirements of a particular Homeowners Association's Governing Documents. In addition, changes in statutory and case law may modify or nullify provisions of this document or its enforcement or may create rights or duties not anticipated by this document. Users of this sample form document are advised to periodically review applicable statutes and court rulings to ensure its compliance with all applicable laws.

I. There ☐ is/are ☐ is/are no lawsuit(s) pending against the Association. The nature of the lawsuit(s) is: ____
____
____
____.

J. The Association ☐ does ☐ does not provide insurance coverage for the benefit of Unit Owners as per the attached summary from the Association's insurance agent.

K. The Board ☐ has ☐ has no knowledge of alterations or improvements to the Unit or to the Limited Common Elements assigned to the Unit or any portion of the Condominium Development that violate any provision of the Declaration, Bylaws, or Rules of the Association. Known violations are: ________________
____
____
____.

L. The Board ☐ has ☐ has not received notice from a governmental authority concerning violations of health or building codes with respect to the Unit, the Limited Common Elements assigned to the Unit, or any other portion of the Condominium Development. Notices received are: ____________________
____
____
____.

M. The remaining term of any leasehold estate that affects the Condominium Development is ____________________ and the provisions governing an extension or a renewal of the lease are: ______________________________
____
____
____.

N. The Association's managing agent is:

Name: ____

Mailing Address: ______________________________________

Telephone Number: _______________ Facsimile Number: _______________

O. Association fees resulting from the transfer of the Unit are $ _______________.

P. Required contribution, if any, to the capital reserves account is $____________.

DRAFTER'S DICTUM – This document is a sample form for illustrative purposes and may or may not conform to the specific requirements of a particular Homeowners Association's Governing Documents. In addition, changes in statutory and case law may modify or nullify provisions of this document or its enforcement or may create rights or duties not anticipated by this document. Users of this sample form document are advised to periodically review applicable statutes and court rulings to ensure its compliance with all applicable laws.

Q. The following documents are attached:

1. Operating Budget;
2. Balance Sheet; and
3. Insurance Summary.

NOTICE: This Condominium Resale Certificate must be prepared no more than three (3) months before the date it is delivered to a prospective buyer of the Unit.

____
Tejas Estates Condominium Association, Inc.

By: ______________________________________

Title: ______________________________________

Mailing Address: ______________________________

Date: ______________________________________

Email ______________________________________

DRAFTER'S DICTUM – This document is a sample form for illustrative purposes and may or may not conform to the specific requirements of a particular Homeowners Association's Governing Documents. In addition, changes in statutory and case law may modify or nullify provisions of this document or its enforcement or may create rights or duties not anticipated by this document. Users of this sample form document are advised to periodically review applicable statutes and court rulings to ensure its compliance with all applicable laws.

Appendix O: Sample Resale Certificate Form in Accordance with Chapter 207 of the Texas Property Code (for use by Subdivision Associations)

TEJAS ESTATES HOMEOWNERS ASSOCIATION, INC.

SUBDIVISION INFORMATION INCLUDING RESALE CERTIFICATE FOR PROPERTY SUBJECT TO MANDATORY MEMBERSHIP IN A PROPERTY OWNERS ASSOCIATION

(Texas Property Code Section 207.003)

This is a Resale Certificate concerning the real property (including any common areas assigned to the real property) located at 1836 Alamo Drive, Austin, Texas 78701 (Lot 2, Block A of the Tejas Estates Subdivision), Travis County, Texas (the "Property"), and is prepared by the Tejas Estates Homeowners Association, Inc. (the "Association").

A. The Property ☐ is ☐ is not subject to a right of first refusal or other restraint contained in the restrictions or restrictive covenants that restricts the owner's right to transfer the owner's property.

B. The current regular assessment for the Property is $_______ per ____________.

C. A special assessment for the Property that is due after the date this Resale Certificate is prepared is $_______________, which is payable as follows: ____

and is for the following purposes . ____
____.

D. The total of all amounts that are currently due and unpaid to the Association that are attributable to the Property is $_______________.

E. The capital expenditures approved by the Association for its current fiscal year are $_______________.

F. The amount of reserves for capital expenditures is $_______________.

G. Unsatisfied judgments against the Association total $_______________.

DRAFTER'S DICTUM – This document is a sample form for illustrative purposes and may or may not conform to the specific requirements of a particular Homeowners Association's Governing Documents. In addition, changes in statutory and case law may modify or nullify provisions of this document or its enforcement or may create rights or duties not anticipated by this document. Users of this sample form document are advised to periodically review applicable statutes and court rulings to ensure its compliance with all applicable laws.

H. Other than lawsuits relating to unpaid ad valorem taxes of an individual member of the Association, there ☐ is/are ☐ is/are not any lawsuit(s) pending against the Association. The style and cause number of each such pending lawsuit is: ____
____
____
____.

I. The Association's Board ☐ has actual knowledge ☐ has no actual knowledge of conditions on the Property in violation of the restrictions applying to the subdivision or the Bylaws or rules of the Association. Known violations are: __
____
____
____.

J. The Association ☐ has ☐ has not received notice from any governmental authority regarding health or building code violations with respect to the Property or any common areas or common facilities owned or leased by the Association. A summary or copy of each notice is attached.

K. The amount of any administrative transfer fee charged by the Association for a change of ownership of the Property in the subdivision is $______________,
which is payable to: ______________________________
and is for the following purpose: __________________________
____.

L. The Association's managing agent is:

Name: ______________________________________
Mailing Address: ______________________________
Telephone Number:________________ Facsimile Number: ______________

M. The restrictions applicable to the subdivision ☐ do ☐ do not allow foreclosure of the Association's lien on the Property for failure to pay assessments.

N. The following documents are attached, or have already been provided to you.

1. Declaration of Covenants, Conditions, and Restrictions for Tejas Estates

2. Rules Adopted by the Association

3. Bylaws of the Association

DRAFTER'S DICTUM – This document is a sample form for illustrative purposes and may or may not conform to the specific requirements of a particular Homeowners Association's Governing Documents. In addition, changes in statutory and case law may modify or nullify provisions of this document or its enforcement or may create rights or duties not anticipated by this document. Users of this sample form document are advised to periodically review applicable statutes and court rulings to ensure its compliance with all applicable laws.

NOTICE: This Subdivision information may change at any time.

____
Tejas Estates Homeowners Association, Inc.

By: ______________________________________

Title: ______________________________________

Mailing Address: ______________________________________

Date: ______________________________________

Email: ______________________________________

DRAFTER'S DICTUM – This document is a sample form for illustrative purposes and may or may not conform to the specific requirements of a particular Homeowners Association's Governing Documents. In addition, changes in statutory and case law may modify or nullify provisions of this document or its enforcement or may create rights or duties not anticipated by this document. Users of this sample form document are advised to periodically review applicable statutes and court rulings to ensure its compliance with all applicable laws.

Appendix P: Sample Payment Plan Guidelines Policy (for use by Subdivision Associations consisting of fifteen or more Lots)

<u>TEJAS ESTATES HOMEOWNERS ASSOCIATION</u>

PAYMENT PLAN GUIDELINES POLICY
AND APPLICATION OF PAYMENTS SCHEDULE

WHEREAS, Tejas Estates Homeowners Association (the "Association") constitutes a property owners association under the provisions of Chapter 209 of the Texas Property Code (the "Code") and is composed of fifteen (15) or more lots;

WHEREAS, Section 209.0062 of the Code requires the Association to adopt reasonable guidelines that establish an alternative payment schedule by which a member of the Association may make partial payments to the Association for delinquent regular or special assessments or any other amount owed to the Association without accruing additional monetary penalties;

WHEREAS, Section 209.0063 of the Code requires payments made to the Association by its members be applied to a member's account in a particular order of priority, unless such member is in default of a payment plan entered into with the Association;

WHEREAS, the Board of Directors of the Association (the "Board") desires to adopt payment plan guidelines as required under Section 209.0062 of the Code and an application of payments schedule in conformity with Section 209.0063 of the Code.

NOW, THEREFORE, the Board hereby adopts this Payment Plan Guidelines Policy (the "Policy") and Application of Payments Schedule, as set forth below.

<u>PAYMENT PLAN GUIDELINES</u>

1. <u>Eligibility for Payment Plan</u>

Subject to the terms of this Policy, a member of the Association who is delinquent in the payment of any regular or special assessments, or any other amounts owed to the Association, including costs of collection incurred by the Association (hereinafter referred to collectively as the "Assessment Delinquency"), shall be entitled to enter into a payment plan agreement with the Association that allows such member to pay the Assessment Delinquency in installment payments without incurring additional monetary penalties

DRAFTER'S DICTUM – This document is a sample form for illustrative purposes and may or may not conform to the specific requirements of a particular Homeowners Association's Governing Documents. In addition, changes in statutory and case law may modify or nullify provisions of this document or its enforcement or may create rights or duties not anticipated by this document. Users of this sample form document are advised to periodically review applicable statutes and court rulings to ensure its compliance with all applicable laws.

(hereinafter referred to as a "Payment Plan Agreement"). Each such Payment Plan Agreement shall be in accordance with terms of these Payment Plan Guidelines and the requirements of Section 209.0062 of the Code.

Notwithstanding the foregoing, or any provision herein to the contrary, a member of the Association shall be ineligible to pay his or her Assessment Delinquency under a Payment Plan Agreement if such member has failed to honor the terms of a previous Payment Plan Agreement with the Association and it has been less than two (2) years since the member's default under the previous Payment Plan Agreement.

2. Payment Plan Administrative Charges and Interest

In addition to the Assessment Delinquency, a member of the Association who enters into a Payment Plan Agreement shall be required to pay to the Association reasonable costs associated with preparing the Payment Plan Agreement and administering the member's compliance with the Payment Plan Agreement (hereinafter referred to collectively as the "Payment Plan Administrative Charges"). A member of the Association who enters into a Payment Plan Agreement with the Association shall also be required to pay all interest due and payable on the member's Assessment Delinquency in accordance with applicable provisions of the Association's governing documents, which shall continue to accrue on the Assessment Delinquency during the term of Payment Plan Agreement.

3. Available Payment Plan Schedules

The Association has established three alternative installment payment plan schedules (each hereinafter referred to as a "Repayment Schedule"). Any member of the Association who is eligible to enter into a Payment Plan Agreement with the Association shall be entitled to select from any of the Repayment Schedules that he or she qualifies for, which shall be based on the total amount of the Assessment Delinquency owed by the member at the time the Payment Plan Agreement is entered into. The three available Repayment Schedules are as follows:

(a) *Four-Month Repayment Schedule*:

Any member who owes the Association an Assessment Delinquency totaling $400 or less shall be qualified to select the Four-Month Repayment Schedule. Under the Four-Month Repayment Schedule, the member shall pay the Assessment Delinquency, plus any Payment Plan Administrative Charges and accrued interest, in equal monthly installments over a period of four (4) months.

DRAFTER'S DICTUM – This document is a sample form for illustrative purposes and may or may not conform to the specific requirements of a particular Homeowners Association's Governing Documents. In addition, changes in statutory and case law may modify or nullify provisions of this document or its enforcement or may create rights or duties not anticipated by this document. Users of this sample form document are advised to periodically review applicable statutes and court rulings to ensure its compliance with all applicable laws.

(b) *Eight-Month Repayment Schedule*:

Any member who owes the Association an Assessment Delinquency totaling $401–$800 shall be qualified to select either the Four-Month Repayment Schedule or the Eight-Month Repayment Schedule. Under the Eight-Month Repayment Schedule, the member shall pay the Assessment Delinquency, plus any Payment Plan Administrative Charges and accrued interest, in equal monthly installments over a period of eight (8) months.

(c) *Twelve-Month Repayment Schedule*:

Any member who owes the Association an Assessment Delinquency totaling $801 or more shall be qualified to select either the Four-Month Repayment Schedule, the Eight-Month Repayment Schedule, or the Twelve-Month Repayment Schedule. Under the Twelve-Month Repayment Schedule, the member shall pay the Assessment Delinquency, plus any Payment Plan Administrative Charges and accrued interest, in equal monthly installments over a period of twelve (12) months.

4. Payment Plan Agreement

Each Payment Plan Agreement shall be evidenced in writing and executed by both the member and a duly authorized representative of the Association. The Payment Plan Agreement shall specify the total amount of Assessment Delinquency owed to the Association as of the date of the Payment Plan Agreement, the total amount of Payment Plan Administrative Charges and interest to be paid under the Payment Plan Agreement, and the term of the Repayment Schedule.

5. Default of Payment Plan Agreement

Each payment due under any Payment Plan Schedule shall be due and payable to the Association on or before the first (1st) day of each month during the term of the Payment Plan Agreement. Time is of the essence with respect to payments under a Payment Plan Agreement, and the obligation to pay each monthly payment on or before the first (1st) day of each month must be strictly complied with. If a monthly payment made pursuant to a Payment Plan Agreement is returned for insufficient funds and/or if a payment is received after the due day thereof, it shall constitute a material breach of the Payment Plan Agreement. In such event, all unpaid amounts subject to the Payment Plan Agreement shall automatically, without any further notice from the Association, be accelerated and shall be immediately due and payable in full to the Association.

In such event, the member shall be considered in default of the Payment Plan Agreement until he or she pays the full amount of the accelerated Assessment Delinquency, Payment Plan Administrative Charges, and accrued interest subject to the Payment Plan Agreement to the Association (the "Payment Plan Default Period"). In addition, the defaulting member shall be liable for all costs of collection, including attorneys fees, incurred by the Association to collect any remaining unpaid amounts subject to the Payment Plan Agreement, which shall be added to and included within the Assessment Delinquency that must be paid by the defaulting member to the Association under such Payment Plan Agreement. Any payments received by the Association from a member of the Association who is in default under a Payment Plan Agreement with the Association during a Payment Plan Default Period shall be applied to the member's debt or account in the following order of priority:

(1) any attorneys fees or third-party collection costs incurred by the Association in connection with collection of the member's debt;

(2) any other fees and expenses reimbursable to the Association in connection with collection of the member's debt;

(3) any late charges and interest due by the member;

(4) any past-due delinquent assessments (beginning with the oldest);

(5) any current assessments;

(6) any other amount owed to the Association (excluding fines); and

(7) any fines assessed by the Association.

APPLICATION OF PAYMENTS SCHEDULE

In accordance with the terms of Section 209.0063 of the Code, except for payments made to the Association by members who are in default under a Payment Plan Agreement with the Association (as provided above), a payment received by the Association from a member shall be applied to the member's account in the following order of priority:

(1) any delinquent assessments (beginning with the oldest);

(2) any current assessments;

DRAFTER'S DICTUM – This document is a sample form for illustrative purposes and may or may not conform to the specific requirements of a particular Homeowners Association's Governing Documents. In addition, changes in statutory and case law may modify or nullify provisions of this document or its enforcement or may create rights or duties not anticipated by this document. Users of this sample form document are advised to periodically review applicable statutes and court rulings to ensure its compliance with all applicable laws.

(3) any attorneys fees or third-party collection costs incurred by the Association associated solely with collection of unpaid assessments or any other charge that could provide the basis for foreclosure of the Association's assessment lien;

(4) any attorneys fees incurred by the Association that are not associated solely with collection of unpaid assessments or that do not provide a basis for foreclosure of the Association's assessment lien;

(5) any fines assessed by the Association; and

(6) any other amount owed to the Association.

CERTIFICATION

IN WITNESS WHEREOF, the undersigned, Samuel Houston, as the duly elected, qualified, and acting Secretary of Tejas Estates Homeowners Association, Inc., a Texas nonprofit corporation, hereby certifies on behalf of the Association that this Payment Plan Guidelines Policy and Application of Payments Schedule was duly adopted by the Board of Directors of the Association at a meeting of the Board held on September 5, 2015, and shall take effect upon its recording in the Official Public Records of Travis County, Texas.

TEJAS ESTATES HOMEOWNERS
ASSOCIATION, INC.,
a Texas nonprofit corporation

____

BY: Samuel Houston
ITS: Secretary

DRAFTER'S DICTUM – This document is a sample form for illustrative purposes and may or may not conform to the specific requirements of a particular Homeowners Association's Governing Documents. In addition, changes in statutory and case law may modify or nullify provisions of this document or its enforcement or may create rights or duties not anticipated by this document. Users of this sample form document are advised to periodically review applicable statutes and court rulings to ensure its compliance with all applicable laws.

THE STATE OF TEXAS §
COUNTY OF TRAVIS §

This instrument was acknowledged before me on the ____ day of ______________, 2015, by Samuel Houston, Secretary of Tejas Estates Homeowners Association, Inc., a Texas nonprofit corporation.

[SEAL] ________________________________
Notary Public Signature

AFTER RECORDING PLEASE RETURN TO:

Stephen F. Austin, President
Tejas Estates Homeowners Association, Inc.
1836 San Jacinto Boulevard
Austin, Texas 78701

DRAFTER'S DICTUM – This document is a sample form for illustrative purposes and may or may not conform to the specific requirements of a particular Homeowners Association's Governing Documents. In addition, changes in statutory and case law may modify or nullify provisions of this document or its enforcement or may create rights or duties not anticipated by this document. Users of this sample form document are advised to periodically review applicable statutes and court rulings to ensure its compliance with all applicable laws.

Appendix Q: Sample Records Production and Copying Policy (for use by Subdivision Associations)

TEJAS ESTATES HOMEOWNERS ASSOCIATION

RECORDS PRODUCTION AND COPYING POLICY

WHEREAS, Tejas Estates Homeowners Association (the "Association") constitutes a property owners association under the provisions of Chapter 209 of the Texas Property Code (the "Code");

WHEREAS, Section 209.005(i) of the Code requires the Association to adopt a records production and copying policy that prescribes the costs the Association will charge for the compilation, production, and reproduction of information requested by a member of the Association (hereinafter referred to as a "Member") in accordance with the terms of Section 209.005 of the Code; and

WHEREAS, the Board of Directors of the Association (the "Board") desires to adopt such a records production and copying policy as required under Section 209.005(i) of the Code.

NOW, THEREFORE, the Board hereby adopts the Records Production and Copying Policy (the "Policy"), as set forth below.

1. Books and Records Subject to Production

Subject to the terms of this Policy and Section 209.005 of the Texas Property Code (and any amendment thereto), the Association will make its books and records, including financial records, to the extent such books and records are in the possession, custody, or control of the Association, open to and reasonably available for examination by a Member of the Association or a person designated in a written instrument signed by the Member as the Member's agent, attorney, or certified public accountant, in accordance with Section 209.005 of the Code (hereinafter referred to as the "Requesting Party"). A Requesting Party is also entitled to obtain copies of the information contained in the Association's books and records.

Except as provided by Section 209.005(d) of the Code, an attorney's files and records relating to the Association are not records of the Association and are not subject to inspection by a Requesting Party or subject to production in a legal proceeding.

DRAFTER'S DICTUM – This document is a sample form for illustrative purposes and may or may not conform to the specific requirements of a particular Homeowners Association's Governing Documents. In addition, changes in statutory and case law may modify or nullify provisions of this document or its enforcement or may create rights or duties not anticipated by this document. Users of this sample form document are advised to periodically review applicable statutes and court rulings to ensure its compliance with all applicable laws.

In accordance with the provisions of Section 209.005(k) of the Code, and except as otherwise authorized or required pursuant to Section 209.005(l) of the Code, the Association shall not release or allow inspection of any books or records that identify the dedicatory instrument violation history of an individual Member, a Member's personal financial information, including records of payment or nonpayment of amounts due to the Association, a Member's contact information, other than his or her address, or information related to an employee of the Association, including personnel files.

2. Procedures for Requesting Inspection and/or Copying of Association's Records

(A) Request for Information:

To inspect or obtain copies of the Association's records, a Requesting Party must submit a written request for information by certified mail to the Association at its or its designated representative's mailing address as reflected on the most current recorded management certificate for the Association.

The written request for information must describe with sufficient detail the Association's books and records being requested and contain an election either to inspect the books and records before obtaining copies or to have the Association forward copies of the requested books and records to the Requesting Party without any advance inspection.

(B) Inspection of Association's Books and Records:

If an advance inspection of the Association's books and records is requested, within ten (10) business days from the date the Association receives the written request for information, the Association will send to the Requesting Party a written notice specifying the location and alternative dates that such person may inspect during normal business hours the requested books and records to the extent those books and records are in the possession, custody, or control of the Association. The inspection of the requested books and records shall take place at a mutually agreed upon time during normal business hours.

The alternative inspection dates proposed by the Association will be within ten (10) business days from its receipt of the request for information, unless the Association is unable to produce copies of the requested books and records and make them available for inspection within ten (10) business days from receipt of the request for information. In such event, the Association's written notice to the Requesting Party will state that the

Association is unable to produce the information within ten (10) business days from the date it received the request for information and it will specify alternative inspection dates that will occur no later than fifteen (15) business days after the date of the Association's written notice to the Requesting Party.

If the Requesting Party wants to obtain copies of any of the books and records produced for inspection, the Requesting Party must identify the books and records at the inspection that the Association is to copy and forward to the Requesting Party.

(C) Copying of Association's Books and Records:

If copies of identified books and records are requested without an advance inspection of such books and records or are requested following an inspection of such books and records, within ten (10) business days from the date the Association receives the written request or the date of the inspection (as applicable), it will, to the extent such books and records are in its possession, custody, or control, produce copies of the requested books and records for the Requesting Party.

If the Association is unable to produce copies of such requested books or records within ten (10) business days from the written request or inspection, it will provide written notice to the Requesting Party of its inability to produce the requested books and records within ten (10) business days and will state a date by which such copies of such requested books and records will be produced to the Requesting Party, which may not be more than fifteen (15) business days after the date of such notice.

The Association reserves the right to produce copies of the requested books and records in hard copy, electronic form, or any other format reasonably available to it, and the manner of production shall be determined by the Association in its sole discretion.

3. Responsibility for Records Production and Copying Charges

A Member of the Association who, or whose designated representative, submits a request for information to the Association (the "Requesting Member") shall be responsible for the costs, expenses, and charges incurred by the Association in responding to such request for information from such member or his or her designated representative in accordance with the terms of the Texas Administrative Code Title 1, Section 70.3 (and any amendment, modification, update, or increase of such terms) (the "Production and Copying Charges"). As of the effective date of the adoption of this Records Production and Copying Policy, the allowable Production and Copying Charges under Texas Administrative Code Title 1, Section 70.3 are as follows:

(A) Copy Charges:

(i) *Standard paper copy*. Standard paper copy charges consist of the charges for reproducing requested information and records on standard size paper by means of an office machine copier or a computer printer. The charge for standard paper copies is $.10 per page or part of a page. Each side that has recorded information is considered a separate page.

(ii) *Nonstandard copy*. Nonstandard copy charges consist of charges for the costs of materials, other than standard size paper, onto which requested information and records are copied (excluding any applicable additional charges that may be associated with a particular request, such as labor or overhead charges). The charges for nonstandard copies are:

(a)	diskette:	$1.00
(b)	magnetic tape:	actual cost
(c)	data cartridge:	actual cost
(d)	tape cartridge:	actual cost
(e)	CD:	$1.00
(f)	DVD:	$3.00
(g)	JAZ drive:	actual cost
(h)	other electronic media:	actual cost
(i)	VHS video cassette:	$2.50
(j)	audio cassette:	$1.00
(k)	oversize paper copy:	$.50
(l)	specialty paper:	actual cost

(B) Labor Charges:

Labor charges consist of the labor costs incurred in processing a request for information or records, and include the actual time to locate, compile, manipulate data, and reproduce the requested information or record. The charge for labor costs incurred in processing a request for information is $15 an hour.

(C) Overhead Charge:

Whenever a labor charge is incurred in processing a request for information or records, the Association shall also charge a Requesting Member for any other direct and indirect costs incurred in processing a request for information, including an overhead charge to cover such costs as depreciation of capital assets, rent, maintenance and repair, utilities, and administrative overhead. The overhead charge is computed at twenty percent (20%) of the labor charge made to cover any labor costs associated with a particular request. By way of example, if one hour of labor is expended in processing a particular request for information, the overhead charge would be $3.00 ($15.00 for one hour of labor multiplied by 20% or .20).

(D) Miscellaneous Supplies:

The Association shall also charge a Requesting Member for the actual cost of miscellaneous supplies, such as labels, boxes, and other supplies, used to produce the requested information to the Requesting Party.

(E) Postal and Shipping Charges:

The Association shall also charge a Requesting Member for any related postal or shipping expenses that are necessary to transmit the reproduced information to the Requesting Party.

4. Advance Payment of Production and Copying Charges

The Association requires advance payment by the Requesting Member of the estimated amount of Production and Copying Charges to be incurred in responding to a request for information, which will be estimated by using the amounts prescribed by this Policy. Within thirty (30) business days from the date copies of the requested information are delivered to the Requesting Party, the Association will submit a final invoice to the Requesting Member for the actual amount of Production and Copying Charges incurred by the Association in responding to such request for information ("Final Invoice").

If the estimated amount of Production and Copying Charges exceeds the actual amount of such charges, as reflected in the Final Invoice, the Requesting Member shall be entitled to a refund of the excess amount, and the Association will send payment of such excess amount to the Requesting Member within thirty (30) business days from the date the Final Invoice is sent to the Requesting Member.

If the actual amount of Production and Copying Charges, as reflected in the Final Invoice, exceeds the estimated amount of such charges, the additional amount of Production and Copying Charges incurred by the Association must be paid by the Requesting Member within thirty (30) business days from the date the Final Invoice is sent to the Requesting Member. If the Requesting Member does not timely pay the Association the additional amount of Production and Copying Charges, such amount shall be added to the Requesting Member's account as an assessment.

CERTIFICATION

IN WITNESS WHEREOF, the undersigned, Samuel Houston, as the duly elected, qualified, and acting Secretary of Tejas Estates Homeowners Association, Inc., a Texas nonprofit corporation, hereby certifies on behalf of the Association that this Records Production and Copying Policy was duly adopted by the Board of Directors of the Association at a meeting of the Board held on September 5, 2015, and shall take effect upon its recording in the Official Public Records of Travis County, Texas.

TEJAS ESTATES HOMEOWNERS
ASSOCIATION, INC.,
a Texas nonprofit corporation

____
BY: Samuel Houston
ITS: Secretary

DRAFTER'S DICTUM – This document is a sample form for illustrative purposes and may or may not conform to the specific requirements of a particular Homeowners Association's Governing Documents. In addition, changes in statutory and case law may modify or nullify provisions of this document or its enforcement or may create rights or duties not anticipated by this document. Users of this sample form document are advised to periodically review applicable statutes and court rulings to ensure its compliance with all applicable laws.

THE STATE OF TEXAS §
COUNTY OF TRAVIS §

This instrument was acknowledged before me on the ____ day of _______________, 2015, by Samuel Houston, Secretary of Tejas Estates Homeowners Association, Inc., a Texas nonprofit corporation.

[SEAL] ____________________________________
Notary Public Signature

AFTER RECORDING PLEASE RETURN TO:

Stephen F. Austin, President
Tejas Estates Homeowners Association, Inc.
1836 San Jacinto Boulevard
Austin, Texas 78701

DRAFTER'S DICTUM – This document is a sample form for illustrative purposes and may or may not conform to the specific requirements of a particular Homeowners Association's Governing Documents. In addition, changes in statutory and case law may modify or nullify provisions of this document or its enforcement or may create rights or duties not anticipated by this document. Users of this sample form document are advised to periodically review applicable statutes and court rulings to ensure its compliance with all applicable laws.

Appendix R: Sample Document Retention Policy (for use by Subdivision Associations)

<u>TEJAS ESTATES HOMEOWNERS ASSOCIATION</u>

DOCUMENT RETENTION POLICY

WHEREAS, Tejas Estates Homeowners Association (the "Association") constitutes a property owners association under the provisions of Chapter 209 of the Texas Property Code (the "Code") and is composed of fifteen (15) or more lots;

WHEREAS, Section 209.005(m) of the Code provides that the Association must adopt and comply with a document retention policy that includes, at a minimum, the items specified in Section 209.005(m) of the Code; and

WHEREAS, the Board of Directors of the Association (the "Board") desires to adopt a document retention policy as required under Section 209.005(m) of the Code.

NOW, THEREFORE, the Board hereby adopts this Document Retention Policy (the "Policy"), as set forth below.

DOCUMENT RETENTION POLICY

1. <u>Policy</u>:

Books and records are to be retained by the Association for the period of their immediate use, unless longer retention is required for historical reference, contractual or legal requirements, or for compliance with the document retention periods set forth in this Policy. Records that are no longer required, or that have satisfied their recommended period of retention, may be destroyed in an appropriate manner.

The Association's Secretary is responsible for ensuring that the Association's books and records are identified, retained, stored, protected, and subsequently disposed of in accordance with the guidelines set forth in this Policy. Books and records that are required to be retained pursuant to this Policy may be scanned and maintained in an electronic format.

2. <u>Document Retention Periods</u>:

DRAFTER'S DICTUM – This document is a sample form for illustrative purposes and may or may not conform to the specific requirements of a particular Homeowners Association's Governing Documents. In addition, changes in statutory and case law may modify or nullify provisions of this document or its enforcement or may create rights or duties not anticipated by this document. Users of this sample form document are advised to periodically review applicable statutes and court rulings to ensure its compliance with all applicable laws.

The following books and records are to be retained by the Association for the retention periods specified below:

Record Type:	**Retention Period:**
Certificate of Formation (formerly referred to as Articles of Incorporation), Bylaws, and Declarations, and any amendments thereto	**Permanently**
Financial books and records	**7 years**
Account records of current Lot Owners	**5 years**
Contracts with a term of one (1) year or more	**4 years after the expiration of the contract term**
Minutes of Board and Membership Meetings	**7 years**
Tax returns and audit records	**7 years**

CERTIFICATION

IN WITNESS WHEREOF, the undersigned, Samuel Houston, as the duly elected, qualified, and acting Secretary of Tejas Estates Homeowners Association, Inc., a Texas nonprofit corporation, hereby certifies on behalf of the Association that this Document Retention Policy was duly adopted by the Board of Directors of the Association at a meeting of the Board held on September 5, 2015, and shall take effect upon its recording in the Official Public Records of Travis County, Texas.

TEJAS ESTATES HOMEOWNERS
ASSOCIATION, INC.,
a Texas nonprofit corporation

____
BY: Samuel Houston
ITS: Secretary

DRAFTER'S DICTUM – This document is a sample form for illustrative purposes and may or may not conform to the specific requirements of a particular Homeowners Association's Governing Documents. In addition, changes in statutory and case law may modify or nullify provisions of this document or its enforcement or may create rights or duties not anticipated by this document. Users of this sample form document are advised to periodically review applicable statutes and court rulings to ensure its compliance with all applicable laws.

THE STATE OF TEXAS §
COUNTY OF TRAVIS §

This instrument was acknowledged before me on the ____ day of _______________, 2015, by Samuel Houston, Secretary of Tejas Estates Homeowners Association, Inc., a Texas nonprofit corporation.

[SEAL] ______________________________
Notary Public Signature

AFTER RECORDING PLEASE RETURN TO:

Stephen F. Austin, President
Tejas Estates Homeowners Association, Inc.
1836 San Jacinto Boulevard
Austin, Texas 78701

DRAFTER'S DICTUM – This document is a sample form for illustrative purposes and may or may not conform to the specific requirements of a particular Homeowners Association's Governing Documents. In addition, changes in statutory and case law may modify or nullify provisions of this document or its enforcement or may create rights or duties not anticipated by this document. Users of this sample form document are advised to periodically review applicable statutes and court rulings to ensure its compliance with all applicable laws.

Appendix S: Sample Request to Inspect and/or Copy Books and Records (for use by Unit Owners in a Condominium Association)

September 5, 2015

VIA CERTIFIED MAIL, RRR

Tejas Estates Condominium Association
c/o Star of Texas Management
1836 San Jacinto Boulevard
Austin, Texas 78701

Re: Request by David "Davy" Crockett to inspect and/or obtain copies of books and records of the Tejas Estates Condominium Association (the "Association")

Dear Association:

I am the owner of Unit 72 at the Tejas Estates Condominiums and am a member of the Association.

Pursuant to Section 82.114 of the Texas Property Code, I request the Association to make the following books and records of the Association available for inspection and/or copying by me:

(1) Minutes from all regular meetings of the Association's Board of Directors for the 2015 calendar year;

(2) The annual audit report for the calendar years 2014 and 2015; and

(3) Minutes from the annual meeting of the Association's membership for the 2014 calendar year.

Although I am not required to disclose a purpose for my request under Section 82.114 of the Texas Property Code, the purpose of my request to inspect and/or obtain copies of the books and records of the Association is to determine if the Association has been complying with its obligations under the organizational documents and laws governing the Association.

DRAFTER'S DICTUM – This document is a sample form for illustrative purposes and may or may not conform to the specific requirements of a particular Homeowners Association's Governing Documents. In addition, changes in statutory and case law may modify or nullify provisions of this document or its enforcement or may create rights or duties not anticipated by this document. Users of this sample form document are advised to periodically review applicable statutes and court rulings to ensure its compliance with all applicable laws.

If any of the books and records I have requested to inspect exist only electronically or digitally as computer files, please print them out for my inspection or make them available to me on a disc or thumb drive so that I may access them with my own computer.

If you need to speak to me regarding my request, I can be reached at (512) 555-5555 or dcrockett@coonskinhat.com. Otherwise, please let me know as soon as is reasonably possible when the requested books and records will be made available to me.

Thank you for your attention to this matter, and I look forward to hearing from you in the next few days.

Sincerely,

David "Davy" Crockett

DRAFTER'S DICTUM – This document is a sample form for illustrative purposes and may or may not conform to the specific requirements of a particular Homeowners Association's Governing Documents. In addition, changes in statutory and case law may modify or nullify provisions of this document or its enforcement or may create rights or duties not anticipated by this document. Users of this sample form document are advised to periodically review applicable statutes and court rulings to ensure its compliance with all applicable laws.

Appendix T: Sample Request to Inspect and/or Copy Books and Records (for use by Lot Owners in a Subdivision Association)

September 5, 2015

VIA CERTIFIED MAIL, RRR

Tejas Estates Homeowners Association
c/o Star of Texas Management
1836 San Jacinto Boulevard
Austin, Texas 78701

Re: Request by David "Davy" Crockett to inspect and/or obtain copies of books and records of the Tejas Estates Homeowners Association (the "Association")

Dear Association:

I am the owner of 1212 Republic of Texas Avenue, Austin, Texas 78735, and am a member of the Association.

Pursuant to Section 209.005 of the Texas Property Code, I request the Association to make the following books and records of the Association available for inspection by me within ten (10) business days from the receipt of this request:

(1) Minutes from all regular meetings of the Association's Board of Directors for the 2013 calendar year; and

(2) Minutes from all special meetings of the Association's Board of Directors for the 2013 and 2014 calendar years.

I also request the Association to produce copies of the following books and records of the Association to me within ten (10) business days from the receipt of this request:

(1) Minutes from the annual meeting of the Association's membership for the 2012 calendar year; and

DRAFTER'S DICTUM – This document is a sample form for illustrative purposes and may or may not conform to the specific requirements of a particular Homeowners Association's Governing Documents. In addition, changes in statutory and case law may modify or nullify provisions of this document or its enforcement or may create rights or duties not anticipated by this document. Users of this sample form document are advised to periodically review applicable statutes and court rulings to ensure its compliance with all applicable laws.

(2) Minutes from all special meetings of the Association's membership conducted during the 2011, 2012, and 2013 calendar years.

Although I am not required to disclose a purpose for my request under Section 209.005 of the Texas Property Code, the purpose of my request to inspect and/or obtain copies of the books and records of the Association is to determine if the Association has been complying with its obligations under the organizational documents and laws governing the Association.

If any of the books and records I have requested to inspect exist only electronically or digitally as computer files, please print them out for my inspection or make them available to me on a disc or thumb drive so that I may access them with my own computer.

I would ask that you send the copies of the requested books and records to me by mail at my address noted above. If you intend to assess me any charges for the compilation, production, and/or reproduction of the books and records that I have requested copies of, please contact me at (512) 555-5555 or dcrockett@coonskinhat.com so that I may make arrangements to pay such charges. Otherwise, please let me know as soon as is reasonably possible when the requested books and records will be made available to me.

Thank you for your attention to this matter, and I look forward to hearing from you in the next few days.

Sincerely,

David "Davy" Crockett

DRAFTER'S DICTUM – This document is a sample form for illustrative purposes and may or may not conform to the specific requirements of a particular Homeowners Association's Governing Documents. In addition, changes in statutory and case law may modify or nullify provisions of this document or its enforcement or may create rights or duties not anticipated by this document. Users of this sample form document are advised to periodically review applicable statutes and court rulings to ensure its compliance with all applicable laws.

Appendix U: Sample Notice of Past Due Assessments Letter (for use by Condominium Associations)

TEJAS ESTATES CONDOMINIUM ASSOCIATION, INC.
1833 Republic of Texas Avenue
Austin, Texas 78701

September 5, 2015

NOTICE OF PAST DUE ASSESSMENTS

VIA FIRST CLASS AND
CERTIFIED MAIL, RRR

Antonio Santa Anna
3016 Alamo Street, Unit 72
Austin, Texas 78701

RE: Unpaid past due assessments for 3016 Alamo Street, Unit 72, Austin, Texas 78701 (the "Property")

Dear Mr. Santa Anna:

As you are aware, the Property is subject to the Declaration of Covenants, Conditions, and Restrictions for Tejas Estates Condominiums (the "Declaration"), which provides, among other things, that upon acquisition of the Property, the owner becomes a mandatory member of Tejas Estates Condominium Association, Inc. (the "Association") and is obligated to pay assessments levied by the Association (the "Assessments"), which are used to pay for maintenance of the common elements and operation of the Association, among other things.

The purpose of this letter is to inform you that you are delinquent in the payment of Assessments levied against the Property, which to date total $1,200.00. We respectfully request that you pay the total amount due within ten (10) days from the date of this letter.

DRAFTER'S DICTUM – This document is a sample form for illustrative purposes and may or may not conform to the specific requirements of a particular Homeowners Association's Governing Documents. In addition, changes in statutory and case law may modify or nullify provisions of this document or its enforcement or may create rights or duties not anticipated by this document. Users of this sample form document are advised to periodically review applicable statutes and court rulings to ensure its compliance with all applicable laws.

Should you have any questions regarding the above, please feel free to contact the Association's Treasurer, James Bowie, at (512) 555-4343.

Sincerely,

William B. Travis
Property Manager
Tejas Estates Condominium Association, Inc.

DRAFTER'S DICTUM – This document is a sample form for illustrative purposes and may or may not conform to the specific requirements of a particular Homeowners Association's Governing Documents. In addition, changes in statutory and case law may modify or nullify provisions of this document or its enforcement or may create rights or duties not anticipated by this document. Users of this sample form document are advised to periodically review applicable statutes and court rulings to ensure its compliance with all applicable laws.

Appendix V: Sample Notice of Past Due Assessments Letter (for use by Subdivision Associations)

TEJAS ESTATES HOMEOWNERS ASSOCIATION, INC.
1833 Republic of Texas Avenue
Austin, Texas 78701

September 5, 2015

NOTICE OF PAST DUE ASSESSMENTS

VIA FIRST CLASS AND
CERTIFIED MAIL

Antonio Santa Anna
3016 Alamo Street
Austin, Texas 78701

RE: Unpaid past due assessments for 3016 Alamo Street, Austin, Texas 78701 (the "Property")

Dear Mr. Santa Anna:

As you are aware, the Property is subject to the Declaration of Covenants, Conditions, and Restrictions for Tejas Estates (the "Declaration"), which provides, among other things, that upon acquisition of the Property, the owner becomes a mandatory member of Tejas Estates Homeowners Association, Inc. (the "Association") and is obligated to pay assessments levied by the Association (the "Assessments"), which are used to pay for maintenance of the common areas and operation of the Association, among other things.

The purpose of this letter is to inform you that you are delinquent in the payment of Assessments levied against the Property. As of the date of this letter, the outstanding balance owed is $1,836.03, which consists of the following amounts:

DRAFTER'S DICTUM – This document is a sample form for illustrative purposes and may or may not conform to the specific requirements of a particular Homeowners Association's Governing Documents. In addition, changes in statutory and case law may modify or nullify provisions of this document or its enforcement or may create rights or duties not anticipated by this document. Users of this sample form document are advised to periodically review applicable statutes and court rulings to ensure its compliance with all applicable laws.

Past-Due Regular Assessments:	$1,200.00
Past-Due Special Assessments:	$300.00
Late Fees (to date):	$50.00
Accrued Interest (to date):	$11.03
Costs of Collection (to date):	$250.00
Fines:	$25.00
Total:	**$1,836.03**

Demand is hereby made for payment in full of the balance owed. Your account will continue to accrue late fees and interest until the balance is paid in full. This balance does not include Assessments and other amounts accruing after the date of this letter.

You may be eligible to pay off your outstanding balance under an installment payment plan pursuant to the terms of the Association's Payment Plan Guidelines Policy of record. For more information regarding the availability of a payment plan, please contact us. If payment of the outstanding balance in full is not received within thirty (30) days of the date of this notice and you have not otherwise entered into a payment plan to pay off such balance, we will be forced to take further collection actions against your account. Such actions may include the reporting of your delinquent account to the credit bureau, referral of your account to the Association's attorney, the filing of a notice of lien against your property, the filing of a lawsuit, and even the foreclosure of your property by the Association. In the event this matter is turned over to the Association's attorney, you will be liable for all attorneys fees and other costs of collection incurred by the Association.

DRAFTER'S DICTUM – This document is a sample form for illustrative purposes and may or may not conform to the specific requirements of a particular Homeowners Association's Governing Documents. In addition, changes in statutory and case law may modify or nullify provisions of this document or its enforcement or may create rights or duties not anticipated by this document. Users of this sample form document are advised to periodically review applicable statutes and court rulings to ensure its compliance with all applicable laws.

It is our sincere desire to avoid any of the actions described above. We therefore request that you simply bring your account current by remitting payment of the outstanding balance or by contacting us to make arrangements for a payment plan. Should you have any questions regarding the outstanding account balance or to request a payment plan, please contact the Association's Treasurer, James Bowie, at (512) 555-4343.

ACTIVE MILITARY SERVICEMEMBER ADVISORY

Assert and protect your rights as a member of the armed forces of the United States. If you are or your spouse is serving on active military duty, including active military duty as a member of the Texas National Guard or the National Guard of another state or as a member of a reserve component of the armed forces of the United States, please send written notice of the active duty military service to the sender of this notice immediately.

Sincerely,

William B. Travis
Property Manager
Tejas Estates Homeowners Association, Inc.

DRAFTER'S DICTUM – This document is a sample form for illustrative purposes and may or may not conform to the specific requirements of a particular Homeowners Association's Governing Documents. In addition, changes in statutory and case law may modify or nullify provisions of this document or its enforcement or may create rights or duties not anticipated by this document. Users of this sample form document are advised to periodically review applicable statutes and court rulings to ensure its compliance with all applicable laws.

Appendix W: Sample Notice of Assessment Delinquency to Junior Deed of Trust Lienholder (for use by Subdivision Associations)

TEJAS ESTATES HOMEOWNERS ASSOCIATION, INC.
1833 Republic of Texas Avenue
Austin, Texas 78701

September 5, 2015

NOTICE OF PAST DUE ASSESSMENTS
AND INTENT TO FORECLOSE

VIA FIRST CLASS AND
CERTIFIED MAIL

Austin Colony Savings & Loan
1825 Old Three Hundred Way
Austin, Texas 78701

RE: Austin Colony Savings & Loan's Deed of Trust lien against the real property locally known as 3016 Alamo Street, Austin, Texas 78701 (the "Property"), recorded at Document No. 03061836, in the Official Public Records of Travis County, Texas (the "Deed of Trust Lien")

To Whom It May Concern:

Tejas Estates Homeowners Association, Inc. (the "Association") is a property owners association under Chapter 209 of the Texas Property Code that governs the Tejas Estates subdivision development (the "Development") pursuant to the Declaration of Covenants, Conditions, and Restrictions for Tejas Estates (the "Declaration").

The Declaration authorizes the Association to levy assessments against the owners of the lots within the Development to pay for maintenance of the common areas and operation of the Association, among other things. In addition, the Declaration also establishes a contractual lien against each of the lots in the Development to secure payment of levied assessments, late fees, interest, and costs of collection including attorneys fees (the "Assessment Lien").

Antonio Santa Anna, the owner of the Property, has failed to pay assessments, late fees, interest, and/or costs of collection owed by him or her to the Association (the

DRAFTER'S DICTUM – This document is a sample form for illustrative purposes and may or may not conform to the specific requirements of a particular Homeowners Association's Governing Documents. In addition, changes in statutory and case law may modify or nullify provisions of this document or its enforcement or may create rights or duties not anticipated by this document. Users of this sample form document are advised to periodically review applicable statutes and court rulings to ensure its compliance with all applicable laws.

"Assessment Delinquency"). As a result, the Association intends to foreclose its Assessment Lien against the Property in order to satisfy payment of the Assessment Delinquency. The total amount of the Assessment Delinquency as of the date of this notice is $1,836.03.

Austin Colony Savings & Loan ("Austin Colony") has been identified as a holder of a lien of record on the Property that is evidenced by a deed of trust lien, which is inferior or subordinate to the Association's Assessment Lien. Pursuant to Section 209.0091 of the Texas Property Code, the Association is providing you with written notice of the total amount of the Assessment Delinquency giving rise to the foreclosure of its Assessment Lien. Austin Colony may avoid the foreclosure of the Association's Assessment Lien by paying the Association $1,836.03 in full within sixty (60) days from its receipt of this notice.

If you have any questions or would like to make arrangements to pay the Assessment Delinquency, please contact the Association's Treasurer, James Bowie, at (512) 555-4343.

Sincerely,

Stephen F. Austin
President
Tejas Estates Homeowners Association, Inc.

cc: Antonio Santa Anna
owner of 3016 Alamo Street, Austin 78701

DRAFTER'S DICTUM – This document is a sample form for illustrative purposes and may or may not conform to the specific requirements of a particular Homeowners Association's Governing Documents. In addition, changes in statutory and case law may modify or nullify provisions of this document or its enforcement or may create rights or duties not anticipated by this document. Users of this sample form document are advised to periodically review applicable statutes and court rulings to ensure its compliance with all applicable laws.

Appendix X: Sample Notice of Assessment Lien for Non-Payment of Assessments (for use by Condominium Associations)

NOTICE OF ASSESSMENT LIEN AGAINST PROPERTY
FOR SUMS NOT PAID TO PROPERTY OWNERS ASSOCIATION

THE STATE OF TEXAS §
COUNTY OF BEXAR §

WHEREAS, Antonio Santa Anna (the "Owner") is the owner of the real property locally known as 3016 Guadalupe Street, San Antonio, Texas 78205, and legally known as Unit 1, Tejas Estates Condominium, a condominium project in Bexar County, Texas, according to the Declaration of Condominium and amendments thereto, recorded as Document No. 2006139496, Official Public Records, Bexar County, Texas, together with an undivided interest in and to the common elements appurtenant thereto (the "Property");

WHEREAS, the Property is subject to the Condominium Declaration for Tejas Estates Condominium, recorded at Document No. 2006139496, Official Public Records, Bexar County, Texas (the "Declaration");

WHEREAS, under the Declaration and Chapter 82 of the Texas Property Code, Tejas Estates Condominium Association, Inc. (the "Association") has a contractual lien on the Property for unpaid assessments and other sums owed by such Owner to the Association (the "Assessment Lien");

WHEREAS, as of the date of this Notice of Assessment Lien, the Owner has failed to pay to the Association sums totaling $1,200.00;

NOW THEREFORE, the Association hereby files its Notice of Assessment Lien against the Property, as authorized under the Declaration and/or Chapter 82 of the Texas Property Code.

Total Indebtedness. As of the date of this Notice of Assessment Lien, the amount due and owing to the Association for unpaid Assessments and other sums is $1,200.00 (the "Indebtedness"). Such amount will accrue interest and costs of collection, as provided in the Declaration, until paid. Additional amounts assessed against the Property that accrue after the date of this Notice of Assessment Lien and that are not paid shall be automatically added to the Assessment Lien. Moreover, the Association shall not rescind this Notice of Assessment Lien without full payment of the Indebtedness and recording costs incurred to date, plus any additional delinquent sums and attorneys fees incurred hereafter, as well as any recording costs and attorneys fees to be incurred in preparing and reviewing any necessary documents to effectively rescind this Notice of Assessment Lien, as authorized by the Declaration and/or Chapter 82 of the Texas Property Code.

TEJAS ESTATES CONDOMINIUM
ASSOCIATION, INC.,
a Texas nonprofit corporation

____
BY: Stephen F. Austin
ITS: President

THE STATE OF TEXAS §
COUNTY OF BEXAR §

This instrument was acknowledged before me on the ___ day of _______________, 2015, by Stephen F. Austin, President of Tejas Estates Condominium Association, Inc., a Texas nonprofit corporation.

[SEAL] ____________________________________
Notary Public Signature

AFTER RECORDING PLEASE RETURN TO:

Stephen F. Austin, President
Tejas Estates Condominium Association, Inc.
1836 San Jacinto Boulevard
San Antonio, Texas 78205

DRAFTER'S DICTUM – This document is a sample form for illustrative purposes and may or may not conform to the specific requirements of a particular Homeowners Association's Governing Documents. In addition, changes in statutory and case law may modify or nullify provisions of this document or its enforcement or may create rights or duties not anticipated by this document. Users of this sample form document are advised to periodically review applicable statutes and court rulings to ensure its compliance with all applicable laws.

Appendix Y: Sample Notice of Assessment Lien for Non-Payment of Assessments (for use by Subdivision Associations)

NOTICE OF ASSESSMENT LIEN AGAINST PROPERTY
FOR SUMS NOT PAID TO PROPERTY OWNERS ASSOCIATION

THE STATE OF TEXAS §
COUNTY OF BEXAR §

WHEREAS, Antonio Santa Anna (the "Owner") is the owner of the real property locally known as 3016 Alamo Street, San Antonio, Texas 78205, and legally known as Lot 2, Block A, Tejas Estates, a subdivision of record in Bexar County, Texas, according to the map or plat thereof, recorded in Volume 33, Pages 120, Real Property Records, Bexar County, Texas (the "Property");

WHEREAS, the Property is subject to the Declaration of Covenants, Conditions, and Restrictions for Tejas Estates, recorded at Document No. 2007054216, Official Public Records, Bexar County, Texas (the "Declaration");

WHEREAS, under the Declaration, Tejas Estates Homeowners Association, Inc. (the "Association") has a contractual lien on the Property for unpaid assessments and other sums owed by such Owner to the Association (the "Assessment Lien");

WHEREAS, of the date of this Notice of Assessment Lien, the Owner has failed to pay to the Association sums totaling $1,200.00;

NOW THEREFORE, the Association hereby files its Notice of Assessment Lien against the Property, as authorized under the Declaration.

Total Indebtedness. As of the date of this Notice of Assessment Lien, the amount due and owing to the Association for unpaid assessments and other sums is $1,200.00 (the "Indebtedness"). Such amount will accrue interest and costs of collection as provided in the Declaration until paid. Additional amounts assessed against the Property that accrue after the date of this Notice of Assessment Lien and that are not paid shall be automatically added to the Assessment Lien. Moreover, the Association shall not rescind this Notice of Assessment Lien without full payment of the Indebtedness and recording costs incurred to date, plus any additional delinquent sums and attorneys fees incurred hereafter, as well as any recording costs and attorneys fees to be incurred in preparing and reviewing any necessary documents to effectively rescind this Notice of Assessment Lien, as authorized by the Declaration.

DRAFTER'S DICTUM – This document is a sample form for illustrative purposes and may or may not conform to the specific requirements of a particular Homeowners Association's Governing Documents. In addition, changes in statutory and case law may modify or nullify provisions of this document or its enforcement or may create rights or duties not anticipated by this document. Users of this sample form document are advised to periodically review applicable statutes and court rulings to ensure its compliance with all applicable laws.

TEJAS ESTATES HOMEOWNERS
ASSOCIATION, INC.,
a Texas nonprofit corporation

____
BY: Samuel Houston
ITS: President

THE STATE OF TEXAS §
COUNTY OF BEXAR §

This instrument was acknowledged before me on the ___ day of _______________, 2015, by Samuel Houston, President of Tejas Estates Homeowners Association, Inc., a Texas nonprofit corporation.

[SEAL] ______________________________________
Notary Public Signature

AFTER RECORDING PLEASE RETURN TO:

Samuel Houston, President
Tejas Estates Homeowners Association, Inc.
1836 San Jacinto Boulevard
San Antonio, Texas 78205

DRAFTER'S DICTUM – This document is a sample form for illustrative purposes and may or may not conform to the specific requirements of a particular Homeowners Association's Governing Documents. In addition, changes in statutory and case law may modify or nullify provisions of this document or its enforcement or may create rights or duties not anticipated by this document. Users of this sample form document are advised to periodically review applicable statutes and court rulings to ensure its compliance with all applicable laws.

Appendix Z: Sample Release of Notice of Assessment Lien (for use by all Homeowners Associations)

RELEASE OF NOTICE OF ASSESSMENT LIEN

STATE OF TEXAS §
COUNTY OF BEXAR §

WHEREAS, Antonio Santa Anna (the "Owner") is the owner of the property locally known as 3016 Alamo Street, San Antonio, Texas 78205 (the "Property"), and legally known as:

> Lot 2, Block A, Tejas Estates, a subdivision of record in Bexar County, Texas, according to the map or plat thereof, recorded in Volume 33, Pages 120, Real Property Records, Bexar County, Texas;

WHEREAS, the Property is subject to the Declaration of Covenants, Conditions, and Restrictions for Tejas Estates, recorded at Document No. 2007054216, Official Public Records, Bexar County, Texas (the "Declaration"), and any supplements and/or amendments thereto;

WHEREAS, pursuant to the Declaration, Tejas Estates Homeowners Association, Inc. (the "Association") has a contractual lien against the Property for unpaid assessments and other sums owed by such Owner to the Association (the "Assessment Lien");

WHEREAS, the Owner had failed to pay certain sums owed to the Association representing unpaid assessments, fees, and costs of collection, and on January 16, 2015, the Association recorded that certain Notice of Assessment Lien Against Property For Sums Not Paid to Property Owners Association, recorded at Document No. 2009007278, Official Public Records, Bexar County, Texas (the "Notice of Assessment Lien");

WHEREAS, the Owner has now paid all outstanding sums identified in the Notice of Assessment Lien;

NOW THEREFORE, the Association hereby releases such Notice of Assessment Lien, effective upon the recording of this document.

Executed this the _____ day of June, 2015.

DRAFTER'S DICTUM – This document is a sample form for illustrative purposes and may or may not conform to the specific requirements of a particular Homeowners Association's Governing Documents. In addition, changes in statutory and case law may modify or nullify provisions of this document or its enforcement or may create rights or duties not anticipated by this document. Users of this sample form document are advised to periodically review applicable statutes and court rulings to ensure its compliance with all applicable laws.

TEJAS ESTATES HOMEOWNERS
ASSOCIATION, INC.,
a Texas nonprofit corporation

____
BY: Samuel Houston
ITS: President

THE STATE OF TEXAS §
COUNTY OF BEXAR §

This instrument was acknowledged before me on the ___ day of ______________, 2015, by Samuel Houston, President of Tejas Estates Homeowners Association, Inc., a Texas nonprofit corporation.

[SEAL] ____________________________________
Notary Public Signature

AFTER RECORDING PLEASE RETURN TO:

Samuel Houston, President
Tejas Estates Homeowners Association, Inc.
1836 San Jacinto Boulevard
San Antonio, Texas 78205

DRAFTER'S DICTUM – This document is a sample form for illustrative purposes and may or may not conform to the specific requirements of a particular Homeowners Association's Governing Documents. In addition, changes in statutory and case law may modify or nullify provisions of this document or its enforcement or may create rights or duties not anticipated by this document. Users of this sample form document are advised to periodically review applicable statutes and court rulings to ensure its compliance with all applicable laws.

Appendix AA: Sample Architectural Committee Submission Form

TEJAS ESTATES HOMEOWNERS ASSOCIATION, INC.

ARCHITECTURAL REVIEW COMMITTEE APPROVAL APPLICATION

Applicant Name: ______________________ Hm Ph: ______________________

Address: ______________________ Wk Ph: ______________________

Email: ______________________ Cell Ph: ______________________

****

1. Approval Requested (Please check one)

☐ Fence Replacement (Exact)	☐ Landscaping, Walkways	☐ Room/Garage Addition
☐ Fence – NEW	☐ Irrigation	☐ Satellite Dish
☐ Deck or Patio	☐ Pool	☐ Storage/Accessory Building
☐ Deck/Patio Cover	☐ Playscape	☐ Other

****

2. Please Describe Project: ____

____

____

____

****

3. Please submit the following plans and specifications in order to depict the work to be undertaken (submit all, as applicable):

(a) a plot plan showing the location and dimensions of the existing and proposed improvements;

(b) structural design, exterior elevations, exterior materials, colors, textures, and shapes of all improvements to be made;

DRAFTER'S DICTUM – This document is a sample form for illustrative purposes and may or may not conform to the specific requirements of a particular Homeowners Association's Governing Documents. In addition, changes in statutory and case law may modify or nullify provisions of this document or its enforcement or may create rights or duties not anticipated by this document. Users of this sample form document are advised to periodically review applicable statutes and court rulings to ensure its compliance with all applicable laws.

(c) all exterior illumination, including location and method of illumination—no "wash over" of lighting to adjoining property or common areas is permitted;

(d) existing and finished grades at lot corners and at corners of proposed improvements; and

(e) provision for drainage with cut and fill detail if change in lot contour is involved.

****

4. Neighbors' Signatures: Addresses:

______________________________	______________________________
______________________________	______________________________
______________________________	______________________________
______________________________	______________________________
______________________________	______________________________

****

5. Notice to Applicant:

The authority of the Architectural Review Committee ("ARC") is derived from Article 6.1 of the Declaration of Covenants, Conditions, and Restrictions of Tejas Estates (the "Declaration"), which states: "No improvement may be erected, placed or constructed, painted, altered, modified, or remodeled on any Lot without the prior written approval of the Architectural Review Committee."

Applicant acknowledges that all improvements must be constructed in accordance with the Design Guidelines set forth in the Declaration in addition to any guidelines or rules adopted by the Association or ARC from time to time. In addition, all improvements must be constructed in accordance with the laws, rules, regulations, and building codes of governmental authorities having jurisdiction. Approval of this application does not constitute approval by any governmental authority.

Approval of this application does not give Applicant the right to enter upon the property of any other owner or the common area in order to perform the construction contemplated by this application.

The Applicant is solely responsible for ensuring that proposed improvements do not encroach upon a public utility easement located on the Property. Applicant hereby releases the Association, ARC, and each of its Directors, Officers, committee members, and agents from and against any liability caused or occasioned by the location of such improvements. Applicant acknowledges that in the event an improvement encroaches upon a public utility

DRAFTER'S DICTUM – This document is a sample form for illustrative purposes and may or may not conform to the specific requirements of a particular Homeowners Association's Governing Documents. In addition, changes in statutory and case law may modify or nullify provisions of this document or its enforcement or may create rights or duties not anticipated by this document. Users of this sample form document are advised to periodically review applicable statutes and court rulings to ensure its compliance with all applicable laws.

easement located on the Property and a public utility provider requires access to such easement, Applicant may be required to remove such improvements to the extent they encroach upon or interfere with use of the public utility easement.

A copy of the Declaration has been posted on the community web page at www.TejasEstatesHOA.org. If you do not have access to the internet, you may order a copy from the Republic of Texas Property Management. You will be charged a fee for copies.

____________________________ ____________________________

Applicant Signature Date

SUBMIT THIS APPLICATION TO:

Susanna Dickinson

Facsimile: (512) 555-5001 or Susanna.Dickinson@republicoftexasmanagement.com

The application will be routed to the Tejas Estates Architectural Review Committee. Contact the committee with any questions.

****

For ARC Use Only

Complete Application Received–Date

Application Approved–Date

☐ Approved ☐ Disapproved ☐ With Conditions

Application Approved with the following conditions: ____________________

____

____

____

____.

Application Disapproved at this time with the following comments: ________________

____

____

____

____.

DRAFTER'S DICTUM – This document is a sample form for illustrative purposes and may or may not conform to the specific requirements of a particular Homeowners Association's Governing Documents. In addition, changes in statutory and case law may modify or nullify provisions of this document or its enforcement or may create rights or duties not anticipated by this document. Users of this sample form document are advised to periodically review applicable statutes and court rulings to ensure its compliance with all applicable laws.

Appendix BB: Sample Notice of Restrictive Covenant Violation Letter (for use by Condominium Associations)

TEJAS ESTATES CONDOMINIUM ASSOCIATION, INC.
1833 Republic of Texas Avenue
Austin, Texas 78701

September 5, 2015

VIA FIRST CLASS AND
CERTIFIED MAIL, RRR

Antonio Santa Anna
3016 Alamo Street, Unit 18
Austin, Texas 78701

Re: Unit 18 of the Tejas Estates Condominiums, 3016 Alamo Street, Austin, Texas 78701 (the "Unit")

Dear Mr. Santa Anna:

As you are probably aware, the Unit is subject to the Declaration of Covenants, Conditions, and Restrictions for Tejas Estates Condominiums (the "Declaration"), which are contractual obligations assumed by you when you purchased the Unit and are intended to preserve the value and enjoyment of the units in the Tejas Estates Condominiums, including your Unit. This letter is to inform you that the Tejas Estates Condominium Association (the "Association") has observed a violation of the Declaration concerning the Unit. As a courteous reminder from the Association, please be advised that you are in violation of the Declaration in the following manner:

[Violation – Detailed Description]

In order to help us in our efforts to preserve the value and enjoyment of the units, we ask for your cooperation in taking the following action within thirty (30) days from the date of this notice:

[Describe action to remedy violation.]

We hope that you will assist us to resolve this matter and that the Association will not need to take further action. If you have any questions or would like to discuss this matter further, you may contact me at (512) 555-5555 or you may attend the next meeting of the Board of Directors, which is currently scheduled for October 1, 2015.

DRAFTER'S DICTUM – This document is a sample form for illustrative purposes and may or may not conform to the specific requirements of a particular Homeowners Association's Governing Documents. In addition, changes in statutory and case law may modify or nullify provisions of this document or its enforcement or may create rights or duties not anticipated by this document. Users of this sample form document are advised to periodically review applicable statutes and court rulings to ensure its compliance with all applicable laws.

Sincerely,

William B. Travis
Property Manager
Tejas Estates Condominium Association, Inc.

DRAFTER'S DICTUM – This document is a sample form for illustrative purposes and may or may not conform to the specific requirements of a particular Homeowners Association's Governing Documents. In addition, changes in statutory and case law may modify or nullify provisions of this document or its enforcement or may create rights or duties not anticipated by this document. Users of this sample form document are advised to periodically review applicable statutes and court rulings to ensure its compliance with all applicable laws.

Appendix CC: Sample Notice of Restrictive Covenant Violation Letter (for use by Subdivision Associations)

TEJAS HOMEOWNERS ASSOCIATION, INC.
1833 Republic of Texas Avenue
Austin, Texas 78701

September 5, 2015

VIA FIRST CLASS AND
CERTIFIED MAIL

Antonio Santa Anna
3016 Alamo Street
Austin, Texas 78701

Re: 3016 Alamo Street, Austin, Texas 78701 (the "Property")

Dear Mr. Santa Anna:

As you are probably aware, the Property is subject to the Declaration of Covenants, Conditions, and Restrictions for Tejas Estates (the "Declaration"), which are contractual obligations assumed by you when you purchased the Property and are intended to preserve the value of the properties in the Tejas Estates community, including your property, as well as your neighbors' properties. This letter is to inform you that the Tejas Estates Homeowners Association (the "Association") has observed a violation of the Declaration at the Property. As a courteous reminder from the Association, please be advised that you are in violation of the Declaration in the following manner:

[Violation – Detailed Description]

In order to help us in our efforts to preserve the appearance of the community, we ask for your cooperation in taking the following action on or before October 5, 2015:

[Describe action to remedy violation.]

In addition, you are entitled to request a hearing before the Board of Directors for the Association or a designated committee before the thirtieth (30th) day from the date you receive this notice. If the hearing is held before a designated committee, you also have the right to appeal that decision to the Board of Directors by written notice to the Board

> *DRAFTER'S DICTUM* – This document is a sample form for illustrative purposes and may or may not conform to the specific requirements of a particular Homeowners Association's Governing Documents. In addition, changes in statutory and case law may modify or nullify provisions of this document or its enforcement or may create rights or duties not anticipated by this document. Users of this sample form document are advised to periodically review applicable statutes and court rulings to ensure its compliance with all applicable laws.

of Directors within ten (10) days of receiving the committee's decision. All hearing requests must be in writing and may be mailed or faxed to the Tejas Estates Homeowners Association, Attention: William B. Travis, at 1833 Republic of Texas Avenue, Austin, Texas 78701, or to fax number (512) 555-2323.

If you fail to cure the violation described herein within thirty (30) days from the date of this notice, the Association intends to forward this matter to its attorneys for further enforcement action. In such event, the Association will incur attorneys fees for which it will seek reimbursement from you.

We hope that you will assist us to resolve this matter and that no further action by the Association or its attorneys to enforce the Declaration will be necessary. If you have any questions or would like to discuss this matter further, you may contact me at (512) 555-5555.

Sincerely,

William B. Travis
Property Manager
Tejas Estates Homeowners Association, Inc.

ACTIVE MILITARY DUTY ADVISORY

Please be advised that the owner(s) of the Property may have special rights or relief related to this enforcement action under federal law, including the Servicemembers Civil Relief Act (50 U.S.C. app. Section 501 et seq.), if one or more of the owners of the Property is serving on active military duty. If this is the case, please alert the Association immediately.

DRAFTER'S DICTUM – This document is a sample form for illustrative purposes and may or may not conform to the specific requirements of a particular Homeowners Association's Governing Documents. In addition, changes in statutory and case law may modify or nullify provisions of this document or its enforcement or may create rights or duties not anticipated by this document. Users of this sample form document are advised to periodically review applicable statutes and court rulings to ensure its compliance with all applicable laws.

Appendix DD: Sample Notice of Fine or Charge Letter in Accordance with Chapter 82 of the Texas Property Code (for use by Condominium Associations)

TEJAS ESTATES CONDOMINIUM ASSOCIATION, INC.
1833 Republic of Texas Avenue
Austin, Texas 78701

September 5, 2015

VIA FIRST CLASS AND
CERTIFIED MAIL RRR

Antonio Santa Anna
3016 Alamo Street, Unit 18
Austin, Texas 78701

Re: Unit 18 of the Tejas Estates Condominiums, 3016 Alamo Street, Austin, Texas 78701 (the "Unit")

Dear Mr. Santa Anna:

The Tejas Estates Condominium Association (the "Association") has previously notified you that the Unit is subject to the Declaration of Covenants, Conditions, and Restrictions for Tejas Estates Condominiums (the "Declaration"), which are contractual obligations assumed by you when you purchased the Unit and are intended to preserve the value and peaceful enjoyment of the units in the Tejas Estates Condominium, including your Unit. Despite the Association's previous request that you cure certain existing violations of the Declaration concerning the Unit, as further described below, the Association has observed that such violations remain uncorrected. Due to the nature of such continued violations of the Declaration, the Association has elected to assess fines against you as follows:

Unauthorized short-term rental of the Unit:	$100
Failure to maintan exterior of Unit:	$50
Total Fines	$150

DRAFTER'S DICTUM – This document is a sample form for illustrative purposes and may or may not conform to the specific requirements of a particular Homeowners Association's Governing Documents. In addition, changes in statutory and case law may modify or nullify provisions of this document or its enforcement or may create rights or duties not anticipated by this document. Users of this sample form document are advised to periodically review applicable statutes and court rulings to ensure its compliance with all applicable laws.

You may avoid these fines by taking the following action on or before October 5, 2015:

[Describe action to remedy violation.]

You are also entitled to request a hearing before the Board of Directors for the Association to contest such fines, but you must do so no later than thirty (30) days from the date of this notice. All hearing requests must be in writing and may be mailed or faxed to the Tejas Estates Condominium Association, Attention: William B. Travis, at 1833 Republic of Texas Avenue, Austin, Texas 78701 or fax number (512) 555-2323.

If you again refuse to correct the violations described herein within the specified time frame, the Association may assess additional fines and/or forward this matter to its attorneys for further enforcement action. In the event of the latter, the Association will incur attorneys fees for which it will seek reimbursement from you.

We hope that you will voluntarily assist us to resolve this matter and that no further action by the Association or its attorneys to enforce the Declaration will be necessary.

Sincerely,

William B. Travis
Property Manager
Tejas Estates Condominium Association, Inc.

DRAFTER'S DICTUM – This document is a sample form for illustrative purposes and may or may not conform to the specific requirements of a particular Homeowners Association's Governing Documents. In addition, changes in statutory and case law may modify or nullify provisions of this document or its enforcement or may create rights or duties not anticipated by this document. Users of this sample form document are advised to periodically review applicable statutes and court rulings to ensure its compliance with all applicable laws.

Appendix EE: Sample Notice of Fine or Charge Letter in Accordance with Chapter 209 of the Texas Property Code (for use by Subdivision Associations)

TEJAS HOMEOWNERS ASSOCIATION, INC.
1833 Republic of Texas Avenue
Austin, Texas 78701

September 5, 2015

VIA FIRST CLASS AND
CERTIFIED MAIL RRR

Antonio Santa Anna
3016 Alamo Street
Austin, Texas 78701

Re: 3016 Alamo Street, Austin, Texas 78701 (the "Property")

Dear Mr. Santa Anna:

The Tejas Estates Homeowners Association (the "Association") has previously notified you that the Property is subject to the Declaration of Covenants, Conditions, and Restrictions for Tejas Estates (the "Declaration"), which are contractual obligations assumed by you when you purchased the Property and are intended to preserve the value of the properties in the Tejas Estates community, including your property, as well as your neighbors' properties. Despite the Association's previous request that you cure the existing violations of the Declaration at the Property concerning [Violation – Detailed Description], the Association has observed that such violations remain uncorrected. Due to the nature of such continued violation of the Declaration, the Association has elected to assess fines against you as follows:

Failure to repair fence:	$100
Failure to remove trailer from Property:	$50
Total Fines	$150

You are entitled to a reasonable period to cure the specified violation and avoid the assessed fines by taking the following action within thirty (30) days from the date of this notice:

DRAFTER'S DICTUM – This document is a sample form for illustrative purposes and may or may not conform to the specific requirements of a particular Homeowners Association's Governing Documents. In addition, changes in statutory and case law may modify or nullify provisions of this document or its enforcement or may create rights or duties not anticipated by this document. Users of this sample form document are advised to periodically review applicable statutes and court rulings to ensure its compliance with all applicable laws.

[Describe action to remedy violation]

If thirty (30) days is not a reasonably sufficient period of time to complete such corrective actions, please contact the Association's property manager, William B. Travis, to discuss a reasonable time period within which such actions will be completed. If you fail to contact Mr. Travis, the Association will assume that thirty (30) days is reasonably sufficient to complete such corrective actions.

You are also entitled to request a hearing before the Board of Directors for the Association or a designated committee before the thirtieth (30th) day from the date you receive this notice. If the hearing is held before a designated committee, you also have the right to appeal that decision to the Board of Directors by written notice to the Board of Directors within ten (10) days of receiving the committee's decision. All hearing requests must be in writing and may be mailed or faxed to the Tejas Estates Homeowners Association, Attention: William B. Travis, at 1833 Republic of Texas Avenue, Austin, Texas 78701, or to fax number (512) 555-2323.

If you again refuse to correct the violations described herein within the specified time frame, the Association may assess additional fines and/or forward this matter to its attorneys for further enforcement action. In the event of the latter, the Association will incur attorneys fees for which it will seek reimbursement from you.

We hope that you will voluntarily assist us to resolve this matter and that no further action by the Association or its attorneys to enforce the Declaration will be necessary.

Sincerely,

William B. Travis
Property Manager
Tejas Estates Homeowners Association, Inc.

ACTIVE MILITARY DUTY ADVISORY

Please be advised that the owner(s) of the Property may have special rights or relief related to this enforcement action under federal law, including the Servicemembers Civil Relief Act (50 U.S.C. app. Section 501 et seq.), if one or more of the owners of the Property is serving on active military duty. If this is the case, please alert the Association immediately.

DRAFTER'S DICTUM – This document is a sample form for illustrative purposes and may or may not conform to the specific requirements of a particular Homeowners Association's Governing Documents. In addition, changes in statutory and case law may modify or nullify provisions of this document or its enforcement or may create rights or duties not anticipated by this document. Users of this sample form document are advised to periodically review applicable statutes and court rulings to ensure its compliance with all applicable laws.

Appendix FF: Sample Outline for a Chapter 209 Hearing Before the Board of Directors (for use by Subdivision Associations)

Note: A Director or Officer should act as the presiding hearing officer. The hearing officer will provide introductory remarks and administer the hearing agenda.

I. Introduction:

Hearing Officer: "The Board of Directors has convened for the purpose of hearing an appeal by ______________ from a determination by the Homeowners Association that such owner is in violation of the restrictive covenants applicable to his or her property and/or the guidelines or rules of the Homeowners Association (or from the imposition of fines by the Homeowners Association for violation of the restrictive covenants applicable to his or her property and/or the guidelines or rules of the Homeowners Association). The hearing is being conducted as required by Section 209.007 of the Texas Property Code, and it is an opportunity for the appealing party to discuss, verify facts, and attempt to resolve the matter at issue. The Board of Directors would like to resolve the dispute at this hearing. However, the Board of Directors may elect to take the appeal under advisement and conclude the hearing. If the matter is taken under advisement, a final decision will be communicated to the appealing party in writing within fifteen (15) days."

II. Presentation of Facts:

Hearing Officer: "This portion of the hearing is to permit a representative of the Homeowners Association the opportunity to describe the violation and to present photographs or other material relevant to the violation, fines, and/or penalties. After the Homeowners Association's representative has finished his or her presentation, the owner or his or her representative will be given the opportunity to present photographs or other material relevant to the violation, fines, or penalties. The Board of Directors may ask questions during either party's presentation. It is requested that questions by the appealing party be held until completion of the presentation by the Homeowners Association's representative."

[Conduct Presentations]

III. Discussion:

Hearing Officer: "This portion of the hearing is to permit the Board of Directors and the owner to discuss factual disputes relevant to the violation. Discussion regarding any fine or penalty is also appropriate. Discussion should be productive and designed to seek, if possible, an acceptable resolution of the dispute. The Hearing Officer retains the right to conclude this portion of the hearing at any time."

IV. Resolution:

Hearing Officer: "This portion of the hearing is to permit discussion between the Board of Directors and the appealing party regarding the final terms of the settlement if a resolution was agreed upon during the discussion phase of the hearing."

If no settlement is agreed upon, the Hearing Officer may: (1) request that the Board of Directors enter into executive session to discuss the matter; (2) request that the Board of Directors take the matter under advisement and adjourn the hearing; or (3) advise the appealing party of the Board of Directors' decision and adjourn the hearing.

Appendix GG: Links to Texas Homeowners Association Online Resources, Statutes, and Forms

Homeowners Association Resources:

Texas Homeowners Association Law
www.TexasHOALaw.com

Community Associations Institute
www.caionline.org

CAI – Austin Chapter
www.caiaustin.org

CAI – Dallas/Ft. Worth Chapter
www.dfwcai.org

CAI – Greater Houston Chapter
www.caihouston.org

CAI – San Antonio Chapter
www.caisa.org

Links to the Texas Constitution and Statutory Law:

Texas Constitution:
www.statutes.legis.state.tx.us?link=CN

Texas Condominium Act:
www.statutes.legis.state.tx.us/docs/PR/pdf/PR.81.pdf

Texas Uniform Condominium Act:
www.statutes.legis.state.tx.us/docs/PR/pdf/PR.82.pdf

Texas Business Organizations Code:
www.statutes.legis.state.tx.us?link=BO

Texas Nonprofit Corporation Law:
www.statutes.legis.state.tx.us/docs/BO/pdf/BO.22.pdf

Texas Unincorporated Nonprofit Association Act:
www.statutes.legis.state.tx.us/docs/BO/pdf/BO.252.pdf

Chapter 201 of the Texas Property Code:
www.statutes.legis.state.tx.us/docs/PR/pdf/PR.201.pdf

Chapter 202 of the Texas Property Code:
www.statutes.legis.state.tx.us/docs/PR/pdf/PR.202.pdf

Chapter 203 of the Texas Property Code:
www.statutes.legis.state.tx.us/docs/PR/pdf/PR.203.pdf

Chapter 204 of the Texas Property Code:
www.statutes.legis.state.tx.us/docs/PR/pdf/PR.204.pdf

Chapter 205 of the Texas Property Code:
www.statutes.legis.state.tx.us/docs/PR/pdf/PR.205.pdf

Chapter 206 of the Texas Property Code:
www.statutes.legis.state.tx.us/docs/PR/pdf/PR.206.pdf

Chapter 207 of the Texas Property Code:
www.statutes.legis.state.tx.us/docs/PR/pdf/PR.207.pdf

Chapter 208 of the Texas Property Code:
www.statutes.legis.state.tx.us/docs/PR/pdf/PR.208.pdf

Chapter 209 of the Texas Property Code:
www.statutes.legis.state.tx.us/docs/PR/pdf/PR.209.pdf

Chapter 210 of the Texas Property Code:
www.statutes.legis.state.tx.us/docs/PR/pdf/PR.210.pdf

Chapter 211 of the Texas Property Code:
www.statutes.legis.state.tx.us/docs/PR/pdf/PR.211.pdf

Texas Charitable Immunity and Liability Act of 1987:
www.statutes.legis.state.tx.us/docs/CP/pdf/CP.84.pdf

Texas Public Information Act:
www.statutes.legis.state.tx.us/docs/GV/pdf/GV.552.pdf

Texas Open Meetings Act:
www.statutes.legis.state.tx.us/docs/GV/pdf/GV.551.pdf

Texas Debt Collection Practices Act:
www.statutes.legis.state.tx.us/docs/FI/pdf/FI.392.pdf

Texas Fair Housing Act:
www.statutes.legis.state.tx.us/docs/PR/pdf/PR.301.pdf

Texas Community Homes for Disabled Persons Location Act:
www.statutes.legis.state.tx.us/docs/HR/pdf/HR.123.pdf

Federal and Texas Governmental Links:

Texas Secretary of State:
www.sos.state.tx.us

Texas Attorney General:
www.oag.state.tx.us

Texas Workforce Commission:
www.twc.state.tx.us

Texas Comptroller
www.window.state.tx.us

Federal Communications Commission
www.fcc.gov

The Department of Housing and Urban Development
www.hud.gov

Forms:

Proof of Claim – Official Bankruptcy Form:
http://www.uscourts.gov/forms/bankruptcy-forms/proof-claim-0

Periodic Report Forms (for use by Texas Nonprofit Corporations):
www.sos.state.tx.us/corp/forms/802_boc.pdf

Business Organization Code Forms (for use by Texas Nonprofit Corporations and Unincorporated Nonprofit Associations):
www.sos.state.tx.us/corp/forms_boc.shtml

Miscellaneous Resources:

Military Servicemembers Civil Relief Act Centralized Verification Service:
www.servicememberscivilreliefact.com

FCC Fact Sheet on Placement of Antennas published by the Federal Communications Commission:
http://www.fcc.gov/mb/facts/otard.html

Texas Attorney General's Publications: Open Meetings 2008 Handbook and the 2008 Open Meetings Act Made Easy:
www.oag.state.tx.us/open/index.shtml

A Guide for Doing Business with the Secretary of State (for Texas Nonprofit Corporations):
http://www.sos.state.tx.us/corp/forms/boc/boc-np-2010.pdf

SUBJECT INDEX

AUTHOR'S BIOGRAPHY

Gregory S. Cagle graduated from Baylor University School of Law in 1998, where he was a member of the Order of Barristers and Baylor Law Review. Mr. Cagle is a former briefing attorney to the Honorable Justice Dixon W. Holman at the Second District Court of Appeals in Fort Worth, Texas, and is currently a partner at the law firm of Cagle Carpenter Hazlewood in Austin, Texas.

Mr. Cagle concentrates his law practice in civil and complex litigation involving real estate, nonprofit and for-profit corporations, business disputes, construction defects, and residential and commercial property owners associations. Mr. Cagle has extensive litigation experience and has served as lead trial attorney in numerous trials in front of judges and juries. In addition, Mr. Cagle is a certified mediator and is AV peer-review rated by Martindale-Hubble.

Mr. Cagle also has extensive experience in representing and advising property owners associations throughout the State of Texas as general counsel on all aspects of issues involved in the operation and governance of association-governed communities, including management issues, compliance with federal and state laws, interpretation of and compliance with governing documents, architectural review of proposed construction, covenant enforcement, assessment collection, litigation, and dispute resolution. Mr. Cagle is a member of the Community Associations Institute and a fellow in the College of Community Association Lawyers, and he is a frequent speaker and author on topics related to association-governed communities.

More information about Mr. Cagle can be found at www.TexasHOALaw.com.